Handbook of Research on Applied Cybernetics and Systems Science

Snehanshu Saha
PESIT South Campus, India

Abhyuday Mandal
University of Georgia, USA

Anand Narasimhamurthy
BITS Hyderabad, India

Sarasvathi V
PESIT– Bangalore South Campus, India

Shivappa Sangam
UGC, India

A volume in the Advances in Computational
Intelligence and Robotics (ACIR) Book Series

www.igi-global.com

Published in the United States of America by
    IGI Global
    Information Science Reference (an imprint of IGI Global)
    701 E. Chocolate Avenue
    Hershey PA, USA 17033
    Tel: 717-533-8845
    Fax: 717-533-8661
    E-mail: cust@igi-global.com
    Web site: http://www.igi-global.com

Library of Congress Cataloging-in-Publication Data

Names: Saha, Snehanshu, editor.
Title: Handbook of research on applied cybernetics and systems science /
  Snehanshu Saha, Abhyuday Mandal, Anand Narasimhamurthy, V. Sarasvathi, and
  Shivappa Sangam, editors.
Description: Hershey, PA : Information Science Reference, [2017] | Includes
  bibliographical references.
Identifiers: LCCN 2017004264| ISBN 9781522524984 (hardcover) | ISBN
  9781522524991 (ebook)
Subjects: LCSH: Systems engineering--Handbooks, manuals, etc. |
  Cybernetics--Handbooks, manuals, etc.
Classification: LCC TA168 .H3265 2017 | DDC 620.001/135--dc23 LC record available at https://lccn.loc.gov/2017004264

This book is published in the IGI Global book series Advances in Computational Intelligence and Robotics (ACIR) (ISSN: 2327-0411; eISSN: 2327-042X)

British Cataloguing in Publication Data
A Cataloguing in Publication record for this book is available from the British Library.

For electronic access to this publication, please contact: eresources@igi-global.com.

Advances in Computational Intelligence and Robotics (ACIR) Book Series

Ivan Giannoccaro
University of Salento, Italy

ISSN:2327-0411
EISSN:2327-042X

MISSION

While intelligence is traditionally a term applied to humans and human cognition, technology has progressed in such a way to allow for the development of intelligent systems able to simulate many human traits. With this new era of simulated and artificial intelligence, much research is needed in order to continue to advance the field and also to evaluate the ethical and societal concerns of the existence of artificial life and machine learning.

The **Advances in Computational Intelligence and Robotics (ACIR) Book Series** encourages scholarly discourse on all topics pertaining to evolutionary computing, artificial life, computational intelligence, machine learning, and robotics. ACIR presents the latest research being conducted on diverse topics in intelligence technologies with the goal of advancing knowledge and applications in this rapidly evolving field.

COVERAGE

- Cognitive Informatics
- Natural language processing
- Algorithmic Learning
- Computational Logic
- Intelligent control
- Neural Networks
- Evolutionary Computing
- Computer Vision
- Artificial Intelligence
- Brain Simulation

IGI Global is currently accepting manuscripts for publication within this series. To submit a proposal for a volume in this series, please contact our Acquisition Editors at Acquisitions@igi-global.com or visit: http://www.igi-global.com/publish/.

Titles in this Series

For a list of additional titles in this series, please visit: www.igi-global.com/book-series

Advanced Image Processing Techniques and Applications
N. Suresh Kumar (VIT University, India) Arun Kumar Sangaiah (VIT University, India) M. Arun (VIT University, India) and S. Anand (VIT University, India)
Information Science Reference • ©2017 • 439pp • H/C (ISBN: 9781522520535) • US $290.00

Advanced Research on Biologically Inspired Cognitive Architectures
Jordi Vallverdú (Universitat Autònoma de Barcelona, Spain) Manuel Mazzara (Innopolis University, Russia) Max Talanov (Kazan Federal University, Russia) Salvatore Distefano (University of Messina, Italy & Kazan Federal University, Russia) and Robert Lowe (University of Gothenburg, Sweden & University of Skövde, Sweden)
Information Science Reference • ©2017 • 297pp • H/C (ISBN: 9781522519478) • US $195.00

Theoretical and Practical Advancements for Fuzzy System Integration
Deng-Feng Li (Fuzhou University, China)
Information Science Reference • ©2017 • 415pp • H/C (ISBN: 9781522518488) • US $200.00

Multi-Agent-Based Simulations Applied to Biological and Environmental Systems
Diana Francisca Adamatti (Universidade Federal do Rio Grande, Brazil)
Information Science Reference • ©2017 • 406pp • H/C (ISBN: 9781522517566) • US $205.00

Strategic Imperatives and Core Competencies in the Era of Robotics and Artificial Intelligence
Roman Batko (Jagiellonian University, Poland) and Anna Szopa (Jagiellonian University, Poland)
Business Science Reference • ©2017 • 302pp • H/C (ISBN: 9781522516569) • US $185.00

Emerging Research on Applied Fuzzy Sets and Intuitionistic Fuzzy Matrices
Amal Kumar Adak (Jafuly Deshpran High School, India) Debashree Manna (Damda Jr. High School, India) and Monoranjan Bhowmik (Vidyasagar Teacher's Training College, India)
Information Science Reference • ©2017 • 375pp • H/C (ISBN: 9781522509141) • US $205.00

Multi-Core Computer Vision and Image Processing for Intelligent Applications
Mohan S. (Al Yamamah University, Saudi Arabia) and Vani V. (Al Yamamah University, Saudi Arabia)
Information Science Reference • ©2017 • 292pp • H/C (ISBN: 9781522508892) • US $210.00

www.igi-global.com

701 East Chocolate Avenue, Hershey, PA 17033, USA
Tel: 717-533-8845 x100 • Fax: 717-533-8661
E-Mail: cust@igi-global.com • www.igi-global.com

To Raghab Bandyopadhyay

List of Contributors

Table of Contents

Section 3
Machine Learning and Data Sciences

Section 4
Statistical Models and Designs in Computing

Section 5
Scientometrics and Cybernetics

Detailed Table of Contents

Section 1
Signal Processing and Communications

Sobin C. C., IIT Roorkee, India

Vaskar Raychoudhury, IIT Roorkee, India

Snehanshu Saha, PESIT-BSC, India

The amount of data generated by online social networks such as Facebook, Twitter, etc., has recently experienced an enormous growth. Extracting useful information such as community structure, from such large networks is very important in many applications. Community is a collection of nodes, having dense internal connections and sparse external connections. Community detection algorithms aim to group nodes into different communities by extracting similarities and social relations between nodes. Although, many community detection algorithms in literature, they are not scalable enough to handle large volumes of data generated by many of the today's big data applications. So, researchers are focusing on developing parallel community detection algorithms, which can handle networks consisting of millions of edges and vertices. In this article, we present a comprehensive survey of parallel community detection algorithms, which is the first ever survey in this domain, although, multiple papers exist in literature related to sequential community detection algorithms.

Sounak Dey, TCS Research and Innovation, India

Arijit Mukherjee, TCS Research and Innovation, India

The rapid growth in the number of sensors deployed at various scenarios and domains has resulted in the demand of smart applications and services which can take advantage of the sensor ubiquity and the Internet of Things paradigm. However, IoT analytic applications are grossly different from typical IT applications in the sense that in case of IoT, the physical world model is absolutely essential to understand the meaning of sensor data and context. It is also unreasonable to assume that application developers will possess all the necessary skills such as signal processing, algorithms, domain and deployment infrastructures. The scenario is more complicated because of overlapping domains and variety of knowledge. Researchers have attempted to automate parts of the development process, but, the area of feature engineering for sensor signals remain relatively untouched. In this chapter, the authors discuss about the use of semantic modeling for IoT application development with respect to a framework that is capable of largely automating parts of IoT application development.

Chapter 3

Deepayan Bhowmik, Sheffield Hallam University, UK
Mehryar Emambakhsh, Heriot-Watt University, UK

Security is a fundamental issue in today's world. In this chapter we discuss various aspects of security in daily life that can be solved using image processing techniques by grouping in three main categories: visual tracking, biometrics and digital media security. Visual tracking refers to computer vision techniques that analyses the scene to extract features representing objects (e.g., pedestrian) and track them to provide input to analyse any anomalous behaviour. Biometrics is the technology of detecting, extracting and analysing human's physical or behavioural features for identification purposes. Digital media security typically includes multimedia signal processing techniques that can protect copyright by embedding information within the media content using watermarking approaches. Individual topics are discussed referring recent literature.

Chapter 4

Nilanjan De, Calcutta Institute of Engineering and Management, India

Graph operations play a very important role in mathematical chemistry, since some chemically interesting graphs can be obtained from some simpler graphs by different graph operations. In this chapter, some eccentricity based topological indices such as the total eccentricity index, eccentric connectivity index, modified eccentric connectivity index and connective eccentricity index and their respective polynomial versions of corona product of two graphs have been studied and also these indices of some important classes of chemically interesting molecular graphs are determined by specializing the components of corona product of graphs.

Section 2
Systems and Computational Biology

Chapter 5

Nicole A. Lazar, University of Georgia, USA

The analysis of functional magnetic resonance imaging (fMRI) data poses many statistical challenges. The data are massive, noisy, and have a complicated spatial and temporal correlation structure. This chapter introduces the basics of fMRI data collection and surveys common approaches for data analysis.

Chapter 6

James K. Peterson, Clemson University, USA

In this work, the authors develop signaling models based on ideas from homology and discuss how to design a model of signal space which decomposes the incoming signals into classes of progressively higher levels of associative meaning. The tools needed are illustrated with a simple approach using standard linear algebra processing but this is just a simple point of departure into a more complex and potentially more useful signal processing toolbox involving computational homology. These ideas then lead to models of grammar for signals in terms of cascaded barcode signal representations.

Section 3
Machine Learning and Data Sciences

Chapter 7

Prithish Banerjee, West Virginia University, USA
Mark Vere Culp, West Virginia University, USA
Kenneth Jospeh Ryan, West Virginia University, USA
George Michailidis, University of Florida, USA

This chapter presents some popular graph-based semi-supervised approaches. These techniques apply to classification and regression problems and can be extended to big data problems using recently developed anchor graph enhancements. The background necessary for understanding this Chapter includes linear algebra and optimization. No prior knowledge in methods of machine learning is necessary. An empirical demonstration of the techniques for these methods is also provided on real data set benchmarks.

Chapter 8

Kusuma Mohanchandra, Dayananda Sagar College of Engineering, India
Snehanshu Saha, PESIT-South, India

Machine learning techniques, is a crucial tool to build analytical models in EEG data analysis. These models are an excellent choice for analyzing the high variability in EEG signals. The advancement in EEG-based Brain-Computer Interfaces (BCI) demands advanced processing tools and algorithms for exploration of EEG signals. In the context of the EEG-based BCI for speech communication, few classification and clustering techniques is presented in this book chapter. A broad perspective of the techniques and implementation of the weighted k-Nearest Neighbor (k-NN), Support vector machine (SVM), Decision Tree (DT) and Random Forest (RF) is explained and their usage in EEG signal analysis is mentioned. We suggest that these machine learning techniques provides not only potentially valuable control mechanism for BCI but also a deeper understanding of neuropathological mechanisms underlying the brain in ways that are not possible by conventional linear analysis.

Chapter 9

Surbhi Agrawal, PESIT-BSC, India
Kakoli Bora, PESIT-BSC, India
Swati Routh, Jain University, India

In this chapter, authors have discussed few machine learning techniques and their application to perform the supernovae classification. Supernovae has various types, mainly categorized into two important types. Here, focus is given on the classification of Type-Ia supernova. Astronomers use Type-Ia supernovae as "standard candles" to measure distances in the Universe. Classification of supernovae is mainly a matter of concern for the astronomers in the absence of spectra. Through the application of different machine learning techniques on the data set authors have tried to check how well classification of supernovae can be performed using these techniques.

Traditionally supervised learning algorithms are built using labeled training data. Accurate labels are essential to guide the classifier towards an optimal separation between the classes. However, there are several real world scenarios where the class labels at an instance level may be unavailable or imprecise or difficult to obtain, or in situations where the problem is naturally posed as one of classifying instance groups. To tackle these challenges, we draw your attention towards Multi Instance Learning (MIL) algorithms where labels are available at a bag level rather than at an instance level. In this chapter, we motivate the need for MIL algorithms and describe an ensemble based method, wherein the members of the ensemble are lazy learning classifiers using the Citation Nearest Neighbour method. Diversity among the ensemble methods is achieved by optimizing their parameters using a multi-objective optimization method, with the objective being to maximize positive class accuracy and minimize false positive rate. We demonstrate results of the methodology on the standard Musk 1 dataset.

## Chapter 11

With the rapid increment in the clinical text, de-identification of patient Protected Health Information (PHI) has drawn significant attention in recent past. This aims for automatic identification and removal of the patient Protected Health Information from medical records. This paper proposes a supervised machine learning technique for solving the problem of patient data de- identification. In the current paper, we provide an insight into the de-identification task, its major challenges, techniques to address challenges, detailed analysis of the results and direction of future improvement. We extract several features by studying the properties of the datasets and the domain. We build our model based on the 2014 i2b2 (Informatics for Integrating Biology to the Bedside) de-identification challenge. Experiments show that the proposed system is highly accurate in de-identification of the medical records. The system achieves the final recall, precision and F-score of 95.69%, 99.31%, and 97.46%, respectively.

Support Vector Machines is one of the powerful Machine learning algorithms used for numerous applications. Support Vector Machines generate decision boundary between two classes which is characterized by special subset of the training data called as Support Vectors. The advantage of support vector machine over perceptron is that it generates a unique decision boundary with maximum margin. Kernalized version makes it very faster to learn as the data transformation is implicit. Object recognition using multiclass SVM is discussed in the chapter. The experiment uses histogram of visual words and multiclass SVM for image classification.

Computer experiments refer to the study of complex systems using mathematical models and computer simulations. The use of computer experiments becomes popular for studying complex systems in science and engineering. The design and analysis of computer experiments have received broad attention in the past decades. In this chapter, we present several widely used statistical approaches for design and analysis of computer experiments, including space-filling designs and Gaussian process modeling. A special emphasis is given to recently developed design and modeling techniques for computer experiments with quantitative and qualitative factors.

With advances in technologies in the past decade, the amount of data generated and recorded has grown enormously in virtually all fields of industry and science. This extraordinary amount of data provides unprecedented opportunities for data-driven decision-making and knowledge discovery. However, the task of analyzing such large-scale dataset poses significant challenges and calls for innovative statistical methods specifically designed for faster speed and higher efficiency. In this chapter, we review currently available methods for big data, with a focus on the subsampling methods using statistical leveraging and divide and conquer methods.

Section 5
Scientometrics and Cybernetics

Measuring complexity of systems is very important in Cybernetics. An aging human heart has a lower complexity than that of a younger one indicating a higher risk of cardiovascular diseases, pseudo-random sequences used in secure information storage and transmission systems are designed to have high complexity (to resist malicious attacks), brain networks in schizophrenia patients have lower complexity than corresponding networks in a healthy human brain. Such systems are typically modeled as deterministic nonlinear (chaotic) system which is further corrupted with stochastic noise (Gaussian or uniform distribution). After briefly reviewing various complexity measures, this chapter explores characterizing the complexity of deterministic nonlinear chaotic systems (tent, logistic and Hénon maps, Lorenz and Rössler flows) using specific measures such as Lempel-Ziv complexity, Approximate Entropy and Effort-To-Compress. Practical applications to neuron firing model, intra-cranial pressure monitoring, and cardiac aging detection are indicated.

Chapter 16

Pervasive computing has progressed significantly with a growth of embedded systems as a result of recent advances in digital electronics, wireless networking, sensors and RFID technology. These embedded systems are capable of producing enormous amount of data that cannot be handled by human brains. At the same time, there is a growing need for integrating these embedded devices into physical environment in order to achieve a far better capability, scalability, resiliency, safety, security and usability in important sectors such as healthcare, manufacturing, transportation, energy, agriculture, architecture and many more. The confluence of all these recent trends is the vision of distributed cyber-physical systems that will far exceed the performance of traditional embedded systems. Cyber-physical systems are emerging technology that require significant research in design and implementation with a few important challenges to overcome. The goal of this chapter is to present an overview of basic design and architecture of a cyber-physical system along with some specific applications and a brief description of the design process for developers. This chapter also presents a brief discussion of security and privacy issues, the most important challenge of cyber-physical systems.

Chapter 17

The term "Scientometrics" emerges from two significant words –Science and Metrics. It is concerned with metrics used for quantitative analysis of researcher's contribution to various scientific domains. An effective medium to communicate scientific knowledge is via scholarly publications. It provides a platform to propagate research output within and across domains. Thus, there arise need to discover parameters which can measure a researcher's contribution to his field. The most significant metric to measure the impact of a scientific work is citations. The Citation Indexes are utilized as scientometric tool to measure the research output of authors, articles and journals. This book chapter explores the existence of many such scientific parameters at both journal and author level. Further, authors make an earnest attempt to use them to measure the internationality of peer-reviewed journals. They claim that already existing parameters alone are not sufficient for evaluation of internationality and explore new parameters for computing unbiased index both at journal and author level.

Chapter 18

Machine Learning (ML) has assumed a central role in data assimilation and data analysis in the last decade. Many methods exist that cater to the different kinds of data centric applications in terms of complexity and domain. Machine Learning methods have been derived from classical Artificial Intelligence (AI) models but are a lot more reliant on statistical methods. However, ML is a lot broader than inferential statistics. Recent advances in computational neuroscience has identified Electroencephalography (EEG) based Brain Computer Interface (BCI) as one of the key agents for a variety of medical and nonmedical applications. However, efficiency in analysing EEG signals is tremendously difficult to achieve because of three reasons: size of data, extent of computation and poor spatial resolution. The book chapter discusses the Machine Learning based methods employed by the author to classify EEG signals for potentials observed based on varying levels of a subject's attention, measured using a NeuroSky Mindwave Mobile. It reports challenges faced in developing BCIs based on available hardware, signal processing methods and classification methods.

Preface

Cybernetics and Systems Science constitute a fluidly defined academic domain that touches virtually all traditional disciplines, from mathematics, physics and biology to philosophy and the social sciences. Cybernetics is a relatively new area in the field of computer science and computational mathematics while Systems Science is an interdisciplinary research field concerned with the study of general complex systems. The implosion of data and the adaptation of hybrid systems in recently developing "sciences of complexity" have imparted a new edge to Cybernetics and System Science. The present book volume aims to outline recent trends in this domain. The volume is diverse and inclusive in content while maintaining focus on the "systems approach" and practical applications of complex, adaptive and self-regulating systems.

This handbook consists of expository articles written by internationally recognized experts. It is expected to serve as a primer to young researchers in System Sciences. Many of the chapters present a number of open problems and indicate the need for new research to fill the gaps in existing literature. Essentially interdisciplinary in nature, the volume is expected to appeal to a diverse community of young researchers.

We would like to acknowledge the help we received from our colleagues, staff and most importantly, from our family members. We hope the book makes for exciting reading.

Snehanshu Saha
PESIT South Campus, India

Abhyuday Mandal
University of Georgia, USA

Anand Narasimhamurthy
BITS Hyderababd, India

V. Sarasvathi
PESIT South Campus, India

Shivappa Sangam
UGC, India

Section 1
Signal Processing and Communications

Chapter 1
A Survey of Parallel Community Detection Algorithms

Sobin C. C.
IIT Roorkee, India

Vaskar Raychoudhury
IIT Roorkee, India

Snehanshu Saha
PESIT-BSC, India

ABSTRACT

The amount of data generated by online social networks such as Facebook, Twitter, etc., has recently experienced an enormous growth. Extracting useful information such as community structure, from such large networks is very important in many applications. Community is a collection of nodes, having dense internal connections and sparse external connections. Community detection algorithms aim to group nodes into different communities by extracting similarities and social relations between nodes. Although, many community detection algorithms in literature, they are not scalable enough to handle large volumes of data generated by many of the today's big data applications. So, researchers are focusing on developing parallel community detection algorithms, which can handle networks consisting of millions of edges and vertices. In this article, we present a comprehensive survey of parallel community detection algorithms, which is the first ever survey in this domain, although, multiple papers exist in literature related to sequential community detection algorithms.

INTRODUCTION

Today, many applications generate enormous amounts of data. As per the latest statistics (Statista, 2016), Facebook has 1.35 billion daily active users and they share nearly 2.5 million pieces of content in every minute. Similarly, Twitter has 271 million active users, with 300,000 tweets in every minute (ACI, 2016). Analysis of such massive volumes of data helps to uncover much useful information, which can be used for many applications for better decision making. Examples of such applications include, finding similarity in

DOI: 10.4018/978-1-5225-2498-4.ch001

authorship networks, relay selection in delay tolerant networks, identifying users for targeted marketing, etc. Communities can be defined as, densely connected groups of vertices, which share common properties and are sparsely connected to the rest of the nodes in a graph, (Newman, 2003). Community can be used to uncover structural and functional properties of a network. Community detection is a process of identifying communities, (both overlapping and disjoint), in a network. Detecting community structure in large networks is an NP hard problem (Fortunato, 2010). So approximation algorithms are applied to the task of community detection. However, the existing community detection algorithms are sequential in nature and cannot scale to a large extent. Such inefficiency of existing sequential community detection algorithms necessitated the need of developing parallel community detection algorithms, which is the focus of this book chapter.

Community structure exhibits hierarchical properties and hence to represent them dendrograms (Figure 1) are used. Detecting community structure of large network is difficult, not only because of the huge size of the network alone, but also the structure of the large network. For example, Scale-free networks, are networks, in which the degree distribution of the nodes follows a powerlaw distribution, i.e. a few hub nodes have a high degree of connectivity and many of the nodes have a low degree of connectivity. Mathematically, the fraction of the nodes, *P(k)*, in a network, with a degree of *k*, follows a *power law distribution* as follows

$$P(k) \sim k^{-\gamma} \tag{1}$$

Where, $2 < \gamma < 3$. Many networks like collaboration networks, Internet, Airline networks, etc., are *scale-free networks,* which follow a power law distribution. All those networks share a common property that, few nodes have large interconnections to other nodes, where most of the nodes have few interconnections. Although, scale-free networks exhibit community structure naturally, detection procedure is a difficult task. A detailed description of the community and community detection algorithms can be found in the survey by Fortunato (Fortunato, 2010).

Figure 1. Dendrogram representing community structure

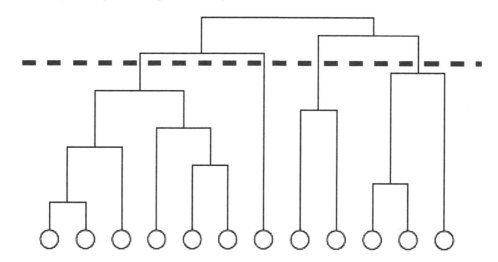

Applications of Community Detection

Community detection algorithms find many applications in real life graphs such as biological networks (Watts, 1998), (Williams, 2000), citation networks (Nascimento, 2003), social networks (Tyler, 2005), mobile healthcare (Yang, 2010), improving performance of WWW (Kleinberg, 1999), supermarket recommendations, ad-hoc networks (Perkins, 2008), etc. In parallel computing, community detection can be used in deciding how to allocate tasks to processors so as to minimize communication overhead between them and enable rapid performance of calculation. Community detection is useful for other reasons too. The central nodes identified in a community module provide function of control and stability. The boundary plays an important role in mediation and lead relationship between different communities. Finally, assuming communities as vertices and inter community edges as the edges between clusters, one can attain coarse grained views of the network. Community detection in various types of networks are listed below.

- **Community Detection in Mobile Social Networks (MoSoN):** MoSoN's are networks formed by humans carrying mobile phones, thereby, forming virtual communities with similar social behavior as inOnline Social Networks (OSNs). MoSoNs combine the advantages of both mobile communications and social networking. Community detection in MoSoNs is challenging because of the time varying nature of the network. As nodes are mobile and connection changes over time, existing static community detection techniques cannot be directly applied on mobile social networks.

- **Community Detection in Evolving Networks:** Many community detection are there in static networks, but few exisits for evolving networks. Complex networks evolve over time, which can be represented using graphs, adding or deleting nodes over time. E.g., in Facebook 700,000 new users added every day and some of the users are deactivating their accounts too. An important feature of complex networks is that they are naturally composed of a group of nodes that are more densely connected with others in the same group, than the rest of the network. Those desely connected node groups are called communities. Time evolving version of social networks is called dynamic networks. Examples include network traffic data, bibliographic data, etc. Clustering is the process of grouping similar objects and clustering for network nodes form communities. A typical approach for evolving networks consists of representing the state of the system at different time stamps so that communities can be identified independently at each time stamp and studied over time. E.g., evolution of graphs can be partitioned into different communities in two different time stamps t_1 and t_2, where $t_2 > t_1$,.Each community of time stamp t_1 may either remains same, disappear, split into sub communities or merge with other communities. Tracking evolution of a given community over time requires clustering algorithm that produces stable clusters, which do not significantly change under very small changes of input data. Most of the existing community detection algorithms change drastically if input is modified.

- **Community Detection in Dynamic Heterogeneous Information Networks:** Information networks are various data/information objects such as individual agents, groups or components which are interconnected or interact with each other to form numerous, large, interconnected and sophisticated networks. Heterogeneous networks are multi-typed networks and the community detection in such networks aims to find the structure of communities with the evolution of time. E.g., in case of bibliographic networks, authors, venues, terms and papers can be different types of objects.

- **Community Detection in Mobile Healthcare:** Mobile healthcare have various applications ranging from remote health monitoring, diagnostic imaging and vaccination for preventing propagation of diseases, etc. Some of theresearchers (Zhang, 2012) exploit social characteristics with the help of community detection algorithms to find out the target vaccination group, vaccination on such a group prevents spreading of diseases based on social relationship details extracted from mobile phone records.
- **Community Detection in Delay Tolerant Networks (DTNs):** Community detection algorithms can be used for designing routing algorithms for DTNs. Detecting community structure helps to select an intelligent relay node (having high centrality or betweenness,etc.) for the destination of a message, so that the message delivery rate can be improved. Bubble Rap (Hui, 2011) is one of the DTN routing algorithms, which use community detection algorithm to partition the network and identifying the social relationships among the nodes, to select the relay nodes for message routing.
- **Community Detection in Biological Networks:** In a biological network, nodes represents biological units such as genes, proteins, and edges represent interaction among genes such as gene flow or social interactions.Although community structure, is ubiquitary in biological networks, detecting community structure from such networks is a difficult task.

Methods of Community Detection

There are various methods applied for community detection, some of them are listed below.

- **Graph Partitioning:** Graph partitioning is the process of dividing the vertices of a graph into equal number of partitions, so that the interconnecting edges are minimized. The graph partitioning is an important task in divide and conquer algorithms, parallel algorithms, and distributes systems, etc. The graph partitioning problem is an NP-complete problem and there are many approximation algorithms exists in literature for finding quality partitions. Initially the graph is divided into a predetermined number of partitions which may not be known in a real time execution. It iteratively swaps the subset of nodes between partitions to optimize the benefit function. The method is not an optimal method for community detection as the number of partitions cannot be predetermined.
- **Hierarchical Clustering:**Hierarchial clustering is often exhibited by social networks, it aims at identifying groups of vertices with high similarity and does not require pre-determined knowledge of the number of clusters. Hierarchial clustering can be further classified as:
  - **Agglomerative Algorithms:** In case of agglomerative algorithms, single-node-clusters, merge iteratively in a bottom up manner based on high similarity.
  - **Divisive Algorithms:** In divisive algorithms, clusters are iteratively split on the basis of low similarity.
- **Partitional Clustering:** The number of clusters is predetermined. They are assigned as points and the distance between the points determine the measure of dissimilarity between the clusters.

Community detection is closely related to graph partitioning. Graph partitioning is a process of dividing the given graph into a given number of partitions, with minimal edges between partitions. The number and size of the partitions are known in advance in case of graph partitioning. Although plenty of good parallel graph partitioning algorithms exist in literature, only few parallel algorithms exist for community detection. This is because of the chances for parallelization is very less on existing sequential algorithms and it is not scalable with respect to the number of threads or data size. Parallel approaches to community detection algorithms will improve the efficiency as well as addressing the issue of scalability.

Quality Metrics for Community

In order to identify whether the communities formed are good or bad and to assess the quality of the partitions formed, many quality metrics are used. The most commonly used ones are summarized below.

- **Modularity**: The metric modularity is proposed by Newman and Girvan (Newman, 2003), which is based on the idea that random graph, or null model is not expected of community structure and hence comparing the density of edges in the original and their expectation to provide information about the partitions. Null model is defined as a graphical model in which the edges are randomly re-wired and manipulated, but the in degree and out degree of the structure is maintained. The modularity metric is calculated using the equation (2), where the summation occurs over all pairs of vertices, A_{ij} is the adjacency matrix, P_{ij} represents the expected number of edges between vertices i & j in the null model. δ equals to 1 (one) if i and j are in the same community, else it is 0 (zero).

$$Q = \frac{1}{2m} \sum_{ij} (A_{ij} - P_{ij}) \delta(C_i, C_j) \qquad (2)$$

- **Modularity Density:** The metric modularity density is an optimization over modularity metric to overcome its natural limitations, such as the tendency of splitting large communities into smaller communities and merging smaller communities, which are less than a threshold to large communities. The modularity density is defined in equation (3). E_{in} is the sum of weights of edges between nodes in the community c_i and E_{in} is the sum of weights of edges from nodes outside the community, c_i.

$$Q_D = \sum_{c_i \in C} \frac{2(E_{in} - E_{out})}{c_i} \qquad (3)$$

- **Normalized Mutual Information:** The metric Normalized Mutual Information (NMI) is an information theoretic quality metric, which measures the similarity between two partitions. NMI metric is defined in equation (4), where H is the entropy function and I is the mutual information.

$$NMI(C_1, C_2) = \frac{2I(C_1, C_2)}{H(C_1) + H(C_2)} \qquad (4)$$

Figure 2. Timeline of existing surveyson community detection algorithms

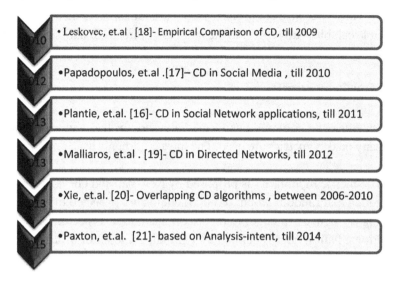

In this section, we have discussed about the community detection methods, applications and quality metrics for detected community structure. Now we will discuss about the existing taxonomies of community detection in literature in next section.

EXISTING COMMUNITY DETECTION TAXONOMIES

In this section, weillustrate the existing taxonomies on sequential Community Detection (CD) algorithms in literature. As a detailed description about the community structure and previous taxonomies were covered in the in the survey by Fortunato (Fortunato, 2010), we shall address some of the latest surveys (Figure 2), on existing sequentialcommunity detection algorithms in the literature.

Plantie, et.al. (2013), proposed a survey of community detection in the area of social network applications. The authors have classified the community detection algorithms based on semantics and type of input,which are published till 2011. They have also listed about community evaluation techniques, which is important in the area of social data mining. Although authors listed the community detection methods using a different classification (based on types of input and output data), the algorithms listed are sequential in nature. Papadopoulos, et.al. (2012), also proposed a survey of community detection in the context of social media and provide a taxonomy for classifying existing community detection algorithms based on methodological principles. The survey also analyzed the performance of existing algorithms in terms of computational complexity and memory requirements. The time span of the survey was till 2010.

Leskovec, et.al. (2010) have classified community detection algorithms, which are published till 2009, based on their performance and the biases of the identified clusters. They have evaluated common objective functions used for identifying the quality of the community structure and analyzed different approximation algorithms which are used for optimizing those objective functions. Malliaros, et.al. (2013) surveyed community clustering and community detection methods in Directed Networks based on methodological principles of the clustering algorithms and the quality of a the cluster in the directed network. The authors have also listed methods for evaluating the resultant graph clusters and some new application domains of directed networks. The time span of the papers covered in the survey was till 2012.

Xie, et.al. (2013), have proposed a survey about fourteen overlapping community detection algorithms, which are published till 2012. Apart from classifying the algorithms, the authors also proposed a framework for analyzingcapabilities of those algorithm to detect overlapping nodes. Such node-level evaluation exposed the issues of under-detection and over-detection, which is an important aspect in the design of efficient community detection algorithms. A recent survey of community detection algorithms was proposed by Paxton, et.al. (2013), based on analysis-intent. The existing community detection algorithms were analyzed into category-based techniques and event based-techniques

Although a number of quality survey papers (listed above) have appeared in literature covering sequential community detection algorithms, there is no survey available for parallel community detection algorithms. So, in this paper, we have surveyed the existing parallel community detection algorithms in the literature based on different classifications, which will help future researchers in their endeavors to design new parallel community detection algorithms.

A NOVEL TAXONOMY OF PARALLEL COMMUNITY DETECTION

In the study of existing parallel algorithms for community detection in large-scale networks, we found that the majority of the algorithms have parallelized a small set of sequential community detection algorithms (henceforth called core algorithms) and differ by adopting different computation and communication models. Standard computation models (hardware platform) are either CPU-based or GPU-based and communication between those computational units is achieved either through shared memory model or through message passing primitives. Researchers while designing a parallel community detection algorithm have to choose from the following three orthogonal design dimensions, the ideal core algorithm, an appropriate computation model, and the perfect communication model (Figure 3).

Figure 3. Design dimensions of parallel community detection algorithms

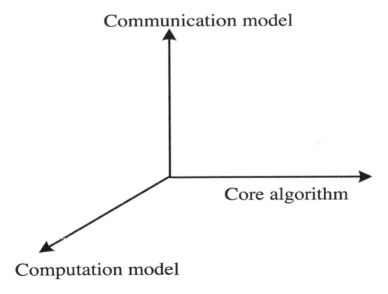

Figure 4. Classification of parallel community detection algorithms

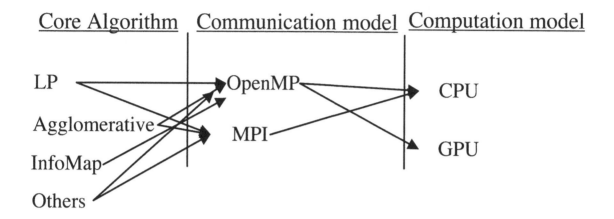

As we have mentioned in the previous section, plenty of survey papers are available covering community detection in various aspects like social media (Papadopoulos, 2012), (Plantie, 2013) and overlapping communities (Xie, 2013), etc. But all the surveys cover sequential community detection algorithms. In this paper a novel taxonomy of parallel community detection algorithms is proposed based on three design dimensions: (1) core algorithm, (2) communication model, and (3) computation model. The core algorithm defines which sequential algorithm is used for parallelization.Communication model defines how different modules of the algorithm communicate with each other in a parallel environment. Finally, computation model decides whether the algorithm is implemented on CPU or GPU.

From Figure 4, it can be inferred that label propagation algorithm can be parallelized using either OpenMP or MPI on both compuatation models. At present, InfoMap algorithm is found to be parallelized using OpenMP in CPU. Louvian method is parallelized using both OpenMP and MPI, but no implementation could be found in literature, other than on CPU.

Classification Based on Core Algorithm

Based on which sequential algorithms are used to generate the parallelized version, the algorithms can be classified into following categories:

- **Label Propagation Method:** In label propagation, nodes are assigned to a label initially and later on, they adopt the most frequent labels in the particular community.
- **Agglomerative Method:** Following a greedy approach, individual vertices form singleton communities and merge among themselves in a *bottom-up* manner to form clusters. Louvain is one of such agglomerative method.
- **InfoMap Algorithm:** InfoMapis a flow-based community detection method, which optimizes the information theoretic objective functions using map equations.

Now we shall discuss about each of the above sequential core algorithms in detail.

Figure 5. Label propagation
(Raghavan, 2007)

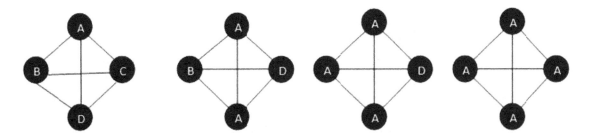

Label Propagation

Raghavan, et al. (2007) have proposed a sequential local community detection algorithm called as *Label Propagation* (LP). Unlike other algorithms in the field of large scale community structures, label propagation, requires no prior information such as size or number of communities. It is a simple and time efficient iterative process, including local updates at each node. The property of local updates and avoidance of global variables make label propagation algorithm easier to parallelize. Initially, every node in the graph is considered as singleton communities and is uniquely labelled. In the subsequent iterations, all the nodes form a list of labels from all neighboring nodes in the community sequentially storing them in a histogram which later provides the frequency of labels. A node takes up the label of the community under which maximum number of its neighbors are included. In case of more than such communities, ties are broken arbitrarily. During initial iterations the method forms small clusters under the same label. These clusters on further iterations speedup and acquire more nodes to their group. Different communities compete for members on reaching borders between them. The algorithm terminates when every community converges and gets satisfied with the labels assigned to them. Figure 5, explains the execution of the algorithm. Initially, all the vertices are of different labels (on the left in the figure) and later on each iteration, each vertex changes the label based on the label of majority of neighbors and finally converges to a community of single label (rightmost in the figure).

Label propagation exhibits a limitation that when the graph structure tends to be bipartite the nodes oscillate between the groups and continuously change labels. The termination of the algorithm usually occurs when there is no change in label of nodes. But with oscillation, termination tends to be problematic. In such cases the iterative process is broken when the nodes attain the label having large number of communities.

Agglomerative Method

Agglomerative methods are hierarchical techniques, which operate in a greedy fashion. In this approach, individual vertices or nodes get progressively merged into clusters, in a bottom-up manner. Initially, every vertex forms its own community and then combines with each other to form clustering of very high modularity in a small amount of time. The metric modularity determines the quality of cluster produced. Higher modularity indicates quality clustering. Modularity may be generally considered as a function of edge weights. Agglomerative methods are designed with a target of either maximizing modularity or minimizing conductance.

Figure 6. Steps involved in Louvain algorithm
(Blondel, 2008)

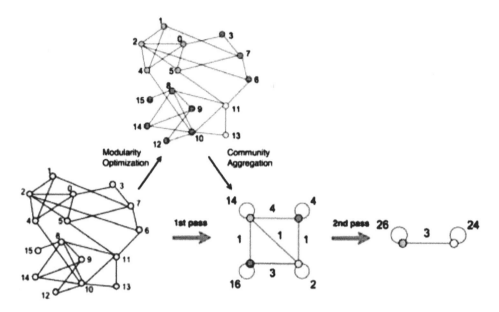

Louvain method, proposed by Blondel, et al. (2008), is an example of such an agglomerative method based on modularity maximization. Modularity is a metric used for measuring the quality of the detected communities. Initially, each vertex forms its own community. The algorithm consists of two phases, with repeated iterations. In the first phase, all the vertices are examined in linear and pre-defined order. In each iteration, the vertices check for gain in modularity while migrating to its neighboring community. If so, the vertices move to the neighboring community and it is assigned under that community. Else, its community remains unchanged. Every iteration in the first phase, checks for a gain in modularity and algorithm terminates when the gain is negligible, i.e. a local maximum modularity is achieved. Once, the first phase is finished, all the detected communities are collapsed into meta-vertices to form a new graph. A self-looping edge is placed in the meta-vertex, with weight as the sum of edge weights of the vertices within the community. Also the edges are placed between meta-vertices with weights equal to the sum of edge weights between two communities. Then the first phase of the algorithm is executed again. The process is continued until maximum modularity value is achieved. The steps involved in Louvain algorithm is illustrated in Figure 6.

The differences between agglomerative and Louvain algorithms are that

- In case of agglomerative techniques, each of the n vertices is considered as a separate community, whereas Louvain considers maximum increase in modularity among nodes and its neighbors.
- Instead of greedy heuristics in case of agglomerative methods, a vertex is reassigned to other community based on the increase in modularity.

Figure 7. Community detection as communication process
(Rosvall, 2007)

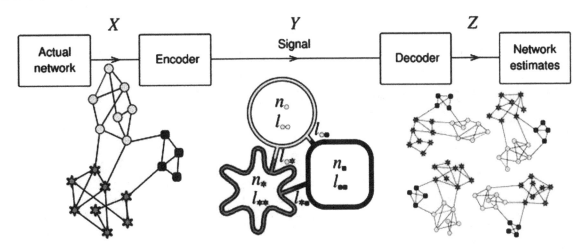

InfoMap Algorithm

Rosvall, et. al. (2007) proposed InfoMap, which is a fast flow based community detection algorithm based on information-theoretic approach. The objective of community detection is to identify the structure of large networks. Using information-theoretic concept, community detection is mapped to finding an efficient compression structure for the network (as in Figure 7). InfoMap uses the concept of map equations and flow is modeled based on a random walk approach similar to page rank. The algorithm is sequential in nature and cannot exploit the advantage of multi-core processing in modern computers. It will be able to process a graph of 5 million vertices and 70 million edges in 45 minutes only.

Classification Based on Communication Model

According to the underlying memory architecture employed in the implementation, the parallel algorithms can be classified as:

- **Shared Memory Based:** Data sharing between the methods occur in the form of shared memory.
- **Distributed Memory Based Using Message Passing:** The algorithms executing in parallel, share data and result asynchronously, i.e. computes data and instructions in their respective threads and communicate with each other through Message Passing Interfaces (MPIs).

Classification Based on Computation Model

Based on whether the algorithm is targeted for implementation in CPU or GPU various parallel algorithms proposed may be classified as:

- **CPU Based:** Certain algorithms are executed in multi-core CPUs which can handle only few software threads at a time.

Figure 8. Classification of parallel community detection algorithms

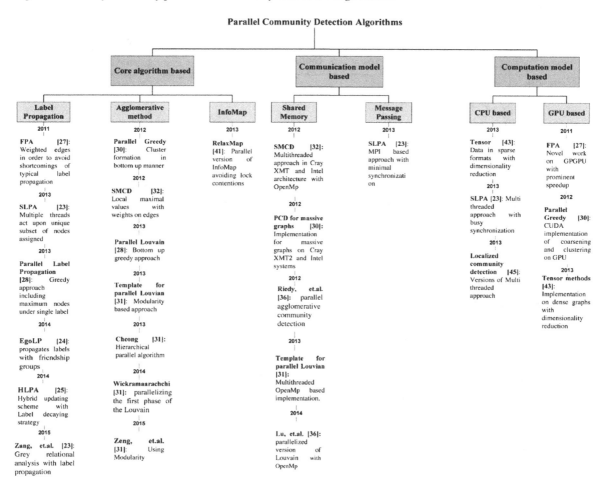

- **GPU Based:** A number of algorithms exploit the capability of the GPU, comprising hundreds of cores, which is able to handle thousands of threads simultaneously.

PARALLEL COMMUNITY DETECTION ALGORITHMS

In this section, we shall discuss the existing parallel community detection algorithms based on the taxonomy (Figure 4).

Core Algorithm Based

In this section we discuss the parallel community detection algorithms based on which sequential algorithm is used for parallelization.

Table 1. Summary of label propagation based parallel algorithms

Algorithm	Remarks
SPLA (Kuzman, Shah & Szymanski, 2013)	MPI-based parallel programming approach
EgoLP (Buzun et al., 2014)	Propagating labels through the network with the help of friendship groups of individual users
HLPA (Wang, Qian, & Wang, 2015)	Hybrid updating scheme,Label decaying strategy
Zhang, et.al. (2015)	Grey relational analysis with label propagation
Soman, et al. (2011)	Edge weights on label propagation algorithm
Parallel Label Propagation (Staudt & Meyerhenke, 2013)	Greedy approach and dominant label in the neighborhood is selected, instead of most frequent label

Parallel Algorithms Based on Label Propagation

A summary of parallel community detection algorithms, which use label propagation as the core sequential algorithm is listed in Table 1.

Kuzmin, et. al. (2013), proposed a parallel overlapping community detection algorithm,called as, Speaker-Listener Label Propagation (SPLA), which parallelizes a variant of label propagation algorithm. Existing clustering algorithm faces problems to extend to parallel versions because of data sharing and increase in data size. Authors uses Message Passing Interface(MPI) based parallel programming approach, in which each processor processes its own data chunk and sends/receives data asynchronously. As a result, increase in data size is not an issue. The network is partitioned into sub-networks. Each thread performs label propagation on the ideally partitioned subset of nodes assigned to it. During the initial phase, each thread receives the subset of nodes assigned to it. A dependency array is formed which provides the information, whether other threads in the system are processed the neighbors of the node in concern. The thread performs label propagation step for every node and new labels are added to the list that it maintains. The process continues with further iterations.The authors also proposed multi-threaded version of SLPA with busy waiting and synchronization. The MPI was implemented on a Blue Green parallel machine and evaluated performance with 1,204 processors.

Buzun, et.al. (2014), have developed, *EgoLP*, a fast community detection algorithm for a billion node social network. The proposed EgoLP method extracts the communities from large social network by propagating labels through the network with the help of friendship groups of the individual users. Initially, each user forms ego-network with their friends or followers and initialize the community labels and start propagating the labels based on predefined interaction rules. Finally, communities are post-processed to remove unstable communities.

HLPA (Wang, 2015), is a hybrid label propagation algorithm for community detection in large-scale networks, which is implemented inthe *Dpark* clustering computing framework. The HLPA algorithm consists of

- **Hybrid Updating Scheme:** Labels are propagated from one side to another, until reach the maximum iteration
- **Label Decaying Strategy:** Is used for preventing monster (more than half of the nodes in the network) and groups of small communities

- Different initialization methods to improve the quality of the detected communities on directed, undirected and bipartite networks.

Zhang, et.al. (2015), proposed a parallel algorithm for detecting overlapping communities by integrating grey relational analysis with label propagation. Overlapping communities are detected by incorporating each vertex with more than one label. With the help of grey relational analysis, the similarity among vertices is computed and using MapReduce, labels are propagated in parallel.

Soman, et al. (2011) have used weights on edges in order to avoid the shortcomings in a typical label propagation algorithm. In order to implement label propagation on the GPGPU based system, different components of the algorithm were mapped into a known data parallel algorithm. Sorting techniques on an array provided the label with maximum weight in the neighborhood. Edge weight becomes the deciding factor in the algorithm, when an edge point in the community structure is considered. The selection of edge weights is done in accordance with the topological structure of the community. The algorithm was able to detect communities for the large data sets like Wiki (100 million edges) and R-MAT(10-40 million edges). The proposed algorithm scales with number of threads also the data size and of near to linear time complexity as O (m (k+d)).

Parallel Label Propagation (Staudt, 2013) is a greedy approach which includes the maximum number of vertices under a particular label. It is suitable for generating locally optimal communities. Although the version may propagate labels well for dense communities it is unlikely to spread across narrow communities.

Parallel Algorithms Based on Agglomerative Method

Although there are many agglomerative community detection algorithms exist in literature, Louvain algorithm is most commonly used as the core sequential algorithm to parallelize. The existing parallel agglomerative community detection algorithms are listed in Table 2.

In the graph coarsening method proposed by Auer, et al. (2012), cluster formulation follow agglomerative techniques in a bottom up manner. In accordance with the algorithm, modularity is initialized to a lower limit. As the method operates in a bottom up fashion, vertices get added to form clusters in loops after checking the change in modularity. Decrease in modularity prompts the function to discard the particular vertex. The authors have proposed a fine grained shared memory parallel graph clustering algorithm and based on that a parallel agglomerative heuristic was developed on both CPU and GPU, which produced a modularity of 0.996 for 14 million vertices and 17 million edges. The algorithm is a fast greedy (bottom-up) modularity maximization on weighted undirected graphs and was scalable with the number of processors. The basic idea is that each vertex is considered as a single separate cluster and merge progressively to increase the modularity. The authors pointed out that the development of local refinement method for clustering, which scales with the number of available processing cores as an open problem.

The parallel version of the Louvain method (Bhowmick, 2013) improved upon agglomerative techniques in the following fronts:

- In case of agglomerative techniques, each of *n* vertices is considered as a separate community, whereas Louvain considers maximum increase in modularity among nodes and its neighbors.

Table 2. Summary of agglomerative parallel algorithms

Algorithm	Remarks
Auer, et al. (Auer & Bisseling, 2012)	Fine grained shared memory parallel graph clustering algorithm
Parallel Louvain method (Bhowmick & Srinivasan, 2013)	Identified the areas in Louvain to paralyze
Scalable Multithreaded Community Detection (Riedy, Bader & Meyerhenke, 2012)	Agglomerative heuristics to achieve local maximum without the intention of an approximate global value
Zeng, et.al. (2015)	Clustering quality is improved by considering ghost vertices for local clustering
Cheong, et.al. (2013)	Hierarchical parallel community detection algorithm
Wickramaarachchi, et al. (2014)	Parallelizing the first phase of the Louvain method
Lu, et al. (2015)	Parallel heuristics for implementing a parallel version of Louvain
Riedy, et. al. (2011)	Greedy approach is used for computing a weighted maximal matching
Que, e.t al. (2013)	Parallel version of the Louvain using Fibonacci hashing techniques

Thus, in each iteration Louvain algorithm achieved a logarithmic decrease instead of a linear one in combining communities together.

- Reassignment of vertices to other communities, according to modularity rather than the greedy approach followed.
- Louvain algorithm exhibits hierarchical property. Subsequent iterations make particular vertices within communities to turn into super-vertices thereby adding more vertices into their communities.

The authors identified the areas of Louvain algorithm which can be parallelized, divided the process into two phases and tested the results using LFR benchmarks. The algorithm is highly scalable and thus reduces the execution time as the amount of processing units increase.Scalable Multithreaded Community Detection (Riedy, 2012) uses agglomerative heuristics to achieve local maximum without the intention of an approximate global value. The algorithm associates positive scores with the edges and computes a weighted maximal matching with those scores. The matched communities are refined to form a community graph. The algorithm terminates when there exist no edges with a positive score. Scores tend to maximize modularity reflecting how edge scores are influenced by the idea of edge forming communities. The algorithm was implemented inthe Cray XMT architecture together with Intel based machines with OpenMP. The algorithm is capable of handling graphs up to 105 million vertices and 33 million edges.The data set used was R-MAT and Live journal friendship network. Staud, et al. (2013) have also proposed an agglomerative heuristic algorithm for community formation in a bottom up greedy approach.

Zeng, et.al. (2015) proposed a parallel community detection algorithm based on Louvain method, which uses modularity as a metric for extracting community structures from large-scale graphs. The algorithm was implemented on distributed memory architecture and the clustering quality is improved by considering ghost vertices for local clustering. The authors have also studied the relation between graph structure property and clustering quality. The proposed algorithm was tested on real-datasets, with up to 16,384 cores.

A hicrarchical parallel community detection algorithm based on Louvain method have been proposed by Cheong, et.al. (2013). The proposed algorithm is implemented on both single and multiple GPU's and applied three levels of parallelism in Louvain method. In the highest level, the network is partitioned into a set of sub-networks and removed links (links join across nodes in different sub-networks) and Louvain method is applied. Now, the resulting networks are combined into a single network with the removed links and again Louvain method is applied to get the community structure.

Wickramaarachchi, et. al. (2014) proposed a distributed parallel community detection algorithm by parallelizing the first phase of the Louvain community detection algorithm. Parallel METIS partitioner is used for performing initial graph clustering. Each of the MPI process picks one of the partitions and run the first iteration of the Louvain algorithm while ignoring the cross partition edges. The resulting graphs are re-numbered and sent to a master process, which will consider the cross partition edges and merges the intermediate graphs into a single graph and further iterations of Louvain algorithm are applied. The algorithm was evaluated on MPI setup with 128 parallel processors. Experiments on random graphs up to 16 million vertices show an increase in speedup up to 5 times to that of the sequential Louvain algorithm.

Lu, et. al. (2014) proposed parallelized version of Louvain method implemented using OpenMP multi-threading. The authors have proposed parallel heuristics for implementing a parallel version of Louvain algorithm such as vertex coloring, vertex following heuristic and maximum label heuristic. Vertex coloring heuristic makes sure that the vertex of the same colors are processed in parallel and prevents processing of adjacent vertices. In case of vertex following heuristic a vertex with a single neighbor, follow the neighbor's community before as part of pre-processing. The minimum vertex label heuristic ensures that if a vertex V is having multiple neighbor communities with maximum modularity gain, then the neighbor vertex having minimum label is selected as a destination community of the vertex V. The above mentioned heuristics are applied for parallelizing the sequential Louvain algorithm. Experiments on real world graphs show that the parallel version achieves speed up to 8 times using 32 threads compared to the sequential algorithm.

Riedy, et. al. (2012) proposed a parallel agglomerative community detection algorithm similar to the sequential algorithm proposed by Clauset, et. al. (2004). The algorithm is able to perform community detection on Intel E7-8870 based server under 500 seconds. The agglomerative community detection algorithms start with unique community for each vertex and communities are merged based on either maximizing modularity or minimizing conductance. The authors considered local optimization criteria for converting disjoint graph partitions into connected communities. As a result community graph is generated which contains vertices, edges and weights are assigned to edges. A positive score is assigned to each edge if it is not already have. A greedy approach is used for computing a weighted maximal matching using the scores. Finally, matched communities were merged into a new community graph. Test set used was UK-2007-05 graph which consists of 105 million vertices and 3.3 billion edges.

Que, e.t al. (2013) proposed a parallel version of the Louvain algorithm for distributed memory systems using Fibonacci hashing techniques. In distributed systems, the changes made at specific vertices are not available to other vertices. The change in connectivity and community structure becomes unavailable for other nodes in the system. Thus, a serial dependence between vertex labels and iterations are performed. The challenges were identified as:

- Calculating modularity gain in the absence of shared memory
- Convergence,as vertices may use obsolete community structure data in a parallel environment.

Parallel Algorithms Based on InfoMap

Bae, et. al. (2013) proposed RelaxMap, a parallel version of existing flow based serial algorithm InfoMap. In addition to providing similar convergence patterns and community structures as the serial algorithm InfoMap, RelaxMap exploits multi-core processor capabilities by relaxing consistency constraints Authors claims that RelaxMap achieves efficiency up to 70 percent up to 12 cores over the sequential algorithm. In Relaxmap, map equations used in InfoMap are parallelized and lock contention was reduced. Only global locking was applied to avoid the inconsistency among the shared states. A basic lock-free parallel algorithm has the drawback that it causes the vertices to make cyclical movements and thus data may converge early. RelaxMap is based on the assumption that real network data being sparse, the vertices are unlikely to influence each other and hence the converging problem was minimized although not totally resolved.

The clustering quality analysis based on Normalized Mutual Information (NMI) provides the following conclusion. The sequential algorithm InfoMap and the parallel counterparts: RelaxMap-1(single thread) and RelaxMap-8 (8 threads) provide clustering of equivalent NMI. However the analysis based on Minimum Description Length (MDL), low MDL value provide better quality, reveals RelaxMap-1 similar to InfoMap and RelaxMap-8 the better one. Similarly, the performance analysis shows that RelaxMap-1 and InfoMap converge in the same number of iterations with similar running times, whereas RelaxMap-8 converges faster and is about 4 to 5 times faster than the others.

We have provided a summary of comparison of parallel community detection algorithms based on the design dimensions in Table 3.

Communication Model Based

In this section, we will discuss the parallel community detection algorithm based on underlying memory architecture.

Shared Memory Based

Several algorithms were formulated based on shared memory (OpenMP based) over Message passing Interface. Directive based parallelization is provided for multiple CPU cores in an OpenMP based algorithm. Bae, et al. (2013), Bhowmick, et al. (2013), Lasalle, et al. (2013), Riedy et al. (2012), Riedy, et al. (2012) proposed algorithms which utilize the faster capability of OpenMP based implementation.

Message Passing Based

In case of Message Passing *Interface* (MPI) based algorithms, each node has its own memory and unable to access other node's memory. It is a very general and asynchronous based approach implemented in distributed memory clusters. The parallel version of Speaker-Listener Label Propagation algorithm (SLPA) (Kuzmin, 2013) is built upon MPI method. A parallel toolkit has been proposed in (Chen, 2014) for measuring the performance of community quality metrics (see Section 1.3).

Table 3. Comparison of parallel community detection algorithms based on design dimensions

Algorithm	Core algorithm				Communication model		Implementation model		Remarks
	LP	Louvain	InfoMap	Others	OpenMP	MPI	CPU	GPU	
[30]		✓			✓			✓	Graph coarsening in bottom up manner
[41]			✓		✓		✓		Map equations are parallelized
[31]		✓			✓		✓		Identified the areas in Louvain to paralyze
[43]				✓	✓		✓	✓	Mixed Membership Stochastic Model (MMSB)
[23]	✓				✓	✓	✓		MPI, Multi-threading
[24]	✓						✓		Propagating labels through the network
[25]	✓						✓		Hybrid updating scheme,Label decaying strategy
[26]	✓						✓		Grey relational analysis with label propagation
[44]				✓	✓		✓		Multiple approaches for parallelizing graph partitioning techniques
[39]		✓				✓	✓		Hashing scheme for data representation and distribution.
[32]		✓			✓		✓		Agglomerative heuristics to achieve local maximum
[33]		✓			✓		✓		Clustering quality is improved by considering ghost vertices for local clustering
[34]		✓						✓	Hierarchical parallel community detection algorithm
[39]		✓			✓		✓		Parallel version of the Louvain using Fibonacci hashing techniques
[37]		✓			✓		✓		Parallel agglomerative, similar to the sequential algorithm proposed by Clauset [38]
[27]	✓				✓			✓	Edge weights, weighted label propagation, multi-core
[28]	✓	✓			✓		✓		Greedy, dominant label in the neighborhood is selected, instead of most frequent label
[47]				✓		✓	✓		Based on propinquity metric,a measure of probable proximity between nodes in a community structure
[35]		✓				✓	✓		Paralyzing the first phase of the Louvain community detection algorithm
[36]		✓			✓		✓		Parallel heuristics such as vertex coloring, vertex following heuristic and maximum label heuristic

Computation Model Based

In this section, the parallel community detection algorithms are classified based on the type of processing unit used for implementation

CPU Implementation

The need for a CPU based implementation arises from the fact that GPU based implementations suffers memory limitations while operating on large data sets. The tensor method proposed by Huang et al. (2013), executed in CPU Dual 8-core Xeon @ 2.0 GHz, data is manipulated in sparse formats consisting of sparse multiplication. In addition, by including randomized methods for dimensionality reduction the authors achieved tremendous gains in terms of running time and memory required for large datasets.

The parallel version of Speaker-Listener Label Propagation algorithm (SLPA) (Kuzmin, 2013) implemented in the CPU is a multi-threaded approach with busy synchronization. The entire network is partitioned into sub networks and assigned to threads. The threads perform label propagation in the subset of nodes assigned to it. Although the partitioning may be done in several ways, the authors suggest that best partitioning results in every thread executing the same amount of time for every node.

Kuzmin, et al. (2013), have proposed three types of implementation based on multi-threading approach. Along with the default multi-threading approach, a single thread approach to analyze non-multi-threaded environment. A multi-threaded approach in which the way nodes form communities differ from the usual was also experimented.

GPU Implementation

In order to overcome the shortcoming to execute a large number of threads simultaneously by a CPU, researchers and designers used GPUs and modeled a number of parallel community detection algorithms.

Graph coarsening and clustering algorithms (Auer, 2012) mainly intended on GPU compares the experimental results of the algorithm on both GPU and CPU. The authors have proposed graph coarsening and clustering algorithm in order to generate a fast and greedy heuristic that maximizes modularity on weighted graphs. Graph coarsening algorithm scaled well with the number of GPUs. It is inferred from the execution of clustering algorithm on both CPU and GPU that the quality of clusters generated by the CPU is much higher than those of the GPU. The GPU version considers all edges for matching irrespective of whether they increase or decrease modularity whereas the CPU version adds only those edges resulting in an increase in modularity. The parallel agglomerative heuristic generated a modularity of 0.996 for 14 million vertices and 17 million edges in about 4.6 seconds.

The algorithm proposed by Soman, et al. (2011) is scalable with a number of GPUs and multi-core architectures and is claimed to be the first and novel work implemented on GPGPUs which provide a large number of threads and cores to implement parallelism. With optimization in algorithm targeted for GPGPU, Algorithms targeted for GPUs tend to be data parallel and hence involve delay in memory read operations. The proposed algorithm following label propagation method provides such delays while reading the labels assigned to neighbors of a particular node. The delay is hidden in the computation involved in determining the dominant label. For a dataset of 1M nodes and 20M edges the algorithm was found to take about 15 seconds to run, whereas for a dataset of 1M nodes and 40M edges it took around 28 seconds. The authors also mention a speedup factor of 8 in comparison with the Power6 processor. Online tensor methods (Huang, 2013) utilize GPU architecture for the dense implementation of their algorithm on dense graphs such as Facebook. Since the method intended is highly parallel, GPUs prove to be ideal with large number of cores although they have less memory space. Code optimization and design of data structures overcome. The GPU based implementation adopts dimensionality reduction which involves the implicit conversion of an observed tensor into its lower dimension.

MISCELLANEOUS

Certain parallel community detection algorithms cannot be directly classified into the categories mentioned so far. Therefore, they need to be mentioned under the unique flag and are gathered under miscellaneous section.

- **Tensor-Based Methods:** In this approach, decomposition or reduction process of tensors, formed from observed data is carried out and inferences collected.
- **Propinquity Based Methods:** In this method, several iterations are performed based on propinquity dynamics to formulate a converged community structure.

Tensor Based Method

Huang, et al, (2013) proposed a probabilistic Mixed Membership Stochastic Model (MMSB) for detecting hidden overlapping communities both with the GPU and CPU based implementations. In this model, tensors were estimated from sub graphs and uses linear algebraic operations (SVD) with iterative stochastic gradient descent method for tensor decomposition.

The authors presented an approach by deploying of tensor decomposition methods which in turn comprises two stages. The GPU based implementation adopts dimensionality reduction which involves the implicit conversion of an observed tensor into its lower dimension. This implementation is highly parallel as GPUs contain a large number of cores. The need for CPU based implementation arises from the fact that GPU based implementations suffers memory limitations while operating on large data sets. The approach was implemented on large synthetic and real datasets with a high accuracy rate and the authors also developed error score based hypothesis testing methodology with p-values and false discovery rates which can be applied upon availability of ground truth communities. The dataset, DBLP graph, used was of 1 million nodes and 16 million edges. Finally, the authors conclude that the GPU based implementations were ideal for dense graphs like Facebook and CPU based implementations were suitable for sparse graphs containing large number of nodes such as Yelp and DBLP.

Propinquity Based Method

Propinquity is a term which is used to describe closeness between people in a given community dataset. It provides us with a measure of probable proximity between nodes in a community structure. Several iterations of reinforcement, between the closely related vertices based on propinquity measure; result in a converged community structure. A different post processing and employment of calculating propinquity values provide efficient results. Zhang, et al. (2009) proposed an algorithm based on propinquity dynamics.

The main problem in community detection is to divide the dataset or graph into sub partitions such that data parallelism may be applied. But the community structure of the graph tends to be overlapping in nature. The Propinquity dynamics algorithm was also able to detect overlapping community structure with an additional post processing procedure. It involves two measures of closeness, which are lsited below.

- **Cutting Threshold:** Determining whether an existing edge should be removed from the structure and
- **Emerging Threshold:** Determining whether a new edge should be added between vertices, optimizing the community structure.

The algorithm was also able to detect overlapping community structure with an additional post processing procedure. The parallel implementation of the algorithm uses the Bulk Synchronous Parallel model (BSP), which make use of data parallelism. Although several existing community detection algorithms exist based on optimizing the objective function, only few techniques were naturally able to generate community structure through heuristics. The proposed technique belongs to such a category. The algorithm has a complexity of O (mk), where m is the number of nodes and k is the number of iterations. The data set used was Wiki pages of 2 million vertices and 11M edges.

OPEN PROBLEMS

In previous sections, we have discussed about the state-of-the art of parallel community detection algorithms. We have listed below some of the open problems that exist in this area, for the benefit of future researchers.

- **Increasing Parallelization Efficiency:** In a multithreaded program, the mode of communication between threads needs to be improved as it may affect the parallel efficiency of the algorithm. Also for reducing lock contention, fine-grained locking structures need to be considered.
- **Merging Different Communication Models in Single Algorithm:** A possibility of combining two communication models needs to be investigated. Such as message passing can be used to communicate between the processors, where multi-threading can be used to increase performance in a single processor.
- **Designing Adaptive Algorithms for Evolving Hardware Platforms:** With increasing improvement in hardware efficiency in forthcoming years, algorithms need to be designed, which can exploit the benefits of more powerful implementation model like GPU, etc.
- **Investigating Parallelizing Options in Other Sequential Algorithms:** Although, plenty of sequential community detection algorithms exist in literature, only few Raghavan, et al. (2007), Blondel, et al. (2008), Rosvall, et. al. (2007) are parallelized yet. Identifying and parallelizing unexplored sequential algorithms will be another area of future research.
- **Detecting Overlapping Communities:** Although many sequential community detection algorithms exist in literature, many are static, not able to handle overlapping communities. Parallel algorithms need to be developed for detecting overlapping communities. Although some pioneer work in this area have been done by Palla, et. al. (2005), for developing overlapping sequential community detection algorithm, researchers have to look for chances of parallelization of overlapping community detection algorithms.
- **Designing Intelligent Algorithms:** All of the community detection algorithms discussed in this article, can be termed as unsupervised methods. Design and development of supervised parallel community detection algorithms are another open problem in this domain. Providing self-learning ability to parallel community detection algorithms will provide results suitable to many of application domains of large-scale networks.

CONCLUSION

Uncovering community structure of large network finds various applications in social media mining, marketing, etc. The existing sequential community detection algorithms cannot handle enormous amount of data as they are not designed for that. The need for developing parallel community detection algorithms arises from the issue of scalability. In this book chapter, we have discussed the existing parallel community detection algorithm in literature and introduce a novel taxonomy for classifying them based on sequential algorithms used, communication model and nature of processing units.

Among different methods identified in literature, Louvain method seems to be more appropriate in implementing the parallel community detection. The system architecture such as CPU or GPU being used for algorithm implementation helps the designer to select among different architecture options. The implementation details regarding whether OpenMP or MPI techniques were used also provides insight into the usage of techniques to be formed while designing parallel algorithms. The details mentioned in this paper help a designer to devise a new parallel community detection algorithm from the suitable sequential algorithms targeting specific system architecture. We have provided a list of open problems for the benefit of future researchers.

ACKNOWLEDGMENT

This work is partially supported by the following Grants: MHRD (GoI) FIG (A) 100579-ECD and DST (GoI) SB/FTP/ETA-23/2013. Further, we would like to thank Mr. Deepak S, M.Tech student, IIT Roorkee for his support.

REFERENCES

Auer, B. F., & Bisseling, R. H. (2012). Graph coarsening and clustering on the GPU. *Graph Partitioning and Graph Clustering*, *588*, 223–240. doi:10.1090/conm/588/11706

Bae, S. H., Halperin, D., West, J., Rosvall, M., & Howe, B. (2013, December). Scalable flow-based community detection for large-scale network analysis. In *2013 IEEE 13th International Conference on Data Mining Workshops* (pp. 303-310). IEEE. doi:10.1109/ICDMW.2013.138

Bhowmick, S., & Srinivasan, S. (2013). A template for parallelizing the louvain method for modularity maximization. In *Dynamics On and Of Complex Networks* (Vol. 2, pp. 111–124). Springer New York. doi:10.1007/978-1-4614-6729-8_6

Blondel, V. D., Guillaume, J. L., Lambiotte, R., & Lefebvre, E. (2008). Fast unfolding of communities in large networks. *Journal of Statistical Mechanics*, *2008*(10), P10008. doi:10.1088/1742-5468/2008/10/P10008

Brandes, U., Delling, D., Gaertler, M., Gorke, R., Hoefer, M., Nikoloski, Z., & Wagner, D. (2008). On modularity clustering. *IEEE Transactions on Knowledge and Data Engineering*, *20*(2), 172–188. doi:10.1109/TKDE.2007.190689

Buzun, N., Korshunov, A., Avanesov, V., Filonenko, I., Kozlov, I., Turdakov, D., & Kim, H. (2014, December). Egolp: Fast and distributed community detection in billion-node social networks. In *2014 IEEE International Conference on Data Mining Workshop* (pp. 533-540). IEEE. doi:10.1109/ICDMW.2014.158

Chen, M., Liu, S., & Szymanski, B. K. (2014, September). Parallel toolkit for measuring the quality of network community structure. In *Network Intelligence Conference (ENIC), 2014 European* (pp. 22-29). IEEE.

Cheong, C. Y., Huynh, H. P., Lo, D., & Goh, R. S. M. (2013, August). Hierarchical parallel algorithm for modularity-based community detection using GPUs. In *European Conference on Parallel Processing* (pp. 775-787). Springer Berlin Heidelberg. doi:10.1007/978-3-642-40047-6_77

Clauset, A., Newman, M. E., & Moore, C. (2004). Finding community structure in very large networks. *Physical Review E: Statistical, Nonlinear, and Soft Matter Physics*, *70*(6), 066111. doi:10.1103/PhysRevE.70.066111 PMID:15697438

Facebook users worldwide. (2016, April 15). Retrieved from http://www.statista.com/statistics/264810/number-of-monthly-active-facebook-users-worldwide/

Fortunato, S. (2010). Community detection in graphs. *Physics Reports*, *486*(3), 75–174. doi:10.1016/j.physrep.2009.11.002

Huang, F., Niranjan, U. N., Hakeem, M. U., & Anandkumar, A. (2013). *Fast detection of overlapping communities via online tensor methods.* arXiv preprint arXiv:1309.0787

Hui, P., Crowcroft, J., & Yoneki, E. (2011). Bubble rap: Social-based forwarding in delay-tolerant networks. *IEEE Transactions on Mobile Computing*, *10*(11), 1576–1589. doi:10.1109/TMC.2010.246

Kleinberg, J. M. (1999). Authoritative sources in a hyperlinked environment. *Journal of the ACM*, *46*(5), 604–632. doi:10.1145/324133.324140

Kuzmin, K., Shah, S. Y., & Szymanski, B. K. (2013, September). Parallel overlapping community detection with SLPA. In *Social Computing (SocialCom), 2013 International Conference on* (pp. 204-212). IEEE. doi:10.1109/SocialCom.2013.37

LaSalle, D., & Karypis, G. (2013, May). Multi-threaded graph partitioning. In *Parallel & Distributed Processing (IPDPS), 2013 IEEE 27th International Symposium on* (pp. 225-236). IEEE. doi:10.1109/IPDPS.2013.50

Le Martelot, E., & Hankin, C. (2013). Fast multi-scale detection of relevant communities in large-scale networks. *The Computer Journal*.

Leskovec, J., Lang, K. J., & Mahoney, M. (2010, April). Empirical comparison of algorithms for network community detection. In *Proceedings of the 19th international conference on World wide web* (pp. 631-640). ACM. doi:10.1145/1772690.1772755

Lu, H., Halappanavar, M., & Kalyanaraman, A. (2015). Parallel heuristics for scalable community detection. *Parallel Computing*, *47*, 19–37. doi:10.1016/j.parco.2015.03.003

Malliaros, F. D., & Vazirgiannis, M. (2013). Clustering and community detection in directed networks: A survey. *Physics Reports*, *533*(4), 95–142. doi:10.1016/j.physrep.2013.08.002

Martelot, E. L., & Hankin, C. (2013). *Fast multi-scale community detection based on local criteria within a multi-threaded algorithm.* arXiv preprint arXiv:1301.0955

Nascimento, M. A., Sander, J., & Pound, J. (2003). Analysis of SIGMODs co-authorship graph. *SIGMOD Record*, *32*(3), 8–10. doi:10.1145/945721.945722

Newman, M. E., & Girvan, M. (2004). Finding and evaluating community structure in networks. *Physical Review E: Statistical, Nonlinear, and Soft Matter Physics*, *69*(2), 026113. doi:10.1103/PhysRevE.69.026113 PMID:14995526

Palla, G., Derényi, I., Farkas, I., & Vicsek, T. (2005). Uncovering the overlapping community structure of complex networks in nature and society. *Nature*, *435*(7043), 814–818. doi:10.1038/nature03607 PMID:15944704

Papadopoulos, S., Kompatsiaris, Y., Vakali, A., & Spyridonos, P. (2012). Community detection in social media. *Data Mining and Knowledge Discovery*, *24*(3), 515–554. doi:10.1007/s10618-011-0224-z

Paxton, N. C., Russell, S., Moskowitz, I. S., & Hyden, P. (2015). A Survey of Community Detection Algorithms Based On Analysis-Intent. In *Cyber Warfare* (pp. 237–263). Springer International Publishing. doi:10.1007/978-3-319-14039-1_12

Perkins, C. E. (2001). *Ad hoc networking* (Vol. 1). Reading, MA: Addison-wesley.

Plantié, M., & Crampes, M. (2013). Survey on social community detection. In *Social media retrieval* (pp. 65–85). Springer London. doi:10.1007/978-1-4471-4555-4_4

Que, X., Checconi, F., Petrini, F., Wang, T., & Yu, W. (2013). *Lightning-fast community detection in social media: A scalable implementation of the louvain algorithm.* Department of Computer Science and Software Engineering, Auburn University, Tech. Rep. AU-CSSE-PASL/13-TR01.

Raghavan, U. N., Albert, R., & Kumara, S. (2007). Near linear time algorithm to detect community structures in large-scale networks. *Physical Review E: Statistical, Nonlinear, and Soft Matter Physics*, *76*(3), 036106. doi:10.1103/PhysRevE.76.036106 PMID:17930305

Riedy, E. J., Meyerhenke, H., Ediger, D., & Bader, D. A. (2011, September). Parallel community detection for massive graphs. In *International Conference on Parallel Processing and Applied Mathematics* (pp. 286-296). Springer Berlin Heidelberg.

Riedy, J., Bader, D. A., & Meyerhenke, H. (2012, May). Scalable multi-threaded community detection in social networks. In *Parallel and Distributed Processing Symposium Workshops & PhD Forum (IP-DPSW), 2012 IEEE 26th International* (pp. 1619-1628). IEEE. doi:10.1109/IPDPSW.2012.203

Rosvall, M., & Bergstrom, C. T. (2007). An information-theoretic framework for resolving community structure in complex networks. *Proceedings of the National Academy of Sciences of the United States of America*, *104*(18), 7327–7331. doi:10.1073/pnas.0611034104 PMID:17452639

Soman, J., & Narang, A. (2011, May). Fast community detection algorithm with gpus and multicore architectures. In *Parallel & Distributed Processing Symposium (IPDPS), 2011 IEEE International* (pp. 568-579). IEEE. doi:10.1109/IPDPS.2011.61

Staudt, C. L., & Meyerhenke, H. (2013, October). Engineering high-performance community detection heuristics for massive graphs. In *2013 42nd International Conference on Parallel Processing* (pp. 180-189). IEEE. doi:10.1109/ICPP.2013.27

Symeon, P., Yiannis, K., Athena, V., & Ploutarchos, S. (2012). Community detection in Social Media Performance and application considerations. *Data Mining and Knowledge Discovery, 24*(3), 515–554. doi:10.1007/s10618-011-0224-z

The Data Explosion in 2014. (2016, April 15). Retrieved from http://aci.info/2014/07/12/the-data-explosion-in-2014-minute-by-minute-infographic/

Tyler, J. R., Wilkinson, D. M., & Huberman, B. A. (2005). E-mail as spectroscopy: Automated discovery of community structure within organizations. *The Information Society, 21*(2), 143–153. doi:10.1080/01972240590925348

Wang, T., Qian, X., & Wang, X. (2015, September). HLPA: A hybrid label propagation algorithm to find communities in large-scale networks. In *2015 IEEE 7th International Conference on Awareness Science and Technology (iCAST)* (pp. 135-140). IEEE. doi:10.1109/ICAwST.2015.7314035

Watts, D. J., & Strogatz, S. H. (1998). Collective dynamics of 'small-world' networks. *Nature, 393*(6684), 440-442.

Wickramaarachchi, C., Frincu, M., Small, P., & Prasanna, V. K. (2014, September). Fast parallel algorithm for unfolding of communities in large graphs. In *High Performance Extreme Computing Conference (HPEC)*, (pp. 1-6). IEEE. doi:10.1109/HPEC.2014.7040973

Williams, R. J., & Martinez, N. D. (2000). Simple rules yield complex food webs. *Nature, 404*(6774), 180–183. doi:10.1038/35004572 PMID:10724169

Xie, J., Kelley, S., & Szymanski, B. K. (2013). Overlapping community detection in networks: The state-of-the-art and comparative study. *ACM Computing Surveys, 45*(4), 43. doi:10.1145/2501654.2501657

Yang, J., Ren, Y., Chen, Y., & Chuah, M. C. (2010). A social community based approach for reducing the propagation of infectious diseases in healthcare. *Mobile Computing and Communications Review, 14*(3), 7–9. doi:10.1145/1923641.1923645

Zeng, J., & Yu, H. (2015, September). Parallel Modularity-based Community Detection on Large-scale Graphs. In *2015 IEEE International Conference on Cluster Computing* (pp. 1-10). IEEE. doi:10.1109/CLUSTER.2015.11

Zhang, B., Cheng, X., Bie, R., & Chen, D. (2012, November). A community based vaccination strategy over mobile phone records. In *Proceedings of the Second ACM Workshop on Mobile Systems, Applications, and Services for HealthCare* (p. 2). ACM doi:10.1145/2396276.2396279

Zhang, Q., Qirong, Q., & Guo, K. (2015, August). Parallel overlapping community discovery based on grey relational analysis. In *2015 IEEE International Conference on Grey Systems and Intelligent Services (GSIS)* (pp. 151-156). IEEE. doi:10.1109/GSIS.2015.7301846

Zhang, Y., Wang, J., Wang, Y., & Zhou, L. (2009, June). Parallel community detection on large networks with propinquity dynamics. In *Proceedings of the 15th ACM SIGKDD international conference on Knowledge discovery and data mining* (pp. 997-1006). ACM. doi:10.1145/1557019.1557127

KEY TERMS AND DEFINITIONS

Community Detection: Communities are densely connected groups of vertices which share common properties within a graph. Four types of criteria define a community: complete mutuality, reachability, vertex degree and comparison of external and internal cohesion.

CPU: A Central Processing Unit (CPU) is a main component of a computer, which can handle only a few threads at a time.

GPU: A Graphics Processing Unit (GPU) comprises of hundreds of cores, which is able to handle thousands of threads simultaneously.

MPI: Message Passing Interface(MPI) is a standard portable message passing system developed for communicating process/threads in a distributed computing environment.

OpenMP: OpenMP is anApplication Programming Interface (MPI), for supporting shared memory based multi-processing applications.

Parallel Algorithms: Algorithms that can be split into different pieces and executed on different processing devices and the result can be combined to form the final result.

Shared Memory: Shared memory is a memory region, which can be accessed by more than one program/processor, which helps them to communicate with each other.

Chapter 2
Towards Automation of IoT Analytics:
An Ontology-Driven Approach

Sounak Dey
TCS Research and Innovation, India

Arijit Mukherjee
TCS Research and Innovation, India

ABSTRACT

The rapid growth in the number of sensors deployed at various scenarios and domains has resulted in the demand of smart applications and services which can take advantage of the sensor ubiquity and the Internet of Things paradigm. However, IoT analytic applications are grossly different from typical IT applications in the sense that in case of IoT, the physical world model is absolutely essential to understand the meaning of sensor data and context. It is also unreasonable to assume that application developers will possess all the necessary skills such as signal processing, algorithms, domain and deployment infrastructures. The scenario is more complicated because of overlapping domains and variety of knowledge. Researchers have attempted to automate parts of the development process, but, the area of feature engineering for sensor signals remain relatively untouched. In this chapter, the authors discuss about the use of semantic modeling for IoT application development with respect to a framework that is capable of largely automating parts of IoT application development.

INTRODUCTION

Nearly two decades ago, in 1999, Prof. Neil Gross predicted: *"In the next century, planet Earth will don an electronic skin. It will use the internet as a scaffold and transmit its sensations"* (Gross, 1999). Seventeen years later, in 2016, we are moving towards a direction of "Internet of Everything", a step forward from the era of "Internet of Things", as number of connected and deployed objects around us are mushrooming at a very high rate. They are predicted to reach a count of 4.9 billion from today to about 25 billion by 2020 (Gartner, 2014). Each of these objects is uniquely addressable and communicates

DOI: 10.4018/978-1-5225-2498-4.ch002

with each other and outer world based on standard communication protocols (INFSO, 2008). This novel paradigm of IoT, or IoE, or more generic *Cyber Physical Systems*, is able to discover context at personal and physical level and is able to answer questions like: who is doing what, when, where; what is happening now; how one is feeling now; and even what is probably going to happen next. These powerful sets of information have high impact on individual users (for assisted living, enhanced learning etc.) as well as industry and business users (like smart transportation, manufacturing, energy and utilities etc.).

However, every good thing comes at a price. This growth in number of smart objects translates into generation of a tremendous volume of data which in turn translates into a huge requirement of data storage, and an efficient and fast communication network. Moreover, all connected objects do not send data in similar format; they are controlled by different stake holders and cater to different use cases involving variety of knowledge domains. There is heterogeneity in terms of hardware and software versions which are again controlled by multiple independent communities. To sum up, the heterogeneity present in the IoT world due to obvious reasons is a major challenge facing researchers in this domain.

The data, produced by these smart objects, are however precious. Data are often referred as "oil" for the not too distant future. But data without any follow-on analysis and some meaningful insight do not have much utility. All useful applications in IoT domain perform this analytics and help end users to visualize the situation/context represented by data in a more meaningful way, thus enabling the user to take some decisions or actions based on the situation.

In order to develop such intelligent and useful IoT applications, one should (i) identify the most appropriate data sources together with the detailed specification of the sources, i.e. the sensors, (ii) properly collect the data, (iii) identify the data format thereof and (iv) understand which part of the data is useful for the application. At the same time, most applications involve usage of multiple algorithms in a sequence to extract a useful insight from the data. To take an informed decision about the algorithms to use and the usage sequence, the application developer requires an in-depth knowledge about algorithms, their usage, complexities, features, side-effects etc. Real-time or near-real-time execution is another common feature for an IoT application, which requires detailed knowledge about the resources involved e.g. edge devices, cloud platforms, gateways, network etc. On the other hand, to build a successful application, the knowledge about the particular domain is as important as the technical aspects. For example, an application in the healthcare domain, targeted towards the smart health paradigm, may require the developer to know certain aspects of the healthcare domain apart from the technical knowledge about processing sensor signals. Needless to say that, it is a tremendous ask for a programmer or developer.

Considering the enormity in the number of connected objects, the volume, velocity and variety of the resultant data, number of algorithms, number of use cases to solve, number of experts from different knowledge domain to be involved, and above all enormous heterogeneity involved at each level, the whole domain of IoT application development cannot be handled manually and thus requirement for machine automation at many levels becomes obvious. In other words, there is a very obvious requirement of modeling the physical world and the knowledge associated with it using semantic techniques.

To enable machines (which can compute) to help us, the knowledge involved at different stages must be captured in a machine-readable and machine-understandable format, and it has already been observed by researchers that Ontology is a useful instrument in this regard. Ontology can capture 'facts' specific to a domain and aims to replace a human domain expert by executing reasoning algorithms on top of the ontology elements. In other words, ontology is a knowledge and information store, represented as a connected graph, to which both machines and human can ask questions, like students normally do to a teacher or patients do to a doctor; more generally, it is similar to a situation where a non-expert asks questions about a domain to an expert. The 'facts' mentioned herein include concepts, concept hierarchies, relations between concepts, instances of concepts, restriction and rules on concepts applicable and relevant to a domain. Analogous to human's reasoning over given facts, computing systems can use a tool called "reasoner" to infer new information from existing ontological knowledge or facts. Typically, in an ontology, facts are expressed using RDF (Resource Descriptor Framework) triplets which takes a tuple form such as <subject, predicate, object> (popularly known as <s, p, o> format). There are different languages like Turtle, N3, OWL2 etc. to express facts and each entity has a global URI so that it is uniquely identifiable and usable globally by anybody or any machine.

A MODEL DRIVEN APPROACH IN IoT APPLICATION DEVELOPMENT

In this chapter, we have insofar discussed the complexity of an IoT application development process given the diversity and heterogeneity associated with this domain. This complexity actually contradicts the goal and vision of IoT. To address such issues a common abstraction layer is an obvious choice where every related stakeholders can talk to each other following their own protocol with the issues related to heterogeneity being tackled by the abstraction layer.

There have been many efforts in this space to create a unified and generic abstraction layer. For example in sensor application development domain, different worldwide sensor communities like W3C SWE-OGC forum have tried to standardize a sensor specification language called SensorML (Botts et al., 2007) which is supposed to be followed by all the sensor manufacturers and users across the world thus removing heterogeneity across sensor world. Similarly, O&M (observation and measurement) is another standard following which sensor observation and measurement data is to be specified (Botts et al., 2006). All these standards have their own UML class diagrams which may be followed and implemented by anybody easily. But all such standards are made purely from software engineering point of view and are supposed to be limited within the concerned domain i.e. sensor. These type of representation models lacks semantics within them i.e. one cannot easily understand what the data specified in O&M format means without guidance from a sensor domain expert. This leads to same set of application development challenges that we have discussed already.

There are different integrated IoT application development platforms which provide services like device management, data storage and management, API based application development framework and a distributed application deployment framework. Some of these frameworks appear in different avatars like PaaS (Platform as a Service), SaaS (Software as a Service), AaaS (Analytics as a Service) etc. where they offer different services for application developers to use and developers do not need to worry about what happens inside. However, they do not actually address the issues like code reusability, need for multiple skills in domain, analytics, programming etc. which are necessary for ease of application development.

Model-driven software development (MDSD) process is a prevalent approach that talks about creating an abstract model and derive an implementation from it (Riedel et al., 2010). OASIS (Oasis, n.d.) uses this approach in their standard meta-model for IT services called TOSCA to address the challenges related to heterogeneous application environments in cloud applications domain (Tosca, 2013). Implementing such idea in IoT application development was proposed in 2014 (Pal et al., 2014). It is possible to create standard models of IoT components like sensors, algorithms, infrastructure etc. which can then be re-used by application developers in actual implementation scenario. If the models are created based on ontologies of each such domain, then from the knowledge engineering point of view, one can infer new and deep insights from underlying concepts of the abstract model. This approach advocates separation of concerns among different stakeholders by introducing re-usable meta-models for IoT system and then automating the development process by stitching required models relevant to a solution, thus augmenting capability of developer and minimizing development time. This Model-driven Development (MDD) framework is capable of addressing issues like algorithm re-use, distributed execution of analytics, generation of analytics and reasoning workflows, a common ontology and semantics for sensor data etc.

USE OF KNOWLEDGE MODELS: AN IoT SCENARIO

To elaborate the use of ontological knowledge models in IoT application development, let us take an example use case of "detecting the heart rate of a human from the PPG signal (photoplethysmograph) using mobile camera." In the smart healthcare paradigm, it is envisaged that normal people will be able to use simple and ubiquitous devices such as mobile phones to monitor their day-to-day physiological parameters, and hence the demand for such applications are actually on the rise. To develop such an application (which is intentionally chosen to be a simple one for easier understanding), a naïve developer needs to be able to answer four top level questions to start with:

1. **What is PPG?** Which requires knowledge from healthcare domain to answer,
2. **How is a PPG Signal Processed in Order to Discover Some Insight From it?** Which involves signal processing domain knowledge,
3. **What are the Algorithms That can be Applied on a PPG Signal?** Requires algorithm domain expertise,
4. **How can a PPG Signal be Processed in a Mobile Camera Itself for Faster Processing?** Which requires knowledge of computational infrastructure.

It is clear that to develop such an application, developer needs help from at least four experts from different domains, leaving apart expertise required to answer many more smaller questions that we have not mentioned at all in above list.

Let us now approach the problem with knowledge models from each of the domains and see how such models can help the developer to figure out a solution to the problem. Figure 1, very simplistically, shows (clockwise from top left corner), ontological models of generic domain knowledge, followed by a healthcare-specific domain knowledge derived from the generic model, a model of infrastructure knowledge and finally algorithm domain knowledge. Relationships shown in generic knowledge model and specific knowledge model are similar except the fact that entities are different in two models: while the first one uses generic entities like *Feature Of interest, Observation, Stimuli, Property, Type* etc., the later one uses specific terms related to healthcare, such as *Heart, Heart Rate, Tachycardia, Physiological parameters, Periodic* etc. The healthcare model also has the fact that: *Heart Rate* is a *periodic* signal and can be captured by *PPG by a camera*. Now the algorithm knowledge model has the fact that: *Fast Fourier Transform* or *FFT* can be applied on a *periodic signal* to convert it from time-domain to frequency-domain. The infrastructure knowledge model mentions that: *mobile phones* have *camera* with a given frame ratio and have some amount of computing capability. Putting all these facts together, an efficient reasoner can infer answers of all of the above four questions and accordingly help the application developer.

Figure 1. Ontological knowledge models to be used in IoT application development

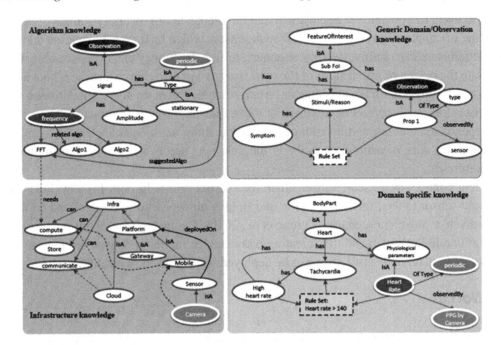

There can be numerous such knowledge models (e.g. for biology, social network, communication etc.) which may be useful in developing cross domain IoT applications. These models, once connected with each other, can help in inferring new facts that are apparently unknown to even domain experts. If the models are enriched properly, they can even suggest certain steps during development, for example, recommending a suitable algorithm for a given type of dataset or signal, or a communication device which has support for a faster network protocol.

However, sensors and algorithms are most common resources that are used in most of the IoT applications. Hence, in this chapter, we have focused in creating authentic and useful knowledge models for these two domains. In next sections, we will discuss how we have tried to achieve this goal.

CREATION OF SENSOR KNOWLEDGE MODEL

The W3C SSN Incubation group (Compton et al., 2012) has identified four most relevant types of use cases related to sensor world, which are:

1. **Data Discovery and Linking**: Related to classification and linking of data created out of sensor observation;
2. **Device discovery and Selection**: Related to searching sensors as per their capabilities and features;
3. **Provenance and Diagnostics**: Related to error in data and sensor network; and
4. **Device Tasking and Operations**: Related to core level programming and controlling of sensor.

The first two of the above points are of utmost importance for IoT application developers and last two are relevant to users responsible for deployment and maintenance of sensors systems.

Most of the IoT application workflows start with sensors which feed raw observation data to the applications. Parameters like quality, velocity, accuracy, format, frequency etc. of sensor observation data directly dictate the design of initial steps of the workflow and in turn they affect the whole application. Thus success of the application largely depends on correct selection of sensors (as mentioned in use-case 2 in above list) along with correct deployment of those sensors for a given scenario. Correct selection of sensor depends upon depth and breadth of knowledge about sensor parameters like capabilities of reading and sending data, measurement methods, measurement precision, battery consumption, deployment expenditure etc.

An efficient context-aware search mechanism for sensors will help both IoT developers who will select the right sensor to feed their application and field engineers who will select and deploy correct sensor for a given deployment scenario (Corcho et al., 2010). Capturing facts about sensors and related parameters in ontological form and thus creating a knowledge model of sensor can play an important role here by recommending best-fit sensor to be deployed or to be used in an application.

Related Works

At the time of this development, no recommendation based sensor selection and search mechanism was readily available. Some efforts were made to capture and describe sensors and related concepts in ontological form. Each of such efforts has pros and cons of its own. As per our study, each of them addresses a focused set of problem and is unable to serve as a reusable and extendable ontology which can be applied to all varieties of sensor and related applications. Issues related to these ontologies are discussed below:

1. **SWAMO**: It has a good presentation of sensor domain (Underbrink et al. 2008). It accommodates real-time sensor information like position, orientation of a sensor etc. Every concept in this ontology is a subclass of "Component" class but that class does not have any clear reference or description; thus making this class to be linked to or aligned to similar concepts in other external ontologies. Conceptually every aspect of a sensor cannot be mapped to "Component". Some classes like "Acceleration" are shown as a subclass of "Position" class which is again conceptually wrong. SWAMO's focus is particularly limited on processes which control sensors. It however enables composition of dynamic and interoperable sensor web services which are essential components of modern semantic web applications. Thus only a part of this work, not all, can be reused for our purpose.
2. **SDO** (Eid et al., 2007): This lightweight ontology re-uses concepts from SUMO (Niles et al., 2001) ontology. This is a desired feature in terms of extension and reusability but it confines itself by describing entities related to sensor observation data only. No other sensor related concept (for e.g. capabilities, range, power consumption etc.) is captured here. Moreover, it is not well maintained.
3. **OntoNym** (Stevenson et al., 2009): This sensor ontology tries to describe sensor and sensor data but it only has 8 classes, 13 object properties and 1 data-type property. This leaves a lot of room for extension but the lack of richness does not make it an ideal candidate for reuse. So this being very lightweight and having less coverage, has not been adopted for our purpose.

Figure 2. Extending OntoSensor: Logical modules

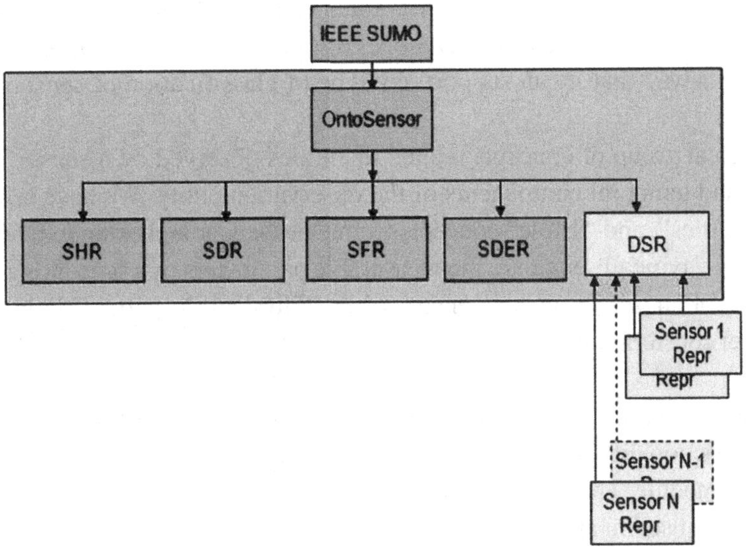

4. **OntoSensor** (Russomanno et al., 2005): Made by University of Memphis, this is another sensor ontology which inherits IEEE SUMO as top level ontology and reuses concepts from SWE SensorML (SWE OGC, 2013), GML and ISO 19115; thus making it a rich and useful-to-reuse ontology. The 'Sensor' and 'Platform' concepts of OntoSensor extend the 'Measurement Device' and 'Transportation Device' concepts respectively from SUMO; while the 'Event' concept extends the 'Process' concept. Via these classes, it covers sensor, its deployment and sensing methods. OntoSensor also covers sensor capabilities and measurable entities. The overall structure and relations defined in OntoSensor, along with features mentioned above, makes it most eligible candidate to extend further to reach to a comprehensive sensor ontology. Though it lacks in detail technical specification of sensor but that is not a must have feature for such a purpose. We have fused some concepts from SDO ontology into OntoSensor to cover up some gaps in description of sensor data entities. In next section, we describe our approach of making such an Ontology by extending OntoSensor.

Working with OntoSensor

As shown in Figure 2, IEEE SUMO is the top level ontology from where OntoSensor has been extended. Structure-wise we have divided the concepts in OntoSensor into five logical modules namely: (i) Sensor Hierarchy Representation (SHR), (ii) Sensor Data Representation (SDR), (iii) Sensor Function Representation (SFR), (iv) Sensor Data Exchange Representation (SDER) and (v) Domain Specific Representation (DSR). Each of these is briefly described below. Though the structure is generic to be used for any sensor but for demonstration purpose we have used *energy meter* as an example sensor here.

1. **SHR** represents the hierarchical class structure or taxonomy of the sensor entity. Classification of a sensor can be made based on various dimensions like (1) its observables, (2) sensor material,

(3) application of sensor (4) its measurement accuracy (5) cost (6) output signal (7) functional principles etc. For example, based on "observables", a probable hierarchy for energy meter can be *Sensor ==> Electrical ==> Electromechanical ==> Induction ==> Energy Meter*. SHR module is made in such a way that it can support any type of classification of sensors, thus making it a generic module.

2. **SDR** is the logical group of concepts related to entities observed by a sensor. This includes thematic, spatial and temporal components of the observation entity. We have re-used "Parameter", "Physical Properties", and "Tuple" concepts from OntoSensor and extended them into larger subtrees. "Parameter" typically encloses the measurable parameters of a sensor (e.g. x, y, z component of acceleration for an accelerometer sensor) while "Physical Properties" hold specifications like accuracy, power consumption of sensor. Figure 3 provides a brief snapshot of SDR for energy meter sensor.

3. **SFR** encapsulates the functionality aspects of a sensor. This includes the Read, Write, Send, Filter, Sleep type of functionality of a sensor. "Action" class of OntoSensor has been extended to create this logical SFR module. These functional entities and their relations will lead to create the semantic web services to be used in applications.

4. Sensor based systems require a secure and flexible bidirectional data communication between functional blocks of the system. Plethora of protocols and proprietary way of data representation are considered for short and long haul communication within sensor based systems. The Sensor Data Exchange Representation (**SDER**) is a logical model to represent communications and data exchange capabilities of sensors, actuators and other physical sensor devices. A snapshot of the ontological implementation of SDER for energy meter sensor is shown in Figure 4 where communication concepts like GPRS, WiFi, MBus, Modbus, Zigbee, SerialPort etc. are included. These concepts however can be imported from or linked to external ontologies.

Figure 3. Sensor data representation: Extending OntoSensor

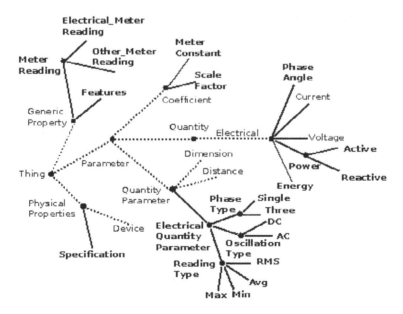

Figure 4. Sensor data exchange representation: Extending OntoSensor

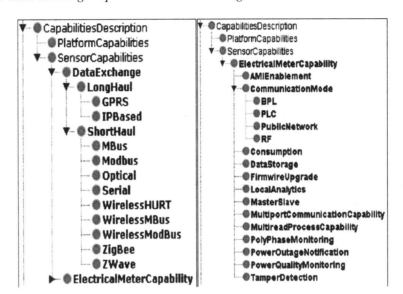

5. **DSR** or Domain Specific Representation is a place holder for capturing concepts which are very specific to a sensor type. Entities and their relations captured in this module are not generic at all. This module has three layers in it: a) *Main Representation* which includes central domain specific concepts, b) *Extended Representation* which is logical extension of *Main Representation* and defines context-aware concepts those have a meaning only in the context of related domain, and finally c) *External Representation* which allows semantic rules, relationships and dependencies between physical resource and external concepts. Examples of some DSR concepts for energy meter sensor are *phase displacement, master-slave mode, user consumption* etc. which carry no meaning for any other sensor.

This implementation of OntoSensor based generic sensor ontology is sufficient for the purpose of storing sensor domain knowledge and then searching those facts. It almost creates room for capturing all possible metadata and observation data of a sensor. Based on this ontology, we have made a sensor data (and metadata) storing and searching system called SensXplore (Dey et al., 2013).

This description of sensor and related searching application are very useful for any general purpose sensor related task. But it failed in case of IoT specific applications. We have already discussed that most IoT applications try to understand the perspective or context of a situation or event in physical real world. They try to find physical reason behind an event and want to help end user to act as per situation or context. Our OntoSensor based sensor ontology does not relate to physical world and physical object of interests.

W3C SSN Incubation group has created a top level structured sensor ontology which accommodates features or properties of physical world objects of interests, their measurable properties and also tries to tell which sensors can measure these properties (Compton et al., 2012). This ontology is based on *Stimulus-Sensor-Observation* aka SSO paradigm (Janowicz et al., 2010) and is made with a goal to use it in modern sensor centric web applications i.e. IoT application. While it maintains modularity in structure and have good pluggability with external ontologies, it also has a good coverage of physical world

Figure 5. SSN: Basic concepts and relations

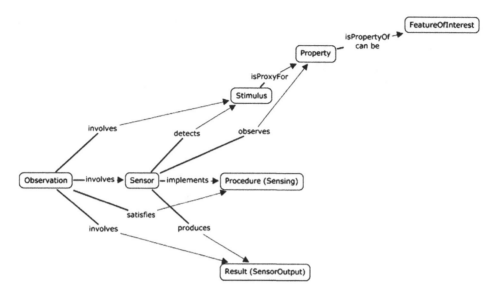

concepts namely *events, stimuli, feature of interest* etc. and sensor related concepts like *measurement parameters, sensing methods, capability* etc. (refer Figure 5). The following section discusses how we have aligned our work with SSO paradigm in order to support IoT use cases.

A Better Approach: Aligning With SSN Ontology

The SSN ontology is aligned with DOLCE UltraLite ontology (DUL, n.d.) which can be used as a common ground for integration and for concept matching with other domain ontologies. Moreover, SSN ontology is able to integrate with other sensor and observation description standards like SWE SensorML, O&M and TML etc. We have imported some external ontology to further enrich SSN ontology. An external ontology named UCUM, located at http://purl.oclc.org/muo/ucum, is imported to introduce some physical measurable entities like *acceleration, temperature, electric current* etc. This ontology has also been used for linking unit of measurements of the observables and capability concepts like accuracy, range etc. In order to cater the time and location information queries, we have imported one Temporal and Spatial ontology into SSN ontology. Figure 6 shows the new structure of sensor ontology. Similar to the case of OntoSensor, here too we have used *energy meter* as an example sensor.

As illustrated in Figure 5, *stimuli* are detectable changes in physical world. As they trigger sensors to measure a change in physical world, they are the reason behind any *observation* or measurement. They trigger changes in values of physical measurable parameters or *properties* around a target physical world object, called *Feature of Interest*. Same *stimuli* however can trigger different sensors. In case of energy meters, example of *Feature of Interest* can be a household, a railway station or a factory (refer Figure 7). On the other hand, *stimuli* can be of unpredictable type like sudden voltage change, power cut etc. or of predictable type like some pre-scheduled run of washing machine in a household which draws a lot of power (refer Figure 8). These *stimuli* act as trigger for energy meter and in turn it measures physical parameters like voltage, current etc. Thus eventually *stimuli* create an *observation* entity. In Figure 9,

Figure 6. Structure for extended ontology for energy meter sensor

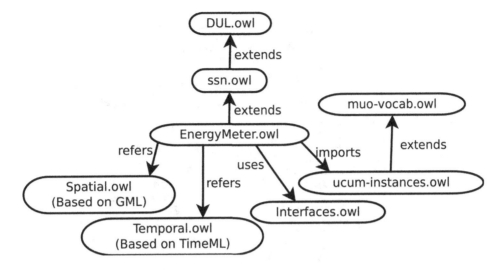

Figure 7. Implementation of "Feature Of Interest" in energy meter scenario

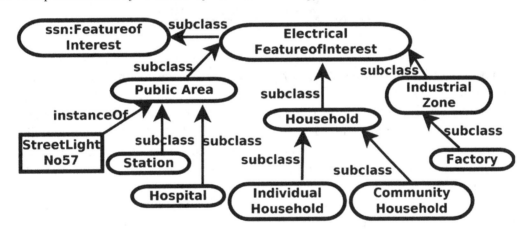

Figure 8. Implementation of "Stimuli" in energy meter scenario

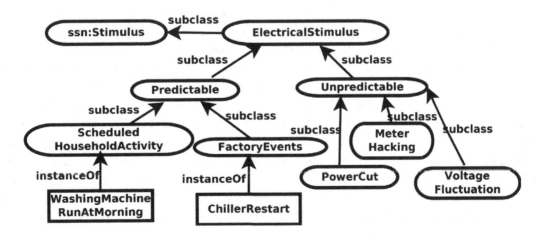

Figure 9. Relation between FOI and Stimuli: energy meter case

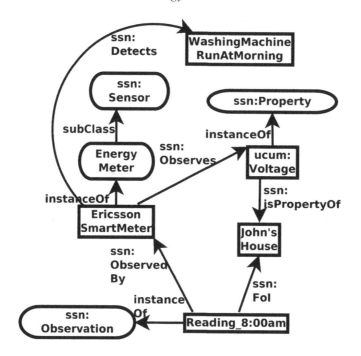

this relation between *stimuli-Feature of Interest-observation* is explained with respect to instances created for energy meter sensor.

Implementation details of other sensor related concepts like observation, measurement properties, measurement capabilities etc. are discussed in details by (Dey et al., 2015). We are not repeating those implementation details here again. One can easily include multiple types of sensors like Image sensor, Motion sensor, Position sensor etc. following the extended SSN ontology structure. Figure 10 illustrates one such example.

Based on this work, we have modified the SensXplore tool. This tool enables registration of new subclasses of sensors (like barometer, accelerometer, energy meter etc.) to be incorporated into the ontology. Figure 11 shows creation of energy meter subclass within the sensor bucket. Once a subclass of sensor is created, then users can create instances of that sensor subclass. For example, if energy meter sensor subclass is created then instances of energy meter namely Kamstrup energy meter, Ericson meter etc. can be created. Similarly for barometer sub class, instance called Omron barometer can be created. In order to create a new instance of a sensor subclass (say energy meter), one have browse through the sensor class hierarchy and have to click on desired sensor subclass i.e. energy meter class to get a web based user interface (refer Figure 12) that shows all the properties of sensor class along with additional properties of respective energy meter subclass. By filling up values for all these properties one new instance of energy meter subclass can be created. Once the energy meter instances are created they can be deployed at different households (which are feature-of-interests) via SensXplore tool and then one can geographically search those energy meters using the geo-search mechanisms provided in this tool. Output of the search will be shown visually where sensors will be spotted by red dots on a map (refer Figure 13). Deployment scenarios are typically characterized by entities like feature of interest, stimuli, measurement parameters etc. This tool is capable of recommending which sensor is best fit for a given

Figure 10. Supporting multiple Sensor in Extended SSN ontology

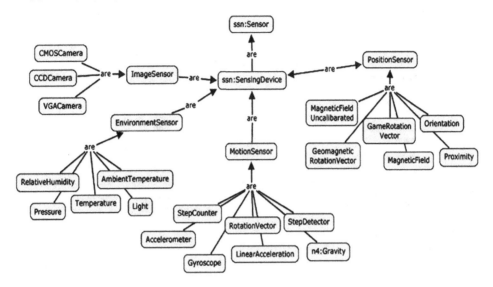

Figure 11. Browsing the sensor hierarchy

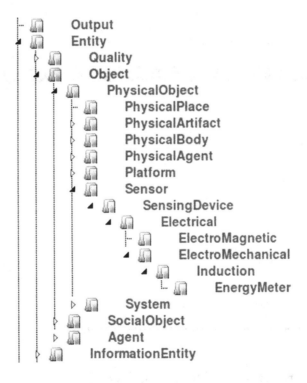

deployment scenario. IoT application developers can also be benefitted by this tool. They can search deployed sensors based on measurable parameters, location, capabilities etc. and can stitch with their application workflow which will be discussed in a relevant section.

In next section, we discuss how to create an efficient algorithm knowledge model and how to use it.

Figure 12. Sensor registration tool

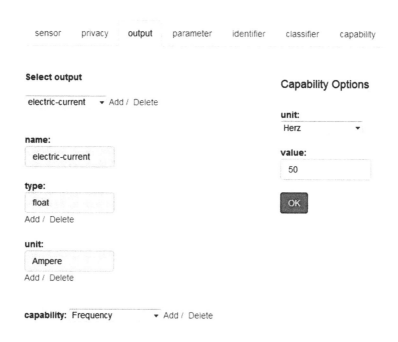

Figure 13. Geographic search of Sensors in SensXplore tool

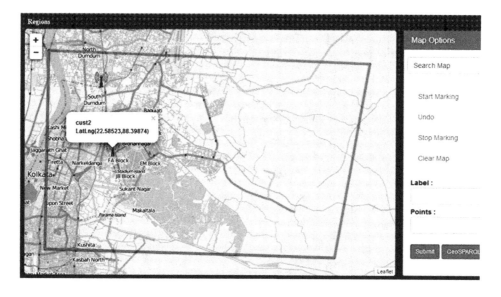

CREATION OF ALGORITHM KNOWLEDGE MODEL

While developing an IoT application, the selection of sensor for collecting data remains the first hurdle. We have discussed above how a sensor knowledge model can help developers in this regard. Our next goal is to create an algorithm knowledge model.

Figure 14. A sample core IoT workflow

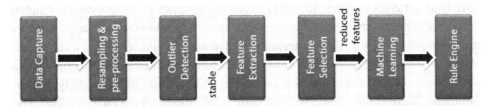

After collecting raw observation data from sensors, it is often required to clean up noise from it. Then a lot of analytic algorithms run sequentially on that clean data to extract some meaningful insights from it. For example, to extract some meaning from sensor data using signal processing, the data has to pass through a set of steps like pre-processing, filtering, outlier detection, feature extraction etc. (Figure 14). For each of these steps there are many algorithms available and developers have to select one from those options. Each algorithm in each such category have their own specialty based on parameters like complexity, accuracy of result, execution time, applicability etc. Selecting right algorithm for each step from this sea of options and stitching them in proper meaningful sequence is not a layman's job. This demands expertise to understand the basic philosophy and knowledge about algorithms and their applicability against a given problem. As most of the analytics on sensor data involve machine learning techniques, we have seen from our experience that maximum development effort is spent to extract right set of features from the data set and then to remove unnecessary or redundant features from the set. Quickly acquiring such expertise for developing an application in IoT domain is a tough job from the developer's point of view and eventually it will slow down the development process. Thus automation in this area is a desired effort.

A knowledge model and corresponding semantic repository of algorithms and features, like we did in the case of sensors, containing detail facts can be a good answer to the above problem. Associated with it there should be a tool which will recommend developers to select right algorithm and stitch them in right sequence in order to make a meaningful sensor data processing workflow aka the core of an IoT application.

Related Works

A few efforts have already been made to address aforesaid area of requirement. We found that there are two types of work in this area: 1) an algorithm repository that comes with a workflow designer tool associated with it, and 2) a workflow designer tool that have an algorithm repository associated with it. Since having a workflow designer tool is necessary to demonstrate the use of algorithm repository so first type of work is very obvious while second type is not very obvious because workflow creation tools are usually generic in design such that they can use algorithms, functions, rules etc. from any arbitrary source.

Algorithmia (Algorithmia, n.d.) is a work that falls in first category mentioned above i.e. it is an algorithm repository associated with a workflow designer. It contains an interface tool for submission of new algorithms in its repository but it lacks depth in terms of variety and count. Also it does not recommend algorithms while creating a workflow. *Caiman* (Reyes-Aldasoro et al., 2011) is another online algorithm repository with very limited set of image processing algorithms focused only for cancer research. The structure of the repository is not very generic. *Stony Brook Algorithm Repository* (Skiena, 1999) is a very comprehensive algorithm repository consisting of about 70 algorithms with practical implementation. Algorithms are from different domains like data structures, computational geometry, graph theory etc. However it does not provide any mechanism of search and recommendation of algorithms and it does not facilitate creation of workflow. There is an algorithm ontology called *OpenTox* (Algorithm ontology, n.d.) created by a community of same name which targets to create models for detecting chemical toxicity; but its structure is not exhaustive and generic enough to accommodate various types of algorithms used in IoT domain. There is only a simple taxonomy of algorithm based on algorithm types and that too is very much focused for toxicity domain. The ontology does not have any relation defined amongst its classes. Kinetic Simulation Algorithm Ontology, in short *KiSAO* (Courtot et al., 2011), is another algorithm ontology that consists description of algorithms for simulation experiments with respect to a very limited set of predefined algorithm characteristics and parameters but it does not have a workflow associated with it.

On the second category of works, *Galaxy* (Blankenberg et al., 2010) is a genome data based workflow creation and execution framework but it has its proprietary execution platform thus restricting variety during workflow designing. Needless to say it does not have an algorithm repository associated with it. *Wotkit* (Blackstock et al., 2012) is another online tool which helps user add sensor, capture and visualize data from it and create custom IoT applications based on widgets exposed as REST APIs. But it does not have feature like processing and analysis of data and does not offer recommendation during workflow creation.

There are some cloud based IoT application development frameworks like *Axeda* (Axeda Machine Cloud, n.d.), *BlueMix* (IBM Bluemix, n.d.), *ThingsWorx* (ThingsWorx, n.d.) etc. which have features like device management and configuration, cloud application development, connectivity service provisioning and management but they lack in having a standard algorithm repository. Moreover semantic search and recommendation feature to be used during workflow designing process is missing. Here is a comparison table between such existing IoT frameworks shown in Figure 15. All of them have some

Figure 15. A feature-wise comparison of IoT frameworks

		Axeda
	Absent	
	Partially matches	
	Present	
	Don't know	
	Value Added Features	
1	Stimuli detection from Observation by various reasoning techniques	
2	Semantic search, ranking, recommendation from repository of re-usable algorithm toolboxes*	
3	Ontology enrichment using structure/unstructured data from web (for 1)	
4	Context help for algorithms from structured data from Web	
5	Workflow designer dashboard	
6	Analytics Services as workflows	
7	Atomic task execution	
8	Workflow Enactment	
9	Distributed workflow orchestration	
10	Automated optimized partitioning/execution for Fog Computing	
11	Stream and Batch mode based optimal workflow partition	

* signal/image processing, statistical, ML, Optimization, reasoning

common features, namely spatio-temporal queries, stream processing, execution support on edge and platform APIs but lacks some features like semantic search, recommendation, ontology enrichment, workflow enactment etc.

Algopedia: The Knowledge Model and Repository for Algorithms

As none of the above works found to be a right starting point for creating an algorithm knowledge model hence we started from scratch. However we have carefully picked up a few classes and properties from these algorithm ontologies to incorporate in ours. The annotated repository of algorithm – we call it *Algopedia* - consists of three distinct parts: an algorithm ontology, an instance repository and a reasoner module. They are described in detail below.

1. **Algorithm Ontology:** The ontology has been created using Protégé 4.0 (A free, open-source ontology editor, n.d.). The top class of the ontology is *Algorithm*. The ontology contains different buckets (aka categories) of algorithms namely *Filtering, Signal Extracting, Machine Learning, Numerical Analysis, Statistical Analysis, Transforms* etc. and are created as subclasses of the *Algorithm* class. The buckets are created as per functionalities of the algorithms i.e. depending on what the algorithms do. Under each of these buckets, there are more subcategories of algorithms (refer Figure 16). The top *Algorithm* class has some generic data type and object type properties like description, authorName, complexity, inputParameters, configParameters, license, usability, profiling information, application areas etc. while sub classes have more specific properties associated with them. Other related entities like *Features, Input and Output Parameter, SignalType, Time* and *Space Complexity* etc. are also defined at the same level of *Algorithm* class. The relations between these entities with *Algorithm* classes are defined using object properties, data-type properties along with associated rules, restrictions and annotations (refer Figure 17). This ontology contains pseudo-codes associated with each algorithm classes. The structure and elements of this ontology provides the basic metadata model for algorithms and is flexible to be enriched with more algorithm categories/sub-categories (i.e. classes), metadata, relations and annotations. Web mining and crowd sourcing from domain experts and users can be a good source for this.

2. **Algorithm Instance Repository:** Based on aforesaid algorithm ontology model and following the pseudo-codes therein, a repository of working code is created. Any coder can implement a code instance for a given algorithm by following steps in corresponding pseudo-code from the ontology. Next, he/she can submit that code sample in the instance repository along with proper annotations and metadata like author's name, data set on which it is tested, profiling information if any etc. Let's explain this with an example. Say, an algorithm domain expert has created one algorithm class Filter and its subclass *BandPassFilter* and respective pseudo-codes. These are stored in Algopedia ontology. If somebody writes a python implementation named *bandpass_filter.py* based on *BandPassFilter* pseudo-code then that particular *.py* file goes to algorithm instance repository. Different languages like C, R, Java etc. can be used to implement same *BandPassFilter* pseudo-code and each of them can have different code complexities; the repository will accommodate each of them and all of them will be identified as instances of the class *BandPassFilter*. This instance repository can again be enriched by web mining, crowd-sourcing and by feedbacks from users of the instances so that a ranked list of implementations can be generated and be used for recommendation purpose.

Figure 16. Algopedia buckets

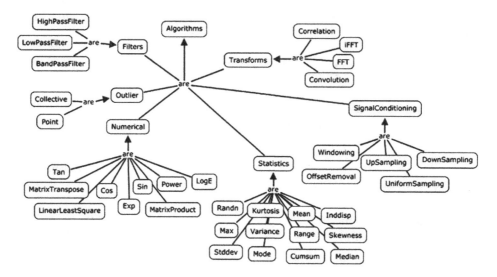

Figure 17. Concepts and relations around "Algorithm" class

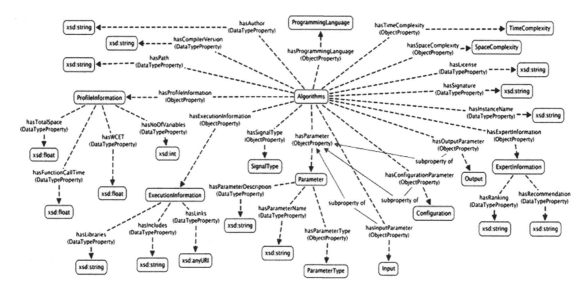

3. **Reasoner:** The reasoner module in Algopedia works both on algorithm ontology and repository. This module

    a. Validates correctness of ontology and repository after a new entry is made by experts or coders or after a round of enrichment via web crawling or crowdsourcing is done.

    b. Can recommend a set of ranked algorithms most suitable for given criteria like signal-type, feature type etc.

Figure 18. Web Interface for Algopedia

Algopedia Web UI

Similar to sensors, we have made another web based tool to allow algorithm code writers to submit their implementations of a pseudo-code in Algopedia repository along with relevant annotation and metadata like author name, library dependencies, compiler version, input/output parameter details etc. This user interface can also be used to edit or modify aforesaid details of instances (refer Figure 18). This user interface is dynamically bound with the underlying Algopedia ontology via REST APIs as listed in table shown in Figure 19. This means: the right panel in Figure 18 is created dynamically as per properties of Algorithm class in ontology. If a new property is added or an existing one is modified, then the changes automatically will reflect back in the user interface. The web services listed in Figure 19 are very much similar to that for sensor ontology.

In next section, we will discuss how these types of knowledge models can be used to create a recommendation based workflow creation in IoT domain.

WORKFLOW CREATION USING KNOWLEDGE MODELS

We have mentioned earlier that most IoT applications basically follow a workflow at their core. This workflow generally starts by collecting sensor observation data and then it processes that data in multiple steps using different algorithms to extract some meaningful insight to be used for further actions. Most of the IoT applications which deal with sensor signal processing follow a common workflow template as shown in Figure 14. It starts with a) data collection from sensors, b) then a set of noise cleaning is done on the data, c) then the data passes through pre-processing stage where it may be converted from frequency domain to time domain, d) next some steps like outlier detection, filtering etc. are done. After these basic steps are over, these workflows often involve classification or clustering model creation using machine learning techniques where one have to extract features out of the processed sensor data set

Figure 19. Sample web services for Sensor and Algorithm knowledge models

Purpose	Method	Relative URI
Concept Hierarchy	GET	tree/classHierarchy
Concept-Instance Hierarchy	GET	tree/classInstanceHierarchy
Concept Template	GET	GPserver/conceptPrototype/{classURI}
Concepts	GET,POST,PUT,DELETE	GPserver/concepts{classURI}
Instance Template	GET	GPserver/instancePrototype/{classURI}
Instances	GET,POST,PUT,DELETE	GPserver/instances/{instanceURI}
Edit Instance	GET	GPserver/editInstance/{instanceURI}
SPARQL Query	GET	query/sparqlQuery/{queryString}

and then select some meaningful features to create a prediction model using supervised or unsupervised learning methods. Model creation and its training part are normally done on trial data. Once the whole workflow along with the model is ready, then one can execute the flow on real time sensor data.

Most of the naïve developers do not have knowledge about the pattern and nature of the data, what to do and not to do with a specific set of data, which algorithm applies best for a certain step or for a certain signal type etc., so it is tedious and time consuming to create one successful workflow. Again, selecting right features from a huge set of features, running right set of model creation algorithm based on the data geometry requires multiple trial cycles and requires hard core machine learning expertise. Readymade knowledge models involving sensors, algorithms, data patterns, features, machine learning techniques along with rule engines can help naïve developers by recommending at each and every steps of such a complicated workflow creation and thus can help save a lot of development time.

We have developed a recommendation based system to create an IoT workflow using the sensor and algorithm knowledge models along with meta-models of feature and machine learning domain knowledge at the backend. We have used a web based tool named Node-Red to demonstrate this system. Here developers can select from a set of custom-made nodes like *SensorSelector, AlgoRecommender, DisplayData, FeatureSelector&Extractor* etc. They can drag and drop one node and can select parameters of their choice within that node. For example, in *AlgoRecommender* node (refer Figure 20), they can select what step they want to execute (say *pre-processing* and then a sub-step called *transform*), what type of data is coming into that step (say *periodic stationary*) etc. Based on these parameters, the algorithm knowledge model will recommend most suitable set of algorithms available and developer can select one from that set (say *FFT*).

In a similar fashion, *FeatureSelector&Extractor* node can work with support of corresponding knowledge models. We have created a repository of more than eighty signal features which are most commonly used in sensor signal analytics and have classified them into time and frequency domain. Example of time domain features are RMS, zero crossing rate, low energy frame rate, running average of amplitude, sum of absolute differences, intensity etc. while example of frequency domain features

Figure 20. A snapshot of Algo-recommender node

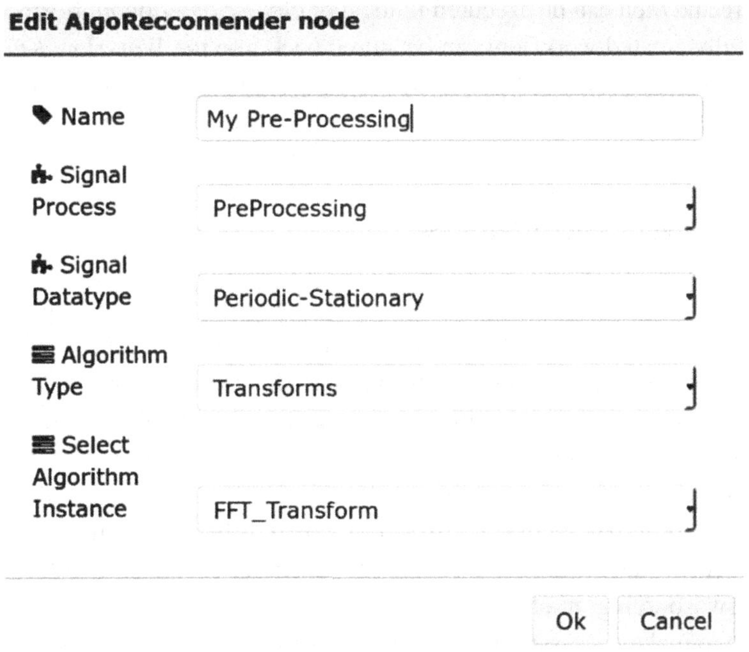

are spectral entropy, spectral flux, spectral roll off, bandwidth, phase deviation etc. This node helps in reducing the dimensionality of the features by performing a set of optimization techniques and finally recommending a reduced set of features to developer. During model creation phase, system recommends a list of possible learning algorithms for the user to select any one of them (like SVM); corresponding configuration parameters (like window size, cluster number etc.) are also to be supplied to create the model.

The drag and drop facility in Node-Red will enable developers to undergo multiple trial and error loops until they reach their desired solution. Without recommendation and in absence of backend knowledge models, these multiple trials would take days rather months to come up with a working solution. Once

Figure 21. Sample MDD nodes and a sample workflow created in Node-RED platform

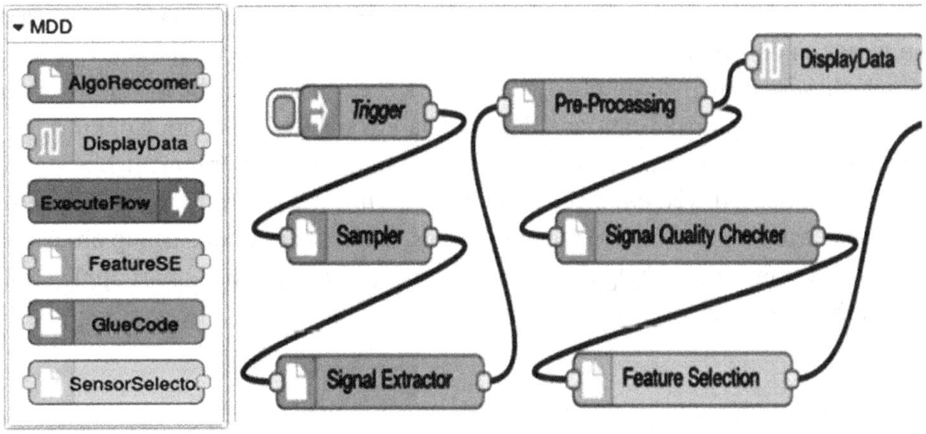

a workflow is complete by stitching all the nodes together (as shown in Figure 21), it can be converted into a JSON structure and then can be executed in local or cloud execution platform with real time sensor data. A successfully created workflow can be stored back into the *Workflow Knowledge Model* for further reuse by other developers who try to create similar applications. The whole mechanism of the workflow creation platform is described in more detail by (Dey et al., 2015).

FUTURE WORKS AND CONCLUSION

In this chapter, we have discussed how a model driven approach for application development can be realized in IoT domain and how ontologies can help create such reusable knowledge models. So far we have designed the sensor and algorithm knowledge models and used them successfully to create a web-based application development platform which can provide recommendations to the developer using the knowledge models. However, this is an initial prototype and there is ample scope of work left in this area. Both algorithm and sensor knowledge models can be enriched by crowd sourced information from users. This information may include qualifications such as better lifetime, better battery usage or better reliability for sensors, and time/space complexity, memory footprint, functional qualities etc. for algorithms. Such crowdsourcing, in effect, will increase the reliability and use of these models in IoT community. We have to make necessary arrangements to enable crowd-sourcing within our system. At present, knowledge models are exposed to application world by RESTFul web services. More such web APIs are to be made for ease of development. A scope of improvement is to make such web services compatible with semantic web service standards like OWL-S. While creating a workflow, we can incorporate the *Design by Contract* paradigm of software development, using which the system can itself identify whether a node with certain output can be stitched with a next node that expects a certain input. This is not only limited to syntactic matching but also semantic matching so that the workflow makes sense.

A typical smart IoT application captures raw data from sensors, and then tries to extract some meaningful information from the data by running some analytics. Based on some rules, the application then tries to derive the actual insight from the information and we call this acquiring knowledge. Finally based on that knowledge, the application tries to take decision for a given situation. This final step is the most crucial in the sense that the accumulated knowledge and the reasoning method in the application should be correct enough to take the appropriate decision. As of now, this final layer, which is often called the *layer of wisdom*, does not have any proper methodology to take into account the experience of a real practitioner in a certain domain, for example the experience of a doctor. But extensive research is going on across the world on data and decision sciences, using numerous approaches such as *deep learning* and *deep QA*, which we feel are two complimentary approaches – one based on the discovery on intricate patterns and relationships within the data, and the other based on the accumulation of knowledge through books, journals, literature etc. If and when the success in building a proper human-like learning system is achieved, the much-needed wisdom layer on analytics will take its proper shape. Until that time, a staged automation is what we may be looking at – such as, automated signal cleanup process, automated extraction of signal features etc. to help the industry create more and more smart applications in order to help people in their daily activities.

REFERENCES

A free, open-source ontology editor and framework for building intelligent systems. (n.d.). Retrieved March 31, 2016, from http://protege.stanford.edu/

Algorithm ontology. (n.d.). Retrieved March 31, 2016, from http://www.opentox.org/dev/apis/api-1.1/Algorithms

Algorithmia - Open Marketplace for Algorithms. (n.d.). Retrieved March 31, 2016, from https://algorithmia.com/

Axeda Machine Cloud | PTC. (n.d.). Retrieved March 31, 2016, from http://www.ptc.com/axeda/product/iot-platform

Blackstock, M., & Lea, R. (2012). IoT Mashups with the WoTKit. In *Internet of Things (IOT), 3rd International Conference on the. IEEE*, (pp. 159–166). doi:10.1109/IOT.2012.6402318

Blankenberg, D., Kuster, G. V., Coraor, N., Ananda, G., Lazarus, R., Mangan, M.,... Taylor, J. (2010). Galaxy: a web-based genome analysis tool for experimentalists. In Current protocols in molecular biology (pp. 19–10). doi:10.1002/0471142727.mb1910s89

Botts, M., Percivall, G., Reed, C., & Davidson, J. (2006). OGC® sensor web enablement: Overview and high level architecture. In GeoSensor networks (pp. 175-190). Springer Berlin Heidelberg.

Botts, M., & Robin, A. (2007). *OpenGIS sensor model language (SensorML) implementation specification*. OpenGIS Implementation Specification OGC, 7(000).

Compton, M., Barnaghi, P., Bermudez, L., García-Castro, R., Corcho, O., Cox, S., & Taylor, K. et al. (2012). The SSN ontology of the W3C semantic sensor network incubator group. *Web Semantics: Science, Services, and Agents on the World Wide Web*, 17, 25–32. doi:10.1016/j.websem.2012.05.003

Corcho, O., & García-Castro, R. (2010). Five challenges for the semantic sensor web. In Semantic Web (vol. 1, no. 1, pp. 121–125).

Courtot, M., Juty, N., Knupfer, C., Waltemath, D., Zhukova, A., Drager, A., & Hastings, J. et al. (2011). Controlled vocabularies and semantics in systems biology. *Molecular Systems Biology*, 7(1), 543. doi:10.1038/msb.2011.77 PMID:22027554

Dey, S., Dasgupta, R., Pal, A., & Misra, P. (2013). Semantic Web Challenge Competition ISWC. *Sensxplore: A tool for sensor discovery using semantics with focus on smart metering*. Retrieved March 31, 2016, from http://challenge.semanticweb.org/2013/submissions/swc2013_submission_8.pdf

Dey, S., Jaiswal, D., Dasgupta, R., & Mukherjee, A. (2015). Organization and Management of Semantic Sensor Information using SSN Ontology: Energy Meter Use Case. *Proceedings of the 7th IEEE International Conference on Sensing Technology*. doi:10.1109/ICSensT.2015.7438444

Dey, S., Jaiswal, D., Pal, H. S., & Mukherjee, A. (2015). A Semantic Algorithm Repository and Workflow Designer Tool: Signal Processing Use Case. In *International Conference on IoT as a Service, IoT360 Summit, Rome*.

DG INFSO & EPoSS. (2008). Internet of things in 2020: Roadmap for the future. INFSO D, 4.

DUL. (n.d.). Retrieved March 31, 2016, http://www.loa-cnr.it/ontologies/DUL.owl

Eid, M., Liscano, R., & El Saddik, A. (2007). *A universal ontology for sensor networks data.* doi:10.1109/CIMSA.2007.4362539

Gross, N. (1999). *21st Century Internet, Bloomberg Business Week.* Retrieved March 31, 2016, from http://www.businessweek.com/1999/99_35/b3644024.htm

IBM Bluemix is the cloud platform that helps developers rapidly build, manage and run web and mobile applications. (n.d.). Retrieved March 31, 2016, from www.ibm.com/software/bluemix/welcome/solutions2.html

Janowicz, K., & Compton, M. (2010, November). The stimulus-sensor-observation ontology design pattern and its integration into the semantic sensor network ontology. In *Proceedings of the 3rd International Conference on Semantic Sensor Networks* (vol. 668, pp. 64-78). CEUR-WS. org.

Niles, I., & Pease, A. (2001). Towards a standard upper ontology. In *Proceedings of the international conference on Formal Ontology in Information Systems.* ACM.

NodeRED. (n.d.). Retrieved March 31, 2016, from http://nodered.org/

OASIS – Organization for the Advancement of Structured Information Standards. (n.d.). Retrieved March 31, 2016, from https://www.oasis-open.org/

Pal, A., Mukherjee, A., & Balamuralidhar, P. (2014). Model Driven Development for Internet of Things: Towards Easing the Concerns of Application Developers. *International Conference on IoT as a Service, IoT360 Summit.*

Press Release. Gartner. (2014). *Gartner Says 4.9 Billion Connected Things Will Be in Use in 2015.* Retrieved March 31, 2016, from http://www.gartner.com/newsroom/id/2905717

Reyes-Aldasoro, C. C., Griffiths, M. K., Savas, D., & Tozer, G. M. (2011). Caiman: An online algorithm repository for cancer image analysis. *Computer Methods and Programs in Biomedicine, 103*(2), 97–103. doi:10.1016/j.cmpb.2010.07.007 PMID:20691494

Riedel, T., Yordanov, D., Fantana, N., Scholz, M., & Decker, C. (2010, June). A model driven internet of things. In *Networked Sensing Systems (INSS), 2010 Seventh International Conference on* (pp. 265-268). IEEE. doi:10.1109/INSS.2010.5573154

Russomanno, D. J., Kothari, C., & Thomas, O. (2005). Sensor ontologies: from shallow to deep models. In *System Theory, SSST'05. Proceedings of the Thirty-Seventh Southeastern Symposium on* (pp. 107–112). doi:10.1109/SSST.2005.1460887

Skiena, S. (1999). Who is interested in algorithms and why? Lessons from the stony brook algorithms repository. ACM SIGACT News, 30(3), 65–74.

Stevenson, G. G., Knox, S., Dobson, S., & Nixon, P. (2009). Ontonym: a collection of upper ontologies for developing pervasive systems. In *Proceedings of the 1st Workshop on Context, Information and Ontologies.* ACM. doi:10.1145/1552262.1552271

SWE-OGC. (2013). *Sensorml, o&m and tml standard.* Retrieved March 31, 2016, from http://www. opengeospatial.org/standards/

ThingWorx | ThingWorx. (n.d.). Retrieved March 31, 2016, from http://www.thingworx.com/

TOSCA - Topology and Orchestration Specification for Cloud Applications. V1.0. (2013). Retrieved March 31, 2016, from http://docs.oasis-open.org/tosca/TOSCA/v1.0/os/TOSCA-v1.0-os.html

Underbrink, A., Witt, K., Stanley, J., & Mandl, D. (2008). Autonomous mission operations for sensor webs, In *AGU Fall Meeting Abstracts* (vol. 1, 2008, p. 05).

Chapter 3
Image Processing for Surveillance and Security

Deepayan Bhowmik
Sheffield Hallam University, UK

Mehryar Emambakhsh
Heriot-Watt University, UK

ABSTRACT

Security is a fundamental issue in today's world. In this chapter we discuss various aspects of security in daily life that can be solved using image processing techniques by grouping in three main categories: visual tracking, biometrics and digital media security. Visual tracking refers to computer vision techniques that analyses the scene to extract features representing objects (e.g., pedestrian) and track them to provide input to analyse any anomalous behaviour. Biometrics is the technology of detecting, extracting and analysing human's physical or behavioural features for identification purposes. Digital media security typically includes multimedia signal processing techniques that can protect copyright by embedding information within the media content using watermarking approaches. Individual topics are discussed referring recent literature.

INTRODUCTION

Surveillance and security are the integral part of today's life particularly when million's of CCTVs are in action covering many public places including, airports, railway stations, high streets, market places, shopping complexes, theaters and many more to name. At the same time, in today's digital world we capture, store and share millions of images, videos and other creative contents. Development in network infrastructure and media compression technology influenced a paradigm shift in entertainment content consumption such as video streaming, and on-demand video services. However all these scenarios pose several challenges in image processing community in addressing digital security in everyday life.

The security and surveillance are often treated separately in the image and signal processing research domain. While computer vision techniques deal with challenges in visual tracking, anomaly detection or biometric identifications, multimedia signal processing community is more concern with digital

DOI: 10.4018/978-1-5225-2498-4.ch003

media security and digital right management using data hiding techniques (e.g., watermarking). In this book chapter we attempted to discuss image processing approaches proposed in the literature addressing various digital security related issues, from surveillance to media security. To the best knowledge of the authors' there is no such attempt made in the literature that brings together such range of topics under one common theme.

The chapter is broadly categorised in three sections: a) visual tracking, b) biometric and c) multimedia security. We restricted our discussion of the individual topics with respect to image processing techniques.

IMAGE PROCESSING FOR VISUAL TRACKING

Automatic detection, tracking and anomaly identification occupy a considerable space in computer vision research and have many applications including intelligent surveillance, human-computer interaction (HCI), human-robot interaction (HRI), augmented reality (AR), medical applications and visual vehicle navigation etc. More importantly, recently there is a great deal of interest in robust visual tracking algorithms due to the increased need of automated video analysis relating safety in public places such as railway station, airport, shopping areas, religious festivals or governmental offices. This poses fundamental challenges in computer vision which involves input from image processing research along with input from machine learning community. In this section we discussed fundamental steps for visual tracking by dissecting the algorithms available in recent literature.

Image analysis for tracking consists of three key steps: 1) detection of interesting moving objects; 2) tracking moving objects in time lapsed frames and 3) analysis of tracked objects for behavioural study such as recognition, prediction and anomaly detection. One can broadly dissect the visual tracking algorithms in four different categories (Yilmaz et al., 2006; Haering et al., 2008; Yang et al., 2011): a) Object representation, b) Feature selection, c) Object detection and d) Object tracking. These categories can also be grouped and fitted into a classical image processing pyramid of low level, medium level, intermediate level and high level algorithms, based on the complexity and the type of data they process (Figure 1).

Object Representation

Shape Representation

Objects in a scene can be represented by their shape of appearance. Example of shape representations are: i) Points where objects can be represented by a point, e.g., centroid (Veenman et al., 2001) or by a set of points (Serby et al., 2004) to track objects that engage a smaller region of the image space; ii) Primitive geometric shapes where objects can be represented by various geometric shapes such as rectangle, ellipse (Comaniciu et al., 2003) or parametric ellipsoid (Limprasert et al., 2013) for tracking purposes; iii) Object silhouette and contour where the contour of object boundary and the contour region is called as silhouette and used in tracking (Yilmaz et al., 2004). iv) Articulated shape models where targets are composed of combination of connected body parts, e.g., human subject can be articulated with the torso, head, arm, leg etc... (Husz et al., 2011). Individual body parts are represented using cylinders or ellipses; and v) Skeletal models where skeletons are extracted from object silhouettes by applying medial axis transform and used in object recognition (Ali and Aggarwal, 2001) or tracking (Schwarz et al., 2012).

Figure 1. Image processing pyramid of visual tracking algorithms

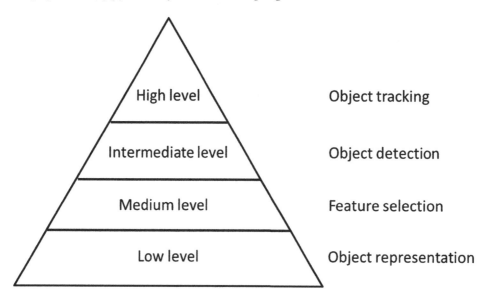

Appearance Representation

Alternatively the objects can be represented by their appearances combined with the shape model for tracking purposes. Example appearance models are: i) Probability densities of object appearance features (e.g., color, texture) can estimated for the region of interest from their shape representation. Example probability density estimation algorithms are mixture of Gaussian (Paragios and Deriche, 2002) or histograms (Comaniciu et al., 2003); ii) Templates are used e.g., for object recognition and tracking, and can be formed from the geometrical shapes or silhouettes (Dufour et al., 2002); and iii) Active appearance model are generated simultaneously by statistical shape models and appearances, which can generalise the object e.g., face (Edwards et al., 1998). While the shape can be defined by object representation (e.g., contour), the appearance can be defined from colour, texture or gradients.

Feature Selection

A single feature or combination of features are crucial for visual tracking, in order to uniquely identify a target object in image space or world coordinates. Features can be affected by many factors including viewpoint, occlusion, illumination, texture, or articulation. Commonly used visual features are:

Colour

Various color spaces, e.g., RGB (Red, Green, Blue) and HSV (Hue, Saturation, Value) have been used to represent object features. The object color can be influenced by two physical phenomena (Yilmaz et al., 2006): 1) spectral distribution of the source and 2) surface reflectance of the target object. Comaniciu et al. (Comaniciu et al., 2003) used color histograms in mean-shift based object tracking.

Edge

Edge features can be generated by capturing sudden intensity changes and are usually less sensitive to illumination changes when compared to using colour feature selection. The Canny edge detector (Canny, 1986) is one of most used edge detectors to date.

Texture

Texture selection measures the intensity variation of an object's surface to quantify smoothness and regularity (Shotton et al., 2009). Various algorithms have been proposed to investigate texture patterns using filters (Laws, 1980), wavelets (Mallat, 1989) or local binary patterns descriptors (Ojala et al., 2002). Similar to edge feature selection, this is also less sensitive to illumination changes.

Gradient

The directional change in intensity or colour is captured in gradient feature and has been proven to be more robust particularly for human detection e.g., Histogram of Oriented Gradients (HOG) by Dalal and Triggs (Dalal and Triggs, 2005).

Spatio-Temporal

Local spatio-temporal features capture the salient and motion characteristics in video and is usually invariant to spatio-temporal shifts, scales or background clutter. For example optical flow (Horn and Schunck, 1981) defines the translation of each pixel in a region and is used as feature in motion-based segmentation and tracking algorithms.

Object Detection

Object detection methods are necessary in order to perform object tracking, and are applied in every frame in the target video. In some cases, temporal cues are used to reduce false detection. Various types of detectors have been proposed in the literature including:

Point Detector

Objects are represented by interest points with expressive texture. Commonly used algorithms are invariant to changes in illumination, camera viewpoint, rotation or scaling. Examples of popular point detectors include Harris detector (Harris and Stephens, 1988), KLT (Kanade-Lucas-Tomasi) detector (Shi and Tomasi, 1994), and SIFT (Scale-invariant feature transform) detector (Lowe, 2004).

Background Subtraction

These algorithms model the pixels to be either part of the background or part of the foreground. Any considerable change signifies as moving object detection. Example background subtraction algorithms can be found in (KaewTraKulPong and Bowden, 2002) and (Zivkovic and van der Heijden, 2006).

Segmentation

These algorithms partition the image into perceptually (e.g., by colour or texture) similar regions. Segmented regions can be identified as a target object which can later be used in tracking. Various algorithms have been proposed, including mean-shift clustering (Comaniciu and Meer, 2002), segmentation using graph-cuts (Boykov and Funka-Lea, 2006), and active contours (Yilmaz et al., 2004).

Supervised Learning

Object detection using sequences of different object views or illuminations can be achieved in supervised learning algorithms as opposed to template matching. Supervised learning is a classification problem. Object detection algorithms are often trained and tested with given object feature set and associated object classes. Adaptive boosting (Adaboost) (Freund and Schapire, 1997) and Support Vector Machines (SVM) (Boser et al., 1992) are two classic examples. An example of a popular pedestrian detector (Dalal and Triggs, 2005) is shown in Figure 2.

Figure 2. Example of a pedestrian detector using HOG
(Dalal & Triggs, 2005)

Object Tracking

Object tracking algorithms generate the trajectory of the targets over time in a video sequence. Object detection and tracking are often performed either separately e.g., detecting target objects in every frame and then track by correspondence over frames; or jointly e.g., correspondence is estimated by iteratively updating object information (e.g., points of interest or location) using processing outputs from previous frames. Many tracking algorithms can be found in the literature, and can be grouped into the following categories:

Point Tracking

Point tracking is performed by correspondence of detected objects represented by points. Based on the correspondence type, this can again be classified as 1) deterministic e.g., Greedy Optimal Assignment (GOA) Tracker (Veenman et al., 2001) or 2) statistical e.g., Kalman filter (Broida and Chellappa, 1986), Particle Filter (PF) or Sequential Monte Carlo (SMC) (Arulampalam et al., 2002), Joint Probability Data Association Filter (JPDAF) (Bar-Shalom and Foreman, 1988), Multiple Hypothesis Tracking (MHT) (Blackman, 2004) or Probability Hypothesis Density (PHD) Filter (Vo and Ma, 2006).

Silhouette Tracking

Tracking algorithms often consider silhouettes to represent complex object shapes e.g., a human body cannot be described by simple geometric shapes, and corresponding target object regions in successive frames. For example Kang et al. (Kang et al., 2004) used histogram of colour and edges as object models and used in tracking.

Kernel Tracking

Kernel tracking algorithms depend on the motion of an object often defined by a region in subsequent frames. Mean-shift (Comaniciu et al., 2003), Kanade-Lucas-Tomasi (KLT) feature tracker (Shi and Tomasi, 1994), Support Vector Machine (SVM) tracker (Avidan, 2004) are few examples of kernel tracking. An example of mean-shift tracking (Comaniciu et al., 2003) is shown in Figure 3.

Figure 3. Example of color histogram based mean-shift tracking

Biometrics Authentication

Biometrics is a combination of two Greek words (Jain et al., 2004): bios, meaning life, and metrikos, meaning measure. The main motivation of storing a person's biometric data is to reuse it for the recognition purposes. Therefore, there are generally at least two sessions involved at a biometrics data storage process: a) data acquisition stage, in which the raw data is obtained and biometric data is stored; and b) authentication stage acquired data for the target subject is compared with the available dataset to check the person's identity. The biometric data obtained at the first stage is usually known as the gallery, while the one from the second stage is known as the probe.

A good biometric system should be (Jain et al., 2004, 2006):

- **Consistent:** The observed physical or behavioural biometrics features captured from a subject should not significantly change, when the probe data acquisition is performed, i.e., the data should not lose its similarity with the data stored in the gallery for the same class labels, and should maintain its dissimilarity with the samples from other subjects.
- **Discriminative:** The biometric data should not be similar between different people to maintain its reliability in recognising a subject correctly.
- **Easily Obtainable:** The imaging or in general, data acquisition procedure should be easy and practical for both the subject, whose biometric data is obtained and the biometrics system customer, who utilises the data capture device.
- **Robust:** Another key feature of a good biometrics is its robustness. The biometric features should not be easily manipulated or changed by the subject. The biometrics system should be prepared to detect such change. Otherwise, the subject might be wrongly classified as another person or might not be correctly verified.
- **Secure:** As the acquired data is completely private for a subject, it should be very safely and securely stored. Also, the biometrics data should be properly coded and encrypted to avoid any spoofing attacks as much as possible.
- **Maintainable:** Although the storage costs are annually becoming lower and lower, the size of data should not be too large. This is not just to reduce the storage expenses, but to reduce the processing time of the data.
- **Fast:** The data acquisition and process procedures should be as quick as possible. Slow processing time is inconvenient for both sides of a biometrics system, i.e the subject and device customer.

There are two widely used approaches to evaluate the performance of a biometrics system. The first one is by using the receiver operator characteristic (ROC) curve. In the case of a verification scenario (or open-set recognition (Scheirer et al., 2013), in which the subject might not necessarily have a corresponding sample in the dataset), based on the matching scores computed over the samples in a biometrics test session, a subject can be selected as legitimate or an impostor. The decision making is usually performed by assigning a threshold on the subject's biometrics matching scores (Jain et al., 2006). All biometric systems produce some degree of errors in their output decisions. Therefore, if the decision making threshold is varied from 0 to 1 over a normalised set of matching scores, a subject's biometrics verification rate can be computed. Plotting these thresholds (false alarm rate (FAR) or false positive rate(FPR)) against the output verification rate (true positive rate (TPR)) or sometimes against FNR, produces the ROC curve. For the former, the more concave the ROC curve means a better verification rate. An important point on an ROC curve is when FAR and TPR are equal. This point is called equal error rate (EER) and is usually reported to show the biometrics system's verification performance. Also, detection error trade-off (DET) is a modified version of an ROC curve used to quantitatively describe the performance of a biometrics system.

The second approach is based on the cumulative matching characteristic (CMC) curve. The CMC curve is usually used for the identification scenarios (or in close-set recognition (Scheirer et al., 2013), in which the test subject has a corresponding sample in the gallery). It is the probability of correctly assigning the right class label to a test sample, when the matching scores are sorted per gallery samples (Jain et al., 2006). Therefore, the classification rate at the ith rank means the probability of assigning the correct label to the test samples, after the i smallest matching scores are evaluated. For the CMC curves, usually the classification rate of the first rank is reported. It corresponds to the probability of the equality of test subject's label to the smallest matching score.

While fingerprints, irises, pupils, faces, palmprints, voice and gait are the most common biometric modalities, they all suffer from certain issues. For example, fingerprints and palmprints are vulnerable to dirt and scratches (Jain et al., 2004), while iris and pupil recognition performance can be deteriorated by blinking, occlusions or contact lenses (Jain et al., 2006). In addition, gait and voice can be inconsistent and vary over time.

As high resolution cameras have become cheaper, the face has become one of the most reliable biometrics. However, make up, lighting conditions, expressions, pose and occlusions are also commonly known issues associated with face recognition procedures. In order to reduce the sensitivity of face recognition algorithms to lighting and pose, 3D face recognition was introduced. Numerous 3D capturing devices and technologies, such as structured-light based (Savran et al., 2008), Minolta Vivid 900 laser (Phillips et al., 2005) and Photometric Stereo imaging (Zafeiriou et al., 2011), have been utilised to perform data acquisition at biometric sessions.

Figure 4. Different steps of a 3D face recognition algorithm

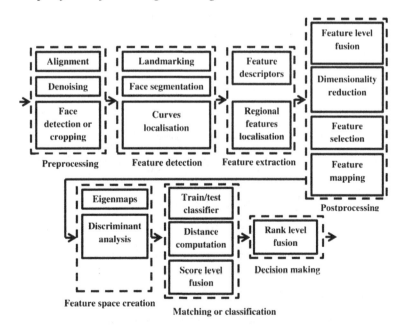

A typical face recognition algorithm is shown in Figure 4. The preprocessing section of a face recognition algorithm usually consists of pose correction, denoising and face detection. Then, in the feature detection step, some informative sets of points, which can be consistently detected on the facial surface, are used for feature extraction. After that, the feature space is post-processed. Some of the well-known algorithms used for feature space post-processing are feature selection, mapping, dimensionality reduction algorithms. Multiple sets of features can be fused at this step to increase the classification accuracy.

The next step is denoted as feature space creation, in which the feature space can further be manipulated to make it more robust. There are numerous algorithms for this task, such as principal component or discriminant analysis algorithms. Then, the matching or classification methods are applied to the feature space and, finally, the decision making is performed. Depending the capabilities of a face recognition algorithm, some of these steps might be omitted. For instance, if the feature detection or extraction step is rotation invariant, using an alignment algorithm might not be necessary.

Nose as a Biometric

Although capturing the 3D faces enables solving several issues associated with the 2D face recognition, the algorithms are still sensitive to facial expressions, occlusions, pose and noise. As an example, Figure 5 shows the matching errors for the face of subject 1, in 5 different cases: neutral, occluded, rotated, noisy and with facial expression, demonstrating sensitivity of holistic facial matching algorithms to facial deformities. The matching is performed using the iterative closest point (ICP) algorithm (Best and McKay, 1992).

Figure 5. Matching results using five different probe samples of subject 1 in the gallery with variations caused by occlusion, pose, noise and expression

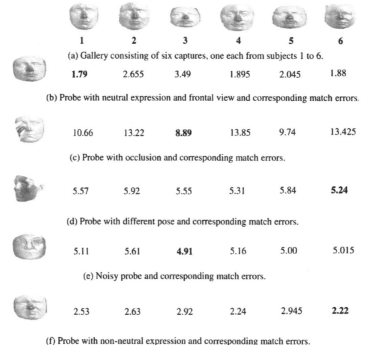

| 1 | 2 | 3 | 4 | 5 | 6 |

(a) Gallery consisting of six captures, one each from subjects 1 to 6.

| **1.79** | 2.655 | 3.49 | 1.895 | 2.045 | 1.88 |

(b) Probe with neutral expression and frontal view and corresponding match errors.

| 10.66 | 13.22 | **8.89** | 13.85 | 9.74 | 13.425 |

(c) Probe with occlusion and corresponding match errors.

| 5.57 | 5.92 | 5.55 | 5.31 | 5.84 | **5.24** |

(d) Probe with different pose and corresponding match errors.

| 5.11 | 5.61 | **4.91** | 5.16 | 5.00 | 5.015 |

(e) Noisy probe and corresponding match errors.

| 2.53 | 2.63 | 2.92 | 2.24 | 2.945 | **2.22** |

(f) Probe with non-neutral expression and corresponding match errors.

Figure 6. Matching results using the nasal regions of five different probe samples of subject 1 in the gallery with variations caused by occlusion, pose, noise and expression

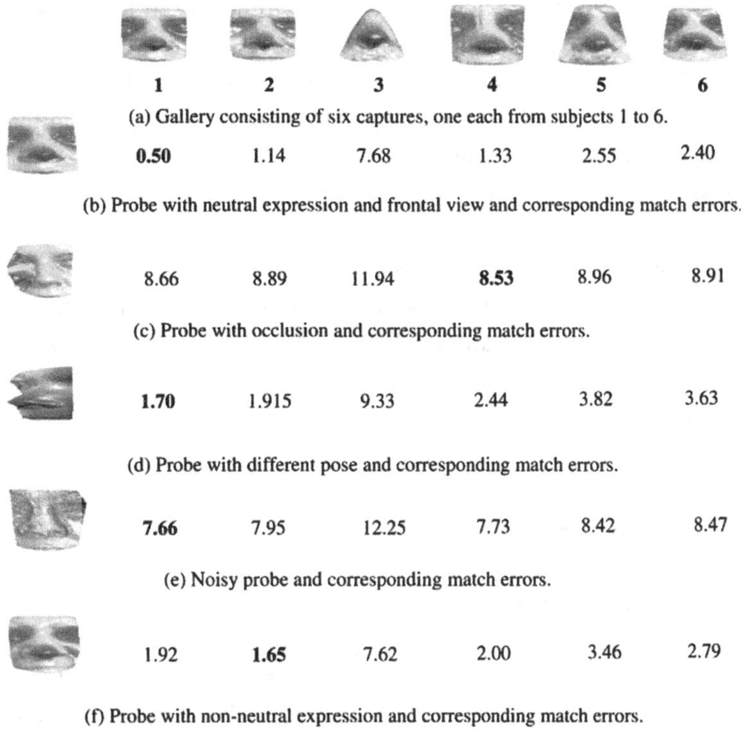

(a) Gallery consisting of six captures, one each from subjects 1 to 6.

1	2	3	4	5	6
0.50	1.14	7.68	1.33	2.55	2.40

(b) Probe with neutral expression and frontal view and corresponding match errors.

8.66	8.89	11.94	**8.53**	8.96	8.91

(c) Probe with occlusion and corresponding match errors.

1.70	1.915	9.33	2.44	3.82	3.63

(d) Probe with different pose and corresponding match errors.

7.66	7.95	12.25	7.73	8.42	8.47

(e) Noisy probe and corresponding match errors.

1.92	**1.65**	7.62	2.00	3.46	2.79

(f) Probe with non-neutral expression and corresponding match errors.

As a solution to this, 3D face recognition can be performed using the nasal region. The most fundamental reason of choosing the nose region for recognising people is its small variations in different expressions. Compared to other parts of the face, like the cheeks, eyes, forehead and mouth, it is much less changed in non-neutral expressions. Moreover, since the nose tip is usually the closest point to the camera and its convexity is more salient than other parts of the face, the nose can be easily segmented on the face. Furthermore, hiding the nose in real biometric sessions is nearly impossible, without attracting suspicion.

The results of a similar experiment performed over the nasal region is illustrated in Figure 6 for the same subjects. Similarly, the identity of the neutral face has been correctly recognised as the lowest matching error is produced by ICP for subject 1. However, for other problematic cases, the nasal region has been able to lead to the correct identity at lower ranks. For example, for the facial expression case in Figure 6-f, although the matching error is lowest for the wrong subject, the second lowest matching error correspond to the correct subject label. However, for the whole face experiment in Figure 6-f, it occurs in the third rank.

There are a few papers which have focused specifically on 3D nose recognition (Drira et al., 2009; Dibeklio˘ glu et al., 2009) where the 3D information of the nose region is utilised. Drira et al. present another approach for 3D face recognition using the nose region (Drira et al., 2009) demonstrating better performance. Their method utilises the geodesic contours, used in (Bronstein et al., 2005), only on the nose region. After denoising and nose segmentation (by fitting a sphere with radius 100 mm on the nose tip), the concentric contours are found on the nose surface using Dijkstra algorithm (Dijkstra, 1959). Dibeklioglu et al. first perform different curvature calculations on the face surface and then segment the nose region (Dibeklio˘ glu et al., 2009). Then, the ICP algorithm is used for recognition.

Moorhouse et al. introduced another approach for 3D nose recognition (Moorhouse et al., 2009). Colour information in YCbCr domain is clustered by GMM and curvature calculation is used for landmark detection and nose segmentation. Unlike the previous three 3D nose recognition papers, instead of using laser scanners, photometric stereo imaging is utlised to make the dataset. Four different features are evaluated on the nose surface: geometric ratios, the Fourier descriptors (FD) of the ridge, combination of these features and eigennoses.

A combination of the nasal region, forehead and eyes are used for a 2D/3D face recognition by Mian et al. (Mian et al., 2007). A modified ICP algorithm is used for matching, in conjunction with a pattern rejector based on spherical face representation (SFR) and scale-invariant feature transform (SIFT). As a result high recognition ranks are achieved, in particular for neutral probes.

Finally, in the section bellow we describe an example of a highly successful face recognition algorithm based on the 3D nasal curves.

Face Recognition Using the Nasal Curves

Preprocessing and Segmentation

The face is first denoised using a 2.3×2.3 median filtering. Principal component analysis (PCA) is then iteratively performed over the point clouds to correct the pose (Mian et al., 2007). Then the convex areas are located by thresholding the shape index map. The centroid of the largest connected component in the convex map is selected as the nose tip location. The nasal region is then cropped using the method proposed in (Emambakhsh et al., 2013), by intersecting two horizontal and one vertical cylinder.

Nasal Region Landmarking

The resulting nasal region (L(X)) is shown in Figure 7. In addition to the nose tip L9, three other landmarks are detected: nasal root (L1) and nasal alar groove (L5 and L13). In order to detect L1, several orthogonal planes to the nasal region are intersected with the nasal region. The angle between the ith plane and the y-axis is denoted as αi. Therefore, the normal vector for the orthogonal plane will be [cos αi, sin αi, 0], which passes L9. This results in the blue curves shown in Figure 8. For each curve, the global minimum is detected, shown in green in Figure 8. Connecting these points creates a new curve, whose global maximum corresponds to the nasal root L1.

The algorithm proposed in (Segundo et al., 2010) is used to detect L5 and L13. First, an orthogonal plane passing through L9 with normal vector [0, 1, 0] is intersected with the nasal region. Then the minima of the left and right sides of L9 over the intersected curve are detected by computing the first and second differentiation of the curve.

The locations of L1, L5 and L13 are used to create the other landmarks shown in Figure 7. These are simply found by equally dividing the connecting lines between the landmarks and then mapping the middle points to the nasal region.

Figure 7. The locations of the landmarks and their names

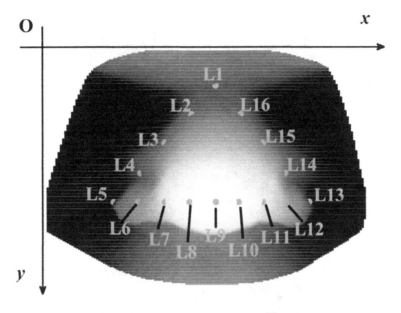

Figure 8. L1 detection procedure: the blue lines are the planes' intersections, the green curve is each intersection's minimum and L1 is given by the maximum value of the minima, shown with a red dot

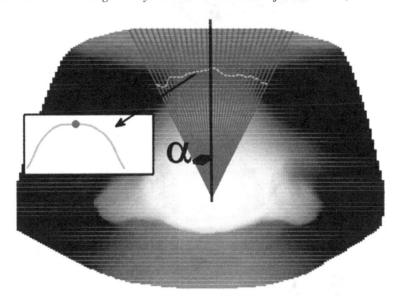

Nasal Curves and Feature Selection

The found landmarks are used to create the nasal curves shown in Figure 9. The depth map components of each curves is extracted and concatenated to form the feature space. The facial curves are excellent feature descriptors containing rich information in lower dimensional space than the original 3D point cloud. However, some of these curves are more sensitive to the facial expression while some are more robust.

Figure 9. The nasal curves: (a) Frontal and (b) side view

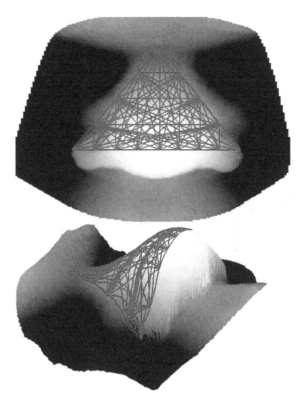

Figure 10. Rank-one recognition rate against the number of nasal curves selected by the FSFS algorithm. The sets of curves for selected feature sets are also shown, with the largest image (second from right) showing the 28 curves that produced the highest recognition rate (Emambakhsh et al., 2013).

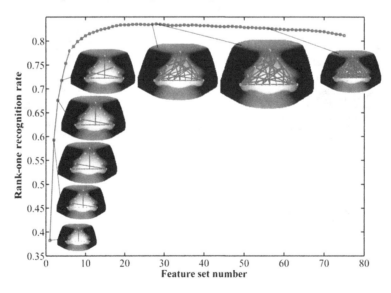

In order to detect those expression robust curves, the forward sequential feature selection (FSFS) is used to select the most robust feature set. For each selected feature set, the rank-one recognition rate is computed. At each iteration, the feature set combination which generates the highest recognition rate is stored. The one vs. all scenario is performed for the matching step using a city-block (CB) distance computation. The feature selection at different iterations of FSFS is shown in Figure 10. While the distribution of these curves is relatively even over the nasal surface, it is slightly denser on the nasal cartilage, which is less flexible due to its bony structure. This method demonstrated a significant improvement over existing methods using standard datasets (Emambakhsh et al., 2013).

Multimedia Security

As digital technologies have shown a rapid growth within the last decade, content protection now plays a major role within content management systems. Of the current systems, digital watermarking provides a robust and maintainable solution to enhance media security. Evidence of popularity of watermarking is clearly visible as watermarking research has resulted in 14685 image & video watermarking papers published in last 20 years and 1818 (12.4%) alone in 2014-15 (Scopus, 2016). This section discusses common watermarking philosophies, applications and recent researches in the domain.

Definition, Properties, Applications and Attacks

By definition a digital watermark is the copyright or author identification information which is embedded directly in the digital media in such a way that it is imperceptible, robust and secure. The watermarking research is considerably mature by now, after its major inception in mid nineties and offers digital protection to a wide spectrum of application as shown in Figure 11. Cox et al. (Cox et al., 2000) listed various applications of watermarking including broadcast monitoring, owner identification, proof of ownership, authentication, transactional watermarking, copy control and covert communication. A few of them are followed in the watermarking industry (Digital Watermarking Alliance, 2016) with few additions such as Audience measurement and improved auditing. Image quality evaluation methods were proposed in the literature where a watermark is embedded either in the discrete wavelet transform (DWT) (Wang et al., 2007) or discrete cosine transform (DCT) (Nezhadarya et al., 2009) frequency domain and the degradation of the extracted watermark was used to determine the quality without any reference to the original image. Uehira et al. (Uehira et al., 2016) proposed a new application of image displays to invisible optoelectronic watermarking systems where a paired installer is used to transfer auxiliary data using watermark code patterns. The authors used flat-panel image display and smart phones to establish an optical link between them, enabling the viewer to receive auxiliary data on their smart devices. An improved management of medical application was proposed in (Tsai et al., 2015) where watermarking techniques were used to embed patient data such as identity (ID), serial number or region of interest to ensure the image association with the correct patient and to indicate its relationship to other images in a series. Yamada et al. (Yamada et al., 2016) developed a real-time watermarking system for video-on-demand services where frame images are watermarked, unique to the user, when a server receives request from a user. The system aims to deter piracy. Another application includes a method for providing royalty payments for content distributed via a network (Levy and Stager, 2012).

Figure 11. Watermarking applications

SI No.	Name	Description
		Watermarking Applications
1	Broadcast monitoring	Passive monitoring by the automatic watermark detection of broadcasted watermarked media.
2	Copyright identification	Resolving copyright issues of digital media by using watermark information as copyright data.
3	Content authentication	Authentication of original art work, performance and protection against digital forgery.
4	Access control	Access control applications, such as, Pay-TV.
5	Copy control	Disabling copy of CD / DVD etc. by watermarked permission.
6	Packaging and tracking	Transaction tracking and protection against forged consumable items including pharmaceutical products by embedding watermark on packaging.
7	Medical record authentication	Authentication of digitally preserved patient's medical record, including blood sample, X-ray, ECG etc.
8	Insurance / Banking document authentication	Digital authentication of insurance claim, banking, financial, mortgage and corporate documents.
9	Media piracy control	Tracking of the source of media piracy.
10	Ownership identification	Supproting legitimate claim, such as, royalty by the media owner.
11	Transaction tracking	Tracking of media ownership in a buyer-seller scenario.
12	Meta-data hiding	Hiding meta-data within the media instead of a big header.
13	Video summary creation	Instant retrieval of video summary by embedding the summary within the host video.
14	Video hosting authentication	Piracy control by video authentication at video hosting servers, including youtube, megavideo etc.

Figure 12. Watermarking properties and associated applications

Properties	Description	Applications
	General Properties of Digital Watermarking	
Imperceptibility	The watermark should not noticeably distort or degrade the host data in order to preserve the quality of the marked document.	1, 2, 3, 4, 14.
Robustness	To measure robustness the watermark must be reliably detectable against signal processing schemes including data compression.	
Fragility	These kinds of watermark are embedded in host data in such a way that they do not survive in the case of any modification even copying.	7, 8.
Tamper-resistance	The tamper-resistance property is focused on the intentional attacks in contrast to robustness.	3, 5, 9, 10, 11, 14.
False positive rate	The probability of identifying an un-watermarked piece of data as containing a watermark by a detector is called the false positive rate.	6.
Data payload	The amount of information present in watermarked media is called data payload.	12, 13.

Figure 13. Types of watermarking techniques

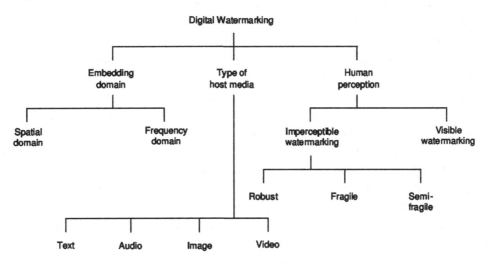

Figure 14. Watermark types

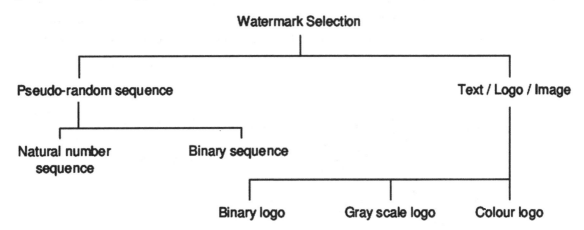

Digital watermarking comprises elements from a variety of disciplines including image processing, video processing, telecommunication, computer science, cryptography, remote sensing and geographical information systems etc. Watermarking systems are often characterized by a set of common properties and the importance of each property depends on the application requirements. A list of such properties and corresponding example applications(Cox et al., 2002; Barni and Bartolini, 2004) are shown in Figure 12, where last column of the figure shows the associated applications' number from Figure 11.

Based on the embedding method, the watermarking techniques can be categorized as shown in Figure 13. The watermark embedding can be done in the spatial domain or in the frequency domain. The latter have been a much popular choice as frequency decomposition characterizes the host media to represent the human eye characteristics and eye perception towards the media. Therefore frequency domain watermarking can provide better insight to reduce embedding distortion or increase the robustness (Cox et al., 1997). Now, depending on the type of host media, watermarking can be divided into four different categories: audio, image and video watermarking. Again, based on the human perception the watermarking schemes can be categorized as visible or imperceptible (invisible) watermarking and the latter can also be categorized as robust, fragile or semi-fragile watermarking. In case of a robust watermarking scheme, the watermark is expected to be sustained even after a compression or any other intentional attack, whereas in the case of a fragile scheme (Fridrich et al., 2000) the watermark information is usually destroyed to any alteration or attack to the media, in order to authenticate the image integrity. A semi-fragile scheme (Lin & Chang, 2000) represents properties from both the above mentioned categories and the watermark information is robust to certain type of attacks while fragile to other type of attacks.

Watermark represents the owner's identity. Hence the selection of the watermark is considered important and varies according to application requirements. Early days of watermarking scheme often used a pseudo-random number to embed the watermark and authenticity of the media is examined by the presence or absence of the watermark. In recent literature a message or logo based watermark (Kundur and Hatzinakos, 2004) has been preferred by the researchers and in this case authentication is done by extracting the hidden message or logo to identify the legitimate owner. Figure 14 shows the different types of watermark used in this field.

Main requirements of the watermarking schemes are either 1) to retain the watermark information after any intentional attacks or natural image/video processing operation, or 2) to identify any tampering (fragile watermarking) of the target media. Any process that modifies the host media affecting the watermark information, is called attack on watermarking. Various types of attacks can be grouped together as follows: 1) signal processing, 2) geometric, 3) enhancement, 4) printing-scanning-capturing,

Figure 15. Attack characterization

Watermarking attack characterisation													
Attacks \ Applications	Comm. n/w adaptation	Display device adaptation	Image editing	Medical record	Intentional Attacks	Packaging / Tracking	Broadcast monitoring	Copy control	Meta-data hiding	Video editing	Video summary	Insurance / Banking document	Video hosting authentication
Image:													
Signal Processing													
JPEG	■	■							■				
JPEG 2000	■	■							■				
Geometric													
Horizontal Flip					■				■				
Rotation					■				■				
Cropping			■		■				■				
Scaling			■		■				■				
Row / Column removal				■	■								
Enhancement													
Low pass filtering					■				■			■	
Shrpening					■				■				
Histogram modification					■				■				
Gamma correction					■				■				
Color quantisation					■				■				
Restoration					■				■				
Noise addition					■				■				
Printing-Scanning						■						■	
Printing-Capturing						■						■	
Oracle Attack					■								
Fragile watermarking				■					■				
Semi-Fragile watermarking				■					■				
Video:													
Signal Processing													
Motion JPEG 2000	■	■						■	■				
MPEG-2	■	■						■	■				
MPEG-4	■	■						■	■				
MC-EZBC	■	■						■	■				
H.264/AVC	■	■						■	■				
H.264/SVC	■	■						■	■				
H.264/MVC	■	■						■	■				
Linear / Non-linear adaptive filtering									■				
Geometric													
Desynchronisation					■					■			■
Cropping					■					■			
Row / Column removal					■								
Chrominance attack					■				■	■			■
Trasncoding	■	■											

5) oracle, 6) chrominance, 7) transcoding attacks etc. The attack characterization with respect to image and video watermarking and related applications are shown in Figure 15.

While watermarking schemes in general are evaluated in terms of imperceptibility (Asikuzzaman et al., 2014; Koz and Alatan, 2008), robustness against various intentional (Fallahpour et al., 2014) and unintentional (e.g., compression (Sttz et al., 2014), filtering (Zhu et al., 2014) or geometric (Zhang et al., 2011)) attacks and fragility (Chan et al., 2015), security of the watermarking schemes are also reported in (Bianchi and Piva, 2013; Adelsbach et al., 2004). The security of the watermark can be defined as the ability to properly conceal the watermark information in such way that it is secret to the unauthorized users. The security of the watermarking schemes are usually implemented using two different approaches (Adelsbach et al., 2004):

- Asymmetric watermarking which uses two different keys for watermark embedding and detection and
- Zero-knowledge watermark detection using cryptographic techniques where the watermark detection process is substituted by cryptographical protocol.

Cryptographical scrambling of the watermark logo is also used in order to secure the watermark (Kundur and Hatzinakos, 2004) in addition to the other security measures, such as, key based coefficient selection, random filter parameter selection etc. These are particularly useful when the attacker has access to the watermark detector.

Watermarking Process

The watermarking procedure, in its basic form, consists of two main processes: 1) Embedding and 2) Extraction and authentication. At this point, for simplicity, we describe these processes with reference to the image watermarking.

Embedding

This process insert or embed the watermark information within the host image by modifying all or selected pixel values (spatial domain); or coefficients (frequency domain), in such a way that the watermark is imperceptible to human eye and is achieved by minimizing the embedding distortion to the host image. The system block for the embedding process is shown in Figure 16 and can be expressed as:

Figure 16. Watermark embedding process

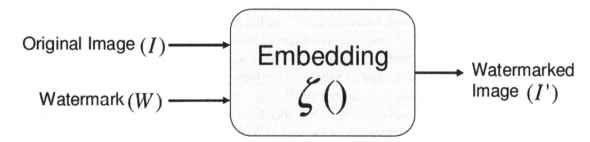

$$I' = \zeta\left(I, W\right),$$ (1)

where I is the watermarked image, I is the original host image, W is the watermark information and $\zeta()$ is the embedding function.

The embedding function can further be categorized in sub-processes: 1) forward transform (for frequency domain), 2) pixel / coefficient selection, 3) embedding method (additive, multiplicative, quantization etc.) and 4) inverse transform.

Finally the performance of the watermark embedding is measured by comparing the watermarked image (I) with the original unmarked image (I) and is calculated by various metrics: 1) peak signal to noise ratio (PSNR), 2) weighted PSNR (wPSNR) (Kwon and Lee, 2001), 3) structural similarity measure (SSIM) (Wang et al., 2004), 4) just noticeable difference (JND) (Watson, 1993) and 5) subjective quality measurement (Koumaras, 2008).

- **PSNR:** This is one of the most commonly used visual quality metric which is based on the root mean square error (RMSE) of the two images with dimension of X × Y as in Eq. (2) and Eq. (3).

$$PSNR = 20\log_{10}\left(\frac{255}{RMSE}\right)$$ (2)

$$RMSE = \sqrt{\frac{1}{X \times Y}\sum\sum\left(I\left(m,n\right) - I'\left(m,n\right)\right)^2}$$ (3)

- **wPSNR:** On contrary to error measurement in spatial domain as in the previous metric, this metric measures PSNR in wavelet transform domain with weighting factors at different frequency decomposition level. The host and processed images are firstly wavelet decomposed and then squared error is computed at every subband. Finally wPSNR is calculated using cumulative squared error with weighting parameters for each subband. The weights for various subbands are adjusted in such way that wPSNR has the highest correlation with the subjective score.
- **SSIM:** This quality measurement metric assumes that human visual system is highly adapted for extracting structural information from a scene. Unlike PSNR, where average error between two images taken into consideration, SSIM focuses on a quality assessment based on the degradation of structural information. The structural information in the scene is calculated using local luminance and contrast rather an average luminance and contrast.
- **JND:** In this metric the host and test images are DCT transformed and Just Noticeable Differences are measured using thresholds. The thresholds are decided based on 1) luminance masking and 2) contrast masking of the transformed images. The threshold for luminance pattern relies on the mean luminance of the local image region, whereas the contrast masking is calculated within a block and particular DCT coefficient using a visual masking algorithm.
- **Subjective:** Although various objective metrics have been proposed to measure the visual quality, often by modeling the human visual system or subjective visual tests, the subjective test offers best visual quality measurement. Subjective tests procedures are recommended by ITU (Koumaras, 2008) which defines the specification of the screen, luminance of the test room, distance of the

Figure 17. Watermark extraction and authentication process

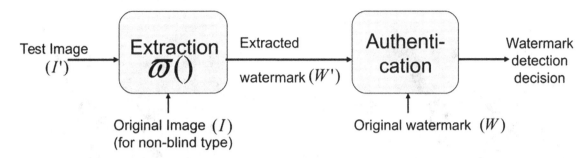

observer from the screen, scoring techniques, test types such as double stimulus continuous quality test (DSCQT) or double stimulus impairment scale test (DSIST) etc. The tests are carried out with multiple viewer and the mean opinion score (MOS) represents the visual quality of the test image. However the subjective tests are often time consuming and difficult to perform and hence researchers prefer objective metrics to measure the visual quality.

Among these metrics, due its simplicity, the most common method of evaluating the embedding performance in watermarking research is PSNR. It is also observed that most of the metrics behaves in a similar fashion when compared with any embedding distortion measured by PSNR of 35dB or above.

Extraction and Authentication

As the process name suggested, it consists of two subprocess: 1) extraction of watermark and 2) authentication of the extracted watermark. The watermark extraction follows a reverse embedding algorithm, but with a similar input parameter set. Now based on the watermark extraction criteria any watermarking method can be categorized in: 1) non-blind type and 2) blind type. For the first category, a copy of the original un-watermarked image is required during extraction whereas in the latter case, the watermark is extracted from the test image itself. The extraction process can be written in the simplified form as:

$$W = (I, I'), \tag{4}$$

where W is the extracted watermark, I is the test image, I is the original image and () is the extraction function.

Once the watermark is extracted from the test image, the authentication is performed by comparing with the original input watermark information. Common authentication methods are defined by finding the closeness between the two in a vector space, by calculating the similarity correlation or Hamming distance. A complete system diagram of extraction and authentication process is shown in Figure 17. An example of image watermark embedding and extraction processes are shown in Figure 18 and Figure 19, respectively. The figure also shows the difference image demonstrating how the watermark information is distributed within the textured region so that it is imperceptible to human vision.

Figure 18. An image watermark embedding and extraction example: Embedding

Original image   Watermark   Watermarked image

Figure 19. An image watermark embedding and extraction example: Extraction

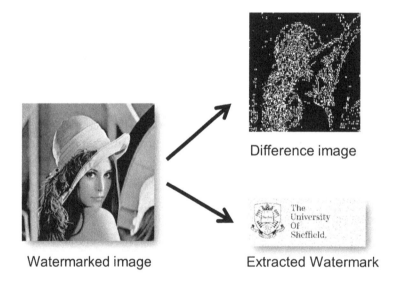

Difference image

Watermarked image   Extracted Watermark

Recent Research Trends

The visual quality of host media (often known as imperceptibility) and robustness are widely considered as the two main properties vital for a good digital watermarking system. They are complimentary to each other and hence challenging to attain the right balance between them. Frequency-based watermarking, more precisely wavelet domain watermarking, methodologies are highly favoured in the current research era. The wavelet domain is also compliant within many image coding, e.g., JPEG2000 (Taubman and Marcellin, 2002) and video coding, e.g., Motion JPEG2000, Motion-Compensated Embedded Zeroblock Coding (MC-EZBC) (Chen and Woods, 2004), schemes, leading to smooth adaptability within modern frameworks. Due to the multi-resolution decomposition and the property to retain spatial synchronisation, which are not provided by other transforms (the Discrete Cosine Transform (DCT) for example), the Discrete Wavelet Transform (DWT) provides an ideal choice for robust watermarking (Bhatnagar and Q.M. J. Wuand B. Raman, 2012; Piper et al., 2005; Bhowmik and Abhayaratne, 2008; Soheili, 2010; Bhowmik and Abhayaratne, 2007; Abhayaratne and Bhowmik, 2013; Feng and Yang, 2005; Xia et al., 1998; Xie and Arce, 1998; Barni et al., 2001; Kundur and Hatzinakos, 2004; Kim and Moon, 1999; Marusic et al., 2003; Zhang and Mo, 2001).

When designing a watermarking scheme there are numerous features to consider, including the wavelet kernel, embedding coefficients and wavelet subband selection. Each of these particular features can sufficiently impact the overall watermark characteristics (Bhowmik and Abhayaratne, 2014) and is largely dependant upon the target application requirements:

1. **Wavelet Kernel Selection:** An appropriate choice of wavelet kernel must be determined within the watermarking framework. There have been previous studies to show that the performance of watermark robustness and imperceptibility is dependant on the wavelet kernels (Bhowmik and Abhayaratne, 2007, 2008, 2009). The orthogonal Daubechie wavelets are a favourable choice with many early watermarking schemes (Feng and Yang, 2005; Xia et al., 1998; Xie and Arce, 1998; Barni et al., 2001; Kundur and Hatzinakos, 2004), although the later introduction of bi-orthogonal wavelets within the field of digital watermarking has increased their usage (Kim and Moon, 1999; Marusic et al., 2003; Zhang and Mo, 2001).

2. **Host Coefficient Selection:** Various approaches exist to choose suitable transform coefficients for embedding a watermark. In current methods, coefficient selection is determined by the threshold values based upon the coefficient magnitude (Kim and Moon, 1999) or a pixel masking approach based upon HVS (Barni et al., 2001) or the median of 3 coefficients in a 3×1 overlapping window (Xie and Arce, 1998) or simply by selecting all the coefficients (Xia et al., 1998; Feng and Yang, 2005; Kundur and Hatzinakos, 2004).

3. **Wavelet Subband Selection:** The choice of subband bears a large importance when determining the balance between robustness of the watermark and imperceptibility. Embedding within the high frequency domain subbands (Huo and Gao, 2006; Barni et al., 2001; Feng and Yang, 2005; Kundur and Hatzinakos, 2004; Xia et al., 1998) can often provide great imperceptibility but with limited watermark robustness capabilities. Contradictory schemes embed data only within the low frequency subbands (Xie and Arce, 1998; Zhang and Mo, 2001) aimed towards providing a high robustness. Spread spectrum domain embedding (Dey et al., 2012; Kim and Moon, 1999; Chen et al., 2003) modifies data across all frequency subbands, ensuring a balance of both low and high frequency watermarking characteristics. The number of decomposition levels is also an important factor. Previous studies have researched watermarking schemes using two (Huo and Gao, 2006; Feng and Yang, 2005; Xia et al., 1998), three (Marusic et al., 2003; Zhang and Mo, 2001) and four or more (Barni et al., 2001; Kundur and Hatzinakos, 2004) wavelet decomposition levels.

4. An extension of image watermarking to video is the easiest option for any video watermarking scheme. Frame-by-frame video watermarking (Hartung and Girod, 1998; Cox et al., 1997) and 3D wavelet based video watermarking schemes (Campisi, 2005; Kim et al., 2004) are available in the literature. However a direct extension of the image watermarking schemes without consideration of motion, produces flicker and other motion related mismatch. The watermarking algorithms along with MCTF, which decomposes motion information, provides a better solution to this problem (Vinod and Bora, 2006).

CONCLUSION

In this chapter, we discussed various image processing techniques used in visual surveillance and security applications covering visual tracking, biometric application and digital media security. Individual categories provided a general introduction to the topic, discussed the commonly used techniques by dissecting the approaches proposed in the literature. Suitable examples are also provided for better understanding. The comprehensive bibliography is useful for the readers interested in further research.

REFERENCES

Abhayaratne, C., & Bhowmik, D. (2013). Scalable watermark extraction for real-time authentication of JPEG 2000 images. *Journal of Real-Time Image Processing*, *8*(3), 307–325. doi:10.1007/s11554-011-0218-5

Adelsbach, A., Katzenbeisser, S., & Sadeghi, A. R. (2004). Cryptography meets watermarking: Detecting watermarks with minimal or zero knowledge disclosure.*Proc. European Signal Processing Conference (EUSIPCO)*, *1*, 446–449.

Ali, A., & Aggarwal, J. K. (2001). Segmentation and recognition of continuous human activity.*Proc. IEEE Workshop on Detection and Recognition of Events in Video*, 28–35. doi:10.1109/EVENT.2001.938863

Arulampalam, M. S., Maskell, S., Gordon, N., & Clapp, T. (2002). A tutorial on particle filters for online nonlinear/non-Gaussian Bayesian tracking. *IEEE Transactions on Signal Processing*, *50*(2), 174–188. doi:10.1109/78.978374

Asikuzzaman, M., Alam, M. J., Lambert, A. J., & Pickering, M. R. (2014). Imperceptible and robust blind video watermarking using chrominance embedding: A set of approaches in the DT CWT domain. *IEEE Transactions on Information Forensics and Security*, *9*(9), 1502–1517. doi:10.1109/TIFS.2014.2338274

Avidan, S. (2004). Support vector tracking. *IEEE Transactions on Pattern Analysis and Machine Intelligence*, *26*(8), 1064–1072. doi:10.1109/TPAMI.2004.53 PMID:15641735

Bar-Shalom, Y., & Foreman, T. (1988). *Tracking and Data Association*. Academic Press Inc.

Barni & Bartolini. (2004). *Watermarking Systems Engineering (Signal Processing and Communications, 21)*. Boca Raton, FL: CRC Press, Inc.

Barni, M., Bartolini, F., & Piva, A. (2001). Improved wavelet-based watermarking through pixel-wise masking. *IEEE Transactions on Image Processing*, *10*(5), 783–791. doi:10.1109/83.918570 PMID:18249667

Besl, P. J., & McKay, N. D. (1992). A method for registration of 3-D shapes. *IEEE Transactions on Pattern Analysis and Machine Intelligence*, *14*(2), 239–256. doi:10.1109/34.121791

Bhatnagar, G., Wuand, Q. M. J., & Raman, B. (2012). Robust gray-scale logo watermarking in wavelet domain.*Computers & Electrical Engineering*,*38*(5), 1164–1176. doi:10.1016/j.compeleceng.2012.02.002

Bhowmik, D., & Abhayaratne, C. (2007). Morphological wavelet domain image watermarking.*Proc. European Signal Processing Conference (EUSIPCO)*, 2539–2543.

Bhowmik, D., & Abhayaratne, C. (2009). Embedding distortion modeling for non-orthonormal wavelet based watermarking schemes. *Proc. SPIE Wavelet App. in Industrial Processing VI, 7248.* doi:10.1117/12.810719

Bhowmik, D., & Abhayaratne, C. (2008). A generalised model for distortion performance analysis of wavelet based watermarking. In *Digital Watermarking* (pp. 363–378). Springer.

Bhowmik, D., & Abhayaratne, C. (2014). On Robustness Against JPEG2000: A Performance Evaluation of Wavelet-Based Watermarking Techniques. *Multimedia Systems, 20*(2), 239–252. doi:10.1007/s00530-013-0334-0

Bianchi, T., & Piva, A. (2013). Secure watermarking for multimedia content protection: A review of its benefits and open issues. *IEEE Signal Processing Magazine, 30*(2), 87–96. doi:10.1109/MSP.2012.2228342

Blackman, S. S. (2004). Multiple hypothesis tracking for multiple target tracking. *IEEE Aerospace and Electronic Systems Magazine, 19*(1), 5–18. doi:10.1109/MAES.2004.1263228

Boser, B. E., Guyon, I. M., & Vapnik, V. N. (1992). A training algorithm for optimal margin classifiers. *Proc. Fifth Annual Workshop on Computational Learning Theory, COLT '92,* 144–152. doi:10.1145/130385.130401

Boykov, Y., & Funka-Lea, G. (2006). Graph cuts and efficient N-D image segmentation. *International Journal of Computer Vision, 70*(2), 109–131. doi:10.1007/s11263-006-7934-5

Broida, T. J., & Chellappa, R. (1986). Estimation of object motion parameters from noisy images. *IEEE Transactions on Pattern Analysis and Machine Intelligence, PAMI-8*(1), 90–99. doi:10.1109/TPAMI.1986.4767755 PMID:21869326

Bronstein, A. M., Bronstein, M. M., & Kimmel, R. (2005). Three-dimensional face recognition. *International Journal of Computer Vision, 64*(1), 5–30. doi:10.1007/s11263-005-1085-y

Campisi, P. (2005). Video watermarking in the 3D-DWT domain using quantization-based methods. *Multimedia Signal Processing, IEEE 7th Workshop on,* 1–4.

Canny, J. (1986). A computational approach to edge detection. *IEEE Transactions on Pattern Analysis and Machine Intelligence, PAMI-8*(6), 679–698. doi:10.1109/TPAMI.1986.4767851 PMID:21869365

Chan, H. T., Hwang, W. J., & Cheng, C. J. (2015). Digital hologram authentication using a hadamard-based reversible fragile watermarking algorithm. *Journal of Display Technology, 11*(2), 193–203. doi:10.1109/JDT.2014.2367528

Chen & Woods. (2004). Bidirectional MC-EZBC with lifting implementation. *Circuits and Systems for Video Technology. IEEE Transactions on, 14*(10), 1183–1194.

Chen, T.-S., Chen, J., & Chen, J.-G. (2003). A simple and efficient watermarking technique based on JPEG2000 codec. *Proc. Int'l Symp. on Multimedia Software Eng.,* 80–87. doi:10.1109/MMSE.2003.1254425

Comaniciu, D., & Meer, P. (2002). Mean shift: A robust approach toward feature space analysis. *IEEE Transactions on Pattern Analysis and Machine Intelligence, 24*(5), 603–619. doi:10.1109/34.1000236

Comaniciu, D., Ramesh, V., & Meer, P. (2003). Kernel-based object tracking. *IEEE Transactions on Pattern Analysis and Machine Intelligence*, *25*(5), 564–577. doi:10.1109/TPAMI.2003.1195991

Cox, I. J., Kilian, J., Leighton, F. T., & Shamoon, T. (1997). Secure spread spectrum watermarking for multimedia. *IEEE Transactions on Image Processing*, *6*(12), 1673–1687. doi:10.1109/83.650120 PMID:18285237

Cox, I. J., Miller, M. L., & Bloom, J. A. (2002). Watermarking applications and their properties. *Information Technology: Coding and Computing, 2000. Proceedings. International Conference on*, 6–10.

Cox, I. J., Miller, M. L., & Bloom, J. A. (2002). *Digital watermarking*. San Francisco, CA: Morgan Kaufmann Publishers Inc.

Dalal, N., & Triggs, B. (2005). Histograms of oriented gradients for human detection.*Proc. IEEE CVPR*, *1*, 886–893. doi:10.1109/CVPR.2005.177

Dey, N., Pal, M., & Das, A. (2012). A session based blind watermarking technique within the ROI of retinal fundus images for authentication using dwt, spread spectrum and harris corner detection. *International Journal of Modern Engineering Research*, *2*, 749–757.

Dibeklioˇglu, G�¨okberk, & Akarun. (2009). Nasal region-based 3D face recognition under pose and expression variations. *3rd International Conference on Advances in Biometrics*, 309–318.

Digital Watermarking Alliance. (2016). Retrieved from www.digitalwatermarkingalliance.org/applications.asp

Dijkstra, E. W. (1959). A note on two problems in connexion with graphs. *Numerische Mathematik*, *1*(1), 269–271. doi:10.1007/BF01386390

Drira, H., Amor, B. B., Daoudi, M., & Srivastava, A. (2009). Nasal region contribution in 3D face biometrics using shape analysis framework.*3rd International Conference on Advances in Biometrics*, 357–366. doi:10.1007/978-3-642-01793-3_37

Dufour, R. M., Miller, E. L., & Galatsanos, N. P. (2002). Template matching based object recognition with unknown geometric parameters. *IEEE Transactions on Image Processing*, *11*(12), 1385–1396. doi:10.1109/TIP.2002.806245 PMID:18249707

Edwards, G. J., Taylor, C. J., & Cootes, T. F. (1998). Interpreting face images using active appearance models.*Proc. IEEE International Conference on Automatic Face and Gesture Recognition*, 300–305. doi:10.1109/AFGR.1998.670965

Emambakhsh, M., Evans, A. N., & Smith, M. (2013). Using nasal curves matching for expression robust 3D nose recognition.*6th IEEE International Conference on Biometrics: Theory, Applications and Systems (BTAS)*, 1–6. doi:10.1109/BTAS.2013.6712732

Fallahpour, M., Shirmohammadi, S., Semsarzadeh, M., & Zhao, J. (2014). Tampering detection in compressed digital video using watermarking. *IEEE Transactions on Instrumentation and Measurement*, *63*(5), 1057–1072. doi:10.1109/TIM.2014.2299371

Feng, X. C., & Yang, Y. (2005). A new watermarking method based on DWT. *Proc. Int'l Conf. on Computational Intelligence and Security, Lect. Notes in Comp. Sci. (LNCS), 3802*, 1122–1126. doi:10.1007/11596981_168

Freund, Y., & Schapire, R. E. (1997). A decision-theoretic generalization of on-line learning and an application to boosting. *Journal of Computer and System Sciences, 55*(1), 119–139. doi:10.1006/jcss.1997.1504

Fridrich, J., Goljan, M., & Baldoza, A. C. (2000). New fragile authentication watermark for images. *Proc. IEEE ICIP, 1*, 446–449.

Haering, N., Venetianer, P. L., & Lipton, A. (2008). The evolution of video surveillance: An overview. *Machine Vision and Applications, 19*(5-6), 279–290. doi:10.1007/s00138-008-0152-0

Harris, C., & Stephens, M. (1988). A combined corner and edge detector.*Proc. of Fourth Alvey Vision Conference*, 147–151.

Hartung, F., & Girod, B. (1998). Watermarking of uncompressed and compressed video. *Signal Processing, 66*(3), 283–301. doi:10.1016/S0165-1684(98)00011-5

Horn, B. K. P., & Schunck, B. G. (1981). Determining optical flow. *Artificial Intelligence, 17*(1-3), 185–203. doi:10.1016/0004-3702(81)90024-2

Huo, F., & Gao, X. (2006). A wavelet based image watermarking scheme.*Proc. IEEE ICIP*, 2573–2576.

Husz, Z. L., Wallace, A. M., & Green, P. R. (2011). Tracking with a hierarchical partitioned particle filter and movement modelling. *IEEE Transactions on Systems, Man, and Cybernetics. Part B, Cybernetics, 41*(6), 1571–1584. doi:10.1109/TSMCB.2011.2157680 PMID:21724518

Jain, A. K., Ross, A., & Pankanti, S. (2006). Biometrics: A tool for information security. *IEEE Transactions on Information Forensics and Security, 1*(2), 125–143. doi:10.1109/TIFS.2006.873653

Jain, A. N., Ross, A., & Prabhakar, S. (2004). An introduction to biometric recognition. *IEEE Transactions on Circuits and Systems for Video Technology, 14*(1), 4–20. doi:10.1109/TCSVT.2003.818349

Pong & Bowden. (2002). An improved adaptive background mixture model for real-time tracking with shadow detection. In P. Remagnino, G. A. Jones, N. Paragios, & C. S. Regazzoni (Eds.), *Video-Based Surveillance Systems* (pp. 135–144). Springer, US.

Kang, Cohen, & Medioni. (2004). Object reacquisition using invariant appearance model. *Proc. of International Conference on Pattern Recognition (ICPR), 4*, 759–762.

Kim, J. R., & Moon, Y. S. (1999). A robust wavelet-based digital watermarking using level-adaptive thresholding.*Proc. IEEE ICIP, 2*, 226–230.

Kim, Lee, Moon, Cho, Lim, Kwon, & Lee. (2004). A new digital video watermarking using the dual watermark images and 3D DWT. TENCON 2004. IEEE Region 10 Conference, 291–294.

Koumaras, H. G. (2008). *Subjective video quality assessment methods for multimedia applications.* Technical Report ITU-R BT.500-11, Geneva, Switzerland.

Koz, A., & Alatan, A. A. (2008). Oblivious spatio-temporal watermarking of digital video by exploiting the human visual system. *IEEE Transactions on Circuits and Systems for Video Technology*, *18*(3), 326–337. doi:10.1109/TCSVT.2008.918446

Kundur, D., & Hatzinakos, D. (2004). Toward robust logo watermarking using multiresolution image fusion principles. *IEEE Transactions on Multimedia*, *6*(1), 185–198. doi:10.1109/TMM.2003.819747

Kwon, O., & Lee, C. (2001). Objective method for assessment of video quality using wavelets.*Proc. IEEE Int'l Symp. on Industrial Electronics (ISIE 2001)*, 1, 292–295.

Laws, K. (1980). *Textured image segmentation* (PhD Thesis). Electrical Engineering, University of Southern California.

Levy & Stager. (2012). *Digital watermarking applications*. US Patent App. 13/590,940.

Limprasert, W., Wallace, A., & Michaelson, G. (2013). Real-time people tracking in a camera network. *IEEE Journal on Emerging and Selected Topics in Circuits and Systems*, *3*(2), 263–271. doi:10.1109/JETCAS.2013.2256820

Lin, C. Y., & Chang, S. F. (2000). Semifragile watermarking for authenticating JPEG visual content. *Proc. SPIE Security, Steganography, and Watermarking of Multimedia Contents*, 3971, 140–151.

Lowe, D. G. (2004). Distinctive image features from scale-invariant keypoints. *International Journal of Computer Vision*, *60*(2), 91–110. doi:10.1023/B:VISI.0000029664.99615.94

Mallat, S. G. (1989). A theory for multiresolution signal decomposition: The wavelet representation. *IEEE Transactions on Pattern Analysis and Machine Intelligence*, *11*(7), 674–693. doi:10.1109/34.192463

Marusic, Tay, Deng, & Palaniswami. (2003). A study of biorthogonal wavelets in digital watermarking. *Proceedings of International Conference on Image Processing*, 2, II–463. doi:10.1109/ICIP.2003.1246717

Mian, Bennamoun, & Owens. (2007). An efficient multimodal 2D-3D hybrid approach to automatic face recognition. *Pattern Analysis and Machine Intelligence, IEEE Transactions on*, *29*(11), 1927–1943.

Moorhouse, A., Evans, A. N., Atkinson, G. A., Sun, J., & Smith, M. L. (2009). The nose on your face may not be so plain: Using the nose as a biometric.*3rd IET International Conference on Crime Detection and Prevention (ICDP)*, 1–6. doi:10.1049/ic.2009.0231

Nezhadarya, E., Wang, Z. J., & Ward, R. K. (2009). Image quality monitoring using spread spectrum watermarking.*Proc. IEEE ICIP*, 2233–2236. doi:10.1109/ICIP.2009.5413955

Ojala, T., Pietikainen, M., & Maenpaa, T. (2002). Multiresolution gray-scale and rotation invariant texture classification with local binary patterns. *IEEE Transactions on Pattern Analysis and Machine Intelligence*, *24*(7), 971–987. doi:10.1109/TPAMI.2002.1017623

Paragios, N., & Deriche, R. (2002). Geodesic active regions and level set methods for supervised texture segmentation.*International Journal of Computer Vision*, *46*(3), 223–247. doi:10.1023/A:1014080923068

Phillips, P. J., Flynn, P. J., Scruggs, T., Bowyer, K. W., Jin Chang, K., Hoffman, J., … Worek, W. (2005). Overview of the face recognition grand challenge. *IEEE Conference on Computer Vision and Pattern Recognition (CVPR)*, 947– 954. doi:10.1109/CVPR.2005.268

Piper, A., Safavi-Naini, R., & Mertins, A. (2005). Resolution and quality scalable spread spectrum image watermarking.*Proceedings of the 7th workshop on Multimedia and security*, 79–90. doi:10.1145/1073170.1073186

Alÿuz, Dibeklioğlu, Çeliktutan, Gökberk, Sankur, & Akarun. (2008). Bosphorus database for 3D face analysis. Biometrics and Identity Management, 5372, 47–56.

Scheirer, W. J., de Rezende Rocha, A., Sapkota, A., & Boult, T. E. (2013). Toward open set recognition. *IEEE Transactions on Pattern Analysis and Machine Intelligence*, *35*(7), 1757–1772. doi:10.1109/TPAMI.2012.256 PMID:23682001

Scopus. (2016). Retrieved from www.scopus.com

Schwarz, L. A., Mkhitaryan, A., Mateus, D., & Navab, N. (2012). Human skeleton tracking from depth data using geodesic distances and optical flow. *Image and Vision Computing*, *30*(3), 217–226. doi:10.1016/j.imavis.2011.12.001

Segundo, Silva, Bellon, & Queirolo. (2010). Automatic face segmentation and facial landmark detection in range images. *Systems, Man, and Cybernetics, Part B: Cybernetics, IEEE Transactions on*, *40*(5),1319–1330.

Serby, D., Meier, E. K., & Van Gool, L. (2004). Probabilistic object tracking using multiple features. *Proc. International Conference on Pattern Recognition*, 2, 184–187.

Shi, J., & Tomasi, C. (1994). Good features to track.*Proc. IEEE CVPR*, 593–600.

Shotton, J., Winn, J., Rother, C., & Criminisi, A. (2009). TextonBoost for image understanding: Multi-class object recognition and segmentation by jointly modeling texture, layout, and context. *International Journal of Computer Vision*, *81*(1), 2–23. doi:10.1007/s11263-007-0109-1

Soheili, M. R. (2010). Blind Wavelet Based Logo Watermarking Resisting to Cropping. *Proc. 20ᵀʰ International Conference on Pattern Recognition*, 1449–1452. doi:10.1109/ICPR.2010.358

Sttz, T., Autrusseau, F., & Uhl, A. (2014). Non-blind structure-preserving substitution watermarking of h.264/cavlc inter-frames. *IEEE Transactions on Multimedia*, *16*(5), 1337–1349. doi:10.1109/TMM.2014.2310595

Taubman, D. S., & Marcellin, M. W. (2002). *JPEG2000 Image Compression Fundamentals, Standards and Practice*. Springer. doi:10.1007/978-1-4615-0799-4

Tsai, J.-M., Chen, I.-T., Huang, Y.-F., & Lin, C.-C. (2015). Watermarking technique for improved management of digital medical images. *Journal of Discrete Mathematical Sciences and Cryptography*, *18*(6), 785–799. doi:10.1080/09720529.2015.1023532

Uehira, K., Suzuki, K., & Ikeda, H. (2016). Does optoelectronic watermark technology migrate into business and industry in the near future? applications of optoelectronic watermarking technology to new business and industry systems utilizing flat-panel displays and smart devices. *IEEE Transactions on Industry Applications*, *52*(1), 511–520. doi:10.1109/TIA.2015.2480769

Veenman, C. J., Reinders, M. J. T., & Backer, E. (2001). Resolving motion correspondence for densely moving points. *IEEE Transactions on Pattern Analysis and Machine Intelligence*, *23*(1), 54–72. doi:10.1109/34.899946

Vinod & Bora. (2006). Motion-compensated inter-frame collusion attack on video watermarking and a countermeasure. *IEE Proceedings-Information Security*, *153*(2), 61–73.

Vo, B.-N., & Ma, W.-K. (2006). The Gaussian mixture probability hypothesis density filter. *IEEE Transactions on Signal Processing*, *54*(11), 4091–4104. doi:10.1109/TSP.2006.881190

Wang, S., Zheng, D., Zhao, J., Tam, W. J., & Speranza, F. (2007). An image quality evaluation method based on digital watermarking. *IEEE Transactions on Circuits and Systems for Video Technology*, *17*(1), 98–105. doi:10.1109/TCSVT.2006.887086

Wang, Z., Bovik, A. C., Sheikh, H. R., & Simoncelli, E. P. (2004). Image quality assessment: From error visibility to structural similarity. *IEEE Transactions on Image Processing*, *13*(4), 600–612. doi:10.1109/TIP.2003.819861 PMID:15376593

Watson, A. B. (1993). Visual optimization of dct quantization matrices for individual images. Proc. American Institute of Aeronautics and Astronautics (AIAA) Computing in Aerospace, 9, 286–291. doi:10.2514/6.1993-4512

Xia, X., Boncelet, C. G., & Arce, G. R. (1998). Wavelet transform based watermark for digital images. *Optics Express*, *3*(12), 497–511. doi:10.1364/OE.3.000497 PMID:19384401

Xie, L., & Arce, G. R. (1998). Joint wavelet compression and authentication watermarking.*Proc. IEEE ICIP*, 2, 427–431.

Yamada, T., Maeta, M., & Mizushima, F. (2016). Video watermark application for embedding recipient id in real-time-encoding vod server. *Journal of Real-Time Image Processing*, *11*(1), 211–222. doi:10.1007/s11554-013-0335-4

Yang, H., Shao, L., Zheng, F., Wang, L., & Song, Z. (2011). Recent advances and trends in visual tracking: A review. *Neurocomputing*, *74*(18), 3823–3831. doi:10.1016/j.neucom.2011.07.024

Yilmaz, A., Xin Li, , & Shah, M. (2004). Contour-based object tracking with occlusion handling in video acquired using mobile cameras. *IEEE Transactions on Pattern Analysis and Machine Intelligence*, *26*(11), 1531–1536. doi:10.1109/TPAMI.2004.96 PMID:15521500

Yilmaz, A., Javed, O., & Shah, M. (2006). Object tracking: A survey. *ACM Computing Surveys*, *38*(4), 13, es. doi:10.1145/1177352.1177355

Zafeiriou, S., Hansen, M., Atkinson, G., Argyriou, V., Petrou, M., Smith, M., & Smith, L. (2011). The Photoface database.*IEEE Conference on Computer Vision and Pattern Recognition Workshops (CVPRW)*, 132–139.

Zhang, H., Shu, H., Coatrieux, G., Zhu, J., Wu, Q. M. J., Zhang, Y., & Luo, L. et al. (2011). Affine legendre moment invariants for image watermarking robust to geometric distortions. *IEEE Transactions on Image Processing*, *20*(8), 2189–2199. doi:10.1109/TIP.2011.2118216 PMID:21342852

Zhang, Z., & Mo, Y. L. (2001). Embedding strategy of image watermarking in wavelet transform domain.*Proc. SPIE Image Compression and Encryption Tech.*, 4551-1, 127–131. doi:10.1117/12.442900

Zhu, X., Ding, J., Dong, H., Hu, K., & Zhang, X. (2014). Normalized correlation-based quantization modulation for robust watermarking. *IEEE Transactions on Multimedia*, *16*(7), 1888–1904. doi:10.1109/TMM.2014.2340695

Zivkovic, Z., & van der Heijden, F. (2006). Efficient adaptive density estimation per image pixel for the task of background subtraction. *Pattern Recognition Letters*, *27*(7), 773–780. doi:10.1016/j.patrec.2005.11.005

Chapter 4

Application of Corona Product of Graphs in Computing Topological Indices of Some Special Chemical Graphs

Nilanjan De

Calcutta Institute of Engineering and Management, India

ABSTRACT

Graph operations play a very important role in mathematical chemistry, since some chemically interesting graphs can be obtained from some simpler graphs by different graph operations. In this chapter, some eccentricity based topological indices such as the total eccentricity index, eccentric connectivity index, modified eccentric connectivity index and connective eccentricity index and their respective polynomial versions of corona product of two graphs have been studied and also these indices of some important classes of chemically interesting molecular graphs are determined by specializing the components of corona product of graphs.

INTRODUCTION

Chemical graph theory is a branch of mathematical chemistry in which different tools from graph theory are used to model the chemical phenomenon mathematically. Molecules and molecular compounds are modeled as molecular graphs, in which the vertices correspond to the atoms and the edges correspond to the chemical bonds between the atoms. A topological index is a numeric value which is a graph invariant and correlates the physico-chemical properties of a molecular graph. Topological indices are used for studying quantitative structure-activity relationship (QSAR) and quantatitive structure-property relationship (QSPR) for predicting different properties of chemical compounds and their biological activities. In chemistry, biochemistry and nanotechnology different topological indices are found to be useful in isomer discrimination, QSAR, QSPR and pharmaceutical drug design. Usage of topological indices in biology and chemistry began in 1947 when chemist Harold Wiener introduced the wiener index to study

DOI: 10.4018/978-1-5225-2498-4.ch004

the correlations between physico-chemical properties of organic compounds such as alkanes, alcohols, amines etc (Wiener, 1947). There are several studies regarding different topological indices of special molecular graphs of which we mention a few.

The Let G be a simple connected graph with vertex set $V(G)$ and edge set $E(G)$. Let n and m be the number of vertices and edges of G respectively. Let $u, v \in V(G)$, then the distance $d(u, v)$ between u and v is defined as the length of a minimum path connecting u and v. Also for a given vertex v of $V(G)$ its eccentricity $\varepsilon(v)$ is the largest distance from v to any other vertices of G. For different terminology and notation, we refer the reader to Harary (1969). Topological indices can be classified into different categories such as, vertex degree based topological indices, vertex eccentricity based topological indices, vertex degree cum eccentricity based topological indices, distance based topological indices etc. In this study we have mainly concentrated on vertex degree cum eccentricity based topological indices such as Eccentric Connectivity index, Modified Eccentric Connectivity index, Connective Eccentric index.

BACKGROUND

Different topological indices have been defined and many of them have found applications as means to model chemical, pharmaceutical and other properties of molecules. Thus topological indices are convenient means of translating chemical constitution into numerical values. There are various types of topological indices; among these in this chapter we consider mainly vertex degree cum eccentricity based topological indices. The total eccentricity index of a graph is defined as

$$\zeta(G) = \sum_{i=1}^{n} \varepsilon_G(v_i).$$

Fathalikhani et al. (2014) have studied total eccentricity of some graph operations. Some studies on total eccentricity index are also found in literature (Dankelmann, Goddard & Swart, 2004; De, Nayeem & Pal, 2014, 2015).The eccentric connectivity index of a graph G was proposed by Sharma, Goswami and Madan (1997) and is defined as

$$\xi^c(G) = \sum_{i=1}^{n} d_G(v_i)\varepsilon_G(v_i).$$

A lot of results related to chemical and mathematical study on eccentric connectivity index have been obtained, for details see (Zhou & Du, 2010; Yang & Xia, 2010; Das & Trinajstic, 2011; Zhang & Hua, 2010; Ghorbani & Hemmasi, 2009; Dureja & Madan, 2007; Ashrafi, Ghorbani & Hossein-Zadeh, 2011; Doslic, Saheli & Vukicevic, 2010).

Let $\delta_G(v_i) = \sum\limits_{v_j \in N(v_i)} d_G(v_j)$ i.e. sum of degrees of the neighbor vertices of G, so that $|N(v_i)| = d_G(v_i)$.

One modified version of eccentric connectivity index is defined as (Ashrafi & Ghorbani, 2010):

$$\xi_c(G) = \sum_{i=1}^{n} \delta_G(v_i)\varepsilon_G(v_i).$$

For different study of this index readers are refer to Alaeiyan, Asadpour and Mojarad (2013) and De, Nayeem, and Pal (2014). One of these type of topological index was named as the connective eccentricity index of a graph G. The connective eccentric index was introduced by Gupta, Sing and Madan (2000) and is defined as

$$C^{\xi}(G) = \sum_{v \in V(G)} \frac{d_G(v)}{\varepsilon_G(v)}.$$

In Ghorbani (2011), Ghorbani computed some bounds of connective eccentricity index and also calculate this index for two infinite classes of dendrimers. In De (2012), the present authors, presented some bounds for this connective eccentric index in terms of different graph invariants. Ghorbani and Malekjani in Ghorbani and Malekjani (2012), compute the eccentric connectivity index and the connective eccentric index of an infinite family of fullerenes. Yu and Feng in 2013, derived some upper or lower bounds for the connective eccentric index and investigate the maximal and the minimal values of connective eccentricity index among all n-vertex graphs with fixed number of pendent vertices. Very recently, the present author, in De, Pal, and Nayeem (2014a, 2014b, 2014c), calculated connective eccentric index of some graph operations and of some particular thorny graphs and for V-phenylenic nanotorus. In this regard reader should note that, both connective eccentric index and connective eccentricity index represent the same topological index.

According to suggestion of the *International Academy of Mathematical Chemistry,* to identify weather any topological index is useful for predicting physico-chemical parameters or not, the value of the topological index for different octane isomers are correlated with some different physic-chemical parameters such as boiling point (representative for intermolecular, van der Waals-type interactions), melting point, heat capacities, entropy, density, heat of vaporization, enthalpy of formation, motor octane number, molar refraction, acentric factor, total surface area, octanol-water partition coefficient, and molar volume. Generally, octane isomers are chooses as they are convenient for such studies as the number of their structural isomers is large (18) enough to make the statistical conclusion reliable. Also octane isomers are selected because experimental data are easily available for all such isomers. A dataset of octane isomers, found at http://www.moleculardescriptors.eu/dataset/dataset.htm. To compare these topological indices such as the modified eccentric connectivity index (MECI) eccentric connectivity index (ECI), total eccentricity index (TEI) and connective eccentricity index (CEI) in terms of degeneracy and intercorrelation, we compute its value for octane isomers as given in Table 1. Intercorrelation of these topological indices is given in Table 2.

Let G_1 and G_2 be two simple connected graphs with n_i number of vertices and e_i number of edges respectively, for $i \in \{1, 2\}$. The corona product of $G_1 \circ G_2$ of these two graphs is obtained by taking one copy of G_1 and n_1 copies of G_2; and by joining each vertex of the i-th copy of G_2 to the i-th vertex of G_1, where $1 \leq i \leq n_1$. The corona product of G_1 and G_2 has total number of $(n_1 n_2 + n_1)$ vertices and $(e_1 + n_1 e_2 + n_1 n_2)$ edges. Clearly, the corona product operation of two graphs is not commutative. For details studies of corona product of graphs for different topological indices, interested readers refer to [39-45].

Table 1. Different topological indices of octane isomers

Molecules	MECI	ECI	TEI	CEI
Octane	136	74	44	2.352
2-methyl-heptane	126	65	39	3.167
3-methyl-heptane	121	63	38	3.25
4-methyl-heptane	118	61	37	3.383
3-ethyl-hexane	107	54	33	3.767
2,2-dimethyl-hexane	132	56	34	3.633
2,3-dimethyl-hexane	117	54	33	3.767
2,4-dimethyl-hexane	117	54	33	3.767
2,5-dimethyl-hexane	114	56	34	3.633
3,3-dimethyl-hexane	114	52	32	5.4
3,4-dimethyl-hexane	112	52	32	3.9
2-methyl-3-ethyl-pentane	93	43	27	4.833
3-methyl-3-ethyl-pentane	95	41	26	5.083
2,2,3-trimethyl-pentane	107	43	27	4.833
2,2,4-trimethyl-pentane	115	45	28	4.583
2,3,3-trimethyl-pentane	103	41	26	5.083
2,3,4-trimethyl-pentane	101	43	43	4.833
2,2,3,3-tetramethylbutane	100	34	34	6

Table 2. Intercorrelation of indices

	MECI	ECI	TEI	CEI
MECI	1	0.737	0.325	0.628
ECI	-	1	0.426	0.866
TEI	-	-	1	0.34
CEI	-	-	-	1

Figure 1. Corona product of two graphs

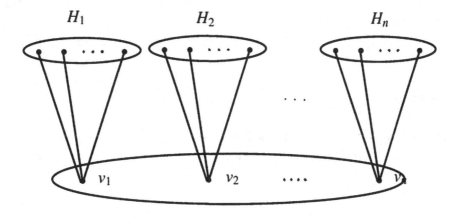

Let the vertices of G_1 are denoted by $V(G_1) = \{u_1, u_2,, u_{n_1}\}$ and the vertices of the i-th copy of G_2 are denoted by $V(G_2^i) = \{v_1^i, v_2^i,, v_{n_2}^i\}$ for $i = 1, 2,, n_1$. Thus the vertex and edge sets of $G_1 \circ G_2$ are given by

$$V(G_1 \circ G_2) = V(G_1) \bigcup_{i=1,2,,n_1} V(G_{2,i})$$

and $E(G_1 \circ G_2) = E(G_1) \bigcup_{i=1,2,,n_1} E(G_{2,i}) \cup \{u_i, v_j : u_i \in V(G_1), v_j^i \in V(G_{2,i})\}$.

First we start with following important Lemma.

Lemma:1 The degree, eccentricity and neighborhood degree sum of the vertices of $G_1 \circ G_2$ are given as follows

  (a) If $u_i \in V(G_1)$, then

      (i) $d_{G_1 \circ G_2}(u_i) = d_{G_1}(u_i) + n_2$,

      (ii) $\varepsilon_{G_1 \circ G_2}(u_i) = \varepsilon_{G_1}(u_i) + 1$ and

      (iii) $\delta_{G_1 \circ G_2}(u_i) = \delta_{G_1}(u_i) + n_2 d_{G_1}(u_i) + 2m_2 + n_2$.

  (b) If $u_i \in V(G_1)$, then

      (i) $d_{G_1 \circ G_2}(v_j^i) = d_{G_1}(v_j) + 1$,

      (ii) $\varepsilon_{G_1 \circ G_2}(v_j^i) = \varepsilon_{G_1}(u_i) + 2$ and

      (iii) $\delta_{G_1 \circ G_2}(v_j^i) = \delta_{G_1}(v_j) + d_{G_2}(v_j) + d_{G_1}(u_i) + n_2$.

In this chapter, the author find the eccentric connectivity index and modified eccentric connectivity index and their respective polynomial versions of corona product of two graphs. Finally, we calculate the eccentric connectivity index and modified eccentric connectivity index of some particular type of graphs by specializing the components of corona product of graphs.

MAIN RESULTS

The corona product operation is binary and noncommutative. All the graphs considered here are connected, finite and simple. Let G_1 and G_2 be two simple connected graphs, so that their vertex sets and edge sets are represented as $V(G_i)$ and $E(G_i)$ respectively, for $i \in \{1, 2\}$. The corona product of two graphs is given in Figure 1.

Total Eccentricity Index

The total eccentricity index of a graph is defined as the sum of the eccentricity of all the vertices of the graph. In the following first the total eccentricity index of corona product of graphs are derived.

Theorem 1 The total eccentricity index of $G_1 \circ G_2$ is given by

$$\zeta(G_1 \circ G_2) = (1 + n_2)\zeta(G_1) + n_1(1 + 2n_2). \tag{1}$$

Proof. From definition of corona product of graphs, total eccentricity index and using lemma 1, we have

$$\zeta(G_1 \circ G_2) = \sum_{i=1}^{n_1} \varepsilon_{G_1 \circ G_2}(u_i) + \sum_{i=1}^{n_1}\sum_{j=1}^{n_2} \varepsilon_{G_1 \circ G_2}(v_j^i)$$

$$= \sum_{i=1}^{n_1} \left\{ \varepsilon_{G_1}(u_i) + 1 \right\} + \sum_{i=1}^{n_1}\sum_{j=1}^{n_2} \left\{ \varepsilon_{G_1}(u_i) + 2 \right\}$$

$$= \sum_{i=1}^{n_1} \varepsilon_{G_1}(u_i) + n_1 + n_2 \sum_{i=1}^{n_1} \varepsilon_{G_1}(u_i) + 2n_1 n_2$$

$$= \zeta(G_1) + n_1 + n_2 \zeta(G_1) + 2n_1 n_2. \quad \square$$

The total eccentricity polynomials of G are defined as

$$\theta(G, x) = \sum_{i=1}^{n} x^{\varepsilon_G(v_i)}.$$

It is easy to see that the total eccentricity index of a graph can be obtained from the corresponding polynomials by evaluating their first derivatives at $x = 1$. In the following the total eccentricity polynomial of corona product of graphs is given.

Theorem 2 The total eccentricity polynomial of $G_1 \circ G_2$ is given by

$$\theta(G_1 \circ G_2, x) = x\theta(G_1, x) + x^2 n_2 \theta(G_1, x). \tag{2}$$

Proof. From definition of corona product of graphs, total eccentricity polynomial and using lemma 1, we have

$$\theta(G_1 \circ G_2, x) = \sum_{i=1}^{n_1} x^{\varepsilon_{G_1 \circ G_2}(u_i)} + \sum_{i=1}^{n_1}\sum_{j=1}^{n_2} x^{\varepsilon_{G_1 \circ G_2}(v_j^i)}$$

$$= \sum_{i=1}^{n_1} x^{\left\{ \varepsilon_{G_1}(u_i) + 1 \right\}} + \sum_{i=1}^{n_1}\sum_{j=1}^{n_2} x^{\left\{ \varepsilon_{G_1}(u_i) + 2 \right\}}$$

$$= x\sum_{i=1}^{n_1} x^{\varepsilon_{G_1}(u_i)} + n_2 x^2 \sum_{i=1}^{n_1} x^{\varepsilon_{G_1}(u_i)}$$

$$= x\theta(G_1, x) + x^2 n_2 \theta(G_1, x).$$

Hence the desired result follows. □

Eccentric Connectivity Index

The eccentric connectivity index of a graph is defined as the sum of the products of eccentricity with the degree of vertices over all vertices of the graph. In the following the eccentric connectivity index of corona product of graphs is given.

Theorem 3 The eccentric connectivity index of $G_1 \circ G_2$ is given by

$$\xi^c(G_1 \circ G_2) = \xi^c(G_1) + 2(n_2 + m_2)\zeta(G_1) + 2m_1 + 4n_1 m_2 + 3n_1 n_2 . \tag{3}$$

Proof. From definition of corona product of graphs, eccentric connectivity index and using lemma 1, we have

$$\xi^c(G_1 \circ G_2) = \sum_{i=1}^{n_1} d_{G_1 \circ G_2}(u_i)\varepsilon_{G_1 \circ G_2}(u_i) + \sum_{i=1}^{n_1}\sum_{j=1}^{n_2} d_{G_1 \circ G_2}(v_j^i)\varepsilon_{G_1 \circ G_2}(v_j^i)$$

$$= \xi_1^C(G_1 \circ G_2) + \xi_2^C(G_1 \circ G_2)$$

Now, $\xi_1^c(G_1 \circ G_2) = \sum_{i=1}^{n_1} d_{G_1 \circ G_2}(u_i)\varepsilon_{G_1 \circ G_2}(u_i)$

$$= \sum_{i=1}^{n_1} \left\{ d_{G_1}(u_i) + n_2 \right\}\left\{ \varepsilon_{G_1}(u_i) + 1 \right\}$$

$$= \sum_{i=1}^{n_1} d_{G_1}(u_i)\varepsilon_{G_1}(u_i) + n_2 \sum_{i=1}^{n_1} \varepsilon_{G_1}(u_i) + \sum_{i=1}^{n_1} d_{G_1}(u_i) + n_1 n_2$$

$$= \xi^C(G_1) + n_2\zeta(G_1) + 2m_1 + n_1 n_2 .$$

Also, $\xi_2^c(G_1 \circ G_2) = \sum_{i=1}^{n_1}\sum_{j=1}^{n_2} d_{G_1 \circ G_2}(v_j^i)\varepsilon_{G_1 \circ G_2}(v_j^i)$

$$= \sum_{i=1}^{n_1}\sum_{j=1}^{n_2} \left\{ d_{G_2}(v_j) + 1 \right\}\left\{ \varepsilon_{G_1}(u_i) + 2 \right\}$$

$$= \sum_{i=1}^{n_1} \varepsilon_{G_1}(u_i)\sum_{j=1}^{n_2} d_{G_2}(v_j) + n_2 \sum_{i=1}^{n_1} \varepsilon_{G_1}(u_i) + 2n_1 \sum_{j=1}^{n_2} d_{G_2}(v_j) + 2n_1 n_2$$

$$= (n_2 + 2m_2)\zeta(G_1) + 4n_1 m_2 + 2n_1 n_2 .$$

Adding $\xi_1^c(G_1 \circ G_2)$ and $\xi_2^c(G_1 \circ G_2)$, the desired result can be proved. □

Luo and Wu computed the eccentric connectivity index of corona product graph as a particular case of cluster product of graphs in Luo and Wu (2014), which coincides with Theorem 3.

The eccentric connectivity polynomials of G is defined as $\xi^c(G,x) = \sum_{i=1}^{n} d_G(v_i) x^{\varepsilon_G(v_i)}$. It is easy to see that the eccentric connectivity index of a graph can be obtained from the corresponding polynomials by evaluating their first derivatives at $x = 1$. In the following theorem we use the same reasoning

Theorem 4 The eccentric connectivity polynomial of $G_1 \circ G_2$ is given by

$$ECP(G_1 \circ G_2, x) = xECP(G_1, x) + x\big((1+x)n_2 + 2m_2 x\big)\theta(G_1, x).$$
(4)

In the next section exact relation for the modified eccentric connectivity index of corona product of graphs are presented.

Modified Eccentric Connectivity Index

The modified eccentric connectivity index of a graph is defined as the sum of the products of eccentricity with the total degree of neighboring vertices over all vertices of the graph. In this section exact relation for the modified eccentric connectivity index of corona product of graphs are presented.

Theorem 5 The modified eccentric connectivity index of $G_1 \circ G_2$ is given by

$$\xi_c(G_1 \circ G_2) = \xi_c(G_1) + 2n_2\xi^c(G_1) + (n_2 + n_2^2 + 4m_2)\zeta(G_1) + M_1(G_1) + (\zeta(G_1) + 2n_1)M_1(G_2)$$

$$+6n_1m_2 + 6n_2m_1 + n_1n_2(2n_2 + 1)$$
(5)

Proof. From definition of corona product of graphs and modified eccentric connectivity index, we have

$$\xi_c(G_1 \circ G_2) = \sum_{i=1}^{n_1} \delta_{G_1 \circ G_2}(u_i)\varepsilon_{G_1 \circ G_2}(u_i) + \sum_{i=1}^{n_1}\sum_{j=1}^{n_2} \delta_{G_1 \circ G_2}(v_j^i)\varepsilon_{G_1 \circ G_2}(v_j^i)$$

$$= \xi_c^{-1}(G_1 \circ G_2) + \xi_c^{-2}(G_1 \circ G_2)$$

Now, using lemma 1 we have

$$\xi_c^{-1}(G_1 \circ G_2) = \sum_{i=1}^{n_1} \delta_{G_1 \circ G_2}(u_i)\varepsilon_{G_1 \circ G_2}(u_i)$$

$$= \sum_{i=1}^{n_1} \big\{\delta_{G_1}(u_i) + n_2 d_{G_1}(u_i) + 2m_2 + n_2\big\}\big\{\varepsilon_{G_1}(u_i) + 1\big\}$$

$$= \sum_{i=1}^{n_1} \delta_{G_1}(u_i)\varepsilon_{G_1}(u_i) + n_2\sum_{i=1}^{n_1} d_{G_1}(u_i)\varepsilon_{G_1}(u_i) + (2m_2 + n_2)\sum_{i=1}^{n_1} \varepsilon_{G_1}(u_i) + \sum_{i=1}^{n_1} \delta_{G_1}(u_i)$$

$$+n_2\sum_{i=1}^{n_1} d_{G_1}(u_i) + (2m_2 + n_2)n_1$$

$$= \xi_c(G_1) + n_2\xi^c(G_1) + (2m_2 + n_2)\zeta(G_1) + M_1(G_1) + 2n_2m_1 + n_1(2m_2 + n_2).$$

Also, $\xi_c^2(G_1 \circ G_2) = \sum_{i=1}^{n_1} \sum_{j=1}^{n_2} \delta_{G_1 \circ G_2}(v_j^i) \varepsilon_{G_1 \circ G_2}(v_j^i)$

$$= \sum_{i=1}^{n_1} \sum_{j=1}^{n_2} \left\{ \delta_{G_1}(v_j) + d_{G_2}(v_j) + d_{G_1}(u_i) + n_2 \right\} \left\{ \varepsilon_{G_1}(u_i) + 2 \right\}$$

$$= \sum_{i=1}^{n_1} \varepsilon_{G_1}(u_i) \sum_{j=1}^{n_2} \delta_{G_2}(v_j) + \sum_{i=1}^{n_1} \varepsilon_{G_1}(u_i) \sum_{i=1}^{n_2} d_{G_2}(v_j) + n_2 \sum_{i=1}^{n_1} d_{G_1}(u_i) \varepsilon_{G_1}(u_i)$$

$$+ n_2^2 \sum_{i=1}^{n_1} \varepsilon_{G_1}(u_i) + 2 \sum_{i=1}^{n_1} \sum_{j=1}^{n_2} \delta_{G_2}(v_j) + 2 \sum_{i=1}^{n_1} \sum_{j=1}^{n_2} d_{G_2}(v_j) + 2 n_2 \sum_{i=1}^{n_1} d_{G_1}(u_i) + 2 n_1 n_2^2$$

$$= \zeta(G_1) M_1(G_2) + 2 m_2 \zeta(G_1) + n_2 \xi^c(G_1) + n_2^2 \zeta(G_1) + 2 n_1 M_1(G_2)$$

$$+ 4 n_1 m_2 + 4 n_2 m_1 + 2 n_1 n_2^2.$$

The expression for the modified eccentric connectivity index of $G_1 \circ G_2$ follows by summing $\xi_c^1(G_1 \circ G_2)$ and $\xi_c^2(G_1 \circ G_2)$. $\square$

The modified eccentric connectivity polynomials of G are defined as

$$\xi_c(G, x) = \sum_{i=1}^{n} \delta_G(v_i) x^{\varepsilon_G(v_i)}$$

so that, the modified eccentric connectivity index of a graph can be obtained from this polynomial by evaluating their first derivatives at $x = 1$. In the following we calculate the modified eccentric connectivity polynomial of $G_1 \circ G_2$ using the previous process. Similar to the last theorem, in the following result we use the same arguments to obtain the modified eccentric connectivity polynomial of corona product of graphs.

Theorem 6 The modified eccentric connectivity polynomial of $G_1 \circ G_2$ is given by

$$MECP(G_1 \circ G_2, x) = xMECP(G_1, x) + x(1+x)n_2 ECP(G_1, x) + x\big(xM_1(G_2) + 2(1+x)m_2 + n_2(n_2 x + 1)\big)\theta(G_1, x)$$

$$(6)$$

The Connective Eccentricity Index

The connective eccentricity index of a graph is defined as the sum of the ratios of degree with the eccentricity of vertices over all vertices of the graph. In the following we calculate the connective eccentricity index of $G_1 \circ G_2$ using the previous process.

Theorem 7 The connective eccentricity index of $G_1 \circ G_2$ is given by

$$C^\xi(G_1 \circ G_2) = m_1 + \frac{5}{6} n_1 n_2 + \frac{2}{3} n_1 m_2 \qquad (7)$$

when all the vertices of G are well connected.

Proof: From definition of corona product of graphs, connective eccentric index and using lemma 1, we have

$$C^\xi(G_1 \circ G_2) = \sum_{i=1}^{n_1} \frac{d_{G_1 \circ G_2}(u_i)}{\varepsilon_{G_1 \circ G_2}(u_i)} + \sum_{i=1}^{n_1} \sum_{j=1}^{n_2} \frac{d_{G_1 \circ G_2}(v_j^i)}{\varepsilon_{G_1 \circ G_2}(v_j^i)}$$

$$= \sum_{i=1}^{n_1} \frac{\left\{d_{G_1}(u_i) + n_2\right\}}{\left\{\varepsilon_{G_1}(u_i) + 1\right\}} + \sum_{i=1}^{n_1} \sum_{j=1}^{n_2} \frac{\left\{d_{G_2}(v_j) + 1\right\}}{\left\{\varepsilon_{G_1}(u_i) + 2\right\}}$$

$$= \frac{1}{2} \sum_{i=1}^{n_1} \left\{d_{G_1}(u_i) + n_2\right\} + \frac{1}{3} \sum_{i=1}^{n_1} \sum_{j=1}^{n_2} \left\{d_{G_2}(v_j) + 1\right\}$$

$$= \frac{1}{2}(2m_1 + n_1 n_2) + \frac{1}{3} n_1(2m_2 + n_2).$$

This completes the proof. □

Applications

Corona product of graphs appears in chemical literature as plerographs of the usual hydrogen-suppressed molecular graphs known as kenographs (see Milicevic and Trinajstic (2006) for definitions and more information). Interesting classes of graphs can be obtained by specializing the first component or the second component in the corona product of two graphs. In the following the total eccentricity index, eccentric connectivity index, modified eccentric connectivity index and connective eccentric index of different chemically interesting graphs are studied by specializing the first or second component in the corona product of two graphs

Thorny Graph

Let G be a given graph with vertex set $\{v_1, v_2, ..., v_n\}$ and $\{p_1, p_2, ..., p_n\}$ be the set of non-negative integers. Then, the thorn graph of G denoted by $G^*(p_1, p_2, ..., p_n)$ is obtained by attaching p_i new vertices of degree one adjacent to p_i for each i. This thorn graphs was introduced by Gutman in 1998 and a number of study on thorn graphs for different topological indices are made by several researchers in the recent past (Bonchev & Klein, 2002; Walikar et al., 2006; Zhou & Vukicevic, 2009; Li, 2011; Heydari & Gutman, 2010; Zhou, 2005; Vukicevic, Zhou & Trinajstic, 2007. 2005). Recently, the present author [28-30] studied different eccentricity related topological indices on thorn graphs. For any given graph G, the t-thorny graph or the t-fold bristled graph is obtained by attaching t-vertices of degree one to each vertex of G (See Figure 2). This graph can be obtained as corona product of G and complement of complete graph on t-vertices $\overline{K}_t$. Thus the expressions of the connective eccentricity index of different t-thorny graphs can be obtained by calculating connective eccentric index of corona product of that graphs with $\overline{K}_t$. Obviously, the connective eccentricity index of different t-thorny graphs can also be obtained from the previous theorems by putting $p_i = t$ for $1 \le i \le |V(G)|$.

Corollary 1 The total eccentricity index of the t-thorn graph G^t is computed as follows

$$\zeta(G^t) = (t+1)\zeta(G) + n(2t+1).$$

Example 1 The total eccentricity index of t-thorny graph or the t-fold bristled graph of C_n and P_n are given by

$$\zeta(C_n \circ \overline{K_t}) = \begin{cases} n^2, \text{ when } n \text{ is even} \\ n(n-1), \text{ when } n \text{ is odd} \end{cases}$$

$$\zeta(P_n \circ \overline{K_t}) = \begin{cases} n^2, \text{ when } n \text{ is even} \\ n(n-1), \text{ when } n \text{ is odd} \end{cases}$$

Similarly, the following result follows.

Example 2 Let H be an arbitrary graph with n vertices, the following results follows

(i) $\zeta(P_m \odot H) = \begin{cases} m(2n+1) + (n+1)(\dfrac{3}{4}m^2 - \dfrac{1}{2}m), \text{ if } m \text{ is even} \\ m(2n+1) + (n+1)(\dfrac{3}{4}m^2 - \dfrac{1}{2}m - \dfrac{1}{4}), \text{ if } m \text{ is odd} \end{cases}$

(ii) $\zeta(C_m \odot H) = \begin{cases} m(2n+1) + \dfrac{1}{2}m^2(n+1), \text{ if } m \text{ is even} \\ m(2n+1) + \dfrac{1}{2}m(m-1)(n+1), \text{ if } m \text{ is odd} \end{cases}$

Corollary 2 The eccentric connectivity index of t-fold Bristled Graph G^t is given by

$$\xi^c(G^t) = \xi^c(G) + 2t\zeta(G) + 2m + 3nt.$$

Example 3 The eccentric connectivity index of t-thorny graph or the t-fold bristled graph of C_n and P_n are given by

$$\xi^c(C_n \circ \overline{K_t}) = \begin{cases} n^2, \text{ when } n \text{ is even} \\ n(n-1), \text{ when } n \text{ is odd} \end{cases}$$

$$\xi_c(P_n \circ \overline{K_t}) = \begin{cases} n^2, \text{ when } n \text{ is even} \\ n(n-1), \text{ when } n \text{ is odd} \end{cases}$$

Similar to eccentric connectivity index, the modified eccentric connectivity index of t-thorny graph is obtained from *Theorem 2* as follows.

Corollary 3 The modified eccentric connectivity index of G^t is given by

$$\xi_c(G^t) = \xi_c(G) + 2t\xi^c(G) + t(t+1)\zeta(G) + M_1(G) + 6mt + nt + 2nt^2$$

Example 4 The modified eccentric connectivity index of t-thorny graph or the t-fold bristled graph of C_n and P_n are given by

$$\xi_c(C_n \circ \overline{K_t}) = \begin{cases} n^2, \text{ when } n \text{ is even} \\ n(n-1), \text{ when } n \text{ is odd} \end{cases}$$

$$\xi_c(P_n \circ \overline{K_t}) = \begin{cases} n^2, \text{ when } n \text{ is even} \\ n(n-1), \text{ when } n \text{ is odd} \end{cases}$$

Now, in the following we find connective eccentricity index of different t-thorny graphs from corona product of graphs.

Corollary 4 The connective eccentricity index of t-thorny complete graph is given by

$$C^\xi(K_n^t) = \frac{1}{2}n(n-1+t) + \frac{nt}{3}.$$

Proof. From definition of corona product of graphs, we have the following

$$C^\xi(K_n^t) = C^\xi(K_n \circ \overline{K_t}) = \sum_{u \in V(K_n)} \frac{d_{K_n \circ \bar{K_t}}(u)}{\varepsilon_{K_n \circ \bar{K_t}}(u)} + n \sum_{u \in V(\overline{K_t})} \frac{d_{K_n \circ \bar{K_t}}(u)}{\varepsilon_{K_n \circ \bar{K_t}}(u)}$$

$$= \sum_{u \in V(K_n)} \frac{d_{K_n}(u) + t}{\varepsilon_{K_n}(u) + 1} + n \sum_{u \in V(\overline{K_t})} \frac{d_{\bar{K_t}}(u) + 1}{\varepsilon_{K_n}(u) + 2}$$

$$= \sum_{u \in V(K_n)} \frac{(n-1)+t}{1+1} + n \sum_{u \in V(\bar{K_t})} \frac{0+1}{1+2} = \frac{1}{2}n(n-1+t) + \frac{nt}{3}$$

This completes the proof. $\square$

Similarly the following results follow from direct calculation.

Corollary 5 The connective eccentricity index of t-thorny complete bipartite graph is given by

$$C^\xi(K_{m,n}^t) = \frac{2}{3}mn + \frac{7}{12}nt.$$

Corollary 6 The connective eccentricity index of t-thorn star S_n^t is

$$C^\xi(S_n^t) = \frac{5}{6}(n-1) + \frac{t}{4} + \frac{7nt}{12}.$$

Figure 2. t-thorny graph or t fold bristled graph of Pn and Cn

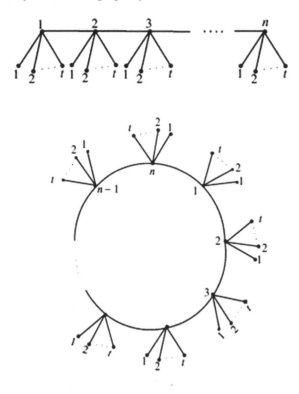

Corollary 7 The connective eccentricity index of t-thorny ring $C_{n,t}$ is given by

$$C^{\xi}(C_n^t) = \begin{cases} \dfrac{4n(t-2)(n+3)}{(n+2)(n+4)} + \dfrac{4n}{(n+2)}, if \ n \ is \ even \\ \dfrac{4n(t-2)(n+2)}{(n+1)(n+3)} + \dfrac{4n}{(n+1)}, if \ n \ is \ odd \end{cases}.$$

Corollary 8 The connective eccentricity index of t-thorny path P_m^t is given by

$$C^{\xi}(P_m^t) = \begin{cases} \displaystyle\sum_{i=0}^{n-1} \dfrac{2t+4}{n+i+2} + \sum_{i=0}^{n} \dfrac{2t}{n+i+3} + \dfrac{2t+2}{2n+2}, when \ m \ is \ even \\ \displaystyle\sum_{i=1}^{n-1} \dfrac{2t+4}{n+i+1} + \dfrac{t+2}{n+1} + \dfrac{t}{n+2} + \sum_{i=1}^{n-1} \dfrac{2t}{n+i+2} + \dfrac{2t+2}{2n+1}, when \ m \ is \ odd \end{cases}.$$

A particular thorny graph, the n-sunlet graph is obtained by attaching n pendent edges to the cycle C_n, so that it contains $2n$ vertices and edges. Let it denoted by SL_n and thus $SL_n = C_n \circ \overline{K_1}$. So, the following result follows.

Example 5 The total eccentricity index, eccentric connectivity index and modified eccentric connectivity index of SL_n is given by

1. $\zeta(SL_n) = \begin{cases} 4n, \text{ when } n \text{ is even} \\ 4n-1, \text{ when } n \text{ is odd} \end{cases}$

2. $\xi^c(SL_n) = \begin{cases} 2n^2 + 5n, \text{ when } n \text{ is even} \\ 2n(n-1) + 5n, \text{ when } n \text{ is odd} \end{cases}$

3. $\xi_c(SL_n) = \begin{cases} 2n^2 + 5n, \text{ when } n \text{ is even} \\ 2n(n-1) + 5n, \text{ when } n \text{ is odd} \end{cases}$

Example 6 The total eccentricity index, eccentric connectivity index, modified eccentric connectivity index and connective eccentric index of star graph (See Figure 3) is given by

1. $\zeta(K_1 \circ \overline{K_{n-1}}) = (2n-1)$
2. $\xi^c(K_1 \circ \overline{K_{n-1}}) = 3(n-1)$
3. $\xi_c(K_1 \circ \overline{K_{n-1}}) = 2n^2 - 3n + 1$
4. $C^{\xi}(K_1 \circ \overline{K_{n-1}}) = \dfrac{3}{2}(n-1)$.

Example 7 The total eccentricity index, eccentric connectivity index, modified eccentric connectivity index and connective eccentric index of bistar $B_{n,n}$ is given by

1. $\zeta(P_2 \circ \overline{K_n}) = 6n + 4$
2. $\xi^c(P_2 \circ \overline{K_n}) = 10n + 4$
3. $\xi_c(P_2 \circ \overline{K_n}) = 6n^2 + 14n + 4$
4. $C^{\xi}(P_2 \circ \overline{K_n}) = \dfrac{5}{3}n + 1$.

Suspension of a Graph

The suspension of a graph G is defined as corona product of K_1 and G. So from previous theorems the following result follows

Corollary 9 The total eccentricity index, eccentric connectivity index and modified eccentric connectivity index and connective eccentric index of suspension of G are given by

1. $\zeta(K_1 \circ G) = 2n + 1$
2. $\xi^c(K_1 \circ G) = 3n + 4m$
3. $\xi_c(K_1 \circ G) = 2M_1(G) + 2n^2 + n + 6m$
4. $C^{\xi}(K_1 \circ G) = \dfrac{3n}{2} + m$.

Example 8 The wheel graph W_n on *(n+1)* vertices is the suspension of C_n (See Fig. 3). So its total eccentricity index, eccentric connectivity index and modified eccentric connectivity index and connective eccentric index are given by

1. $\zeta(K_1 \circ C_n) = 2n + 1$
2. $\xi^C(K_1 \circ C_n) = 7n$
3. $\xi_c(K_1 \circ C_n) = 2n^2 + 15n$
4. $C^{\xi}(K_1 \circ C_n) = \dfrac{5n}{2}$.

Figure 3. Star, Fan, Wheel graph on (n+1) vertices

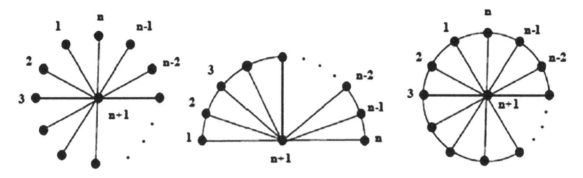

Example 9 The fan graph F_n on *(n+1)* vertices is the suspension of P_n (See Figure 3). So its total eccentricity index, eccentric connectivity index and modified eccentric connectivity index and connective eccentric index are given by

1. $\zeta(K_1 \circ P_n) = 2n + 1$
2. $\xi^c(K_1 \circ P_n) = 7n - 4$
3. $\xi_c(K_1 \circ P_n) = 2n^2 + 15n - 18$
4. $C^\xi(K_1 \circ P_n) = \dfrac{5n}{2} - 1$.

Bottleneck Graphs

The bottleneck graph B is the corona product of K_2 and G. So from the previous theorems the following result follows

Corollary 10 The total eccentricity index, eccentric connectivity index and modified eccentric connectivity index and connective eccentric index of bottleneck Graph B is given by

1. $\zeta(B) = 6n + 4$
2. $\xi^c(B) = 4n + 18m + 4$
3. $\xi_c(B) = 6M_1(G) + 6n^2 + 14n + 20m + 4$
4. $C^\xi(B) = \dfrac{5n}{3} + \dfrac{4m}{3} + 1$.

Figure 4. The bridge graph B_n.and $T_{n,3}$.

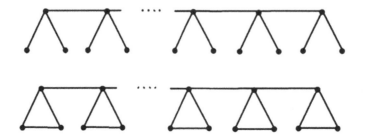

Bridge Graphs

The bridge graph with respect to the vertices $v_1, v_2,, v_n$ is denoted by $B(G_1, G_2,, G_n; v_1, v_2,, v_n)$ where $G_1, G_2,, G_n$ be a set of finite pair wise disjoint graphs. The bridge graph is obtained by joining the vertices v_i and v_{i+1} of G_i and G_{i+1} by an edge, for all $i = 1, 2, ., (n-1)$. In particular, if $G_1 \cong G_2 \cong \cong G_n \cong G$ and $v_1 = v_2 == v_n = v$, then the bridge graph is denoted by $G_n(G, v)$. Now we consider three particular type of bridge graphs as in Luo and Wu (2014), named as $B_n = G_n(P_3, v)$, $T_{m,k} = G_m(C_k, u)$ and $J_{n,m+1} = G_n(P_3, v)$ (See Figure 4). According to definition of corona product of graphs the bridge graphs $B_n = P_n \circ \overline{K}_2$, $T_{m,k} = P_m \circ K_2$ and $J_{n,m+1} = P_n \circ C_m$. So the eccentric connectivity index of these bridge graphs is given as follows.

Example 10

1. $\xi^c(B_n) = \begin{cases} \dfrac{9}{2} n^2 + 3n, & \text{when } n \text{ is even} \\ \dfrac{9}{2} n^2 + 3n - \dfrac{3}{2}, & \text{when } n \text{ is odd} \end{cases}$

2. $\xi^c(T_{m,3}) = \begin{cases} 6m^2 + 6m, & \text{when } m \text{ is even} \\ 6m^2 + 6m - 2, & \text{when } m \text{ is odd} \end{cases}$

3. $\xi^c(J_{n,m+1}) = \begin{cases} 3n^2(m + \dfrac{1}{2}) + 5mn - n, & \text{when } n \text{ is even} \\ 3n^2(m + \dfrac{1}{2}) + 5mn - n - m - \dfrac{1}{2}, & \text{when } n \text{ is odd} \end{cases}$

Similarly, the modified eccentric connectivity index of the bridge graphs $P_n \circ \overline{K}_2$, $P_m \circ K_2$ and $P_n \circ C_m$ are obtained as follows.

Example 11

1. $\xi_c(B_n) = \begin{cases} \dfrac{27}{2} n^2 + 3n - 2, & \text{when } n \text{ is even} \\ \dfrac{27}{2} n^2 + 3n - \dfrac{13}{2}, & \text{when } n \text{ is odd} \end{cases}$

2. $\xi^c(T_{m,3}) = \begin{cases} 18m^2 + 10m - 2, & \text{when } m \text{ is even} \\ 18m^2 + 10m - 8, & \text{when } m \text{ is odd} \end{cases}$

3.

$\xi^c(J_{n,m+1}) = \begin{cases} 11n^2 + 3mn^2 + 2nm^2 + 7nm - 4n - 2m + 2 + \dfrac{1}{4}n(3n-2)(m^2 + 5m + 4n), & \text{when } n \text{ is even} \\ 11n^2 + 3mn^2 + 2nm^2 + 7nm - 4n - 3m + 1 + \dfrac{1}{4}n(3n^2 - 2n - 1)(m^2 + 5m + 4n), & \text{when } n \text{ is odd} \end{cases}$

CONCLUSION

In this chapter, the behavior of the total eccentricity index, eccentric connectivity index, modified eccentric connectivity index and connective eccentric index under corona product of graphs have studied and also these results are applied by specializing the component of corona product to compute these indices for some classes of special classes of graphs. Nevertheless, there are still many classes of graphs not covered by our approach. So it is interesting to find explicit formulas for the eccentric-distance sum index of various classes of chemical graphs and nano-structures. In order to achieve that goal, further research into mathematical properties of the vertex eccentric related index will be necessary.

REFERENCES

Alaeiyan, M., Asadpour, J., & Mojarad, R. (2013). A Numerical Method for MEC Polynomial and MEC Index of One-Pentagonal Carbon Nanocones. *Fullerenes, Nanotubes and Carbon Nanostructures*, 21(10), 825-835.

Alizadeh, Y., Iranmanesh, A., Doslić, T., & Azari, M. (2014). The edge Wiener index of suspensions, bottlenecks, and thorny graphs. *Glasnik Matematicki Series III*, 49(69), 1–12. doi:10.3336/gm.49.1.01

Ashrafi, A. R., & Ghorbani, M. (2010). A Study of fullerenes by MEC polynomials. *Electronic Materials Letters*, 6(2), 87–90.

Ashrafi, A. R., Ghorbani, M., & Hossein-Zadeh, M. A. (2011). The eccentric connectivity polynomial of some graph operations. *Serdica Journal of Computing*, 5, 101–116.

Bian, H., Ma, X., & Vumar, E. (2012). The Wiener-type indices of the corona of two graphs. *Ars Combinatoria*, 107, 193–199.

Bonchev, D., & Klein, D. J. (2002). On the Wiener number of thorn trees, stars, rings, and rods. *Croatica Chemica Acta*, 75, 613–620.

Dankelmann, P., Goddard, W., & Swart, C. S. (2004). The average eccentricity of a graph and its subgraphs. *Utilitas Mathematica*, 65, 41–51.

Das, K. C., & Trinajstić, N. (2011). Relationship between the eccentric connectivity index and Zagreb indices. *Computers & Mathematics with Applications (Oxford, England)*, 62(4), 1758–1764. doi:10.1016/j.camwa.2011.06.017

De, N. (2012). Bounds for connective eccentric index. *International Journal of Contemporary Mathematical Sciences*, 7(44), 2161–2166.

De, N. (2012). On eccentric connectivity index and polynomial of thorn graph. *Applications of Mathematics*, 3, 931–934.

De, N. (2012). Augmented Eccentric Connectivity Index of Some Thorn Graphs. *International Journal of Applied Mathematical Research, 1*(4), 671–680. doi:10.14419/ijamr.v1i4.326

De, N., Nayeem, S. M. A., & Pal, A. (2014). Total eccentricity index of the generalized hierarchical product of graphs. *International Journal of Applied and Computational Mathematics, 1*. doi:10.1007/s40819-014-0016-4

De, N., Nayeem, S. M. A., & Pal, A. (2014). Bounds for modified eccentric connectivity index. *Advanced Modeling and Optimization, 16*(1), 133–142.

De, N., Nayeem, S. M. A., & Pal, A. (2014). Computing modified eccentric connectivity index and connective eccentric index of V-phenylenic nanotorus. *Studia Universitatis Babes-Bolyai Chemia, 59*(4), 129–137.

De, N., Nayeem, S. M. A., & Pal, A. (2014). Connective eccentricity index of some thorny Graphs. *Annals of Pure and Applied Mathematics, 7*(1), 59–64.

De, N., Nayeem, S. M. A., & Pal, A. (2014). Modified Eccentric Connectivity of Generalized Thorn Graphs. *International Journal of Computer Mathematics, 2014*, 1–8. doi:10.1155/2014/436140

De, N., Nayeem, S. M. A., & Pal, A. (2015). Modified eccentric connectivity index and polynomial of Corona product of graphs. *International Journal of Computers and Applications, 132*(9), 1–5. doi:10.5120/ijca2015907536

De, N., Pal, A., & Nayeem, S. M. A. (2014). On some bounds and exact formulae for connective eccentric indices of graphs under some graph operations. *International Journal of Combinatorics, 2014*, 1–5. doi:10.1155/2014/579257

De, N., Pal, A., & Nayeem, S. M. A. (2015). Total eccentricity index of some composite graphs. *Malaya Journal of Matematik, 3*(4), 523–529.

Doslić, T., & Saheli, M. (2014). Eccentric connectivity index of composite graphs. *Utilitas Mathematica, 95*, 3–22.

Došlić, T., Saheli, M., & Vukičević, D. (2010). Eccentric connectivity index: Extremal graphs and Values. *Iranian Journal of Mathematical Chemistry, 1*, 45–56.

Dureja, H., & Madan, A. K. (2007). Superaugmented eccentric connectivity indices: New generation highly discriminating topological descriptors for QSAR/QSPR modeling. *Medicinal Chemistry Research, 16*(7-9), 331–341. doi:10.1007/s00044-007-9032-9

Fathalikhani, K., Faramarzi, H., & Yousefi-Azari, H. (2014). Total eccentricity of some graph operations. *Electronic Notes in Discrete Mathematics, 45*, 125–131. doi:10.1016/j.endm.2013.11.025

Ghorbani, M. (2011). Connective Eccentric Index of Fullerenes. *Journal of Mathematical Nanoscience, 1*, 43–52.

Ghorbani, M., & Hemmasi, M. (2009). Eccentric connectivity polynomial of C_{12n+4} fullerenes. *Digest Journal of Nanomaterials and Biostructures, 4*, 545–547.

Ghorbani, M., & Malekjani, K. (2012). A new method for computing the eccentric connectivity index of fullerenes. *Serdica Journal of Computing, 6*, 299–308.

Gupta, S., Singh, M., & Madan, A. K. (2000). Connective eccentricity Index: A novel topological descriptor for predicting biological activity. *Journal of Molecular Graphics & Modelling, 18*(1), 18–25. doi:10.1016/S1093-3263(00)00027-9 PMID:10935202

Gutman, I. (1998). Distance in thorny graph. *Publ. Inst. Math. (Beograd), 63*, 31–36.

Harary, F. (1969). *Graph Theory*. Addison-Wesely.

Heydari, A., & Gutman, I. (2010). On the terminal Wiener index of thorn graphs. *Kragujevac Journal of Mathematics, 32*, 57–64.

Li, S. (2011). Zagreb polynomials of thorn graphs. *Kragujevac Journal of Science, 33*, 33–38.

Luo, Z., & Wu, J. (2014). Zagreb eccentricity indices of the generalized hierarchical product graphs and their applications. *Journal of Applied Mathematics, 2014*, 1–8. doi:10.1155/2014/241712

Miličević, A., & Trinajstić, N. (2006). Combinatorial enumeration in chemistry. In A. Hincliffe (Ed.), *Chemical Modelling: Applications and Theory* (Vol. 4). Cambridge, UK: RSC Publishing.

Pattabiraman, K., & Kandan, P. (2014). Weighted PI index of corona product of graphs. *Discrete Mathematics. Algorithms and Applications, 06*. doi:10.1142/S1793830914500554

Sharma, V., Goswami, R., & Madan, A. K. (1997). Eccentric connectivity index: A novel highly discriminating topological descriptor for structure-property and structure-activity studies. *Journal of Chemical Information and Modeling, 37*, 273–282.

Vukiþeviü, D., Nikoliü, S., & Trinajstiü, N. (2005). On the Schultz Index of Thorn Graphs, Internet Electron. J. Mol. Des., 4, 501-514.

Vukičević, D., Zhou, B., & Trinajstić, N. (2007). Altered Wiener Indices of Thorn Trees. *Croatica Chemica Acta, 80*, 283–285.

Walikar, H. B., Ramane, H. S., Sindagi, L., Shirakol, S. S., & Gutman, I. (2006). Hosoya polynomial of thorn trees, rods, rings, and stars. *Kragujevac Journal of Science, 28*, 47–56.

Wiener, H. (1947). Structural determination of paraffin boiling points. *Journal of the American Chemical Society, 69*(1), 17–20. doi:10.1021/ja01193a005 PMID:20291038

Yang, J., & Xia, F. (2010). The Eccentric Connectivity Index of Dendrimers. *International Journal of Contemporary Mathematical Sciences, 5*, 2231–2236.

Yarahmadi, Z., & Ashrafi, A. R. (2012). The Szeged, Vertex PI, first and second Zagreb Indices of corona Product of Graphs. *Filomat, 26*(3), 467–472. doi:10.2298/FIL1203467Y

Yu, G., & Feng, L. (2013). On Connective Eccentricity Index of Graphs. MATCH Communications in Mathematical and in Computer Chemistry, 69, 611-628.

Zhang, L., & Hua, H. (2010). The Eccentric Connectivity Index of Unicyclic Graphs. *International Journal of Contemporary Mathematical Sciences*, 5, 2257–2262.

Zhou, B. (2005). On modified Wiener indices of thorn trees. *Kragujevac Journal of Science*, 27, 5–9.

Zhou, B., & Du, Z. (2010). On eccentric connectivity index. *MATCH Communications in Mathematical and in Computer Chemistry*, 63(1), 181–198.

Zhou, B., & Vukičević, D. (2009). On Wiener-type polynomials of thorn graphs. *Journal of Chemometrics*, 23(12), 600–604. doi:10.1002/cem.1258

Section 2
Systems and Computational Biology

Chapter 5
Statistical Analysis of Functional Magnetic Resonance Imaging Data

Nicole A. Lazar
University of Georgia, USA

ABSTRACT

The analysis of functional magnetic resonance imaging (fMRI) data poses many statistical challenges. The data are massive, noisy, and have a complicated spatial and temporal correlation structure. This chapter introduces the basics of fMRI data collection and surveys common approaches for data analysis.

INTRODUCTION

Human beings have long been interested in how we ourselves work and function. Of particular fascination has been the working of the human brain. Through the ages we have had opportunity to learn about how our brain functions, mostly haphazardly as the result of illness or accident: a Roman gladiator who suffered amnesia after a blow to the skull; an elderly person who had a stroke, lost the use of one side of the body, but gradually recovered much of the original functionality; savants who were unable to speak but were musical or mathematical prodigies. From all of these isolated incidents, together with postmortem dissections of the brains of healthy individuals, scientists were able to build models of how the brain functions, how information is processed, and what specific regions in the brain are responsible for different types of tasks.

It is only relatively recently, however, that technological advances have allowed us to study the function of the human brain – healthy or diseased – in something closer to real time. Neuroimaging techniques such as positron emission tomography (PET), electroencephalography (EEG), magnetoencephalography (MEG), and functional magnetic resonance imaging (fMRI) have brought a wealth of new knowledge and new understanding to cognitive neuroscientists. Statisticians have been an important part of this exciting endeavor.

DOI: 10.4018/978-1-5225-2498-4.ch005

Consider fMRI as an example. With this imaging modality, the subject is put into a magnetic resonance machine – a large powerful magnet – and is asked to perform some task, for example to tap his or her fingers in a particular pattern, or to do a simple math problem. While the subject is carrying out the task, a complex array of machinery takes images of the brain in action; actually, the neuronal activity itself is not measured, but rather an indirect measure called the blood-oxygenation level dependent, or BOLD, signal, which is related to the oxygen requirements of the brain when it processes information. In general terms, parts of the brain that are responding to a stimulus or performing a cognitive task require more oxygen than those that are not. Hence, the blood that is delivered to different areas of the brain will differ in the ratio of oxygenated to deoxygenated hemoglobin. Oxygenated and deoxygenated hemoglobin, in turn, have different magnetic properties. Functional MRI takes advantage of that difference through the measured BOLD signal.

This is obviously a complicated process, and the data that result in the end are also complicated, in ways that make them interesting and challenging for statistical analysis. Some of the crucial features of fMRI data are:

1. They are very noisy. Some noise is intrinsic – it comes from the scanner itself. This type of noise can usually be estimated rather easily and can often be corrected for. Other noise comes from the subject. For instance, breathing and heartbeat introduce systematic noise, as they move the brain within the skull and affect blood flow to the brain. fMRI has very good spatial resolution; measurements are taken on the millimeter scale. As a result, however, even small amounts of movement on the part of the subject contaminate the data, shifting the measured signal from one location to another. Subject-related noise, particularly motion, is harder to handle, but there are procedures in place for this as well.

2. They are massive in scale. For a single subject, the magnetic resonance machine may scan the whole brain 100–200 times over the course of an experiment. Each such three-dimensional volume is made up of hundreds of thousands of volume elements, or voxels, little cubes of length 3 mm per side, typically. That is, for each subject in a study, the data may consist of hundreds of thousands of time series, and each time series may have 100-200 measurements. Of course most studies also include multiple subjects, sometimes divided into groups (for example, patients and controls). That is a lot of data; computational challenges are one important consequence.

3. They are correlated both temporally and spatially. Temporal correlation arises because the entire sequence of the brain response – the so-called hemodynamic response function – to a stimulus is slower than the time it takes to collect an image; hence, the measured signal at a given time point is affected by the signal that was measured in previous time points, and in turn affects signals measured at later time points. As for spatial correlation, all of the voxels are in the same brain; what takes place at one location is affected by - and affects - other locations. The spatial dependence is particularly interesting from a statistical perspective. Whereas many standard spatial statistics models assume that the closer in space two locations are, the more strongly correlated they are, with the strength of the dependence decreasing quickly with distance, the brain does not work that way at all. The brain has two hemispheres, and while one hemisphere tends to be dominant for specific types of processing, there will also be similar functions on the other side - language and visual processing for instance take place in both hemispheres. The result is that locations that are physically far from each other - on different sides of the brain - can still be very highly correlated if they take on similar functional roles.

The goal of this chapter is to introduce the reader to the fundamentals of fMRI data collection and analysis. This field is rapidly developing, as new methods for the statistical analysis of these interesting data sets are deployed. Hence it is impossible to be comprehensive or completely up-to-date. Rather, the aim is to provide a high-level survey of some of the statistical questions that arise in the analysis of these data, and the approaches that have been considered to answer these questions.

DATA COLLECTION

For a complete discussion of the data collection principles of MR imaging in general, and fMRI more specifically, see Huettel et al. (2004).

The magnetic resonance machine is a very powerful magnet – 3 Tesla (T) is common in research settings. For comparison, the natural magnetic field of the Earth is 25 to 65 microteslas. Within the scanner it is possible to manipulate the magnetic field using gradients, that cause local changes and allow for the localization of signal in the tissue (see Hashemi et al., 2004 for a comprehensive treatment of MRI physics). That is, to within millimeter precision the level of the BOLD response is known. The spatial resolution of fMRI is thus very good, especially in comparison to other popular imaging techniques. It's worth noting, however, that in terms of the underlying neuronal structure, it is actually quite poor. A single voxel contains many hundreds of thousands of neurons, which means that the scale of the observed data is orders of magnitude larger than the level at which one might ideally wish to perform inference.

Increased brain activation requires oxygen; hence when a subject is exposed to a stimulus or is performing some cognitive task, the parts of the brain that are involved have increased demands for oxygen, although not apparently for blood. The result is a change in the oxygenation level of the hemoglobin in the relevant areas – the ratio of deoxygenated to oxygenated hemoglobin changes. Furthermore, deoxygenated and oxygenated hemoglobin have different magnetic properties: oxygenated blood is diamagnetic, i.e. it is repulsed from a magnetic field; deoxygenated blood is paramagnetic, and is attracted to a magnetic field. Ultimately, oxygenated blood in strong fields shows a stronger MR signal than does deoxygenated blood. This is the basis of the blood oxygenation level dependent, or BOLD, signal that is actually measured in fMRI; it is an indirect measure of brain activation.

The hemodynamic response function describes the response to presentation of a stimulus. A stylized version of the function is in Figure 1. As can be seen, after stimulus there is a delay of 1–2 seconds before the blood flow starts to increase, reaching a peak after about six seconds. This is quite slow in comparison to the neuronal activity itself, which takes place at millisecond timing. If no additional stimulus is given, the response starts to decay again. Research has revealed that there is often a "dip" before return to baseline levels. A common model for the hemodynamic response function is the sum of two Gamma density functions, with parameters that control the time of the initial rise, the time to peak, the post-decay dip, and return to baseline. Manipulation of those parameters allows one to increase the initial lag, make the peak response higher or lower, include the dip at the end, or not, and so forth.

In general, it will take several seconds to perform a scan of the entire brain (depending on certain parameters that are largely under the control of the experimenter). Since the neuronal responses are much faster than that – on the order of milliseconds – the temporal resolution of fMRI is quite poor.

The intricate nature of neuroimaging studies thus implies two different levels of experimental design that are relevant for the collection of fMRI data. The finer level involves the scanner itself – the calibration of the machine and the design of the particular imaging sequences by which the data will be

Figure 1. Example of idealized hemodynamic response function (HRF) modeled as the sum of two Gamma density functions

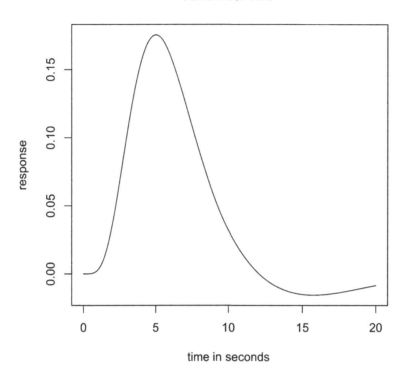

acquired. This is more of an engineering question than a statistical one, and won't be considered further (see Huettel et al., 2004, for details). The second, coarser level is more traditional experimental design from a statistical perspective: how should stimuli be presented so that the questions of scientific interest can be answered from the collected data. Two main types of design are prevalent in fMRI studies, and they support two different sorts of scientific question.

One type is the "block design" in which periods of some task, or multiple tasks, are interspersed with periods of rest. A schematic is shown in Figure 2. For the first 20 scans of the study, the subject is at rest, perhaps fixating on a central crosshair in the middle of a screen mounted inside the scanner. For the next 20 scans, the subject is performing a task or being presented with a stimulus. These blocks of rest and stimulus/task alternate over the course of the experiment. Such a design is effective for activation detection using the subtraction paradigm, which compares levels of BOLD response in times of rest to times of stimulus. "Active" voxels are those which show a difference in the level of response. The repeated stimulus presentation leads to a convolution of multiple hemodynamic response functions of the type shown in Figure 1; this in turn yields the "boxcar" shape of the time series which is characteristic of task-reactive voxels. When the stimulus ends, there is again a lag as the hemodynamic response decays back to baseline levels.

The second main type of design is "event-related." Here, stimuli are not presented over an extended (multiple seconds) period of time, but rather are given individually and sporadically, separated by rest periods of variable length. That is, the stimulus or task appears irregularly and in an unpredictable fashion.

Figure 2. Block design along with theoretical time course for a task-related voxel

Block design experiment

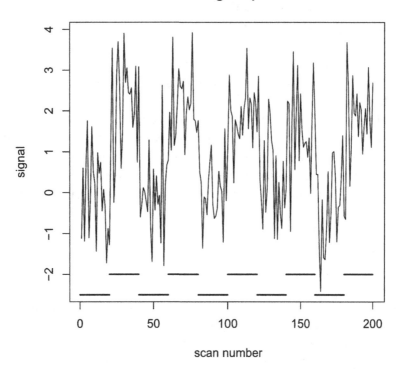

This sort of design is useful for estimation of the hemodynamic response function, but less efficient for activation detection. By contrast, the block design does not permit estimation, because it is difficult to deconvolve the pieces of the cumulative BOLD response into individual estimated functions.

Mixed designs have also been proposed (Kao et al., 2009). These combine periods of block-like stimulus presentation with event-related presentations, and are generally designed to optimize a weighted function of different criteria (estimation, activation detection, appropriate balance of stimulus types, etc).

In more recent years, a third type of study – resting state fMRI – has become more popular. Resting state fMRI, as the name implies, does not involve any task or stimulus presentation at all. Rather, subjects remain in the scanner for some length of time in a state of alert rest. Subjects should not fall asleep, but neither are they given any particular tasks to carry out. The goal of such a paradigm is to understand background or ambient thought, and is instructive for the building of networks between brain regions. Resting state fMRI will not be considered explicitly in the rest of this chapter. See Fox and Raichle (2007) or Cole et al. (2010) for introductions to this type of fMRI study.

Finally, prior to any statistical analysis, it is standard (although somewhat controversial among statisticians) for the data to undergo a series of preprocessing steps. These range from corrections for "scanner drift" (changes in the signal that occur over time simply because of changing temperature of the magnet) to adjustments for the subject's heartbeat and respiration, which introduce systematic signal on top of the signal of interest. Perhaps most controversial are two common preprocessing steps: (1) spatial smoothing, which applies a spatial kernel (often Gaussian) to the data, in an effort to make them appear "more normal" and hence more amenable to certain statistical analyses; (2) warping to a common atlas, such as MNI or Talairach space, to allow for combination and comparison of subjects, since the brain is idiosyncratic in size, shape, and to a certain extent layout. Both of these preprocessing steps introduce additional spatial correlation of a largely poorly-understood nature into the data. Recent work by Rowe and colleagues (Bruce et al., 2011; Nencka et al., 2009; Rowe et al., 2009) provides a mathematical framework for understanding the effects of preprocessing. Among the important contributions of this research is a return to a more raw form of the measured data, as they are collected from the scanner. This brings the statistical analysis, which is currently many steps removed from the measurements of interest, closer to their source.

From these initial principles, it is evident that BOLD fMRI yields an indirect measurement of neuronal activity, which is the true effect of interest. Furthermore, measurement at both the spatial and temporal scale is far removed from the neuronal level. Hence even before taking account of other features of the data, we have a proxy measure that spatially and temporally agglomerates in such a way that much of the information of interest is lost or simply unattainable. This is not, however, the end of the complications.

STATISTICAL ISSUES

It should be apparent from the above that fMRI data pose many interesting challenges from an analysis perspective. At the most basic level, of an individual voxel within the brain of an individual subject, one can consider parametric or nonparametric tests and one can ignore the temporal correlation (which will obviously result in a flawed analysis, but has the virtue of being simple to implement and explain) or incorporate it via time series modeling. Of course a single voxel is not of interest in and of itself, since it has no intrinsic biological or other meaning, so analysis of potentially all of the voxels in the brain is what is needed. This brings in the spatial dependence as well, which can also be ignored or included in the analysis, and modeled in a wide variety of different ways. If spatial correlation is ignored completely, and each voxel treated as an independent unit of inference (the so-called "massively univariate" approach), the result is a serious multiple testing problem, which has spurred many years of research in the statistics community. The spatial and temporal correlations can be modeled together to some extent, although this will create problems of identification and computation, or they can be modeled separately, which is unrealistic. The problems, then, are myriad, which might explain the wide variety of statistics and machine learning techniques that have been applied to the data.

The challenges don't stop there, of course, because rarely is a researcher interested in just a single subject. Rather interest is on the group level, and more generally still, on the comparison of groups – healthy controls versus people with schizophrenia; men versus women; children with autism versus children without; elderly subjects with or without various types of age-related cognitive impairments. The ways in which one passes from single-subject analysis to multi-subject to multi-group vary, but often will involve a (frequentist or Bayesian) hierarchical model.

Another focus of much recent research in fMRI data analysis is connectivity, as opposed to activation detection. Here, one is interested in constructing and assessing networks that connect voxels or different brain regions, and comparing those across groups. Different types of connectivity have been defined in the literature, in particular functional and effective connectivities (Friston, 2011). Functional connectivity is usually taken to refer to correlation (or, more generally, statistical dependence) between regions, whereas effective connectivity deals with the influence of one region on another (which is more of a causal statement). Questions center on existence and strength of connections between the various nodes in the brain network, in addition to direction of influence when this can be inferred from the data. As with detection, it is possible to approach connectivity from a wide range of statistics and machine learning perspectives.

OVERVIEW OF APPROACHES TO STATISTICAL ANALYSIS

Single Subject

We start with consideration of a traditional single subject analysis based on the subtraction paradigm, or the idea that activations of interest can be detected via a contrast of the BOLD signal between a rest and a task condition. For simplicity of exposition, we will assume a block design, although similar strategies can work for event-related studies as well.

In the simplest formulation, then, at each voxel the investigator is interested in comparing the level of BOLD response during times of rest and times of stimulus. Carrying out the comparison at each voxel individually implies that spatial correlation is ignored. If, in addition, temporal correlation is ignored then at each location the contrast in BOLD signal can be summarized by a two-sample t-statistic. The mean level of activation during task times is compared to that during rest times, all scaled by an estimate of variability, which can be a pooled or unpooled variance estimator. Degrees of freedom will be related to the length of the time course, hence typically greater than 100, and one can use approximate normality for inferential purposes. That is, at each voxel calculate

$$t = \frac{(\bar{X}_{task} - \bar{X}_{rest})}{sd}$$

Where $\bar{X}_{task}$ is the mean of the measured BOLD response from images taken when the task was being performed (or stimulus being presented); $\bar{X}_{rest}$ is the mean of the measured response from images taken while the subject was at rest; and sd is some suitable estimate of variability.

The problems with this simplistic approach are apparent and numerous. The data within a voxel are of course temporally correlated; proceeding as if the measurements are independent distorts results. Carrying out analysis on the voxel level and ignoring the spatial correlation both induces a massive multiple testing problem and results in a loss of information, since dependence among neighboring points could lead to sharper inference. The t-test itself is based on the assumption that the underlying data are normally distributed, or at least approximately so. The simple analysis also ignores the nature of the hemodynamic response, particularly the delay in the rise of the BOLD signal after stimulus presentation.

Each individual decision involves some inaccuracy or is of questionable validity. Nonetheless this incorrect analysis is informative. Indeed, with suitable corrections for multiple testing, this approach gives results that are in line with researcher expectations. In addition, it offers a starting point from which a better, more sophisticated model can be built. Let's start with the nature of the hemodynamic response. It is commonplace in the literature to convolve the stimulus response trail with a function that models the hemodynamic response; an example of such a model is the sum of two Gamma probability density functions (see Figure 1). When the stimulus trail for an event-related design is convolved with such a function, the "spikes" that represent events are softened to look like the prototypical hemodynamic response function. When this convolution is performed on a block design trail, the result is a more gradual rise and fall of the blocks, which mimics the delay in the response following stimulus presentation, and the slow decay once the stimulus is turned off. A simple t-test will no longer work with this convolved stimulus trail, however one can instead correlate the two time series. In the case of the raw stimulus presentation trail, the two analyses coincide, so this is a true and useful generalization.

Temporal correlation is easily incorporated via time series models of low order - AR(1) for example is often used, although this is still too simplistic to truly capture the nature of the dependence in the data. With this change, the analysis shifts from a simple two-sample t-test or correlation analysis to a general linear model, which is probably the most widely-used analysis for subject-level fMRI data (see, for example, Worsley & Friston, 1995).

The questions of spatial structure and multiplicity are not as readily addressed. The spatial dependence in fMRI data is complicated and not amenable to the standard models of spatial statistics, which arose for the most part in a geosciences context. Whereas the typical spatial model assumes that as locations become more separated from each other physically, the correlation between observations at those sites becomes smaller (often at an exponential rate), brain space behaves differently. While it is true to some extent that voxels that are close to each other physically have similar behavior, this comes with several caveats. First, brain activation tends to be regional; that is, there are regions that react to particular stimuli or are involved in particular tasks. Within those regions, if they are task-relevant, one might expect behavior akin to a standard spatial model. But the borders of regions also tend to be sharp, so there is not necessarily a gradual decline in dependence. Instead, the dependence will drop off suddenly, so that a voxel inside a region and a neighboring voxel outside that region will not exhibit strong positive correlation. Second, the brain is made up of two hemispheres, which have some amount of redundancy in function. For example, there are regions for visual processing in both hemispheres; likewise for verbal, motor, and many other supporting functions. One can reasonably expect to find task-relevant voxels responding in both hemispheres. These voxels are physically far from each other, yet strongly correlated, and even more correlated than they are with task-irrelevant voxels that are more proximal. For this reason, researchers have defined functional distance for brain data as well as the more common physical distance (for instance, Bowman, 2007; although this paper analyzes data from positron emission tomography and not fMRI, the underlying issue is the same). We need to account for both of these in spatial modeling of fMRI data, yet it is not altogether clear how to do this.

As for multiple testing corrections, this is not unrelated to the spatial question. Evidently one should account for spatial correlation in correcting for multiple testing. The "true" amount of independent information is not the total number of voxels, because of the spatial correlation, nor is it 1, since the measured signal differs from voxel to voxel, but rather somewhere in between. General methods for the control of Type I error, and in particular the Bonferroni correction for control of the family wise error rate, are much too conservative when such a large number of tests is conducted. Other approaches have therefore become more popular in the fMRI literature. Three of the most prominent are contiguity cluster thresholding (Forman et al., 1995), random field theory (Worsley, 2003), and procedures for the control of the false discovery rate (Benjamini & Hochberg, 1995; Genovese et al., 2002).

All procedures for handling the multiplicity problem in imaging data are looking for the cutoff point on the curve of ordered p-values that will separate the voxel-level hypothesis tests that should be rejected (voxel declared active) from those that should not. The different approaches, including those that try to incorporate dependence structure, place the cutoff in different ways and at different locations.

Once we move beyond the basics of data analysis, there are various more subtle questions with which we have to contend. To give just one example, we can consider the issue of masking, that is, removing from the analysis those voxels in the image that contain measurements from the air surrounding the head, rather than from the brain. It is standard for many analyses to mask these voxels out, in part to ameliorate the multiple testing problems. On the other hand, retaining the air voxels in the analysis can be a useful diagnostic, since a method that reveals a lot of apparent activation outside of the brain is clearly flawed. Furthermore for some methods of analysis it is actually important to keep the air voxels in; removing them can create edge effects or other artifacts (see for instance Ye et al., 2009).

Although the general linear model at the voxel level is perhaps the most commonly used statistical analysis, it should be evident even from this brief overview, that the data are challenging and rich, and admit a wide variety of statistical analyses. And indeed, a dizzying array of analysis paths and techniques has been suggested to be applied to fMRI, and more are put forth on a regular basis. Among the more popular approaches are clustering, principal components analysis (PCA), independent components analysis (ICA), Bayesian models (which more easily admit the incorporation of temporal and spatial information), and locally spatial analyses. Methods from machine learning are also used – entropy and mutual information, image analysis techniques, and so forth.

Multiple Subjects

A traditional analysis of fMRI data for multiple subjects takes a so-called "two-step approach." The first step creates a statistical parametric map for each subject, using one of the methods described in the previous section. These will most often be maps of t, F, or $\hat{\beta}$ (coefficients from a linear model) statistics. These are used as the basis for the second step, which combines the individual maps in some way. Often, a simple or weighted average is used, as in meta-analysis. In the fMRI context, each subject is thought of as a "study" and standard meta-analytic approaches can be brought to bear at each voxel.

Alternatively, any of a large number of procedures that have been proposed in the statistics literature over the years for the combination of independent pieces of information can be used, again at the voxel level. See Lazar et al. (2002) for a survey of some of these and their use in the creation of fMRI-based group maps. In brief, whereas the meta-analysis methods are built on the combination of test statistics or effect sizes, another class of procedures combines p-values across the individual subject maps at each voxel. A popular and powerful method is due to Fisher (1950):

$$T_F = -2 \log \sum_{i=1}^{n} p_i$$

where n is the number of subjects in a study, and p_i is the p-value for subject i. In the fMRI setting, the T_F statistic would be calculated in this way at each voxel separately, resulting in a group map of T_F values. Under the omnibus null hypothesis of no activation of interest at a voxel across all subjects, T_F is distributed as χ^2_{2n}. Rejection of the null follows for large values of T_F and these can be used to identify regions (voxels) that show large signal for the group as a whole. An interesting feature of the T_F statistic is that it can be influenced by one extremely small p-value, i.e. a highly significant result for just a single subject in the group. While in many settings this might be a drawback, for functional neuroimaging data this characteristic is actually advantageous, as it induces a type of natural spatial smoothing; activation does not have to be in precisely the same voxel for all subjects, as it does for the meta-analysis approaches. This obviates the need for spatial smoothing at the preprocessing stage.

An example of a Fisher T_F map is shown in Figure 3. Shown is a group map created from the individual p-value maps of 16 individuals with schizophrenia, who were asked to perform an eye movement task in the scanner. Warmer colors indicate areas with high values of the T_F statistic, in other words regions of high activation across the group. Note that not necessarily all of the 16 subjects contribute strongly to all of the "hot spots." In particular, it is evident that each of the four main clusters has a few red voxel loci (where presumably more of the group had strong activation) surrounded by gradually decreasing activation represented by the orange and yellow. This is the inherent smoothing operation described earlier. Whereas individual subject maps exhibit a great deal of variability, and typically do not display such connected and coherent regions, the combining operation highlights brain areas that are task relevant.

Multiple Groups

A common approach for comparing multiple (often two) groups of subjects extends the two-step analysis in a hierarchical fashion, essentially building a linear model with main effects for group. Subjects are considered to be nested within group. The estimated coefficients for the regression model, or contrasts between those coefficients, are used to determine voxel locations at which the groups differ. Analysis is voxel-based and massively univariate, having now gone through many levels of preprocessing and data manipulation, the effects of which are not well understood.

Figure 3. Fisher group activation map on an eye-movement task for 16 subjects with schizophrenia

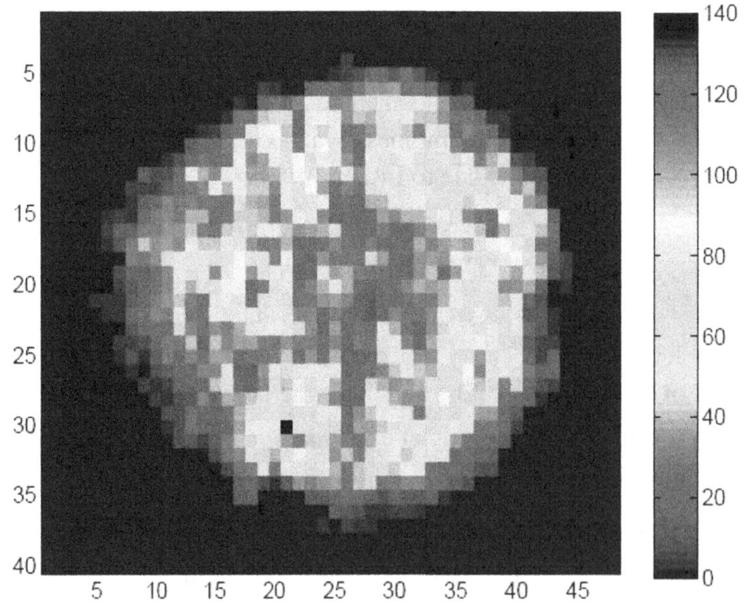

For a more accurate representation of this figure, please see the electronic version.

Alternatively, given a set of group maps we can consider computer vision methods for the comparison of images to provide a different analysis perspective. Analysis can still proceed on a voxel by voxel basis, for instance by calculating the distance between equivalent voxels in each of the group maps and summing over all voxels. But it is also possible to calculate distances between groups of voxels, allowing for a more holistic analysis. Many suitable distances have been proposed; Van der Weken et al. (2004) gives a detailed description and comparison of different distance measures for image comparison. One drawback of this approach is that the distance distributions are not known, so it is not easy to evaluate whether or not a particular distance between two images is "large" or not. This is the typical problem of assessing the statistical significance of a result. Bootstrap (Efron & Tibshirani, 1998) may be applicable; this is still an open area of research. Some of the distance measures can be readily extended to more than two images, which increases the flexibility of this approach.

DISCUSSION

Functional MRI data are statistically rich and complex. They present many challenges to statisticians, computer scientists, and applied mathematicians; these challenges have been an impetus to interdisciplinary collaboration and methods development alike. There are many open questions still, especially around issues of discovery and analysis of brain networks. Furthermore, many of the pressing questions in modern science – reproducibility and validity of published results prominently among them – are highly relevant in the neuroimaging context as well. Although there have been successes and much excitement, the intricacies of the data and the scientific questions demand a sober and reasoned approach.

REFERENCES

Benjamini, Y., & Hochberg, Y. (1995). Controlling the false discovery rate: A practical and powerful approach to multiple testing. *Journal of the Royal Statistical Society. Series B. Methodological, 57*, 289–300.

Bowman, F. D. (2007). Spatiotemporal models for region of interest analyses of functional neuroimaging data. *Journal of the American Statistical Association, 102*(478), 442–453. doi:10.1198/016214506000001347

Bruce, I. P., Karaman, M. M., & Rowe, D. B. (2011). A statistical examination of SENSE image reconstruction via an isomorphism representation. *NeuroImage, 29*, 1267–1287. PMID:21908127

Cole, D. M., Smith, S. M., & Beckmann, C. F. (2010). Advances and pitfalls in the analysis and interpretation of resting-state FMRI data. *Frontiers in Systems Neuroscience, 4*, 1–15. PMID:20407579

Efron, B., & Tibshirani, R. J. (1998). *An Introduction to the Bootstrap*. Boca Raton, FL: Chapman & Hall/CRC Press.

Fisher, R. A. (1950). *Statistical Methods for Research Workers* (11th ed.). London: Oliver and Boyd.

Forman, S. D., Cohen, J. D., Fitzgerald, M., Eddy, W. F., Mintun, M. A., & Noll, D. C. (1995). Improved assessment of significant change in functional magnetic resonance imaging (fMRI): Use of a cluster size threshold. *Magnetic Resonance in Medicine, 33*(5), 636–647. doi:10.1002/mrm.1910330508 PMID:7596267

Fox, M. D., & Raichle, M. E. (2007). Spontaneous fluctuations in brain activity observed with functional magnetic resonance imaging. *Nature Reviews. Neuroscience, 8*(9), 700–711. doi:10.1038/nrn2201 PMID:17704812

Friston, K. J. (2011). Functional and effective connectivity: A review. *Brain Connectivity, 1*(1), 13–36. doi:10.1089/brain.2011.0008 PMID:22432952

Genovese, C. R., Lazar, N. A., & Nichols, T. E. (2002). Thresholding of statistical maps in functional neuroimaging using the false discovery rate. *NeuroImage, 15*(4), 870–878. doi:10.1006/nimg.2001.1037 PMID:11906227

Hashemi, R. H., Bradley, W. G., & Lisanti, C. J. (2004). *MRI: The Basics* (2nd ed.). Philadelphia, PA: Lippincott Williams & Wilkins.

Huettel, S. A., Song, A. W., & McCarthy, G. (2004). *Functional Magnetic Resonance Imaging*. Sunderland, MA: Sinauer.

Kao, M.-H., Mandal, A., Lazar, N., & Stufken, J. (2009). Multi-objective optimal experimental design for event-related fMRI studies. *NeuroImage, 44*(3), 849–856. doi:10.1016/j.neuroimage.2008.09.025 PMID:18948212

Lazar, N. A., Luna, B., Sweeney, J. A., & Eddy, W. F. (2002). Combining brains: A survey of methods for statistical pooling of information. *NeuroImage, 16*(2), 538–550. doi:10.1006/nimg.2002.1107 PMID:12030836

Nencka, A. S., Hahn, A. D., & Rowe, D. B. (2009). A Mathematical Model for Understanding the Statistical effects of k-space (AMMUST-k) preprocessing on observed voxel measurements in fcMRI and fMRI. *Journal of Neuroscience Methods, 181*(2), 268–282. doi:10.1016/j.jneumeth.2009.05.007 PMID:19463854

Rowe, D. B., Hahn, A. D., & Nencka, A. S. (2009). Functional magnetic resonance imaging brain activation directly from k-space. *Magnetic Resonance Imaging, 27*(10), 1370–1381. doi:10.1016/j.mri.2009.05.048 PMID:19608365

Van der Weken, D., Nachtegael, M., & Kerre, E. E. (2004). Using similarity measures and homogeneity for the comparison of images. *Image and Vision Computing, 22*(9), 695–702. doi:10.1016/j.imavis.2004.03.002

Worsley, K. J. (2003). Detecting activation in fMRI data. *Statistical Methods in Medical Research, 12*(5), 401–418. doi:10.1191/0962280203sm340ra PMID:14599003

Worsley, K. J., & Friston, K. J. (1995). Analysis of fMRI time-series revisited again. *NeuroImage, 2*(3), 173–181. doi:10.1006/nimg.1995.1023 PMID:9343600

Ye, J., Lazar, N. A., & Li, Y. (2009). Geostatistical analysis in clustering fMRI time series. *Statistics in Medicine, 28*(19), 2490–2508. doi:10.1002/sim.3626 PMID:19521974

Chapter 6
Modeling Associations:
Sensor Fusion and Signaling Bar Codes

James K. Peterson
Clemson University, USA

ABSTRACT

In this work, the authors develop signaling models based on ideas from homology and discuss how to design a model of signal space which decomposes the incoming signals into classes of progressively higher levels of associative meaning. The tools needed are illustrated with a simple approach using standard linear algebra processing but this is just a simple point of departure into a more complex and potentially more useful signal processing toolbox involving computational homology. These ideas then lead to models of grammar for signals in terms of cascaded barcode signal representations.

INTRODUCTION

We discuss how to model the signals that come into a complex system which must then be parsed into an appropriate meaning so that the output of the system can be targeted appropriately. There are a lot of ideas about this in the world of complex biological systems and it is difficult to understand the process by which higher level meaning is extracted from raw signals. There are clearly specialized neural architectures in all biological organisms that have evolved to do this. By studying them, it is possible to gain valuable insights into how to design artificial systems that can perform associative learning better. Progress in a complicated problem like this often comes from looking at the problem in the proper abstract way. So that is what the focus is here: a fairly abstract vision of how to decompose a signal into interesting pieces is introduced and then over time, these ideas are tied into a framework for the design of engineering systems that are perhaps more capable at understanding how to handle a complex input and parse its meaning.

The problem of signal fusion is well known. A good example is how is speech understood? Raw auditory signals that a baby hears are not randomly organized. Instead, what the baby hears are short sounds separated at perhaps 10 millisecond intervals. The cortex in vertebrates is initially the same whether it

DOI: 10.4018/978-1-5225-2498-4.ch006

is eventually going to become auditory, visual, motor or other. It is exposure to environmental signals that shapes how a particular cortical area processes information.

Hence, at first, the baby is exposed to patterns of sound separated by short amounts of relative silence. This exposure, in a sense, primes the cortical architecture responsible for processing auditory information to pay attention to this pattern of on and off. Effectively, the cortical processing tunes the *time constants* of the cortical neural architecture.

This is a network of computational nodes (here they are biological neurons) combined into a graph using edges which themselves perform various computations. The *time constants* then refer to the way in which the edges and nodes interact to focus on the signal. The specialized architecture of the cortex is organized as a series of stacked *cans* which are laid one on top of the other in a vertical chain. The tuning we have spoken of amounts to aligning the bottom most can in this chain to optimally notice the primary on and off sound patterns. The results of this computation are passed upward to the next can in the chain whose architecture is designed to notice the time constants associated with groupings of the first level of on and off patterns. If the first on patterns are called phonemes, the next level of processing focuses on groups of phonemes which might be called word primitives. It is posited that as the processing moves upward through the chain of cans, higher and higher levels of meaning in the signal are extracted. Of course, the cortex really consists of large sheets of chains of cans organized much like the springs in a mattress and there is also a lot of crosstalk between the chains. We discuss this a bit more in Section 6 and actually show some of neural circuits involved, but for now just retain the idea that the signals that come into a complex system, need to be analyzed and higher levels of associated meaning must be found so that the system creates an appropriate output or response to the environmental input received.

For example, suppose you embed approximately 10^6 sensors into the fuselage of an airplane all of which provide information on a millisecond level to control programs. How do you parse that vast array of information to make an intelligent decision about what the data is telling you? Statistical techniques are tricky as many times the important data is a rare event which is lost in averaging. The amount of computation to process the data is intense and most of the data being processed is not relevant to the operational state of the aircraft. There is a great need to extract higher level meaning from the complex signal the sensors are generating.

Note that it is very difficult to define many of these terms even though we all know what they mean. What is a quantitative definition of *higher level meaning*? The term is at the heart of how we might model associations that develop between disparate sensor modalities. Our example so far was auditory, but in truth, decisions on what an organism should do are based are taking data from what the sensory suites of the organism gathers (perhaps sound, vision, pressure etc.) and combining these so as to generate an output the organism can use to benefit its state. In the sections below, we outline a set of ideas that may give us a more quantitative way to think about the idea of *generalization* in an engineering context. We start with looking at this idea using standard tools from linear algebra in Section 2. We then discuss how the way we are decomposing the signal leads to the idea of *barcodes* as signal targets in Section 3. Families of signals can then be combined in such a way as to generate a *grammar* of signals and we look at that in Section 4. We then look at all of this more abstractly in Section 5 where we introduce some new points of view based on mathematical ideas from homology. These ideas are then connected back to the kind of laminar processing seen in cortex in Section 6 and Section 7 which contains a number of conjectures about how the circuitry for generalization might be organized. We finish with a general discussion of computation in neural systems as we think it is relevant to complex engineering design in Section 8 with our conclusions given in Section 9.

SIGNALING MODELS

We begin with an example from the analysis of a typical $Ax = b$ computation which we will use to motivate a different way to look at how to model the complicated interaction of multiple signals in a complex system. Our example will be coded in **Octave** which is a free and open source interactive programming environment which is essentially compatible with **MatLab**.

Consider the matrix A constructed from three independent vectors V_1, V_2 and V_3.

Listing 1. Solution: MatLab Code

```
>> V1 = [1;2;3;-4;5;-2;1;10;4;-5];
>> V2 = [-1;12;7;8;8;3;-2;14;1;6];
>> V3 = [4;9;-3;1;-7;4;6;4;19;8];
>> V4 = 2*V1;
>> V5 = 7*V2;
>> V6 = 8*V3;
>> V7 = 2*V1 + 4*V2 - 8*V3;
>> V8 = 13*V2;
>> V9 = 22*V3;
>> V10 = -3*V1-4*V2;
>> A = [V1,V2,V3,V4,V5,V6,V7,V8,V9,V10]
A =
```

```
    1    -1     4     2    -7    32   -34   -13    88     1
    2    12     9     4    84    72   -20   156   198   -54
    3     7    -3     6    49   -24    58    91   -66   -37
   -4     8     1    -8    56     8    16   104    22   -20
    5     8    -7    10    56   -56    98   104  -154   -47
   -2     3     4    -4    21    32   -24    39    88    -6
    1    -2     6     2   -14    48   -54   -26   132     5
   10    14     4    20    98    32    44   182    88   -86
    4     1    19     8     7   152  -140    13   418   -16
   -5     6     8   -10    42    64   -50    78   176    -9
```

We then use partial pivoting to find the *LU* decomposition of *A* using simple code we have built to help illustrate these ideas. The code we use is **GePivTwo** which is setup to handle a square matrix.

To understand what this code does, we note $A(1:\mathbf{n},1)$ is the first column of *A*. Applying the absolute value function **abs** to that takes the absolute value of each entry in that column. Then applying **max** to that finds the value of the maximum (returned as **maxc**) and the position of the maximum (returned as **r**). Next, $A(2:\mathbf{n},2)$ is column 2 of *A* from the row 2 position down; i.e. rows 2 to **n** of column 2. Applying **abs** to that takes the absolute value of each entry in portion of the column. Then applying **max** to that finds the value of the max and its position as usual (returned as **maxc**) and **r**). So if the column was from 2 to 8 and **r** was 7 it would mean the entry in row 7 is the biggest one in absolute value. But we are doing this for a vector of size 7 as we stripped off the first entry. So what is returned is **r** = 6 which we want to adjust back to the original row number of *A* which is 7. Note, we get this by $\mathbf{q} = \mathbf{r} + \mathbf{k} - 1$

$= 6 + 1 = 7$. So we want to swap row 24 and row 7. The vector **piv** keeps track of the row swaps in a common sense way and since the process of the *LU* decomposition construction destroys *A*, we create a new version of *A* using the swaps and return it as **A piv**. Code like this is always tricky when you have rows of zeros. So we note if **maxc** is zero and if it is we swap it to the bottom.

Listing 2. The LU decomposition with pivoting

```
function [Apiv,L,U,piv] = GePivTwo(A)
%
% A is nxn matrix
% L is nxn lower triangular matrix
% U is nxn upper triangular matrix
% piv is a nx1 integer vector to hold variable order
% permutations
% Apiv is the original A with all the row swaps
%
[n,n] = size(A);
Apiv = A;
piv = 1:n;
for k=1:n-1
    [maxc,r] = max(abs(A(k:n,k)));
    if maxc > 0
        q = r+k-1;
        % this line swaps the k and q positions in piv
        % after this, piv position k has value q and piv
        % position q has value k
        piv([k q]) = piv([q k]);
        % then we swap row k and q in A
        A([k q],:) = A([q k],:);
        Apiv([k q],:) = Apiv([q k],:);
        if A(k,k) ~=0
            A(k+1:n,k) = A(k+1:n,k)/A(k,k);
            A(k+1:n,k+1:n) = A(k+1:n,k+1:n) - A(k+1:n,k)*A(k,k+1:n);
        end
    else
        fprintf("column %d is zero\n",k);
        fprintf("Swap this row to the bottom\n");
        piv([k n]) = piv([n k]);
        A([k n],:) = A([n k],:);
        Apiv([k n],:) = Apiv([n k],:);
    end
end
L = eye(n,n) + tril(A,-1);
U = triu(A);
end
```

Running this code on A, we print out the swap vector **piv** so you can see how the efficiency of the LU construction is significantly enhanced by the swapping process. We also print out the swapped original matrix as $Apiv$.

Listing 3. Find the LU decomposition of A

```
%find LU decomp of A with pivoting.
%Apiv is the original A with rows swap
%according to the scheme given by
%the permutation vector piv
>> [Apiv,L,U,piv] = GePivTwo(A);
piv =
      8    4    9   10    2    5    6    7    1    3
Apiv =
      10   14    4   20   98   32    44   182    88   -86
      -4    8    1   -8   56    8    16   104    22   -20
       4    1   19    8    7  152  -140    13   418   -16
      -5    6    8  -10   42   64   -50    78   176    -9
       2   12    9    4   84   72   -20   156   198   -54
       5    8   -7   10   56  -56    98   104  -154   -47
      -2    3    4   -4   21   32   -24    39    88    -6
       1   -2    6    2  -14   48   -54   -26   132     5
       1   -1    4    2   -7   32   -34   -13    88     1
       3    7   -3    6   49  -24    58    91   -66   -37

>> U
U =
     10.0   14.0    4.0   20.0   98.0    32.00    44.00   182.0    88.00   -86.0
      0.0   13.6    2.6    0.0   95.2    20.80    33.60   176.8    57.20   -54.4
      0.0    0.0   18.2    0.0    0.0   146.24  -146.24     0.0   402.15    -0.0
      0.0    0.0    0.0    0.0    0.0     0.00     0.00    -0.0    -0.00    -0.0
      0.0    0.0    0.0    0.0    0.0     0.00    -0.00    -0.0     0.00     0.0
      0.0    0.0    0.0    0.0    0.0     0.00    -0.00     0.0     0.00    -0.0
      0.0    0.0    0.0    0.0    0.0     0.00    -0.00    -0.0    -0.00     0.0
      0.0    0.0    0.0    0.0    0.0     0.00     0.00    -0.0    -0.00     0.0
      0.0    0.0    0.0    0.0    0.0     0.00     0.00     0.0    -0.00     0.0
      0.0    0.0    0.0    0.0    0.0     0.00     0.00     0.0     0.00    -0.0
```

We see that U has 7 zero rows which tells us that only 3 of the vectors V_i used to construct A are linearly independent and so the dimension of the kernel K is 7. We find the kernel using the code **Get-KernelTwo** which is a bit complicated as we need to handle zero rows in our calculations. The code is below. First, we test to see if the kernel is 0 by seeing if all the diagonal entries of U are not zero. If so, we simple return the dimension **dimK** is 0 and the kernel is the appropriately sized zero vector. Then if we know that there are zero rows, we find out where they are. Now, we could have more than one and they could be sprinkled around in *U* so first we do a loop to find them and save these row numbers in the vector **skiprow**. If **skiprow**(*j*) is 1, that will tells us to handle it special. Once we have found the zero rows, we swap them to the bottom of the matrix after we have set the component *x*(*j*) for that zero row to be 1. We also have inserted some diagnostic prints in this code, so you can see how it is progressing as we loop through *A*.

Listing 4. The code to find the kernel of A

```
function [dimK,K] = GetKernelTwo(U)
%
% U = Upper Triangular matrix from
% LU decomposition of A
% We find ker(A)
[n,n] = size(U);
UOrig = U;
for i = 1:n
    test(i) = abs(U(i,i)) > 1.0e-12;
end
if min(test) > 0.5
   K = zeros(n,1);
   dimK = 0;
else
   skiprow = zeros(n,1);
   x = zeros(n,1);
   b = zeros(n,1);
   z = zeros(n,1);
   I = eye(n,n);
   E = [ ];
   K = [ ];
   count = n+1;
   nullcount = 0;
   % check for all zero rows at the top
   fprintf('scan for zero rows\n');
   for j = 1:n
       fprintf('scanning row %d\n',j);
       % see if a row is all zeros
       % r is column where max occurs
       % maxc is value of max
       [maxc,r] = max(abs(U(j,:)));
       if maxc < 1.0e-12
          %fprintf('row %d is all zeros\n',j);
          skiprow(j) = 1;
          x(j) = 1.0;
```

```
        end
    end
    % swap zero rows to the bottom
    for j = 1:n
        if skiprow(j) == 1
            % then we swap row j and n in U
            U([j n],:) = U([n j],:);
        end
end
U
% now all zero rows are at the bottom
% and the x(j)'s are set to be 1 for
% each zero row
for j = n:-1:2
if (abs(U(j,j)) >= 1.0e-12)
    fprintf('pivot is not zero for row = %d\n',j);
    for k = 1:j-1
        E(k,:) = K(j,:)/U(j,j);
    end
    K(j,:) = K(j,:)/U(j,j);
    for p = 1:j-1
        K(p,:) = -U(p,j)*E(p,:) + K(p,:);
    end
    E(1:j-1,:) = 0;
else
    nullcount = nullcount + 1;
    E = [E,b];
    count = count - 1;
    K = [I(:,count),K];
    K(1:j-1,1) = - x(j)*U(1:j-1,j);
    end
end
if abs(U(1,1)) > 1.0e-12
    fprintf('pivot is not zero for row = 1\n');
    K(1,:) = K(1,:)/U(1,1);
    end
    [row,dimK] = size(K);
    end
end
```

Now we find the kernel of $\bs{A}$.

Listing 5. Finding the kernel of A

```
>> [dimK2,K2] = GetKernelTwo(U);
scan for zero rows
scanning row 1
scanning row 2
scanning row 3
scanning row 4
scanning row 5
scanning row 6
scanning row 7
scanning row 8
scanning row 9
scanning row 10

pivot is not zero for row = 3
pivot is not zero for row = 2
pivot is not zero for row = 1


>> K2
K2 =
        -2.00    -0.00     0.00    -2.00     0.00     0.00     3.00
         0.00    -7.00     0.00    -4.00   -13.00     0.00     4.00
        -0.00    -0.00    -8.00     8.00    -0.00   -22.00     0.00
         1.00    -0.00    -0.00    -0.00    -0.00    -0.00     0.00
         0.00     1.00    -0.00    -0.00     0.00     0.00     0.00
         0.00     0.00     1.00     0.00     0.00    -0.00    -0.00
         0.00     0.00     0.00     1.00    -0.00    -0.00     0.00
         0.00     0.00     0.00     0.00     1.00     0.00    -0.00
         0.00     0.00     0.00     0.00     0.00     1.00    -0.00
         0.00     0.00     0.00     0.00     0.00     0.00     1.00
```

The kernel of A is a 7 dimensional subspace of $\Re^{10}$ whose basis is given by the columns of K. We know the standard unit vectors e_1 to e_3 are mapped by A into the range vectors V_1 to V_3. Hence, we know we can write any x in the input space as

$$x = \sum_{i=1}^{3} \langle x, e_i \rangle e_i + \sum_{j=1}^{7} \langle x, K_j \rangle K_j$$

The second sum is clearly in the subspace K and we can use the first sum to define $x_p = \sum_{i=1}^{3} \langle x, e_i \rangle e_i$. We can define an equivalence relationship between vectors x and y by saying x is related to y, $x \sim y$ if and only if $x - y$ lies in K. The collection of all vectors equivalent to x under the relationship $\sim$ is called the equivalence class of x which is denoted by $[x]$; i.e.

$$[x] = x_p + K$$

This is the first step. Next, the projection of e_1 to e_3 onto the kernel can easily be calculated; you can think of these vectors as the inverse range basis.

Listing 6. Projecting the Inverse Range Basis to the kernel

```matlab
I = eye(10,10);
%Get the projection of e1 into K
W1 = zeros(10,1);
for i=1:7
    W1 = W1+dot(I(:,1),K(:,i))*K(:,i);
end

%Get the projection of e2 into K
W2 = zeros(10,1);
for i=1:7
    W2 = W2+dot(I(:,2),K(:,i))*K(:,i);
end

%get the projection of e3 into K
W3 = zeros(10,1);
for i=1:7
    W3 = W3+dot(I(:,3),K(:,i))*K(:,i);
end
```

The vectors W_1 to W_3 are simply projected to K and this is not an orthogonal projection. In this case, these vectors are linearly independent. This is an easy check using the code **Overdetermined**. Our vectors here are ten dimensional, so to check independence we need the *LU* decomposition of a system of 10 equations in 3 unknowns. Once we have the *LU* decomposition which are 10×3 matrices, we need to compute the kernel which requires special code for the overdetermined case.

Listing 7. The LU decomposition for an overdetermined system

```matlab
function [L,U,dimK,K] = Overdetermined(A)
%
% A is nxm matrix with n > m
% L is nxn lower triangular
% U is nxn upper triangular
%
[m,n] = size(A);
% row reduce on columns of A
for k=1:n-1
```

```
% find multiplier
if (A(k,k) ~= 0)
A(k+1:n,k) = A(k+1:n,k)/A(k,k);
 % zero out column
A(k+1:n,k+1:n) = A(k+1:n,k+1:n) - A(k+1:n,k)*A(k,k+1:n);
else
 break;
end
end
L = eye(m,n) + tril(A,-1);
U = triu(A);
[dimK,K] = GetKernelOver(U);
end
```

The kernel calculation code for the overdetermined case is the function **GetKernelOver**.

Listing 8. Kernel Calculation Code for the overdetermined case

```
function [dimK,K] = GetKernelOver(U)
%
% U = Upper Triangular matrix from
% LU decomposition of A
% A is not square and is mxn with
% m > n so this is an overdetermined
% system
% We find ker(A)
[m,n] = size(U);

if abs(U(n,n)) > 1.0e-12
    K = zeros(n,1);
    dimK = 0;
else
    x = zeros(n,1);
    b = zeros(n,1);
    I = eye(n,n);
    E = [ ];
    K = [ ];
    count = n+1;
    nullcount = 0;
    for j = n:-1:2
          if (abs(U(j,j)) >= 1.0e-12)
              E(1:j-1,:) = K(j,:)/U(j,j);
              K(j,:) = K(j,:)/U(j,j);
              for p = 1:j-1
```

```
                    K(p,:) = -U(p,j)*E(p,:) + K(p,:);
              end
              E(1:j-1,:) = 0;
           else
           nullcount = nullcount + 1;
           E = [E,b];
           count = count - 1;
           x(j) = 1;
           K = [I(:,count),K];
              K(1:j-1,1) = - x(j)*U(1:j-1,j);
           end
        end
     K(1,:) = K(1,:)/U(1,1);
     [row,dimK] = size(K);
     end
end
```

With these tools, we can check the linear independence of the columns of **B**. By inspection of the upper triangular part, **U**, we see all the W_i vectors are linearly independent.

Listing 9. Checking the linear independence of W1 through W3

```
>> B = [W1,W2,W3];
>> [LB,UB,dimKB,KB] = Overdetermined(B);

>> UB
UB =
       17.00000       20.00000      -16.00000
        0.00000      226.47059      -13.17647
        0.00000        0.00000      596.17455
        0.00000        0.00000        0.00000
        0.00000        0.00000        0.00000
        0.00000        0.00000        0.00000
        0.00000        0.00000        0.00000
        0.00000        0.00000        0.00000
        0.00000        0.00000        0.00000
        0.00000        0.00000        0.00000
```

The vector x_p was a linear combination of the vectors e_1 through e_3. Note each e_i can be written as

$$e_i = (e_i - W_i) + W_i$$

Now look at the projection of W_1, W_2 and W_3 onto the subspace spanned by K_4 through K_7.

Listing 10. Projecting the W_i vectors to the span of K_4 to K_7

```
% Get the projection of W1 onto span K4, K5, K6, K7
Z1 = zeros(10,1);
for i=4:7
    Z1 = Z1+dot(W1,K(:,i))*K(:,i);
end

% Get the projection of W2 onto span K4, K5, K6, K7
Z2 = zeros(10,1);
for i=4:7
    Z2= Z2+dot(W2,K(:,i))*K(:,i);
end

% Get the projection of W3 onto span K4, K5, K6, K7
Z3 = zeros(10,1);
for i=4:7
    Z3= Z3+dot(W3,K(:,i))*K(:,i);
end
```

The vectors Z_1 through Z_3 live in the subspace spanned by K_4 through K_7. The vectors W_i - Z_i live outside that subspace but are still in the kernel. So now we have a collection of vectors:

- $\{e_1 - W_1, e_2 - W_2, e_3 - W_3\}$ is a basis for the part of x_p not in K. Call this subspace $E - W$. This is 3 dimensional.
- $\{W_1 - Z_1, W_2 - Z_2, W_3 - Z_3\}$ is a basis for the part of the projection of x_p found in K but outside the subspace spanned by $\{Z_1, Z_2, Z_3\}$. Call this subspace $W - Z$ and call the subspace spanned by the Z_i, Z. By construction Z is a subspace of the span of $\{K_4, K_5, K_6, K_7\}$.
- $\{Z_1, Z_2, Z_3\}$, which as discussed is a subspace of the span of $\{K_4, K_5, K_6, K_7\}$. Since each the vectors that span Z are independent, this part is 3 dimensional also.
- Thus, 6 dimensions of the 7 dimensional space K have been used up by this projection process. One of the vectors K_4 to K_7 spans the one dimensional subspace of K left. We will call this vector Ω and the subspace generated by Ω, K_Ω.

From the discussions above, it is clear we have found a decomposition of the input space of the form

$$\Re^{10} = (E - W) \oplus (W - Z) \oplus Z \oplus K_\Omega$$

We can check to see if we have found a good basis for the input space $\Re^{10}$. A good candidate would be

$$I_B = \{\{e_1 - W_1, e_2 - W_2, e_3 - W_3\}, \{W_1 - Z_1, W_2 - Z_2, W_3 - Z_3\}, \{Z_1, Z_2, Z_3\}, K_7\}$$

Listing 11. Checking to see if I_B is a basis for the input space

```
>> IB = [I(:,1)-W1, I(:,2)-W2, I(:,3)-W3, W1-Z1,...
W2-Z2, W3-Z3, Z1, Z2, Z3, K(:,7)];
>> [LIB,UIB] = GE(IB);
>> UIB
UIB =
% first five
-16.00      -20.00       16.00      -873.00     -5772.00
  0.00     -224.00       12.00     -3780.75    -44410.00
  0.00        0.00     -594.36      8604.46     17704.89
  0.00        0.00        0.00       -41.91      -170.27
  0.00        0.00        0.00         0.00      -925.75
  0.00        0.00        0.00         0.00         0.00
  0.00        0.00        0.00         0.00         0.00
  0.00        0.00        0.00         0.00         0.00
  0.00        0.00        0.00         0.00         0.00
  0.00        0.00        0.00         0.00         0.00

% second five
   10640.00       890.00      5792.00    -10656.00      3.00
   13036.00      3779.50     44635.00    -13048.00      0.25
 -325253.64     -8603.53    -17704.84    325849.00      3.01
     163.33        42.06       170.25      -163.32      0.38
    -237.07        -0.42       925.81       237.07     -1.02
   -3875.13         0.51        -0.04      3875.16      1.35
       0.00         0.13         0.00        -0.01      0.42
       0.00         0.00         0.08        -0.01      0.32
       0.00         0.00         0.00         0.05     -0.00
       0.00         0.00         0.00         0.00      1.00
```

We see this is a basis for the input space, $\Re^{10}$. So given x in $\Re^{10}$ as an input, $x = x_p + x_k$ where x_p is in the span of e_1 to e_3 and x_k is in K. Then the equivalence class

$$[x] = x_p + K$$

is the first decomposition of the input signal x. Thus at this point, we can say the input space can be written as the direct sum

$$\Re^{10} = \Re^3 \oplus K$$

We know $e_1 \Rightarrow V_1$, $e_2 \Rightarrow V_2$ and $e_3 \Rightarrow V_3$, under A. Further, we have seen we can project e_1 to e_3 onto K giving vectors W_1 to W_3. So we can say

$$x_p = y_p + W$$

where W is the span of W_1 to W_3 and y_p is in K / W. We further decompose the signal using the vectors Z_1, Z_2 and Z_3 which are the projections of the W_i onto the subspace spanned by K_4 through K_7. The subspace determined by the vectors Z_i is called Z for convenience. Then, the differences $W_i - Z_i$ lie outside of the span of by K_4 through K_7 which we will denote by L. Then we have

$$y_p = z_p + Z$$

where z_p is in the part of Z not in L. We see L is three dimensional. Putting it all together, we have

$$\begin{aligned}
x &= x_p + K \\
&= y_p + W + K / W \\
&= z_p + Z + (W - Z) + K / (W - Z) / Z
\end{aligned}$$

That is

$$\begin{aligned}
\Re^{10} &= \Re^4 \oplus \Re^3 \oplus \Re^3 \oplus \Re^1 \\
&= \left\langle e_i - W_i \right\rangle \oplus \left\langle W_i - Z_i \right\rangle \oplus \left\langle Z_i \right\rangle \oplus \left\langle \Omega \right\rangle
\end{aligned}$$

SIGNAL DECOMPOSITION AND BAR CODES

Hence, a signal $\bs{x}$ in $\Re^{10}$ has a representation (C_1, C_2, C_3, C_4). Let's use the notation $\left\langle\left\langle B_1, B_2, ..., B_n \right\rangle\right\rangle$ to denote the span of the vectors $\{B_1, ..., B_n\}$. Then

ℭℭℬℭℬ ℭℬℛ SBCPT

$$\begin{aligned}
C_1 &\in \left\langle\left\langle e_1 - W_1, e_2 - W_2, e_3 - W_3 \right\rangle\right\rangle \\
C_2 &\in \left\langle\left\langle W_1 - Z_1, W_2 - Z_2, W_3 - Z_3 \right\rangle\right\rangle \\
C_3 &\in \left\langle\left\langle Z_1, Z_2, Z_3 \right\rangle\right\rangle \\
C_4 &\in \left\langle\left\langle \Omega \right\rangle\right\rangle
\end{aligned}$$

Next, truncate and discretize the signals on each axis of $\Re^{10}$ into *[-N, N]* for a choice of positive integer *N*. Then

$$\begin{aligned}
C_1 &\in [-N, N]^3 \\
C_2 &\in [-N, N]^3 \\
C_3 &\in [-N, N]^3 \\
C_1 &\in [-N, N].
\end{aligned}$$

For example, say $N = 10$ and we have $s_1 = (-3, 5, 2)$, $s_2 = (1, 5, -8)$, $s_3 = (0, 0, 3)$ and $s_4 = -4$. Now convert to a positive integer by taking the integer j in each slot and converting to $j + 10$. This maps the integers from $-N$ to N into the integers in $[0, 2N]$. This gives

$$C_1 = (-3, 5, 2) \rightarrow (7, 15, 12)$$
$$C_2 = (1, 5, -8) \rightarrow (11, 15, 12)$$
$$C_3 = (0, 0, 3) \rightarrow (10, 10, 13)$$
$$C_4 = -4 \rightarrow 6$$

This leads to the **bar code** which consists of 4 codes which can be determined a variety of ways. Here, we take the integer entry, say -13 which was the raw value, convert to $[0, 20]$ and then use the value 7 to set a 1 in the column associated with that value. This gives us a 20×10 matrix which we call a bar code, B_x which consists of 4 blocks of messages, M_1 to M_4.

$B_x =$

M_1			M_2			M_3			M_4
0	0	0	0	0	0	0	0	0	0
0	0	0	0	0	0	0	0	0	0
0	0	0	0	0	0	0	0	0	0
0	0	0	0	0	0	0	0	0	0
0	0	0	0	0	0	0	0	0	0
0	0	0	0	0	0	0	0	0	0
1	0	0	0	0	0	0	0	0	0
0	0	0	0	0	0	0	0	0	0
0	0	0	0	0	0	0	0	0	0
0	0	0	0	0	0	1	1	1	0
0	0	0	1	0	0	0	0	0	0
0	0	1	0	0	1	0	0	0	0
0	0	0	0	0	0	0	0	0	1
0	0	0	0	0	0	0	0	0	0
0	1	0	0	1	0	0	0	0	0
0	0	0	0	0	0	0	0	0	0
0	0	0	0	0	0	0	0	0	0
0	0	0	0	0	0	0	0	0	0
0	0	0	0	0	0	0	0	0	0
0	0	0	0	0	0	0	0	0	0

Hence, the signal x is mapped into a bar code B_x. This is an example of a signal decomposition determined by this particular matrix A. A nice way to interpret this decomposition strategy, is to go back to the original matrix A. The input space is $\Re^{10}$ and imagine that we have 10 independent signals T_1 to

T_{10} which we can identify with the generic basis vectors e_1 to e_{10}. The only combinations of these 10 signals that are valid for the purpose of generating a signal response are the linearly independent vectors V_1, V_2, and V_3. The 7 dimensional kernel we see represents the fact that most signals do not occur in useful combinations for the purpose of triggering a response. The useful signals x then have a decomposition as we have discussed. From that we can build a model of the probability of signal response. Let p_x denote the number of columns that a different from 10 (the original 0 response in the raw discretization) in the barcode B. Then we define the **probability** of signal response, P to be

$$\mathsf{P}_x = 10 p_x$$

This is a simple model, but it says that there is a guaranteed response if all 10 columns do not contain a 10 component which indicates the barcode is fully generated. For each column that does not contain a 10, we reduce the probability of response by 10%.

We can take this a step further. The mapping *[-N,N]* could be replaced by a mapping into Z_k, the set of integers mod k. For example, we could take the original signal decomposition and do a different discretization. Letting $\lfloor t \rfloor$ denote the floor of the real number t, we first do this:

$$\mathsf{C}_1 = (s_1, s_2, s_3) \rightarrow (\lfloor s_1 \rfloor, \lfloor s_2 \rfloor, \lfloor s_3 \rfloor)$$
$$\mathsf{C}_2 = (s_4, s_5, s_6) \rightarrow (\lfloor s_4 \rfloor, \lfloor s_5 \rfloor, \lfloor s_6 \rfloor)$$
$$\mathsf{C}_3 = (s_7, s_8, s_9) \rightarrow (\lfloor s_7 \rfloor, \lfloor s_8 \rfloor, \lfloor s_9 \rfloor)$$
$$\mathsf{C}_4 = (s_{10}) \rightarrow (\lfloor s_{10} \rfloor)$$

Now we have replaced all the raw signal components by integers. Assume next, that

$$(\lfloor s_1 \rfloor, \lfloor s_2 \rfloor, \lfloor s_3 \rfloor) \in (Z_7, Z_7, Z_7)$$
$$(\lfloor s_4 \rfloor, \lfloor s_5 \rfloor, \lfloor s_6 \rfloor) \in (Z_9, Z_9, Z_9)$$
$$(\lfloor s_7 \rfloor, \lfloor s_8 \rfloor, \lfloor s_9 \rfloor) \in (Z_4, Z_4, Z_4)$$
$$\lfloor s_{10} \rfloor \in Z_5$$

Then, after processing where the integer $\lfloor m \rfloor \rightarrow m \% k$ (which in **Octave** would be implemented by **mod**(m,k) which would return the proper value even if m were negative; i.e. **mod**(-22,3) returns 2). Hence, in this case we would have

$$(\lfloor s_1 \rfloor, \lfloor s_2 \rfloor, \lfloor s_3 \rfloor) \rightarrow (\lfloor s_1 \rfloor \% 7, \lfloor s_2 \rfloor \% 7, \lfloor s_3 \rfloor \% 7) = (\lfloor -3 \rfloor \% 7, \lfloor 5 \rfloor \% 7, \lfloor 2 \rfloor \% 7) = (4, 5, 2)$$
$$(\lfloor s_4 \rfloor, \lfloor s_5 \rfloor, \lfloor s_6 \rfloor) \rightarrow (\lfloor s_4 \rfloor \% 9, \lfloor s_5 \rfloor \% 9, \lfloor s_6 \rfloor \% 9) = (\lfloor 1 \rfloor \% 9, \lfloor 5 \rfloor \% 9, \lfloor -8 \rfloor \% 9) = (1, 5, 1)$$
$$(\lfloor s_7 \rfloor, \lfloor s_8 \rfloor, \lfloor s_9 \rfloor) \rightarrow (\lfloor s_7 \rfloor \% 4, \lfloor s_8 \rfloor \% 4, \lfloor s_9 \rfloor \% 4) = (\lfloor 0 \rfloor \% 4, \lfloor 0 \rfloor \% 4, \lfloor 3 \rfloor \% 4) = (0, 0, 3)$$
$$\lfloor s_{10} \rfloor \rightarrow \lfloor s_{10} \rfloor \% 5 = \lfloor -4 \rfloor \% 5 = (1)$$

In this case, the resulting bar code is not a matrix as the columns are of different sizes.

$$
B_x =
\begin{array}{|ccc|ccc|ccc|c|}
\hline
\multicolumn{3}{|c|}{M_1} & \multicolumn{3}{c|}{M_2} & \multicolumn{3}{c|}{M_3} & M_4 \\
\hline
0 & 0 & 0 & 0 & 0 & 0 & 0 & 0 & 0 & 0 \\
0 & 0 & 1 & 1 & 0 & 1 & 0 & 0 & 0 & 0 \\
0 & 0 & 0 & 0 & 0 & 0 & 0 & 0 & 1 & 1 \\
1 & 0 & 0 & 0 & 0 & 0 & 0 & 0 & 0 & 0 \\
0 & 1 & 0 & 0 & 1 & 0 &   &   &   & 0 \\
0 & 0 & 0 & 0 & 0 & 0 &   &   &   &   \\
0 & 0 & 0 & 0 & 0 & 0 &   &   &   &   \\
  &   &   & 0 & 0 & 0 &   &   &   &   \\
  &   &   & 0 & 0 & 0 &   &   &   &   \\
\hline
\end{array}
$$

It helps to see this visually. In Figure 1, we denote the *active* part of the code in each column with a closed circle. There are four blocks here, so we use four colours.

In a Z_7 column, there are 6 ways to fill the column with just one 1 and a seventh choice which is all zeros. For our example, there are $73 \times 9^3 \times 4^3 \times 5$ or $343 \times 729 \times 64 \times 5 \approx 80$ million valid signals. Some of these signals have columns that are all zeros. There are $6^3 \times 8^3 \times 3^3 \times 4$ or $216 \times 512 \times 27 \times 4 \approx 12$ million signals having no zero columns which is about 15%. There are also signals which has at least one zero column. The calculations for how many there are of these are quite complicated in our example as our columns are not equal sizes. But just to give you the feel of it, let's look at how many ways there are to have one column of zeros. There are $^{10}C_1 = 10$ ways to have one column be all zeros. The probability of activating a target here is 90% in this case where there are 10 columns.

- Column 1, 2 or 3 is zero giving $6^2 \times 8^3 \times 4^3 \times 4$ or $36 \times 512 \times 64 \times 4 \approx 5$ million signals.
- Column 4, 5 or 6 is zero giving $6^3 \times 8^2 \times 4^3 \times 4$ or $216 \times 64 \times 64 \times 4 \approx 3.5$ million signals.

Figure 1. A visual barcode

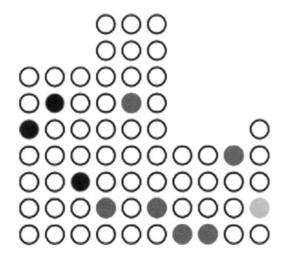

The barcode for a particular signal is shown with filled in circles for the active part of the decomposition. Filled circles at the bottom indicate zero values for that column.

- Column 7, 8 or 9 is zero giving $6^3 \times 8^3 \times 4^2 \times 4$ or $216 \times 512 \times 16 \times 4 \approx 7.0$ million signals.
- Column 10 is zero giving $6^3 \times 8^3 \times 4^3$ or $216 \times 512 \times 64 \approx 7.0$ million signals.

Thus, there are about 22.5 million signals with one column of zeros or about 28%. The remaining possibilities of signals having more than one zero column fill out the remainder of the signals. We see that about 85% of the signals correspond to signals with at least one column of zeros. A non-valid signal might correspond to actions that should not be taken. If we assume that all signals with nonzero components potentially correspond to an action, albeit one we may not wish to take, we note we have a correspondence mapping of the form

$$x \in \Re^{10} \to \mathsf{T} \cup \mathsf{T}^c$$

where T is the set of signal targets with all nonzero columns and T^c are the rest of the signals. Signals in T should not be used to create target responses. Hence, a signal processing error that related in such an improper signal being used to create a target response would be a type of security violation. A simple decomposition component calculation error could take an invalid signal and inappropriately add a 1 to enough columns to cause the signal to create a target activation signal. This would mean a part of the signal space that should not be used to create responses is actually being used to do that.

SIGNAL GRAMMARS

The signal processing we have seen so far can be extended to chains of such processing. If we concatenate p signal decomposition engines together, we form a chain

$$x \to \mathsf{B}_1 \to \mathsf{B}_2 \to \cdots \to \mathsf{B}_p$$

We will be analysing this chain of barcodes for the case of just three concatenated decompositions but it should be clear how to extend the ideas. We strongly recommend you read Rot and Andrian (2004) for ideas on how to think about signals as generated a type of signal grammar which is *read* which is designed to be parsed by the complex system the signals operate in to generate useful outputs. The signal family which generates the barcode family B_1 generates target outputs for each viable signal; that is, a signal whose barcode has no zero columns in it. We will stick to our example for now. This first family of barcodes is represented by the direct sum

$$x \in (Z_7 \oplus Z_7 \oplus Z_7) \oplus (Z_9 \oplus Z_9 \oplus Z_9) \oplus (Z_4 \oplus Z_4 \oplus Z_4) \oplus (Z_5)$$

This family of barcodes can be used to generate another family of signals in a variety of ways and this will generate another family of barcodes. For convenience of discussion, let's assume this intermediate step gives signals y which satisfy

Figure 2. A barcode sentence

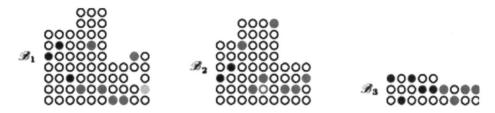

Three barcodes are shown. This corresponds to a sentence in a signaling grammar: the subject is $x \in \mathscr{B}_1$ which is $(Z_7 \oplus Z_7 \oplus Z_7) \oplus (Z_9 \oplus Z_9 \oplus Z_9) \oplus (Z_4 \oplus Z_4 \oplus Z_4) \oplus (Z_5)$, the verb is $y \in \mathscr{B}_2$ which is $(Z_6 \oplus Z_6) \oplus (Z_8 \oplus Z_8 \oplus Z_8 \oplus Z_8) \oplus (Z_4 \oplus Z_4 \oplus Z_4)$ and the object is $z \in \mathscr{B}_3$ which is $(Z_3 \oplus Z_3 \oplus Z_3 \oplus Z_3 \oplus Z_3) \oplus (Z_2 \oplus Z_2 \oplus Z_2 \oplus Z_2)$ .. Of course, these are just sample decompositions for the three barcode families.

$$y \in (Z_6 \oplus Z_6) \oplus (Z_8 \oplus Z_8 \oplus Z_8 \oplus Z_8) \oplus (Z_4 \oplus Z_4 \oplus Z_4)$$

This second family of barcodes, B_2 then generates a third family of signals, z, satisfying

$$z \in (Z_3 \oplus Z_3 \oplus Z_3 \oplus Z_3 \oplus Z_3) \oplus (Z_2 \oplus Z_2 \oplus Z_2 \oplus Z_2)$$

We illustrate this process in Figure 2 where we show the first barcode from B_1 is $((4,5,2), (1,5,1), (0,0,3), (1))$, the second barcode from B_2 is $((2,3), (5,1,2,7), (1,1,2))$ and the third barcode from B_3 is $((2,0,2,1,1), (1,1,0,1))$.

The first family of signals which is parsed into the first group of barcodes is thus interpreted as generating a second family of signals. Given $x \in \mathsf{B}_1$, this signal can be remapped into $\Re^{10}$ using its decomposition or another algorithm entirely can be used to generate the second family. For example, if $x = ((5.6, 7), (2,6,3), (2,1,3), (4))$, the first triples components all come from Z_7. Hence, given a level M for the second level signal, we map this is the interval $[-M, M]$ using the following steps:

- For $j \in Z_7$, we note $-3 \le (j - 3) \le 3$ and so by using $j - 3$ we reintroduce negative values into the second signal.
- The signal range is to be $[-M, M]$, so we could use the table where a random value in each of these intervals is chosen for the signal generated by the first block of x. We can do a similar thing for the other blocks. This gives a secondary signal which is in $[-M, M]^{10}$ in our example.

$$j - 3 = -3 \rightarrow \left[-\frac{6M}{7}, -M \right]$$

$$j - 3 = -2 \rightarrow \left[-\frac{4M}{7}, -\frac{6M}{7} \right)$$

$$j - 3 = -1 \rightarrow \left[-\frac{2M}{7}, -\frac{4M}{7} \right)$$

$$j - 3 = 0 \rightarrow \left[-\frac{2M}{7}, \frac{2M}{7} \right)$$

$$j - 3 = 1 \rightarrow \left[\frac{2M}{7}, \frac{4M}{7} \right)$$

$$j - 3 = 2 \rightarrow \left[\frac{4M}{7}, \frac{6M}{7} \right)$$

$$j - 3 = 3 \rightarrow \left[\frac{6M}{7}, M \right]$$

- This secondary signal is then parsed into the new decomposition $y \in \mathbf{B}_2$ which is in $[-K, K]^9$ in our example, where K is chosen as we like.

In our example, this process terminates here as we are only looking at a simple sentence of the form **Subject - Verb - Object**. Once the secondary signal is parsed into $[-K, K]^9$, this generates the final piece, the **Object** of the sentence. This is then used to generate the final target for the initial signal x.

Note, using a grammatical construction is a way to insure that a signal x is parsed without error. Our intended target is the outcome from the tertiary signal z and errors in x and/or y have a lower probability altering the correct final output wanted for z.

SIGNAL DECOMPOSITION FROM HOMOLOGY

Let's go back and look at our example a bit more abstractly. First, let's do a detour into what are called *winding numbers*. Consider a simple circle in the plane parameterized by $x(t) = \cos(t)$, $y(t) = \sin(t)$ for $0 \leq t \leq 2\pi$. From the centre of the circle, draw a vector to a point outside the circle. The variable t then represents the angle from the positive x axis measure counterclockwise (ccw) to this line. You can imagine that the picture we draw would be very similar even if we chose an anchor point different from the centre. We would still have a well-defined angle t. If we choose an arbitrary starting angle t_0, the angle we measure as we move ccw around the circle would be start at t_0 and would end right back at the start point with the new angle $t_0 + 2\pi$. Hence, there is no way around the fact that as we move ccw around the circle, the angle we measure has a discontinuity. To allow for more generality later, let this angle be denoted by $\theta(t)$ which in our simple example is just $\theta(t) = t$; but, we will generalize this soon. This is just a motivational example. Since $\tan(\theta(t)) = y(t) / x(t)$, we have the general equation for the rate of change of the angle:

$$\theta'(t) = \frac{-y(t)x'(t) + x(t)y'(t)}{x^2(t) + y^2(t)}$$

Of course, here this reduces to $\theta'(t) = 1$ as we really just have $\theta(t) = t$ which has a very simple derivative! Then, recalling how you do a line integral around a closed path in the plane, we have

$$\frac{1}{2\pi}\int_C \frac{-y(t)x'(t) + x(t)y'(t)}{x^2(t) + y^2(t)}dt = \frac{1}{2\pi}\int_0^{2\pi} 1 dt = 1$$

On the other hand, suppose we put the anchor point of our angle measurement system outside the circle. So imagine the reference line for the angle $\theta(t)$ to be moved from a vector starting at the origin of the circle to a point outside the circle to a new vector starting outside the circle. For convenience, assume this new vector is in quadrant one. At the point this vector is rooted, it determines a local coordinate system for the plane whose positive x axis direction is given by the bottom of the usual reference triangle we draw at this point. In Figure 3, we show a typical setup. Note the angles measured start at θ_1, increase to θ_2 and then decrease back to θ_1. Then, since the angles are now measured from the base point (x_0, y_0) outside the circle, we set up the line integral a bit different. We find the change in angle is now zero and there is no discontinuous jump in the angle.

$$\frac{1}{2\pi}\int_C \frac{-(y(t) - y_0)x'(t) + (x(t) - x_0)y'(t)}{(x(t) - x_0)^2 + (y(t) - y_0)^2}dt = 0$$

In general, if we try to measure the angle using a point inside the circle, we always get $+1$ for this integral and if we try to measure the angle from a reference point outside the circle we get 0. This integer we are calculating is called the *winding number* associated with the particular curve given by our

Figure 3. Angle measurements from outside the circle

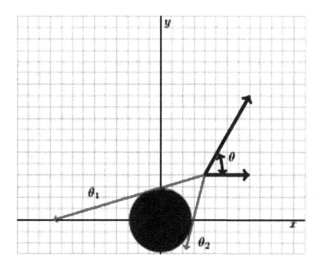

The angle reference system is outside the circle. The angle θ_1 is the first angle needed for the circle and the angle θ_2 is the last.

circle. Now, if we had a parameterized curve in the plane given by the pair of functions $(x(t), y(t))$, the line integrals we have just used still are a good way to define the change in angle as we move around the curve. This more general curve is called the path Γ and we define the *winding number* of the path Γ relative to a point P to mean we are measuring the change in angle as we move around the curve Γ from its start point to its finish. The most interesting curves are the ones that are closed. So if functions that determine Γ are defined on *[a, b]*, a closed curve means $(x(a), y(a)) = (x(b), y(b))$. Hence, closed curves are nice analogues of the simplest possible closed curve - the circle at the origin. The winding number, $W(\Gamma, P)$, is defined to be

$$W(\Gamma, P) = \frac{1}{2\pi} \int_{\Gamma} \frac{-(y(t) - y_0)x'(t) + (x(t) - x_0)y'(t)}{(x(t) - x_0)^2 + (y(t) - y_0)^2} dt$$

where the coordinates of P are (x_0, y_0).

Now let's back up a bit. In Figure 3, we found the change in angle as we moved around the circle was zero giving us a winding number of zero because we had placed the angle measurement systems reference outside the circle. Another way of saying this is that $W(\Gamma, P) = 0$ for Γ being the circle centred at the origin when P is outside the circle. A little thought tells you that this should be true for more arbitrary paths Γ although, of course, there is lots of detail we are leaving out as well as subtleties. Now look at Figure 3 again and think of the circle and its interior as a collection of points we cannot probe with our paths Γ. We can form closed loops around any point P in the plane in general and we can *deform* these closed paths into new closed paths that let P pop out of the inside of Γ as long as we are free to alter the path. Altering the path means we find new parameterizations $(x(t), y(t))$ which pass through new points in the plane. We are free to do this kind of alteration as freely as we want as long as we don't pick a P inside the grey circle. Think about it. If we had a closed path Γ that enclosed a point P inside the grey circle, then we cannot deform this Γ into a new path that excludes P from its interior because we are not allowed to let the points $(x(t), y(t))$ on the new path enter the grey circle's interior. So we can probe for the existence of this collection of point which have been excluded by looking at the winding numbers of paths Γ. Paths Γ whose winding numbers relative to a point P inside the grey circle will all have nonzero winding numbers. Another way of saying this is that if P is not inside the grey circle, there are paths Γ with P not in their interior and so their winding number is zero. But for P inside the grey circle, we cannot find any closed paths Γ whose interior excludes P and hence their winding numbers are always not zero (in our simple thought experiment, they are +1).

From the above discussions, we see it is reasonable to use winding number as a tool to detect **holes** in the plane. We could imagine the plane studded with a finite number of circles at different centres which correspond to regions of interest to us for some reason. If we calculate the winding numbers of test paths Γ which are closed all around the plane, the test paths that enclose a hole will all have a nonzero winding number. There is also no reason to have the holes be circle in the plane. The holes could correspond to the interiors of any closed path Γ. Further, although our example has been laid out in the plane, we would like to look at how to detect holes in $\Re^3$, $\Re^4$ and so forth. Unfortunately, the idea of winding number is intrinsically something for the plane, so this extension requires a more abstract approach.

Essentially, we can do the following chain of steps. We will list these for an example like our first one for $Ax = b$ in our earlier discussions.

- Most of the closed paths in $\Re^2$ are not important but the ones that are form a subspace in the collection of all closed paths which can be written as a coset, $[\gamma] + G_1$ where γ is the closed path and G_1 is the subspace of uninteresting paths.

- The coset $[\gamma] + G_1$ is a smaller collection that has found the holes in our data, so to speak. These one dimensional holes could align to form two dimensional holes. In this case we would have a new coset $[\xi] + G_2$ where G_2 is the subspace of paths in $[\gamma] + G_1$ which align to form a two dimensional hole: i.e. the first hole is a coin, and the next coset finds the stacks of two coins that are present.

- Continuing in this fashion, the 3D holes are given by another coset $[\alpha] + G_3$ and the fourth dimensional holes by a last coset $[\beta] + G_3$.

- Hence, we have a decomposition: closed paths Γ have a representation as

$$\Gamma = (\gamma, \xi, \alpha, \beta)$$

The situation from this point of view is much more complicated than our simple $Ax = b$ problem. These are paths, not vectors, and even the decompositions into $(\gamma, \xi, \alpha, \beta)$ are now equivalence classes of paths. However, there is a way to make this all work out and it turns out that the equivalence classes of paths can often be identified with our much simpler spaces like $(Z_7, Z_7, Z_7) \oplus (Z_9, Z_9, Z_9) \oplus (Z_4, Z_4, Z_4) \oplus Z^5$ from the $Ax - b$ experiment. To train yourself for this point of view, you need to study a fair bit of mathematics and we encourage you to do so. The standard mathematics and engineering curriculum does not cover a lot of modeling and computation these days, but with maturity you can get started. For modeling which blends calculus, ordinary and partial differential equations and computation with science, you can look at (Peterson, 2016a) for material up to calculus of two variables, (Peterson, 2016b) for additional training in nonlinear models and computations and (Peterson, 2016c) for partial differential equation models that discuss in detail the ones that help us model how neurons work in a typical neural system. Engineers and mathematics majors usually get some additional training in what is called analysis and abstract algebra and that will serve you well if you want to read up on these ideas of winding numbers in the plane and how you extend the ideas to $\Re^n$. The first books we read in this area was the book on *Algebraic Topology* (Fulton, 1995) which requires you to be focused and ready to learn new ways to think.

Hence, in these introductory sections, we have not used the full power of the approach we see in algebraic topology, but instead, we snuck on these ideas using the $Ax = b$ example.

We have a template in mind for the construction of an interesting model of signal decomposition based on all these ideas. The outline is this:

1. Decide how large the range space and kernel of your signal space should be. You can then choose appropriate linearly independent vectors to serve as the useful signals for the space. Note in our example, the range was 3 dimensional and the kernel was 7 dimensional. Roughly speaking each projection to an underlying subspace as we have described peels off 3 dimensions of the kernel.

So if our example, this terminated with a last subspace of 1 dimension which we cannot do another projection into. This lead to a 4 piece coset decomposition which, from our discussions above, allows us to model signal bar codes having 4 blocks. However, it is easy to design a new $Ax = b$ system have a 101 dimensional kernel which would lead to a coset decomposition have 33 levels with a 2 dimensional subspace of the kernel left over. Thus, we can design as many levels of decomposition as we wish.

2. Once the $Ax = b$ design is chosen, we can map the signal space into any type of Z_k space we wish using standard **mod** functions.

3. The coset at level k, which is algebraic topology corresponds to a k dimensional *can* or stack of coins, is interpreted by us as a partial signal message. As we have discussed, each coset fills in a column of the signal's message bar code and we can model efficacy of the message completion by noting how many columns in the bar code are not filled in.

Now our simple approach to these sorts of decompositions is not the best, although it is a nice starting point. Our decompositions are tied to the $Ax = b$ framework we start with and have a number of weaknesses. First, the size of the kernel is tied to the choice of output space. So if we had say 12 signals, the maximum number of linearly independent vectors in $\Re^{12}$ would be 12, and the resulting $Ax = b$ problem we formulate must map these vectors in $\Re^{12}$ into $\Re^{12}$. In general, we are thinking of the signaling problem as massively overdetermined so we easily have 1000's of signals to combine. Hence, we can design A to be 12×100 or with even more columns and the decompositions we have discussed will generate roughly eight 12 dimensional cosets in the kernel of A. But notice our decompositions are tied to the interplay between the structure of the range of A and the kernel of A.

A great advantage of the ideas from homology is this. Instead of linear independence of signals, we focus on the idea of a finite free group. This means we take a finite number of objects which can be anything really and look at all possible integer combinations of them. For example, the finite objects could be five people, Jim, Saha, Tony, Pauli and Qaitlin, and an apple and an orange. Any combination such as 22 **Jim** - 33 **Saha** + 1023 **Tony** - 456 **Pauli** + 38 **Qaitlin** – 213 **Apple** + 4103456 **Orange** is an allowed combination. Since the order in which we perform these combinations does not matter, this is a commutative process and so we call the set of such possible combinations a **finite free abelian group**. With the right way to interpret paths in this group, we can calculate the cosets we have discussed earlier in this section by looking at closed paths with zero and nonzero winding numbers. Of course, it is not so simple as the concept of winding number is harder to understand, but we can prove that any such finite free abelian **F** group can be identified as

$$\mathsf{F} = G_1 \oplus G_2 \oplus G_3 \oplus G_4$$

where each G_i is a group. This sort of decomposition is called the Betti Node Decomposition (BND) and the proof of this statement is done very nicely in (Kaczynski, Mischaikow, Mrozek, 2004) using programming code and induction. If each group G_i is generated by g_i, the decomposition can be rewritten as

$$\mathsf{F} = \langle\langle g_1 \rangle\rangle \oplus \langle\langle g_2 \rangle\rangle \oplus \langle\langle g_3 \rangle\rangle \oplus \langle\langle g_4 \rangle\rangle$$

Hence, the decompositions we have been discussing with the $Ax = b$ framework are a simple example of the Betti Group Decomposition. The general Betti Group Decomposition is much nicer than ours as it is not tied at all to the notions of linear independence and the connection between the kernel of A and the range of A. Now for signal processing purposes, we start with a finite number of signals, $\mathcal{S}_1$ to $\mathcal{S}_p$ and find the BND for the finite free abelian group generated by these signals.

LAMINAR PROCESSING AND PERSISTENT HOMOLOGY

Some form of laminar processing is often used when an animal tries to make sense out of disparate raw sensory signals to develop a usual output to be sent to drive actions and behaviours. We do not have to look at human neuroanatomy to study this sort of thing and indeed, there are great advantages to studying simpler systems. But for the moment, let's look at some building blocks of information processing in the human cortex. What we are going to show you is laid out in a lot more detail in (Peterson, 2016d) but for our purposes, we can be brief.

A model of isocortex models of cortical processing is given in (Raizada & Grossberg, 2003) which is a good starting point. There are other approaches, of course, but we will focus on this model here. A

Figure 4. The structure of a cortical column

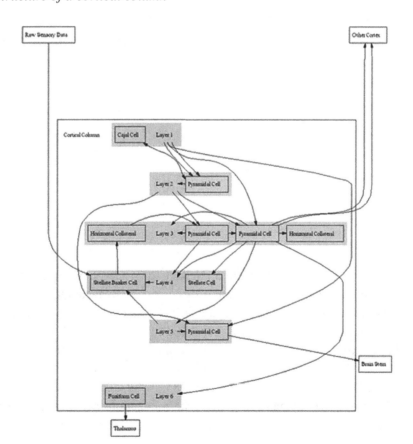

Figure 5. Generic overview

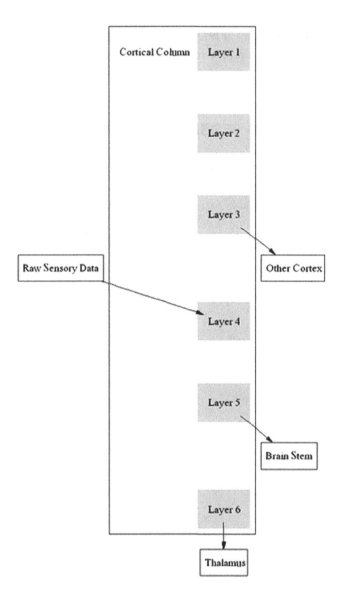

good discussion of auditory processing is given in (Nelken, 2004) and how information from multiple cortical areas can be combined into a useful signal is discussed in (Beauchamp, 2005). But for the moment, let's stick to one cortex at a time. The Raizada article uses clues from visual processing to gain insight into how virgin cortical tissue (isocortex) is wired to allow for its shaping via environmental input. Clues and theoretical models for auditory cortex can then be found in the survey paper of (Merzenich, 2001). We begin with a general view of a typical cortical column taken from the standard references of (Brodal, 1992; Diamond, Scheibel, & Elson, 1985; Nolte, 2002). A typical cortical column of six layers is shown in Figure 4 with details of some of the connections between the layers are shown in Figure 5. This column is oriented vertically with layer one closest to the skull and layer six furthest in.

We show layer four having a connection to primary sensory data. The six layers of the cortical column consist of specific cell types and mixtures which are Layer One: the Molecular layer; Layer Two, the external Granule Layer; Layer Three, the external Pyramidal Layer which has output to other cortex areas; Layer Four, the Internal Granule Layer which collects primary sensory input or input from other brain areas; Layer Five, the Internal Pyramidal Layer which outputs to the motor cortex; and Layer Six, the Multiform Layer which outputs to the thalamus brain areas. Now we can make some general observations about the cortical architecture. First, layers three and five contain pyramidal cells which collect information from layers above themselves and send their processed output for higher level processing. Layer three outputs to motor areas and layer five, to other parts of the cerebral cortex. Layer six contains cells whose output is sent to the thalamus or other brain areas. Layer four is a collection layer which collates input from primary sensory modalities or from other cortical and brain areas. We see illustrations of the general cortical column structure in Figure 5 and Figure 4. The cortical columns are organized into larger vertical structures following a simple stacked protocol: sensory data → cortical column 1 → cortical column 2 → cortical column 3 and so forth. For convenience, our models will be shown with three stacked columns. The output from the last column is then sent to other cortex, thalamus and the brain stem. A useful model of generic cortex, isocortex, is that given in Grossberg (2003), Grossberg and Seitz (2003) and Raizada and Grossberg (2003). Two fundamental cortical circuits are introduced in these works: the *on - center, off – surround* (OCOS) and the *folded feedback pathway* (FFP) seen in Figure 6 and Figure 7. In Figure 6, we see the *On - Center, Off – Surround* control structure that is part of the cortical column control circuitry. Outputs from the thalamus (perhaps from the nuclei of the Lateral Geniculate Body) filter upward into the column at the bottom of the picture. At the top of the figure, the three circles that are not filled in represent neurons in layer four whose outputs will be sent to other parts of the column. There are two thalamic output lines: the first is a direct connection to the input layer four, while the second is an indirect connection to layer six itself. This connection then connects to a layer of inhibitory neurons which are shown as circles filled in with black. The middle layer four output neuron is thus innervated by both inhibitory and excitatory inputs while the left and right layer four output neurons only receive inhibitory impulses.

Hence, the *center* is excited and the part of the circuit that is off the center, is inhibited. We could say the *surround is off*. It is common to call this type of activation the *off surround*. Next consider a stacked cortical column consisting of two columns, column one and column two. There are cortico-cortical feedback axons originating in layer six of column two which input into layer one of column one. From layer one, the input connects to the dendrites of layer five pyramidal neurons which connects to the thalamic neuron in layer six. Hence, the *higher level cortical input* is fed back into the previous column layer six and then can excite column one's fourth layer via the on - center, off -surround circuit discussed previously. This description is summarized in Figure 7.

We call this type of feedback a *folded feedback pathway*. For convenience, we use the abbreviations OCOS and FFP to indicate the on - center, off - surround and folded feedback pathway, respectively. The layer six - four OCOS is connected to the layer two - three circuit as shown in Figure 8. Note that the layer four output is forwarded to layer two - three and then sent back to layer six so as to contribute to the standard OCOS layer six - layer four circuit. Hence, we can describe this as another FFP circuit. Finally, the output from layer six is forwarded into the thalamic pathways using a standard OCOS circuit. This provides a way for layer six neurons to modulate the thalamic outputs which influence the cortex. This is shown in Figure 9. (Raizada & Grossberg, 2003) as seen in Figure 10.

Figure 6. The On - center, off - surround control structure

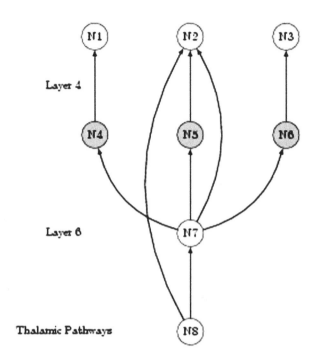

Figure 7. The folded feedback pathway control structure

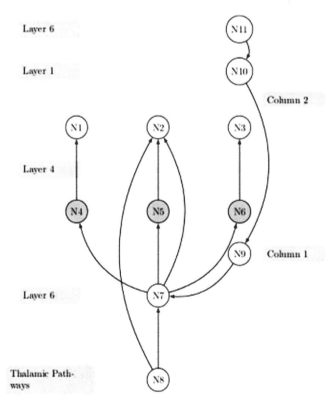

Figure 8. The layer six - four connections to layer two – three are another FFP

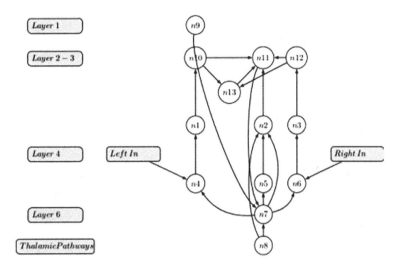

Figure 9. The layer six to Thalamic OCOS

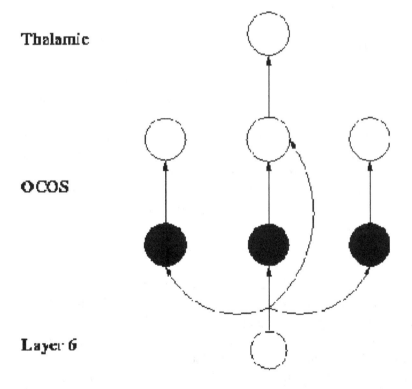

The FFP and OCOS cortical circuits can also be combined into a multi-column model. It is known that cortical outputs dynamically assemble into spatially and temporally localized phase locked structures. A review of such functional connectivity appears in (Andrew Fingelkurts, Alexander Fingelkurts, and Kähkönen, 2005).

Figure 10. The OCOS/ FFP cortical model

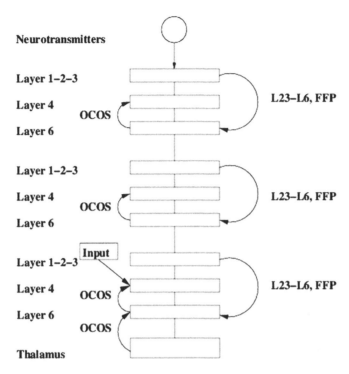

It is reasonable to think that cortical architectures are attempts by the evolutionary processes to evolve a computational approach to association. In order to perform this sensor fusion also called association, animals have evolved various types of neural circuitry. For example, in birds there is the *nidopallidium caudolaterale* (Herrold et al., 2011) and the structure of the auditory cortex (Wang, Brzozowsha-Prechtl, Karten, 2010) and the honeybee is sometimes used as a model of cognition (Menzel, 2012). The newly discovered genome of Ctenophores (Moroz et al., 2014) has made us understand that there was probably a second neural system evolution. In fact, a study of different organisms leads us to design principles for the neural systems that have arisen to solve various problems as discussed in (Sanes & Zipursky, 2010) and (Sprecher & Reichert, 2003). However all animals need to do sensor fusion and this is what we wish to develop a model for which we believe will give us new tools and approaches for developing sensor fusion models for association that are nicely robust in the engineering domain. We are therefore interested in ways to model how associations are made in a functioning neural system so that we can translate these ideas into engineering design principles.

Thus, whether the brain model is from a small animal such as a ctenophore, a spider or a more complex organism such as a squid or human, we feel there is a lot of commonality in how a functioning brain takes raw sensory input and transforms it into outputs which help the organism thrive. This laminar processing motif can be seen in other organisms, not exactly of course, but it is there in principle. There is actually a debate at various levels about the existence of minicolumns in the cortical structures, but we think there is compelling evidence for it as seen in (Buxhoeveden & Casanova, 2002a) and (Buxhoeveden & Casanova, 2002b), although a dissenting view is presented in (Horton & Adams, 2005).

LAMINAR PROCESSING AS A DECOMPOSITION ALGORITHM IMPLEMENTATION

In what follows, we outline a quantitative approach to how associations are formed and indicate graph based neural models that can take advantage of this formalism. A partial sketch of the modeling process is as follows. We have taken an $\Re^n$ sensory input signal and discretized it using **mod** computations into a subspace decomposition. The signal x is mapped into a bar code $\mathbf{B}_x$ with message blocks given by

$$\mathbf{C}_1 = (\lfloor s_1 \rfloor, \lfloor s_2 \rfloor, \lfloor s_3 \rfloor) \in (Z_7, Z_7, Z_7)$$
$$\mathbf{C}_2 = (\lfloor s_4 \rfloor, \lfloor s_5 \rfloor, \lfloor s_6 \rfloor) \in (Z_9, Z_9, Z_9)$$
$$\mathbf{C}_3 = (\lfloor s_7 \rfloor, \lfloor s_8 \rfloor, \lfloor s_9 \rfloor) \in (Z_4, Z_4, Z_4)$$
$$\mathbf{C}_4 = \lfloor s_{10} \rfloor \in Z_5$$

which tells us the input space $\mathbf{J} = \Re^{10}$ has the decomposition

$$\mathbf{J} = (Z_7 \oplus Z_7 \oplus Z_7) \oplus (Z_9 \oplus Z_9 \oplus Z_9) \oplus (Z_4 \oplus Z_4 \oplus Z_4) \oplus (Z_5)$$

We have an engineering perspective here. We believe we understand the signal structure enough to posit the kind of decomposition we want using a simple $Ax = b$ paradigm. In general, if you do not know this, you would have to analyze the signal carefully to determine the appropriate decomposition. The tools to do this come from a particular type of computational homology, called persistent homology, which we will not discuss here in detail. But, we can give a broad overview to give you some perspective. To apply this type of tool, a given R^n sensory input signal collection is discretized into chunks of data. The data is treated as the building blocks of a path through $\Re^n$ space and the closed paths which have winding number zero are removed as a coset from the full sets of paths that are closed with nonzero winding numbers. Then extensions to these ideas are used to find the additional cosets of the decomposition to give the full Betti Node Decomposition (BND) associated with this particular choice of discretization of the signal space. Denote the BND for discretization choice d by Φ_d, where

$$\Phi_d = \sum_{i=1}^{N} \oplus G_i^d$$

where we label the decomposition cosets with a superscript d to indicate they can change with the choice of d. If you repeat this process for progressively smaller values of d, you get a family of BND's, Φ^j where the superscript j indicates this is the BND for the discretization choice d_j. We are looking at a sequence of strictly decreasing values $d_1 > d_2 > d_3 \ldots$ and as the value d_j decreases, we typically see a sudden addition of a decomposition coset as the topological hole is suddenly discovered because the discretization level is small enough to notice its presence. The choice of discretization value is, of course, guided by the underlying science or engineering. The computational part of this approach is demanding. The coset decompositions are discovered by solving $Ax = b$ problems over the integers Z. This means standard things like row operations to find the *LU* decomposition are complicated as we can only multiple integers to do the work. This means that we quickly run into issues with overflow as two 64 bit integers when multiplied together create an integer beyond the capability of this integer type to store. Hence, we are forced to do the integer arithmetic using arbitrary precision integer libraries. Integers like this are essentially stored as a sort of growing list which means more storage is needed and multiply operations take more time. However, this can be done. The best introduction we know is in (Kaczynski, Mischaikow, Mrozek, 2004) from 2004 and the code is *C++* code which is called from MatLab. Better implementations are being worked on so we can take advantage of multicore architectures and so forth. But that is another story. Thus, this approach gives rise to the sequence Φ^j.

Our approach based on the simple $Ax = b$ decomposition ideas we went over earlier, were able to take a signal *x* and find its barcode representation. However, in the persistent homology approach, we find the right BND first and then given a signal *x*, we must decompose the signal into its coset representation. This can be done using algorithms in (Kaczynski, Mischaikow, Mrozek, 2004) to generate the representation $x \in \sum_{i=1}^{N} \oplus G_i$. We invite you to read more about this – albeit, remember our cautions about the mathematical maturity you should possess before you do so! This technique to experimentally explore what the group decomposition could be for a given set of $\Re^n$ data is further discussed and refined in Carlsson (2009), Lafon and Lee (2006), and Singh et al. (2008) (Edelsbrunner, Letscher, Zomorordian, 2002; Li, Xie, Yi, 2012).

For human cortical processing, we note the neural architectures for cortical processing as suggested by (Raizada & Grossberg, 2003) and others, use an on center - off surround type processing element to focus attention on the relevant aspect of the incoming signal. This can be thought of as the outer part of the circuit determines the subgroup placement G_i with the focusing part of the circuit finding the particular equivalence class giving the representation $[j] + G_i$ where [j] is the equivalence class the input belongs to at that level. The BND captures the idea that a signal gives rise to progressively more *complicated* representations. Hence, it is possible that modeling association with a Betti node approach could have value in understanding how associations are formed via computation. Indeed this addresses the question of what the function of the cortical column might be. We posit the minicolumn structure arose in many species as a solution to sensor fusion because the Betti node graph model is an efficient solution to the problem of finding associations. Note this gives a function to the minicolumn which answers the objections of (Horton & Adams, 2005). Indeed, a signal *x* into a Betti node $\sum_{i=1}^{n} \oplus G_i$ corresponds to the decomposition $(x_1, \ldots, x_n)$ with $x_i \in G_i$, and the signal decomposes into the tree shown in Table 1.

We note the levels *i* in the above tree correlate with higher levels of associations. Also, this helps explain how understanding of *meaning* has discontinuous jumps as a signal input might suddenly cross the threshold to move to a new representation $(x_1, \ldots, x_n)$ with x_i changing to $x_i' \in G_i$ due to the new information. These changes are integer valued and so are essentially quantal as the integer values we use are simply integer scales of information processing units we pick.

From the engineering perspective, we can build the following model. We assume a cortical column of *N* cans as described by the simple circuitry of (Raizada and Grossberg, 2003) each corresponds to a $\sum_{i=1}^{N} \oplus G_i$. We can easily design appropriate $Ax = b$ architectures to give rise to any particular decomposition like this as we have discussed or we can use the more general algorithms of (Kaczynski,

Table 1.

$[x_1] + G_1$	x_1 is a coset of the quotient space S/G_1, the level 1 representation
$[x_2] + G_2$	x_2 is a coset of the quotient space G_1/G_2, the level 2 representation x_2 is a chain of level 1 representations
$[x_3] + G_3$	x_3 is a coset of the quotient space G_2/G_3, the level 3 representation x_3 is a chain of level 2 representations
$\vdots$	$\vdots$
$[x_n] + G_n$	x_n is a coset of the quotient space G_{n-1}/G_n, the level n representation x_n is a chain of level *n-1* representations

Mischaikow, and Mrozek, 2004) to find the more general finite abelian group decomposition of the incoming signals. Each can therefore corresponds to a G_i computation; in essence, the outer neuron node calculations correspond to finding the modded out subgroup and the inner neuron node calculations give the particular equivalence class. If you study Figures 6 to 10 you can see how this is done. Given the $\sum \oplus\, G_i$, this tells us by fiat the barcode that comes from the direct sum decomposition of the signal x. Since these calculations are giving rise to BND information, we will call the computations performed on the signals, **Betti** calculations and the engine which does this sort of nodal processing will be called a **Betti** node or BN. This is in contrast to the kind of information processing that is done by a traditional neuron in a cognitive model.

COMPUTATION IN NEURAL SYSTEMS

Although our interest is in complex engineering systems, it is worthwhile to talk about cognitive models at this point since they are models built from graphs at which processing is done in both the nodes and the edges. Such a model certainly fits many complex engineering systems as long as we define what our edge and nodal processing functions are. In any event, such a graph based model must process concurrent signals and now we want to show how the decomposition ideas fit into this framework.

We note brain models connect computational nodes to other computational nodes using edges between the nodes. The proper background and motivation for this approach in a neurobiological setting are discussed in (Peterson, 2015) and complete descriptions of how this can be implemented in MatLab code with additional background is in (Peterson, 2016d). Using that approach, we model the neural circuitry of a brain using a directed graph architecture $\mathcal{G}(N, E)$ consisting of computational nodes N and edge functions E which mediate the transfer of information between two nodes. Hence, if N_i and N_j are two computational nodes, then $E_{i \rightarrow j}$ would be the corresponding edge function that handles information transfer from node N_i and node N_j. We organize the directed graph using interactions between neural modules (visual cortex, thalamus, etc.) which are themselves subgraphs of the entire circuit. Once a direct graph is chosen to represent neural circuitry, the addition of new neural modules is easily handled as a subgraph addition. Although connectivity is time dependent, we can think of a useful brain model as a sequence of such graphs of nodes and edges. For simulation purposes, this means there is a finite sequence of times, $\{t_1, t_2, \ldots, t_n\}$ and associated graphs $\mathcal{G}_i(N_i, E_i)$, where the subscript i denotes the time point t_i. In between these times, the graph has fixed connectivity and we can use a variety of tools to train the graph to meet input to output objectives. At each time point, we can therefore build our cognitive model using many different approaches as detailed in, e.g. (Sherman, 2004), (Friston, 2005), (Russo & Nestler 2013), (Friston, 2010) and (Maia & Frank 2011) among others. In the graph context, the update equations for a given node then are given as an input/output pair. For the node N_i, let y_i and Y_i denote the input and output from the node, respectively. Then we have

$$y_i(t+1) = I_i + \sum_{j \in \mathcal{B}(i)} E_{j \to i}(t) Y_j(t) \text{ where } Y_i(t+1) = \sigma_i(t)(y_i(t))$$

where $\boldsymbol{I}_i$ is a possible external input, $\mathcal{B}(i)$ is the list of nodes which connect to the input side of node $\boldsymbol{N}_i$ and $\sigma_i(t)$ is the function which processes the inputs to the node into outputs. Note if these objects are not scalars, then the addition and multiplication operations and the nodal processing need to be defined appropriately. This processing function is mutable over time t because second messenger systems are altering how information is processing each time tick. Hence, our model consists of a graph $\mathcal{G}$ which captures the connectivity or topology of the brain model on top of which is laid the instructions for information processing via the time dependent node and edge processing functions. Some ways to approximate the nodal processing for faster computation that is stateless are given in (Peterson, 2015) but that is not our interest here.

We have already mentioned, we can replace an entire cortical column of traditional neuron nodal processing by a **Betti** node, BN. If a lateral input goes into a cortical can at level i, we would treat this as an input from a G_i value in one can to the G_j level of another can. Obvious care would have to be taken at moving elements from one subgroup level to another, but with a little though it is easy to see various ways to do this, which we won't discuss here in detail. But, as a simple example, we could replace the cortical modules in such a graph model by BN's allowing a cortical sheet of many interconnected traditional neuronal nodes to be replaced by the decompositions of the form $\sum_{j=1}^{N} \oplus G_i$ which we can denote by Φ_i. If the cortical sheet consists of an $m \times n$ array of cortical cans, Θ_{ij}, each cortical can is replaced by a BN calculation Φ_{ij} and we see we assume the correspondence.

$$\Theta_{ij} \Rightarrow \sum_{k=1}^{n_{ij}} \oplus G_{ij}$$

where we use G_{ij} to represent $G^{\Phi_{ij}}$ with lateral inputs between the cortical cans corresponding to links between BN's $\sum_{k=1}^{n_{ij}} \oplus G_{ij}$ at approximately the same level. This allows us to construct a new way of doing information processing in a brain model. A new training algorithm would amount to using an iterative scheme to alter the $\sum_{k=1}^{n_{ij}} \oplus G_{ij}$ choices in various ways including changing the generators to achieve goals.

CONCLUSION

We have shown you some new approaches to how to understand sensor fusion by decomposing the signal space into useful subspaces. The decomposition naturally leads to an interpretation in terms of progressively higher levels of meaning. Our focus here was on fairly easy to understand approaches based on traditional linear algebra processing using $Ax = b$ manipulations that should be easily accessible. However, a better approach is to use the decomposition of a finite free abelian group which requires much more mathematical background. We have not done more with this than a basic discussion to whet your appetite and hopefully encourage you to read more. These ideas of signal decomposition are nicely general ways of looking at the problem of understanding how higher orders of meaning are extracted from primary sensory data. The same ideas can be applied to the families of cytokine and chemokine signaling molecules to help us understand central nervous infection (Peterson, Kesson, King, 2016c) and also to the development of a better model of how anesthesia affects consciousness levels (Peterson, 2016d). So these ideas are not limited to a strictly engineering perspective. There is currently a large interest in tools to extract higher order meaning from signals roughly described as deep learning algorithms. The signal decomposition ideas presented here could lead to some new approaches to deep learning and what is interesting is that the tools we would use with the BN's would not be differentiable in nature and in general not set in a metric space. Non metric space algorithms for learning are discussed in (Schlief and Tino, 2015) but there is much more to learn.

The models presented here give us at any instant of time, generate a graph architecture $\mathcal{G}(N, E)$ for the purpose of sensor fusion to build higher levels of meaning. The graph can be used to add as much detail as we wish and so from a certain perspective, if we construct a sequence of graphs $\mathcal{G}^k(N_k, E_k)$, we have a quantitative way of asking what happens as we move outward in this sequence. Do we approach a stable mathematical structure $\mathcal{G}^\infty$? Each graph $\mathcal{G}^k(N_k, E_k)$ defines a topological space $\mathcal{B}$ which in turn can be used to determine conditions under which the graph sequence is a Cauchy Sequence in $\mathcal{B}$. We note the graph models are quite complicated mathematically as they are a mixture of edge processing functions and nodes that can be simple sigmoidal units to full Betti computational units. A full Betti node cortical architecture would consist of a full sheet of Betti nodes with corresponding connections. Since these graphs are discrete in nature, it is not clear how to define the local topological structures which as n grows gives rise to global properties. A clue to how to do this is in the theory of *Loop Quantum Gravity* (Rovelli & Vidotto, 2013) as it also deals with the question of local to global structure arising from graphs of simple processing units.

REFERENCES

Beauchamp, M. (2005). See me, hear me, touch me: Multisensory integration in lateral occipital - temporal cortex. *Current Opinion in Neurobiology*, *15*(2), 145–153. doi:10.1016/j.conb.2005.03.011 PMID:15831395

Brodal, P. (1992). *The Central Nervous System: Structure and Function.* New York: Oxford University Press.

Buxhoeveden, D., & Casanova, M. (2002). The minicolumn hypothesis in neuroscience. *Brain, 125*(5), 935–951. doi:10.1093/brain/awf110 PMID:11960884

Buxhoeveden, D., & Casanova, M. (2002). The Minicolumn and the Evolution of the Brain. *Brain, Behavior and Evolution, 60*(3), 125–151. doi:10.1159/000065935 PMID:12417819

Carlsson, G. (2009). Toploogy and Data. *Bulletin (New Series) of the American Mathematical Society, 46*(2), 255–308.

Diamond, M., Scheibel, A., & Elson, L. (1985). *The Human Brain Coloring Book*. New York: Barnes and Noble Books.

Edelsbrunner, H., Letscher, D., & Zomorodian,. (2002). A. Topological persistence and Simplification. *Discrete & Computational Geometry, 28*(4), 511–533. doi:10.1007/s00454-002-2885-2

Fingelkurts, A., Fingelkurts, A., & Kähkönen, S. (2005). Functional connectivity in the brain – is it an elusive concept? *Neuroscience and Biobehavioral Reviews, 28*(8), 827–836. doi:10.1016/j.neubiorev.2004.10.009 PMID:15642624

Friston, K. (2005). A Theory of cortical responses. *Phil. Trans. R. Soc. B., 360*(1456), 815–836. doi:10.1098/rstb.2005.1622 PMID:15937014

Friston, K. (2010). The free-energy principle: A unified brain theory? *Nature Reviews. Neuroscience, 11*(2), 127–138. doi:10.1038/nrn2787 PMID:20068583

Fulton, W. (1995). *Algebraic Topology: A First Course. Graduate Texts in Mathematics*. New York: Springer. doi:10.1007/978-1-4612-4180-5

Grossberg, S. (2003). *How Does The Cerebral Cortex Work? Development, Learning, Attention and 3D Vision by Laminar Circuits of Visual Cortex*. Technical Report TR-2003-005, Boston University, CAS/CS.

Grossberg, S., & Seitz, A. (2003). *Laminar Development of Receptive Fields, Maps, and Columns in Visual Cortex: The Coordinating Role of the Subplate*. Technical Report 02-006, Boston University, CAS/CS.

Herrold, C., Palomero-Gallagher, N., Hellman, B., Kröner, S., Theiss, C., Güntürkün, O., & Zilles, K. (2011). The receptor architecture of the pigeons nidopalladium caudolaterale: And avian analague to the mammalian prefrontal cortex. *Brain Structure & Function, 216*(3), 239–254. doi:10.1007/s00429-011-0301-5 PMID:21293877

Horton, J., & Adams, D. (2005). The cortical column: A structure without a function. *Phil. Trans. Royal Society B, 360*(1456), 837–862. doi:10.1098/rstb.2005.1623 PMID:15937015

Kaczynski, T., Mischaikow, K., & Mrozek, M. (2004). *Computational Homology*. Springer. doi:10.1007/b97315

Lafon, S., & Lee, A. (2006). Diffusion Maps and Coarse-Graining: A Unifed Framework for Dimensionality Reduction, Graph Partitioning, and Data Set Parameterization. *IEEE Transactions on Pattern Analysis and Machine Intelligence, 28*(9), 1393–1403. doi:10.1109/TPAMI.2006.184 PMID:16929727

Li, X., Xie, Z., & Yi, D. (2012). A Fast Algorithm for Constructing Topological Structure in Large Data. Homology. *Homotopy and Applications, I*(14), 221–238. doi:10.4310/HHA.2012.v14.n1.a11

Maia, T., & Frank, M. (2011). From reinforcement learning models to psychiatric and neurological disorders. *Nature Neuroscience, 14*(2), 154–162. doi:10.1038/nn.2723 PMID:21270784

Menzel, R. (2012). The honeybee as a model for understanding the basis of cognition. *Nature Reviews. Neuroscience, 13*(11), 758–768. doi:10.1038/nrn3357 PMID:23080415

Merzenich, M. (2001). Cortical Plasticity Contributing to Child Development. In J. McClelland & R. Siegler (Eds.), *Mechanisms of Cognitive Development: Behavioral and Neural Perspectives* (pp. 67–96). Lawrence Erlbaum Associates, Publishers.

Moroz, L., Kocot, K., Citarella, M., Dosung, S., Norekian, T., Povolotskaya, I., & Kohn, A. et al. (2014). The ctenophore genome and the evolutionary origins of neural systems. *Nature, 510*(7503), 109–120. doi:10.1038/nature13400 PMID:24847885

Nelken, I. (2004). Processing of complex stimuli and natural scences in the auditory cortex. *Current Opinion in Neurobiology, 14*(4), 474–480. doi:10.1016/j.conb.2004.06.005 PMID:15321068

Nolte. J., (2002). *The Human Brain: An Introduction to Its Functional Anatomy*. Mosby, A Division of Elsevier Science.

Peterson, J. (2015a). Computation In Networks. *Computational Cognitive Science, 1*(1), 1. doi:10.1186/s40469-015-0003-z

Peterson, J. (2015b). Nodal Computation Approximations in Asynchronous Cognitive Models. *Computational Cognitive Science, 1*(1), 4. doi:10.1186/s40469-015-0004-y

Peterson, J. (2016). *BioInformation Processing: A Primer On Computational Cognitive Science*. Singapore: Springer Series on Cognitive Science and Technology. doi:10.1007/978-981-287-871-7

Peterson J. (in press). *Zombies, Predatory Wasps and Consciousness*. Academic Press.

Peterson, J., Kesson, A. M., & King, N. J. C. (in press). *Viral Infections and Central Nervous System Infection Models*. Academic Press.

Raizada, R., & Grossberg, S. (2003). Towards a theory of the laminar architecture of cerebral cortex: Computational clues from the visual system. *Cerebral Cortex, 13*(1), 100–113. doi:10.1093/cercor/13.1.100 PMID:12466221

Rot, A., & von Andrian, U. (2004). Chemokines in innate and adaptive host defense: Basic chemokinese grammar for immune cells. *Annual Review of Immunology, 22*, 891–928.

Rovelli, C., & Vidotto, F. (2013). *An Elementary introduciton to Quantum Gravity and Spinfoam Theory*. Retrieved from http://www.cpt.univ-mrs.fr/˜rovelli/IntroductionLQG.pdf

Russo, S., & Nestler, E. (2013). The brain reward circuitry in mood disorders. *Nature Reviews. Neuroscience, 14*(9), 609–625. doi:10.1038/nrn3381 PMID:23942470

Sanes, J., & Zipursky, S. (2010). Design Principles of Insect and Vertebrate Visual Systems. *Neuron, 66*(1), 15–36. doi:10.1016/j.neuron.2010.01.018 PMID:20399726

Schlief, F., & Tino, P. (2004). Indefinity Proximity Learning: A Review. *Neural Computation*, *27*(10), 2039–2096. doi:10.1162/NECO_a_00770

Sherman, S. (2004). Interneurons and triadic circuitry of the thalamus. *Trends in Neurosciences*, *27*(11), 670–675. doi:10.1016/j.tins.2004.08.003 PMID:15474167

Singh, G., Memoli, F., Ishkhanov, T., Sapiro, G., Carlsson, G., & Ringach, D. (2008). Topological analysis of population activity in visual cortex. *Journal of Vision (Charlottesville, Va.)*, *8*(8), 1–18. doi:10.1167/8.8.11 PMID:18831634

Sprecher, S., & Reichert, H. (2003). The urbilaterian brain: Developmental insights into the evolutionary origin of the brain in insects and vertebrates. *Arthropod Structure & Development*, *32*(1), 141–156. doi:10.1016/S1467-8039(03)00007-0 PMID:18089000

Wang, Y., Brzozowsha-Prechtl, A., & Karten, H. (2010). Laminary and columnar auditory cortex in avian brain. *Proceedings of the National Academy of Sciences of the United States of America*, *107*(28), 12676–12681. doi:10.1073/pnas.1006645107 PMID:20616034

Section 3
Machine Learning and Data Sciences

Chapter 7
Graph–Based Semi–Supervised Learning With Big Data

Prithish Banerjee
West Virginia University, USA

Kenneth Jospeh Ryan
West Virginia University, USA

Mark Vere Culp
West Virginia University, USA

George Michailidis
University of Florida, USA

ABSTRACT

This chapter presents some popular graph-based semi-supervised approaches. These techniques apply to classification and regression problems and can be extended to big data problems using recently developed anchor graph enhancements. The background necessary for understanding this Chapter includes linear algebra and optimization. No prior knowledge in methods of machine learning is necessary. An empirical demonstration of the techniques for these methods is also provided on real data set benchmarks.

1. INTRODUCTION

Automation and learning in the era of "Big Data" are the cornerstones of modern machine learning methods. The main idea is to predict new data points given a sequence of 'training' points. In many cases, these approaches are viewed as adapting to the prediction problem at hand by effectively emphasizing predictive characteristics within the training points and ignoring (or down weighting) other less meaningful noise within the data. This is all done on-the-fly in real time, so there is also the need for the automation of this type of learning process. This ability is often viewed as a learning paradigm and has deep roots within statistics and computer science (Hastie et al., 2009). In order to do this task, one must have methods that are (i) computationally efficient (e.g., all the parameters can be quickly estimated from the training points) and (ii) well-grounded in theory. Machine learning is the field attributed to providing data driven algorithms and models for exploring the data to make these predictions in real applications. Machine learning approaches tend to show promise in several practical applications including but not limited to those listed.

DOI: 10.4018/978-1-5225-2498-4.ch007

- **Cybernetics and System Science:** Artificial intelligence (AI) and machine learning are some of modern research methods used in the field of cybernetics and system science. Automated biometrics recognition systems provide a clear example of how machine learning methods paired with AI help advance this important field. The goal is to uniquely identify a person in a fully automated fashion based on their biometric traits such as fingerprint, iris, and facial image match scores or other biometric modalities (Jain et al., 2004). In movies, such identification of the suspect is usually shown instantaneously, but this task in reality is daunting primarily due to the quality and sheer volume of the biometric data that must be processed in order to form a match. Calibrating uncertainty of matches and providing probabilistic feedback in real time on big data are a direct application of machine learning and are already having a profound practical impact on this field (Kung et al., 2005; Palaniappan & Mandic, 2007).

- **Speech Recognition:** This problem involves identification of certain dialects and languages for communication. The data typically consist of different speech recordings that are quantified into a matrix by a linguistics expert (Deng et al., 2013).

- **Text Categorization:** Filtering out spam emails, categorizing user messages, and recommending internet articles are some of the tasks that one hopes computationally efficient algorithm can achieve (Sebastiani, 2002). Another pertinent and seemingly simpler problem is that of determining whether or not a text message is 'interesting.' Individuals cannot manually perform this relevant task in real time given the volume of information available at a given time point, so machine learning has gained traction in this content area.

- **Neuroscience:** Mapping out the network of dendrons, exons, and cell bodies is a non-trivial and time-consuming process (Lao et al., 2004; Richiardi et al., 2013), but is necessary to better understand the functioning of the brain. Machine learning approaches have had a significant impact on this challenging and practical problem.

This Chapter focuses on semi-supervised learning from a machine learning point-of-view with graphs. Semi-supervised learning in general is widely regarded as a compromise between unsupervised and supervised learning. Elements of these two extreme learning paradigms are summarized below.

- **Unsupervised Learning:** Suppose an $n{\times}p$ data matrix $\mathbf{X}$ is generated by some application. Each row is an observation, and each column is a variable. For example, the rows often represent different text documents in text categorization, and a column represents some common numerical summary, e.g., the number of times a keyword appears in a document. The goal in unsupervised learning is to hunt for patterns within the data that are informative about the application domain. In the text example, the documents could be papers about climate change that are published in a well-known journal, and the researcher's goal may be to determine what word frequencies scientists use most often to describe the current-state of climate change. Different methods tend to dig for patterns within the data and usually involve some form of clustering (Tryon, 1939; Everitt and Hothorn, 2011), ranking (Page et al., 1999), or dimensionality reduction (Pudil and Novovičová, 1998).

- **Supervised Learning:** An $n{\times}p$ data matrix $\mathbf{X}$ may still be collected, but unlike unsupervised learning, an $n{\times}1$ response vector $\mathbf{y}$ is also observed. In this case, the data come in pairs $(\mathbf{x}_1, y_1), \ldots, (\mathbf{x}_n, y_n)$, where vector $\mathbf{x}_i \in \mathbb{R}^p$ is stored as the ith row of $\mathbf{X}$ for $i=1,\ldots,n$. The goal is to determine how $\mathbf{X}$ can be used to predict, describe, or make inferences about the response vector $\mathbf{y}$. Performance metrics are introduced to measure how well one can assess the prediction of the response y_0 for a new data point $\mathbf{x}_0$. An easy-to-understand example comes from text categorization. Suppose one wishes to identify whether or not an email is 'spam.' The response is the email type, i.e., 'spam' or 'not spam,' and the goal would be to train and apply a learner to categorize emails as they arrive in real time. This spam application is an example of *classification*, where the response y_0 takes values from a finite discrete set. On the other hand, if $y_0 \in \mathbb{R}$ or $\mathbf{y}_0 \in \mathbb{R}^d$, then the problem is a *regression* application.

Semi-supervised learning might also involve an $n\times p$ feature data set $\mathbf{X}$ and a response vector $\mathbf{y}$, but unlike supervised learning, responses are observed for a proper subset of the observations $L \subset \{1,\dots,n\}$ (labeled set) and missing for the remaining observations $U=\{1,\dots,n\}-L$ (unlabeled set). This problem is partially unsupervised in that many rows of $\mathbf{X}$ will have no available response labeling.

This Chapter has the following progression. Before presenting a graph-based approach for semi-supervised learning in Section 3, necessary background information on supervised learning is first given in Section 2. The presentation of graph-based semi-supervised learning begins with some easy-to-follow graphical examples in Section 3.1 and an optimization perspective in Section 3.2. This is followed-up with an in-depth discussion of computational issues associated with these methods in Section 3.3. A sparse graph result using anchor points is then presented in Section 4. The sparse graph substantially lowers the computational burden with larger n or p, but maintains solid performance as seen in the empirical demonstrations of Section 5. Section 6 concludes this Chapter with some final comments and new research directions.

2. STATISTICAL MACHINE LEARNING PROBLEM SETUP

Statistical machine learning addresses the issue of predicting new data points given a training set of data points. Let $y_i \in \mathbb{R}$ and $\mathbf{x}_i \in \mathbb{R}^p$ be the response and feature vector for observation $i=1,\dots,n$. The response vector is $\mathbf{y} = (y_1,\dots,y_n)^T$, and the $n\times p$ matrix of feature data $\mathbf{X}$ simply stacks the $\mathbf{x}_1,\dots,\mathbf{x}_n$ as row vectors. The goal in machine learning under this setup is to construct a function $f : \mathbb{R}^p \to \mathbb{R}$ for the prediction of a new y_0 given its feature information $\mathbf{x}_0$. In order to make this endpoint well defined, we might first assume that the data $(\mathbf{x}_0, y_0), (\mathbf{x}_1, y_1),\dots,(\mathbf{x}_n, y_n)$ are independent and identically distributed from some measurable joint distribution P, and this assumption is made throughout this chapter for ease of exposition.

The function f can be chosen as the minimizer of some prediction error metric, typically motivated by some justifiable loss function. In a regression context, the squared error loss function $L(y_0, f(\mathbf{x}_0)) = (y_0 - f(\mathbf{x}_0))^2$, which measures the square of the deviation between a response and the function f, is widely considered to be the default choice and results in the expected squared error prediction metric

$$\mathbb{E}\left[\left(y_0 - f(\mathbf{x}_0)\right)^2\right] = \int \left(y_0 - f(\mathbf{x}_0)\right)^2 dP. \tag{1}$$

Other loss functions that generalize prediction metric (1) will be considered later in this Chapter. The integral (1) is taken over the unknown response y_0 and its feature data $\mathbf{x}_0$. As such, it is common to consider the conditional pointwise minimization problem

$$f(\mathbf{x}_0) = \arg\min_{a \in \mathbb{R}} \mathbb{E}\left[(y_0 - a)^2 \mid \mathbf{x}_0\right]$$

having solution

$$f(\mathbf{x}_0) = \mathbb{E}[y_0 \mid \mathbf{x}_0]. \tag{2}$$

Many approaches produce an estimated function $\hat{f}$ that approximates (2). The global fit of an ordinary least squares (OLS) linear regression

$$\mathbb{E}[y_0 \mid \mathbf{x}_0] \approx \mathbf{x}_0^T \left(\mathbf{X}^T\mathbf{X}\right)^{-1} \mathbf{X}^T\mathbf{y} \tag{3}$$

provides one such approximation, and the local averaging of k-Nearest Neighbors (k-NN)

$$\mathbb{E}[y_0 \mid \mathbf{x}_0] \approx \text{Average}(\{y_i : \mathbf{x}_i \in N_k(\mathbf{x}_0)\})$$

is another well-known yet different approximation approach, where $N_k(\mathbf{x}_0) \subset \{\mathbf{x}_1, \ldots, \mathbf{x}_n\}$ such that $\left|N_k(\mathbf{x}_0)\right| = k$ is the neighborhood of $\mathbf{x}_0$. Both approaches have a tuning parameter that trades-off the bias and variance of prediction errors. For example, k-NN exhibits low bias and high variance with $k=1$ and high bias and low variance with $k=N$, so its tuning parameter k spans the trade-off. In linear regression (3), the trade-off is subtler, but the choice of p (the number of columns in $\mathbf{X}$) does indeed span the bias and variance trade-off. In general, it is sensible to use cross-validation to estimate the values of tuning parameters in order to enhance performance, possibly on an empirical version of the underlying theoretical performance metric. This Chapter lines-up with this use of cross-validation, although rationales for other approaches are found in the literature (Efron, 1983; Bowman, 1984; Browne et al., 1993; Hastie et al, 2009).

For ease of presentation throughout this Chapter, an aggregate loss function

$$\mathcal{L}(\mathbf{y}, \mathbf{f}) = \sum_{i=1}^{n} L(y_i, f_i) \tag{4}$$

is often assumed, where $L : \mathbb{R} \times \mathbb{R} \to \mathbb{R}$ is the observation-level loss function for predicting response y_i with $\mathbf{f}_i$ for $i=1,\ldots,n$. Many techniques can also be motivated as the solution to a penalized optimization problem of the form

$$\min_{\mathbf{f}} \mathcal{L}(\mathbf{y}, \mathbf{f}) + \lambda \mathbb{J}(\mathbf{f}) \tag{5}$$

where $\mathcal{L} : \mathbb{R}^n \times \mathbb{R}^n \rightarrow \mathbb{R}$ is an aggregate loss function (4), λ is the Lagrangian multiplier referred as smoothing parameter, and $\mathbb{J}(\mathbf{f})$ is a penalization function that varies rapidly over small regions. Clearly, OLS linear regression (3) follows by assuming $\mathbf{f} = \mathbf{X}\beta$ with a squared error loss function, $\underline{\beta} \in \mathbb{R}^p$, and $\lambda = 0$. The connection between an optimization (5) and k-NN is subtler, but to see it, use the indicator function $\mathcal{I}_{\{\cdot\}}$ to define a two-sided local kernel

$$K_k\left(\mathbf{x}_i, \mathbf{x}_j\right) = \mathcal{I}_{\{\mathbf{x}_i \in N_k(\mathbf{x}_j) \text{ or } \mathbf{x}_j \in N_k(\mathbf{x}_i)\}}. \tag{6}$$

(A one-sided, non-symmetric kernel could also be used depending on the implementation of k-NN). The prediction function at $\mathbf{x}_0$ then solves

$$\hat{f}(\mathbf{x}_0) = \arg\min_{a \in \mathbb{R}} \sum_{i=1}^{n} K_k(\mathbf{x}_i, \mathbf{x}_0)(y_i - a)^2 \tag{7}$$

The generic prediction (7) can be applied to each training data point $\mathbf{x}_i$ to get $\hat{f}(\mathbf{x}_i)$ for $i = 1, .., n$, so the corresponding $n \times 1$ vector $\hat{\mathbf{f}} = \left(\hat{f}(\mathbf{x}_1), ... \hat{f}(\mathbf{x}_n)\right)^T$ solves

$$\hat{\mathbf{f}} = \arg\min_{\mathbf{f}} (\mathbf{y} - \mathbf{f})^T \mathbf{W}(\mathbf{y} - \mathbf{f}) + \mathbf{f}^T \Delta \mathbf{f}, \tag{8}$$

where $\mathbf{W}$ with components $W_{ij} = K_k\left(\mathbf{x}_i, \mathbf{x}_j\right)$ is the Gram matrix for the kernel and the Laplacian matrix $\Delta = \text{diag}\left(\mathbf{W}\vec{\mathbf{1}}\right) - \mathbf{W} = \mathbf{D} - \mathbf{W}$ defines the penalty term. Thus, k-NN is indeed a special case of (5). Generalizations of (5) are of particular note and elaborated on next.

In the case of the linear regression, it is common to consider more general penalty functions for $\lambda > 0$, e.g., *Ridge Regression* $\mathbb{J}(\mathbf{f}) = \underline{\beta}^T \underline{\beta}$, *Lasso* $\mathbb{J}(\mathbf{f}) = \sum_{j=1}^{p} |\beta_j|$, and *Elastic Net* a convex combination of ridge and lasso regression penalty terms. OLS linear regression clearly optimizes over the column space $\mathcal{C}(\mathbf{X})$ of $\mathbf{X}$ since $\hat{\mathbf{f}} \in \mathcal{C}(\mathbf{X})$.

Generalizing away from $\mathcal{C}(\mathbf{X})$ brings another interesting idea. Suppose $\hat{f}$ has expansion $\hat{f}(\mathbf{x}) = \sum_{j=1}^{\tilde{p}} \hat{\beta}_j h_j(\mathbf{x}) = \mathbf{h}(\mathbf{x})^T \underline{\hat{\beta}}$, where vector $\mathbf{h}(\mathbf{x})^T = \left(h_1(\mathbf{x}), ..., h_{\tilde{p}}(\mathbf{x})\right)$ is computed from a set of $\tilde{p}$ basis functions $h_j : \mathbb{R}^p \rightarrow \mathbb{R}$. Construction of basis functions requires the specification of knot points, which can be a tedious task. This motivates the concept of a $p = 1$ smoothing spline

$$\hat{\mathbf{f}}_\lambda = \arg\min_{\mathbf{f}: f'' \text{ exits}} (\mathbf{y} - \mathbf{f})^T (\mathbf{y} - \mathbf{f}) + \lambda \int \left(f''(\mathbf{x})\right)^2 d\mathbf{x}.$$

It is evident that $\lambda = 0$ leads to OLS linear regression with low bias and high variance, whereas $\lambda = \infty$ produces the opposite extreme of high bias with low variance.

The *Reinsch* form of the smoothing spline

$$\min_{\mathbf{f}} (\mathbf{y} - \mathbf{f})^T (\mathbf{y} - \mathbf{f}) + \lambda \mathbf{f}^T \mathbf{P} \mathbf{f} \qquad (9)$$

with some positive semi-definite penalty matrix $\mathbf{P}$ is also of note. It is well-known that a smoothing spline can be generalized in terms of a Hilbert space optimization problem where one specifies a Hilbert space consisting of twice differentiable functions f'' whose f and f' are absolutely continuous (Heckman, 1995). This line of thought leads to a more general approach for large p that begins with the representer inner product kernel $\tilde{K}(\mathbf{x}_i, \mathbf{x}_j)$, the endowed Hilbert space $\mathcal{H}_{\tilde{K}}$, and the appropriate inner product. This inner product is chosen by construction, so the kernel function is the representer for $\mathcal{H}_{\tilde{K}}$. The optimization of $\mathbf{f}$ is

$$\min_{\mathbf{f} \in \mathcal{H}_{\tilde{K}}} \mathcal{L}(\mathbf{y}, \mathbf{f}) + \lambda \left\| \mathbf{f} \right\|^2_{\mathcal{H}_{\tilde{K}}} \qquad (10)$$

and is achieved on finite data with $\hat{\mathbf{f}} = \tilde{\mathbf{K}} \hat{\underline{\alpha}}$, where

$$\hat{\underline{\alpha}} = \arg\min_{\underline{\alpha} \in \mathbb{R}^n} \mathcal{L}(\mathbf{y}, \tilde{\mathbf{K}}\underline{\alpha}) + \lambda \underline{\alpha}^T \tilde{\mathbf{K}}\underline{\alpha}. \qquad (11)$$

The finite representation (11) of (10) is a special case of (5) and is made possible because of a mathematical theorem that is often referred to in non-technical terms as the 'kernel trick' in the literature. A further generalization of (8) is observed when the Gram matrix $\mathbf{W}$ is taken from a Gaussian kernel

$$K_\sigma \left(\mathbf{x}_i, \mathbf{x}_j \right) = \exp\left(\frac{-\left\| \mathbf{x}_i - \mathbf{x}_j \right\|^2_2}{2\sigma^2} \right). \qquad (12)$$

Optimizations (5) and (8)-(10) motivate many popular supervised techniques and are extended to semi-supervised learning next in Section 3.

3. AN OVERVIEW OF SEMI-SUPERVISED LEARNING

Semi-supervised learning is a class of machine learning approaches with commonalities to supervised and unsupervised learning. It is the extension of supervised learning that involves training with feature data observations where a proper subset of some (or possibly many or pretty much all) of these observations have a missing response. A practical motivation for semi-supervised learning is that acquiring responses may be relatively costly or time consuming, so it may be infeasible to obtain a large number of responses in certain applications. On the other hand, it may be possible to obtain the feature data $\mathbf{X}$ in a relatively inexpensive and easy manner. The ultimate goal of this practical machine learning area is to routinely outperform supervised (and sometimes unsupervised) learning approaches in terms of common performance metrics. The probability a response was observed is assumed to be independent of the response and feature data throughout this Chapter. This so-called MCAR or Missing Completely at Random assumption is often assumed in semi-supervised learning although it is rarely acknowledged (Lafferty & Wasserman, 2008).

The available data set partitions into two subsets based on whether or not the response was observed for a given observation. The random subset of observations with responses is called the *labeled set* (i.e., $L=\{i: y_i$ is observed$\}$), whereas that without responses is called the *unlabeled set* (i.e., $U=\{1,\ldots,n\}-L$). It is often tacitly assumed that the data were subsequently sorted so that the first $|L|$ observations are labeled. If $\mathbf{Y}_L \in \mathbb{R}^{|L|}$ is the (known) labeled response vector and $\mathbf{Y}_U \in \mathbb{R}^{|U|}$ is the (unknown) unlabeled response vector, then the data have the partition

$$\mathbf{Y}\left(\mathbf{Y}_U\right) = \begin{pmatrix} \mathbf{Y}_L \\ \mathbf{Y}_U \end{pmatrix}, \quad \mathbf{X} = \begin{pmatrix} \mathbf{X}_L \\ \mathbf{X}_U \end{pmatrix}.$$

Supervised techniques are trained from data $\mathbf{X}_L, \mathbf{Y}_L$, whereas semi-supervised techniques are trained from $\mathbf{X}_L, \mathbf{Y}_L, \mathbf{X}_U$. Thus, semi-supervised learning offers additional flexibility. In some of the examples to come, a semi-supervised function of $\mathbf{X}_L, \mathbf{Y}_L, \mathbf{X}_U$ has the superior prediction performance. In other situations, the best estimate of function $f : \mathbb{R}^p \to \mathbb{R}$ from Section 2 may in fact be a supervised function of $\mathbf{X}_L, \mathbf{Y}_L$, but these situations can be mitigated by cross-validation estimation of tuning parameters. In this regard, Section 6 describes *safe* semi-supervised functions of $\mathbf{X}_L, \mathbf{Y}_L, \mathbf{X}_U$ that default to a supervised function of $\mathbf{X}_L, \mathbf{Y}_L$ if a tuning parameter is set to one of its boundary values. It also is worth noting that the unknown or latent variables $\mathbf{Y}_U$ can be treated as additional decision variables in optimization problems used to define a semi-supervised function of $\mathbf{X}_L, \mathbf{Y}_L, \mathbf{X}_U$, and this joint training optimization approach can make the extension of a supervised optimization (5) to one for semi-supervised learning appear relatively seamless.

There is a spectrum of ideas on how to learn from labeled and unlabeled data (Chapelle et al., 2006b). The heuristic method of self-learning (also known as self-training, self-labeling, or decision-directed learning) is one of the earliest attempts to formally incorporate unlabeled data during training. The idea is to repeatedly train on the full data using a wrapper algorithm with the unlabeled responses set to their predicted values from the prior iteration, i.e., set $\hat{\mathbf{f}}_U^{(0)} = \vec{\mathbf{0}}$ and repeat

$$\hat{\mathbf{f}}^{(i+1)} = \phi\left(\mathbf{Y}\left(\hat{\mathbf{f}}_U^{(i)}\right), \mathbf{X}\right),$$

where $\phi(\mathbf{y}, \mathbf{X})$ is an arbitrary supervised learner trained from data $(\mathbf{y}, \mathbf{X})$. Earlier heuristic versions of this approach were introduced in late 1960s (Scudder, 1965). Although this method seems heuristic, recent work has related these approaches to fixed-point optimization and Lipchitz continuity. This form of continuity can provide rigorous explanations as to why self-training is expected to work (Culp & Michailidis, 2008; Culp, 2011a).

Some other prior work in semi-supervised learning was cast as a transductive inference problem (Vapnik and Chervonenkis, 1974). This idea is based on an intuitive belief that predicting the unlabeled observations at hand (i.e., available during training) should be easier than predicting arbitrary data, which motivates some semi-supervised approaches. Other earlier attempts include semi-supervised extensions of Fisher's linear discriminate rule (Hosmer Jr, 1973; McLachlan & Ganesalingam, 1982), EM algorithm based (Dempster et al., 1977), multinomial mixture models (Cooper & Freeman, 1970), and Gaussian mixture model based PAC or Probability Approximately Correct learning ideas (Ratsaby & Venkatesh, 1995). With the rising popularity of support vector machines (SVMs), transductive SVMs emerged as an extension to standard SVMs for semi-supervised learning (Joachims, 1999). Transductive SVMs and semi-supervised SVMs (S3VMS) find an imputed labeling for all the unlabeled data, and a separating hyperplane, such that maximum margin, is achieved on the labeled data and (imputed) unlabeled data (Chapelle et al., 2006a; Ji et al., 2008; Li et al., 2010). Graph-based approaches, which are of the focus of this Chapter, are another common class of semi-supervised learning methods (Chapelle et al., 2006b) and are introduced next by first describing the issue of graph construction.

3.1 Proximity Graph Construction

Semi-supervised graph-based methods have attracted interest in recent years (Chapelle et al., 2006b; Liu et al., 2010; Culp & Ryan, 2013). Most notably, they can capture non-linear structures within the feature space often referred to as *manifolds* and use manifolds if they help predict the response. Proximity graphs can be observed directly, e.g., the data are represented via a connection or a network between close neighboring points such as a social network, a webpage hit set, a citation network, or a protein interaction network. In other cases, graphs can be constructed from a feature data matrix $\mathbf{X}$. In either case, existing graph-based semi-supervised methods are designed to bring out the heterogeneous nature of a network.

Proximity graphs can be constructed from a feature data matrix $\mathbf{X}$ as follows. First, a distance metric such as Euclidean distance is selected, and a k-NN metric is then often applied to induce sparsity by setting all the distances beyond the k nearest neighbors to ∞. Dissimilarities are then converted to a similarity graph usually by way of some local kernel function. Let $\mathbf{G} = (\mathbf{V}, \mathcal{E})$ be the resulting *proximity graph*, where the nodes $\mathbf{V} = \{1, \ldots, n\}$ represent the observations and the similarity between pairs of nodes are directly given by a collection of weighted edges $\mathcal{E}$. Methods to come use the corresponding $n \times n$ adjacency matrix $\mathbf{W} = [w_{ij}]$ or graph for short, where w_{ij} is the weight on the edge between observations i and j in graph $\mathbf{G}$. The Gram matrix in the k-NN method using kernel (6) is an example of a proximity graph used by supervised techniques. Semi-supervised learning has an advantage here since the unlabeled data can provide important gap-filling structural connectivity. Whether a graph is observed directly or constructed from a model matrix $\mathbf{X}$, it emits the partitioning

$$\mathbf{W} = \begin{pmatrix} \mathbf{W}_{LL} & \mathbf{W}_{LU} \\ \mathbf{W}_{UL} & \mathbf{W}_{UU} \end{pmatrix}, \tag{13}$$

where $\mathbf{W}_{LL}$ directly contains labeled-to-labeled adjacencies, $\mathbf{W}_{LU} = \mathbf{W}_{UL}^T$ labeled-to-unlabeled adjacencies, and $\mathbf{W}_{UU}$ unlabeled-to-unlabeled adjacencies.

A natural question is "Why should we use a proximity graph?" As motivation, consider the simulated Swiss roll data from Culp (2011b) and its feature data plotted here in Figure 1(a). The data having the appearance of a Swiss roll manifold are embedded in a 3D space. In order for semi-supervised learning to work in this setting, we must relate the conditional density of $y_0|\mathbf{x}_0$ to the marginal density of $\mathbf{x}_0$. Take

Figure 1. (a) Swiss Roll data set with response regions in a 3D lattice (b) A sparse proximity graph approximates the Swiss Roll

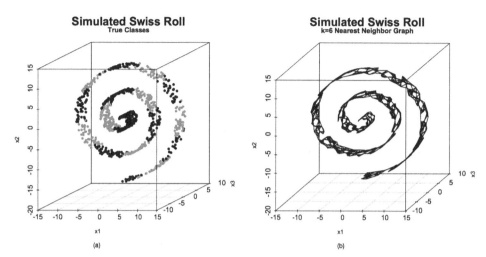

for example the binary gray and black responses in Figure 1(a); these were generated deterministically along chunks of the Swiss roll.

It is evident from Figure 1(a) that the observed feature data has a non-Euclidean structure. For example, some observations in an inner layer of the roll have a smaller Euclidean distance to observations in an outer layer than to observations in the same chunk of constant responses along the roll. In order to capture this structure, we need to effectively walk along the spiral path, and proximity graphs are useful for this endpoint. A k-NN graph method with $k=6$ was applied in Figure 1(b). Adjacency matrix $\mathbf{W}$ was computed from this 6-NN graph with a local kernel.

We make the following observation from the Swiss roll example. If manifolds exist within the feature data, then the graph-based approach does indeed make sense. The Swiss roll is a situation where knowing the manifold can aid in classification, so constructing a proximity graph from $\mathbf{X}$ is useful for such problems. However, an even more glaring example can occur when the feature data cluster into unconnected manifolds such that the majority category (in classification) or the expected response (in regression) differs dramatically from manifold to manifold. Take for example the unlabeled maze in Figure 2. The response differs on the two sides of the maze. With this type of case in mind, some have invoked the so-called *cluster assumption*, i.e., two points lie on the same manifold if a network-based distance between them is very low, but such distances between points on separate manifolds are usually large. The two sides of the maze are the manifolds, and in terms of language from graph theory, they also correspond to the two *connected components* in the graph $\mathbf{W}$ constructed from this 487×2 data matrix $\mathbf{X}$. In general, a graph-based semi-supervised method relies on the unlabeled data being useful to implicitly discover feature data manifolds that are predictive of the response. These types of graph-based functions certainly do not exhaust all possible semi-supervised functions of $\mathbf{X}_L, \mathbf{Y}_L, \mathbf{X}_U$. Combining a graph-based semi-supervised function of $\mathbf{X}_L, \mathbf{Y}_L, \mathbf{X}_U$ with other types of semi-supervised functions of $\mathbf{X}_L, \mathbf{Y}_L, \mathbf{X}_U$ (to improve performance in scenarios that are not a simple Swiss roll or rat maze) is discussed during the concluding remarks of Section 6.

Figure 2. A 2D Rat Maze Data Set with n=487, |L|=2. The binary gray or black responses satisfy the cluster assumption.

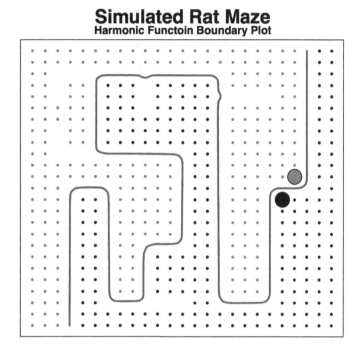

3.2 Semi-Supervised Optimization

Semi-supervised optimization typically involves generalizing (5) to account for the unlabeled data during training. The techniques of how to generalize this optimization problem vary. One such example, of primary use in this Chapter, is labeled loss

$$\min_{\mathbf{f}} \mathcal{L}(\mathbf{Y}_L, \mathbf{f}_L) + \lambda \mathbb{J}(\mathbf{f}) \tag{14}$$

which incorporates the unlabeled data through the penalty function (Culp & Ryan, 2013). Another example is joint training

$$\min_{\mathbf{f}, \mathbf{Y}_U} \mathcal{L}\left(\mathbf{Y}\left(\mathbf{Y}_U\right), \mathbf{f}_L\right) + \lambda \mathbb{J}(\mathbf{f}) + \gamma \mathbb{P}\left(\mathbf{Y}_U\right) \tag{15}$$

where the (unknown) unlabeled responses are treated as additional decision variables during the optimization, $\mathbb{J}(\mathbf{f})$ is a penalty term independent of $\mathbf{Y}_U$, $\mathbb{P}(\mathbf{Y}_U)$ is a penalty term independent of $\mathbf{f}$, and $\lambda > 0$ and $\gamma > 0$ are smoothing parameters.

For ease of presentation, the remainder of this Chapter focuses on the labeled loss optimization with a penalty of the form $\mathbb{J}(\mathbf{f}) = \mathbf{f}^T \mathbf{B} \mathbf{f}$ for some $n \times n$ (symmetric) positive semi-definite matrix $\mathbf{B}$. Similar to graph $\mathbf{W}$ with partitions (13),

$$\mathbf{B} = \begin{pmatrix} \mathbf{B}_{LL} & \mathbf{B}_{LU} \\ \mathbf{B}_{UL} & \mathbf{B}_{UU} \end{pmatrix}$$

and its submatrix $\mathbf{B}_{LU} = \mathbf{B}_{UL}^T$ must be nonzero in order for the unlabeled data to have an effect. Theorem 1 is a general result regarding labeled loss and an arbitrary positive semi-definite matrix $\mathbf{B}$.

Theorem 1. Let $\mathbf{B}$ be an arbitrary $n{\times}n$ positive semi-definite penalty matrix such that $\mathbf{B}_{UU}$ is positive definite. The solution to

$$\min_{\mathbf{f}} \mathcal{L}\left(\mathbf{Y}_L, \mathbf{f}_L\right) + \lambda \mathbf{f}^T \mathbf{B} \mathbf{f} \tag{16}$$

is

$$\hat{\mathbf{f}}_U = -\mathbf{B}_{UU}^{-1} \mathbf{B}_{UL} \hat{\mathbf{f}}_L \tag{17}$$

where $\hat{\mathbf{f}}_L$ solves

$$\min_{\mathbf{f}_L} \mathcal{L}\left(\mathbf{Y}_L, \mathbf{f}_L\right) + \lambda \mathbf{f}_L^T \mathbf{B}_{LL}^* \mathbf{f}_L \tag{18}$$

with $\mathbf{B}_{LL}^* = \mathbf{B}_{LL} - \mathbf{B}_{LU} \mathbf{B}_{UU}^{-1} \mathbf{B}_{UL}$.

Proof: The labeled loss optimization (16) can be written as

$$\min_{\mathbf{f}} \mathcal{L}\left(\mathbf{Y}_L, \mathbf{f}_L\right) + \lambda \left(\mathbf{f}_L^T \mathbf{B}_{LL} \mathbf{f}_L + 2\mathbf{f}_U^T \mathbf{B}_{UL} \mathbf{f}_L + \mathbf{f}_U^T \mathbf{B}_{UU} \mathbf{f}_U\right)$$

Differentiating this objective function with respect to $\mathbf{f}_U$ for any $\mathbf{f}_L$ implies

$$\Rightarrow \mathbf{B}_{UL} \hat{\mathbf{f}}_L + \mathbf{B}_{UU} \hat{\mathbf{f}}_U = \vec{\mathbf{0}}$$
$$\Rightarrow \hat{\mathbf{f}}_U = -\mathbf{B}_{UU}^{-1} \mathbf{B}_{UL} \hat{\mathbf{f}}_L$$

For this specific $\hat{\mathbf{f}}_U$,

$$\begin{aligned} \mathbf{f}^T \mathbf{B} \mathbf{f} &= \mathbf{f}_L^T \mathbf{B}_{LL} \mathbf{f}_L + 2\mathbf{f}_U^T \mathbf{B}_{UL} \mathbf{f}_L + \mathbf{f}_U^T \mathbf{B}_{UU} \mathbf{f}_U \\ &= \mathbf{f}_L^T \mathbf{B}_{LL} \mathbf{f}_L - 2\mathbf{f}_L^T \mathbf{B}_{LU} \mathbf{B}_{UU}^{-1} \mathbf{B}_{UL} \mathbf{f}_L + \mathbf{f}_L^T \mathbf{B}_{LU} \mathbf{B}_{UU}^{-1} \mathbf{B}_{UL} \mathbf{f}_L \\ &= \mathbf{f}_L^T \mathbf{B}_{LL}^* \mathbf{f}_L. \quad\quad \square \end{aligned}$$

Theorem 1 establishes that the loss function only influences the labeled estimates and the unlabeled estimates are a linear combination of those labeled cases irrespective of loss function. Specific choices of $\mathbf{B}$ often depend on the graph $\mathbf{W}$ in practice. A simplification of Theorem 1 can be found in Culp and Ryan (2013), and a more general result is given in Culp et al. (2016).

In practice, the general idea for choosing $\mathbf{B}$ involves constructing penalty matrices designed from the graph $\mathbf{W}$, where $\mathbf{W}$ as discussed in Section 3.1 is usually either observed directly or is constructed from $\mathbf{X}$. Section 3.1 also gave examples on how to construct feature data graphs which are useful when the feature data contains manifold(s). Proximity graphs provide the connected networks among the nodes (feature data points) that share some possibly non-Euclidean geometrical structure. Two common choices of $\mathbf{B}$ include the normalized and unnormalized Laplacian matrices

$$\Delta = \begin{cases} \mathbf{I} - \mathbf{D}^{-1/2}\mathbf{W}\mathbf{D}^{-1/2} & \text{Normalized} \\ \mathbf{D} - \mathbf{W} & \text{Unnormalized,} \end{cases}$$

where $\mathbf{D} = \mathrm{diag}\left(\mathbf{W}\vec{\mathbf{1}}\right)$ is the diagonal degree matrix. Either Laplacian matrix is a sensible choice for characterizing the graph $\mathbf{W}$ in labeled loss optimization (14), and it is unclear which is better in practice.

If the penalty $\mathbb{J}(\mathbf{f}) = \mathbf{f}^T \Delta \mathbf{f}$, then optimization (14) becomes

$$\min_{\mathbf{f}} \mathcal{L}\left(\mathbf{Y}_L, \mathbf{f}_L\right) + \lambda \mathbf{f}^T \Delta \mathbf{f} \tag{19}$$

and by Theorem 1, the solution for $\mathbf{f}_U$ in is $\hat{\mathbf{f}}_U = -\Delta_{UU}^{-1}\Delta_{UL}\hat{\mathbf{f}}_L$, where $\hat{\mathbf{f}}_L$ solves (18). This estimator is an example of a *harmonic function* in graph-based semi-supervised learning (Culp & Ryan, 2013). Its $\hat{\mathbf{f}}_U = \mathbf{S}\hat{\mathbf{f}}_L$, where $\mathbf{S} = -\Delta_{UU}^{-1}\Delta_{UL}$ is a stochastic matrix. In other words, the components of $\hat{\mathbf{f}}_U$ are probability-weighted averages of predicted values $\hat{\mathbf{f}}_L$ on the labeled set and have a Markov Chain interpretation (Culp & Ryan, 2013).

A Laplacian-based penalty (normalized or unnormalized) will propagate a class majority (in classification) or an average response (in regression) by manifold in a logical manner (Culp & Ryan, 2013). This is advantageous from a performance standpoint if the cluster assumption is satisfied. For example, the harmonic classification border in Figure 2 correctly navigates the maze and separates the two manifolds in this simple example where the response is constant on each manifold. Furthermore, this prediction border is independent of the choice of the observation level loss function $L(\bullet,\bullet)$ in the rat maze example as long as $L(\bullet,\bullet)$ satisfies $L(c_1,c_1)<L(c_2,c_3)$ for any scalars c_1,c_2,c_3 such that $c_2 \neq c_3$.

Unlike $\hat{\mathbf{f}}_U$, the choice of a loss function is required in order to determine $\hat{\mathbf{f}}_L$ in situations that are not as trivial as the rat maze. The squared error loss function is commonly used in a regression context with $y_i \in \mathbb{R}$. In this case, optimization (18) simplifies to $\min_{\mathbf{f}_L} \left\| \mathbf{Y}_L - \mathbf{f}_L \right\|_2^2 + \lambda \mathbf{f}_L^T \Delta_{LL}^* \mathbf{f}_L$, where $\Delta_{LL}^* = \Delta_{LL} - \Delta_{LU}\Delta_{UU}^{-1}\Delta_{UL}$, and differentiating this functional with respect to $\mathbf{f}_L$ and equating to $\vec{\mathbf{0}}$ implies

$$\Rightarrow -\left(\mathbf{Y}_L - \hat{\mathbf{f}}_L\right) + \lambda \Delta_{LL}^* \hat{\mathbf{f}}_L = \vec{\mathbf{0}}$$
$$\Rightarrow \hat{\mathbf{f}}_L = \left(\mathbf{I} + \lambda \Delta_{LL}^*\right)^{-1} \mathbf{Y}_L$$

Therefore, the solution to optimization (19) with squared error loss is

$$\begin{pmatrix} \hat{\mathbf{f}}_L \\ \hat{\mathbf{f}}_U \end{pmatrix} = \begin{pmatrix} \left(\mathbf{I} + \lambda \Delta_{LL}^*\right)^{-1} \\ -\Delta_{UU}^{-1}\Delta_{UL}\left(\mathbf{I} + \lambda \Delta_{LL}^*\right)^{-1} \end{pmatrix} \mathbf{Y}_L$$

Another common example is the logistic loss in classification when responses are restricted to $y_i \in \{0,1\}$. In this case, optimization (19) reduces to

$$\min_{\mathbf{f}_L} \left\{ \sum_{i \in L} \log\left(1 + \exp\left(-2\left(2y_i - 1\right)f_i\right)\right) + \lambda \mathbf{f}_L^T \Delta_{LL}^* \mathbf{f}_L \right\}. \tag{20}$$

Algorithm 1 summarizes a method for iteratively solving penalized logistic loss optimization (20) and is a based on the derivation given next. First, differentiating (20) with respect to f_i for $i \in L$ yields

$$\sum_{i \in A_0} \frac{2\exp\left(2f_i\right)}{\exp\left(2f_i\right)+1} + \sum_{i \in A_1} \frac{-2\exp\left(-2f_i\right)}{\exp\left(-2f_i\right)+1} + 2\lambda\left(\Delta_{LL}^* f_L\right)_i = 0$$

where sets $A_0 = \{i \in L: y_i = 0\}$ and $A_1 = \{i \in L: y_i = 1\}$. Then the rearranged score equation

$$\sum_{i \in L} \left\{ \left(1 - y_i\right)g\left(f_i\right) - y_i\left(1 - g\left(f_i\right)\right) + \lambda\left(\Delta_{LL}^* \mathbf{f}_L\right)_i \right\} = 0$$

with $g\left(f_i\right) = \exp\left(2f_i\right)/\left(\exp\left(2f_i\right)+1\right)$ simplifies to

$$\mathbf{s}\left(\mathbf{f}_L\right) = -\left(\mathbf{Y}_L - \mathbf{g}\left(\mathbf{f}_L\right)\right) + \lambda \Delta_{LL}^* \mathbf{f}_L = \vec{\mathbf{0}}, \tag{21}$$

so Newton's method can be used to solve the gradient score with ℓth iteration

$$\mathbf{f}_L^{(\ell)} = \mathbf{f}_L^{(\ell-1)} - \left(\nabla\mathbf{s}\left(\mathbf{f}_L\right)\Big|_{\mathbf{f}_L = \mathbf{f}^{(\ell-1)}}\right)^{-1}\mathbf{s}\left(\mathbf{f}_L^{(\ell-1)}\right) \tag{22}$$

given some initialization $\mathbf{f}_L^{(0)}$. It follows that $\nabla\mathbf{s}\left(\mathbf{f}_L^{(\ell)}\right) = \omega^{(\ell)} + \lambda\Delta_{LL}^*$, where

$$\omega^{(\ell)} = \mathrm{diag}\left(\mathbf{g}\left(\mathbf{f}_L^{(\ell)}\right)\left(\vec{\mathbf{1}} - \mathbf{g}\left(\mathbf{f}_L^{(\ell)}\right)\right)\right).$$

For this final part of the derivation, define $\mathbf{S}^{(\ell-1)} = \left(\omega^{(\ell-1)} + \lambda\Delta_{LL}^*\right)^{-1}\omega^{(\ell-1)}$. Putting this gradient equation together with (21) and (22) yields

$$\mathbf{f}_L^{(\ell)} = \mathbf{f}_L^{(\ell-1)} - \mathbf{S}^{(\ell-1)}\left(\omega^{(\ell-1)}\right)^{-1}\left(\mathbf{Y}_L - \mathbf{g}\left(\mathbf{f}_L^{(\ell-1)}\right) - \lambda\Delta_{LL}^*\mathbf{f}_L^{(\ell-1)}\right)$$

$$\mathbf{f}_L^{(\ell)} = \mathbf{S}^{(\ell-1)}\mathbf{f}_L^{(\ell-1)} - \mathbf{S}^{(\ell-1)}\left(\omega^{(\ell-1)}\right)^{-1}\left(\mathbf{Y}_L - \mathbf{g}\left(\mathbf{f}_L^{(\ell-1)}\right)\right)$$

$$\mathbf{f}_L^{(\ell)} = \mathbf{S}^{(\ell-1)}\mathbf{Z}^{(\ell-1)} \text{ with } \mathbf{Z}^{(\ell-1)} = \mathbf{f}_L^{(\ell-1)} - \left(\omega^{(\ell-1)}\right)^{-1}\left(\mathbf{Y}_L - \mathbf{g}\left(\mathbf{f}_L^{(\ell-1)}\right)\right),$$

and so Algorithm 1 follows as a method for iteratively solving (20).

Algorithm 1: Logistic loss

1: **Input** smoothing parameter $\lambda > 0$, $|L| \times |L|$ matrix Δ_{LL}^*, initial vector $\mathbf{f}_L^{(0)} \in \mathbb{R}^{|L|}$

2: **Repeat For** $\ell = 1, 2, \ldots$

3: $\quad \mathbf{Z} = \mathbf{f}_L^{(\ell-1)} - \left(\omega^{(\ell-1)}\right)^{-1}\left(\mathbf{Y}_L - \mathbf{g}\left(\mathbf{f}_L^{(\ell-1)}\right)\right)$

4: $\quad \mathbf{f}_L^{(\ell)} = \left(\omega^{(\ell-1)} + \lambda\Delta_{LL}^*\right)^{-1}\omega^{(\ell-1)}\mathbf{Z}$

5: **Until** $\mathbf{f}_L^{(\ell)}$ converges

6: **Output** $\mathbf{f}_L^{(\ell)}$

It is observed that the loss function is optimized only on the labeled observations L, and we typically expect $|L|$ to be small. So, the choice or complexity of the loss function is not expected to have a significant impact on the computational burden of any resulting semi-supervised approaches. Next, Section 3.3 elaborates on the computational complexities involving graph construction algorithms and will in-turn motivate the anchor based graph construction mechanism of Section 4.

3.3 Computational Issues

We have thus far reviewed literature on two important aspects of the graph-based semi-supervised learning framework: (i) proximity graph construction in Section 3.1 and (ii) optimization of an objective function in Section 3.2. A concern about this framework is the issue of scaling with large n. As for (i), the time complexity for computing the graph $\mathbf{W}$ is $\mathcal{O}\left(n^2\right)$ with many graph construction algorithms, and the choice of graph kernel is also important. Commonly used graph kernels include (6) and (12) which involve the optimization of parameters k, λ, σ. It is noted that $k < 7$ is usually adequate, and many implementations default to $k = 5$ since σ tends to offset the k parameter. As for (ii), there are $\left\lceil |L|/t \right\rceil t \approx |L|$ calls to the graph fitting function at each point in a (σ, λ)-grid used during t-fold cross-validation, and graph-fitting optimization is $\mathcal{O}\left(|U||L| + |U|^3\right)$ under squared error loss (Zhu et al., 2003; Zhou et al., 2004; Belkin et al., 2006). Simplifying the computational burden of (i) graph construction and (ii) graph fitting is important, but care is required in order to not to sacrifice performance.

Table 1. Comparison of BLAS routines in R when p=5 and |L|=300

n	R Framework	Graph Construction (sec)	Optimization (sec)
10,000	R with reference BLAS	45.78	25.49
10,000	R + OpenBLAS	23.08	10.08
10,000	R + vecLib	21.55	08.35
60,000	R with reference BLAS	NA	NA
60,000	R + OpenBLAS	NA	NA
60,000	R + vecLib	NA	NA

Graph-based semi-supervised learning approaches often require several matrix operations which becomes tedious with increased n, $|L|$, or $|U|$. The reference BLAS (Basic Linear Algebra Subprograms) typically handles the matrix operations in R or C++ and speeds up the real computations, but is more tedious to program. Some open source BLAS routines, including OpenBLAS and Apple's optimized BLAS routine vecLib, are also readily available. Consider simulated examples where the components of the $n \times 5$ dimensional feature data $\mathbf{X}$ with $n \in \{10,000, 60,000\}$ are a random sample from the standard normal distribution, and the labels for the first $|L|=300$ observations are a random sample from the discrete uniform distribution on the set $\{\pm 1\}$. In the case of $n=60,000$, the graph construction and optimization were outside of our computational reach. The results in Table 1 give some justification as for why this Chapter turns its attention to the graph construction problem in Section 4.

4. ANCHOR GRAPHS IN SEMI-SUPERVISED LEARNING

Classification and regression problems involving the prediction of the response y_0 for a new observation $\mathbf{x}_0$ are challenging yet relevant from a practical standpoint. The graph-based semi-supervised methods of Section 3 used manifolds in the feature data $\mathbf{X}$ to predict y_0 from $\mathbf{x}_0$ as follows. First, the proximity graphs $\mathbf{W}$ of Section 3.1 incorporated the unlabeled latent network to adequately bring out the heterogeneous nature within the full (labeled and unlabeled) feature data matrix $\mathbf{X}$, and this proximity graph $\mathbf{W}$ was a fundamental component of the semi-supervised optimization frameworks in Section 3.2. Section 3.3 examined the issue of scalability and computational complexity that arises for these graph-based semi-supervised techniques as say n increases. This leads into the focus of this Section, i.e., a familiar performance versus speed trade-off: (a) get the best performance by optimizing a computationally intense problem versus (b) get (hopefully) comparable performance results faster by optimizing a problem requiring substantially less computation.

Anchor graphs can be made to strike a good compromise within this trade-off for graph-based semi-supervised learning. This Chapter extends the work of Liu et al. (2010) by presenting a clear description of their anchor graph construction and pairing it with a labeled loss optimization framework that applies to and performs well in large n regression and classification settings. The anchor graph concept uses $m < n$ *anchor points* spread throughout the feature space to approximate the empirical distribution of the rows of $\mathbf{X}$. The fundamental matter of selecting the anchor points is the topic of Section 4.1. Given m anchor points in $\mathbb{R}^p$, the *Local Anchor Embedding* or LAE Algorithm of Section 4.2 outputs an $n \times m$ matrix $\mathbf{Z}$ with non-negative components such that $\mathbf{Z}\vec{\mathbf{1}} = \vec{\mathbf{1}}$ that is used to construct an anchor graph.

As long as the selection of the anchors points is handled judiciously, the anchor graph parameter m will be seen to span the performance versus speed trade-off with small (large) m erring toward computational speed (performance). In terms of graph construction for semi-supervised learning, the matrix $\mathbf{Z}$ will be transformed into an *$m \times m$ reduced combinatorial Laplacian matrix* in Section 4.3 This in-turn will also reduce the computational burden of the optimization phase through a reformulated problem to come in Section 4.4 that optimizes a smaller $m \times 1$ vector β instead of the $n \times 1$ vector $\mathbf{f}$. The concept of this reformulated problem is the use of the linear approximation $\mathbf{f} \approx \mathbf{Z}\beta$ in labeled loss optimization (14). A complexity analysis in Section 4.4 will show that small m results in a huge computational saving in both the graph construction and optimization phases of graph-based semi-supervised learning. There is yet another subtle, but substantial computational savings due to anchor graphs during cross-validation. Recall the earlier discussion from Section 3.1 of constructing the $n \times n$ graph $\mathbf{W}$ and the need to pick a kernel function and its bandwidth parameter σ, e.g., see Gaussian kernel (12). It turns out that the anchor graph of Liu et al. (2010) eliminates the σ parameter and the need to select a kernel.

The two moons example in Figure 3 is used throughout this Section to illustrate the concept of anchor graphs. In this example, there are $|L|=6$ labeled and $|U|=994$ unlabeled cases of feature data in $\mathbb{R}^p$ with $p=2$. The labeled cases are all black on the upper moon and gray on the lower moon, so we might prefer the entire upper (lower) moon to be predicted as black (gray) in this simple example of binary classification. It is worth noting that any of the graph-based semi-supervised techniques from Section 3 will likely result in this preferred classification out-of-the-box, depending on the implementation of cross-validation and its ability to accurately estimate tuning parameters. See Culp and Ryan (2013) for a description of using unlabeled data during the necessary cross-validation phase. The two moons example

Figure 3. A two moons example with |L|=6 and |U|=994. The moon determines the true binary classification (black or gray).

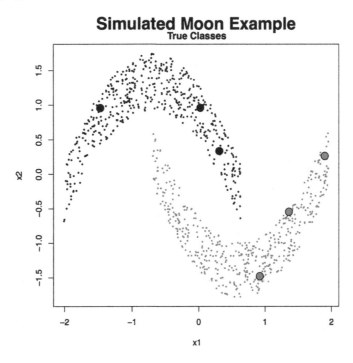

will also illustrate a key shortcoming of an anchor graph in that it does not necessarily produce this perfect classification without sufficiently large *m* (and hence additional computational time). In practice, real data sets rarely (if ever) conform to such perfect manifold assumptions like the two moons, but the performance versus computational speed trade-off will be seen to favor the use of anchor graphs on some real data set benchmarks later in Section 5.

4.1 Anchor Points

The anchor graph first simplifies graph construction by restricting attention to *m<n anchor points* or *anchors*. The idea is to first choose a small set (relative to *n*) of *m* representative anchors $\mathbf{v}_1,\ldots,\mathbf{v}_m$ such that $\mathbf{v}_j \in \mathbb{R}^p$ for all *j=1,...,m*. Let **V** be the *m×p* matrix that stacks the anchors as row vectors. Each anchor represents a neighborhood about a possibly large set of observations in **X** and are then used for graph construction. Distance calculations are restricted to distances between rows in **X** and **V** and results in an *n×m* distance matrix. Recall from Section 3.1 that proximity graph construction involved computation of a distance matrix for all *n* observations, so this can greatly simplify graph construction. In order to use this, the labeled loss functional (14) with the combinatorial Laplacian regularizer must be adapted for processing a non-square distance matrix; this is the topic of Section 4.2.

The number of anchors and their locations are critical, and a poor choice can lead to inaccurate graphs as empirically demonstrated by revisiting the two moons example in Figure 4. In the Figure 4(a), the *m=6* anchors (labeled 1-6 in the figure) are the *|L|=6* labeled observations. The left horn of the lower moon is misclassified as black because the labeled cases are all away from the horns. This matter is nearly resolved with a much better classification in Figure 4(b). There are two misclassified cases when *m=150* anchors are a random sample of the rows from **X**. Notice the jagged nature of both classification borders. This is a direct property of the underlying anchor graph construction and is expected to be more pronounced as *p* increases.

Figure 4. Two moons from Figure 3 revisited. (a) Labeled cases are anchors m=|L|=6. (b) Randomly selected rows of **X** *are anchors m=150.*

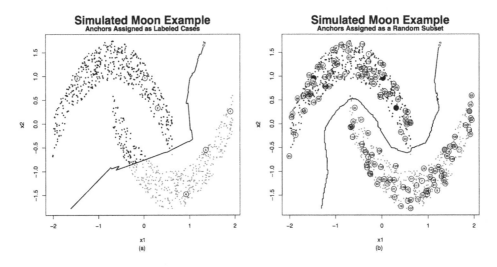

Figure 5. The two moons from Figures 3 and 4 revisited. Anchors are the m=150 centroids from (a) k-means and (b) Hierarchical clustering.

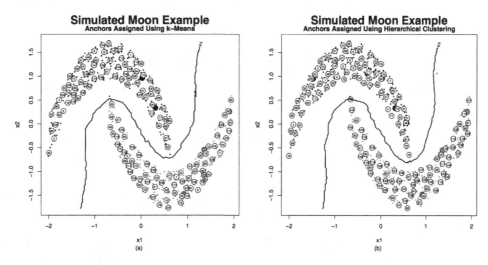

Clearly, the anchor points should be chosen as a set of points that adequately represent the empirical marginal distribution of the rows of **X**. Typically, the centroids from a clustering algorithm are a good choice for anchor points. Unlike the traditional use of clustering methods where the number of clusters is usually rather small, many clusters may be required in this anchor point application in order to adequately describe any manifolds in the feature data **X**. For example, return to the two moons in Figure 5 for demonstrations of anchor point selection by way of k-means cluster centers in Figure 5(a) and hierarchical cluster centers in Figure 5(b). Each attempt with $m/n=30\%$ misclassifies one observation. Notice again the jaggedness of the classification boundaries.

While an adequately large number of anchor points is necessary for representative graph construction, a larger number of anchors may be computationally inefficient. In this Chapter, we used $m = \lceil 0.3n \rceil \times \mathcal{I}_{\{n<1,667\}} + 500 \times \mathcal{I}_{\{n\geq1,667\}}$ because it was a good compromise of speed versus performance.

4.2 Local Anchor Embedding

This section concerns the construction of an $n \times m$ matrix **Z** from the $n \times p$ feature data matrix **X**, such that row i of **Z** is comprised of the weights for an optimized probability weighted average of the s closest anchor points to feature data $\mathbf{x}_i$ for $i=1,\ldots,n$. No direct edges/connections exist between the feature data points $\mathbf{x}_1,\ldots,\mathbf{x}_n$. Instead, the connectivity among the feature data points are through their common anchors, e.g., if $\mathbf{Z}_{ij} \approx \mathbf{Z}_{i'j} \approx 1$ then $\mathbf{x}_i$ and $\mathbf{x}_{i'}$ are both close to anchor point $\mathbf{v}_j$. The construction of such a **Z** given by Liu et al. (2010) eliminates the need for a graph kernel like (12), but introduces the need for a Local Anchor Embedding (LAE) algorithm. Before introducing the actual steps of this algorithm, their LAE algorithm is first introduced conceptually, so its purpose is clear to the reader. Given inputs of an arbitrary $\mathbf{x} \in \mathbb{R}^p$ and a set of m anchors from Section 4.1, the purpose of the LAE algorithm is to output an m-length vector **z** like the one outputted from the following simple two-step procedure.

Step 1: Determine a subset of the anchor points $\{\mathbf{v}_1,...,\mathbf{v}_m\}$ of size s that are closest to $\mathbf{x} \in \mathbb{R}^p$ and denote their indices by $\langle\mathbf{x}\rangle \subset \pi_m = \{1,...,m\}$. Thus, $|\langle\mathbf{x}\rangle| = s$, and if $i \in \langle\mathbf{x}\rangle$ and $i' \in \pi_m$ such that $i' \notin \langle\mathbf{x}\rangle$, then $\|\mathbf{x} - \mathbf{v}_i\|_2^2 \leq \|\mathbf{x} - \mathbf{v}_{i'}\|_2^2$.

Step 2: Let $\mathbf{V}_{\langle\mathbf{x}\rangle}$ be the $p \times s$ submatrix of $\mathbf{V}^T$ consisting of the s anchors closest to $\mathbf{x}$ appended as column vectors and define the simplex $\mathbb{S} = \left\{\mathbf{z} \in \mathbb{R}^s : \vec{\mathbf{1}}^T\mathbf{z} = 1, \ z_i \geq 0\right\}$. The optimization

$$\mathbf{z}_{\langle\mathbf{x}\rangle} = \arg\min_{\mathbf{u}\in\mathbb{S}} g(\mathbf{u}), \text{ where } g(\mathbf{u}) = g(\mathbf{x},\mathbf{u}) = \frac{1}{2}\left\|\mathbf{x} - \mathbf{V}_{\langle\mathbf{x}\rangle}\mathbf{u}\right\|_2^2 \tag{23}$$

solves for an s-length vector $\mathbf{z}_{\langle\mathbf{x}\rangle}$. The outputted m-length vector $\mathbf{z}$ takes its entry $\mathbf{z}_i$ from the corresponding entry in $\mathbf{z}_{\langle\mathbf{x}\rangle}$ if $i \in \langle\mathbf{x}\rangle$ and $\mathbf{z}_i=0$ otherwise for $i=1,...,m$.

If Steps 1 and 2 above are applied sequentially to the rows of $\mathbf{X}$ and the outputted $\mathbf{z}$'s are stacked as row vectors into a matrix, then the matrix $\mathbf{Z}$ mentioned earlier results. The LAE algorithm, which uses an iterative numerical approach to carry out Step 2 given above, is given below in Algorithm 4. The inner workings of Algorithm 4 are complex, but a conceptual understanding of Algorithm 4 is intuitive from geometric and optimization perspectives. Both perspectives are given next to provide deeper insight.

Geometric Examples of the LAE Algorithm

A geometric perspective of the LAE algorithm involves the convex polytope of all possible probability weighted averages of the s closest anchors to an arbitrary data vector $\mathbf{x}$. This convex polytope may include the data vector $\mathbf{x}$ in which case $\mathbf{x} = \sum_{i=1}^m \mathbf{z}_i \mathbf{v}_i = \sum_{i\in\langle\mathbf{x}\rangle} \mathbf{z}_i \mathbf{v}_i$. This happens in Figure 6(a). The data point $\mathbf{x}=(2,3)$ denoted by an empty circle is contained in the convex polygon with edges defined by the anchors 1,2,4 having Cartesian coordinates (1,2),(2,5),(7,2). Anchor 3 with coordinates (3,4) does not define an edge of this polygon since it is contained within the convex hull. The set $\langle\mathbf{x}\rangle = \{1,3,2,4\}$, and matrix

$$\mathbf{V}_{\langle\mathbf{x}\rangle} = \begin{pmatrix} 1 & 32 & 7 \\ 2 & 45 & 2 \end{pmatrix}.$$

The vector of probability weights $\mathbf{z}_{\langle\mathbf{x}\rangle} = (0.53, 0.2, 0.21, 0.06)^T$ was obtained manually by brute force and can be used to approximate $\mathbf{x}$, i.e.,

$$\mathbf{V}_{\langle\mathbf{x}\rangle}\mathbf{z}_{\langle\mathbf{x}\rangle} = 0.53\begin{pmatrix}1\\2\end{pmatrix} + 0.21\begin{pmatrix}3\\4\end{pmatrix} + 0.20\begin{pmatrix}2\\5\end{pmatrix} + 0.06\begin{pmatrix}7\\2\end{pmatrix} = \begin{pmatrix}1.98\\3.02\end{pmatrix} \approx \begin{pmatrix}2\\3\end{pmatrix} = \mathbf{x}$$

Figure 6. Geometric examples with p=2 and s=4 of the LAE algorithm. The empty circle is the inputted data point **x**. *Vector* $\mathbf{V}^T\mathbf{z}$ *based on the LAE output* **z** *is (a) the data point* **x** *when contained in the polygon of the anchors and (b) a point on the boundary of this polygon (i.e., the black dot) otherwise.*

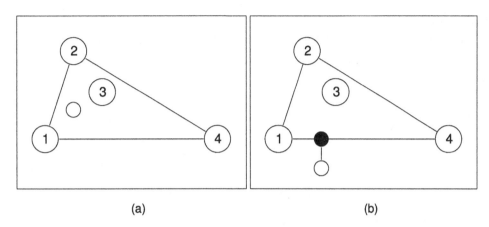

(a)   (b)

with corresponding criterion error $g\left(\mathbf{z}_{\langle \mathbf{x} \rangle}\right) = 8 \times 10^{-4}$. The LAE algorithm iteratively approximates $\mathbf{z}_{\langle \mathbf{x} \rangle} = (0.532781, 0.1967257, 0.2049202, 0.06557314)^T$ with a better error criterion value of $g\left(\mathbf{z}_{\langle \mathbf{x} \rangle}\right) = 3.25 \times 10^{-10}$.

The first example above is a circumstance where the LAE method works in an ideal fashion. Suppose instead that the point **x** is outside of the convex polytope of its *s* nearest anchors. Now, **x** can no longer be recovered exactly as a probability weighted average of its *s* closest anchors. In this case, the LAE algorithm uses a simplex projection to enforce the constraint that solution **z**=**z**(**x**) from optimization is in simplex $\mathbb{S}$, and the LAE algorithm effectively finds a vector on the boundary of the convex polygon as close as possible to **x** in Figure 6(b). The setup of this second example is the same as the first, except **x**=(2.5,1). The corresponding linear combination that approximates **x** is

$$\mathbf{V}_{\langle \mathbf{x} \rangle}\mathbf{z}_{\langle \mathbf{x} \rangle} = 0.75\begin{pmatrix}1\\2\end{pmatrix} + 0.00\begin{pmatrix}2\\5\end{pmatrix} + 0.00\begin{pmatrix}3\\4\end{pmatrix} + 0.25\begin{pmatrix}7\\2\end{pmatrix} = \begin{pmatrix}2.5\\2.0\end{pmatrix}$$

with an error criterion value of $g\left(\mathbf{z}_{\langle \mathbf{x} \rangle}\right) = 1.0$.

Logically, the second example in Figure 6(b) provides a natural solution to the problem of dealing with observations outside of the convex polygon of *s*=4 local anchor points in $\mathbb{R}^p$ when *p*=2. From a machine learning perspective, this idea still has practical shortcomings. Most importantly, vector $\mathbf{V}_{\langle \mathbf{x} \rangle}\mathbf{z}_{\langle \mathbf{x} \rangle}$ in the second example is a linear combination of just anchors 1 and 4 even though anchor 4 is the farthest from **x**. In some circumstances, anchor point 4 may not necessarily be on the same manifold as **x** and anchors 1-3, so this might put weight on responses from the wrong manifold when constructing predictions. As a result, classification borders (and regression fits) are jagged (e.g., recall discussions of Figures 3-5), and misclassifications may occur on the boundaries of manifolds. The problem is only further compounded by the curse of dimensionality since larger p only increases the odds that points are on the edge and thus fall outside of a convex polytope of s anchors in $\mathbb{R}^p$ when $p>2$.

Algorithm 2: Accelerated gradient descent

1: **Input** starting vectors $\mathbf{v}^{(0)}, \mathbf{u}^{(0)} \in \mathbb{R}^s$, a β-Lipschitz differentiable convex function $h : \mathbb{R}^s \to \mathbb{R}$, and scalar $\beta>0$

2: **Initialize** $\lambda=\gamma=k=0$

3: **Repeat**

4: $\mathbf{u}^{(k+1)} = \mathbf{v}^{(k)} - \dfrac{1}{\beta} \nabla h \left(\mathbf{v}^{(k)} \right)$

5: $\mathbf{v}^{(k+1)} = (1 - \gamma)\mathbf{u}^{(k+1)} + \gamma \mathbf{u}^{(k+1)}$

6: **Set** $\gamma=1-\lambda$, $\lambda = \dfrac{1 + \sqrt{1 + 4\lambda^2}}{2}$, $\gamma=\gamma/\lambda$ and $k=k+1$

7: **Until** $\mathbf{v}^{(k)}$ converges

8: **Output** vector $\mathbf{v}^{(k)}$

Optimization Overview of the LAE Algorithms

The LAE algorithm is now presented as a hybridized accelerated gradient descent approach that iteratively enforces that its solutions are on simplex $\mathbb{S}$. Direct or approximate calculation of a Hessian matrix is typically required when quadratic programming to solve (23), but is computationally expensive. An iterative first-order optimization method based on a *simplex projection* with an *accelerated gradient descent* can reduce the computational burden. Interest lies in optimization function $g : \mathbb{R}^s \to \mathbb{R}^+$ from (23) at a given $\mathbf{x} \in \mathbb{R}^p$, and an accelerated gradient descent method can imply a faster convergence than regular gradient descent methods (Nesterov, 2005) if this function satisfies the following two sufficient conditions.

1.   Function $g(\mathbf{z})$ at any fixed $\mathbf{x} \in \mathbb{R}^p$ is convex and continuously differentiable with respect to $\mathbf{z}$.
2.   Function $g(\mathbf{z})$ at any fixed $\mathbf{x} \in \mathbb{R}^p$ is β-Lipschitz, i.e., the gradient

$$\nabla g \left(\mathbf{z}_{\langle \mathbf{x} \rangle} \right) = \mathbf{V}_{\langle \mathbf{x} \rangle}^T \mathbf{V}_{\langle \mathbf{x} \rangle} \mathbf{z}_{\langle \mathbf{x} \rangle} - \mathbf{V}_{\langle \mathbf{x} \rangle}^T \mathbf{x}$$

satisfies $\left\| \nabla g \left(\mathbf{z}_1 \right) - \nabla g \left(\mathbf{z}_2 \right) \right\|_1^1 \leq \beta \left\| \mathbf{z}_1 - \mathbf{z}_2 \right\|_1^1$ for any $\mathbf{z}_1, \mathbf{z}_2 \in \mathbb{R}^s$.

Algorithm 2 is the accelerated gradient descent proposed by Yuri Nesterov. Since its output is not constrained to be within simplex $\mathbb{S}$, the projection onto $\mathbb{S}$ outputted by Algorithm 3, i.e.,

$$\breve{\mathbf{z}} = \arg \min_{\mathbf{u} \in \mathbb{S}} \left\| \mathbf{z} - \mathbf{u} \right\|_2^2,$$

is used in the LAE algorithm of Liu et al. (2010) to force approximate solutions to (23) to be within $\mathbb{S}$.

Algorithm 3: Simplex projection

1: **Input** vector $\mathbf{z} \in \mathbb{R}^s$

2: **Sort** the components of $\mathbf{z}$ into $z_{[1]} \geq z_{[2]} \geq \cdots \geq z_{[s]}$

3: **Find** $\delta = \max \left\{ i \in \pi_s : z_{[i]} - \frac{1}{i} \left(\sum_{j=1}^{i} z_{[j]} - 1 \right) > 0 \right\}$

4: **Compute** $\tau = \frac{1}{\delta} \left(\sum_{j=1}^{\delta} z_{[j]} - 1 \right)$

5: **Output** vector $\bar{\mathbf{z}} \in \mathbb{S}$ with $\breve{z}_i = \max\{ z_i - \tau, 0 \}$ for $i = 1, \ldots, s$

Now, recall the non-negative matrix $\mathbf{Z}$ whose ith row consists of the probability weights associating each feature data vector $\mathbf{x}_i$ for $i = 1, \ldots, n$ to its s nearest anchors. When the input is $\mathbf{x}_i$, the LAE algorithm 4 outputs the ith row of $\mathbf{Z}$ for $i = 1, \ldots, n$. Its Step 6 is a simplex projection, and you can see the elements of accelerated gradient descent in Steps 11 and 12. Step 7 looks to reduce the step size $1/\beta$ until the objective evaluated at the approximate solution within the simplex is no worse than the previous iteration based on a first order linear approximation plus a positive threshold.

Algorithm 4: Local anchor embedding

1: **Input** $\mathbf{x} \in \mathbb{R}^p$, $\mathbf{V} \in \mathbb{R}^{m \times p}$, and s (a positive integer not exceeding m)

2: **Find** s rows in $\mathbf{V}$ closest to $\mathbf{x}$ and save their index set $\langle \mathbf{x} \rangle \subset \pi_m$

3: **Initialize** $\mathbf{u}^{(0)} = \mathbf{z}^{(0)}_{\langle \mathbf{x} \rangle} = \vec{\mathbf{1}} / s \in \mathbb{S}$, $\lambda = \gamma = 0$, $\beta = 1$

4: **Repeat For** $k = 0, 1, \ldots$

5:     **Repeat**

6:          $\breve{\mathbf{z}} = \arg\min_{\mathbf{u} \in \mathbb{S}} \left\| \mathbf{u}^{(k)} - \frac{1}{\beta} \nabla g\left(\mathbf{u}^{(k)} \right) - \mathbf{u} \right\|_2^2$

7:          **If** $g\left(\breve{\mathbf{z}} \right) \leq g\left(\mathbf{u}^{(k)} \right) + \nabla g\left(\mathbf{u}^{(k)} \right)^T \left(\breve{\mathbf{z}} - \mathbf{u}^{(k)} \right) + \frac{1}{\beta} \left\| \breve{\mathbf{z}} - \mathbf{u}^{(k)} \right\|_2^2 / 2$

8:          **Break Inner Repeat; Else** $\beta = 2\beta$

9:     **End Repeat**

10:      $\mathbf{z}^{(k+1)}_{\langle \mathbf{x} \rangle} = \breve{\mathbf{z}}$

11:      $\mathbf{u}^{(k+1)} = (1 - \gamma)\mathbf{z}^{(k+1)}_{\langle \mathbf{x} \rangle} + \gamma \mathbf{z}^{(k)}_{\langle \mathbf{x} \rangle}$

12:      **Set** $\gamma = 1 - \lambda$, $\lambda = \frac{1 + \sqrt{1 + 4\lambda^2}}{2}$, $\gamma = \gamma/\lambda$

13: **Until** $\mathbf{z}^{(k)}_{\langle \mathbf{x} \rangle}$ converges

14: **Output** vector $\mathbf{z} \in \mathbb{R}^p$ such that $\mathbf{z}_{\langle \mathbf{x} \rangle} = \mathbf{z}^{(k)}_{\langle \mathbf{x} \rangle} \in \mathbb{S}$ and $\mathbf{z}_{\pi_p - \langle \mathbf{x} \rangle} = \vec{\mathbf{0}}$

4.3 Graph Design

In the previous Section 4.2, the LAE algorithm was documented and deconstructed. This method outputs a non-negative $n \times m$ matrix $\mathbf{Z}$ that reduces the dimension of $\mathbf{X}$ using m anchor points. A next logical step is to construct an adjacency matrix $\mathbf{W}$ and its corresponding graph Laplacian Δ from $\mathbf{Z}$; recall these topics from Sections 3.1 and 3.2. The anchor-based graph adjacency matrix is simply

$$\mathbf{W} = \mathbf{Z}\Lambda^{-1}\mathbf{Z}^T$$

where $\Lambda = \mathrm{diag}\left(\vec{\mathbf{1}}^T\mathbf{Z}\right)$ is the diagonal matrix consisting of the column sums of $\mathbf{Z}$. This graph forms edges through the anchors. In Figure 7(a), edges are drawn between observation $\mathbf{x}_i$ and anchor $\mathbf{v}_j$ if $j \in \langle\mathbf{x}\rangle$ such that $\mathbf{V}_{ij}>0$. In Figure 7(b), edges are now drawn between observations $\mathbf{x}_i$ and $\mathbf{x}_j$ if $\mathbf{W}_{ij}>0$. The panels look quite similar.

The (unnormalized) graph Laplacian

$$\Delta = \mathbf{D} - \mathbf{W} = \mathbf{I} - \mathbf{Z}\Lambda^{-1}\mathbf{Z}^T$$

follows by construction, since $\mathbf{D} = \mathrm{diag}\left(\mathbf{W}\vec{\mathbf{1}}\right) = \mathbf{I}$ because $\Lambda^{-1}\mathbf{Z}^T\vec{\mathbf{1}} = \vec{\mathbf{1}}$ and $\mathbf{Z}$ has rows summing to one. This leads to an adjacency matrix well suited for semi-supervised learning in large n situations because it possesses the following three desirable properties.

1. The $n{\times}n$ anchor-based graph adjacency matrix $\mathbf{W}$ has non-negative components, so its Laplacian Δ is necessarily positive semi-definite.
2. The sparse weight matrix $\mathbf{Z}$ often results in a sparse adjacency matrix $\mathbf{W}$ in practice because most pairs of data points do not share a common set of nearest anchors.
3. Memory and computation savings result because the $n{\times}m$ matrix $\mathbf{Z}$ is all that is needed to construct the $n{\times}n$ matrix $\mathbf{W}$. However, this can be taken a step further, by computing and storing the smaller $m{\times}m$ *reduced Laplacian* matrix $\mathbf{Z}^T\Delta\mathbf{Z}$ directly, i.e., the graph $\mathbf{W}$ is never computed in practice.

Figure 7. The two moons from Figures 3-5 revisited. (a) Anchor graph edges connect anchors m=150 and observations n=1,000. (b) Edges from graph $\mathbf{W}$ connect observations.

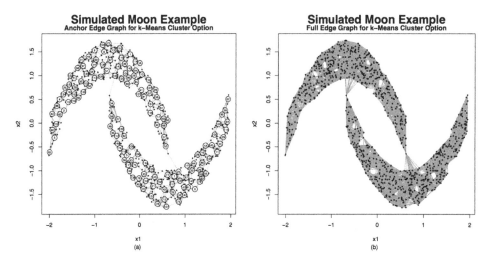

A heuristic classifier was proposed to obtain classifications using the reduced Laplacian (Liu et al., 2010). Next, this Chapter pursues a more promising optimization framework.

4.4 Regression and Classification With Anchor Graphs

The labeled loss optimization functional (16) is now used to fit the function $\mathbf{f}$. In the special case of $\mathbf{f}=\mathbf{Z}\beta$ with Laplacian $\Delta = \mathbf{I} - \mathbf{Z}\Lambda^{-1}\mathbf{Z}^T$, labeled loss optimization

$$\min_{\mathbf{f}} \mathcal{L}\left(\mathbf{Y}_L, \mathbf{f}_L\right) + \lambda \mathbf{f}^T \Delta \mathbf{f}$$

reduces to

$$\min_{\underline{\beta}} \mathcal{L}\left(\mathbf{Y}_L, \mathbf{Z}_L \underline{\beta}\right) + \lambda \underline{\beta}^T \mathbf{Z}^T \Delta \mathbf{Z} \underline{\beta}. \tag{24}$$

The solution to (24) with squared error loss is generalized ridge regression

$$\hat{\underline{\beta}} = \left(\mathbf{Z}_L^T \mathbf{Z}_L + \lambda \mathbf{Z}^T \Delta \mathbf{Z}\right)^{-1} \mathbf{Z}_L^T \mathbf{Y}_L.$$

Logistic loss follows by applying Algorithm 1 with $\mathbf{f}=\mathbf{Z}\beta$ and $\Delta = \mathbf{I} - \mathbf{Z}\Lambda^{-1}\mathbf{Z}^T$. The λ parameter controls the semi-supervised smoothness assumption, i.e., $\lambda=0$ the graph is not used while $\lambda>0$ allows the graph to influence the fitted function $\hat{\mathbf{f}} = \mathbf{Z}\hat{\underline{\beta}}$. A prediction $\mathbf{z}^T \hat{\underline{\beta}}$ is computed by applying the LAE algorithm to arbitrary $\mathbf{x}$ to get vector $\mathbf{z}=\mathbf{z}(\mathbf{x})$, and this was used to determine the classification borders in Figure 5 where either category is equally likely.

The anchor graph methodology of this Section 4 is computationally efficient with a faster convergence rate than other existing graph-based methodologies (Hein et al., 2005; Karlen et al., 2008). One of the main contributions of this method is the use of the $m \times m$ reduced Laplacian matrix $\mathbf{Z}^T \Delta \mathbf{Z}$ in place of the $n \times n$ Laplacian matrix Δ during optimization. The complexity of the required matrix inverse in the anchor graph method is $\mathcal{O}\left\{m^3 + m^2 n\right\}$ with $m \ll n$. This is clearly faster than the computation of (19) with squared error loss whose order is $\mathcal{O}\left\{| L \| U | + | U |^3\right\}$, so the anchor graph method is promising for large n scenarios from a computational perspective. Table 2 rounds out the computational experiment from Section 3.3. The entries in Table 2 are an order of magnitude smaller than the corresponding entries in Table 1 and document the computational efficiency due to anchor graphs.

The classifier is applied to the simulated two moon example using 3-fold cross-validation to estimate λ in Figure 8(a). The classification border misclassifies one observation. Furthermore, the fit is jagged which relates directly to LAE algorithm being applied to observations on the edge of a moon (refer to Section 4.2). The k-NN graph with $k=6$ version of labeled logistic loss (Algorithm 1) was also fit with the Laplace kernel $K_\sigma(\mathbf{x}_i, \mathbf{x}_j)=\exp(-D_{ij}/\sigma)$. The parameters (σ, λ) were estimated using 3-fold cross-validation. The resulting prediction border in Figure 8(b) is smoother with no misclassification errors.

Table 2. Comparison of BLAS routines in R for the anchor graph p=5 and |L|=300

n	R Framework	Graph Construction (sec)	Optimization (sec)
10,000	R with reference BLAS	3.41	14.71
10,000	R + OpenBLAS	1.78	0.92
10,000	R + vecLib	1.46	0.86
60,000	R with reference BLAS	22.74	88.11
60,000	R + OpenBLAS	14.56	8.48
60,000	R + vecLib	12.74	5.91

Figure 8. The two moons from Figures 3-5,7 revisited. Prediction borders are superimposed under logistic loss with (a) Anchor graph optimization (24) and (b) Labeled loss optimization (14).

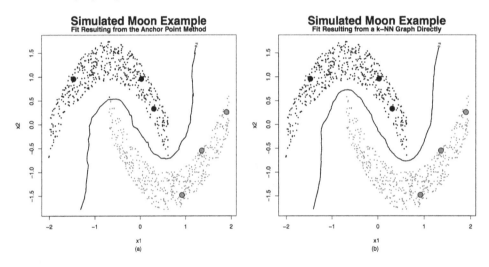

5. EMPIRICAL DEMONSTRATIONS

The competitiveness of three semi-supervised approaches using labeled loss is established on three publicly available data sets summarized in Table 3. Two versions of label loss optimization (14) were fit with a k-NN graph (with k=6) using cosine distance generated from the Laplace kernel function. The two versions only differed in their choice of penalty matrix: (i) Laplacian and (ii) normalized Laplacian. Lagrangian parameter λ and kernel parameter σ were estimated using 3-fold cross-validation. The efficient semi-supervised anchor graph approach was fit as the third technique for comparison with s=5.

Table 3. Data sets

Data Set	(n,m,p)	Type	Reference
Meat Spectrometry	(215,100,64)	Regression	Faraway (2016)
Power Plant	(9568,4,500)	Regression	Lichman (2013)
Sonar	(208,60,62)	Classification	Lichman (2013)

Figure 9. Performance (left) and time (right) for real data set benchmarks from Table 3. The graph-based semi-supervised techniques are (1) k-NN with Laplacian, (2) k-NN with normalized Laplacian, and (3) anchor graph.

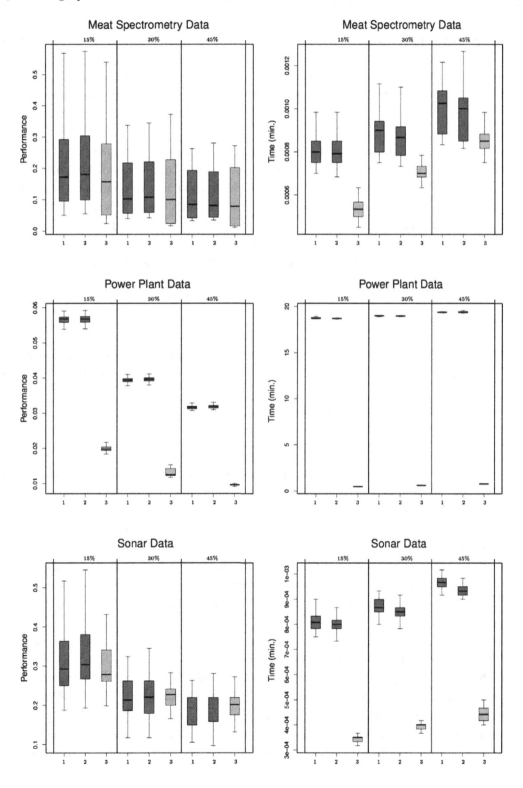

Its λ parameter was estimated via 3-fold cross-validation. In the context of regression, the squared error version was applied. The performance metric was unlabeled root-mean-squared error divided by the standard error of the response. In the context of classification, logistic loss versions were applied with a classification error performance metric.

Much work on computational efficiency was done to fit the semi-supervised technique quickly in memory. Since all three approaches were based on inverting a symmetric matrix at some point, a Cholesky decomposition and efficient storage of matrices (e.g., only store the upper triangle of the penalty matrix) were used in conjunction with optimized LAPACK/ATLAS C-routines to substantially boost speed. An even larger speedup for the k-NN graph-based approaches was due to the *Stagewise Cross Validation* (SCV) scheme of Culp et al. (2016).

Performance results and computation times in Figure 9 were based on 50 randomly selected labeled sets at each labeled percentage $100|L|/\min\{n, 1500\}=15, 30, 45\%$. The anchor method maintains strong performance compared to the other semi-supervised techniques in all cases and is substantially better for the power plan data. A performance boost due to the anchor graph method is not typical or expected in general. The performance difference between the unnormalized and normalized Laplacians is negligible. In terms of time comparisons, the linearity of the anchor graph proved to speed-up the procedure substantially relative to the k-NN graph approaches, especially for the larger power plant data set.

6. DISCUSSION

Motivation for graph-based semi-supervised techniques typically stems from generalizing a supervised optimization problem. Several supervised minimization problems involve an objective function of the form

"Loss Function" $+$ "Lagrangian Parameter" $\times$ "Penalty Function."

The choice of loss function depends on the application under examination, but almost always differs based on the response variable type. The main idea is for the loss function to increase as the function deviates from the response. Squared error loss and logistic loss were studied in this Chapter, but many others could be considered (Hastie et al., 2009). The penalty function accounts for smoothness of the function to be estimated. This is usually constructed in a way so that larger values of the Lagrangian parameter shrink the function towards an extreme endpoint with lower variability and higher bias. For example, ridge regression with a quadratic penalty achieves this trade-off by shrinking the function towards zero, and smoothing splines also achieves this trade-off by shrinking towards a simple linear regression alternative which has lower variance than a non-parametric spline fit. The Lagrangian parameter trades-off predicting the responses well (low bias) versus achieving a stable or smooth estimate (low variance). In practice, estimation of this parameter is critical for the success of a machine learning approach and is almost always optimized via t-fold cross-validation.

The graph-based semi-supervised techniques presented in this Chapter were centered around a labeled loss functional as a natural extension to a supervised optimization problem. The goal of this effort was to allow the unlabeled data to influence the fit, and this was accomplished by modifying the smoothness of the fit via the penalty function. This changes the behavior of the fit, especially in cases where manifolds could influence the underlying learning process. Penalty functions were constructed to capture these manifolds via a k-NN graph operator. Two k-NN graph-based approaches were presented. One was based on the combinatorial Laplacian, and the other was based on the normalized Laplacian. Both regularizers have been extensively studied. The role of the Lagrangian tuning parameter still spans the bias/variance trade-off, and the low variance end produces a stable estimator on each manifold, i.e., the function is shrunk towards the mean response in regression (or the majority category in classification) of the manifold. The presented techniques have the advantage of incorporating unlabeled data through a proximity graph, but the disadvantage of the additional computational burden can be dramatic.

An anchor graph approach was presented to approximate these graph-based operators and directly address the computational issues associated with fitting graph operators to big data. This had several advantages. First, an accelerated gradient descent approach summarized in the Local Anchor Embedding or LAE algorithm was shown to dramatically speed up the underlying construction of the graph. Second, a kernel tuning parameter that must be dealt with for k-NN graph approaches was removed from the problem and streamlined cross-validation. Third, the approach was demonstrated to perform as good as or better than the k-NN graph approaches in some practical applications. The downside of the approach was centered upon the formulation of odd neighborhood structures due to observations that may lie outside of the underlying convex polytopes used to produce the anchor graph. This problem is exacerbated with increased p.

A joint training generalization provides a natural way to incorporate unlabeled data deeper into the semi-supervised graph-based problem (15). Joint training differs from labeled loss optimization in that the loss function side of the supervised optimization problem is modified to better account for the unlabeled data. This is done through a latent unlabeled response vector and a new penalty function for the latent unlabeled response vector (Culp & Ryan, 2013) Shrinking in this manner has shown some general advantages when extrapolations are present within the latent unlabeled responses (Ryan and Culp, 2015). As the penalty function increases, techniques optimized under this framework tend to shrink unlabeled predictions towards the grand mean (or towards a supervised estimator) instead of towards the manifold mean. Practically, this approach adds a natural robustness to noise in the data or poorly specified manifolds. Such examples are quite common in practice.

Another interesting generalization not discussed in this Chapter is a *safe* semi-supervised framework (Culp et al., 2016). In many practical settings, noise in the response or feature data can corrupt the manifold structures within big data. Labeled loss semi-supervised learning approaches are known to be quite sensitive to these circumstances (Singh et al., 2009). In-fact, they can tend to perform much worse than corresponding supervised approaches. One-way to correct for this is to formulate a semi-parametric approach $\eta = \mathbf{f} + \mathbf{X}\beta$. The optimization problem is then modified to optimize over $\mathbf{f}$ and β simultaneously. A ridge penalty on β can also be added to the penalty function. Essentially, learning is broken into two phases: (i) accounting for as much of the response as possible with the term $\mathbf{X}\beta$ and then (ii) allowing the manifold, graph-based semi-supervised approach to account for non-Euclidean structures in the linear regression residuals $\mathbf{y} - \mathbf{X}\beta$. This hybridized approach to semi-supervised learning that incorporates the graph-based methods from this Chapter with linear regression tends to perform quite strongly in regression applications and consistently beats some of the strongest supervised competitors.

ACKNOWLEDGMENT

The work of Mark Vere Culp was supported in part by the NSF CAREER/DMS-1255045 grant. The opinions and views expressed in this paper are those of the authors and do not reflect the opinions or views at the NSF.

REFERENCES

Belkin, M., Niyogi, P., & Sindhwani, V. (2006). Manifold regularization: A geometric framework for learning from labeled and unlabeled examples. *Journal of Machine Learning Research*, 7, 2399–2434.

Bowman, A. W. (1984). An alternative method of cross-validation for the smoothing of density estimates. *Biometrika*, *71*(2), 353–360. doi:10.1093/biomet/71.2.353

Browne, M. W., Cudeck, R., Bollen, K. A., & Long, J. S. (1993). Alternative ways of assessing model fit. *Sage Focus Editions*, *154*, 136–136.

Chapelle, O., Chi, M., & Zien, A. (2006). A continuation method for semi-supervised SVMs. *Proceedings of the 23rd International Conference on Machine Learning*, 185–192.

Chapelle, O., Schölkopf, B., & Zien, A. (Eds.). (2006). *Semi-Supervised Learning*. MIT Press. Retrieved from http://www.kyb.tuebingen.mpg.de/ssl-book

Cooper, D. B., & Freeman, J. H. (1970). On the asymptotic improvement in the out-come of supervised learning provided by additional nonsupervised learning. *IEEE Transactions on Computers*, *100*(11), 1055–1063. doi:10.1109/T-C.1970.222832

Culp, M. (2011a). On propagated scoring for semisupervised additive models. *Journal of the American Statistical Association*, *106*(493), 248–259. doi:10.1198/jasa.2011.tm09316

Culp, M. (2011b). spa: A semi-supervised R package for semi-parametric graph-based estimation. *Journal of Statistical Software*, *40*(10), 1–29. doi:10.18637/jss.v040.i10

Culp, M., & Michailidis, G. (2008). Graph-based semisupervised learning. *IEEE Transactions on Pattern Analysis and Machine Intelligence*, *30*(1), 174–179. doi:10.1109/TPAMI.2007.70765 PMID:18000333

Culp, M. V., & Ryan, K. J. (2013). Joint harmonic functions and their supervised connections. *Journal of Machine Learning Research*, *14*, 3721–3752.

Culp, M. V., Ryan, K. J., & Banerjee, P. (2016). On safe semi-supervised learning. *IEEE Pattern Analysis and Machine Intelligence*.

Dempster, A. P., Laird, N. M., & Rubin, D. B. (1977). Maximum likelihood from incomplete data via the EM algorithm. *Journal of the Royal Statistical Society. Series B. Methodological*, 1–38.

Deng, L., Li, J., Huang, J., Yao, K., Yu, D., Seide, F., & Acero, A. et al. (2013). Recent advances in deep learning for speech research at Microsoft. *IEEE International Conference on Acoustics, Speech, and Signal Processing (ICASSP)*, 8604–8608. doi:10.1109/ICASSP.2013.6639345

Efron, B. (1983). Estimating the error rate of a prediction rule: Improvement on cross-validation. *Journal of the American Statistical Association*, 78(382), 316–331. doi:10.1080/01621459.1983.10477973

Everitt, B., & Hothorn, T. (2011). *An Introduction to Applied Multivariate Analysis with R*. Springer Science & Business Media. doi:10.1007/978-1-4419-9650-3

Faraway, J. (2016). *Faraway: Functions and Datasets for Books by Julian Faraway*. Retrieved from https://CRAN.R-project.org/package=faraway

Hastie, T., Tibshirani, R., & Friedman, J. (Eds.). (2009). The Elements of Statistical Learning (Data Mining, Inference and Prediction, Second Edition). Springer.

Heckman, G. (1995). *Harmonic Analysis and Special Functions on Symmetric Spaces*. Academic Press.

Hein, M., Audibert, J., & von Luxburg, U. (2005). From graphs to manifolds–weak and strong point- wise consistency of graph Laplacians. In *Proceedings of the 18th Annual Conference on Learning Theory*, (pp. 470–485). New York, NY: Springer. doi:10.1007/11503415_32

Hosmer, D. W. Jr. (1973). A comparison of iterative maximum likelihood estimates of the parameters of a mixture of two normal distributions under three different types of sample. *Biometrics*, 29(4), 761–770. doi:10.2307/2529141

Jain, A. K., Ross, A., & Prabhakar, S. (2004). An introduction to biometric recognition. *IEEE Transactions on Circuits and Systems for Video Technology*, 14(1), 4–20. doi:10.1109/TCSVT.2003.818349

Ji, J., Shao, F., Sun, R., Zhang, N., & Liu, G. (2008). A TSVM based semi-supervised approach to SAR image segmentation. *IEEE International Workshop on Education Technology and Training and International Workshop on Geoscience and Remote Sensing*, 1, 495–498. doi:10.1109/ETTandGRS.2008.13

Joachims, T. (1999). *Transductive inference for text classification using support vector machines* (Vol. 99). ICML.

Karlen, M., Weston, J., Erkan, A., & Collobert, R. (2008). Large scale manifold transduction. In *Proceedings of the 25th International Conference on Machine Learning*, (pp. 448–455). ACM.

Kung, S. Y., Mak, M. W., & Lin, S. H. (2005). *Biometric Authentication: A Machine Learning Approach*. Prentice Hall Professional Technical Reference.

Lafferty, J., & Wasserman, L. (2008). *Statistical analysis of semi-supervised regression*. In J. C. Platt, D. Koller, Y. Singer, & S. T. Roweis (Eds.), Advances in Neural Information Processing Systems (Vol. 20, pp. 801–808). Curran Associates, Inc.

Lao, Z., Shen, D., Xue, Z., Karacali, B., Resnick, S. M., & Davatzikos, C. (2004). Morphological classification of brains via high-dimensional shape transformations and machine learning methods. *NeuroImage*, 21(1), 46–57. doi:10.1016/j.neuroimage.2003.09.027 PMID:14741641

Li, Y. F., Kwok, J. T., & Zhou, Z. H. (2010). Cost-sensitive semi-supervised support vector machine. *Proceedings of the National Conference on Artificial Intelligence*, 1, 500.

Lichman, M. (2013). *UCI machine learning repository*. Retrieved from http://archive.ics.uci.edu/ml

Liu, W., He, J., & Chang, S. (2010). Large graph construction for scalable semi-supervised learning. *Proceedings of the 27th International Conference on Machine Learning*, 679– 687.

McLachlan, G. J., & Ganesalingam, S. (1982). Updating a discriminant function on the basis of unclassified data. *Communications in Statistics–Simulation and Computation*, *11*(6), 753–767. doi:10.1080/03610918208812293

Nesterov, Y. (2005). Smooth minimization of non-smooth functions. *Mathematical Programming*, *103*(1), 127–152. doi:10.1007/s10107-004-0552-5

Page, L., Brin, S., Motwani, R., & Winograd, T. (1999). *The PageRank citation ranking: Bringing order to the web*. Academic Press.

Palaniappan, R., & Mandic, D. P. (2007). Biometrics from brain electrical activity: A machine learning approach. *IEEE Transactions on Pattern Analysis and Machine Intelligence*, *29*(4), 738–742. doi:10.1109/TPAMI.2007.1013 PMID:17299228

Pudil, P., & Novovičová, J. (1998). Novel methods for feature subset selection with respect to problem knowledge. In Feature Extraction, Construction and Selection, (pp. 101–116). Springer. doi:10.1007/978-1-4615-5725-8_7

Ratsaby, J., & Venkatesh, S. S. (1995). Learning from a mixture of labeled and unlabeled examples with parametric side information. In *Proceedings of the Eighth Annual Conference on Computational Learning Theory*, (pp. 412–417). ACM. doi:10.1145/225298.225348

Richiardi, J., Achard, S., Bunke, H., & Van De Ville, D. (2013). Machine learning with brain graphs: Predictive modeling approaches for functional imaging in systems neuroscience. *IEEE Signal Processing Magazine*, *30*(3), 58–70. doi:10.1109/MSP.2012.2233865

Ryan, K. J., & Culp, M. V. (2015). On semi-supervised linear regression in covariate shift problems. *Journal of Machine Learning Research*, *16*, 3183–3217. Retrieved from http://jmlr.org/papers/v16/ryan15a.html

Scudder, H. J. (1965). Probability of error of some adaptive pattern-recognition machines. *IEEE Transactions on Information Theory*, *11*(3), 363–371. doi:10.1109/TIT.1965.1053799

Sebastiani, F. (2002). Machine learning in automated text categorization. *ACM Computing Surveys*, *34*(1), 1–47. doi:10.1145/505282.505283

Singh, A., Nowak, R., & Zhu, X. (2009). *Unlabeled data: Now it helps, now it doesn't*. In D. Koller, D. Schuurmans, Y. Bengio, & L. Bottou (Eds.), Advances in Neural Information Processing Systems (Vol. 21, pp. 1513–1520). Curran Associates, Inc.

Tryon. (1939). *Cluster analysis: Correlation profile and orthometric (factor) analysis for the isolation of unities in mind and personality*. Edwards Brother, Incorporated, Lithoprinters and Publishers.

Vapnik, V. N., & Chervonenkis, A. Y. (1974). *Theory of Pattern Recognition* [in Russian]. Nauka.

Zhou, D., Bousquet, O., Lal, T. N., Weston, J., & Schölkopf, B. (2004). Learning with local and global consistency. *Advances in Neural Information Processing Systems*, *16*(16), 321–328.

Zhu, X., Ghahramani, Z., & Lafferty, J. (2003). *Semi-supervised learning using Gaussian fields and harmonic functions* (Vol. 3). ICML.

Chapter 8
Machine Learning Methods as a Test Bed for EEG Analysis in BCI Paradigms

Kusuma Mohanchandra
Dayananda Sagar College of Engineering, India

Snehanshu Saha
PESIT-South, India

ABSTRACT

Machine learning techniques, is a crucial tool to build analytical models in EEG data analysis. These models are an excellent choice for analyzing the high variability in EEG signals. The advancement in EEG-based Brain-Computer Interfaces (BCI) demands advanced processing tools and algorithms for exploration of EEG signals. In the context of the EEG-based BCI for speech communication, few classification and clustering techniques is presented in this book chapter. A broad perspective of the techniques and implementation of the weighted k-Nearest Neighbor (k-NN), Support vector machine (SVM), Decision Tree (DT) and Random Forest (RF) is explained and their usage in EEG signal analysis is mentioned. We suggest that these machine learning techniques provides not only potentially valuable control mechanism for BCI but also a deeper understanding of neuropathological mechanisms underlying the brain in ways that are not possible by conventional linear analysis.

INTRODUCTION

EEG-based brain-computer interface (BCI) has assumed a significant role towards aiding the study and understanding of neuroscience, machine learning, and rehabilitation in the recent years. BCI could be interpreted as a platform for direct communication between a human brain and a computer bypassing the normal neurophysiology pathways. The primary goal of BCI is to restore communication in severely paralyzed population. However, the BCI for speech communication has its applications extended to silent speech communication, cognitive biometrics, and synthetic telepathy (Mohanchandra, Saha, & Lingaraju, 2015). Electroencephalography (EEG) is a non-invasive interface,

DOI: 10.4018/978-1-5225-2498-4.ch008

which has high potential due to its superior temporal resolution, ease of handling, portability, and low set-up cost. A general method for designing BCI is to use EEG signals extracted during mental tasks. EEG is the recording of the brain's spontaneous electrical activity from multiple electrodes placed on the scalp. EEG can be altered by motor imagery (Mohanchandra, Saha, & Deshmukh, 2014, pp. 434 - 439) and can be used by patients with severe motor impairments to communicate with their environment and to assist them. Such a direct connection between the brain and the computer is known as an EEG-based BCI.

An extensive exploration of the voluminous literature reveals a gap in the ability to provide speech communication using brain signals to produce meaningful words. Scientific endeavor is directed in the direction of developing a BCI-to-speech communication using the neural activity of the brain through subvocalized speech. Subvocalized speech is talking silently in the mind without moving any articulatory muscle or producing overt activities. The electrical signals generated by the human brain during subvocalized speech are captured, analyzed and interpreted as speech. The book chapter intends to dwell upon the characterization of subvocalized speech, captured via EEG signals. Since EEG signals suffer from poor spatial resolution (Kusuma, & Snehanshu, 2014, pp. 64-71), classification of mental activities using subvocalized speech is a challenging problem and according to the authors, the final frontier of machine learning. EEG signals suffer from the curse of dimensionality due to the intrinsic biological and electromagnetic complexities. Therefore, selecting a representative feature subset which would reduce the size of the dataset without compromising the quality of the information is a research problem worth attention. The problem this chapter would detail on involves efficient classification of subvocalized speech by novel subset selection method minimizing loss of information.

The EEG is acquired through multichannel sensors for a couple of seconds that leads to a large dataset. The deployment of multiple sensors leads to a significant volume of data. Gathering and maintaining the huge amount of data is a challenge and extracting useful information from them is even more demanding. Machine learning is a solution to this problem which helps researchers to evaluate the data in real-time. The machine learning algorithm is used to discover and learn knowledge from the input data. The category and bulk of the data affect the learning and prediction performance of the algorithms. Machine learning algorithms are characterized as supervised and unsupervised methods, also known as predictive and descriptive, respectively.

Supervised methods are built on the training set of the features and corresponding class labels known with confidence. The algorithm is trained on this set of features, and the result is applied to other features of which the target label is not mentioned. In contrast, unsupervised methods do not label data into classes. Unsupervised algorithms require some initial input to one or more of the adjustable parameters, and the solution obtained depend on the input given. It is to be noted that, the success of any predictive or analytic algorithm depends on efficient feature selection paradigms. Feature selection is a dimensionality reduction that efficiently identifies and generates discriminatory features among different classes of data as a compressed feature vector.

This book chapter is arranged as follows. Section 2, illustrates the broad outlook of the data and the methods used for experimentation. Section 2.2, presents the formation and evaluation of the Subset Selection Method (SSM), for feature selection. The SSM algorithm selects a subset of features that has significant variances which have impressive characteristics. The features with low variances are omitted from the feature space as they represent outliers and noise. The algorithm is tested on the EEG signals of subvocalized speech.

Figure 1. Functional model of the EEG-based BCI system

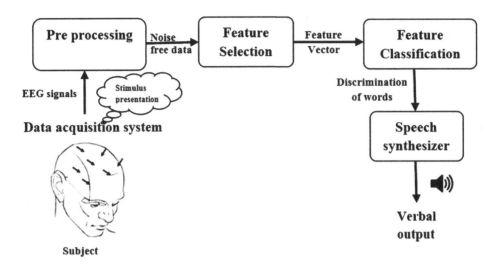

In this chapter, we contemplate on few well-known classifiers and clustering methods in the BCI community. A study of their uses for classification of the EEG signals of subvocalized words is carried out. These classifiers have several advantages that make them promising classifiers in BCI design. The classifiers used are the weighted k-Nearest Neighbor (k-NN), Support vector machine (SVM), Decision Tree (DT) and Random Forest (RF). In section 2.3, the theory of k-NN, SVM, DT and RF is briefly explained. The results obtained from the classifiers are presented in section 3. Finally, section 4, outlines the discussion of the results obtained and the summary of the work carried out.

METHODS

The architecture used in the BCI speech communication system is shown in Figure 1. The data acquisition system captures the EEG data from the electrodes at specific locations on the scalp for input to the BCI system. The preprocessing module involves amplification, analog filtering, A/D conversion, and artifact removal, thereby improving the signal-to-noise ratio of the EEG signal. Next, in the feature selection stage, the dependent discriminatory features of each subvocalized word are extracted from the pre-processed signals. These features form a feature vector, upon which the classification is done. In the classification stage, feature patterns are identified to determine various linguistic categories of the subvocalized words spoken by the user. Once the classification into such categories is done, the words are quickly recognized, and the speech synthesizer produces the speech sounds.

Data Acquisition

The EEG data is recorded using a Neuroscan 64-channel cap-based EEG device with the standard 10-20 montage placements. Vertical eye movements were detected using separate channels, placed above and below the subject's right eye. Horizontal eye movements were recorded by different electrodes put on either side of the eyes. In this study, meaningful words, catering to the basic needs of a person, are considered. The EEG data is extracted during subvocalization of the word, i.e. when the subject talks silently in his mind without any overt physical manifestation of speech. The experiment involved three volunteer participants referred to as subject1 through subject3. The five words selected are 'water', 'help', 'thanks', 'food', and 'stop' - referred as word1, word2, word3, word4, and word5, respectively, in subsequent modules. All volunteer subjects were right-handed male students between the ages of 20 and 25. All subjects are normal and underwent the EEG process without any neurological antecedents. The EEG data was analyzed offline using Neuroscan's SCAN 4.5 software. The signals are filtered between 0.5 Hz and 40 Hz using a band-pass filter and down-sampled to 250 Hz.

Feature Selection

Feature selection is a kind of dimensionality reduction that efficiently identifies and generates discriminatory features among different classes of data as a trampled feature vector. In the current work, EEG is measured from 64 channels with a 2-second epoch for each word, contributing to a huge amount of data. Hence, the need for dimension reduction is crucial in EEG data analysis. Due to volume conduction of the brain signals, the electric potential observed at the scalp becomes more widespread. Therefore, the channels are highly correlated. Prominent signals are measured by scalp electrodes located above the active cerebral area involved in the mental processing. So, in multi-channel EEG data, groups of channels are interrelated. The reason for this multi-pronged data analysis is that more than one channel might be measuring the same EEG potential evoked by the mental processing. However, to avoid the redundancy of information, a group of channels can be replaced with a new single variable/channel. In our work, the representative feature SSM, using pair-wise cross-correlation among the features, is used to reduce the size of the dataset with minimal loss of information. The desired outcome from the SSM, based on principal representative features (*PRF*), is to project the feature space onto a smaller subspace that represents the data with significant discrimination. This exercise facilitates analysis, as explained in the subsequent discussion.

Algorithm 1: Compute the most informative subspace in a space S of EEG signals
Input: Observation matrix X containing m channels and N samples per channel.
Output: Feature vector containing n significant variances.
Function ComputeVariance(X) // Calculates the variance for each trial of data
      Calculate the empirical mean of each row of data // for each channel
      Subtract the mean of the data from the original dataset
      Compute the covariance matrix of the dataset
      Compute the variance and *PRF* of the covariance matrix
      Sort the variance and the associated *PRF* in decreasing order
      Return n significant characteristic variances as the feature vector
end function

The subset method generates a new set of variables, called *PRF*. Each *PRF* is a linear combination of the original variables. All the *PRF*s are orthogonal to each other, so there is no redundant information. This relationship is ascertained by a simple pairwise cross-correlation coefficient computation. The *PRF*s as a whole form an orthogonal basis for the space of the data. The coefficients are calculated so that the first *PRF* defines the maximum variance. The second *PRF* is calculated to have the second highest variance, and, importantly, is uncorrelated with the first *PRF*. Subsequent *PRF*s exhibit decreasing contribution of variance and is uncorrelated with all other *PRF*s. The full set of *PRF*s is as large as the original set of variables. However, it is common that the cumulative sum of the variances of the first few *PRF*s exceeds 80% of the total variance of the original data as observed in our experimental procedure. Only the first few variances can be considered; the remaining is discarded, thus reducing the dimensionality of the data. The output generated by the SSM based on principal features is described in algorithm (1).

The algorithm is explained in detail as follows. Let $X \in R^{m \, x \, N}$ denote the original matrix, where m and N represent the number of channels and number of samples per channel respectively. Let $Y \in R^{mxN}$ denote the transformed matrix derived from a linear transformation P on X. The sample mean M, of each channel, given by $M = \frac{1}{N}\sum_{i=1}^{N} X_i$, is subtracted from every measurement of each channel. For m channels, the covariance matrix C is computed, which is an m × m square symmetrical matrix. The elements of C are defined as:

$$C_{ik} = C_{ki} = \frac{1}{N-1}\sum_{t=1}^{N}(X_{it} - M_i)(X_{kt} - M_k) \tag{1}$$

Where X is the data set with N samples, and M_i denotes the mean of channel *i*. The entry C_{ik} in C for i≠k is called the covariance of X_i and X_k. C is positive definite (Johnson, 1970) since it is of the form XX^T.

The SSM based on principal features finds an orthonormal m *x* m matrix P that transforms X into Y such that, X = PY.

$$\begin{bmatrix} x_1 \\ x_2 \\ \vdots \\ x_m \end{bmatrix} = \begin{bmatrix} u_1 & u_2 & \cdots & u_m \end{bmatrix} \begin{bmatrix} y_1 \\ y_2 \\ \vdots \\ y_m \end{bmatrix} \tag{2}$$

Each row in P is a set of new basis vectors for expressing the columns of X. The new variables y_1, y_2,....,y_m are uncorrelated and are arranged in decreasing order. Each observation of x_i is transformed to y_i, by rotation and scaling, to align a basis with the axis of maximum variance, such that $x_i = Py_i$. The x_i is rendered into m new uncorrelated variables y_i. Obtaining the principal feature axes involves computing the Eigen analysis of the covariance matrix C. The Eigen value λ_i is found by solving the characteristic equation, $|C - \lambda I| = 0$. The Eigen value denotes the amount of variability captured along that dimension. The eigenvectors are the columns of matrix P such that

$$c = PDP^T where, D = \begin{bmatrix} \lambda_1 & 0 & 0 & 0 \\ 0 & \lambda_2 & 0 & 0 \\ 0 & 0 & \lambda_3 & 0 \\ 0 & 0 & 0 & \lambda_4 \end{bmatrix} \tag{3}$$

Table 1. The Principal components, Variance, Relative Variance (RV) and Cumulative Variance (CV) for word1 (first 10 values)

PC	Variance	RV (%)	CV(%)
1	288.44347	86.42	86.42
2	17.23578	5.16	91.58
3	13.28826	3.98	95.57
4	8.39055	3.11	98.68
5	3.91906	0.57	99.25
6	1.00867	0.30	99.56
7	0.46584	0.14	99.70
8	0.30191	0.09	99.79
9	0.13911	0.04	99.83
10	0.10133	0.03	99.86

Figure 2. Two dimension PRFs plot, reveals the relationship between variables in different subspaces

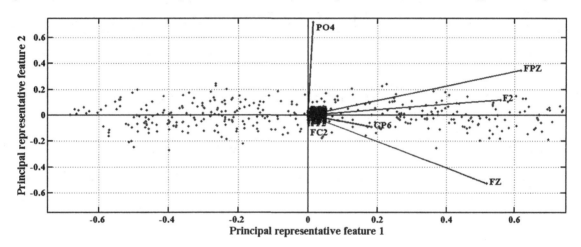

The vectors $u_1, u_2, \ldots u_m$ are the unit vectors corresponding to the columns of the orthogonal matrix P. The unit vectors $u_1, u_2, \ldots u_m$ are called the *PRF* vectors. They are derived in decreasing order of importance. The first *PRF* u_1 determines the new variable y_1 as shown in Equation (4). Thus, y_1 is a linear combination of the original variables $x_1, x_2, \ldots x_m$ where $a_1, a_2, \ldots, a_m$ are the entries in *PRF* vector u_1. Similarly, u_2 determines the variable y_2 and so on.

$$y_1 = a_1x_1 + a_2x_2 + \ldots\ldots\ldots + a_mx_m \tag{4}$$

Hence, the SSM based on principal features generates a subset of features endowed with large representative variances, thus embodying impressive structure while the features with lower variances represent noise and are omitted from the feature space.

Table 2. The coefficients of the first four PRFs are shown. The channels from the frontal region and the channels with prominent variance selected from the PRF matrix are shown.

Channels	Coefficients of *PRF*- 1	Coefficients of *PRF*- 2	Coefficients of *PRF*-3	Coefficients of *PRF*- 4
FP1	0.0022	0.0616	0.0317	0.0801
FPZ	**0.6193**	**-0.3484**	**-0.4277**	**0.1128**
FP2	0.0016	0.0775	0.0188	0.0778
AF3	0.0018	0.0563	0.0327	0.0806
AF4	0.0016	0.0603	0.0200	0.0737
F7	0.0008	0.0324	0.0163	0.0588
F5	0.0028	0.0494	0.0314	0.0547
F3	0.0038	0.0509	0.0569	0.0717
F1	0.0026	0.0563	0.0405	0.0818
FZ	**0.5202**	**0.5275**	**0.4171**	**0.4084**
F2	**0.5587**	**-0.1185**	-0.0903	**-0.2703**
CP6	**0.1829**	0.0911	**0.4793**	**-0.7529**
PO4	0.0151	**-0.7200**	**0.6110**	**0.2819**
FC2	0.0013	0.0434	0.0254	0.0710

Table 3. Range (Mean ± Standard Deviation) of the first four features (variances) across 50 trials of EEG signals for the five subvocalized words is shown

Features \ words	word1	word2	word3	word4	word5
Feature 1	232.07±0.20	424.73 ± 0.28	143.12 ± 0.20	807.84 ± 0.09	322.01 ± 0.34
Feature 2	15.38 ± 0.23	20.00 ± 0.16	17.12 ± 0.29	28.44 ± 0.11	14.56 ± 0.29
Feature 3	8.05 ± 0.34	10.66 ± 0.24	8.89 ± 0.17	9.96 ± 0.25	9.02 ± 0.24
Feature 4	5.33 ± 0.18	5.70 ± 0.30	5.14 ± 0.17	5.72 ± 0.36	4.89 ± 0.14

Table 1 shows the variance of the covariance matrix, computed using the SSM based on principal features. The cumulative variance (CV) illustrates that the first four variances explain 99% of the total variance. The remaining components contribute less than 1% each. Therefore, the first four components are chosen to form the feature vector, and the remaining variances are discarded. The remaining variance values are relatively small and are all about the same size, and hence, can be discarded.

The first two *PRF*s are typically responsible for the bulk of the variance. They display most of the variance in the data and give the direction of the maximum spread of the data. The first *PRF* gives the direction of the maximum spread of the data. The second gives the direction of the maximum spread, perpendicular to the first direction. The loading plot in Figure 2 reveals the relationships between variables/channels in the space of the first two *PRF*s. An intense loading for *PRF*- 1 is observed in channels FPZ, F2, CP6, and FZ. Similarly, an intense loading for *PRF*-2 is found in electrode channels PO4 and FC2.

In Table 2, a significant difference in the values is observed for FPZ, FZ, F2, and CP6 of *PRF*-1. Also, note that the majority of the variance in the dataset is along the aforementioned channels. So, the information from these channels alone is just sufficient to infer the result. Therefore, the information from the remaining channels can be discarded, thus reducing the computational burden on the system. The *PRF*-1 expressed as a linear combination of the original variables is shown in Equation (5).

$$PRF1 = 0.0022*FP1+0.6192*FPZ+0.0016*FP2+ 0.0018*AF3+0.0016*AF4+0.0008*F7+0.0028*F5+... \tag{5}$$

The study shows significant differences in the variance across different words (shown in Table 3). These variances correspond to the EEG change due to a particular component of mental rehearsal of different words. These features from the training set and the testing set were fed to the classifier, in the form of feature vectors, for classification of the test data.

Feature Classification

Classification or clustering algorithms are typically deployed on a dataset that are reduced dimensionally and free from noise. A few important Machine learning algorithms that would feature in the book chapter are: K-nearest neighbor (KNN), weighted KNN, Support Vector Machine (SVM), Decision Tree (DT) and Random Forest.

k-Nearest Neighbor (k-NN)

The *k*-NN is one of the simplest and versatile algorithms. It is used in a variety of applications ranging from biomedical signal processing, computer vision to proteomics. The *k*-NN is a non-parametric algorithm; it means that it does not make any theoretical assumptions on the underlying data distribution. The *k*-NN is also called as a lazy algorithm as it does not use the training data to do any generalization. So, the training phase is very fast. Lack of generalization means, that the *k*-NN does not construct any general internal model, but simply keeps all the instances of the training data during the testing phase (Mohanchandra, Snehanshu, Murthy, & Lingaraju, 2015, pp. 313-329). The classification of new cases is based on a similarity/distance measure against the entire training data set. Though the training phase is minimal, the testing phase is costly in terms of both time and memory. In the worst case, more time is consumed as all data points might take part in decision making.

The training data ensures a set of feature vectors from the feature space and class label associated with each vector. In the simplest case, it is a binary classifier with a positive or a negative class. The *k*-NN classifies the feature vectors (Zhang, Berg, Maire, & Malik, 2006, pp. 2126-2136) based on closest training examples in the feature space. But *k*-NN algorithm works equally well for multi-class problems. The advantage of the *k*-NN method over other supervised learning methods is its ability to deal with multiple class problems (Yazdani, Ebrahimi, & Hoffmann, 2009, pp. 327-330). The k-NN classifies the feature vector based on the majority votes of its neighbors. It is assigned to the class that has lesser distance amongst its *k* nearest neighbors. The *k* is a positive integer that decides the number of neighbors that contribute to the classification. The Euclidean function is used as a metric to measure the distance between the query point, and the training samples. Other measures include Manhattan, Minkowski, Mahalanobis, City-block, and Chebyshev measures.

The k-NN is described as follows: Let $T = \left\{ (x_i, y_i), i = 1, 2, ..., N \right\}$ be a training set of the data, where $x_i \in R^m$ is the training vector in the m-dimensional feature space and y_i is the corresponding class label. Given a query x_q, its unknown class y_q is predicted by the following steps. Firstly, a set of k nearest neighbors for the query x_q is identified. Denote the set as $T' = \left\{ (x_j, y_j), j = 1, 2, ..., k \right\}$ arranged in the ascending order of their Euclidean distance $d(x_q, x_j)$ between x_q and x_j shown in equation(6),

$$d\left(x_q, x_j \right) = \sqrt{(x_q - x_j)^T (x_q - x_j)} \tag{6}$$

Secondly, the class label of the query feature is predicted by the majority voting of its nearest neighbors. Let y^q denote the number of observations that belong to class y from the group of the nearest neighbors. Then,

$$y^q = \arg \max_y \sum_{(x_j, y_j \in T')} \delta(y = y_j) \tag{7}$$

where y is the class label, y_j is the class label for the jth nearest neighbor among its k nearest neighbors. The Dirac delta function, $\delta(y = y_j)$ takes a value of one if $y = y_j$ and zero otherwise. The new observation is predicted as belonging to class y, by considering the maximum class represented in the k nearest neighbors.

In k-NN, k is usually chosen as an odd number if the number of classes is binary. The optimal choice of the value of k is highly data dependent. For a small value of k, the noise will have a higher influence on the classification result. A large value of k conceals the effect of noise but makes it computationally expensive. Although, the algorithm is quite accurate and robust to noisy data, the time required for classifying the query data is high. The classification time of the k-NN algorithm is proportional to the number of features and the number of training instances. Also, the k neighbors have equal influence on the prediction irrespective of their relative distance from the query point.

A distance weighted k-NN algorithm is proposed as a refinement of the k-NN algorithm. A set of weights w, one for each nearest neighbor can be defined by the comparative nearness of each neighbor on the query point. Greater weights are given to closer neighbors and smaller weights to the farther ones. The weight is defined as,

$$w_j = \frac{1}{d\left(x_q, x_j \right)^2} \tag{8}$$

The $d(x_q, x_j)$ is the distance between the query point x_q and the jth nearest neighbor among its k nearest neighbors. Normalize the weight values in the range 0 to 1. Assign the weight w_j to each instance x_j in the training set. Then, the classification of the query feature is made by the majority weighted voting as shown in equation (9),

Figure 3. **A** *k-NN classifier for the value of k=3 and k=5. The purple circle is the query point.*

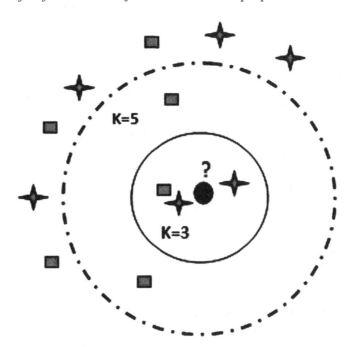

$$y^q = \arg \max_{y} \sum_{(x_j, y_j \in T')} w_j \delta(y = y_j) \tag{9}$$

The nearest neighbor gets a weight value of one and the farthest neighbor a weight of zero. In the current work, Euclidean distance is used as a distance metric, and the value of *k* is chosen as three after repeated cross-validation. The vector is directly predicted and assigned to the class of its nearest neighbor.

The training model assigns a corresponding class label for the feature vectors. During the classification phase, the unlabeled feature vector is classified by assigning a class label of the majority *k* training samples nearest to the query point (Phyu, 2009, pp. 18-20). In Figure 3 the test sample (purple circle) should be either classified to the class of green squares or the class of red stars. If k = 3, it looks for three nearest neighbors. In the example shown, it is assigned to the class of red stars because there are two stars and only one square inside the inner circle. If k = 5, it looks for five nearest neighbors. The test sample is allocated to the class of green squares as there are three squares and two stars inside the outer circle.

Support Vector Machine (SVM)

SVM is a significant supervised machine learning technique applied for classification or regression analysis (Kotsiantis, Zaharakis, & Pintelas, 2007). The SVM is a binary classifier, which extends into a multiclass classifier by fusing several of its kinds. The SVM finds an optimal classification hyperplane that separates clusters of feature vectors belonging to different classes. The features belonging to the first class are on one side of the plane and features belonging to the second class are on the other side of the hyperplane. There is an apparent gap that is as wide as possible. The features near the hyperplane are the support vectors.

An SVM is a supervised learning model that classifies the data by finding the best hyperplane (Burges, 1998, pp. 121-167) that separates all data points of one class from those of the other class. The best hyperplane for an SVM is the one with the maximum margin between the two classes. The margin is the width of the slab parallel to the hyperplane that has no interior data points. Given the features of the data, the support vector machine is first trained to compute a model to distinguish the data from two classes. The trained model is then used to classify the new incoming data. The details are given in Algorithm (2).

Algorithm 2: Classify the EEG signals (one-against-all) based on the feature vector
Input: feature vector for 5 different classes (train, test)
Output: classified label
Function BuildMultiSVM(train, test)
      training set $(x_i, y_i, i=1,2,..,5)$
for K ∈ { 1: I } do // number of classes

compute SVM solution w and b for all x_i with input labels y_i, such that $\phi(w) = 1/2 \|w\|^2$, is minimized
      given the constraint $y_i(w^T x_i + b) \geq 1$
binarize the group such that the current class is +1 and all other classes are -1
compute output $f_i = <w, x_i> + b$ for all x_i in +1 class
set $y_i = \text{sgn}(f_i)$ for every K ∈ I, $y_i = +1$
end for
for J ∈ {1:size(test)} // classify test cases
for k ∈ {1:I} // number of Classes
if (models(k)==test(j))
break;
end if
end for
return k;
end for
end function

For a specified set of training data (x_i, y_i), where i = 1... N, and $x_i \in R^d$ and $y_i \in \{+1,-1\}$ (representing two different classes of the subvocalized word), train a classifier f(x) such that:

$$f(x_i) \begin{cases} \geq 0 & y_i = +1 \\ < 0 & y_i = -1 \end{cases} \qquad (10)$$

The linear classifier is of the form $f(x_i) = w^T x_i + b$, (dot product) where w is the normal to the hyperplane, known as weight vector, and b is the bias. For a linear classifier, the w is learned from the training data and is needed for classifying the new incoming data. The support vectors are the data points x_i on the boundary, for which $y_i f(x_i) = 1$. The optimal hyperplane can be represented as l$w^T x_i$ + bl= 1. The distance between a support vector x_i and the hyperplane can be written as shown in Equation (11). For a canonical hyperplane, the numerator is equal to one. Therefore, the distance from the hyperplane to the support vectors is $1/\|w\|$

$$\text{distance} = \frac{\left| w^T x_i + b \right|}{\left\| w \right\|} = \frac{1}{\left\| w \right\|} \tag{11}$$

The margin M is twice the distance from the hyperplane to the support vectors. Therefore, $M = 2 / \left\| w \right\|$. To find the best separating hyperplane, estimate w and b that maximize the margin $2 / \left\| w \right\|$, such that for $y_i = +1$, $w^T x_i + b \geq 1$ and for $y_i = -1$, $w^T x_i + b \leq -1$ or equivalently, minimize $\frac{1}{2} \left\| w \right\|^2$ subject to the constraint $y_i(w^T x_i + b) \geq 1$. Learning an SVM can be formulated as a convex quadratic optimization problem, subject to linear inequality constraints for a unique solution. The objective function (Hsu, & Lin, 2002, pp. 415-425) of this problem is formulated as:

$$\min_{w \in R^d} J(w) = \frac{1}{2} \left\| w \right\|^2, s.t \left\{ y_i(w^T x_i + b) \geq 1, i = 1, 2, \dots N \right. \tag{12}$$

We can express the inequality constraint as $C_i(w) = y_i(w^T x_i + b) - 1$. The Lagrangian function is used as the method to find the solution for constrained optimization problems with one or more equalities. However, when the function has inequality constraints, we need to extend the method to Karush-Kuhn-Tucker (KKT) conditions. The KKT defines the necessary conditions for a local minimum of constrained optimization. The necessary conditions define the properties of the gradients of the objective and constraint functions. According to the KKT dual complementarity condition, $\alpha_i C_i(x) = 0$, the objective function of Equation (12) can be expressed by a Lagrangian function as shown in Equation (13).

$$\min \quad L(w, b, \alpha_i) = \frac{1}{2} \left\| w \right\|^2 - \sum_{i=1}^{d} \alpha_i [y_i(w^T x_i + b) - 1] s.t \alpha_i \geq 0, i = 1, 2, \dots N \tag{13}$$

The scalar quantity α_i is the Lagrange multiplier for the corresponding data point x_i. The optimal condition for the Lagrange function is at some point w when no first order feasible descent direction exists (saddle point). At this point w, there exists a scalar α_i such that,

$$\frac{\partial L}{\partial w} = 0 \Rightarrow w = \sum_{i=1}^{d} \alpha_i y_i x_i \tag{14}$$

And

$$\frac{\partial L}{\partial b} = 0 \Rightarrow \sum_{i=1}^{d} \alpha_i y_i = 0 \tag{15}$$

If we exploit the definition of w from Equation (14) and substitute it in the Lagrangian Equation (13), then simplify, we get

$$L(w,b,\alpha_i) = \sum_{i=1}^{d}\alpha_i - \frac{1}{2}\sum_{i,j=1}^{d}\alpha_i\alpha_j y_i y_j x_i^T x_j - b\sum_{i=1}^{d}\alpha_i y_i \tag{16}$$

However, from Equation (15) the last term in Equation (16) must be zero. Positioning the constraints $\alpha_i \geq 0$ and the constraint given in Equation (15), we obtain the dual optimization problem shown in Equation (17).

$$\max \quad W(\alpha) = \sum_{i=1}^{d}\alpha_i - \frac{1}{2}\sum_{i,j=1}^{d}\alpha_i\alpha_j y_i y_j x_i^T x_j, s.t \sum_{i=1}^{d}\alpha_i y_i = 0 \, and \, \alpha_i \geq 0 \forall i \tag{17}$$

The optimal value of α, substituted in Equation (14), gives the optimal value of w in terms of α. There exists a Lagrange multiplier α_i for every training data point x_i. Suppose we have to fit our model's parameters to a training set, and now wish to make a prediction at a new input point, x. We would then calculate the linear discriminate function $g(x) = w^T x + b$, and predict y = 1 if and only if this quantity is greater than zero. Using Equation (14), the discrimination function can be written as:

$$w^T x + b = \left(\sum_{i=1}^{d}\alpha_i y_i x_i\right)^T x + b$$

$$w^T x + b = \sum_{i=1}^{d}\alpha_i y_i < x_i, x > + b \tag{18}$$

The prediction of the class labels from the Equation (18) depends on the inner product between the input point x and the support vectors x_i of the training set. In the solution, the points that have $\alpha_i > 0$ are called the support vectors.

In general, if the problem does not have a simple hyperplane as a separating criterion, we need non-linear separators. A non-linear classifier can be created by applying the kernel trick. A kernel function maps the data points onto a higher dimensional space, hoping to improve the separateness of data. The kernel function is expressed as a dot product in an infinite dimensional feature space. Therefore, the dot product between the input point x and the support vectors x_i in Equation (18) can be computed by a kernel function. Using kernels, the discriminate function g(x) with support vectors x_i can be written as:

$$g(x) = w^T x + b = \sum_{i=1}^{d}\alpha_i y_i k(x_i, x) + b \tag{19}$$

Using the kernel function, the algorithm can be carried into a higher dimension space without explicitly mapping the input points into this space. This is highly desirable as sometimes our higher dimensional feature space could even have infinite dimension, and thus, be infeasible to compute. With the kernel functions, it is possible to operate in a theoretical feature space of infinite dimension. Some standard kernel functions include the polynomial function, the radial basis function, and the Gaussian functions.

In the present work, a one-against-all multiclass SVM, with the default linear kernel, was constructed to discriminate the 5 subvocalized words competently. The feature classification, using the SVM classifier, is described in the algorithm (2). Linear kernel SVM was used as the data is found to be linearly separable. The linearity of the data was verified using the perceptron learning algorithm. The one-against-all model constructs N (N=5 in the present work) binary SVM classifiers, each of which separates one class from the rest. The jth SVM is trained with the features of the jth class and labeled as a positive class; all of the others are labeled as a negative class. The N classes can be linearly separated such that the jth hyperplane puts the jth class on its positive side and the rest of the classes on its negative side. However, the drawback of this method is that when the results from the multiple classifiers are combined into the final decision, the outputs of the decision functions are directly compared, without considering the competence of the classifiers (Liu, & Zheng, 2005, pp. 849-854). Another drawback of the SVM is that there is no definite method to select the best suitable kernel for the problem at hand.

Decision Tree (DT)

A Decision Tree is a classifier that separates the feature space into rectangular regions through multiple comparisons with feature specific thresholds (Aydemir, & Kayikcioglu, 2014, pp. 68-75). In EEG signal analysis using DT, there are two phases: i) construct the tree to reduce the features ii) pruning the tree to avoid over-fitting. In the construction phase, the DT is iteratively built from the root to the leaves. At each node, the split criterion is calculated with the associated training examples. An optimized split criterion is identified at each node. The feature selection criterion at each node is based on information gain, Gini index or Gain ratio. In the present work, we use Gini index as an optimization criterion for selecting the features at each node. The Gini index is defined as:

$$Gini(s) = 1 - \sum_j P_j^2 \tag{20}$$

Gini index is an impurity based criterion that measures the divergences between the probabilities distribution of the target attribute's values. P_j is the probability that the feature belongs to class j. The Gini index is maximum when all the classes in the data have equal probability. The value of Gini index varies between 0 and 1 regardless of the number of classes. The tree growing phase continues until the maximum tree depth is reached. In the pruning phase, a stopping criterion is applied allowing the DT, to over-fit the training set. Subsequently, the over-fitted tree is reduced to a smaller tree by removing the branches that do not contribute to the accuracy. The pruning method improves the generalization performance of a decision tree, especially in noisy domains. In the current work, the pruning with m-estimate (m=2) was used.

Random Forest (RF)

Random Forest (RF) is an ensemble learning algorithm constructed by combining multiple decision trees (Breiman, 2001, pp. 5-32). The decision trees are built as base classifiers during the training time utilizing both bagging and random subspace selection method for tree building. The accuracy of the RF ensemble classifier depends on the diversity and accuracy of base classifiers. The upper boundary of the generalization error given by

$$E^* \le \frac{\rho(1 - S^2)}{S^2} \qquad (21)$$

where E* is the generalization error, ρ is the mean correlation of the base classifiers, and S is the accuracy of the classifiers. To achieve low generalization error, the individual base classifiers should have high accuracy with low correlation between them. The RF uses two randomization processes during the construction to ensure the diversity of the DTs. In the first step of bagging, a unique training set is compiled for each tree through random sub-sampling and replacement, also called the bootstrapping. Secondly, only a random subset of features is used for the calculation of the split thresholds at each node of the DT. This is known as the random subspace selection method. By injecting randomness in random forests the ability to rank different features and acquiring a measure of feature importance is gained. These two methods combined cause diversity in the decision trees assuring low correlation for individual trees. By averaging over a large ensemble of DTs, smoothes the single tree classification model and prevents over-fitting. The second step of bagging is called the aggregating step. In this, the class assignment of the RF classifier is chosen by a majority vote of all decisions.

The Gini impurity (GI) criterion is used for the rating of features. The rating is based on the mean improvement in GI per feature. The dissimilarity of GI between two subsequent nodes is calculated and summed up for each feature separately. Feature with high mean improvement is rated high as they discriminate the classes efficiently.

The formation of RF is explained as follows: Let $T_R = \{(X_1, y_1), (X_2, y_2), \ldots \ldots \ldots, (X_m, y_m)\}$ be the training dataset and each data has N features. Then, the input feature vector $X_i = \{x_{i1}, x_{i2}, \ldots \ldots, x_{iN}\}$ and y_i is the class label, where i = 1,2,….m.

Suppose, we want D number of decision trees in the RF. Create D number of feature sets of the same size as the original feature set T_R by random selection and replacement. This will result in $\{T_{R1}, T_{R2}, \ldots \ldots, T_{RD}\}$ feature sets. This is called as bootstrapping. Due to "selection and replacement", every feature set can have either duplicate features or missing features. This is called Bagging. Subsequently, in the random subspace method, the RF creates D trees with n random sub-features selected out of N features to form each tree, where n is the square root of N.

Next, to classify the test data $P = \{x_1, x_2, \ldots, x_N\}$ it should be passed through each tree to produce D outputs $Y = \{y_1, y_2, \ldots \ldots, y_D\}$. Finally, prediction of the class is made based on the majority vote on this test data.

After creating the RF (D trees), for each (Xi, yi) in the original training dataset T_R, select all T_{Ri} that does not contain (Xi, yi). This subset of the feature set is called out-of-bag (OOB) set. OOB estimate of the generalization error is the error rate of the OOB class on the training set T_R.

To achieve good performance, we need to optimize two important parameters in the RF algorithm. One is the number of input variables M tried at each split, and the other is the number of trees (D) grown for each forest. The default value of M is the square root of the number of features provided as input to the classifier. To select an appropriate value of D, we initially build the forest with a default parameter of M, and then the average Out of Bag (OOB) error is examined for different forest sizes. Figure 4 illustrates the change of OOB error with increasing forest size (D) under default M (M=8). It is observed that the

Figure 4. The average OOB error for different forest sizes with default M value. The forest size should be greater than 120 for a stable OOB error of 0.784.

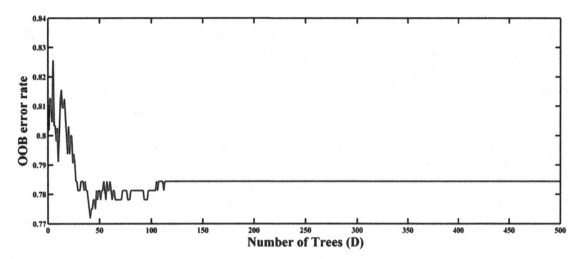

Figure 5. The average OOB error for different values of M with D = 500 is plotted. The optimal value of M with the least OOB error occurs near the default M (M=8) parameter.

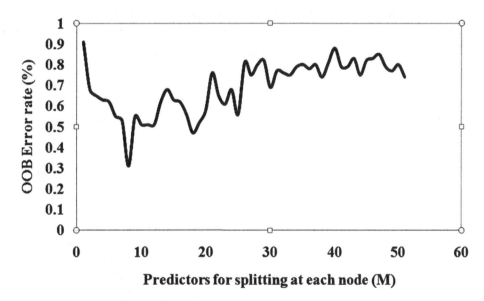

OOB error tends to be stable at 0.784 when D reaches 120 trees. As RF works better for greater D, we selected the forest size as 500 in our experiment. After D is set, forests are built with varying values of M from 1 to 50. Figure 5 shows the OOB error with different M values. The optimal value of M with the least OOB error occurs near the default parameter of M = 8. Based on the results, a final RF model is generated using the parameters D = 500 and M = 8.

EXPERIMENT RESULTS

The k-NN, Decision Tree, SVM and RF classifiers were used to evaluate the performance of the designed BCI model in classifying the EEG signals of subvocalized words. The data set has 50 trials of each word, measured for two seconds, from a 64-channel EEG headset. A total of 250 trials, measured for five subvocalized words, were used for evaluating the possibility of recognizing the subvocalized word from the EEG signals. The classifiers were tested on the same dataset and the identical feature set.

The subset selection method (SSM), based on principal features, was applied to the preprocessed EEG signals of five subvocalized words. Due to the vast dimension of the dataset, the SSM, based on principal features, was used to project the data to reduce the dimension while preserving maximum useful information. An optimal number of coefficients, contributing to 99% of the variance (4 features), were selected as features for each trial of the EEG signal. The features (mean ± standard deviation) are shown in Table 3. A major difference in the variance across each word facilitates classifying the EEG signals of the subvocalized word appropriately. Figure 6 shows the separation of feature space of different trials of SSM features of the five subvocalized words. The features selected, using the SSM based on principal features, were used to build the classifier. To develop a generalized, robust classifier that performs well when new samples are input, we choose a five-fold cross-validation data re-sampling technique for training and testing the classifier. In this procedure, the data is split into five equal-sized subsamples. Four subsamples of the data are used for training the classifier, and one subsample is used for testing. This procedure is repeated five times using a different subsample for testing in each case. Based on the results obtained, the precision, recall, F-measure, and accuracy are calculated. The average performance over five folds is taken as the actual estimate of the classifier's performance.

Figure 6. The diagram shows the nonlinear mapping of different trials of SSM features of the five subvocalized words

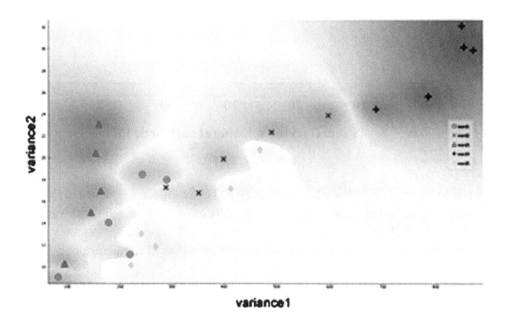

Performance Evaluation

The classifier performance is determined by computing the precision, recall, F-measure, and classification accuracy drawn from the "confusion matrix". The confusion matrix illustrates the true positive (TP), false negative (FN), false positive (FP), and true negative (TN) of the classified data. The metrics are calculated using the following formulae:

$$Recall = TP/ (TP+FN) \tag{22}$$

$$Precision = TP/(TP+FP) \tag{23}$$

$$F\text{-measure} = 2((precision * recall) / (precision + recall)) \tag{24}$$

$$Accuracy = (TP+TN)/ (TP+TN+FP+FN) \tag{25}$$

The Table 4 presents the precision, recall, F-measure, and average accuracy obtained by the SVM classifier in classifying the different subvocalized words. The recall represents the ability of the test to retrieve the correct information. With the SVM classifier, a recall of 0.6 was achieved which means 60% of the activity was detected (TP), but 40% of the activity was undetected (FN). Precision identifies the percentage of the selected information that is correct. A precision of 0.5 detected 50% of the activity correctly (TP), but the remaining 50% of the activity was mistaken as belonging to the same class (FP). Higher recall indicates that most of the relevant information was extracted, and higher precision means that substantially more relevant than irrelevant information was retrieved. The precision and recall are inversely related. Often it is possible to increase one at the cost of reducing the other. The feature selection and classifier model used in data analysis affect the level of recall and precision. The balanced F-measure is a combined measure that assesses the precision-recall tradeoff. It is the average of the two parameters and varies between a best value of 1 and a worst value of 0. The SVM classifier projected the following results. The F-measure ranged between 0.27 and 0.75. The classification accuracy varied between 60 and 92 percent across different subvocalized words, which appreciably, is good.

The Table 5 presents a comparative classification result obtained using k-NN, DT, SVM and RF classifiers. The last column of Table 5 presents the average classification accuracy across all class obtained using the features of subset selection method. The statistical analysis shows that the multiclass SVM outperforms all the other classifiers. The SVM gets the highest precision, F-measure, and classification

Table 4. Recall, Precision, F-measure, and accuracy assessment for different words using multiclass SVM for three subjects

Task	Recall	Precision	F-measure	Classification accuracy
word 1	0.60	0.50	0.55	0.80
word 2	0.40	0.40	0.40	0.76
word 3	0.20	0.50	0.28	0.80
word 4	0.60	1.00	0.75	0.92
word 5	0.40	0.20	0.27	0.60

Table 5. The performance of different classifiers for a feature vector consisting of 4 features across all the subvocalized words and across all the subjects

Method	Recall	Precision	F-measure	Classification accuracy
k-NN	0.60	0.33	0.43	0.68
Decision Tree	0.40	0.50	0.44	0.79
SVM	0.50	1.00	0.67	0.88
Random Forest	0.30	0.50	0.38	0.85

accuracy. The RF classifier performed better than k-NN and decision tree and is the second best classifier among the four classifiers used. The results demonstrate that there is a significant potential for the use of subvocalized speech in EEG-based direct speech communication.

The plot of classification accuracy against the increasing number of features used in the feature vector to discriminate the subvocalized speech of word1 is shown in Figure 7. It is observed that the classification accuracy increases as the number of features increases and remains constant after the fourth value. So in the current work, only four discriminating features are used to form a feature vector.

DISCUSSION

In this chapter, we deal with the comparison of different classifiers in predicting the EEG signals of five subvocalized words. The main concern is to evaluate the complexity of the input data and help in discriminating the features and entail in decision making. An attempt is made to identify an efficient classification method. The result of the subset selection method proposed for feature extraction of the subvocalized words is evaluated. A few well-known classifiers in the BCI community such as the weighted k-NN, SVM, DT and RF classifiers are tested.

Figure 7. The graph shows the variation in classification accuracy versus the number of features used in the feature vector to discriminate the subvocalized speech of word1

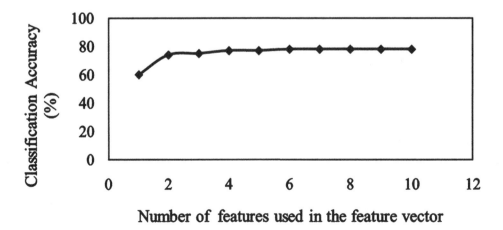

Experiments were carried out to assess the functioning of the classifiers for multiclass classification of the subvocalized words. Though the results of classification accuracy vary from subject to subject, the average accuracy reached by the multiclass SVM outperforms all the other classifiers and makes it suitable for the application. The computational simplicity of the SVM makes it suitable for real-time use. The result obtained from the RF classifier is encouraging. Since the RF is intrinsically multiclass and robust to outliers, it can also be used for real-time analysis.

In general, there is no single best classifier or a best feature extraction method that outperforms all others. For each subject, the combination of a classifier, feature and model parameters should be tuned together, and finally the method with the best performance on the training data set should be selected as the final model for testing on unseen data.

Lastly, we emphasize that classification is just one step in our framework, and to get an acceptable performance other steps are also necessary. Acquisition of the data, pre-processing, feature extraction, and feature selection all change the distribution of the data in the feature space and have an important role in getting good results. Therefore, a BCI system should be viewed as a unit consisting of different blocks in which all the block settings and parameters should be adjusted jointly for each subject.

REFERENCES

Aydemir, O., & Kayikcioglu, T. (2014). Decision tree structure based classification of EEG signals recorded during two dimensional cursor movement imagery. *Journal of Neuroscience Methods*, *229*, 68–75. doi:10.1016/j.jneumeth.2014.04.007 PMID:24751647

Breiman, L. (2001). Random forests. *Machine Learning*, *45*(1), 5–32. doi:10.1023/A:1010933404324

Burges, C. J. (1998). A tutorial on support vector machines for pattern recognition. *Data Mining and Knowledge Discovery*, *2*(2), 121–167. doi:10.1023/A:1009715923555

Hsu, C. W., & Lin, C. J. (2002). 'A comparison of methods for multiclass support vector machines'. *Neural Networks. IEEE Transactions on*, *13*(2), 415–425.

Johnson, C. R. (1970). Positive definite matrices. *The American Mathematical Monthly*, *77*(3), 259–264. doi:10.2307/2317709

Kotsiantis, S. B., Zaharakis, I. D., & Pintelas, P. E. (2007). *Supervised machine learning: A review of classification techniques. Frontiers in Artificial Intelligence and Applications, Emerging Artificial Intelligence Applications in Computer Engineering: Real Word AI Systems with Applications in EHealth, HCI, Information Retrieval and Pervasive Technologies* (Vol. 160). IOS Press.

Liu, Y., & Zheng, Y. F. (2005, August). One-against-all multi-class SVM classification using reliability measures. In *Neural Networks, 2005. IJCNN'05. Proceedings. 2005 IEEE International Joint Conference on* (Vol. 2, pp. 849-854). IEEE.

Mohanchandra, Saha, Murthy, & Lingaraju. (2015). Distinct adoption of k-nearest neighbour and support vector machine in classifying EEG signals of mental tasks. *International Journal of Intelligent Engineering Informatics,3*(4), 313-329.

Mohanchandra, K., & Saha, S. (2014). Optimal Channel Selection for Robust EEG Single-trial Analysis. *AASRI Conference on Circuit and Signal Processing (CSP 2014)*, 9, 64-71. doi:10.1016/j.aasri.2014.09.012

Mohanchandra, K., Saha, S., & Deshmukh, R. (2014). Twofold classification of motor imagery using common spatial pattern. *International Conference on Contemporary Computing and Informatics (IC3I), IEEE, 2014*, 434 - 439. doi:10.1109/IC3I.2014.7019636

Mohanchandra, K., Saha, S., & Lingaraju, G. M. (2015). *EEG based brain computer interface for speech communication: principles and applications. Intelligent Systems Reference Library, Brain-Computer Interfaces: Current Trends and Applications* (Vol. 74). Berlin: Springer-Verlag GmbH; doi:10.1007/978-3-319-10978-7

Phyu, T. N. (2009). Survey of classification techniques in data mining. *Proceedings of the International MultiConference of Engineers and Computer Scientists,* 1, 18-20.

Yazdani, A., Ebrahimi, T., & Hoffmann, U. (2009). Classification of EEG signals using Dempster Shafer theory and a k-nearest neighbor classifier. *NER 2009: 4th International Conference on Neural Engineering*, 327-330. doi:10.1109/NER.2009.5109299

Zhang, H., Berg, A. C., Maire, M., & Malik, J. (2006). SVM-KNN: Discriminative nearest neighbor classification for visual category recognition. *Computer Society Conference on Computer Vision and Pattern Recognition*, 2, 2126-2136. doi:10.1109/CVPR.2006.301

Chapter 9
Machine Learning Approaches for Supernovae Classification

Surbhi Agrawal
PESIT-BSC, India

Kakoli Bora
PESIT-BSC, India

Swati Routh
Jain University, India

ABSTRACT

In this chapter, authors have discussed few machine learning techniques and their application to perform the supernovae classification. Supernovae has various types, mainly categorized into two important types. Here, focus is given on the classification of Type-Ia supernova. Astronomers use Type-Ia supernovae as "standard candles" to measure distances in the Universe. Classification of supernovae is mainly a matter of concern for the astronomers in the absence of spectra. Through the application of different machine learning techniques on the data set authors have tried to check how well classification of supernovae can be performed using these techniques. Data set used is available at Riess et al. (2007) (astro-ph/0611572).

INTRODUCTION

Cosmology is a data starved science. With the advancement of technology and new advanced technological telescopes and other such instruments, here we have a flood of data. Data which is not easy as well to be interpreted, very complex data. So, astronomical area requires various techniques which help in dealing with the problem of interpretation and analysis of such vast complex data. Out of several astronomical problems, here we have taken one such problem i.e. the problem of supernovae (SNe) classification using certain machine learning algorithms. But the question is why we need to classify supernovae or why is it important?

A supernova is a violent explosion of a star, whose brightness for an amazingly short period of time, matches that of the galaxy in which it occurs. This explosion can be due to the nuclear fusion in a de-

DOI: 10.4018/978-1-5225-2498-4.ch009

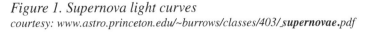

Figure 1. Supernova light curves
courtesy: www.astro.princeton.edu/~burrows/classes/403/_supernovae.pdf

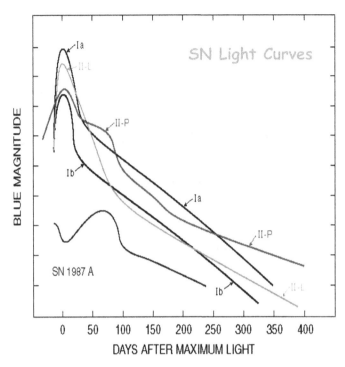

generated star or by the collapse of the core of a massive star, both leads in the generation of massive amount of energy. The shock waves due to explosion can lead to the formation of new stars and also helps astronomers indicate the astronomical distances. Supernovae are classified according to the presence or absence of certain features in their orbital spectra. According to Rudolph Minkowski there are two main classes of supernova, the Type-I and the Type-II. Type-I is further subdivided into three classes i.e. the Type-Ia, the Type-Ib and the Type-Ic. Similarly, Type II supernova are further sub-classified as Type II-P, Type II-L and Type IIn. The detail classification of these two types of supernova is discussed in the following section. Astronomers face lot of problem in classifying them because a supernova changes itself over the time. At one instance a supernovae belonging to a particular type, may get transformed into the supernovae of other type. Hence, at different time of observation, it may belong to different type. Also, when this spectra is not available, it poses a great challenge to classify them. They have to rely only on photometric measurements for their classification. This poses a big challenge in front of astronomers to do their studies. Figure 1 shows the supernova classification from their light curves.

Machine learning methods help researchers to analyze the data in real time. Here, we build a model from the input data. A learning algorithm is used to discover and learn knowledge from the data. These methods can be supervised (that rely on training set of objects for which target property is known) or unsupervised (require some kind of initial input data but unknown class).

In this chapter, classification of Type Ia supernova are taking in considerations from a supernova dataset defined in Davis et.al (2007), Reiss et al. (2007) and Wood Vessey et al. (2007) using several machine learning algorithms. To solve this problem, the dataset is classified in two classes which may aid astronomers in the classification of new supernovae with high accuracy. The chapter is further organized as - background, Machine learning techniques, results and conclusion.

BACKGROUND

Current models of the universe posit the existence of a ubiquitous energy field of unknown composition that comprises about 73% of all mass-energy and yet that can only be detected through subtle effects. Cosmologists have dubbed this mysterious field dark energy, and over the past decade, it has become an accepted part of the standard cosmology and a focus of observational efforts. More than that: it is fair to say that understanding dark energy has become the central problem in modern cosmology. In (Christopher et.al.,2009) describe two classes of methods for making sharp statistical inferences about the equation of state from observations of Type-Ia Supernovae (SNe). The dark energy pressure and density are expressed in terms of co-moving distance, r, from which they calculated reconstruction equation, w, which is very important to express various cosmological models. First, they derive a technique for testing hypotheses about w, the equation of state that requires no assumptions about its form and can distinguish among competing theories. The technique is based on combining shape constraints on r, features of the functions in the null hypothesis, and any desired cosmological assumptions. Second, they develop a framework for nonparametric estimation of w with corresponding assessment of uncertainty. Given a sequence of parametric models for w of increasing dimension, we use the forward operator $T(\cdot)$ to convert it to a sequence of models for r and use the data to select among them.

Kernel principal component analysis (KPCA) with 1NN (K=1 for K nearest neighbor) was proposed in (Emile E.O.Ishida,2012), in order to perform the supernovae photometry classification. Dimensionality reduction was done using PCA and KNN algorithm was applied thereafter. The study concluded that for a dark energy survey sample, 15% of the original set will be classified with the purity of >=90%.

In (Djorgovski et.al.,2012), an automatic classification method was proposed for astronomical catalog with missing data. Bayesian networks (BNs), a probabilistic graphical model that is able to predict missing values in the observed data and dependency relationships between variables is used. To learn a Bayesian network from incomplete data, an iterative algorithm that utilizes sampling methods and expectation maximization algorithm to estimate the distributions and probabilistic dependencies of variables from data with missing values, was deployed. The goal was to extrapolate values of missing features from the observed ones. In this work, the authors used Gaussian node inference which is commonly used for continuous data. Each variable is modeled with a Gaussian distribution where its parameters are linear combinations of the parameters of the parent nodes in the Bayesian. In (Joseph W. R et. al.,2012), a semi-supervised method to classify photometric supernova typing was used. The nonlinear dimensionality reduction was performed on the supernova light curves using diffusion map followed by random forest classification on a spectroscopically confirmed trained set to learn a model that can predict types of each newly observed data. It was observed that despite collecting data on a smaller number of supernovae, deeper magnitude-limited spectroscopic surveys are better for producing training sets. For Type-Ia supernovae it was observed that there was 44% increase in purity and 30% increase in efficiency. When redshift is incorporated, it leads to a 5% improvement in Type Ia purity and 13% improvement in Type Ia efficiency. Next, they used K2 algorithm, a greedy search strategy to learn the structure of the BN. Finally, Random Forest (RF) classifier was implemented which produced reasonably accurate results. In (Karpenka N.V et.al.,,2013), authors proposed another classification method, which was mainly a two-step method. Initially, binary classification was performed to check, whether supernova is Type-Ia or not. They used neural network approach to identify whether the supernova is Type-Ia or not. In the first phase, SN light curve flux measurements were fitted individually using Gaussian likelihood function.

Then from each fit the parameter vector having mean & standard deviations along with flux measurements. Maximum likelihood value and Bayesian evidence were used as input for neural network training.

CATEGORIZATION OF SUPERNOVA

The basic classification of supernova is done depending upon the shape of their light curves and the nature of their spectra. But there are different ways of classifying the supernovae-

1. **Based on Presence of Hydrogen in Spectra:** If hydrogen is not present in the spectra then it belongs to the Type I supernova; otherwise, it is the Type II.
2. **Based on Type of Explosion:** There are two types of explosions that may takes place in the star- *thermonuclear* and *core-collapse*. Core collapse, happens at the final phase in the evolution of a massive star, whereas thermonuclear explosions are found in white dwarfs.

The detailed classification of supernova is given below where both types are discussed in correspondence to each other. The classification is the basic classification depending on Type I & Type II. According to (Phillip,P.,2013), it was considered that the two classes (Type I & Type II) are categorized based on the explosion method. According to that belief, Type I belongs to thermonuclear explosion & Type II belongs to core-collapse. But, with recent research studies, it has been observed that both types may belong to both categories.

Type I Supernova

Supernova are classified as Type I if their light curves exhibit sharp maxima and then die away smoothly and gradually. The spectra of Type I supernovae are hydrogen poor. As discussed earlier they have three more types- Type-Ia, Type-Ib and Type-Ic.

According to (Fraser,2016) and (TypeI and TypeII Supernovae,2016), Type Ia supernova are created when we have binary star where one star is a white dwarf and the companion can be any other type of star, like a red giant, main sequence star, or even another white dwarf. The white dwarf pulls off matter from its companion star and the process continues till the mass exceeds the Chandrasekhar limit of 1.4 solar masses.(Phillip P,2013),The Chandrashekahar limit/mass is the maximum mass at which a self-gravitating object with zero temperature can be supported by electron degeneracy method). This causes it to explode. Type-Ia is due to the thermonuclear explosion and has strong silicon absorption lines at 615 nm and this type is mainly used to measure the astronomical distances. This is the only supernova that appears in all type of galaxies. Type-Ib has strong helium absorption lines and no silicon lines; Type-Ic has no silicon and no helium absorption lines. Type-Ib and Type-Ic are core collapse supernova like Type II without hydrogen lines. The reason of Type-Ib and Type-Ic to fall in core collapse is that they produce little Ni (Phillips M.M.,1993) and are found within or near star formation regions. Core collapse explosion mechanism happens in massive stars for which hydrogen is exhausted and sometimes even He (as in case of Type-Ic). Both the mechanisms are shown in Figure 2a & 2b.

Some of the supernova are determined using their spectroscopic properties and some using light curves.

Figure 2. (a) Core collapse mechanism (b) Thermonuclear mechanism
courtsey: *http://www-astro.physics.ox.ac.uk/~podsi/sn_podsi.pdf*

 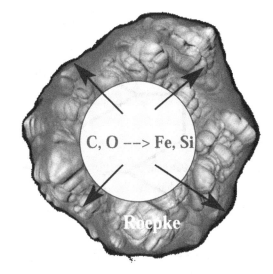

Type II Supernova

Type-II is generally due to core collapse explosion mechanism. These supernovae are modeled as implosion-explosion events of a massive star. An evolved massive star is organized in the manner of an onion, with layers of different elements undergoing fusion. The outermost layer consists of hydrogen, followed by helium, carbon, oxygen, and so forth. According to (Fraser,2016), a massive star, with 8-25 times the mass of the Sun, can fuse heavier elements at its core. When it runs out of hydrogen, it switches to helium, and then carbon, oxygen, etc., all the way up the periodic table of elements. When it reaches iron, however, the fusion reaction takes more energy than it produces. The outer layer of the star collapses inward in a fraction of a second, and then detonates as a Type II supernova. Finally the process left with a dense neutron star as a remnant. This show a characteristic plateau in their light curves a few months after initiation. They have less sharp peaks at maxima and peak at about 1 billion solar luminosities. They die away more sharply than the Type I. It has visible strong hydrogen and helium absorption lines. If the massive star have more than 25 times mass of the Sun, the force of the material falling inward collapses the core into a black hole. The main characteristics of Type II supernova is the presence of hydrogen lines in its spectra. These lines have P Cygni profiles and are usually very broad, which indicates rapid expansion velocities for the material in the supernova.

Type II supernova are sub-divided based on the shape of their light curves. Type II-Linear (Type II-L) supernova has fairly rapid, linear decay after maximum light. Type II-plateau (Type II-P) remains bright for a certain period of time after maximum light i.e. they shows a long phase that lasts approximately 100d and here light curves are almost constant(plateau phase). Type II-L is rarely found and doesn't show the plateau phase, but decreases logarithmically after their light curve is peaked. As they drop on logarithmic scale, more or less linearly, hence L stands for "Linear". In Type II-narrow (Type IIn) supernova, hydrogen lines had a vague or no P Cygni profile, and instead displayed a narrow component superimposed on a much broader base. Some type Ib/Ic and IIn supernova with explosion energies E $>10^{52}$ erg are often called *hypernovae*.

Figure 3. Classification of supernova

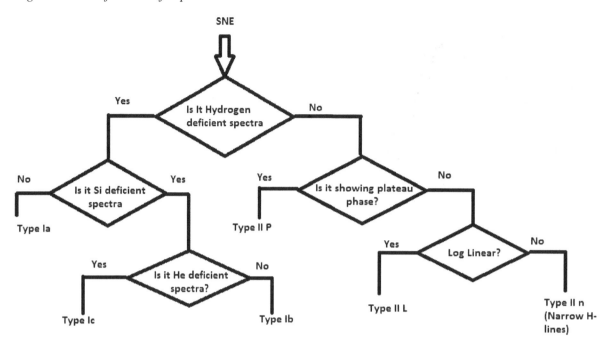

The classification of supernova is shown in Figure 3 with the following flowchart as-

MACHINE LEARNING TECHNIQUES

Machine learning is a discipline that constructs and study algorithms to build a model from input data. The type and the volume of the dataset will affect the learning and prediction performance. Machine learning algorithms are classified into *supervised* and *unsupervised* methods, also known as predictive and descriptive, respectively. Supervised methods are also known as classification methods. For them class labels or category is known. Through the data set for which labels are known, machine is made to learn using a learning strategy, which uses parametric or non-parametric approach to get the data. In *parametric* model, there are fixed number of parameters and the probability density function is specified as $p(x|\theta)$ which determines the probability of pattern x for the given parameter θ (generally a parameter vector). In *nonparametric* model, there are no fixed number of parameters, hence cannot be parameterized. Parametric models are basically probabilistic models like Bayesian model, Maximum Aposteriori Classifiers etc. and non- parametric where directly decision boundaries are determined like Decision Trees, KNN etc. These models (parametric and nonparametric mainly talks about the distribution of data in the data set, which helps to take the decision upon the use of appropriate classifiers.

If class labels are not known (unsupervised case), and data is taken from different distributions it is hard to assess. In these cases, some distance measure, like Euclidian distance, is considered between two data points, and if this distance is 0 or nearly 0, the two points are considered as similar. All the similar points are kept in the same group, which is called as cluster. Likewise the clusters are devised. While clustering main aim is to keep high intracluster similarity and low intercluster similarity. There are several ways in which clustering can be done. It can be density based, distance based, grid based etc. Shapes of the cluster also can be spherical, ellipsoidal or any other based on the type of clustering being performed. Most basic type of clustering is distance based, on the basis of which K-means algorithm is devised which is most popular algorithm. Other clustering algorithms to name a few are K- medoids, DBScan, Denclue etc. Each has its own advantages and limitations. They have to be selected based on the dataset for which categorization has to be performed. Data analytics uses machine learning methods to make decision for a system.

According to (Nicholas,2010), supervised methods rely on a *training set* of objects for which the target property, for example a classification, is known with confidence. The method is trained on this set of objects, and the resulting mapping is applied to further objects for which the target property is not available. These additional objects constitute the *testing set*. Typically in astronomy, the target property is spectroscopic, and the input attributes are photometric, thus one can predict properties that would normally require a spectrum for the generally much larger sample of photometric objects.

On the other hand, unsupervised methods do not require a *training set*. These algorithms usually require some prior information of one or more of the adjustable parameters, and the solution obtained can depend on this input.

In between supervised & unsupervised algorithms there is one more type of model- *semi-supervised* method is there that aims to capture the best from both of the above methods by retaining the ability to discover new classes within the data, and also incorporating information from a training set when available.

Below are few supervised learning techniques which have been used for classification of supernovae.

Decision Tree

A decision tree classifier is a machine learning approach which constructs a tree that can be used for classification or regression. Each of the nodes are based on a feature (attribute) of the data set, the first node is called as root node, which can be any important feature and hence considered as best predictor. Every other node of the tree is then split into child nodes based on certain splitting criteria or decision rule, which identify the allegiance of the particular object (data) to the feature class. The final result is a tree with decision nodes and leaf nodes where leaf nodes represent the classes of classification. Typically an impurity measure is defined for each node and the criterion for splitting a node is based on increase in purity of child nodes as compared to the parent node i.e. splits that produce child nodes which have significantly less impurity as compared to the parent node are favored. The Gini index (for CART) and entropy are two popular impurity measures. Entropy is used to interpret as a descriptor of information gain from that node. One significant advantage of decision tree is that both categorical and numerical data can be handled, a disadvantage is that decision trees tend to overfit the training data.

The core algorithm for building decision trees is known as ID3 given by J. R. Quinlan. ID3 employs a top-down, greedy search through the space of possible branches with no backtracking and uses *Entropy* and *Information Gain* to construct a decision tree. Below is the ID3 algorithm(Decision Trees,2015)-

ID3 Algorithm

Characterization of the model:

- X is a set of feature vectors, also called feature space.

- C is a set of classes.
- c: X --> C is the ideal classifier for X.
- D is a set of examples.

Construction of a decision tree T to approximate c., based on D

Algorithm ID3(D, Attributes, Target)

- Create a node t for the tree.
- Label t with the most common value of Target in D.
- If all examples in D are positive, return the single-node tree t, with label say, "+".
- If all examples in D are negative, return the single-node tree t, with label say, "–".
- If Attributes is empty, return the single-node tree t.
- Otherwise:*
  - ○ Let A* be the attribute from Attributes that best classifies examples in D.
  - ○ Assign t the decision attribute A*.
  - ○ For each possible value "a" in A* do:
    - ▪ Add a new tree branch below t, corresponding to the test A* = "a".
    - ▪ Let D_a be the subset of D that has value "a" for A*.
    - ▪ **If** D_a is empty: Then add a leaf node with label of the most common value of Target in D. **Else** add the subtree ID3(D_a, Attributes {A*}, Target).
- Return t.

K-Nearest Neighbor

K-NN classifies an unknown instance with the most common class among K closest instances. It is an instance-based classifier that compares new incoming instance with the data already stored in memory. K-Nearest Neighbors algorithm (or K-NN for short) is a non-parametric method used for classification and regression. Using a suitable distance or similarity function, K-NN relates new problem instances to the existing ones in the memory. K neighbors are located and majority vote outcome decides the classification. Occasionally, the high degree of local sensitivity makes the method susceptible to noise in the training data. If K = 1, then the object is assigned to the class of that single nearest neighbor. If K > 1, then the object is assigned to the class which has K number of similar nearest neighbor. According to (Veksler, 2013), in theory if infinite number of samples available, the larger the K values, the better is the classification, which gives smoother boundary. As per theoretical properties if K < sqrt(n), where n is number of objects to be classified, classification produces better results. One can choose K through cross validation also. The algorithm usually uses *Euclidian distance, Manhattan distance* or *Minkowski distance* to find the nearest neighbor for continuous variables. In the instance of categorical variables the Hamming distance must be used. This algorithm works well for larger dataset. It can be applied to the data from any distribution. A shortcoming of the K-NN algorithm is its sensitivity to the local structure of the data.

Linear Discriminant Analysis

LDA is commonly used for both dimensionality reduction and data classification. The basic LDA classifier attempts to find a linear boundary that best separates the data. LDA maximizes the ratio of between-class variance to the within-class variance in any dataset guarantying maximal separability. This yields the optimal Bayes' classification (i.e. under the rule of assigning the class having highest posterior probability) under the assumption that covariance is same for all classes. According to (Balakrishnama S. et. Al,1998), there are two different approaches used to classify test vectors. They are *Class dependent transformation* and *class independent transformation.*

- **Class Dependent Transformation:** This approach involves maximizing the ratio of between-class variance to within-class variance so that adequate class separability is obtained. This approach uses two optimizing criterion to transform the data sets.
- **Class Independent Transformation:** This approach involves maximizing the ratio of overall variance to within-class variance. This approach uses only one optimizing criterion to transform the data sets. In this type of LDA, each class is considered as a separate class against all other classes.
- The choice of type of LDA depends on the dataset as well as the goal of classification. For good discrimination of the classes, we prefer class dependent transformation and for general classification problem, class independent transformation is preferred.

In present implementation, an enhanced version of LDA (often called Regularized Discriminant Analysis) is used. This involves Eigen-decomposition of the sample covariance matrices and transformation of the data and class centroid. Finally the classification is performed using the nearest centroid in the transformed space also taking into account prior probabilities.

Naïve Bayes

Naïve Bayes classifier is based on Bayes theorem. It is a supervised learning method as well as a statistical method for classification. It allows us to capture uncertainty about a probabilistic model in a better way by determining probabilities of the outcome. It can solve both diagnostic and predictive problems. It can perform the classification of arbitrary number of independent variables and is generally used when data is high-dimensional. Data to be classified can be either categorical or numerical. A small amount of training data is sufficient to estimate necessary parameters. The method assumes independent distribution for attributes and thus estimates $P(X \mid Y_i) = P(X_1 \mid Y_i) * P(X_2 \mid Y_i) * ... * P(X_n \mid Y_i)$; where $X_1, X_2, ... X_n$ are 'n' input variables and Y_i are 'i' different classes. Although this assumption is often violated in practice (hence the name Naïve), Naïve Bayes often performs well. This classifier provides practical learning algorithm and prior knowledge and observed data can be combined. It calculates explicit probabilities for hypothesis and X_b, Y_b it is robust to noise in input data. It is computationally fast and space efficient.

Random Forest

Random forest is an ensemble of various decision trees. Each tree enunciates a classification and decision is taken based upon mean prediction on them (regression) or majority voting (classification). When a new object from the data set needs to be classified, data is kept down at each of the trees. Classification implies a tree voting for that class. Random forest works efficiently with large datasets. It gives accurate results even in the cases of missing data. The training algorithm for random forests applies the general technique of bootstrap aggregating, or bagging, to tree learners. Grow each tree in the forest on an independent bootstrap sample from the training data. At each node select 'm' variables at random out of all 'M' possible variables; find the best possible split on the selected 'm' variables.

Given a training set $X = x_1, x_2 ... x_n$ with responses $Y = y_1, y_2 ... y_n$, bagging selects a random sample of the training set with replacement iteratively and fits trees to these samples. For b = 1, ..., B: Sample, with replacement, n training examples from X, Y; call these X_b, Y_b. Next, we train a decision or regression tree on X_b, Y_b. Post-training, predictions for unseen samples x' can be made by averaging the predictions from all the individual regression trees on x': or by considering the majority votes in the case of decision trees.

Support Vector Machine

SVM classifiers are candidate classifiers for binary class discrimination. The basic formulation is designed for the linear classification problem; the algorithm yields an optimal hyperplane i.e. one that maintains largest minimum distance from the training data, defined as the margin. It can also perform non-linear classification via the use of kernels, which involves the computation of inner products of all pairs of data in the feature space; this implicitly transforms the data into a different space where a separating hyperplane can be found. One advantage of the SVM is that the optimization problem is convex. The result may not be transparent always which is a drawback of this method.

SUPERNOVAE DATA SOURCE AND CLASSIFICATION

The selection of classification algorithm not only depends on the dataset, but also the application for which it is employed. There is, therefore, no simple method to select the best optimal algorithm. Our problem is to identify Type Ia supernova from the given dataset in (Davis M.S. et al.,2007) which contains 292 different supernova information. Since the classification is binary classification, as one need to identify Type Ia supernova from the list of 292 supernovas, the best resulting algorithms are used for this purpose. The algorithms used for classification are Naïve Bayes, LDA, SVM, KNN, Random Forest and Decision Tree.

The dataset used is retrieved from (Davis M.S. et al.,2007). These data are a combination of the ESSENCE, SNLS and nearby supernova data reported in Wood-Vasey et al. (2007) and the new Gold dataset from Riess et al.(2007). The final dataset used is combination of ESSENCE / SNLS / nearby dataset from Table 4 of Wood-Vasey et al. (2007), using only the supernova that passed the light-curve-fit quality criteria. It has also considered the HST data from Table 6 of Riess et al. (2007), using only the supernovae classified as gold. These were combined for Davis et al. (2007) and the data are provided

Table 1. Results of Type -Ia supernova classification

Algorithm	Accuracy (%)
Naïve Bayes	98.86
Decision Tree	98.86
LDA	65.90
KNN	96.59
Random Forest	97.72
SVM	65.90

in 4 columns: redshift, distance modulus, uncertainty in the distance modulus and quality as "Gold" or "Silver". The supernova with quality labeled as "Gold" are Type Ia with *high confidence* and those with label "Silver" are *Likely but uncertain SNe Ia*. In the dataset, all the supernova with redshift value less than **0.023** and quality value **Silver** are discarded.

RESULTS AND ANALYSIS

The experimental study was setup to evaluate performance of various machine learning algorithms to identify Type-Ia supernova from the above mentioned dataset. The data set mentioned above is tested on 6 major classification algorithms namely Naïve Bayes, Decision tree, LDA, KNN, Random Forest and SVM respectively. A ten-fold cross validation procedure was carried out to make the best use of data, that is, the entire data was divided into ten bins in which one of the bins was considered as test-bin while the remaining 9 bins were taken as training data. We observe the following results and conclude that the outcome of the experiment is encouraging, considering the complex nature of the data. Table 1 shows the result of classification.

Performance analysis of the algorithms on the dataset is as follows.

1. Naïve Bayes' and Decision Tree top the accuracy table with the accuracy of 98.86%.
2. Random Forest ranks 2 with accuracy of 97.72% and KNN occupies 3rd position with 96.59% accuracy.
3. The dramatic change was observed in the case of SVM, which occupied the last position with LDA with an accuracy of 65.9%. The geometric boundary constraints inhibit the performance of the two classifiers.

Overall, we can conclude Naïve Bayes', Decision Tree and Random Forest perform exceptionally well with the datasets, while KNN acts as an average case.

FUTURE RESEARCH DIRECTIONS

Supernova classification is an emerging problem that scientists, astronomers and astrophysicists are working on to solve using various statistical techniques. In the absence of spectra, how this problem can be solved. In this chapter, Type-Ia supernova are classified using machine learning techniques based on redshift value and distance modulus. The same techniques can be applied to solve the overall supernova classification problem. It can help us to differentiate Type I supernova from Type II, Type Ib from Type Ic or so on. Machine learning techniques along with various statistical methods help us to solve such problems.

CONCLUSION

In this chapter, we have compared few classification techniques to identify Type Ia supernova. Here it is seen that Naive Bayes, Decision Tree and Random Forest algorithms gave best result among all. This work is relevant to astroinformatics, especially for classification of supernova, star-galaxy classification etc. The dataset used is a well-known which is the combination of ESSENCE, SNLS and nearby supernova data.

Supernovas are discovered in regular intervals. A supernova will occur about once every 50 years in a galaxy the size of the Milky Way. In other words, we can say a star explodes every second or so somewhere in the universe, and some of those aren't too far from Earth. A huge task of categorizing those manually may be translated into a simple automated system using this work. The new data can be appended to the dataset with discovered but non-categorized supernova. The machine learning algorithms could then perform the task of classification, as demonstrated earlier with reasonably acceptable accuracy. A significant portion of time could thus be saved.

REFERENCES

Balakrishnama, S., & Ganapathiraju, A. (1998). *Linear Discriminant Analysis- A brief tutorial*. Retrieved on 04-05-16 from https://www.isip.piconepress.com/publications/reports/1998/isip/lda/lda_theory.pdf

Ball & Brunner. (2010). *Overview of Data Mining and Machine Learning methods*. Retrieved on 25-04-16, from http://ned.ipac.caltech.edu/level5/March11/Ball/Ball2.html

Cain, F. (2016). *What are the Different Kinds of Supernovae?* Retrieved on 20-04-2016, from http://www.universetoday.com/127865/what-are-the-different-kinds-of-supernovae/

Davis, T. M., Mortsell, E., Sollerman, J., Becker, A. C., Blondin, S., Challis, P., & Zenteno, A. et al. (2007). Scrutinizing Exotic Cosmological Models Using ESSENCE Supernova Data Combined with Other Cosmological Probes. *The Astrophysical Journal*, 666(2), 716–725. doi:10.1086/519988

Decision Trees. (2015). Retrieved on 03-05-16 from www.uni-weimar.de/medien/.../unit-en-decision-trees-algorithms.pdf

Djorgovski, S. G., Mahabal, A. A., Donalek, C., Graham, M. J., Drak, A. J., Moghaddam, B., & Turmon, M. (2012). *Flashes in a Star Stream: Automated Classification of Astronomical Transient Events*. Retrieved from https://arxiv.org/ftp/arxiv/papers/1209/1209.1681.pdf

Genovese, C. R., Freeman, P., Wasserman, L., Nichol, R. C., & Miller, C. (2009). Inference for the Dark Energy equation of state using Type Ia Supernova data. *The Annals of Applied Statistics*, *3*(1), 144–178. doi:10.1214/08-AOAS229

Ishida, E. E. O. (2012). Kernel PCA for Supernovae Photometric Classification. *Proceedings of the International Astronomical Union*, *10*(H16), 683–684. doi:10.1017/S1743921314012897

Karpenka, N. V., Feroz, F., & Hobson, M. P. (2013). *A simple and robust method for automated photometric classification of supernovae using neural networks*. MNRAS429,1278–1285. Retrieved from http://arxiv.org/find/astro-ph/1/au:+Souza_R/0/1/0/all/0/1

Phillips. (1993). Article. *Astrophys. J., 413*, L105.

Richards, Homrighausen, Freeman, Schafer, Poznanski. (2012). Semi-supervised learning for Photometric Supernova Classification. *Monthly Notices of the Royal Astronomical Society*, *419*, 1121–1135. doi:10.1111/j.1365-2966.2011.19768.x

Riess, , Strolger, L.-G., Casertano, S., Ferguson, H. C., Mobasher, B., Gold, B., & Stern, D. et al. (2007). New Hubble Space Telescope Discoveries of Type Ia Supernovae at z > 1: Narrowing Constraints on the Early Behavior of Dark Energy. *The Astrophysical Journal*, *659*(1), 98–121. doi:10.1086/510378

Supernovae and Gamma-Ray Bursts. (2013). Dept. of Astrophysics, University of Oxford. Retrieved from http://www-astro.physics.ox.ac.uk/~podsi/sn_podsi.pdf

Type I and Type II Supernovae. (2016). Retrieved from http://hyperphysics.phy-astr.gsu.edu/hbase/astro/snovcn.html#c3

Type Ia supernova data used by Davis, Mörtsell, Sollerman, et al. (2007). Retrieved from http://dark.dark-cosmology.dk/~tamarad/SN/

Veksler, O. (2013). *k Nearest Neigbors*. Retrieved on 04-05-16 from www.csd.uwo.ca/courses/CS9840a/Lecture2_knn.pdf

Wood-Vassey,. (2007). Observational Constraints on the Nature of the Dark Energy: First Cosmological Results from the ESSENCE Supernova Survey. *The Astrophysical Journal*, *666*(2), 694–715. doi:10.1086/518642

Chapter 10

Supervised Learning in Absence of Accurate Class Labels:
A Multi-Instance Learning Approach

Ramasubramanian Sundararajan
GE Global Research, India

Hima Patel
GE Global Research, India

Manisha Srivastava
GE Global Research, India

ABSTRACT

Traditionally supervised learning algorithms are built using labeled training data. Accurate labels are essential to guide the classifier towards an optimal separation between the classes. However, there are several real world scenarios where the class labels at an instance level may be unavailable or imprecise or difficult to obtain, or in situations where the problem is naturally posed as one of classifying instance groups. To tackle these challenges, we draw your attention towards Multi Instance Learning (MIL) algorithms where labels are available at a bag level rather than at an instance level. In this chapter, we motivate the need for MIL algorithms and describe an ensemble based method, wherein the members of the ensemble are lazy learning classifiers using the Citation Nearest Neighbour method. Diversity among the ensemble methods is achieved by optimizing their parameters using a multi-objective optimization method, with the objective being to maximize positive class accuracy and minimize false positive rate. We demonstrate results of the methodology on the standard Musk 1 dataset.

DOI: 10.4018/978-1-5225-2498-4.ch010

1. INTRODUCTION

Supervised learning algorithms usually have a set of input samples and corresponding labels associated with that data. The goal of building a classifier is then to find a suitable boundary that can predict correct labels on test or unseen data. A lot of research has been carried out to build robust supervised learning algorithms that can battle the challenges of nonlinear separations, class imbalances etc.

However, the implicit assumption is that there exists a set of labels for the training data. This assumption may sometimes be expensive or not practical in the real world. In this chapter, we would like to draw your attention towards a set of algorithms where labels are not available at an instance level but rather at a coarser level – "bag" level. A bag is nothing but a collection of instances or individual data points. A bag is labeled positive if it contains at least one positive instance (which may or may not be specifically identified), and negative otherwise. This class of problems is known as multi-instance learning (MIL) problems.

This setting is applicable in a number of problems where traditional two-class classifiers may face one or more of the following difficulties:

Precise Labeling Unavailable

Getting precisely labeled instances is difficult or time-consuming, whereas a precise labeling at a coarser level can be more easily obtained for a larger sample of instances.

Consider the problem of automatically identifying patients who suffer from a certain ailment, based on detection of certain abnormalities in medical images acquired through any appropriate modality (X-ray, CT, MRI, microscopy etc.). Building a model for such automatic identification usually involves creating a labeled sample for training, i.e., having an expert mark out these abnormalities in patients who have the said ailment, and creating a training dataset that contains both these images as well as those from normal patients. The model itself is usually some sort of classifier that operates either on images, or regions of interest thereof, or on individual pixels. This method is very well understood and applied in practice.

However, while obtaining ground truth, i.e., labeled examples, certain practical difficulties exist. For instance, the expert may not mark all abnormalities in an image comprehensively and accurately. Another situation could be, if the expert is marking out pink/red colored rod-shaped objects in a microscopy image of a sputum smear slide to indicate the presence of Mycobacterium Tuberculosis, he/she may just mark a few to convey that the patient has the disease, rather than marking every one of them. Also, the marking may be a single pixel inside the object, or an approximate bounding box, rather than a perfect contour of the bacterium. In some cases, the expert may simply mark the image/patient as abnormal rather than mark out the specific region of abnormality, especially in cases where the abnormal region is of diffuse character (e.g. late stage Pneumoconiosis on PA chest x-rays).

These practical issues consequently introduce some noise in the labels either through unmarked or approximately marked abnormalities. The level of granularity at which the label can be considered reliable is the image/patient itself.

From a traditional classification approach, this throws up two options:

1. Learn at a pixel/ROI level in the presence of label noise. While some classifiers are relatively robust to label noise, their accuracy is generally poorer than when they are learnt without noise. This

means that, in cases where the patient has very few regions of abnormality, any error will lead to a misdiagnosis, which is not ideal.

2. Learn at a patient level, by characterizing each image (or set of images corresponding to a patient) using a single feature set and then training the classifier using these features and the patient level class labels. The trouble with this approach is that the features themselves are likely to characterize both normal and abnormal regions of the image; depending on the size of the abnormality relative to the size of the image and the nature of the features themselves, the performance of the classifier built using this approach is likely to vary considerably.

A third option, which is proposed in the computer aided diagnosis (CAD) literature pertains to multi-instance learning. The idea is to consider each image (or images pertaining to a patient) as a bag of instances. The individual instances in the bag may either be pixels or regions of interest (identified using a method with high sensitivity but not necessarily a low false positive rate). These instance bags are labeled using the patient labels. Application of MIL in these scenarios allows for classification of patients as normal / abnormal based on labels at one or more, but not all images for a given patient.

In this chapter, we describe a generic algorithm for building an ensemble based method for multi instance learning. Here the members of the ensemble are lazy learning classifiers learnt using the Citation Nearest Neighbour method. Diversity among the ensemble members is achieved by optimizing their parameters using a multiobjective optimization algorithm, with the objectives being to maximize positive class accuracy and minimize false positive rate.

The organization of this chapter is as follows: Section 2 briefly describes the prior work in this area. Section 3 describes the proposed method. Section 4 describes an application of this method to a benchmark dataset, along with some results. Section 5 concludes with some directions for further work.

2. LITERATURE REVIEW

The MIL problem was first discussed in Dietterich et al. (1997), who also proposed a learning algorithm based on axis-parallel rectangles to solve it. Subsequently, a number of other researchers in the area have proposed MIL algorithms, notably Wang and Zucker (2000); Zhang and Zhou (2009); Zhou and Zhang (2007); Maron and Lozano-Perez (1998); Viola et al. (2006); Andrews et al. (2002). For a survey of MIL algorithms, please refer to Babenko (2008); Zhou (2004). In our algorithm, we specifically focus on extending the lazy learning approach proposed in Wang and Zucker (2000).

Applications of MIL to real-life problems have been explored in the literature as well. Examples are primarily to be found in the computer-aided diagnostics and image classification area in the form of both papers D. Wu and Boyer (2009); Fung et al. (2007); Bi and Liang (2007)) and patents Bi and Liang (2010); Krishnapuram et al. (2009); Rao et al. (2011).

The idea of using ensembles for classification in general has been explored extensively in the literature. While Zhang and Zhou (2009); Zhou and Zhang (2007) discuss the use of ensembles in the MIL context, the method by which the ensemble elements are combined is fairly straightforward (simple voting scheme). Bi and Liang (2007) propose the use of a cascaded ensemble of linear SVMs combined using an AND-OR framework, but with the key difference that all elements in the cascade are optimized simultaneously and the execution order of the classifiers is not decided a priori.

We approach the ensemble construction problem from the generalized standpoint suggested in Wolpert (1992) – it is possible that each classifier in the ensemble has learnt a different aspect of the underlying problem; however, combining them may require an additional layer of complexity. We therefore use the stacked generalization approach Wolpert (1992), wherein a second layer classifier is used to combine the outputs of the first layer ensemble of classifiers. This second layer classifier operates like a single-instance learner, and can therefore be built using any of a variety of standard classifier methods, such as support vector machines, random forests and so on Breiman et al. (1984); Breiman and Schapire (2001); Cristianini and Shawe-Taylor (2000).

3. METHODOLOGY

Consider a set of instance bags $\{B^1; B^2, ..., B^N\}$, where each bag B^i contains instances $\{X_1^i, ..., X_{N_i}^i\}$ and is labeled $Y^i \in \{-1, +1\}$ – we shall refer to them as positive and negative bags. The specific instance-level labels y_j^i for X_j^i may be unknown, except that Y^i is set to 1 if at least one of Y_j^i is 1, and -1 otherwise. The task of the proposed algorithm is to predict the true label Y^{new} for an unseen bag B^{new}. Let the prediction be denoted by $\hat{Y}^{new}$.

The broad steps followed by the proposed classifier are as follows (see Figure 1):

1. Use an ensemble of multi instance classifiers that use the Citation Nearest Neighbour technique. Let the classifiers be denoted by $C_{(j)}, j = 1, ..., J$, and the predictions from these classifiers for B^{new} be denoted by $\hat{Y}^{new}_{(j)} = C_{(j)}(B^{new})$. Each classifier uses a different set of parameters, so that diversity among the ensemble is maintained.

Figure 1. Proposed multi instance learning classifier

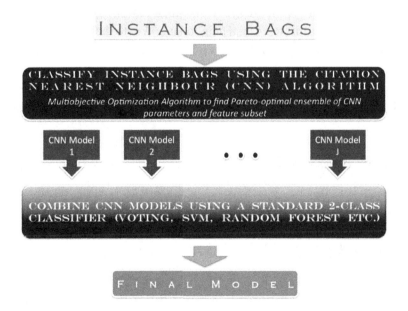

Algorithm 1. Prediction on an unseen bag

Input: *Training sample: Train =* $\{B^1, B^2, ..., B^N\}$ *, where each bag* B^i *contains instances* $\{X_1^i, ..., X_{N_i}^i\}$ *and is labeled* $Y_i \in \{-1, +1\}$
CNN classifiers: $C_{(1)}, ...C_{(J)}$
Final classifier: F
Unseen instance bag: B^{new}
Output: *Prediction for* B^{new} *:* $\hat{Y}^{new}$
begin
1. Apply each CNN classifier $C_{(j)}, j = 1...J$ *to* B^{new} *. Let*
$\hat{Y}_j^{new} = C_{(j)}(Train, B^{new})$
be the prediction from the jth *CNN classifier.*
2. Combine the predictions using the final classifier F. Let
$\hat{Y}^{new} = F(\hat{Y}_{(1)}^{new}, ..\hat{Y}_{(J)}^{new})$
be the final prediction for B^{new}
3. Return $\hat{Y}^{new}$
end

2. Combine the predictions $\hat{Y}^{new}_{(1)}$ ...., $\hat{Y}^{new}_{(J)}$ using a normal classifier F and return the final prediction, i.e., $\hat{Y}^{new} = F(\hat{Y}^{new}_{(1)}, ..., \hat{Y}^{new}_{(J)})$.

In the following subsections, we describe how this classifier is built. Section 3.1 describes the Citation Nearest Neighbour (CNN) classifier for multi-instance learning. Section 3.2 describes how an ensemble of CNN classifiers is built, and the predictions of the ensemble combined to get the final prediction.

3.1. Citation Nearest Neighbor Algorithm

Our proposed algorithm uses a customized version of a simple, yet effective lazy learning method, namely the Citation Nearest Neighbour (CNN) technique, originally proposed in Wang and Zucker (2000).

The CNN technique is simply a nearest neighbour technique with an additional inversion step. We find references, i.e., the neighbours of a test bag and note their labels. Similarly, we find citers, i.e., those training bags that would consider this test bag a neighbour and note their labels as well. We then arrive at a final result based on whether the positive bags in references and citers put together outnumber the negative bags.

The distance between bags is normally calculated using a metric called the minimal Hausdorff distance. Given two bags $A^1 = \{a_1^1, ..., a_p^1\}$ and $A^2 = \{a_1^2, ..., a_q^2\}$, the Hausdorff distance is defined as:

$$H(A^1, A^2) = \max(h(A^1, A^2), h(A^2, A^1)) \tag{1}$$

where

$$h(A_1, A_2) = \max_{a \in A^1} \min_{b \in A^2} d(a_j, b_k) \tag{2}$$

where $d(a,b)$ is an appropriately defined distance metric between two instances a and b. However, this metric is quite sensitive to the presence of any outlying point in either bag, whose minimum distance from any of the instances in the other bag may be quite high. Therefore, a modified version of Equation (2) is used:

$$h_{(d)}(A^1, A^2) = d^{th} \max_{a \in A^1} \min_{b \in A^2} d(a_j, b_k) \tag{3}$$

when d = p (number of instances in bag A), equations (2) and (3) are equivalent. When d = 1, the minimum of individual point distances between the two bags decide the inter-bag distance.

Given a test bag, let X_R be the number of references, i.e., training sample bags that can be considered as neighbours (i.e., having low Hausdorff distance) to the test bag. This can be found by defining a neighborhood size N_R – this means that the training bags within N_R distance from the test bag are to be considered as references.

Algorithm 2. Citation Nearest Neighbor (CNN) Classifier

Input: *Training Sample: Train = { B^1,..B^T }, where each bag B^i contains instances $\{X^i_1, ...X^i_N\}$ and is labeled $Y^i \in \{-1, +1\}$. Each individual instance X^i_l is described by an m dimensional feature $\left(X^i_{l(1)}, ..., X^i_{l(m)}\right)$.*

Threshold defining references: η_R

Threshold defining citers: η_C
Rank used in Hausdorff distance: d
Feature Subset: $S \subseteq \{1, ..m\}$
Threshold for classification: θ

Unseen instance bag: B^{tst}

Output: *Prediction for $\hat{B}^{tst}$: $\hat{Y}^{tst}$*
begin
function $\hat{Y}^{tst} = CNN(Train, \eta_R, \eta_C, d, S, \theta, B^{tst})$

1. Calculate the $\Lambda_{(T+1)XT}$ matrix of pairwise distances between instance bags, where:

a. If $i \leq T$, **then** $\Lambda_{i,j} = H(B^i, B^j)$, **else** $\Lambda_{i,j} = H(B^i, B^{tst})$

b. The Hausdorff distance $H(A^1, A^2) = \max(h_{(d)}(A^1, A^2), h_{(d)}(A^2, A^1))$ (see equation 3)

c. The distance metric $d(a,b)$ between instance pairs of two bags is to be calculated on the feature subset S

2. $\chi_R^+ = 0, \chi_C^+ = 0, \chi_R^- = 0, \chi_C^- = 0$

3. For each B^i i = 1 to N:

a. IF $\Lambda_{T+1,i}$ is within the η_R smallest values in $\Lambda_{T+1,.}$ and $Y^i = +1$, **then** $\chi_R^+ = \chi_R^+ + 1$

b. IF $\Lambda_{T+1,i}$ is within the η_R smallest values in $\Lambda_{T+1,.}$ and $Y^i = -1$, **then** $\chi_R^- = \chi_R^- + 1$

c. IF $\Lambda_{T+1,i}$ is within the η_R smallest values in $\Lambda_{.,i}$ and $Y^i = +1$, **then** $\chi_C^+ = \chi_C^+ + 1$

d. IF $\Lambda_{T+1,i}$ is within the η_R smallest values in $\Lambda_{.,i}$ and $Y^i = -1$, **then** $\chi_C^- = \chi_C^- + 1$

4. Calculate the classifier score for this example as:

$Score = \dfrac{\chi_R^+ + \chi_C^+}{\chi_R^+ + \chi_C^+ + \chi_R^- + \chi_C^-}$

5. IF $Score \geq \theta$, **then** $\hat{Y}^{tst} = +1$ **else** $\hat{Y}^{tst} = -1$

6. Return $\hat{Y}^{tst}$
end

Similarly, let X_C be the number of citers, i.e., training sample bags that would consider the test bag their neighbor – this means that the training bags for which the test bag falls within the lowest X_C distances from them are to be considered as citers.

Note that the two concepts are not identical – the test bag may be closest to a particular training bag, but from the standpoint of that training bag, there may be other training bags that are closer to it than the test bag.

Now, let $X_R{}^+$ and $X_R{}^-$ be the number of positively and negatively labeled bags among the references, and $X_C{}^+$ and $X_C{}^-$ be the number of positively and negatively labeled bags among the citers. The predicted label for the test bag B^{new} is +1 if:

$$\frac{X_R^+ + X_C^+}{X^R + X^C} \geq \theta \text{, where } \theta = 0.5 \text{ typically} \tag{4}$$

and, -1 otherwise. In other words, if there are more positively labeled references and citers for the test bag, its predicted label is positive. See Algorithm 1 and 3 for pseudo-codes for overall scheme for prediction on an unseen instance bag and CNN classifiers.

3.1.1. Customizing CNN Model

Optimizing the CNN model typically involves finding the number of references and citers to use (in other words, fix N_R and N_C), as well as the value of the rank d in the Hausdorff distance calculation (empirically, d = 1 has been found to be effective in most cases).

However, we consider the following additional customizations:

1. In problems where we also know the instance labels (but where it is still beneficial to solve the problem as one of multiple instance learning), we could give higher importance to proximity with a positively labeled instance inside a positively labeled bag. Since the logic behind the CNN algorithm is that the positive examples across bags are likely to fall close to each other in the feature space, this customizations may allow us to exploit such proximity to a greater extent.
2. While comparing the labels of references and citers put together, we could give higher importance to positive bags than negative ones. This may be useful in situations where the cost of misclassification is asymmetric or where the user is primarily interested in optimizing the accuracy on the positive class, while keeping false positives below an acceptable limit.
3. In situations where the feature set describing each instance is quite large, there is the problem of feature selection in order to arrive at a parsimonious model with good generalization ability.

Given the above customizations, it is intuitive that one would need to have a process whereby these parameters are appropriately set for the problem in question. Given that our ultimate objective is to create a classifier that can predict the true label of an unseen test instance bag B^{new} with high accuracy, the ideal combination of parameters ought to be one that maximizes this generalization ability.

In order to estimate generalization ability, we typically use the cross-validation technique. In other words, we take out some of the instance bags in the training sample (known as the training subsample) to use for training, train a model on this part, and test the model on the remaining instance bags (known

Algorithm 3. Leave-one-out validation for CNN Classifier

Input: *Training sample: Train = $\{B^1, B^2, ..., B^N\}$, where each bag B^i contains instances $\{X^i_1, ..., X^i_{N_i}\}$ and is labeled $Y_i \in \{-1, +1\}$.*

Each individual instance X^i_l is described by an m-dimensional feature vector $(X^i_{l(1)}, ..., X^i_{l(m)})$.

Threshold defining references: η_R

Threshold defining citers: η_C
Rank used in Hausdorff distance: d
Feature subset: $S \subseteq \{1...m\}$
Threshold for classification: θ

Output: *Class +1 (positive) accuracy: Acc^+*

Class -1 (negative) accuracy: Acc^-

Validation outputs: $\hat{Y}^i$, i = 1...N.
begin
function $(Acc^+, Acc^-, \hat{Y}^1, ...\hat{Y}^N) = LOO(Train, \eta_R, \eta_C, d, S, \theta)$

1. Initialize $n^+ = 0$, $n^- = 0$, $a^+ = 0, a^- = 0$
2. **For** *i = 1,...,N*

 (a) Set Training subsample: $TS^i = Train - B^i$

 (b) Set validation subsample: B^i

 (c) **If** $Y^i = +1$ **then** $n^+ = n^+ + 1$ **else** $n^- = n^- + 1$

 (d) Call $\hat{Y}^i = CNN(TS^i, \eta_R, \eta_C, d, S, \theta, B^i)$ (see Algorithm 2)

 (e) **If** $Y^i = \hat{Y}^i$ **and** $Y^i = +1$ **then** $a^+ = a^+ + 1$

 (f) **If** $Y^i = \hat{Y}^i$ **and** $Y^i = -1$ **then** $a^- = a^- + 1$

3. *Calculate* $Acc^+ = \dfrac{a^+}{n^+}, Acc^- = \dfrac{a^-}{n^-}$

4. **Return** $(Acc^+, Acc^-, \hat{Y}^1, ...\hat{Y}^N)$
end

---

as the validation subsample) as a way of checking its performance on un-seen examples. However, in order to avoid sample bias, we need to do this repeatedly and choose different ways to split the training sample into training and validation subsamples.

A systematic way to do this would be to split the dataset into roughly equal sized chunks (say k chunks). In each iteration, one of the chunks is used as the validation subsample while the other chunks together comprise the training subsample. By doing this with each chunk in turn, we ensure that all examples in the training subsample are used in the validation subsample at some point or another. The average performance of the validation subsamples across these iterations is used as a measure of generalization ability (performance on unseen examples). This approach is referred to as k-fold validation in the literature.

An extreme case of this procedure is one where each split contains only one example in the validation subsample – this method of splitting is repeated as many times as the number of examples in the training sample, and the average performance on the validation subsamples across all these splits is reported as an estimate of generalization ability. This approach is called the leave-one-out strategy (see Algorithm 3). Depending on the size of the dataset (i.e., the number of instance bags), one can choose either the k-fold validation technique or the leave-one-out strategy.

The customization process can therefore be described as follows:

1. Consider a set of potential combinations of parameters for the CNN model. These include N_R, N_C, d, relative importance of positive to negative bags while calculating the final label (θ), subset of features to use while calculating the distance metric etc.

2. For each potential combination, estimate the generalization ability using the leave-one-out or similar method.
3. Choose the parameter combination that achieves the best generalization ability.

3.2 Building the Ensemble of CNN Classifiers

When we consider the method described in Section 3.1.1, above to customize a CNN model, two things become obvious:

- The number of parameters to tune is sufficiently large that the problem of searching through all combinations of parameters may be non-trivial from a computational perspective. Therefore, one may need a smart search algorithm to identify the best combination of parameters from a large possible set.
- Typically, one wishes to identify a model that maximizes the likelihood of identifying a positively labeled bag correctly, while also minimizing the likelihood of false positives (i.e., negatively labeled bags incorrectly identified). Different parameter combinations are likely to optimize these two metrics in different ways, as they will have different views of the problem space.

There is merit in combining diverse views of the same problem to arrive at a more balanced view overall; therefore, we build an ensemble of CNN classifiers.

We accomplish this by using a multi-objective search heuristic such as NGSA-II Deb et al. (2002) to find the optimal CNN parameters. The search algorithm is asked to find the best set of parameters that optimize the following objectives:

1. Maximize the likelihood of classifying a positive instance bag correctly
2. Maximize the likelihood of classifying a negative instance bag correctly

These two objectives are estimated using the leave-one-out method described in Section 3.1.1. Note that these two objectives may be in conflict in any problem where perfect separability between the classes is not achievable at the given level of solution complexity. Therefore, the multi-objective search algorithm will throw up a set of candidate solutions, each of which optimizes these two objectives at varying degrees of relative importance.

Theoretically, the best possible set is known as a Pareto frontier of solutions. Any solution in the Pareto frontier cannot be considered superior to another in the frontier (i.e. if it improves on one objective, it loses on another simultaneously), but can be considered superior to all other solutions available. (Note that in this case, when we use the word solution, we refer to a parameter set for the CNN algorithm, and by performance, we refer to the ability to identify positive and negative bags correctly, as measured using the leave-one-out method.)

In practice, a multi-objective optimizer such as NGSA-II will try and arrive at a good approximation to the Pareto frontier, and will output a diverse set of solutions (i.e., parameter combinations for CNN) that optimize the two objectives at varying degrees of relative importance. These solutions constitute the ensemble we wished to construct. The method of combining these solutions is described in Section 3.2.1. Algorithm 4 gives the pseudo code for the same.

Algorithm 4. Optimizing the parameters for CNN using a multi-objective optimization algorithm

---

Input: *Training sample: Train =* $\{B^1, B^2, ..., B^N\}$ *, where each bag* B^i *contains instances* $\{X_1^i, ..., X_{N_i}^i\}$ *and is labeled* $Y_i \in \{-1, +1\}$

Output: *CNN classifiers:* $C_{(1)}, ..., C_{(J)}$

begin

function $(C_{(1)}, ..., C_{(J)}) = MOO(Train)$

Formulation The problem of finding the optimal ensemble of CNN classifiers is stated as follows:

$\max Acc^+(C, Train)$

$\max Acc^-(C, Train)$

where *(5)*

$C = (\eta_R, \eta_C, d, S, \theta)$ *See Algorithm2*

$(Acc^+, Acc^-, \hat{Y}^1, ..., \hat{Y}^N) = LOO(Train, \eta_R, \eta_C, d, S, \theta)$ *See Algorithm3*

Each candidate solution (CNN classifier) is parameterized in terms of the following variables (see Algorithm 2): $(\eta_R, \eta_C, d, S, \theta)$. The goodness of each candidate solution is the leave-one-out validation performance of the classifier, in terms of accuracy in identifying positive and negative bags (see Algorithm 3).

Result A Pareto-optimal set of candidate solutions $C_{(1)}, ..., C_{(J)}$, where every pair $C_{(i)}, C_{(j)}$ of solutions is such that, if $Acc_{(i)}^+ > Acc_{(j)}^+$, then $Acc_{(i)}^- < Acc_{(j)}^-$ and vice-versa. This means that, without any additional information that allows us to choose betweenaccuracy on positive bags versus accuracy on negative bags, we cannot choose between any of the solutions in the Pareto-optimal set.

end

3.2.1. Combining the CNN Classifiers in the Ensemble

As described earlier, we construct an ensemble of CNN models in order to capture diverse views of the problem to be solved. However, the task lies before us to combine these views. The simplest method of combination would be to let all the models vote on a test instance bag, and let the majority decide the label. However, it is possible that the optimal method of combination of these diverse views (as represented by the CNN models in the ensemble) calls for a greater degree of complexity than a voting scheme.

Therefore, we propose the use of the stacked generalization method Wolpert (1992), wherein we build a second level classifier F, which will combine the predictions of the various CNN models in order to return the final prediction. F can be any two-class classifier such as a support vector machine, random forest etc. See Algorithm 5.

In order to train this classifier, we use the predictions obtained from each member of the ensemble for each instance bag through the validation method described in Section 3.1.1. One can also choose to optimize the parameters of this classifier using the NSGA-II or similar algorithm, as described in Section 3.2 above.

4. EMPIRICAL VALIDATION

We demonstrate the utility of our proposed method on the Musk 1 dataset taken from the UCI Machine Learning repository. This dataset describes a set of 92 molecules of which 47 are judged by human experts to be musks and the remaining 45 molecules are judged to be non-musks. The goal is to learn to predict whether new molecules will be musks or non-musks. However, the 166 features that describe these molecules depend upon the exact shape, or conformation, of the molecule. Because bonds can rotate, a single molecule can adopt many different shapes. To generate this data set, the low-energy conformations

Algorithm 5. Building a stacked ensemble of CNN classifiers

Input: *Training sample*: $Train = \{B^1, B^2 \ldots B^n\}$, where each bag B^i contains instances $\{X_1^i \ldots X_{N_i}^i\}$ and is labeled $Y^i \in \{-1, +1\}$

Output: *CNN Classifiers*: $C_{(1)} \ldots C_{(J)}$

Final classifier: F

begin

function $(C_{(1)} \ldots C_{(J)}, F) = StackEns(Train)$

CNN classifiers Call a multiobjective optimization algorithm (e.g. NSGA-II) to find an optimal ensemble of CNN classifiers (see Algorithm 4):

$(C_{(1)} \ldots C_{(J)}) = MOO(Train)$

Training sample for stacked ensemble Construct the training sample for generating the seconf stage classifier, i.e., construct $T2_{N \times J}$ where $T2_{.j}$ is the set of leave-one-out predictions $(\hat{Y}_{(j)}^1 \ldots \hat{Y}_{(j)}^N)$ obtained for classifier $C_{(j)}$, through the following function call (see Algorithm 3):

$(Acc_{(j)}^+, Acc_{(j)}^-, \hat{Y}_{(j)}^1 \ldots \hat{Y}_{(j)}^N) = LOO(Train, \eta_{R(j)}, \eta_{C(j)}, d_{(j)}, S_{(j)}, \theta_{(j)})$

Each row $T2_{i.}$ is associated with the class label Y^i for bag B^i.

Final classifier Build a standard 2-class classifier F using the labeled training set $T2$ generated above.

Return $(C_{(1)} \ldots C_{(J)}, F)$

end

---

of the molecules were generated and then filtered to remove highly similar conformations. This left 476 conformations. Then, a feature vector was extracted that describes each conformation.

This many-to-one relationship between feature vectors and molecules lends itself naturally to a multiple instance problem. When learning a classifier for this data, the classifier should classify a molecule as musk if any of its conformations is classified as musk. A molecule should be classified as non-musk if none of its conformations is classified as a musk, refer Bache and Lichman (2013).

4.1. CNN Models

The solution parameters to be optimized are the CNN model parameters, as well as the feature subset used to compute distance between instances. Since this is a large-scale multi-objective optimization problem with objectives where the gradient is ill-defined, we use a direct search method such as a multi-objective genetic algorithm to solve it. Specifically, we use the Non-dominated Sorting Genetic Algorithm II (NSGA-II) to optimize the CKNN parameters and feature subset Deb et al. (2002), Deb (2001).

Table 1. Citation Nearest Neighbour algorithm results arrived at using the NSGA-II optimization method

Class 0 accuracy	Class 1 accuracy	# Models
100%	91.49%	12
95.56%	95.74%	42
93.33%	97.87%	16
84.44%	100%	30

Table 2. Selection of solutions arrived at using the stacked ensemble

Class 0 accuracy	Class 1 accuracy	#Models
100%	93.61%	76
97.78%	100%	24

The fitness functions (Class +1 and Class 1 accuracy) are calculated for each solution (i.e., CKNN parameters and feature subset) by considering the average performance on cross-validation samples obtained using the leave-one-out method. This method has been shown to give good estimates of generalization ability Vapnik (1998), and would therefore help us in arriving at the best possible model.

Since NSGA-II is a multi-objective optimization method, its purpose is to generate a Pareto frontier of solutions (CKNN models), namely those which represent the best possible trade-off between the various objectives (Class +1 and Class 1 accuracy). Table 1 gives a summary of the results.

4.2. Stacked Ensemble

We find that the results of the CNN algorithm, tuned as described in Section 4.1 above, do not yet approach the performance level desired by us. We therefore consider using an ensemble approach, whereby we combine the predictions of the various CNN models arrived at in the final generation of the NSGA-II run. Since these models approximate the Pareto frontier, it is possible that their combination would allow us to come up with a hybrid model that does even better on both objectives. Also, we wish to keep unrestricted, the method of combination of the CKNN predictions; therefore, we use the stacked generalization approach proposed in Wolpert (1992).

We therefore model the second level learning problem as one of mapping the predictions from the last generation of CKNN models to the desired sequence labels. We choose a Support Vector Machine classifier Cristianini and Shawe-Taylor (2000); Hsu et al. (2000) with a Radial Basis function kernel in order to combine the predictions. In order to optimize the and C parameters of the SVM model, as well as pick the optimal subset of CKNN models whose predictions are to be combined, we again use the NSGA-II algorithm as described in Section 4.1.

4.3. Experimental Results

Since NSGA-II generates a Pareto frontier of solutions, a sample of three solutions of the stacked ensemble model is given in Table 2. These results suggest that the stacking layer improves the trade-off between accuracy on the two classes.

CONCLUSION AND DIRECTIONS FOR FUTURE WORK

We have described a multi instance learning based methodology to tackle the problem of label deficiency. One obvious area of further work is to test it on a diverse set of problems and benchmark it against methods such as those proposed in Dietterich et al. (1997); Zhou and Zhang (2007), as a way of validating the effectiveness of the proposed method. Furthermore, we have noticed that, for problems with large feature sizes, the computational effort required to arrive at a solution can be quite high. Use of Hadoop – Map Reduce, Tensor Flow or other such big data architectures need to be explored further to make this computationally efficient.

REFERENCES

Andrews, S., Tsochantaridis, I., & Hofmann, T. (2002). Support vector machines for multiple-instance learning. Advances in Neural Information Processing Systems, 15.

Babenko, B. (2008). *Multiple instance learning: algorithms and applications. Technical report.* San Diego, CA: University of California.

Bache, K., & Lichman, M. (2013). *UCI machine learning repository.* Retrieved from http://archive.ics. uci.edu/ml

Bi, J., & Liang, J. (2007). Multiple instance learning of pulmonary embolism detection with geodesic distance along vascular structure. *Proceedings of IEEE Conference on Computer Vision and Pattern Recognition.* doi:10.1109/CVPR.2007.383141

Bi, J., & Liang, J. (2010). *Method of multiple instance learning and classification with correlations in object detection.* US Patent No. US7822252 B2.

Bi, J., Wu, D., & Boyer, K. (2009). A min-max framework of cascaded classifier with multiple instance learning for computer aided diagnosis. *Proceedings of IEEE International Conference on Computer Vision and Pattern Recognition.*

Breiman, L., Friedman, J. H., Olshem, R. A., & Stone, C. J. (1984). *Classification and Regression Trees.* London: CRC Press.

Breiman, L., & Schapire, E. (2001). Random forests. *Machine Learning.*

Cristianini, N., & Shawe-Taylor, J. (2000). *An Introduction to Support Vector Machines.* Cambridge University Press.

Deb, K. (2001). *Multi-objective optimization using evolutionary algorithms.* John Wiley and Sons.

Deb, K., Pratap, A., Agarwal, S., & Meyarivan, T. (2002). A fast and elitist multiobjective genetic algorithm: Nsga-ii. *IEEE Transactions on Evolutionary Computation, 6*(2), 182–197. doi:10.1109/4235.996017

Dietterich, T. G., Lathrop, R. H., & Lozano-Perez, T. (1997). Solving the multiple-instance problem with axis-parallel rectangles. *Artificial Intelligence, 89*(1-2), 31–71. doi:10.1016/S0004-3702(96)00034-3

Fung, G., Dundar, M., Krishnapuram, B., & Rao, R. B. (2007). Multiple instance learning for computer aided diagnosis. Advances in Neural Information Processing Systems.

Hsu, Chang, & Lin. (2000). *A practical guide to support vector classification.* Academic Press.

Krishnapuram, B., Raykar, V. C., Dundar, M., & Bharat Rao, R. (2009). *System and method for multiple-instance learning for computer aided diagnosis.* US Patent No. US20090080731 A1.

Maron, O., & Lozano-Perez, T. (1998). A framework for multiple-instance learning. Advances in Neural Information Processing Systems, 10.

Rao, Dundar, Krishnapuram, & Fung. (1998). *System and method for multiple instance learning for computer aided detection*. US Patent No. US7986827 B2.

Vapnik. (2011). *Statistical Learning Theory*. John Wiley & Sons.

Viola, P., Platt, J. C., & Zhang, C. (2006). Multiple instance boosting for object detection. Advances in Neural Information Processing Systems, 18.

Wang, J., & Zucker, J.-D. (2000). Solving the multiple instance problem - a lazy learning approach. *17th International Conference on Machine Learning*.

Wolpert, D. H. (1992). Stacked generalization. *Neural Networks*, *5*(2), 241–259. doi:10.1016/S0893-6080(05)80023-1

Zhang, M.-L., & Zhou, Z.-H. (2009). Multi-instance clustering with applications to multi-instance predic-tion. *Applied Intelligence*, *31*(1), 47–68. doi:10.1007/s10489-007-0111-x

Zhou. (2004). *Multi-instance learning: A survey. Technical report*. Nanjing University.

Zhou, Z.-H., & Zhang, M.-L. (2007). Solving multi-instance problems with classifier ensemble based on constructive clustering. *Knowledge and Information Systems*, *11*(2), 155–170. doi:10.1007/s10115-006-0029-3

Chapter 11
Patient Data De–Identification:
A Conditional Random–Field–Based Supervised Approach

Shweta Yadav
Indian Institute of Technology Patna, India

Sriparna Saha
Indian Institute of Technology Patna, India

Asif Ekbal
Indian Institute of Technology Patna, India

Parth S Pathak
ezDI, LLC, India

Pushpak Bhattacharyya
Indian Institute of Technology Patna, India

ABSTRACT

With the rapid increment in the clinical text, de-identification of patient Protected Health Information (PHI) has drawn significant attention in recent past. This aims for automatic identification and removal of the patient Protected Health Information from medical records. This paper proposes a supervised machine learning technique for solving the problem of patient data de- identification. In the current paper, we provide an insight into the de-identification task, its major challenges, techniques to address challenges, detailed analysis of the results and direction of future improvement. We extract several features by studying the properties of the datasets and the domain. We build our model based on the 2014 i2b2 (Informatics for Integrating Biology to the Bedside) de-identification challenge. Experiments show that the proposed system is highly accurate in de-identification of the medical records. The system achieves the final recall, precision and F-score of 95.69%, 99.31%, and 97.46%, respectively.

INTRODUCTION

With the start of the golden era in the medical interpretation, the vast amount of information in the clinical domain is increasing at a rapid rate. In the past decade, with the development of the health information technology and health data documentation, there has been progress in how heath care is performed (Berner et al., 2005).

DOI: 10.4018/978-1-5225-2498-4.ch011

With the widespread use of health information technology, there has been huge pace in the increment of clinical data in addition to the fast adoption of the Electronic Clinical Records and with the conversion of narrative data to the electronic form. The amount of information can be improved further with the minimization of the medical error. This requires the development of some sophisticated tools for Medical Language Processing (MLP). Most medical records are in the narrative forms which are formed as the result of transcription of dictations, direct entry by providers, or use of speech recognition applications. However, their use in this form is restricted to any organization or research, as medical records have a sufficient number of personal health information or protected health information (PHI). According to Health Insurance Portability and Accountability Act (HIPAA), 1996, the PHI terms need to be enclosed and protected. This has lead to de- identification problem. Paragraph 164.514 of the Administrative Simplification Regulations promulgated under the Health Insurance Portability and Accountability Act (HIPAA) states that for data to be treated as de-identified, it must clear one of two hurdles (HIPPA ACT 1996).

1. An expert must determine and document "that the risk is very small that the information could be used, alone or in combination with other reasonably available information, by an anticipated recipient to identify an individual who is a subject of the information."
2. Or, the data must be purged from a specified list of seventeen categories of possible identifiers relating to the patient or relatives, household members and employers, and any other information that may make it possible to identify the individual.

Studies showed that there was a significant drop in the patient consent request reducing the participation rate and also, this is quite infeasible for the huge population. Even, in the case when a patient provides the permission, documents must be tracked to stop any unauthorized disclosure. This emerging problem of consent, waiver, and tracking can be effectively handled if the patient personal health information is properly de-identified facilitating the clinical NLP research (Wolf & Bennett, 2006).

De-identification task is more specifically defined as the step where the private information is removed or replaced while keeping the record as it is (Stubbs et al., 2015). De-identification is a type of traditional named entity recognition (NER) problem, with the property of defining a term to be PHI type or not. The main aim of de-identification challenge as pointed out earlier is to remove the PHI terms maintaining data integrity as much as possible. Every record is enclosed in the RECORD_ tags and is provided a unique ID which is randomly generated. Figure 1 shows Sample Discharge Summary Excerpt; a sample discharge summary from the training dataset where the goal is to identify the PHI (private health information) terms. In this summary, some the PHI terms are doctors' name ("Dr. Do Little"), patient name ("John Doe") and hospital name ("ABHG", "SBHG"). A TEXT_ tag encloses the text of different records. Each PHI instance is enclosed within PHI_ tags and the PHI TYPE represents the category of the PHI term as shown in Figure 1.

As shown in Figure 1, the task is to enclose the PHI terms such as ("Dr. Do Little", "John Doe", "ABHG", "SBHG"). This task can be seen as the typical sequence labeling task where for e.g. "Dr. Do Little" should be labeled as whole with Doctor. Here, we present an example where input forms the sequence of words and output is the label sequence and its corresponding de-identified sentence. "BIO" notation was followed to label the NE where "B" represents the beginning of label sequence, "I" denotes intermediate of label sequence and "O" represents others.

Figure 1. Sample discharge summary excerpt

```
<RECORD ID="641">
<TEXT>
<PHI TYPE="HOSPITAL">SBHG</PHI>
HISTORY OF PRESENT ILLNESS:
Mr. <PHI TYPE="PATIENT">Doe</PHI> is a XX-year-old white male with a history of
diabetes mellitus , inferior myocardial infarction , who underwent open repair of his
increased diverticulum <PHI TYPE="DATE">January 1st</PHI> at <PHI
TYPE="HOSPITAL"> ABHG</PHI> .
No cardiopulmonary resuscitation was performed as per the patient and family wishes
DISCHARGE SUMMARY
ARF32 FA
DISCHARGE SUMMARY NAME:
UNIT NUMBER:
<PHI TYPE="PATIENT">JOHN DOE</PHI>
ADMISSION DATE:
<PHI TYPE="DATE">01/01/1900 </PHI>
DISCHARGE DATE:
<PHI TYPE="DATE">01/02/1900 </PHI>
DD:
<PHI TYPE="DOCTOR">Dr.  Do little</PHI>, M.D.
</RECORD>
```

Table 1. Example of PDI task following BIO notation

Sentence	Mr.	John	D	Doe	is	xx-year-old	white	male
Named Identity	O	B-Doctor	I-Doctor	I-Doctor	O	O	O	O
De-Identified Sentence	Mr.	XYZ_Doctor			is	xx-year-old	White	male

In the past few years, de-identification of the clinical record has become the booming research area. Sixth Message Understanding Conference (MUC) had defined the Named Entity Recognition (NER) problem with an objective to identify the relevant entities from the text. NER forms an important task in NLP. Similarly, in the medical domain, NER is very crucial in the identification of the clinical terms by which we can get insights to the problem, medication, procedure, and examination.

Major research works for entity extraction in the medical domain had used machine learning and rule-based concepts. MedLEE (Friedman et al., 1996) is one such system in clinical domain proposed by Carol Friedman et al. at Columbia University. Aronson (2001) developed MetaMap system at National Library of Medicine. Another system cTAKES (Savova et al., 2010), developed using Unstructured Information Management Architecture (UIMA) framework and OpenNLP, a widely accepted system.

Recently, the Medical Natural Language Processing Community had organized a number of challenges for NER task. The earliest shared task is organized by Center of Informatics for Integrating Biology and the Bedside (i2b2) in 2009 on medical name recognition (Uzuner et al., 2010). In 2010, i2b2 shared task was conducted with the aim to identify the medical problems, test entities and various treatments from the clinical records (Uzuner et al., 2011). Since then, Conference and Labs of the Evaluation Forum (CLEF) had organized a challenge in 2013 with the aim of solving disorder mention recognition and normalization (Goeuriot et al., 2013). Very recently, i2b2 in 2014 (Stubbs et al., 2015) had organized a challenge for patient data de-identification problem and CUI (concept unique identifier) detection. Semantic Evaluation (SemEval) 2014 also came up with the disorder mention recognition and the normalization. With a large number of challenges organized almost every year, it had drawn the attention of many researchers to solve these real-life challenging problems.

Different approaches have been used to solve this problem ranging from machine learning techniques (Stubbs et al., 2015; Yang et al., 2015), rule-based system (Beckwith et al., 2006; Berman et al., 2003) to the hybrid system. Rule-based systems are designed over dictionaries with the rules that are designed manually to recognize the PHI terms from the text. Building a system using rules lacks generalization capability as well as it consumes more time and skill for developing rules. Rule-based systems are seen to provide good performance for the PHI terms those appear less often. This has lead to the development of some machine learning techniques for automatic extraction of PHI terms from the text which makes the process more generalized. The only drawback of machine learning based approach is the requirement of having large annotated corpus which can be developed manually.

Generally, the NER problem is the sequence labeling problem where the aim is to identify the proper output sequence of the entities. Thus, for the given input sequence of words, we need to obtain the best labeled- sequence. Researchers have primarily used supervised machine learning algorithms to solve this kind of medical NER problem. The algorithms used for extracting medical entities are Conditional Random Fields (CRFs) (Lafferty et al., 2001), Maximum Entropy (ME) (McCallum et al., 2000), and Structural Support Vector Machines (SSVMs) (Xue et al., 2008). Among these different classifiers, Conditional Random Field had drawn a huge attention for solving the sequence labeling task. Top best system (Yang et al., 2015) of de-identification task had used CRF as the underlying classifier because of the property of CRF to properly map the relationships between their surrounding tokens. Supervised machine learning techniques are able to capture the handcrafted features very effectively. Some of the prominent features which have been used are orthographic features that capture the word structures, syntactic features like Part of Speech (PoS), and semantic features as well as the discourse features. These features are typically used for solving any NER problems. Many other domain specific features could be generated for further improving the performance of the system.

In the current work, we develop a supervised machine learning based classification framework for solving the patient de-identification problem. The proposed method is evaluated on the i2b2 2014 dataset. It concerned identifying four different PHI categories, namely PATIENT, DOCTOR, HOSPITAL names and DATE from the medical records. Taking into account the effectiveness of applying CRF in solving the NER problem, CRF was adopted to train the model. Diverse features are extracted and CRF based model was trained using this huge collection of features. Several experiments were carried out with different cross folds. Results of the proposed system are shown for different cross-validation settings like 5,6,7,8,9,10 fold cross validations.

This task suffers from various challenges as similar to any NLP task. One such challenge is the ambiguity problem where we found that due to the lexical similarity PHI terms mostly overlap with the non-PHI terms. An example includes Brown (Doctor name) which is a PHI term vs. brown (Colour name) which is a non-PHI term. Another major challenge is the occurrence of some out-of-vocabulary PHI terms which are not present in the dictionaries. These words act like the foreign words which can be misspelled. Gazetteers list, dictionaries are the mostly used for solving any NER problem but the contribution of these types of words lowers the performance and creates some errors. Results obtained prove that the proposed system outperforms the existing systems in identifying four different PHI terms.

The remaining paper is organized as follows. Next immediate section discusses the background of de-identification task and its significance. This is followed by a section which provides the insight to the related work. Next section discussed the methodology adopted for the de-identification which is followed by the details of experiments and their analysis. Finally, we conclude in the last section.

BACKGROUND AND SIGNIFICANCE

Most of the works done in biomedical Natural Language Processing (NLP) domain can be distinguished into two different types on the basis of the text, biomedical text and clinical text (Meystre et al., 2010). Biomedical texts are the texts that appear in the journals, articles, posters etc. On the other hand, the clinical texts are mostly the texts written by the doctors in the form of prescriptions for the patients. This text comprises of the patient information like his/her name, age, gender, the procedure that was applied to him/her and what are his/her medical histories. These texts also provide insights to the findings made during procedure and the medication provided to them.

The clinical text is the whole range of narrative found in the patient records. These texts vary from the short-segment which gives the chief complaints to the long-text comprising of the history of the patients. There is another class of text which is discussed in the literature very often (Coorevits et al., 2013). While some of the texts are similar to that of biomedical texts for example internal research reports, the others appear to be like clinical texts for example patient notes. As these narratives are rarely exposed outside the organizations, there is a very sparse study on them.

There is one obvious question that what distinguishes clinical text from the biomedical text and why processing of these poses a challenge to the NLP society. Firstly, in the clinical texts, a large number of grammatical errors can be found which may have occurred at the telegraphic phrase. Other segments in clinical documents which create some problem are discharged summaries and the lab test reports. Moreover, clinical documents suffer from the problems like abbreviations and acronyms. These lexical structures are often overloaded i.e., there is a multiple rendering for the same word set. Literature shows that almost 33% of the times, acronyms are overloaded which makes it prone to the ambiguity problem (Liu et al., 2001). There is a huge problem due to the spelling mistake, which is observed most commonly in the notes lacking spelling support. US Veterans Administration (VA) has one of the largest EHR systems with only the basic text support. Even in their corpus, there are lots of abbreviations and acronym problem. Furthermore, the clinical data consists of different types of characters which appear anywhere within the text. Another problem that is raised is to change the unstructured narrative text into the structured; templates along with pseudo-tables are in general used in the method of conversion (Meystre et al., 2010). Template having a narrative structure for patient history or the discharge summary that is common among the medical society provides benefits to NLP. Explicit templates are formatted text with the fields specific to the institution are filled by the user. These different variations in template make this domain quite challenging.

There are many methodologies adopted to cover different types of questions related to clinical research domain (Dehghan et al., 2015), (Liu et al., 2015), (He et al., 2015). Although, the pharmaceutical industry covers the clinical trails and therapy but nowadays, these industries are spreading the horizon of solving the medication issues like drug interaction, disease prevention through the proper investigation of diseases. These include the course of the disease and various other factors like, what were the different criteria for diagnosis, how the patient education affected his/her health and his/her surveillance. With the rapid and booming research interest in the clinical domain, the studies have also spread to obtain the role of different gene pathways in the identification of their relations in the development of diseases. Some clinical research focuses on improving the health care with lowering the health care cost, thus providing the benefits to the mass. As such, it is highly important to have a proper study of the clinical records in solving the major unsolved and challenging problems of the society with the NLP system.

De-identification task forms one such challenge which aims to identify the noun phrases or part of a noun phrase automatically from the text. In the traditional named entity recognition task, originated by the MUC challenge, the focus was to identify the person, organization, location names from the newspaper type electronic text. Generally, de-identification task is the task of identifying and enclosing patient personal health information like not just identifying the persons but also identifying the type of person (Patient, Doctor), Organizations (Hospital), Location (Streets, Country), ages, dates but not in the term of years. Apart from these, structures of the text too vary a lot. While in newswire or journalistic domain, lots of clues can be obtained from their titles, abstract and cases while in the patient records, due to its semi-structured form the task becomes quite challenging.

LITERATURE SURVEY

De-identification task is a type of the traditional Named Entity Recognition (NER) problem. Message Understanding Conference had been the center for the evaluation of NER system in several domains. MUC had organized several challenges to identify several named entities like person, location, organization, time, dates etc. For the MUC-6 NER task, a total of 15 teams participated in the challenge submitting 20 different systems. The best F-Measure value reported was 96.42% (Sundheim, 1997). In the MUC-7 challenge, 14 systems were submitted from 12 different teams obtaining the highest F-Measure value of 93.39% (Chinchor, 2001). National Institute of Standards and Technology (NIST) organized two different tasks, Information Extraction Named Entity task and the Automatic Content Extraction (ACE) tasks. Both of these tasks were evaluated on the newswire domain.

In the biomedical domain, Critical Assessment of Information Extraction Systems in Biology (BioCreAtIvE) (Hirschman et al.,2005), organized several biomedical challenges including the entity extraction task, where the task is to identify different entities like gene name, protein name from the given biomedical text derived from the PubMed, PMC. PubMed and PMC are huge repositories consisting of almost 3.5 million biomedical literature. For the evaluation, TREC Genomics Track was considered. The BioNLP 2009 challenge (Kim et al., 2009) focuses on event extraction primarily on the protein and gene event extractions. The same challenge was also focussed on BioNLP 11(Pyysalo et al., 2011) and BioNLP 13 shared task (Nedellec et al., 2013), where data was used from MEDLINE. Another task BioASQ was organized for entity extraction using data from PubMed. Several challenges have been organized for entity extraction. Recently, i2b2 had organized the task for the de-identification of the clinical terms in the years 2006 and 2014 (Stubbs et al., 2015). Here, the challenge was to identify the certain PHI terms.

In the 2006 shared task, a total of 889 patient records were used. This challenge got sixteen submissions from seven different teams. The challenge had used longitudinal records of each patient rather than the individual records. It was observed that longitudinal records contain more personal information of patients rather than an individual record. Completely identifying the patient information from individual records is a problematic task. This makes the de-identification using the longitudinal records a more complicated task. The submitted systems identified the task as a token classification task (using Support Vector Machine) while some distinguished it as the sequence labeling task (using Hidden Markov Model, Conditional Random Field).

Wellner et al. (2007) in i2b2-2006 challenge built the best system based on CRF. They used some lexical and semantics features. They adapted two important NER systems, one based on the CRF, Carafe, and other Lingpipe, HMM-based implementation. The carafe was seen to be highly effective in capturing the PHI terms. Szarvas et al. (2007) adopted an iterative method for named-entity de-identification. They treat de-identification as a classification task and use machine learning based decision tree with local features and dictionaries. Aramaki et al. (2006) also used CRF as their classifier with the features such as local, external and global features. The global feature includes the features which capture position, the length of a sentence and also several tokens in the previous sentence. External features include the dictionary for location, person name, and dates. They performed two-phase learning wherein the first phase, they learned their system using local features and in the second phase, they include first phase features set in addition to the most frequent label. They identified that sentence feature is very informative in identifying dates, IDs and patient because of the appearance of this PHI in beginning of the records while the external feature was useful in identifying dates, locations, doctors and patients.

While many systems have used CRF based classifier, some submitted systems also used SVM. Hara (2006) developed a hybrid system making use of rules. The rules identified the patterns for the PHI terms such as phone numbers, IDs, and dates. They train SVM on the global and local features which were found to be very helpful in identifying the PHI terms such as a hospital, patient, location, doctors, and age. In addition to these features, their system included the section heading which is closed to the target, category of the sentence, the surface form of target, the root, PoS tag and orthography features. The system used two types of the ordered tree, dependency tree and "n-grams trees" making use of the Boosting Algorithm for Classification Trees (BACT). With this information and in addition of chunking technique, they identified the position and the text span of PHI terms such as a patient, doctor, location, and hospital. The results show that performance is degraded with the incorporation of sentence feature.

In 2014 patient de-identification task, machine learning technique was more prominent. According to the 2014 i2b2/UTHealth shared task, the challenge was to de-identify the data in a stricter way as compared to the HIPAA standards in the form of additional categories. The task was to identify the 25 PHI categories with the associated subcategories from the clinical records like professions, time and dates, facilities etc. These tasks also consider the longitudinal records. Yang et al. (2015) submitted the system in the i2b2-2014 challenge and they reported the accuracy of 93.60%. This was the best performing system. They developed a hybrid model which used both the machine learning and the rule-based technique to extract the PHI terms. They exploited the various features like linguistic features, syntactic feature and different word surface oriented features which were further improved by using the task-specific features. They also used the regular expression pattern to identify the PHI terms like date, ID.

The second best system (Dehghan et al., 2015) from Manchester used a combined system developed using the knowledge-based technique as well as the rule-based system. The rules were defined to obtain the orthographic features, different patterns. They used CRF as the underlined classifier to obtain the PHI terms. For some categories like PATIENT, DOCTOR, HOSPITAL, the initial annotation was extracted at the patient level and dictionary was created for the patient. At the last stage, the outputs of the rule-based system, as well as the CRF based model, were integrated on the basis of some rules. These systems were highly efficient in obtaining the PHI terms such as the DATE, DOCTORS, and PATIENT.

System (Liu et al., 2015) from Harbin Institute of Technology Shenzhen Graduate School in i2b2 challenge used two different variations of the CRF. They define one CRF system working at the token level while another CRF system that works at the character level. They performed feature engineering and used the features such as bag-of-words, section relevant features, lexical features, semantic features. Apart from the two different CRF outputs, the third output was obtained by developing the rules using the Rule-based system. The final outputs of all the three systems were merged on the basis of the output overlapping. If there was no overlapping i.e., if all the three systems obtained the same PHI tag, then that tag was accepted else the tag was obtained on the basis of the preference. They give the first preference to the rule based system, then the character-level system and lastly to the token-level based CRF system.

Another submitted system from Harbin Institute of Technology (He et al., 2015) used OpenNLP system to pre-process their data, sentence splitting, and tokenizer. They trained their system using CRF making use of features such as lexical, syntactic and orthographic features. They did not use external features such as dictionaries to identify the terms. The system developed by Kaiser Permanente (Torii et al., 2014) adapted the MIST tool. They include some additional rules that used lexicon for Location and Profession and different regular expressions for the categories such as Phone Numbers, ZIP and Organization. In addition to MIST system, the team learned NER model using Stanford NER system. The system then merges the overlapped identified entities. They reported the F-Measure value of 92.21%.

Through the literature survey, we found that hybrid systems (both the rule-based system as well as the machine learning based) perform well when compared with the individual techniques. It is reported that among top ten ranked systems, seven systems have adopted the rule-based technique. MedEx (Xu et al., 2010) forms one such system proposed at Vanderbilt University that utilizes the biomedical dictionary to identify the important medical concepts.

Overall, the best systems report high recall and precision, often greater than 90%, and sometimes as high as 99%. Nevertheless, no study has evaluated the performance of automated de-identification for all PHI classes (Meystre et al., 2010). Only a handful of studies provide details on over-scrubbing (non-PHI wrongly identified as PHI) and none of them investigate the effect of de-identification on subsequent IE tasks. It is indeed possible that de-identification has an adverse effect on IE accuracy (Meystre et al., 2010). Over-scrubbing errors could overlap with useful information, for example, if a disease name is erroneously recognized as a person name, it will be removed and lost to subsequent IE applications. Second, NLP techniques such as part-of-speech tagging and parsing may be less effective on modified texts.

It can be concluded that though a lot of systems have evolved in the recent past, but still there is a need to develop a more accurate automated de-identification system.

METHODS

Supervised machine learning based classification frameworks have been developed to detect the PHI tokens from the medical records. Similar to any entity extraction technique, de-identification task is also considered to be the sequence labeling task. The proposed system architecture is divided into four different modules. The first module deals with the pre-processing of data. The second module represents the feature engineering part where features are generated. Training of the model through Conditional Random Field (CRF) is done in the third module. The fourth module represents the de-identification of the PHI terms. Detailed descriptions of the methodology adopted for the system are given below. Figure 2 represents the Proposed System Architecture.

Pre-Processing of the Medical Records

Datasets provided with the i2b2 de-identification challenge were untokenized; this necessitates the use of the pre-processing module for the process of tokenization. The pre-processing was performed in three different stages. The first stage of the pre-processing module deals with the sentence splitting. The second

Figure 2. Proposed system architecture

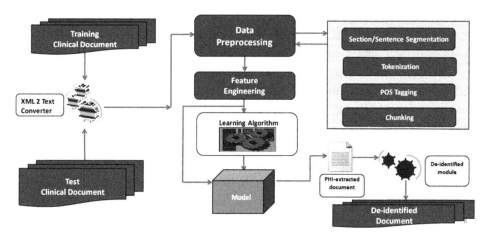

module focuses on the tokenization of the medical records. The last and final stages are used to identify the rules for tokens such that when they are divided, they should match some patterns.

Apart from this process, pre-processing steps also include shallow parsing and Part of Speech (PoS) tagging to obtain the word lemma, chunk and part-of-speech of the corresponding words. Additionally, we extracted some of the document- level features, for example obtaining the different sections (HISTORY OF PATIENT ILLNESS, MEDICATIONS etc.) and position of the sentence in the text (beginning of the text, end of the text) using some of the hand-crafted rules.

Feature Generation

This module focuses on developing some prominent features. The features were developed, such as the linguistic, syntactic features as well as word surface-oriented features in order to capture the semantics of the PHI terms. The features were further enhanced by embedding the feature set by the task-specific features. The list of the extracted features for the PHI recognition task is given below:

- **Token Features:** Some features are generated during the pre-processing step like word lemma, word chunk and the Part-of-Speech tag of the current word.
- **Bag-of-Word Feature:** It includes the unigrams, bigrams, trigrams of the target token within the window size of [-2, 2]. An *n*-gram is a contiguous sequence of *n* items from a given sequence of text or speech. An *n*-gram of size 1 is referred to as an unigram, size 2 is a bigram and size 3 is a trigram.
- **Contextual Features:** This feature is the combined feature which includes the lemma, chunk, POS tag of the surrounding tokens. We consider the window size of [-3, 3]. These features give the context knowledge for each word.
- **Combined POS-Token Feature:** The combination of POS tag within the context of [-1, 1] and the current token $\{w_0p_{-1}, w_0p_0, w_0p_1\}$ is formed, where w_0 represents the current word, and p_{-1}, p_0 and p_1 represent the previous POS tag, current POS tag and the next POS tags respectively.
- **Affixes:** This feature includes prefix and suffix of the word. It refers to the fixed length characters stripped either from the left most part or the rightmost part of the token. For example, the suffix

Table 2. Some of the orthographic features with their examples in uses

Feature	Example	Feature	Example
InitCap	David	CapMixAlpha	EpoR
InCap	mAb	DigitSpecial	12-4
DigitOnly	12,23	AlphaDigitAlpha	IL34S,EIB
DigitAlpha	28BC	CapLowAlpha	Srs, Ras, Epo
Hyphen	–	DigitCommaDigit	2,34
CapsAndDigits	28Houston	LowMixAlpha	mAB,mRNA
StopWord	at, on	AllCaps	DHC
AlphaDigit	s72	EndwithDot	Dr., Mr.

and prefix of word 'health' are h, he, hea, heal and h, th, lth, alth respectively. Here, we set the length to size 4.

- **Sentence Information Feature:** This feature includes the structure of the sentence. It includes the information regarding length of the sentence, whether the sentence has any delimiters like '.', '?', '!', whether there is any bracket unmatched.

- **Orthographic Feature:** Several orthographic features were developed to capture the capitalization and digit information. These are very useful information to capture the entity extraction. Symbol such as the ',' is found to be very crucial in detecting the boundaries of the NEs. Table 2 lists some of the orthographic features with their examples in uses.

- **Word Normalization:** Two different variants of this feature were developed. The first feature is used to capture the words which are in plural form, verb, alphanumeric letters, hyphen, and digit. This feature actually converts the words to its root form. Another feature represents the orthographic construction of the words. This feature is termed as the word shape feature where each word is mapped to its respective class. Words are normalized by converting every uppercase character by 'A', lowercase character is changed to 'a' and every digit by '0'. For example, if the token is 'Medical-49', its normalized form would be 'Aaaaaaa-00'.

- **Word Class Feature:** This feature is generated motivated by the fact that similar entities reside within the similar class. This feature is the enhancement of the word normalization feature. After the word conversion, the squeezing operation is performed where the consecutive sequence of words is converted into the single character. For example for the word 'Medical-49', its word class form would be 'Aa-0'.

- **Section Feature:** This binary feature was generated after extracting the sections from the training set manually. Top 16 sections were extracted with their probabilities of carrying the relevant PHI terms. These sections were generated manually and form very effective feature in the identification of the PHI terms.

- **Gazetteer List:** For the identification of the PHI terms, task related term list helps in improving the performance of the system. These lists include the headings which give very strong remarks about the occurrence of the PHI terms. Example: 'Transcribed by', 'Dictated by'. These sections carry information about the occurrence of the DOCTOR name. Apart from this, the dictionary was used for the names like the common names across countries, full name and the abbreviation of the common US locations for e.g. "New York" and "NY". We used the list of names for the days, months.

- In addition, some lexical clues were identified for each individual PHI category. These are the types of the trigger words that give an indication regarding the presence of the particular PHI terms for example 'Dr.', 'M.D' in the case of DOCTOR, 'Mr.', 'Mrs' in the case of the patient. These lexical clues are obtained from the neighboring contexts of the target PHI terms. These are filtered on the basis of occurrence and their importance with the target PHI categories.

- **General Entity Information:** The Stanford Named Entity Recognizer (http://nlp.stanford.edu/ software/CRF-NER.shtml) was used to obtain the named entity tag of the corresponding token.

- **Discourse Features:** This feature plays a very important role in the identification of the terms that are very much related to section headings and their positions of occurrence in the sentence. For example the strong contextual clues words like 'CC:' and 'Dictated by'.

Classification: CRF Classifier

We trained our system using the Conditional Random Field algorithm. This algorithm is very popular in the domain of entity recognition because of its ability to tackle the sequence labeling task very efficiently. CRF is categorized under the class of statistical modeling. They are mainly applied for the structural prediction which is formed by the combination of classification and graphical modeling methods. CRF integrates the performance of the graphical models to compactly model multivariate data and classification methods to perform prediction using a large set of input features.

The CRF-classifier works on the Markov Assumption that given the observation sequence of the token $x_1, x_2, x_3, \ldots \ldots x_n$, the corresponding label-sequence $y_1, y_2, y_3 \ldots \ldots y_n$ is predicted by the CRF. It maximizes the conditional probability for every y in the possible set of label sequence. Mathematically, CRF can be represented as

$$\exp(\sum_{j} \gamma_j t_j(y_{(i-1)}, y_i, x, i) + \sum_{k} \mu_k s_k(y_i, x, i)) \tag{1}$$

Here, $t_j(y_{(i-1)}, y_i, x, i)$ represents the transition feature function for the whole set of observation sequence. i and $(i-1)$ denote the position of the labels in the label sequence. Here $s_k(y_i, x, i)$ represents the state feature function at the label position i and observation sequence. γ_j and μ_k are the parameters estimated from the training dataset. While defining the feature function, the real valued feature set of the observation is constructed as $b(x, i)$. It expresses empirical distribution characteristics of the training data in order to hold the model distribution.

There are various other algorithms that can handle the sequence labeling task like Maximum Entropy Markov Model (MEMM) and Hidden Markov Model (HMM). The main advantage of CRF over HMM is that it is conditional in nature, which helps in relaxation of the independence assumption as needed by the HMM. Apart from that, CRF is very much efficient in handling the label bias problem. Label bias problem is due to the directed graphical model that is exhibited by MEMM and HMM. It was observed that CRF outperforms the other models in a number of tasks such as speech recognition, bioinformatics.

De-identification task targets to automatically extract the PHI terms with the proper boundary identification. As CRF being the better performer than other models, this work used CRF as an underline base classifier. The open source toolkit CRF++ was used to carry out our experiments. BIO notation was followed to label the PHI terms which occur in sequence. Here 'B' identifies the beginning of the PHI token, 'I' represents that the PHI token is within the sequence. 'O' is used to identify that token belongs to none of the PHI term categories.

For the classifier learning, whole feature set discussed in the previous section was used. CRF modeling is done by considering all the PHI categories through learning by the training phase and predicting the output of the model built during the test phase.

De-Identification of PHI Terms

In order to hide the patient personal information, de- identification of the PHI terms is highly necessary. A template was adopted through which we convert all PATIENT, HOSPITAL, DOCTOR names present into a generic format like XYZ_PATIENT, XYZ_HOSPITAL, XYZ_DOCTOR, respectively and all the dates into the format 00-00_DATE. Thus, capturing the information required without compromising the personal details. We represent this below in Figure 3 by considering the original document and the de-identified document. Figure 3 shows De-Identification Process.

Figure 3. De-identification process

PHI Extracted Document

```
<RECORD ID="001">
<TEXT>
<PHI
TYPE="HOSPITAL">ABHG</PHI>
Report Status:
Unsigned Please do not go above this box
important format codes are contained.
DISCHARGE SUMMARY
ARF32 FA
DISCHARGE SUMMARY NAME:
UNIT NUMBER:
<PHI TYPE="PATIENT">JOHN
DOE</PHI>
ADMISSION DATE:
<PHI TYPE="DATE">01/02/1900
</PHI>
DISCHARGE DATE:
<PHI TYPE="DATE">01/31/1997
</PHI>
DD:
<PHI TYPE="DOCTOR">Do
Little</PHI>, M.D.
</RECORD>
```

De-identified module

De-identified Document

```
<RECORD ID="641">
<TEXT>
<PHI TYPE="HOSPITAL">
[XYZ_HOSPITAL] </PHI>
Report Status:
Unsigned Please do not go above this box
important format codes are contained.
DISCHARGE SUMMARY
ARF32 FA
DISCHARGE SUMMARY NAME:
UNIT NUMBER:
<PHI TYPE="PATIENT">
[XYZ_PATIENT] </PHI>
ADMISSION DATE:
<PHI TYPE="DATE"> [00-00_DATE]
</PHI>
DISCHARGE DATE:
<PHI TYPE="DATE"> [00-00_DATE]
</PHI>
DD:
<PHI TYPE="DOCTOR">
[XYZ_DOCTOR] </PHI>, M.D.
</RECORD>
```

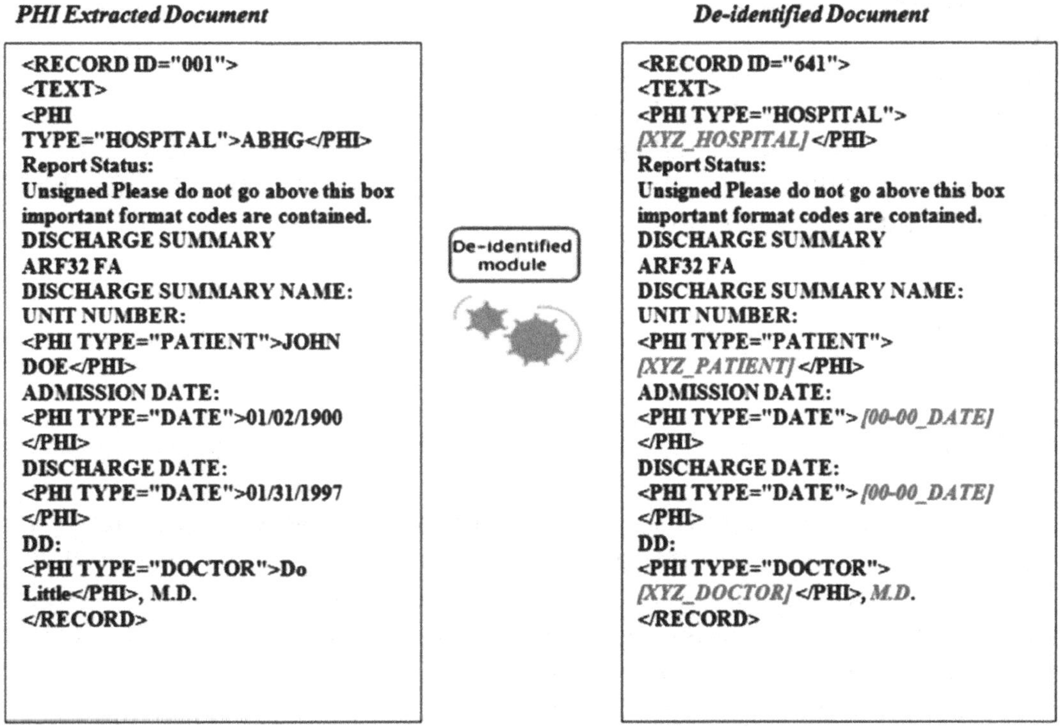

DATASET AND EXPERIMENTS

Dataset

The 2014 i2b2 challenge dataset was used in the current paper, which was taken from the Research Patient Data Repository of Partners' Healthcare. A total of 1304 medical records basically of longitudinal nature were manually annotated. These records were obtained from 297 patients following the annotation guidelines. The dataset was divided into two parts where the first part consists of 790 records of 188 patients that were used as the training dataset and 514 records of 109 patients were test dataset.

i2b2-2014 challenge dataset compromises of 17,045 PHI relevant instances in the training dataset, while the test dataset consists of total 11,462 PHI instances. To ensure the patient confidentiality as much as possible, the challenge aims to identify HIPAA- PHI categories firstly with the added subcategories. They were annotated using seven main PHI categories with the twenty- five associated subcategories. While our experiments cover the seven main PHI categories, i2b2 challenge covers almost all HIPAA defined categories and subcategories. The list of categories, as well as subcategories that were needed to be identified, is as follows:

- NAME (subtypes: PATIENT, DOCTOR,USERNAME)
- PROFESSION
- LOCATION (subtypes: HOSPITAL, DEPARTMENT, ORGANIZATION, ROOM, STREET, CITY, STATE, COUNTRY, ZIP)
- AGE
- DATE
- CONTACT(subtypes: PHONE,FAX,EMAIL,URL,IPADDRESS)
- Ids(SUBTYPES: MEDICAL RECORD NUMBER, HEALTH PLAN NUMBER, SOCIAL SECURITY NUMBER, ACCOUNT NUMBER, VECHILE ID, DEVICE ID, LICENCE NUMBER, BIOMETRIC ID)

In this work, the aim was to identify four different PHI subtypes; PATIENT, DOCTOR, HOSPITAL name and DATE from the above-defined categories. The experiment was performed with only the training dataset.

Evaluation

The system was evaluated by using 10 fold cross-validation on the training data. For evaluating the classifier's performance, we have used the most popular evaluation metrics; recall, precision, and F-Measure. Recall also known as sensitivity is defined as the ratio of total number retrieved relevant documents to the number of relevant records. Precision represents the positive prediction and is the ratio of retrieved relevant records to the total number of documents.

Recall and precision are represented as follows

$$recall = \frac{Total\ number\ of\ correctly\ predicted\ NE}{Total\ number\ of\ actual\ NE\ present\ in\ the\ gold\ data} \tag{2}$$

$$precision = \frac{Total\ number\ of\ correctly\ retrieved\ NE}{Total\ number\ of\ NE\ retrieved\ by\ the\ system} \qquad (3)$$

F-Measure considers both the precision and recall. It is defined as the harmonic mean of recall and precision. We defined F-Measure value as follows:

$$f_\alpha = \frac{(1+\alpha^2)(recall * precision)}{\alpha^2 * precision + recall} \qquad (4)$$

Here we set the value of $\alpha = 1$.

Experimental Results

Table 3. reports the extensive results of 10-fold cross validation: Recall, Precision and F-score values for individual entities. The system was developed using the handcrafted feature set trained on CRF. It was an interesting observation that with the set of whole features learned using CRF, the system performs quite well. The system was evaluated using 5,6,7,8,9,10 fold cross validation. Here, the performance of the proposed system with10 fold cross validation is reported.

Table 3 shows that overall system has achieved good recall values as compared to precision values. But there are some interesting observations regarding the recognition of individual entities. If the comparison is done on the performance among 3 important PHI terms; Hospital name, Doctor Name & Patient name then Doctor class is having the highest precision and recall values of 99.70% and 93.80% respectively. Precision and recall values for Date are quite good, but the performance can be further improved by introducing some more date based patterns. The recall value for the hospital is low as compared to all the PHI terms introduced here; the one possible reason behind this is to use abbreviation instead of full hospital names.

The report shows that the system is accurate in predicting the PHI terms with the high degree of precision. The detailed error analysis is performed on the obtained results.

Table 4 shows different error cases. Here, X or Y represents any class like PATIENT, DOCTOR, HOSPITAL, and DATE. "B_X" or "B_Y" represents the beginning of the token, "I_X" or "I_Y" represents the intermediate of the token and "O" denotes others.

Table 3. Results of 10-fold cross validation: Recall, precision & F-score values for individual entities

Class	Recall	Precision	F-Score
Overall	0.9569	0.9931	0.9746
Hospital	0.9056	0.9769	0.9399
Doctor	0.9380	0.9970	0.9666
Patient	0.9355	0.9831	0.9587
Date	0.9905	0.9984	0.9944

Table 4. Different error cases

Case	Actual Labels	Classified Labels
MISSED ENTITY	B_X I_X	O
ACTUAL ENTITY	B_X I_X	B_Y I_Y
WRONG BOUNDARY	B_X I_X	B_X O
OVER PREDICT	O	B_X I_X

Table 5 mentions about case 1: missed entity error. Here the system was unable to identify the entity. In the following e.g. 'DO' which in actual represents the Doctor name was predicted as others. The reason for the error is the short words or the abbreviated words. 'DO' is the abbreviated form of doctor name 'DO D LITTLE' which is missed by the system.

Table 6 presents the case 2: actual entity error. Here the entity was predicted but was not able to classify it in the proper class. For example in the following sentence, 'FOR' was captured as the B-DOCTOR while it should be others.

Table 7 represents the case 3: wrong boundary error. This case represents the boundary detection problem, where the system was able to capture the token properly but was not able to properly identify the boundary of the token. In the below example 'LITTLE' was not identified as the boundary of the system.

Table 8 represents the case 4: over predicted error. Last error occurred due to the over prediction where non-entity was categorized as the entity. For example here 'DO LITTLE' was categorized as the entity and was tagged by the DOCTOR. It might be because our system is unable to properly identify the context.

Table 5. CASE 1: Missed entity error

Words	DR.	DO	2	.	DO	D	LITTLE	,	M.D	.
Actual	O	B-DOCTOR	O	O	B-DOCTOR	I-DOCTOR	I-DOCTOR	O	O	O
Predicted	O	O	O	O	B-DOCTOR	I-DOCTOR	I-DOCTOR	O	O	O

Table 67. CASE 2: Actual entity error

Words	Dictating	For	DO	LITTLE	,	M.D	.
Actual	O	O	B-DOCTOR	I-DOCTOR	O	O	O
Predicted	O	B-DOCTOR	I-DOCTOR	I-DOCTOR	O	O	O

Table 7. CASE 3: Wrong boundary error

Words	HE	WILL	FOLLOW-UP	WITH	DR.	DO	LITTLE
Actual	O	O	O	O	O	B-DOCTOR	I-DOCTOR
Predicted	O	O	O	O	O	B-DOCTOR	O

Table 8. CASE 4: Over predict error

Words	DO	LITTLE	THORACOSCOPIC	EXAM	BX	DRAINAGE	.
Actual	O	O	O	O	O	O	O
Predicted	B-DOCTOR	I-DOCTOR	O	O	O	O	O

From the confusion matrix presented in Table 3, it was identified that mainly case 1 type of the error was more dominated.

- DOCTOR was tagged as O where there are the following forms: < D1 > M.D., < D2 > M.D., < D3> M.D.
- Misclassification has occurred when Hospital name is written in short for example CMC, FIH, OLH, HGMC etc.
- Most of the misclassification errors occurred when the patient name was preceded by the Mr., Mrs., Ms.
- Dates of the forms like 11th of April, January 25, Veterans Day were not captured properly.

CONCLUSION

In this paper, a clinical de-identification system is developed that aims to identify the Protected Health Information and to classify them into the predefined categories present in the clinical records. The proposed approach for de-identification is purely based on a popular machine learning technique. A variety of domain independent features, semantic, lexical features were designed for the system to be domain adaptable. Various others features extracted from localization dictionaries were combined in order to further enhance the performance of the system. The proposed system achieves encouraging performance. The system obtained the overall F-Measure of 97.46%, in identifying PATIENT, HOSPITAL, DOCTOR names and DATE.

However, a lot of issues are yet to be resolved. One such issue is to resolve abbreviation problem which is identified as a non-PHI term. In addition, it would be interesting to observe the performance of the proposed system on other type of PHI mentions.

FUTURE WORK

In future, this work can be extended using deep neural network architecture to identify the PHI terms from the medical records. Another major challenge is to deal ambiguity and abbreviation problem to properly distinguish PHI terms with non-PHI terms which can be another future work.

REFERENCES

Aramaki, E., Imai, T., Miyo, K., & Ohe, K. (2006, November). Automatic deidentification by using sentence features and label consistency. In *i2b2 Workshop on Challenges in Natural Language Processing for Clinical Data* (pp. 10-11).

Aronson, A. R. (2001). Effective mapping of biomedical text to the UMLS Metathesaurus: the MetaMap program. In *Proceedings of the AMIA Symposium* (p.17). American Medical Informatics Association.

Beck, T., Gollapudi, S., Brunak, S., Graf, N., Lemke, H. U., Dash, D., & Brookes, A. J. et al. (2012). Knowledge engineering for health: A new discipline required to bridge the ICT gap between research and healthcare. *Human Mutation, 33*(5), 797–802. doi:10.1002/humu.22066 PMID:22392843

Beckwith, B. A., Mahaadevan, R., Balis, U. J., & Kuo, F. (2006). Development and evaluation of an open source software tool for deidentification of pathology reports. *BMC Medical Informatics and Decision Making, 6*(1), 1. doi:10.1186/1472-6947-6-12 PMID:16515714

Berner, E. S., Detmer, D. E., & Simborg, D. (2005). Will the wave finally break? A brief view of the adoption of electronic medical records in the United States. *Journal of the American Medical Informatics Association, 12*(1), 3–7. doi:10.1197/jamia.M1664 PMID:15492029

BioASQ. (n.d.). *BioASQ project, Data*. Retrieved January 07, 2015, from http://www.bioasq.org/participate/data

Chinchor. (2001, January 12). *Named Entity Scores– English, in: Message Understanding Conference Proceedings*. Retrieved January 06, 2015, from http://www.itl.nist.gov/iaui/894.02/related_projects/muc/proceedings/ne_english_score_report.html

Coorevits, P., Sundgren, M., Klein, G. O., Bahr, A., Claerhout, B., Daniel, C., & De, et al.. (2013). Electronic health records: New opportunities for clinical research. *The Association for the Publication of the Journal of Internal Medicine, 274*(6), 547–560. doi:10.1111/joim.12119 PMID:23952476

Dehghan, A., Kovacevic, A., Karystianis, G., Keane, J. A., & Nenadic, G. (2015). Combining knowledge- and data-driven methods for de-identification of clinical narratives. *Journal of Biomedical Informatics, 58*, S53–S59. doi:10.1016/j.jbi.2015.06.029 PMID:26210359

Deleger, L., Molnar, K., Savova, G., Xia, F., Lingren, T., Li, Q., & Solti, I. et al. (2013). Large-scale evaluation of automated clinical note de-identification and its impact on information extraction. *Journal of the American Medical Informatics Association, 20*(1), 84–94. doi:10.1136/amiajnl-2012-001012 PMID:22859645

Friedman, C., Shagina, L., Socratous, S. A., & Zeng, X. (1996). A WEB-based version of MedLEE: A medical language extraction and encoding system. In *Proceedings of the AMIA Annual Fall Symposium* (p. 938). American Medical Informatics Association.

Goeuriot, L., Jones, G.J., Kelly, L., Leveling, J., Hanbury, A., Müller, H., Salantera, S., Suominen, H. and Zuccon, G. (2013). ShARe/CLEF eHealth Evaluation Lab 2013, Task 3: Information retrieval to address patients' questions when reading clinical reports. *CLEF 2013 Online Working Notes, 8138*.

Hara, K. (2006, November). Applying a SVM based Chunker and a text classifier to the deid challenge. In *i2b2 Workshop on challenges in natural language processing for clinical data* (pp. 10-11).

He, B., Guan, Y., Cheng, J., Cen, K., & Hua, W. (2015). CRFs based de-identification of medical records. *Journal of Biomedical Informatics*, 58. PMID:26315662

Health Insurance Portability and Accountability Act. P.L. 104e191, 42 U.S.C. 1996.

Hirschman, L., Yeh, A., Blaschke, C., & Valencia, A. (2005). Overview of BioCreAtIvE: Critical assessment of information extraction for biology. *BMC Bioinformatics*, 6(Suppl 1), S1. doi:10.1186/1471-2105-6-S1-S1 PMID:15960821

Kim, J. D., Ohta, T., Pyysalo, S., Kano, Y., & Tsujii, J. I. (2009, June). Overview of BioNLP'09 shared task on event extraction. In *Proceedings of the Workshop on Current Trends in Biomedical Natural Language Processing: Shared Task* (pp. 1-9). Association for Computational Linguistics. doi:10.3115/1572340.1572342

Lafferty, J., McCallum, A., & Pereira, F. C. (2001). *Conditional random fields: Probabilistic models for segmenting and labeling sequence data*. Academic Press.

Liu, H., Lussier, Y. A., & Friedman, C. (2001). Disambiguating ambiguous biomedical terms in biomedical narrative text: An unsupervised method. *Journal of Biomedical Informatics*, *34*(4), 249–261. doi:10.1006/jbin.2001.1023 PMID:11977807

Liu, Z., Chen, Y., Tang, B., Wang, X., Chen, Q., Li, H., & Zhu, S. et al. (2015). Automatic de-identification of electronic medical records using token-level and character-level conditional random fields. *Journal of Biomedical Informatics*, 58. PMID:26122526

McCallum, A., Freitag, D., & Pereira, F. C. (2000, June). *Maximum Entropy Markov Models for Information Extraction and Segmentation* (Vol. 17). ICML.

Meystre, S. M., Friedlin, F. J., South, B. R., Shen, S., & Samore, M. H. (2010). Automatic de-identification of textual documents in the electronic health record: A review of recent research. *BMC Med Res Methodol BMC Medical Research Methodology*, *10*(1), 70. doi:10.1186/1471-2288-10-70 PMID:20678228

Nédellec, C., Bossy, R., Kim, J. D., Kim, J. J., Ohta, T., Pyysalo, S., & Zweigenbaum, P. (2013, August). Overview of BioNLP shared task 2013. In *Proceedings of the BioNLP Shared Task 2013 Workshop* (pp. 1-7).

Pyysalo, S., Ohta, T., Rak, R., Sullivan, D., Mao, C., Wang, C., & Ananiadou, S. et al. (2012). Overview of the ID, EPI and REL tasks of BioNLP Shared Task 2011. *BMC Bioinformatics*, *13*(11), 1. PMID:22759456

Savova, G. K., Masanz, J. J., Ogren, P. V., Zheng, J., Sohn, S., Kipper-Schuler, K. C., & Chute, C. G. (2010). Mayo clinical Text Analysis and Knowledge Extraction System (cTAKES): Architecture, component evaluation and applications. *Journal of the American Medical Informatics Association*, *17*(5), 507–513. doi:10.1136/jamia.2009.001560 PMID:20819853

Stubbs, A., Kotfila, C., & Uzuner, Ö. (2015). Automated systems for the de-identification of longitudinal clinical narratives: Overview of 2014 i2b2/UTHealth shared task Track 1. *Journal of Biomedical Informatics*, *58*, S11–S19. doi:10.1016/j.jbi.2015.06.007 PMID:26225918

Sundheim, B. M. (1996, May). Overview of results of the MUC-6 evaluation. In *Proceedings of a workshop on held at Vienna, Virginia* (pp. 423-442). Association for Computational Linguistics. doi:10.3115/1119018.1119073

Szarvas, G., Farkas, R., & Busa-Fekete, R. (2007). State-of-the-art anonymization of medical records using an iterative machine learning framework. *Journal of the American Medical Informatics Association, 14*(5), 574–580. doi:10.1197/jamia.M2441 PMID:17823086

Torii, M., Fan, J. W., Yang, W. L., Lee, T., Wiley, M. T., Zisook, D., & Huang, Y. (2014, November). De-identification and risk factor detection in medical records. Seventh i2b2 Shared Task and Workshop: Challenges in Natural Language Processing for Clinical Data.

Uzuner, Ö., Solti, I., & Cadag, E. (2010). Extracting medication information from clinical text. *Journal of the American Medical Informatics Association, 17*(5), 514–518. doi:10.1136/jamia.2010.003947 PMID:20819854

Uzuner, Ö., South, B. R., Shen, S., & DuVall, S. L. (2011). 2010 i2b2/VA challenge on concepts, assertions, and relations in clinical text. *Journal of the American Medical Informatics Association, 18*(5), 552–556. doi:10.1136/amiajnl-2011-000203 PMID:21685143

Wellner, B., Huyck, M., Mardis, S., Aberdeen, J., Morgan, A., Peshkin, L., & Hirschman, L. et al. (2007). Rapidly Retargetable Approaches to De-identification in Medical Records. *Journal of the American Medical Informatics Association, 14*(5), 564–573. doi:10.1197/jamia.M2435 PMID:17600096

Wolf, M. S., & Bennett, C. L. (2006). Local perspective of the impact of the HIPAA privacy rule on research. *Cancer, 106*(2), 474–479. doi:10.1002/cncr.21599 PMID:16342254

Xu, H., Stenner, S. P., Doan, S., Johnson, K. B., Waitman, L. R., & Denny, J. C. (2010). MedEx: A medication information extraction system for clinical narratives. *Journal of the American Medical Informatics Association, 17*(1), 19–24. doi:10.1197/jamia.M3378 PMID:20064797

Xue, H., Chen, S., & Yang, Q. (2008). Structural support vector machine. *Advances in Neural Networks-ISNN, 2008*, 501–511.

Yang, H., & Garibaldi, J. M. (2015). Automatic detection of protected health information from clinic narratives. *Journal of Biomedical Informatics, 58*. PMID:26231070

KEY TERMS AND DEFINITIONS

Classification: Classification in the machine learning is defined as the supervised learning technique where problem is to identify the class of the new observation with the already developed observations through the labeled data.

Conditional Random Field (CRF): An undirected probabilistic graphic model categorized under statistical modeling method used for structured prediction in machine learning and pattern recognition.

Health Insurance Portability and Accountability Act (HIPAA): An act formulated in 1996 for the secure transmission and usability of the private health information electronically.

Machine Learning: A field of computer science that exploits the development of the algorithms for making a prediction on the data on the basis of its learning.

Medical Natural Language Processing: A domain of natural language processing that focuses on text mining of the medical records like clinical texts.

Named Entity Recognition (NER): An entity extraction task which aims to identify and retrieve the text carrying relevant information into some predefined categories.

Natural Language Processing (NLP): A domain of computer science, computational linguistics and artificial intelligence that focuses on computers understand to human languages or natural language.

Support Vector Machine (SVM): A supervised learning model used in the classification that learns from the data by developing a model that maximizes the error margin.

Chapter 12
Support Vector Machines and Applications

Vandana M. Ladwani
PESIT-BSC, India

ABSTRACT

Support Vector Machines is one of the powerful Machine learning algorithms used for numerous applications. Support Vector Machines generate decision boundary between two classes which is characterized by special subset of the training data called as Support Vectors. The advantage of support vector machine over perceptron is that it generates a unique decision boundary with maximum margin. Kernalized version makes it very faster to learn as the data transformation is implicit. Object recognition using multiclass SVM is discussed in the chapter. The experiment uses histogram of visual words and multiclass SVM for image classification.

INTRODUCTION TO PATTERN RECOGNITION

What is Pattern Recognition

Pattern recognition deals with discovering the classes in a dataset. The dataset consists of objects of different classes. Objects can be images, signals or any other details of the data depending on the application. Pattern recognition can be used in various areas such as character recognition, anomaly detection, face recognition, signal classification, medical decision making etc. Pattern recognition is the fundamental building block of intelligent system.

Features

Features represent the distinguishing information retrieved from the data. This information helps to differentiate between the data from various classes. For character data the features can be pixel intensities. For signal classification the features can be energy levels at different frequency. Feature detection itself is a vast area. Features impact the classification performance. Classification model is trained learns boundaries between various classes using these features

DOI: 10.4018/978-1-5225-2498-4.ch012

Classification

Classification is the task of distinguishing the data into different classes to which it belongs. For classification data is preprocessed then appropriate features are extracted and depending upon the application and the data available supervised, unsupervised or semi-supervised classification is used.

Supervised, Unsupervised, and Semi-Supervised Classification

In case of supervised classification training data has the correct label for the class to which is belongs to.Features are extracted from the training data, these features along with the labels are presented to the classifier, using a learning algorithm the classifier learns the decision boundaries between various classes. Features are extracted from the test data and then presented to the classifier and the classifier predicts the label for it. Unsupervised learning is used for clustering, in case of unsupervised learning dataset no information regarding which class the data belongs to and even the number of classes dataset contains. Unsupervised learning assigns the patterns to the various classes based on the similarity of the features. Semi-supervised learning on the other hand has data points with labels as well as data points for which the class is not known. Semi-supervised helps to cluster the unlabeled data by using the constraints derived from the labeled data.

WHY SUPPORT VECTOR MACHINES

Support Vector Machine Introduction

Support vector machine is one the most powerful machine learning algorithms used for classification or regression tasks. Support Vector Machines are used in various applications such as face recognition, medical decision making, regression tasks etc. with high accuracy.

Perceptron Algorithm

If we consider a 2 dimensional data the linear discriminant function is given as

$$w1x1 + w2x2 + b = 0$$

Where b represents the bias term.For a multidimensional case the equation of linear discriminant function is $f(x) = w^t x + b = 0$ This represents a hyperplane.

Perceptron algorithm tries to find this hyperplane and uses the hyperplane for classifying the linearly separable data. All the data points satisfying the relation $w^t x + b > 0$ lie to one side of the hyperplane, whereas data points satisfying the relation $w^t x + b < 0$ belong to other side of the hyperplane.

Figure 1. Separators for multiple classes

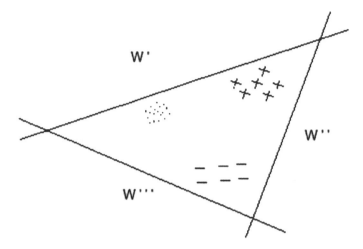

Multiclass Perceptron

Perceptron can also be used for multiclass classification.

In case of multiclass perceptron we have a separator for each of the class. The separator for a set of data points from a particular class is the one farthest from that class.

Let us consider data from three classes as depicted in Figure 1.Separators for the data labeled _,. , x are W' W'' and W ''' respectively.Class label is predicted as per the separator that satisfies the following condition

$$W = \mathrm{argmax}\left(W^{T}X\right)$$

The problem with the perceptron is that it converges to a separator but the separator need not be unique.

Support Vector Machines versus Perceptron

Consider the example as shown in Figure 2.There are two possible classifiers detected labelled 1 and 2

We observe both perform better with respect to the training data presented but if some of the data points lie outside the training data set classifier 2 performs better as compared to the classifier 1. In case of classifier 1 the separation between two class boundaries is minimal so classifier 2 gives better generalization performance due to obvious reason that it has enough margins from both the classes.The goal of support vector machines is to find out such a classifier that maximizes the margin.

Figure 2. Illustration of two separators for the linearly separable data

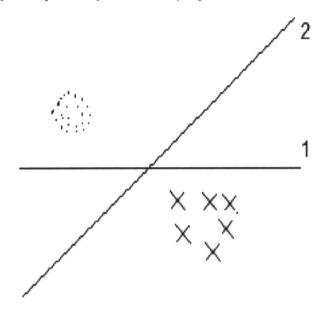

HARD MARGIN SVM

Hard Margin Primal Formulation

Support vector machines guarantees to give a unique solution in contrast to the perceptron.Support vector machine for separable case is also termed as hard margin SVM.Some candidate hyperplanes can be scaled versions of the others.For example:

$2x1 + 3x2 = 5$

$4x1 + 6x2 = 10$

Both the equations represent the same hyperplane. So we need to get rid of the scaling factor.

The hyperplane is scaled such that distance of nearest point of class1 and class2 from hyperplane is +1 and -1.So the total margin is given as $\dfrac{2}{w}$ Points belonging class1 satisfy the equation

$$w^T x + w_0 \geq 1$$

And points belonging to class2 satisfy the rule

$$w^T x + w_0 \leq -1$$

The optimization problem is maximize the margin which is same as minimizing the following objective function

$$\frac{1}{2} \, \mathrm{w}^2$$

Subject to the constraint

$$Y_{label} \left(\mathrm{w}^T \mathrm{x} + \mathrm{w}_0 \right) \geq 1$$

Where Y_{label} is +1 for class1 and -1 for class2. This is a constrained optimization problem. Lagrangian function for the problem is given as

$$L \left(\left(\mathrm{w}_0, \mathrm{w}, \pm \right) = \frac{1}{2} \mathrm{w}^T \mathrm{w} + \sum_i \pm_i \left(1 - Y_{ilabel} \left(\mathrm{w}^T \mathrm{x} + \mathrm{w}_0 \right) \right) \right)$$

The KKT conditions are given as

$$\frac{\partial}{\partial \mathrm{w}} L \left(\mathrm{w}, \mathrm{w}_0 \gg \right) = 0 \rightarrow a$$

$$\frac{\partial}{\partial \mathrm{w}_0} L \left(\mathrm{w}, \mathrm{w}_0 \gg \right) = 0 \rightarrow b$$

$$\gg_i \geq 0 \, i = 1, 2, 3, \ldots, N$$

$$\gg_i \left[y_i \left(\mathrm{w}'\mathrm{x}_i + \mathrm{w}_0 \right) - 1 \right] = 0 \, i = 1, 2, 3, \ldots, N$$

$\propto_i, \gg_i$ Represents Lagrange multipliers.

Partial differentiation of equation a and equation b gives

$$\mathrm{w} = \sum_i \propto_i y_{ilabel} \mathrm{x}_i$$

$$\sum_i \propto_i y_{ilabel} = 0$$

Dual Formulation

The dual objective function is given as

$$L\left(\propto\right) = \sum_i \propto_i \quad - \frac{1}{2} \sum_i \propto_i y_{label} x_i^2$$

Max $L\left(\propto\right)$ Subject to

$$\propto_i \ \geq \ 0$$

$$\sum_i \propto_i y_i = 0$$

Application of Multiclass SVM

Object Recognition in Natural Image Using Multiclass SVM

The proposed approach uses multiclass SVM to classify objects. Six categories of objects were considered. Dataset consists of images of bonsai, Buddha, craftsman, chopstick, homer-Simpson and porcupine.

Every image can be considered as set of specific key points like in the image of a human face, eyes, chick etc. form the key points whereas in the image of a vehicle tires, lights can be considered as the key points.

For each image in the training set the key points are detected using SIFT features. Vector quantization is performed which gives a set of centroids. Centroids represent words in the visual dictionary. Then for each training image key points are assigned to the nearest clusters and a histogram which gives number of occurrences of each key point in the image is obtained. This forms a bag of visual words same as bag of words model used for document classification. Feature file includes the features and the labels.

SVM is trained in supervised way. For a test image same features are determined and fed to SVM which predicts the label. Classification accuracy obtained using bag of visual words and SVM is 76%.

KERNEL METHODS

Kernel Trick

The dual formulation for SVM is given as

$$L\left(\propto\right) = \sum_i \propto_i \quad - \frac{1}{2} \sum_i \propto_i y_{label} x_i^2$$

Max $L\left(\propto\right)$ Subject to

$$\propto_i \geq 0$$

$$\sum_i \propto_i y_i = 0$$

This can be written as

$$L\left(\propto\right) = \sum_i \propto_i \ - \frac{1}{2}\sum_{i,j}\pm_i\pm_j y_i y_j x_i^T x_j$$

Linear SVM classifier cannot deal with the non-separable data found as in case of various applications like text, images etc. Solution to this is to use Non Linear classifiers which is a net of collection of linear classifiers example Neural Networks

The other solution is to transform the data to a higher dimensional space where it becomes linearly separable and then use the linear classifiers

If feature transformation to higher dimension is done and linear classifier is used, it may not be generalizable as per the VC theory. The solution to this is to use a kernel function.

Kernel Functions

In the dual representation the objective function for SVM it can be seen that data points appear only as the dot productsKernel function returns the value of dot product between the images of the two arguments

$$k\left(x_1, x_2\right) = < \varnothing\left(x_1\right), \varnothing x_2) >$$

It is not important here to know the transformation function $\varnothing$ Kernel Functions is a class of the functions which helps to operate in the high dimensional space without explicitly transforming each point to the high dimensional space.Few examples of kernels are

Polynomial Kernel

$$k\left(x_1, x_2\right) = \left(1 + x_1.x_2\right)^k$$

Sigmoid Kernel

$$k\left(x_1, x_2\right) = \tanh\left(a.x_1 x_2 + b\right)$$

Gaussian RBF Kernel

$$k\left(x_1, x_2\right) = \exp(- x_1 - x_2{}^2 / \tilde{A}^2$$

Other advanced kernels includeFischer kernel, Graph Kernel String Kernel

Soft Margin SVM With Kernel for XOR Problem

Consider a set of 4 data points that consists of

$$X1 = (1,1), X2 = (1,-1), X3 = (-1,1), X4 = (-1,-1)$$

We want to build SVM based classifier that predicts the labels

$$Y1 = 1, Y2 = -1, Y3 = -1, Y4 = 1$$

Respectively (the label is XOR of the two attributes of the data points)

As it can be observed that for this particular problem no linear classifier can generate the separating hyperplane. For solving this problem we can use either a nonlinear classifier like neural net or transform the data to higher dimensional space where it becomes linearly separable and then use a linear classifier.If kernel trick is used in SVM, no explicit transformation of features is required.To solve the XOR problem, following kernel is used

$$K(X_1, X_2) = (1 + X_1^T X_2)^2$$

Where $X_1 = (x_{11}, x_{12})$ and $X_2 = (x_{21}, x_{22})$ So the implicit feature transformation used for this problem is

$$\varnothing(X_i) = \left[1, x_{i1}^2, \sqrt{2}x_{i1}x_{i2}, x_{i2}^2, \sqrt{2}x_{i1}, \sqrt{2}x_{i2}\right]^T$$

The SVM is used to find the separating hyperplane of maximal margin in the new space. The separating hyperplane becomes a linear function in the transformed space but a nonlinear function in the original space.The primal SVM (soft margin) formulation is given asMinimize

$$\frac{1}{2}w^2 + C\sum_i \frac{3}{4}_i$$

Subject to

$$y_{label}(wX_i - b) \geq 1 - \frac{3}{4}_i$$

$$\frac{3}{4}_i \geq 0$$

Data points can fall into three regionsOutside the margin and on the correct side of the classifierInside the margin and on correct side of the classifierInside the margin but on the wrong side of the classifierThe first case is characterized by $\frac{3}{4}_i = 0$, the second corresponds to $0 < \frac{3}{4}_i \leq 1$ and the third case corresponds to $\frac{3}{4}_i > 1$ SVM for non-linearly separable data is also termed as Soft Margin SVMKernalised Dual formulation is as followsMaximize

$$\sum_i \pm_i - \frac{1}{2} \sum_i \sum_j \pm_i \pm_j y_{labeli} y_{labelj} K(X_i X_j)$$

Subject to

$$\sum_i \pm_i y_{labeli} = 0$$

$$C \geq \pm \geq 0$$

Solving the dual problem for the 4 set of points gives the hyper plane given by

$$x_{i1} \ x_{i2}$$

This simple example illustrates how SVM can be used for classifying nonlinearly separable data without explicitly doing the feature transformation in the higher dimensional space. It behaves as a linear classifier in the transformed space but it is a nonlinear classifier in the original space.

CONCLUSION

SVM is a highly optimal classifier. It has a very good generalization. It is used in numerous applications ranging from face detection verification, Character recognition, anomaly detection, object detection and recognition and content based image retrieval. The only disadvantage of SVM is the difficulty to choose the Kernel Function based on the data. Sometimes we need to experiment with different kernel functions and then use the one that gives best results this result in making the learning process slow.

KEY TERMS AND DEFINITIONS

Kernel Functions: Kernel functions is a class of functions which can be used in SVMs to classify non-separable data without doing explicit feature classification.

Pattern Recognition: Pattern Recognition in the discipline which tries to find the classes in the datasets of the various applications and it is the major building block of artificially intelligent systems.

Perceptron: Perceptron is a learning algorithm which is used to learn the decision boundary for linearly separable data.

Support Vector Machine: Support Vector Machines is a learning algorithm which can be used to classify linearly separable as well as non-separable data.

Section 4
Statistical Models and Designs in Computing

Chapter 13
Design and Analysis of Computer Experiments

Xinwei Deng
Virginia Tech, USA

Ying Hung
Rutgers University, USA

C. Devon Lin
Queen's University, Canada

ABSTRACT

Computer experiments refer to the study of complex systems using mathematical models and computer simulations. The use of computer experiments becomes popular for studying complex systems in science and engineering. The design and analysis of computer experiments have received broad attention in the past decades. In this chapter, we present several widely used statistical approaches for design and analysis of computer experiments, including space-filling designs and Gaussian process modeling. A special emphasis is given to recently developed design and modeling techniques for computer experiments with quantitative and qualitative factors.

1 INTRODUCTION

In many scientific and application areas, physical experimentations can be intensive or very difficult in terms of material, time, and cost. For example, it is almost impossible to conduct experimentation on an earth sized object for the weather forecast. The advance of modern computers and computer-aided design methodologies have given rise to a more economical mode of experimentation called computer experiments. Computer experiments are executed on computers using physical models and numerical methods such as finite-element-based methods and agent-based methods. Due to the complexity and inherent nature of computer models, design and analysis of computer models are quite different from the traditional de- sign and analysis of physical experiments. Computer experiments usually involve complex systems with a large number of input variables (Schmidt, Cruz, & Iyengar, 2005). Moreover,

DOI: 10.4018/978-1-5225-2498-4.ch013

Table 1. A Latin hypercube in three factors x_1, x_2, x_3

x_1	1	2	3	4	5	6
x_2	5	1	3	6	2	4
x_3	3	4	1	2	6	5

computer experiments are often deterministic. It means that replicate observations from executing the computer code with the same inputs will be identical. Thus, the conventional design and analysis of physical experiments would not be appropriate for design and analysis of computer experiments. Because of the deterministic nature of computer experiments, the modeling and analysis of computer experiments will concern more on the bias but not on reducing variance. The de- sign and analysis of computer experiments has received wide attentions in the past decades (Santner, Williams, & Notz, 2003; Fang & Sudjianto, 2006; Sacks, Welch, Mitchell, & Wynn, 1989). The uncertainty quantification and cali- bration of computer experiments also have attracted wide attentions (Kennedy & O'Hagan, 2000; Oakley & O'Hagan, 2002; Higdon, Gattiker, Williams, & Rightley, 2008).

The discussions in this chapter focus on the statistical design and analysis of computer experiments. Existing statistical designs for conducting computer experiments are reviewed in Section 3.2.1. A recent development of statistical designs is introduced in Section 3.2.2 which takes into account a commonly occurred situation where both quantitative and qual- itative variables are involved. Based on the outputs of computer simulations, statistical emulators can be built. Modeling and analysis techniques for building such emulators are reviewed in Section 3.3. Conclusions and remarks are provided in Section 3.4.

2 EXPERIMENTAL DESIGNS FOR COMPUTER EXPERIMENTS

2.1 Space-Filling Designs

Because of the deterministic property of computer experiment outputs, i.e., the same inputs would produce exactly the same outputs, traditional principles used in designing physical experiments (e.g. randomization, blocking, and replication) are irrelevant (Santner, Williams, & Notz, 2003) for designing computer experiments. For example, replication is not required. In fact, it is desirable to avoid replicates when projecting the design onto a subset of factors. This is based on the effect sparsity principle (Wu & Hamada, 2009), which stipulates that only a few out of numerous factors in the system dominate its performance. Thus a good model can be fitted using only these few important factors. Consequently, when projecting the design onto these factors, replication is not required. In addition, designs that facilitate diverse modeling methods would be desirable. Space-filling designs which aim to spread out the design points evenly over the design space are such a class of designs for computer experiments.

Latin hypercube designs (LHDs) are extensively used as space-filling designs in computer experiments (McKay, Beckman, & Conover, 1979) that take into account the deterministic property of experimental outputs. A desirable property of an LHD is its one-dimensional balance, i.e., when an n-point design is projected onto any factor, there are n different levels for that factor. Suppose the n levels of a factor are denoted by 1,..., n. Table 1 illustrates an example of an LHD with three factors in six design points. Figure 1 shows the projections of such a design onto any two factors.

Figure 1. Projections of the Latin hypercube design in Table 1 onto two factors

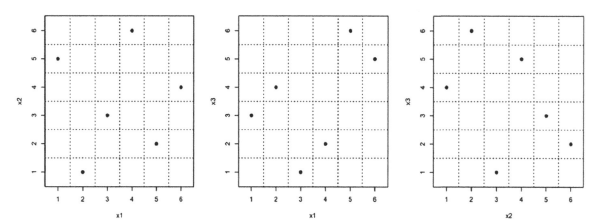

In general, an n-run LHD can be generated using a random permutation of {1,..., n} for each factor. Each permutation leads to a different LHD. For k factors, we can thus obtain (n!)k LHDs. A randomly generated LHD can have a systematic pattern: the variables may be highly correlated or the design may not have good space-filling properties. Therefore, there has been numerous work in the literature to avoid the above problems and obtain a "good" LHD. The idea is to find the best design by optimizing a criterion that describes a desirable property of the design. Iman and Conover (1982), Owen (1994), and Tang (1998) proposed to find designs minimizing correlations among factors. Johnson, Moore, and Ylvisaker (1990) and Morris and Mitchell (1995) proposed to find the best LHD by maximizing the minimum distance between the points so that they can be spread out uniformly over the experimental region. Joseph and Hung (2008) proposed a multi-objective criterion by combining the foregoing two performance measures and the resulting designs are shown to be good in terms of both the correlation and distance criteria. Other approaches of finding optimal LHDs include Owen (1992), Tang (1993), Park (1994), Ye (1998), Ye, Li, and Sudjianto (2000), and Jin, Chen, and Sudjianto (2005). To accommodate computer experiments with different data structures, variants of LHDs have been proposed. For examples, probability-based LHDs are also been proposed in Hung, Amemiya, and Wu (2010) and Hung (2011) for irregular design regions; nested LHDs for conducting multi-fidelity computer experiments have been proposed in Qian (2009); sliced LHDs are also developed in Qian and Wu (2009) for computer experiments with both qualitative and quantitative factors.

Note that, typical LHDs maintain one-dimensional projection property but cannot guarantee good space-filling properties in larger subspaces. In a recent development, Joseph, Gul, and Ba (2015) introduced a so-called maximum projection design that ensures good projections to all subspaces of the factors. A comprehensive review of space-filling designs can be found in Joseph (2016) and Pronzato and Miller (2012).

2.2 Designs With Quantitative and Qualitative Factors

The aforementioned framework for designing computer experiments assumes all input variables are quantitative (Santner, Williams, & Notz, 2003; Fang, Li, & Sudjianto, 2006). However, it is common in practice that both quantitative and qualitative variables are involved in the computer experiments. In the literature, there is few work on how to construct designs for computer experiments with both quantitative and qualitative input variables. Qian (2012) proposed sliced Latin hypercube designs (SLHDs) for such computer experiments. Such a design can be used for constructing design with both quantitative and qualitative variables where the design points in each slice of an SLHD corresponds to one level combinations of the qualitative factors. Huang, Lin, Dennis, Liu, and Yang (2015) considered one kind of sliced Latin hypercube designs with points clustered in the design region for computer experiments with quantitative and qualitative input variables. The run size of such designs can increase dramatically with the number of qualitative factors.

Deng, Hung, and Lin (2015) introduced a new class of designs, marginally coupled designs, for computer experiments with both qualitative and quantitative variables. These designs can maintain an economic run size with attractive space-filling properties. A marginally coupled design has two sub-designs, a design for qualitative factors and a design for quantitative factors. It has two features: the design points for quantitative factors form a Latin hypercube design; and for each level of any qualitative factor of a marginally coupled design, the corresponding design points for quantitative factors form a small Latin hypercube design. The concept of marginally coupled designs is well related to a class of space-filling designs, *sliced Latin hypercubes*, introduced by Qian (2012). A Latin hypercube L of $n = rm$ runs is called a sliced Latin hypercube of r slices if L can be expressed as $L = (L'_1,..., L'_r)'$ where m levels in each column of L_i have exactly one level from each of the m equally-spaced intervals $\{[1/2 + (j - 1)r, 1/2 + jr]: 1 \le j \le m\}$. Given an $n \times p$ Latin hypercube $L = (1_{ij})$, a Latin hypercube design X $= (x_{ij})$ is generated via

$$x_{ij} = \frac{l_{ij} - 1 + u_{ij}}{n}, \quad 1 \le i \le n, 1 \le j \le p$$

where u_{ij}'s are independent random numbers from (0, 1). We say L is a Latin hypercube corresponding to X.

An s-level orthogonal array A of strength t is an $n \times m$ matrix with each column taking s distinct levels and for every $n \times t$ submatrix of A, each of all possible level combinations appears equally often (Hedayat, Sloane, & Stufken, 1999). Such a design is denoted by: $OA(n, s^m, t)$. An $OA(n, s^m, 2)$ say A, is said to be α-resolvable if it can be expressed as: $A = (A'_1,...,A'_{n/(s\alpha)})'$ such that each of $A_1,...,A_{n/(s\alpha)}$ is an $OA(s\alpha, s^m, 1)$. If $\alpha = 1$, the orthogonal array is called completely resolvable.

Let D_1 and D2 be the design for qualitative factors and quantitative factors, respectively. A design D $= (D_1, D_2)$ is called a marginally coupled design if D_2 is a sliced Latin hypercube design with respect to each column of D_1. Typically, an orthogonal array is used for D_1. Example 1 provides a marginally coupled design of 9 runs for two quantitative factors and two qualitative factors.

Example 1: *Consider a computer experiment involving two quantitative variables (x_1, x_2) and two qualitative factors (z_1, z_2) each at three levels. Table 2 presents a marginally coupled design D = (D_1, D_2) of 9 runs for such a computer experiment. Figure 2 displays the scatter plots of x_1 versus x_2. Rows of D_2 corresponding to levels 0,1,2 of z_1 or z_2 are represented by ×, ○, and +. Projected onto x_1 or x_2, three points represented by × or ○ or + are located exactly in each of three intervals [0,1/3), [1/3,2/3), [2/3,1).*

Figure 2. Scatter plots of x1 versus x2 in Example 1, where rows of D2 corresponding to levels 0,1,2 of zi are marked by ×, ○, and +: (a) the levels of z1; (b) the levels of z2

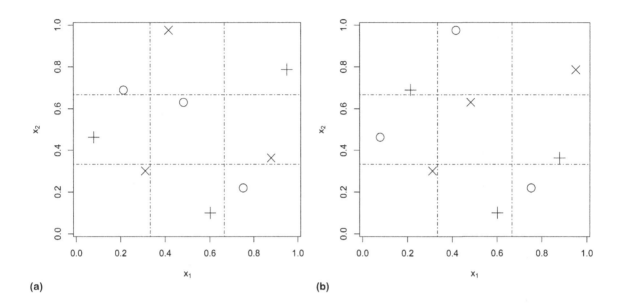

(a)   (b)

An important problem in the study of marginally coupled designs is the existence of such designs. For a given $n \times q$ design D_1, we say a marginally coupled design $D = (D_1, D_2)$ exists if there exists an $n \times p$ design D_2 with $p > 0$ such that D is a marginally coupled design. For D_1 being an $OA(n, s^q, 2)$, Proposition 1 establishes the necessary and sufficient condition of the existence of marginally coupled designs. The proof of Proposition 1 can be found in Deng, Hung, and Lin (2015).

Proposition 1: *Given $D_1 = OA(n, s^q, 2)$, a marginally coupled design exists if and only if D_1 is a completely resolvable orthogonal array.*

Proposition 1 also yields a result, Corollary 1, on the maximum number of columns in an s-level orthogonal array of n runs for which a marginally coupled design exists. This is because an s-level completely resolvable orthogonal array of n runs has at most n/s columns (Suen, 1989).

Corollary 1: *For a marginally coupled design $D = (D_1, D_2)$ with $D_1 = OA(n, s^q, 2)$, let q^* be the maximum value of q such that such a design exists. We have $q^* \leq n/s$.*

The details of construction methods for marginally coupled design can be found in Deng, Hung, and Lin (2015). Recently, He, Lin, and Sun (2016) provides more efficient construction approaches for marginally coupled designs.

Table 2. A marginally coupled design D = (D1, D2)

D_1 0	0	0.311	D_2 0.301
0	1	0.415	0.975
0	2	0.878	0.363
1	0	0.481	0.630
1	1	0.752	0.220
1	2	0.212	0.689
2	0	0.950	0.786
2	1	0.078	0.463
2	2	0.601	0.100

3 MODELING OF COMPUTER EXPERIMENTS

3.1 Gaussian Process Models

Computer experiments, although cheaper than physical experimentations, can still be time consuming and expensive. An approach to reduce the computational time and cost of running computer models is to perform optimization on a meta-model that approximates the original computer model. Kriging is a method widely used for obtaining meta-models (Sacks, Welch, Mitchell, & Wynn, 1989; Santner, Williams, & Notz, 2003; Jin, Chen, & Simpson, 2001). For examples, Pacheco, Amon, and Finger (2003) uses kriging for the thermal design of wearable computers. Cappelleri, Frecker, Simpson, and Snyder (2002) uses kriging for the design of a variable thickness piezoelectric bimorph actuator. The popularity of kriging is as a result of its interpolating property which is desirable in deterministic computer experiments (i.e., no random error in the output) (Sacks, Welch, Mitchell, & Wynn, 1989; Laslett, 1994). A kriging model, known as universal kriging, can be stated as follows. Suppose the true function is y(x), where $x \in \mathbb{R}^p$. The core idea in kriging is to model this function as a realization from a stochastic process:

$$Y(x) = \mu(x) + Z(x) \qquad (2)$$

where

$$\mu(x) = \sum_{i=0}^{m} \mu_i f_i(x)$$

and Z(x) is a weak stationary stochastic process with mean 0 and covariance function $\sigma^2 \psi(h)$. The f_i's are some known functions and μ_i's are unknown parameters. Usually $f_0(x) = 1$. The covariance function is defined as:

$$\text{cov}\left\{Y(x+h), Y(x)\right\} = \sigma^2 \psi(h)$$

where the correlation function $\psi(h)$ is a positive semidefinite function with:

$$\psi(0) = 1$$

and

$$\psi(-h) = \psi(h)$$

In this formulation μ(x) is used to capture some of the known trends, so that Z(x) will be a stationary process. But, in reality, rarely will these trends be known and thus the following special model, known as ordinary kriging, is commonly used (see Currin, Mitchell, Morris, & Ylvisaker, 1991; Welch, Buck, Sacks, Wynn, Mitchell, & Morris, 1992):

$$Y(x) = \mu_0 + Z(x) \tag{3}$$

The meta-model (or the predictor) can be obtained as follows. Suppose we evaluate the function at n points $\{x_1, \cdots, x_n\}$ and let y = $(y_1, \cdots, y_n)'$ be the corresponding function values. values. Then the ordinary kriging predictor is given by:

$$\hat{y}(x) = \hat{\mu}_0 + \psi(x)' \Psi^{-1}(y - \hat{\mu}_0 1_n) \tag{4}$$

where 1_n is a column of 1's of length n, $\psi(x)' = (\psi(x - x_1), ..., \psi(x - x_n))$, Ψ is an n × n matrix with elements $\psi(x_i - x_j)$, and $\hat{\mu}_0 = 1_n' \Psi^{-1} y / 1_n' \Psi^{-1} 1_n$.

It is the best linear unbiased predictor, which minimizes the mean squared prediction error $E\left\{\hat{y}(x) - Y(x)\right\}^2$ under (3). The mean squared error of the predictor in (4) is:

$$s^2(x) = [1 - \psi(x)' \Psi^{-1} \psi(x) + \frac{1 - 1_n' \Psi^{-1}\psi(x))^2}{1_n' \Psi^{-1} 1_n}] \tag{5}$$

With the predictor in (4) and the predicted variance in (5), confidence interval of the pre- diction can be obtained.

It can be easily shown that the predictor in (4) is an interpolating predictor. To evaluate such a predictor, a correlation function has to be specified. A widely used correlation function in computer experiments is the power exponential product correlation function given by (see Santner, Williams, & Notz, 2003):

$$\psi(h) = \exp(-\sum_{j=1}^{p} \theta_j h_j^q), \quad 0 < q \le 2, \tag{6}$$

where $\theta_j > 0$ are correlation parameters. Note that q = 1 and q = 2 correspond to the exponential and Gaussian correlation functions respectively. Other correlation functions, such as Mat´ern correlation functions (Mat´ern, 1986), are also popular in practice. More discussions on the correlation functions can be found in Cressie (1993). Based on (6), the correlation parameters $\theta = (\theta_1, ..., \theta_p)$ can be estimated using the maximum likelihood method assuming the Gaussian process for $Z(x)$ in (3). Then the maximum likelihood estimate is given by:

$$\hat{\theta} = \text{arg min } n \log \hat{\sigma}^2 + \log \det(\Psi), \tag{7}$$

where

$$\hat{\sigma}^2 = \frac{1}{n}(y - \hat{\mu}_0 1_n)' \Psi^{-1}(y - \hat{\mu}_0 1_n).$$

These results can be easily extended to the universal kriging predictor. Other estimation methods such as the penalized likelihood method (Li & Rudjianto, 2005) can also be employed.

Despite the prevalence of the ordinary kriging in many applications, it was observed that the ordinary kriging prediction can be poor if there are some evident trends (Martin & Simpson, 2005) and the prediction accuracy can be improved by selecting the important variables properly (Joseph, Hung, & Sudjianto, 2008). Take data center computer experiments as an example, there are many variables such as the rack power, diffuser flow rate, diffuser height, and hot-air return-vent location (Qian, Wu, & Wu, 2008). Among these variables, only some of them have significant contributions to the temperature distribution. In the literature, there are several methods for variable selection in computer experiments. Welch, Buck, Sacks, Wynn, Mitchell, and Morris (1992) proposed an algorithm to screen important variables sequentially and Linkletter, Bingham, Hengarten, Higdon, and Ye (2006) proposed a Bayesian variable selection procedure. These methods focus on identifying variables with significant impact on the process being studied, which is the main goal in the early stages of experimentation. This is referred to as screening in the experimental design literature (Wu & Hamada, 2009). The variable selection is carried out based on the estimated correlation parameters θ, which can be numerically unstable (Li & Sudjianto, 2005; Joseph, 2006). Therefore, the selected variables may not be reliable.

A recent approach called blind kriging (Joseph, Hung, & Sudjianto, 2008), integrates a Bayesian forward selection procedure into the kriging model. Its objective is to enhance the prediction accuracy with the help of variable selection. This method performs variable selection through the mean function and the Gaussian process part is used to achieve interpolation. It effectively reduces the prediction error and demonstrates the advantages of combining variable selection techniques with kriging. Nevertheless, the iterative Bayesian estimation is computationally intensive. Moreover, studying the selection consistency is crucial because identifying the correct mean function is an important element to ameliorate the prediction accuracy. A new approach known as penalized blind kriging is proposed by Hung (2011b) to overcome the foregoing problems. The idea is to modify the blind kriging by incorporating a variable selection mechanism into kriging via the penalized likelihood functions. Thus, variable selection and modeling are achieved simultaneously.

For complex computer experiments, a large computer model is often run with varying degrees of accuracy, resulting in computer experiments with different levels of fidelity. For example, data from multi-fidelity computer experiments can be modeled by using hierarchical Gaussian process models (Kennedy & O'Hagan, 2000; Qian, Seepersad, Joseph, Allen, & Wu, 2006; Qian & Wu, 2008). The computer experiments also often contain both quantitative and qualitative factors, new Gaussian process models with very flexible correlation structures should be used, instead of those given in (2) and (3). The next section will focus on reviewing several modeling approaches for computer experiments with quantitative and qualitative factors.

3.2 Gaussian Process Models With Quantitative and Qualitative Factors

In many applications, computer experiments often contain both quantitative and qualitative factors. For the example of data center thermal management (Jiang, Deng, Lopez, & Hamann, 2015), the computational fluid-dynamics (CFD) for studying the temperature distribution often contains qualitative factors such as "hot air return vent location" and "power unit type" (Qian, Wu, & Wu, 2008). In the application of epidemiology study (Bhuiyan, Chen, Khan, & Marathe, 2014), the agent-based network method constructs the network with shuffle type as a qualitative factor; in the full-scale embankment over soft soils, finite element modeling considers reinforcement stiffness and column length as qualitative factors (Rowe & Liu, 2015; Liu & Rowe, 2015). The investigation of wear mechanisms of total knee replacements in bioengineering (Han, Santner, Notz, & Bartel, 2009) uses the knee models with qualitative factors such as "prosthesis design" and "force pattern".

However, the standard Gaussian process models in Section 3.3.1 do not work directly for computer experiments with both quantitative and qualitative factors. The is because the correlation function in those models do not take into account the fact that different level combinations of qualitative factors may not have specific distance measurement. To address this issue, two key challenges are (1) how to construct a proper covariance structure for the qualitative factors and (2) how to specify the relationship between the correlation function for qualitative factors and the correlation function for quantitative factors. There are several work focusing on address the first challenge. One approach is to consider a restrictive correlation function (McMillian, Sacks, Welch, & Gao, 1999; Joseph & Delaney, 2007). It can simplify the computational complexity for the model estimation. Another approach is to construct an unrestrictive correlation structure for qualitative factors in Gaussian process models. Qian, Seepersad, Joseph, Allen, and Wu (2006) directly estimated the correlation structure for qualitative factors by adopting semi-definite programming in estimation to ensure the positive-definiteness of the correlation matrix. To overcome the complicated estimation procedure in Qian, Wu, and Wu (2008), a hypersphere parametrization (Pinheiro & Bates, 1996; Rebonato & Jackel, 1999) method is used to model the unrestrictive correlation structure in Zhou, Qian, and Zhou (2011). Zhang and Notz (2015) considered an indicator function method to model the correlation function for the qualitative factors. From the Bayesian modeling aspects, the hierarchical Bayesian Gaussian process models (Han, Santner, Notz, & Bartel, 2009; Swiler, Hough, Qian, Xu, Storlie, & Lee, 2014) have been adopted to accommodate both qualitative and quantitative factors.

For the second challenge of specifying the covariance function for qualitative factors and the correlation function for quantitative factors, the majority of existing work assumes the multiplication between the correlation function of qualitative factors and the correlation function of quantitative factors. Zhou, Qian, and Zhou (2011) introduced a hypersphere parameterization to quantify the correlations of the qualitative factors. Suppose that there are q qualitative factors, $z_1, ..., z_q$, in computer experiments and the jth qualitative factor z_j has m_j levels.

For $j = 1, ..., q$, let $T_j = (\tau_{r,s}^{(j)})$ be an m_j x m_j correlation matrix of the m_j levels of the qualitative factor z_j. Zhou, Qian, and Zhou (2011) apply the hypersphere decomposition to model T_j such that T_j is a positive-definite matrix with unit diagonal elements. Their approach consists of two steps. Step 1 is to find a lower triangular matrix with strictly positive diagonal entries $L_j = (l_{r,s}^{(j)})$ through a Cholesky-type decomposition, that is, $T_j = L_j L'_j$ for $j = 1, ..., q$. In Step 2, each row vector $(l_{r,1}^{(j)}, ..., l_{r,r}^{(j)})$ in L_j is specified as follows: for $r = 1$, $l = 1$ and for $r = 2, ..., m_j$,

$$
\begin{cases}
l_{r,1}^{(j)} = \cos(\varphi_{j,r,1}) \\
l_{r,s}^{(j)} = \sin(\varphi_{j,r,1}) ... \sin(\varphi_{j,r,s-1}) \cos(\varphi_{j,r,s}), \text{ for s=2,...,r-1} \\
l_{r,r}^{(j)} \sin(\varphi_{j,r,1}) ... \sin(\varphi_{j,r,r-2}) \sin(\varphi_{j,r,r-1})
\end{cases}
$$

where $\varphi_{j,r,s} \in (0, \pi)$ and $\tau_{r,r}^{(j)} = \sum_{s=1}^{r} (l_{r,s}^{(j)})^2 = 1$ for $r = 1, ..., m_j$. Combining the hypersphere decomposition for qualitative factors with the Gaussian correlation function for quantitative factors, Zhou, Qian, Zhou (2011) proposed the covariance between any two inputs $w_1 = (x_1, z_1)$ and $w_2 = (x_2, z_2)$ to be:

$$
\phi(Y(w_1), Y(w_2)) = \sigma^2 cor(Z(w_1)Z(w_2)) = \sigma^2(x_1, x_2 \mid \theta) \prod_{j=1}^{q} \tau_{z1j,z2j}^{(j)} \tag{8}
$$

where x_i and z_i represent quantitative and qualitative inputs, respectively, $R(x1, x2|\theta)$ quantifies the correlation between quantitative inputs x_1 and x_2, and $\tau_{z1j,z2j}^{(j)}$ represents the correlation between level z_{1j} and level z_{2j} of the jth qualitative factor. The drawback of the correlation function in (8) is that it may not be very flexible to accommodate the complex effects of qualitative factors on the outputs of computer experiments. For example, a zero value of any $\tau_{z1j,z2j}^{(j)}$ in (8) would result in the overall correlation $\phi(Y(w_1), Y(w_2))$ being zero.

To enhance the flexibility in capturing the correlations between qualitative and quantitative factors, for computer experiments with the p quantitative factors $x = (x_1, ..., x_p)$ and the q qualitative factors $z = (z_1, ..., z_q)$, Deng, Lin, Liu, and Rowe (2016) propose a novel Gaussian process model which models the corresponding response Y as:

$$
Y(x, z_1, ..., z_q) = \mu + G_1(z_1, x) + \cdots + G_q(z_q, x), \tag{9}
$$

where μ is the overall mean, G_j's are independent Gaussian processes with mean zero and the covariance function ϕ_j, for $j = 1, ..., q$. Different from the model in Zhou et al. [52], the additive form is employed in the proposed model in (9) to quantify the contributions of q qualitative input factors to the output. Such an additive form emphasizes the effect of each qualitative factor coupled with quantitative factors. In addition, the additive formulation enables to infer the significance of each individual qualitative factor in the model. Their proposed model in (9) also incorporates interactions between qualitative factors and quantitative factors, and interactions among quantitative factors, although its current form does not take into account the interactions among qualitative factors.

Given the model (9), the response Y follows a Gaussian process with mean zero and the covariance function ϕ specified by:

$$
\begin{aligned}
\phi(Y(w_1), Y(w_2)) &= \mathrm{cov}(Yx_1, z_1), Y(x_2, z_2)) \\
&= \sum_{j=1}^{q} \sigma_j^2 cor(G_j z_1, x_1), G_j(z_{2j} x_2)) \\
&= \sum_{j=1}^{q} \sigma_j^2 \tau_{z1j,z2j}^{(j)} R(x_1, x_2 \mid \theta^{(j)})
\end{aligned}
\tag{10}
$$

where $T_j = (\tau_{r,s}^{(j)})$ is defined as above, σ_j^2 is the variance component associated with G, and $R(x_1, x_2|\theta^{(j)})$ represents the correlation induced by the quantitative parts x_1 and x_2 with the correlation parameter vector $\theta^{(j)}$. One choice for for $R(x_1, x_2|\theta^{(j)})$ is the commonly used Gaussian correlation function in (6).

Recall that the data are (y, w_i), $i = 1,..., n$, where $w_i = (x_i, z_i)$. Denote by $y = (y_1,..., y_n)'$ the resulting outputs with the inputs $w_1,..., w_n$. Under the proposed model in (9), the log-likelihood function is given by:

$$
l(\mu, \theta, \sigma^2, T) = -\frac{1}{2} [\log | \Phi(\theta, \sigma^2, T) | + (y - \mu 1)' \Phi^{-1}(\theta, \sigma^2, T)(y - \mu 1)]
\tag{11}
$$

up to some constant. Here $\Phi(\theta, \sigma^2, T)$ is the covariance matrix of y.

The model in (9) contains the parameters $\mu, \sigma_j^2, \varphi_{j,r,s} (r = 2,..., m_j s < r)$, and $\theta^{(j)}$, for $j = 1,..., q$. Thus there are totally $1 + q + \sum_{j=1}^{q} m_j (m_j - 1) / 2 + pq$ parameters to be estimated. Let $\sigma^2 = (\sigma_1^2,..., \sigma_q^2)$, $T = (T_1,..., T_q)$ and $\theta = (\theta^{(1)},..., \theta^{(q)})$. Furthermore, denote the covariance matrix by $\Phi = \Phi(\theta, \sigma^2, T) = (\phi(y_i(w_i), y_{i'}(w_{i'})))_{n \times n'}$. It is easy to see $\phi(y_i, y_i) = \sum_{j=1}^{q} \sigma_j^2$, and $\phi(y_i, y_{i'})$ is specified by (10) if $i \ne i'$.

One way to obtain the parameter estimates is the maximum likelihood approach, i.e., maximizing the log-likelihood function in (11). That is, given (θ, σ_2, T), the maximum likelihood estimator of μ is given by:

$$
\hat{\mu} = (1'\Phi^{-1}1)^{-1} 1'\Phi^{-1}y .
\tag{12}
$$

Substituting (12) into (11), we obtain that the maximum of (11) is:

$$
l(\hat{\mu}, \theta, \sigma^2, T) = -\frac{1}{2} [\log | \Phi | + y'\Phi^{-1}y) - (1'\Phi^{-1}1)^{-1}(1'\Phi^{-1}y)^2] .
$$

The estimators of θ, σ^2, T can be obtained as:

$$
[\hat{\theta}, \hat{\sigma}^2, \hat{T}] = \mathrm{argmin} \, \log | \Phi | + (y'\Phi^{-1}y) - (1'\Phi^{-1}1)^{-1}(1'\Phi^{-1}y)^2 .
\tag{13}
$$

The minimization problem in (13) requires $\varphi_{j,r,s} \in (0, \pi)$, and $\sigma^j \geq 0$ for $j = 1,..., q$, and can be solved by standard non-linear optimization algorithms in Matlab or R.

The prediction of the proposed additive Gaussian process is similar to the prediction procedure in (3) for the ordinary kriging. The prediction of y at a new location $w_0 = (x_0, z_0)$ is the condition mean, i.e.:

$$E(y(w_0) \mid y_1,..., y_{,}) = \mu + \phi(w_0)' \Phi^{-1}(\theta, \sigma^2, T)(y - \mu 1). \tag{14}$$

where $\phi(w_0) = (\phi(w_0, w_1),..., \phi(w_0, w_n))$. Thus, given the estimates $\hat{\mu}, \hat{\phi}, \hat{\sigma}, \hat{T}$ we have the prediction of y at a new location w_0 is:

$$\hat{y}(w_0) = \hat{\mu} + \phi(w_0)' \Phi^{-1}(\hat{\theta}, \hat{\sigma}^2, \hat{T})(y - \hat{\mu} 1). \tag{15}$$

4 CONCLUSION

This chapter reviews a set of statistical methods for design and analysis of computer experiments. Interpolating models which take into account the deterministic property of computer experiments are discussed. Recent developments on experimental designs and modeling for computer experiments with quantitative and qualitative factors are introduced.

There are several topics deserving further investigation. Space-filling designs are popular in practice, but better designs may well exist. Sequential designs appears to be particularly appropriate for expensive computer experiments. However, studies on constructing sequential designs receive scant attention in the computer experiment literature. On the other hand, the existing techniques in modeling computer experiments can be computationally intensive when the number of observations is large. To overcome this challenge, development of efficient modeling techniques is called for.

ACKNOWLEDGMENT

The research of Deng is supported by NSF-CMMI-1435996 and NSF-CMMI-1233571. The research of Hung is supported by NSF-DMS-1349415 grant. The research of Lin is supported by the Natural Sciences and Engineering Research Council of Canada.

REFERENCES

Bhuiyan, H., Chen, J., Khan, M., & Marathe, M. V. (2014). Fast Parallel Algorithms for Edge-Switching to Achieve a Target Visit Rate in Heterogeneous Graphs. *Parallel Processing (ICPP), 2014 43rd International Conference on IEEE*, 60–69.

Cappelleri, D. J., Frecker, M. I., Simpson, T. W., & Snyder, A. (2002). Design of a PZT Bimorph Actuator Using a Metamodel-Based Approach. *ASME Journal of Mechanical Design, 124*(2), 354–357. doi:10.1115/1.1446866

Cressie, N. A. (1993). *Statistics for Spatial Data*. New York: Wiley.

Currin, C., Mitchell, T. J., Morris, M. D., & Ylvisaker, D. (1991). Bayesian Prediction of Deterministic Functions, with Applications to the Design and Analysis of Computer Experiments. *Journal of the American Statistical Association, 86*(416), 953–963. doi:10.1080/01621459.1991.10475138

Deng, X., Hung, Y., & Lin, C. D. (2015). Design for Computer Experiments with Qualitative and Quantitative Factors. *Statistica Sinica, 25*, 1567–1581.

Deng, X., Lin, C. D., Liu, K. W., & Rowe, R. K. (2016). Additive Gaussian Pro- cess for Computer Models with Qualitative and Quantitative Factors. *Technometrics, 0*. doi:10.1080/00401706.2016.1211554

Fang, K. T., Li, R., & Sudjianto, A. (2006). *Design and Modeling for Computer Experiments*. New York: CRC Press.

Han, G., Santner, T. J., Notz, W. I., & Bartel, D. L. (2009). Prediction for Computer Experiments Having Quantitative and Qualitative Input Variables. *Technometrics, 51*(3), 278–288. doi:10.1198/tech.2009.07132

He, Y., Lin, C. D., & Sun, F. (2016). On Construction of Marginally Coupled De- signs. *Statistica Sinica*.

Hedayat, A. S., Sloane, N. J. A., & Stufken, J. (1999). *Orthogonal Arrays: Theory and Applications*. New York: Springer. doi:10.1007/978-1-4612-1478-6

Higdon, D., Gattiker, J., Williams, B., & Rightley, M. (2008). Computer Model Calibration Using High-Dimensional Output. *Journal of the American Statistical Association, 103*(482), 570–583. doi:10.1198/016214507000000888

Hung, Y. (2011). Adaptive Probability-Based Latin Hypercube Designs. *Journal of the American Statistical Association, 106*(493), 213–219. doi:10.1198/jasa.2011.tm10337

Hung, Y. (2011b). Penalized Blind Kriging in Computer Experiments. *Statistica Sinica, 21*(3), 1171–1190. doi:10.5705/ss.2009.226

Hung, Y., Amemiya, Y., & Wu, C. F. J. (2010). Probability-Based Latin Hypercube Design. *Biometrika, 97*(4), 961–968. doi:10.1093/biomet/asq051

Iman, R. L., & Conover, W. J. (1982). A Distribution-Free Approach to Inducing Rank Correlation Among Input Variables. *Communications in Statistics Part B-Simulation and Computation, 11*(3), 311–334. doi:10.1080/03610918208812265

Jiang, H. J., Deng, X., Lopez, V., & Hamann, H. (2015). Online Updating of Computer Model Output Using Real-time Sensor Data. *Technometrics*.

Jin, R., Chen, W., & Simpson, T. (2001). Comparative Studies of Metamodeling Techniques under Multiple Modeling Criteria. *Journal of Structural and Multidisciplinary Optimization, 23*, 1–13.

Jin, R., Chen, W., & Sudjianto, A. (2005). An Efficient Algorithm for Construct- ing Optimal Design of Computer Experiments. *Journal of Statistical Planning and Inference, 134*(1), 268–287. doi:10.1016/j.jspi.2004.02.014

Johnson, M., Moore, L., & Ylvisaker, D. (1990). Minimax and Maximin Distance Design. *Journal of Statistical Planning and Inference, 26*(2), 131–148. doi:10.1016/0378-3758(90)90122-B

Joseph, V. R. (2006). Limit Kriging. *Technometrics, 48*(4), 458–466. doi:10.1198/004017006000000011

Joseph, V. R. (2016). Space-Filling Designs for Computer Experiments: A Review, (with discussions and rejoinder). *Quality Engineering, 28*(1), 28–44. doi:10.1080/08982112.2015.1100447

Joseph, V. R., & Delaney, J. D. (2007). Functionally Induced Priors for the Analysis of Experiments. *Technometrics, 49*(1), 1–11. doi:10.1198/004017006000000372

Joseph, V. R., Gul, E., & Ba, S. (2015). Maximum Projection Designs for Computer Experiments. *Biometrika, 102*(2), 371–380. doi:10.1093/biomet/asv002

Joseph, V. R., & Hung, Y. (2008). Orthogonal-Maximin Latin Hypercube Designs. *Statistica Sinica, 18*, 171–186.

Joseph, V. R., Hung, Y., & Sudjianto, A. (2008). Blind Kriging: A New Method for Developing Metamodels. *ASME Journal of Mechanical Design, 130*(3), 031102-1–8. doi:10.1115/1.2829873

Kennedy, M. C., & OHagan, A. (2000). Predicting the Output from a Complex Computer Code when Fast Approximations are Available. *Biometrika, 87*(1), 1–13. doi:10.1093/biomet/87.1.1

Laslett, G. M. (1994). Kriging and Splines: An Empirical Comparison of Their Pre- dictive Performance in Some Applications. *Journal of the American Statistical Association, 89*(426), 391–400. doi:10.108 0/01621459.1994.10476759

Li, R., & Sudjianto, A. (2005). Analysis of Computer Experiments Using Penalized Likelihood in Gaussian Kriging Models. *Technometrics, 47*(2), 111–120. doi:10.1198/004017004000000671

Linkletter, C. D., Bingham, D., Hengartner, N., Higdon, D., & Ye, K. Q. (2006). Vari- able Selection for Gaussian Process Models in Computer Experiments. *Technometrics, 48*(4), 478–490. doi:10.1198/004017006000000228

Liu, K.-W., & Rowe, R. K. (2015). Numerical Study of the Effects of Geosynthetic Reinforcement Viscosity on Behaviour of Embankments Supported by Deep-mixing- method (DMM) Columns. *Geotextiles and Geomembranes, 43*(6), 567–578. doi:10.1016/j.geotexmem.2015.04.020

Martin, J. D., & Simpson, T. W. (2005). On the Use of Kriging Models to Approxi- mate Deterministic Computer Models. *AIAA Journal, 43*(4), 853–863. doi:10.2514/1.8650

Mat'ern, B. (1986). *Spatial Variation* (2nd ed.). New York: Springer. doi:10.1007/978-1-4615-7892-5

McKay, M. D., Beckman, R. J., & Conover, W. J. (1979). A Comparison of Three Methods for Selecting Values of Input Variables in the Analysis of Output From a Computer Code. *Technometrics, 21*, 239–245.

McMillian, N. J., Sacks, J., Welch, W. J., & Gao, F. (1999). Analysis of Protein Activity Data by Gaussian Stochastic Process Models. *Journal of Biopharmaceutical Statistics, 9*(1), 145–160. doi:10.1081/ BIP-100101005 PMID:10091915

Morris, M. D., & Mitchell, T. J. (1995). Exploratory Designs for Computer Experi- ments. *Journal of Statistical Planning and Inference, 43*(3), 381–402. doi:10.1016/0378-3758(94)00035-T

Oakley, J., & OHagan, A. (2002). Bayesian Inference for the Uncertainty Distribu- tion of Computer Model Outputs. *Biometrika, 89*(4), 769–784. doi:10.1093/biomet/89.4.769

Owen, A. (1992). Orthogonal Arrays for Computer Experiments, Integration and Vi- sualization. *Statistica Sinica, 2*, 439–452.

Owen, A. (1994). Controlling Correlations in Latin Hypercube Samples. *Journal of the American Statistical Association, 89*(428), 1517–1522. doi:10.1080/01621459.1994.10476891

Pacheco, J. E., Amon, C. H., & Finger, S. (2003). Bayesian Surrogates Applied to Conceptual Stages of the Engineering Design Process. *ASME Journal of Mechanical Design, 125*(4), 664–672. doi:10.1115/1.1631580

Park, J. S. (1994). Optimal Latin-Hypercube Designs for Computer Experiments. *Journal of Statistical Planning and Inference, 39*(1), 95–111. doi:10.1016/0378-3758(94)90115-5

Pinheiro, J. C., & Bates, D. M. (1996). Unconstrained Parametrizations for Variance- Covariance Matrices. *Statistics and Computing, 6*(3), 289–296. doi:10.1007/BF00140873

Pronzato, L., & Mller, W. G. (2012). Design of Computer Experiments: Space Filling and Beyond. *Statistics and Computing, 22*(3), 681–701. doi:10.1007/s11222-011-9242-3

Qian, P. Z. G. (2009). Nested Latin Hypercube Designs. *Biometrika, 96*(4), 957–970. doi:10.1093/biomet/asp045

Qian, P. Z. G. (2012). Sliced Latin Hypercube Designs. *Journal of the American Statistical Association, 107*(497), 393–399. doi:10.1080/01621459.2011.644132

Qian, P. Z. G., & Wu, C. F. J. (2008). Bayesian Hierarchical Modeling for Integrating Low-Accuracy and High-Accuracy Experiments. *Technometrics, 50*(2), 192–204. doi:10.1198/004017008000000082

Qian, P. Z. G., & Wu, C. F. J. (2009). Sliced Space-Filling Designs. *Biometrika, 96*(4), 945–956. doi:10.1093/biomet/asp044

Qian, P. Z. G., Wu, H., & Wu, C. F. J. (2008). Gaussian Process Models for Computer Experiments with Qualitative and Quantitative Factors. *Technometrics, 50*(3), 383–396. doi:10.1198/004017008000000262

Qian, Z., Seepersad, C., Joseph, R., Allen, J., & Wu, C. F. J. (2006). Building Surrogate Models with Detailed and Approximate Simulations. *ASME Journal of Mechanical Design, 128*(4), 668–677. doi:10.1115/1.2179459

Rebonato, R., & Jackel, P. (1999). The Most General Methodology for Creating a Valid Correlation Matrix for Risk Management and Option Pricing Purposes. *The Journal of Risk, 2*(2), 17–27. doi:10.21314/JOR.2000.023

Rowe, R. K., & Liu, K.-W. (2015). 3D Finite Element Modeling of a Full-scale Geosynthetic-Reinforced, Pile-supported Embankment. *Canadian Geotechnical Journal*. doi:10.1139/cgj-2014-0506

Sacks, J., Welch, W. J., Mitchell, T. J., & Wynn, H. P. (1989). Design and Analysis of Computer Experiments. *Statistical Science*, *4*(4), 409–423. doi:10.1214/ss/1177012413

Santner, T. J., Williams, B. J., & Notz, W. I. (2003). *The Design and Analysis of Computer Experiments*. New York: Springer. doi:10.1007/978-1-4757-3799-8

Schmidt, R. R., Cruz, E. E., & Iyengar, M. K. (2005). Challenges of Data Center Thermal Management. *IBM Journal of Research and Development*, *49*(4.5), 709–723. doi:10.1147/rd.494.0709

Suen, C. Y. (1989). Some Resolvable Orthogonal Arrays with Two Symbols. *Communications in Statistics. Theory and Methods*, *18*(10), 3875–3881. doi:10.1080/03610928908830128

Swiler, L. P., Hough, P. D., Qian, P., Xu, X., Storlie, C., & Lee, H. (2014). Surrogate Models for Mixed Discrete-Continuous Variables. In *Constraint Programming and Decision Making* (pp. 181–202). Springer International Publishing. doi:10.1007/978-3-319-04280-0_21

Tang, B. (1993). Orthogonal Array-Based Latin Hypercubes. *Journal of the American Statistical Association*, *88*(424), 1392–1397. doi:10.1080/01621459.1993.10476423

Tang, B. (1998). Selecting Latin Hypercubes Using Correlation Criteria. *Statistica Sinica*, *8*, 965–978.

Welch, W. J., Buck, R. J., Sacks, J., Wynn, H. P., Mitchell, T. J., & Morris, M. D. (1992). Screening, Predicting, and Computer Experiments. *Technometrics*, *34*(1), 15–25. doi:10.2307/1269548

Wu, C. F. J., & Hamada, M. (2009). *Experiments: Planning, Analysis, and Parameter Design Optimization* (2nd ed.). New York: Wiley.

Ye, K. Q. (1998). Orthogonal Column Latin Hypercubes and their Application in Com- puter Experiments. *Journal of the American Statistical Association*, *93*(444), 1430–1439. doi:10.1080/01621459.1998.10473803

Ye, K. Q., Li, W., & Sudjianto, A. (2000). Algorithmic Construction of Optimal Symmetric Latin Hypercube Designs. *Journal of Statistical Planning and Inference*, *90*(1), 145–159. doi:10.1016/S0378-3758(00)00105-1

Zhang, Y., & Notz, W. I. (2015). Computer Experiments with Qualitative and Quan- titative Variables: A Review and Reexamination. *Quality Engineering*, *27*(1), 2–13. doi:10.1080/08982112.2015.968039

Zhou, Q., Qian, P. Z. G., & Zhou, S. (2011). A Simple Approach to Emulation for Computer Models With Qualitative and Quantitative Factors. *Technometrics*, *53*(3), 266–273. doi:10.1198/TECH.2011.10025

Chapter 14
Effective Statistical Methods for Big Data Analytics

Cheng Meng
University of Georgia, USA

Abhyuday Mandal
University of Georgia, USA

Ye Wang
University of Georgia, USA

Wenxuan Zhong
University of Georgia, USA

Xinlian Zhang
University of Georgia, USA

Ping Ma
University of Georgia, USA

ABSTRACT

With advances in technologies in the past decade, the amount of data generated and recorded has grown enormously in virtually all fields of industry and science. This extraordinary amount of data provides unprecedented opportunities for data-driven decision-making and knowledge discovery. However, the task of analyzing such large-scale dataset poses significant challenges and calls for innovative statistical methods specifically designed for faster speed and higher efficiency. In this chapter, we review currently available methods for big data, with a focus on the subsampling methods using statistical leveraging and divide and conquer methods.

1. INTRODUCTION

The rapid development of technologies in the past decade has enabled researchers to generate and collect data with unprecedented sizes and complexities in all fields of science and engineering, from academia to industry. These data pose significant challenges on knowledge discovery. We illustrate these challenges with examples from three different areas below.

- **Higgs Boson Data:** Discovery of the long-awaited *Higgs boson* was announced in July 2012 and was confirmed six months later, leading to a Nobel Prize awarded in 2013 (www.nobelprize.org). A Toroidal LHC Apparatus (ATLAS), a particle detector experiment constructed at the Large Hadron Collider (LHC) in The European Organization for Nuclear Research (CERN) is one of the

DOI: 10.4018/978-1-5225-2498-4.ch014

two LHCs that confirmed the existence of Higgs boson. The ATLAS generates the astronomically large amount of raw data about particle collision events, roughly one petabyte of raw data per second (Scannicchio, 2010). To put it into more tangible terms, one petabyte is enough to store the DNA of the entire population of the USA; one petabyte of average MP3-encoded songs (on mobile phones, roughly one megabyte per minute) would require 2,000 years to play. However, the analysis of the data at the scale of even tens or hundreds of petabytes is almost unmanageable using conventional techniques since the computation cost becomes intimidating or even not affordable at all.

- **Biological Experiments:** RNA-Seq experiments have been used extensively to study transcriptomes (Mortazavi et al., 2008, Nagalakshmi et al., 2008). They serve as one of the best tools so far for novel transcripts detection and transcript quantification in ultra-high resolution, by obtaining tens of millions of short reads. When mapped to the genome and/or to the contigs, RNA-Seq data are summarized by a super-large number of short-read counts. These counts provide a digital measure of the presence and/or prevalence of transcripts under consideration. In any genome-wide analysis, such as the bias correction model proposed by (Li et al., 2010), the sample size goes easily to millions, which renders the standard statistical computation infeasible.

- **State Farm Distracted Driver Detection Data:** Huge datasets are often generated by commercial companies nowadays. A dataset has been released by *State Farm*, the insurance company. *State Farm* is interested in testing whether dashboard cameras can automatically detect drivers engaging in distracted behaviors. Two-dimensional dashboard driver images, each taken in a car with a driver doing something in the car (texting, eating, talking on the phone, applying makeups, reaching behind, *etc.*) are provided. The goal of statistical analysis is to predict the likelihood of what the driver is doing in the picture, i.e. whether computer vision can spot each driver's distracted behavior, such as *if they are not driving attentively, not wearing their seatbelt, or taking a selfie with their friends in the backseat.* In this case, the complexity of big data, i.e. the raw data being in the form of images, poses the first problem before performing any statistical analysis: converting imaging data into the matrix form is needed. In this example, the testing data itself consists of 22,424 images of 26 drivers in 10 scenarios, each with 60 to 90 images, and totaling the size of about 5 GB. The explosion of data generated can be imagined as the time recorded and the number of drivers increases.

This implication of big data goes well beyond the above. Facebook and Twitter generate millions of posts every second; Walmart stores and Amazon are recording thousands of millions of transactions 24 hours 7 day, *etc.* Super large and complicated data sets provide us with unprecedented opportunities for data-driven decision-making and knowledge discoveries. However, the task of analyzing such data calls for innovative statistical methods for addressing the new challenges emerging every day due to the explosion of data.

Without loss of generality, in the rest of this chapter, we will assume that the datasets are already converted to numerical forms. Different statistical techniques will be discussed for analyzing large datasets. These datasets are so large that standard statistical analysis cannot be performed on a typical personal computer (PC). From a statistical point of view, the large data could arise in the following cases, either huge numbers of predictors, huge numbers of sample size or both. In what follows, we will focus on the second scenario. Next, we present the engineering solutions to this problem, point out the advantages and disadvantages, and then introduce the statistical solutions.

1.1. Engineering Solutions

For computer engineers, a straightforward way to reduce computing time is to resort to more powerful computing facilities. Great efforts have been made to solve the problem of big data by designing supercomputers. Many supercomputers have been built rapidly in the past decade, such as Tianhe-2, Bluewater and Blue Gene (Top500.org, 2014). The speed and storage of supercomputers can be hundreds or even thousands of times faster and larger compared to that of a general-purpose PC. However, the main problem with supercomputers is that they consume enormous energy and are not accessible to ordinary users. Thus, although supercomputers can easily deal with large amounts of data very efficiently, they are still not a panacea. Instead, cloud computing can partially address this problem and make computing facilities accessible to ordinary users. Nonetheless, the major bottleneck encountered by cloud computing is the inefficiency of transferring data due to the precious low-bandwidth internet uplinks, not to mention the problems of privacy and security concerns during the transfer process (Gai and Li, 2012). Another relatively new computational facility proposed is the graphic processing unit (GPU), which is powerful in parallel computing. However, a recently conducted comparison found that even high-end GPUs are sometimes outperformed by general-purpose multi-core processors, mainly due to the huge data transferring time (Pratas et al., 2012). In brief, none of the supercomputer, the cloud computing, GPUs solves the big data problem efficiently at this point (Chen and Zhang, 2014). Efficient statistical solutions are required, which makes big data problem manageable on general-purpose PCs.

1.2. Statistical Solutions

The statistical solutions are relatively novel compared to the engineering solutions. New methodologies are still under development. The methods available now can broadly be categorized into three groups: (1) divide and conquer method; (2) fine to coarse method; (3) sampling method. To be specific, we set our context as a dataset of n identically distributed observations and one response variable with p explanatory variables. Our statistical goal will be set for Model Estimation now.

1.2.1. *Divide and Conquer Method*

The divide and conquer method solves big data problems in the following manner. First, the original big dataset is divided into K small blocks that are manageable to the current computing facility unit. Then, the intended statistical analysis is performed on each small block. Finally, an appropriate strategy will be used to combine the results from these K blocks. As a result, the computation for the divide and conquer method can easily be done in parallel. However, the challenge lies in providing strategies for combining the results from smaller blocks. This is trivial for some models, like linear models or generalized linear models, for which the estimation procedures are linear by construction. More specifically, the estimating equations for the full data themselves can be written as a summation of all smaller blocks. The readers are referred to (Li et al., 2013) for more detailed discussion and theoretical properties for resulting estimators for a single parameter case. For other models, including but not limited to nonlinear parametric models (Lin and Xi, 2011), nonparametric models based on kernel regression (Xu et al., 2015), and penalized generalized linear regression models (Chen and Xie, 2014), the divide and conquer method in general still lacks a universal combining strategy which can handle all these cases.

1.2.2. Fine to Coarse Method

Another surprising yet proved to be effective idea proposed much recently is the Fine to Coarse method. To make intended algorithms for the big dataset scalable, statisticians introduced a simple solution: rounding parameters. Hence the continuous real numbers of data are simply rounded from higher decimal places to lower decimal places. A substantial number of observations are degenerated to be identical. This idea was successfully applied to the functional data analysis using smoothing spline ANOVA models. See (Helwig and Ma, 2016) for more details.

1.2.3. Sampling Methods

Another more effective and more general solution to the big data problem is the sampling method. That means that we take a subsample from the original dataset with respect to a carefully designed probability distribution, and use this sample as a surrogate for the original dataset to do model estimation, predictions as well as statistical inference. The most important component of this method is the design of probability distribution for taking the sample.

One naïve choice for the probability distribution is the simple uniform distribution. If we further set the subsample size as n, then it reduces to the procedure of bootstrap (Efrom, 1979, Wu, 1986, Efron, 1992, Shao and Tu, 2012). On the other hand, a great deal of efforts has been spent on developing algorithms for matrix-based machine learning methods and data analyses that construct the random sample in a non-uniform data-dependent fashion (Mahoney, 2011). In particular, a large body of literature specifically pointed out that the subsampling probability distribution using the statistical leverage scores outperforms uniform sampling for different purposes, especially in matrix approximation related problems (Drineas et al., 2006, Mahoney and Drineas, 2009, Drineas et al., 2011). Furthermore, efforts were put on studying the performance of leveraging based estimators from a statistical point of view (Ma et al., 2015, Ma and Sun, 2015).

Overall, the main advantage of the sampling method is its general application to various model settings. Moreover, it will automatically give rise to a random sketch of the full data as a byproduct, which is useful for the purpose of data visualization. However, the nontrivial part of using sampling method is the construction of sampling probability distribution, which plays a crucial role in sampling methods. The rest of this chapter is dedicated to elaborate on the different designs of sampling probability distributions.

2. STATISTICAL FORMULATION OF BID DATA PROBLEM

In this section, we first introduce some general background of the linear model, then discuss the general sampling method which deals with the linear model problem in big data.

2.1. Classical Linear Regression Model

Throughout the chapter, we define y as the response vector, X as the predictor matrix, n as the number of data points and p as the dimension of the predictors.

We start with the classical linear regression model:

$$y = X\beta + \varepsilon \tag{1}$$

where y is a $n \times 1$ vector, X is a $n \times p$ matrix consisting of one intercept and p–1 explanatory variables and β is the $p \times 1$ coefficient vector, ε is the noise term which is assumed to follow a multivariate normal distribution $N(0, \delta 2^1)$.

In linear models, the coefficient vector β can be estimated by calculating the ordinary least square (OLS), that is:

$$\widehat{\beta}_{OLS} = \arg\min_{\beta} \left\| y - X\beta \right\|^2 \tag{2}$$

where $\|.\|$ represents the Euclidean norm on the n-dimensional Euclidean space R^n. When X is full column rank, it can be shown that:

$$\widehat{\beta}_{OLS} = \arg\min_{\beta} \left\| y - X\beta \right\|^2 = \left(X^T X \right)^{-1} X^T y \tag{3}$$

Otherwise, when X is singular, $(X^TX)^{-1}$ should be replaced by a generalized inverse of X^TX. Consequently, the predicted response vector $\hat{y}$ can be represented as:

$$\hat{y} = X \left(X^T X \right)^{-1} X^T y \tag{4}$$

The projection matrix, $X(X^TX)^{-1}X^T$, is often referred to the hat matrix H since it looks like a hat on response vector y to get $\hat{y}$. The hat matrix H plays a crucial role in the subsequent analysis in Section 3.

To get predicted response $\hat{y}$, it suffices to calculate H, i.e. $X(X^TX)^{-1}X^T$. For robustness concern, people usually carry out the required computations by using the singular value decomposition (SVD) instead of calculating the matrix inverse directly (Golub & Van Loan, 2012).

Through some calculations, it can be shown that $H = UU^T$, $\hat{\beta}_{OLS} = \left(X^T X \right)^{-1} X^T y = V\Lambda^{-1}U^T y$.

Box 1. Singular Value Decomposition

Given any $n \times p$ matrix X, we can always decompose it to the form

$$X_{n \times p} = U_{n \times n} \Lambda_{n \times p} V^T_{p \times p},$$

where U and V are both orthonormal matrices and Λ is a diagonal matrix with all the singular values of X on the diagonal.

Algorithm 1: *General Sampling Method in Linear Model*

Step 1 (Subsampling): Take a random sample of size $r > p$ from the full data based on a sampling probability distribution $\left\{ \pi_i \right\}_{i=1}^{n}$ such that $\sum_{i=1}^{n} \pi_i = 1, 0 < \pi_i < 1$. Record the chosen data as $\left\{ y_i^*, X_i^* \right\}_{i=1}^{r}$, along with the sampling probabilities for the chosen data $\left\{ \pi_i^* \right\}_{i=1}^{r}$.

Step 2 (Model-fitting): Use the subsample to fit a weighted least square with weight $\left\{ 1 / \pi_i^* \right\}_{i=1}^{r}$ and obtain the estimator $\tilde{\beta}$ as follows:

$$\tilde{\beta} = argmin_{\beta} \left(y^* - X^* \beta \right)^T W \left(y^* - X^* \beta \right),$$

where $W = Diag \left(\left\{ 1 / \pi_i^* \right\}_{i=1}^{r} \right)$

2.2. General Sampling Method

As mentioned before, in the sampling approach we first choose a small subset of the full data, which we term as "subsampling step," then use this sample to estimate the model parameters, which we term as "model-fitting step." In the linear model setup, this approach can be utilized by sampling a small portion of rows from the input matrix X and then by carrying out linear regression on the sample data. Putting this idea in the framework of the linear model, we come up with the Algorithm 1.

Remark 1: One may wonder why the weighted least square (WLS) instead of ordinary least square (OLS) is used in the second step. This is because the estimator resulting from Algorithm 1 is a conditional asymptotically unbiased estimator for $\hat{\beta}_{OLS}$, i.e., $E \left(\tilde{\beta} | data \right) \approx \hat{\beta}_{OLS}$ and it is also an unbiased estimator for the true parameter, i.e. $E \left(\tilde{\beta} \right) = \beta$ (Ma et al., 2014, Ma et al., 2015). If OLS instead of WLS is used in the second step, the conditional asymptotically unbiasedness property will be lost. However, in that process of pertaining the unbiasedness, one can potentially end up with an estimator with a higher variance. More insights into the gains and losses for estimators result from weighted and unweighted least square estimation for subsample data will be given in Section 4.

Remark 2: Although not explicitly described, asymptotic evaluation of $\tilde{\beta}$ shows that the sampling probability distribution $\left\{ \pi_i \right\}_{i=1}^{n}$ plays an essential role in the property of the resulting $\tilde{\beta}$, especially in estimating the variance of $\tilde{\beta}$. The main goal of the rest of the chapter is to propose a computationally efficient design of $\left\{ \pi_i \right\}_{i=1}^{n}$ for better estimation accuracy.

Algorithm 2: *Uniform Sampling Method in Linear Model*

Step 1 (Subsampling): Take a random sample of size $r>p$ from the full data using a uniform sampling distribution and denote the subsample as $\left\{y_i^*, X_i^*\right\}_{i=1}^r$.

Step 2 (Model-fitting): Using the subsample to fit the least square, obtain the estimator $\tilde{\beta}_{UNIF}$ as follows:

$$\tilde{\beta}_{UNIF} = argmin_\beta \left\|y^* - X^*\beta\right\|^2$$

---

3. LEVERAGE-BASED SAMPLING METHOD

In this section, we introduce two examples of the general sampling methods, the Uniform Sampling Method and Basic Leverage Sampling Method, and give illustrations on the advantages as well as disadvantages of both algorithms.

3.1. Uniform Sampling Method

The most naïve version of the sampling method is to apply the Algorithm 2 with uniform probabilities, i.e. $\pi_i = \dfrac{1}{n}$, for $i=1,2,...,n$. In this particular situation, the WLS in step 2 reduces to the OLS.

This algorithm is easy to understand. Instead of using full data to calculate the least square estimator, we just take a simple random sample from it and calculate the estimator $\tilde{\beta}_{UNIF}$ using the subsample. One obvious advantage of this algorithm is the short computing time, which is $O(rp^2)$. Another advantage, as we mentioned in Remark 1 of Algorithm 1, is the unbiasedness of $\tilde{\beta}_{UNIF}$. However, as implied in Remark 2 of Algorithm 1, the large variance of the estimator is the main drawback of this method. When the sampling size r is small, there is a good chance that the estimator $\hat{\beta}_{UNIF}$ can be totally different from $\hat{\beta}_{OLS}$. This situation can be illustrated by the following example.

In Figure 1, the data points sampled from uniform probabilities did not identify the main linear pattern of the full data, which caused a big difference between $\tilde{\beta}_{UNIF}$ and $\hat{\beta}_{OLS}$. This significant difference is because Uniform Sampling Method ignores the different contribution of different data points for estimating $\hat{\beta}_{OLS}$. A good sampling strategy should take these differences into account. For example, if the subsampled points are spread out, that is, points in the upper right and lower left corners are included, then the fitted line will be much closer to the "truth." Since those points in the upper and lower corner of Figure 1 are high leverage points, it is easy to understand the motivation of the leverage-based sampling method discussed below.

3.2. Leverage Score and Basic Leverage Sampling Method

In the previous subsection, we mentioned that we needed to find the data points that are influential for fitting the regression line. In the statistical literature for model diagnostics, there exists the concept of leverage score to achieve a similar goal (Weisberg, 2005). For the ith data point (y_i, X_i), we define the

Figure 1. Example of the failure of the Uniform Sampling Method. For $i=1,...,2000$, $y=-0.5+x_i+\varepsilon_p$, where x_i is generated from t-distribution with df =6 and $\varepsilon_i \sim N(0,1)$. The small dots are the original data points; big dots are the subsample points. The solid line represents the fitted regression line of the full data, and the dashed line represents the fitted regression line of the subsamples.

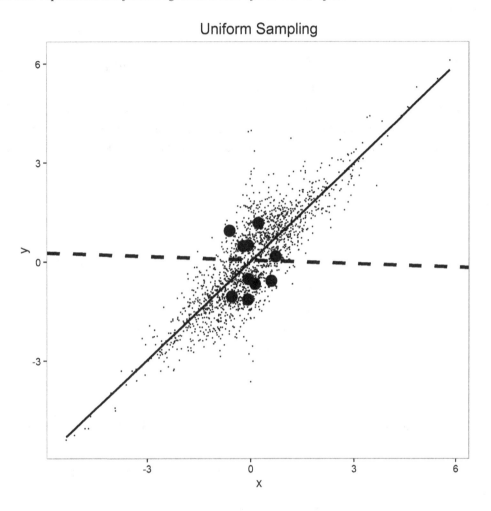

leverage score as $\dfrac{\partial \hat{y}_i}{\partial y_i}$. Intuitively, if the leverage score is large, it means that a small disturbance in y_i results in a big change in $\hat{y}_i$, thus playing a crucial role in model diagnostics.

There is also an elegant explanation for this definition. In Section 2.1, we mentioned about the "hat matrix" H which follows the relationship $\hat{y} = Hy$, i.e.

$$\begin{pmatrix} \hat{y}_1 \\ \hat{y}_2 \\ ... \\ \hat{y}_n \end{pmatrix} = \begin{pmatrix} h_{11} & ... & h_{1n} \\ h_{21} & ... & h_{2n} \\ \vdots & \ddots & \vdots \\ h_{n1} & ... & h_{nn} \end{pmatrix} \begin{pmatrix} y_1 \\ y_2 \\ y_3 \\ y_4 \end{pmatrix} \tag{5}$$

Using this relationship, the leverage score can be written as:

$$\frac{\partial \hat{y}_i}{\partial y_i} = \frac{\partial \left(\sum_{j=1}^{n} h_{ij} y_j \right)}{\partial y_i} = h_{ii}. \tag{6}$$

Hence, the leverage score for the ith data point is just the ith diagonal element of hat matrix H.

Also, it is easy to show that $Var\left(e_i\right) = Var\left(\hat{y}_i - y_i\right) = \left(1 - h_{ii}\right)\sigma^2$, which means the high leverage points have small variances of residuals and that in general $0 < h_{ii} < 1$. This result shows that the regression line tends to pass close to these data points with high leverage scores, indicating their large impact on the regression line. For example, in the univariate linear model, where the design matrix X can be written as

$$X = \begin{bmatrix} 1 & x_1 \\ 1 & x_2 \\ \cdots & \cdots \\ 1 & x_n \end{bmatrix} \tag{7}$$

$$h_{ii} = \frac{1}{n} + \frac{\left(x_i - \bar{x}\right)^2}{\sum_{j=1}^{n}\left(x_j - \bar{x}\right)^2},$$

where $\bar{x} = \dfrac{\sum_{j=1}^{n} x_j}{n}$. In this particular case, the data points with large leverage scores are the data points far away from the mean of the full data, like the points in the upper right corner and lower left corner of Figure 1, confirming our previous guess. This result also meets the general understanding of a high influential point.

When the model matrix X is full column rank, the sum of all the leverage scores of the full data is just the dimension p. Hence, $0 < \pi_i^{BLEV} = \dfrac{h_{ii}}{p} < 1$ with $\sum_{i=1}^{n} \pi_i^{BLEV} = 1$, since

$$\sum_{i=1}^{n} h_{ii} = tr\left(H\right) = tr\left[X\left(X^T X\right)^{-1} X^T\right] = tr\left[\left(X^T X\right)^{-1} X^T X\right] = tr\left(I_p\right) = p \tag{8}$$

These facts motivate the Basic Leverage Sampling Method (BLEV) discussed in Algorithm 3.

This Basic Leverage Sampling Method is another application of the General Sampling Method, in which the sampling probability are substituted by the probability distribution constructed from leverage scores. The computational complexity for BLEV is $O(np^2)$. Same as $\tilde{\beta}_{UNIF}$, $\tilde{\beta}_{BLEV}$ is also a conditional asymptotically unbiased estimator of $\tilde{\beta}_{OLS}$ (Ma et al., 2014, Ma et al., 2015). An example of the BLEV is shown in Figure 3.

Figure 2. Illustration of the leverage scores of the data points from the example in Figure 1. In a univariate linear model, the data points far away from the mean have higher leverage scores.

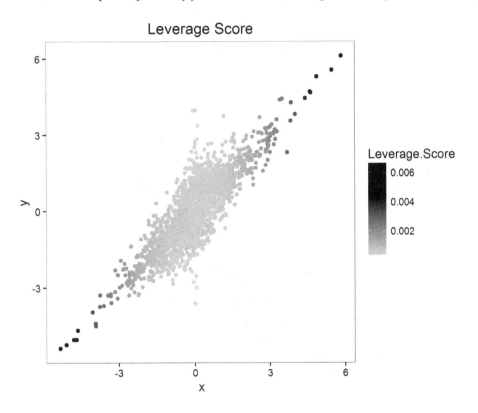

Algorithm 3: *Basic Leverage Sampling Method in Linear Model*

Step 1 (Subsampling): Take a random sample of size $r > p$ from the full data using the probability distribution

$$\left\{ \pi_i^{BLEV} \right\}_{i=1}^n = \left\{ \frac{h_{ii}}{p} \right\}_{i=1}^n \quad \text{and denote it as } \left\{ y_i^*, X_i^* \right\}_{i=1}^r . \text{ Record the corresponding sampling probability as } \left\{ \pi_i^* \right\}_{i=1}^r .$$

Step 2 (Model-fitting): Use the subsample to fit a weighted least square with weight $\left\{ 1 / \pi_i^* \right\}_{i=1}^r$ and obtain the estimator $\tilde{\beta}_{BLEV}$.

Compared to Figure 1, the advantage of BLEV is obvious, since the fitted regression line of the leverage sub-samples is very close to the fitted regression line of the full data. The probability that this scenario occurs equals to the multiplication of the leverage sampling probabilities for the sub-samples, which is 2×10^{-30} in this case. This sub-sample is relatively unlikely to be sampled from uniform probability distribution, since $(1/2000)^{10} = 1 \times 10^{-33}$. In contrast, the sub-sample in Figure 1 is relatively unlikely to be sampled from leverage probability distribution, since the multiplication of the leverage sampling probabilities for the sub-samples in Figure 1 equals to 3.7×10^{-37}, which is much smaller than $(1/2000)^{10}$.

From the example in Figure 1 and Figure 3, the Basic Leverage Sampling Method can be utilized to solve linear model problems in big data intuitively.

Figure 3. An example of the Basic Leverage Sampling Method. The data are the same that in Figure 1. The small dots are the original data; the big dots are the sample. The solid line represents the fitted regression line of the full data, and the dashed line represents the fitted regression line of the subsamples.

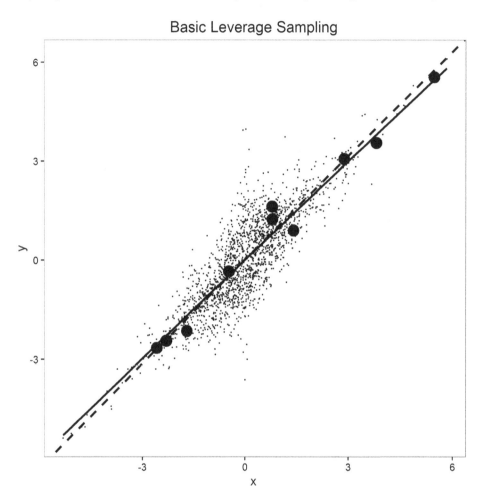

3.3. Disadvantage of Basic Leverage Sampling Method

From the observation in the last subsection, one may assume that BLEV should always have better performance than UNIF. This seems to be true in algorithmic point of view. Prior work has adopted an algorithmic perspective that focuses on providing worst-case run-time bounds for different inputs. It has been shown that leverage-based sampling provides worst-case algorithm results that are uniformly superior to the uniform sampling method (Drineas et al., 2006). However, in a statistical point of view, neither BLEV nor UNIF dominates the other (Ma et al., 2014, Ma et al., 2015). Actually, it has been shown that the variance of estimator $\tilde{\beta}_{BLEV}$ may be inflated by extremely small leverage scores. This could happen when the data distribution has a heavy tail, e.g. a Student-t distribution with small degree of freedom or Cauchy distribution. In such cases, the data points on the tail tend to have enormous leverage scores which dominate the others. For example, consider the case when the dataset has a different distribution in each dimension, the Basic Leverage Sampling Method may fail to capture all the high-influential points. Such a case can be illustrated by the example in Figure 4.

As shown in Figure 4, the high-leverage-score points are only the high influential points for the first dimension, but not for the second dimension. Hence, the subsamples chosen by BLEV are inadequate to predict the second dimension of $\tilde{\beta}_{OLS}$, leading to a bad estimator $\tilde{\beta}_{BLEV}$. That indicates that simply using the leverage score as a sampling probability seems too aggressive.

Furthermore, it poses the interesting question of if we could try different subsampling probabilities and propose even better sampling method than BLEV. These will be discussed in the next section.

4. NOVEL LEVERAGING-BASED SAMPLING METHOD

In this section, we will introduce two novel Leverage-Based Sampling Methods which aims at overcoming the drawback of BLEV.

Figure 4. Illustration of the leverage scores of the 1000 data points from a two-dimensional data set, which the first dimension comes from a Student-t distribution with degree of freedom 4 and the second dimension comes from a standard normal distribution.

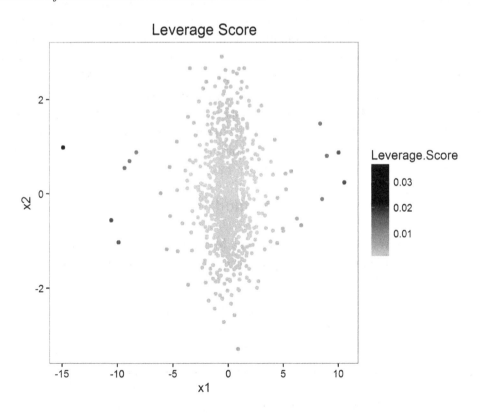

4.1. Shrinkage Leveraging Method

Recall that we want to give large sampling probabilities to the points with large leverage scores since these points are more influential to the fitted regression line. Using the leverage score as the sampling probability is a simple way to accomplish this goal, which generates the Basic Leverage Sampling Method.

In fact, as long as we preserve the ranking of the leverage score, we can still take the benefit of the influential points. We can achieve this goal by comparison between applying the following relatively conservative probability distribution SLEV (shrinkage leveraging) and applying the basic leverage score distribution. Let π_i^{BLEV} denote a distribution defined by the basic leverage scores (i.e., $\pi_i^{BLEV} = \dfrac{h_{ii}}{p}$)

and let $\pi_i^{UNIF} = \dfrac{1}{n}$ denote the uniform distribution; then the sampling probabilities for the shrinkage leveraging can be written as:

$$\pi_i^{SLEV} = \alpha \pi_i^{BLEV} + \left(1 - \alpha\right) \pi_i^{UNIF}, \alpha \in \left(0,1\right) \tag{9}$$

for $i=1,2,\ldots,n$.

Applying these sampling probabilities leads us to the Shrinkage Leverage Sampling Method (SLEV).

The computational complexity for SLEV is $O(np^2)$. The performance of the Shrinkage Leverage Sampling Method depends on how we choose the shrinkage index α. If we choose α very close to 0 or 1, it will just degenerate into the uniform sampling method or basic leverage sampling method. However, if we choose the α more wisely, the SLEV method can overcome the large variance problem. The recommended value of α is falling in the interval [0.8, 0.9] (Ma et al., 2014, Ma et al., 2015). Under this situation, the SLEV can preserve the ranking of the leverage score without containing extremely large or extremely small sampling probabilities, compared to Basic Leverage Sampling probabilities. Furthermore, all these observations also hold if we use the approximate leverage score instead of using the exact leverage score in the method. For these reasons, the SLEV procedure with approximate leverage score is the most recommended method for linear models in big data.

4.2. Unweighted Leverage Sampling Method

Before introducing the Unweighted Leverage Sampling Method, we need to discuss the criteria for judging whether a particular sampling method is good or not. From a statistical point of view, we need a

Algorithm 4: *Shrinkage Leverage Sampling Method in Linear Model*

Step 1 (Subsampling): Take a random sample of size $r>p$ from the full data using the probability distribution $\left\{\pi_i^{SLEV}\right\}_{i=1}^{n}$ and denote it as $\left\{y_i^*, X_i^*\right\}_{i=1}^{r}$. Record the corresponding sampling probability as $\left\{\pi_i^*\right\}_{i=1}^{r}$.

Step 2 (Model-fitting): Use the subsample to fit a weighted least square with weight $\left\{1 / \pi_i^*\right\}_{i=1}^{r}$ and obtain the estimator $\tilde{\beta}_{SLEV}$.

---

comprehensive criterion to consider both bias and variance simultaneously. The mean squared error (MSE) is a reasonable choice. The formula for MSE for $\tilde{\beta}$ is given below.

$$MSE\left(\tilde{\beta} \mid y\right) = E\left\|\tilde{\beta} - \hat{\beta}_{OLS}\right\|^2 \tag{10}$$

Some decomposition analysis will give that

$$MSE\left(\tilde{\beta}\right) = \left\|Bias\left(\tilde{\beta}\right)\right\|^2 + tr\left(Var\left(\tilde{\beta}\right)\right) \tag{11}$$

where we denote $Bias\left(\tilde{\beta}\right) = E\left(\tilde{\beta}\right) - \hat{\beta}_{OLS}$. This decomposition is sometimes termed bias-variance decomposition in the statistics literature.

We know that the estimator generated by UNIF, BLEV and SLEV are all unbiased estimators. This is a very appealing property, and we only need to focus on minimizing the variance of the estimator. However, if our goal is to minimize MSE, it is not necessary to let the estimator be asymptotically unbiased. In other words, an estimator with bias can still be a good estimator if it has a relatively small bias but significantly smaller variance. This is also the main motivation of Unweighted Leverage Sampling Method discussed in Algorithm 5.

It could be theoretically shown that the unweighted leverage estimator is an unbiased estimator to β as well as a conditionally unbiased estimator to the weighted least square estimator $\hat{\beta}_{WLS}$ conditional on given data (Ma et al., 2014, Ma et al., 2015). As a conditionally biased estimator, $\hat{\beta}_{WLS}$ is rarely a concern from an algorithmic perspective. However, from a statistician's point of view, the disadvantage brought by biasedness can be mitigated by the advantage by a significant decrease in variance if our main goal is to minimize MSE. This is exactly the main advantage of an unweighted leverage estimator compared to the Basic Leverage Sampling Method, i.e. it overcomes the inflated variance problem.

5. SOFTWARE IMPLEMENTATION

The key step of our BLEV, SLEV, LEVUNW method is the calculation of leverage scores a design matrix, i.e. applying SVD on it. Almost all the popular statistical software packages are available for this task such as command svd in R base, command svd in MATLAB, subroutine SVD from SAS. The

Algorithm 5: *Unweighted Leverage Sampling Method in Linear Model*

Step 1 (Subsampling): Take a random sample of size $r > p$ from the full data, probability distribution $\left\{\pi_i^{LEVUNW}\right\}_{i=1}^n = \left\{\dfrac{h_{ii}}{p}\right\}_{i=1}^n$

and denote it as $\left\{y_i^*, X_i^*\right\}_{i=1}^r$.

Step 2 (Model-fitting): Use the subsample to fit an ordinary least square and obtain the estimator $\tilde{\beta}_{LEVUNW}$.

Box 2. R Code

```
############################################################
# First, we construct a univariate linear model and set the true
# beta vector as (10,5).
############################################################
setseed=100
set.seed(setseed)
n = 10000
xx = rnorm(n)
y = 10+5*xx+rnorm(n)
############################################################
# Second, we construct the predictor matrix X.
############################################################
X = cbind(1,xx)
############################################################
# Third, we perform SVD for matrix X. Then, we extract the U
# matrix of X. Using U, we extract the leverage scores of all
#observations and put in vector hii.
############################################################
svdx = svd(X)
U = svdx$u
hii = apply(U,1,crossprod)
############################################################
# We construct subsampling probability distribution for BLEV and
# SLEV.
############################################################
blev.prob = hii/2
slev.prob = hii/2*0.9+1/n*0.1
############################################################
# We set the subsample size r.
############################################################
r = 100
############################################################
# Next, perform subsampling using hii as subsampling probability
# distribution and record the subsampling probabilities of the
# subsampled data
############################################################
blev.ind = sample.int(n=n,size=r,replace=TRUE,prob=blev.prob)
slev.ind = sample.int(n=n,size=r,replace=TRUE,prob=slev.prob)
y.blev = y[blev.ind]
y.slev = y[slev.ind]
xx.blev = X[blev.ind,]
xx.slev = X[slev.ind,]
wgt.blev = 1/blev.prob[blev.ind]
wgt.slev = 1/slev.prob[slev.ind]
############################################################
# Now perform WLS on the subsampled data for BLEV and SLEV,
# perform OLS on the subsampled data for LEVUNW
############################################################
lm.blev = lm(y.blev~xx.blev-1, weights = wgt.blev)
lm.slev = lm(y.slev~xx.slev-1, weights = wgt.slev)
lm.levunw = lm(y.blev~xx.blev-1)
bt.blev = lm.blev$coefficients
bt.slev = lm.slev$coefficients
bt.levunw = lm.levunw$coefficients
############################################################
# In order to evaluate the performance of these sampling methods,
# we run the OLS for full data
############################################################
lm.full = lm(y~X-1)
summary(lm.full)
bt = lm.full$coefficients
############################################################
# Finally, we calculate the SE of estimator from this subsampled
# data.
############################################################
SE_blev = crossprod(bt-bt.blev)
SE_slev = crossprod(bt-bt.slev)
SE_levunw = crossprod(bt-bt.levunw)
```

underlying source code for these procedures is all from LAPACK routines or equivalent. For illustration, we provide an R code.

Remark 3: When n gets large enough, calculating SVD poses a challenge in computer memory. In practice, QR decomposition is recommended instead of SVD in this case.

The order of computational cost of all the subsampling methods introduced in this chapter so far are dominated by the SVD of original data matrix X, which will be $O(np^2)$ using one of the earliest algorithms (Golub and Van Loan, 2012) and this is the same magnitude of the time order for solving the original linear problem with full data. Fortunately, there already exists fast approximation algorithms for leverage scores that can be used to achieve this goal, which decreases the running time from $O(np^2)$ to $o(np^2)$ (Drineas et al., 2012). In specific, given an arbitrary $n \times p$ matrix X such that $n \gg p$, and an error parameter $\varepsilon \in (0,1)$, the main algorithm of (Drineas et al., 2012) is based on random projection, and it computes $\tilde{l}_i$ as an approximation of the h_{ii} in the sense that $\left| \tilde{l}_i - h_{ii} \right| \leq \epsilon h_{ii}$ for all $i = 1, \ldots, n$. This algorithm runs in roughly $O(np \log(p)/\varepsilon)$ time, which will be $o(np^2)$ under appropriate settings. See Blendenpik (Avron et al., 2010), LSRN (Meng et al., 2014) as well as (Gittens and Mahoney, 2013) for further upgrading of aforementioned random projection algorithms. It is documented in these studies that if the dimension of input matrix is at least as small as several thousand by several hundred, the run time of the leveraging-based methods can be competitive compared to solving the original linear problem by QR decomposition or SVD with e.g. LAPACK.

6. DEMONSTRATION: TWO CASE STUDIES

To illustrate the performance of the sampling methods on real data, two datasets are considered: an *Illumina HiSeq data set* downloaded from TCGA (http://cancergenome.nih.gov) and the "YearPredictionMSD" dataset, a subset of the Million Song Dataset (http://labrosa.ee.columbia.edu/millionsong/). The former has a strong linear pattern while the latter does not. This property of the dataset will influence the behavior of these methods.

Coefficient estimates were obtained using four subsampling algorithms (UNIF, BLEV, SLEV(0.9) and LEVUNW) for five different subsampling size: $2p$, $4p$, $6p$, $8p$, $10p$. The subsampling size is chosen based on the $n=10p$ rule, which proposed by (Loeppky et al., 2012). For each subsample size, we take 200 hundred subsamples and calculate estimates based on each of the subsampling algorithms. We then calculate the empirical conditional biases and variances with respect to the full sample least square estimate.

6.1. Illumina HiSeq Dataset

Considering an *Illumina HiSeq data set* downloaded from TCGA for 59 cancer patients which contain $n=20,529$ genes. Here, one patient's data are randomly chosen as the response y and use the remaining patients' data as the predictors through a linear model. Thus, the number of predictors in this setup is $p=58$. We first adopt a commonly used transformation for the counts data, i.e. $\log(X+1)$. After transforming the original data, we fit a linear model for the entire data. The adjusted-R^2 is 0.9879, which represents an almost perfect fit. Next, the dataset is fit to a linear model using subsampling methods with five different subsampling sizes. Figure 5 shows the summary of our results.

Figure 5. Empirical results for the Illumina HiSeq data set. The left panel is the empirical conditional squared biases of the UNIF, BLEV, SLEV, LEVUNW; middle panel is the empirical conditional variance; right panel is the empirical conditional MSE. Solid lines for UNIF; dash lines for BLEV; the thick dotted line for LEVUNW; the thin dotted line for SLEV with α= 0.9.

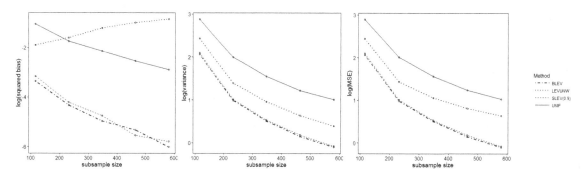

In the left panel of Figure 5, we plot the empirical conditional squared biases of the four methods. Observe that BLEV and SLEV both have smaller squared biases than UNIF and LUVUNW, which indicates that both BLEV and SLEV capture the main linear pattern of the whole dataset more efficiently than UNIF. As mentioned above, compared to $\hat{\beta}_{OLS}$, LUVUNW is a conditionally biased estimator. Thus, as the sample size becomes larger, the squared bias of LUVUNW does not decrease. Since the conditional variance, the dominant part of MSE, of LUVUNW is much smaller than that of UNIF, it still outperforms UNIF when MSE is our final consideration. In this example, BLEV and SLEV have almost the same performance and are consistently better than UNIF and LUVUNW. This is due to the strong linear pattern of the dataset. The phenomenon of a weak linear pattern of the dataset will be strongly influenced by the behavior of these sampling methods could be seen in the next example.

6.2. "YearPredictionMSD" Dataset

In this section, we consider the "YearPredictionMSD" dataset, which is a subset of the Million Song Dataset. This dataset includes 515,345 songs, with 12 features of "timbre." We take these 12 features as well as 78 timbre covariances as predictors, i.e., 90 predictors in total. We take the year of release as the response and fit a linear model to this data set. We tried all four sampling methods on the dataset, and the summary of our results is shown in Figure 6.

The performance of the conditional squared bias of these four methods in this dataset has almost the same pattern as the performance in the Illumina dataset. Interestingly, in the middle panel, the graph shows that the conditional variance of LUVUNW is much better than all the other three methods, which also makes the MSE of LUVUNW decrease much faster than the other methods as the sample size increases. However, because of the large bias of LUVUNW, its best performance on MSE only shows up when the sample size is not too big compared to the entire dataset. The performance of BLEV and SLEV are still quite similar in this example, which is due to the lack of an extremely large leverage score in this dataset. As previously mentioned, if more influential points exist with leverage scores dominating the other data points, SLEV will be more robust than BLEV.

Figure 6. Empirical results for the "YearPredictionMSD" dataset; the notation is the same as that of Figure 5

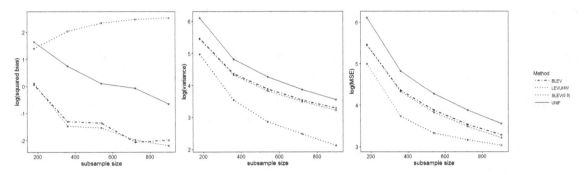

7. SUMMARY

Sampling method, as an effective and general solution for big data problem, becomes more and more attractive. In this chapter, we focus on algorithm leveraging methods for solving large least-squares regression problems. It is a recently proposed popular sampling method, shown to be efficient in sampling influential data points. We compared the performance between Uniform Sampling and Basic Leverage Sampling, then discussed two newly-proposed leverage-based algorithms, Shrinkage Leverage Sampling Method (SLEV) and Leverage Unweighted Sampling Method (LEVUNW), aiming at minimizing MSE. Moreover, our case study provided a detailed evaluation of these algorithms on the real dataset. Based on the empirical results, we have shown that these two new algorithms, SLEV and LEVUNW, providing improved performance. However, there is no universal solution here. Based on the primary goal, careful consideration is needed before applying appropriate method. If the goal is to approximate, we suggest SLEV with either exact or approximate leverage scores. The reason is that SLEV results in much better conditional biases and variance compared to other existing methods according to empirical evidence. On the other hand, if our primary goal is to infer the true and most of the data does not have a relatively good linear pattern, or the sample size is much smaller than the entire data size, LEVUNW is recommended mainly due to its advantage in giving smaller variances. Finally, although not covered in this chapter, the leverage-based sampling method can also be applied to generalized linear models, time series models, variable selections, *etc*. A further refinement of the current methods and even brand new algorithms are under intensive development.

ACKNOWLEDGMENT

This research is partially supported by the NIH grants R01 GM113242 and R01 GM122080, NSF grants DMS-1228288, DMS-1438957, NSF ATD-1440037.

REFERENCES

ATLAS. (n.d.). *Trigger and Data Acquisition System.* Available: http://atlas.cern/discover/detector/trigger-daq

Avron, H., Maymounkov, P., & Toledo, S. (2010). Blendenpik: Supercharging LAPACKs least-squares solver. *SIAM Journal on Scientific Computing, 32*(3), 1217–1236. doi:10.1137/090767911

Chen, C. P., & Zhang, C.-Y. (2014). Data-intensive applications, challenges, techniques and technologies: A survey on Big Data. *Information Sciences, 275,* 314–347. doi:10.1016/j.ins.2014.01.015

Chen, X., & Xie, M. G. (2014). A split-and-conquer approach for analysis of extraordinarily large data. *Statistica Sinica,* 1655–1684.

Drineas, P., Magdon-Ismail, M., Mahoney, M. W., & Woodruff, D. P. (2012). Fast approximation of matrix coherence and statistical leverage. *Journal of Machine Learning Research, 13,* 3475–3506.

Drineas, P., Mahoney, M. W., & Muthukrishnan, S. 2006. Sampling algorithms for l 2 regression and applications. *Proceedings of the seventeenth annual ACM-SIAM symposium on Discrete algorithm,* 1127-1136. doi:10.1145/1109557.1109682

Drineas, P., Mahoney, M. W., Muthukrishnan, S., & Sarl, S. (2011). Faster least squares approximation. *Numerische Mathematik, 117*(2), 219–249. doi:10.1007/s00211-010-0331-6

Efron, B. (1979). Bootstrap methods: Another look at the jackknife. *Annals of Statistics, 7*(1), 1–26. doi:10.1214/aos/1176344552

Gai, K., & Li, S. 2012. Towards cloud computing: a literature review on cloud computing and its development trends. *2012 Fourth International Conference on Multimedia Information Networking and Security,* 142-146. doi:10.1109/MINES.2012.240

Gittens, A., & Mahoney, M. W. (2013). Revisiting the Nystrom method for improved large-scale machine learning. *ICML, 28*(3), 567–575.

Golub, G. H., & Van Loan, C. F. (2012). *Matrix computations.* JHU Press.

Helwig, N. E., & Ma, P. (2016). *Smoothing spline ANOVA for super-large samples: scalable computation via rounding parameters.* arXiv preprint arXiv:1602.05208

Li, J., Jiang, H., & Wong, W. H. (2010). Modeling non-uniformity in short-read rates in RNA-Seq data. *Genome Biology, 11*(5), 1–11. doi:10.1186/gb-2010-11-5-r50 PMID:20459815

Li, R., Lin, D. K., & Li, B. (2013). Statistical inference in massive data sets. *Applied Stochastic Models in Business and Industry, 29,* 399–409.

Lin, N., & Xi, R. (2011). Aggregated estimating equation estimation. *Statistics and Its Interface, 4*(1), 73–83. doi:10.4310/SII.2011.v4.n1.a8

Loeppky, J. L., Sacks, J., & Welch, W. J. (2009). Choosing the Sample Size of a Computer Experiment: A Practical Guide. *Technometrics, 51*(4), 366–376. doi:10.1198/TECH.2009.08040

Ma, P., Mahoney, M., & Yu, B. (2014). A Statistical Perspective on Algorithmic Leveraging. *JMLR: Workshop and Conference Proceedings, 32,* 91-99.

Ma, P., Mahoney, M. W., & Yu, B. (2015). A statistical perspective on algorithmic leveraging. *Journal of Machine Learning Research, 16,* 861–911.

Ma, P., & Sun, X. (2015). Leveraging for big data regression. *Wiley Interdisciplinary Reviews: Computational Statistics, 7*(1), 70–76. doi:10.1002/wics.1324

Mahoney, M. W. (2011). Randomized algorithms for matrices and data. *Foundations and Trends® in Machine Learning, 3,* 123-224.

Mahoney, M. W., & Drineas, P. (2009). CUR matrix decompositions for improved data analysis. *Proceedings of the National Academy of Sciences of the United States of America, 106*(3), 697–702. doi:10.1073/pnas.0803205106 PMID:19139392

Meng, X., Saunders, M. A., & Mahoney, M. W. (2014). LSRN: A parallel iterative solver for strongly over-or underdetermined systems. *SIAM Journal on Scientific Computing, 36*(2), C95–C118. doi:10.1137/120866580 PMID:25419094

Mortazavi, A., Williams, B. A., Mccue, K., Schaeffer, L., & Wold, B. (2008). Mapping and quantifying mammalian transcriptomes by RNA-Seq. *Nature Methods, 5*(7), 621–628. doi:10.1038/nmeth.1226 PMID:18516045

Nagalakshmi, U., Wang, Z., Waern, K., Shou, C., Raha, D., Gerstein, M., & Snyder, M. (2008). The transcriptional landscape of the yeast genome defined by RNA sequencing. *Science, 320*(5881), 1344–1349. doi:10.1126/science.1158441 PMID:18451266

nobelprize.org. (n.d.). *The Nobel Prize in Physics 2013.* Available: http://www.nobelprize.org/nobel_prizes/physics/laureates/2013/

Pratas, F., Trancoso, P., Sousa, L., Stamatakis, A., Shi, G., & Kindratenko, V. (2012). Fine-grain parallelism using multi-core, Cell/BE, and GPU Systems. *Parallel Computing, 38*(8), 365–390. doi:10.1016/j.parco.2011.08.002

Scannicchio, D. (2010). ATLAS trigger and data acquisition: Capabilities and commissioning. *Nuclear Instruments & Methods in Physics Research. Section A, Accelerators, Spectrometers, Detectors and Associated Equipment, 617*(1-3), 306–309. doi:10.1016/j.nima.2009.06.114

Shao, J., & Tu, D. (2012). *The jackknife and bootstrap.* Springer Science & Business Media.

top500.org. (2014). *June 2014.* Available at: https://www.top500.org/lists/2014/06/

Weisberg, S. (2005). *Applied linear regression.* John Wiley & Sons. doi:10.1002/0471704091

Wu, C.-F. J. (1986). Jackknife, bootstrap and other resampling methods in regression analysis. *the Annals of Statistics,* 1261-1295.

Xu, C., Zhang, Y., & Li, R. (2015). *On the Feasibility of Distributed Kernel Regression for Big Data.* arXiv preprint arXiv:1505.00869

Section 5
Scientometrics and Cybernetics

Chapter 15
Measuring Complexity of Chaotic Systems With Cybernetics Applications

Nithin Nagaraj
National Institute of Advanced Studies, India

Karthi Balasubramanian
Amrita University, India

ABSTRACT

Measuring complexity of systems is very important in Cybernetics. An aging human heart has a lower complexity than that of a younger one indicating a higher risk of cardiovascular diseases, pseudo-random sequences used in secure information storage and transmission systems are designed to have high complexity (to resist malicious attacks), brain networks in schizophrenia patients have lower complexity than corresponding networks in a healthy human brain. Such systems are typically modeled as deterministic nonlinear (chaotic) system which is further corrupted with stochastic noise (Gaussian or uniform distribution). After briefly reviewing various complexity measures, this chapter explores characterizing the complexity of deterministic nonlinear chaotic systems (tent, logistic and Hénon maps, Lorenz and Rössler flows) using specific measures such as Lempel-Ziv complexity, Approximate Entropy and Effort-To-Compress. Practical applications to neuron firing model, intra-cranial pressure monitoring, and cardiac aging detection are indicated.

INTRODUCTION

Norbert Weiner defined cybernetics as the 'science of control and communication in the animal and the machine' in 1948. The famous anthropologist Gregory Bateson defined cybernetics as a highly mathematical discipline dealing with "problems of control, recursiveness, and information". There are many parallel traditions of cybernetics, but one that they all have in common is that they all are interested in the study of forms and patterns occurring in physical, biological, economic and social systems with an aim to predict, measure, control, process and communicate. Cybernetics has emerged as a highly inter-

DOI: 10.4018/978-1-5225-2498-4.ch015

disciplinary area of research which is increasingly developing a meta-disciplinary or trans-disciplinary language by which we may better understand the world around us, in order to enable us to regulate and modify it to our needs.

The intersection of cybernetics with complex systems is a primary concern, since complex systems are ubiquitous. Biological systems (e.g. Heart, Brain), ecological systems (populations of species), financial systems (markets), electrical and electronic systems (millions of diodes connected to form an integrated circuit), social networks, computational systems and communication networks (the internet is a connection of millions of computers) are just a few examples of complex systems. Many of these are modeled as deterministic (typically non-linear) or stochastic or a hybrid of the two (with noise invariably added, every real-world system has a stochastic component). It is of vital importance to study these systems to understand their organization, information transmission with or without feedback, information processing and computation, prediction and control of such systems for desired performance.

One of the important steps in modeling, designing and analyzing complex systems in cybernetics is to measure complexity of time series, measurements or observations of the system under study. The main objective of this chapter is to deal exclusively with measuring complexity of complex systems – especially those systems which exhibit complicated behavior and which have potential applications in cybernetics. Such systems are known to exhibit 'Chaos' (a technical term which we will define shortly). After studying complexity of chaotic systems, practical applications of measuring complexity will be demonstrated in three specific cybernetics applications – analyzing a neuron firing model, intra-cranial pressure monitoring, and cardiac aging detection. We shall conclude by pointing to future research directions.

COMPLEX SYSTEMS

A complex system is defined as one in which the individual components that make up the system are by themselves simple but which produces complex behavior due to varied interactions amongst themselves (Northrop, 2010). The study of complex systems has been nascent in the past and has come to prominence only in the last couple of decades. This has been made largely possible by the availability of high-end tools for high speed computation and analysis.

Complex systems possess some basic properties, listed below (Lloyd, 2001).

- They are composed of simple components.
- The interactions among components happen in a non-linear fashion.
- Control of the systems is not centralized.
- The systems show evolution and learning and adapt to improve themselves.

Some examples of naturally occurring complex systems include brain, immune system and respiratory system to name a few. A healthy human heart is known to produce complex beat-to-beat variations. Brain networks in schizophrenia patients have lower complexity than corresponding networks in a healthy human brain. In the physical world, complex systems are frequently encountered in fields like dynamics, information processing, cryptographic protocols, weather prediction, computation and study of population and evolution. For example, pseudo-random sequences used in secure information storage and transmission systems are designed to have high complexity (to resist malicious attacks). What makes complex systems really interesting is that they exhibit some very interesting behavior, even though the underlying equations may well be simple and deterministic.

Enter Chaos

Isaac Newton introduced the method of using differential equations to model the evolution of physical systems. Subsequent generations of scientists have used this procedure with incredible success not just in the physical sciences, but also in the biological sciences, engineering applications and sociology. However, finding analytical solutions to most system of differential equations is a near impossibility and one has to be content with numerical estimation. The solutions for simple systems were found to follow regular motion (steady state or periodic oscillations). However, as the system became more complex (for eg., a system with a huge number of interacting particles like molecules of air colliding in a room), it exhibited complicated behavior. Around 1975, this kind of motion was termed as "Chaos". The word "Chaos" was coined in 1975 by T. Y. Li and J. A. Yorke in their paper (Li & Yorke, 1975) which is a kind of erratic behavior (random looking) from purely deterministic systems. Even simple systems exhibited such complex behavior, which gave a new meaning to the word 'complex'. The key was non-linearity.

Henri Poincaré showed that the dynamics of simple systems (he was studying a highly simplified solar system of three bodies) exhibited "Chaos". He invented a host of techniques which are very useful in analyzing Chaotic systems. Today, the field of dynamical systems comprises the study of anomalous behavior arising out of non-linear deterministic dynamical systems which were previously considered to be experimental error or interfering noise. However, it was the advent of digital computers that enabled scientists to study Chaos in its full glory. Digital computers allow us to study systems (known as maps) that evolve in discrete time as opposed to flows that evolve continuously with time. Even seemingly simple looking 1-dimensional maps exhibit complicated behavior owing to Chaos. One of the simplest ways to "feel" and "understand" chaos in maps is to study number systems.

An Example of Chaos: Number System

We are all familiar with the decimal number system. Counting in base-10 is taught early in our childhood (because we have 10 fingers, this seems to be the natural choice). Furthermore, conversion of fractions to decimals is a routine exercise in early school. It then comes as a surprise that number systems exhibit all the features of chaos which one is typically not aware of.

To illustrate this, consider the algorithm to determine the decimal expansion of the fraction 1/7. By carrying out long division, we find that the decimal expansion of 1/7 is $0.\overline{142857}$ (the over line indicates infinite repetition). If x is a fraction in [0,1], long division can be described as follows. Compute $y = 10x$ and find the integer part of y denoted by $[y]$. In this case $y = 10/7$ and its integer part is $[y] = 1$. Next, find $z = y - [y]$. Here, $z = 10/7 - 1 = 3/7$. Replace x with z and repeat this procedure (an infinite number of times). The decimal expansion is the integer part $[y]$ recorded each time in the above procedure. Thus, long division can be seen as a map $T_{10} : [0,1] \rightarrow [0,1]$ where $x \mapsto T_{10}(x) = 10x - [10x]$ ([.] is the integer part).

Figure 1. The Decimal Map $T_{10} : [0,1] \rightarrow [0,1]$ where $x \mapsto T_{10}(x) = 10x - [10x]$ ([.] is the integer part)

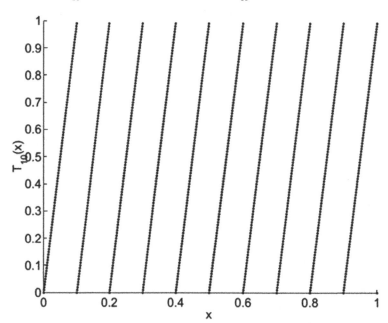

Figure 1 is a plot of the decimal map T_{10}. This map exhibits all the features of Chaos, namely, it has infinity of periodic orbits of all period lengths (these are the rational numbers *p/q* having a recurring decimal expansion), non-periodic or wandering orbits (these are the transcendental numbers like fractional part of π). In our example, 1/7 is a periodic orbit of period length 6 (since the decimal expansion of 1/7 has the same 6 digits recurring). Similarly, $1/3 = 0.333\ldots$ which has period length 1 (the decimal expansion has one digit recurring) and $\frac{1}{4} = 0.25$ which also has period length 1 (the decimal expansion is terminating which can be thought of as the digit zero recurring). There are also numbers which are not purely periodic, but eventually periodic (for eg., $1/6 = 0.1666\ldots$).

Chaos is characterized by "sensitive dependence on initial conditions". This is exhibited by the decimal map T_{10}. Two real numbers that are very close to each other have decimal expansions that are not correlated with each other after a few iterations. For example in the vicinity of the number $1/\pi$, one can find infinitely many real numbers which are recurring, but the number $1/\pi$ itself is non-periodic in its decimal expansion (since it is irrational). Similarly, one can consider the binary map $T_2(x) = 2x - [2x]$ or in general, an N-ary map $T_N(x) = Nx - [Nx]$ where N is an integer greater than 1. All these maps exhibit chaos.

Formally, a system is defined as chaotic if it satisfies a few technical conditions, as described in Devaney (1989). The key ingredients are unpredictability, indecomposability and an element of regularity. Owing to sensitive dependence on initial condition, the chaotic system is unpredictable. It can't be broken into two subsystems which do not interact with each other. Even in the midst of all this random-like behavior, there is an element of 'well-orderedness' which is due to the presence of infinity of periodic orbits which are dense.

Chaos in Biology

One of the first instances of chaos in biological models was provided by Robert May (1976). He observed that for biological populations, there is a tendency for the number of individuals to increase from one generation to the next when the number of individuals in the current generation is small, and for it to decrease when the number of individuals in the current generation to be large. He demonstrated this using the mathematical equation:

$$y_{n+1} = ay_n(1 - y_n).$$

In the above equation, 'n' stands for the population generation number, 'y_n' stands for the number of individuals in the population (size of population) generation 'n' (here 'y_n' is normalized so that the value is always between 0 and 1), and 'a' is a non-linear parameter that can be tuned. Here, 'a' can be thought of as a lumped parameter that is dependent upon all the non-linear factors governing the dynamics of the population (it incorporates environmental conditions such as availability of food). Figure 2 below shows the phase space (a plot of y_n vs. y_{n+1}) as well as the corresponding time-series (populations numbers across successive generations) for different values of 'a'.

Figure 2. The Logistic map (y_{n+1} vs. y_n) on the left and corresponding time series y_n on the right. Top: Period 3 (a=3.83). Middle: Period 8 (a=3.544090). Bottom: Chaos (non-periodic) for a=3.9

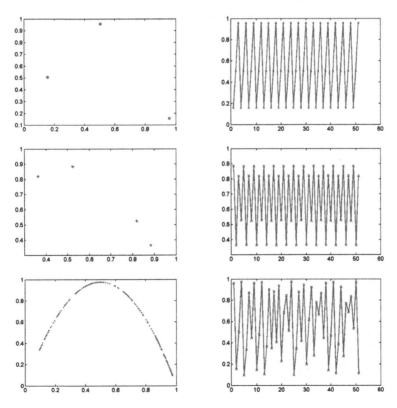

When the value of *a=3.83*, we see that the population size cycles between three distinct values, thereby yielding a period-3 orbit. When the value of '*a*' is set to *3.544090*, the population size cycles between 8 distinct values, thereby yielding a period-8 orbit. For a value of *a=3.9*, there is no periodicity in the population size (as clearly seen in the time-series on the right). This is said to be chaotic as it is does not follow any pattern. Without knowing the equation, just by looking at the chaotic time series, it is impossible to predict what will be the population size in the next generation. The above equation, known as the Logistic equation or Logistic map illustrates the point that biological systems show such complicated 'random-like' behavior, that it becomes very difficult to monitor, predict, analyze and control their behavior. This is the challenge that chaos theory addresses. Real population dynamics studies use much more sophisticated non-linear equations to model, but the intuition gained by the above example stands.

Chaos in the Heart and Brain

It has been discovered that biological systems such as the human heart and the brain, both exhibit chaos. Goldberger (1991), in his seminal paper on heart-beat dynamics, points out that even during bed rest, the heart-rate in healthy individuals is not constant or periodic, but rather shows irregular patterns that are typically associated with a non-linear chaotic system (similar to what was discussed in the previous section for the logistic map with 'a=3.9'). The phase space mapping of the heart rate time series produce 'strange attractors', not limit cycles, thus clearly indicating the presence of underlying chaotic dynamics in the heart rate variability data. One hypothesis is that a heart in a healthy physiological condition is continuously interacting and is a part of multiple complex control mechanisms in the body. These interactions enable the individual to adapt to the changing conditions of the external environment. These highly adaptive and complex mechanisms lead to a very irregular firing rate of pacemaker cells (in the heart's sinus node), thus resulting in a chaotic heart rate variability (Goldberger, 1991).

Figure 3. The human heart and brain exhibit complex behavior. Top: Human heart (left) and a representative ECG signal (right) which exhibits chaotic heart-rate variability. Bottom: Human brain (left) and a representative neuronal spike time series (right) which is chaotic

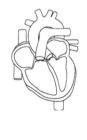
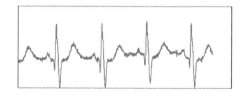

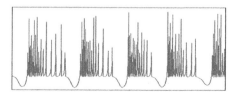

The human brain and the central nervous system is by far one of the most complex biological systems. The human brain is home to 86 billion neurons (Azevedo et al., 2009) and has synaptic connections numbering more than the number of stars in our Milky Way galaxy. The exact functioning of such a highly complex interconnected system has remained largely a mystery. We have very little idea about the way the brain organizes, stores and processes information. Neurons or nerve cells exhibit complicated behavior by producing what are known as 'spike trains', also known as action potentials. These spike trains (time series of synaptic potentials) are known to carry information from one neuron to the next. There is a long history of the search of chaos in the nervous system, some of it is traced in an excellent review article by Korn and Faure (2003). They report several studies in literature which claim to have discovered chaos in the brain, starting from chaos in a single neuron (squid giant axon, spinal giant axons, olfactory bulb, buccal-cerebal neuron, R15 neuron and hippocampal neurons), chaos as a signature of brain health (dopamine producing cells of rodents with brain legions have decreased chaotic dynamics), EEG of human epileptic seizures, higher brain functions - perception and memory, learning, recognition and recall, linguistic capabilities and several such examples. Chaos has been found at almost all levels of hierarchy in the brain and central nervous system. Having taken a brief tour of chaos, we now focus on studying complexity of chaotic systems. Information theory offers useful ways of characterizing complexity, as we shall study in the next section.

INFORMATION AND COMPLEXITY

One of the major scientific advances made in the last century was the discovery that information content of a message can be objectively measured and quantified. This measure of information, called the Shannon entropy ($H(X)$), plays a major role in both theoretical and practical aspects of information theory (Shannon, 1948). Entropy estimation is very useful because it is a direct measure of the amount of compressibility that can be achieved for the given sequence. As per Shannon's Lossless Coding theorem (Shannon, 1948), entropy $H(X)$ gives the bound on the maximum possible lossless compression - in the absence of any noise - that can be achieved by a lossless compression algorithm. A truly random sequence would have maximum entropy and would thus be incompressible. Entropy serves as a useful indicator of *complexity* of the data-set (with higher complexity, less lossless compression is possible).

Shannon's entropy measure is given by the following expression:

$$H(X) = -\sum_{i=1}^{M} p_i \log_2(p_i) \text{ bits/symbol}$$

where X is the symbolic sequence with M distinct symbols (the original time series is quantized to yield a sequence of symbols) and p_i is the probability of the i-th symbol for a block-size of one. Block-size refers to the number of input symbols taken together to compute the probability mass function. With a block size of 1, the calculated entropy is called *'first order entropy'*. With higher block sizes, we get *'higher order entropies'*.

From the above definition, we can see that accurate entropy calculation requires the probability distribution of the source producing the data. In most situations, only data would be available and not the distribution of the source producing it. Hence we calculate the probability distribution based on the data and then estimate the entropy value. This may be termed *'empirically estimated entropy'*.

Entropy may be a good measure, but its estimation is not trivial. To calculate entropy of a time series, it needs to be converted to a symbolic sequence, which requires the use of a partition (that determines the way the data is quantized). The choice of a partition greatly affects the entropy value (Ebeling, Steuer, & Titchener, 2001). Also, noise is another factor that increases entropy. Added to that, entropy value greatly depends on the length of the concerned time series. Due to these limitations of entropy, various other complexity measures such as Kolmogorov complexity, algorithmic complexity, grammar complexity and computational complexity have been proposed in the literature (Chaitin, 1974).

Complexity and Data-Length

One key concern about the use of the various complexity measures is their dependence on data length (Sokunbi, 2014). During the early days, complexity measures like Kolmogorov and Algorithmic complexities were proposed for analysis and classification of stochastic and dynamical systems. These were theoretical measures based on ergodic theorems which made them useful for analyzing lengthy time series. But when applied to short length data, they had their own limitations. Short length time series which were also corrupted with noise could not be effectively analyzed using these measures. This is an important issue to address since we often deal with real-world sequences that are short and noisy.

One of the earliest attempts to deal with shorter length sequences involved the use of lossless data compression algorithms. Data compression algorithms are generally perceived as being of interest for data communication and storage purposes only. However, their use as a complexity measure in the field of data classification and analysis has also been shown to be of great importance. In this regard, Benedetto, Caglioti and Loreto (2002) refer to how lossless compression algorithms like Lempel-Ziv (used by *Gzip, zip, WinZip*) may be used to estimate the complexity of a sequence. When the LZ-77 compression algorithm encodes a sequence of length L with entropy H, into a zipped file of length L_z, then it is known that $\lim_{L\to\infty} \left(\dfrac{L_z}{L} \right) \to H$. Using this, they define relative entropy and find similarities between sequences for automatic identification of unknown sequences using known data as learning sequences. Using such a measure, Benedetto et al. (2002) have been quite successful in applications involving language recognition, authorship attribution and language classification. Even though they were able to work with small unknown sequences for identification, it required long learning sequences to achieve the same. This may not be suitable for applications like biological time series where long sequences may not be practically available.

A Zoo of Complexity Measures

Considering the ubiquitous nature of complex systems, one would be naturally interested in understanding, analyzing, predicting and controlling these complex systems and to this end measuring 'complexity' of these systems comes into the picture. But complexity measurement is easier said than done since it is nearly impossible to define complexity in a unique fashion.

Contemporary researchers in various fields like biology, architecture, engineering, finance, dynamical systems, etc. have defined 'complexity' in different terms according to the field of application. Irrespective of the different ways of defining complexity, there are three basic questions about 'complex' systems that are addressed when we try to quantify 'complexity' of the phenomenon of interest (Lloyd, 2001). These include:

- How hard is it to describe?
- How hard is it to create?
- What is its degree of organization in terms of:
  - Difficulty of describing the organization structure.
  - Knowledge sharing and information flow among the entities.

Using these questions, grouping of complexity measures may be done. The following lists some of the main complexity measures and their foci; the list is by no means exhaustive (Lloyd, 2001).

Difficulty of Description

- Entropy (Dugdale, 1996)
- Algorithmic complexity or algorithmic information content (Chaitin, 1996)
- Rényi entropy (Rényi & Alfréd, 1961)
- Average code-length of codewords of codes like Huffman, Shannon-Fano, Arithmetic and Lempel-Ziv (Sayood, 2012)

Difficulty of Creation

- Computational complexity (Chaitin, 1974)
- Logical depth (Bennett, 1995)
- Thermodynamic depth (Lloyd & Pagels, 1988)

Degree of Organization

- Difficulty of describing the organization structure
- Fractal dimension (Mandelbrot, 1967)
- Stochastic complexity (Rissanen, 1989)
- Grammar complexity (Jiménez-Montaño, 1984)
- Mutual information among the entities.
- Conditional Information (Cover & Thomas, 2012)
- Correlation
- Channel capacity (Mackay, 2003)

The requirement of a complexity measure to overcome the data length constraints, especially in heart beat, EEG and endocrine hormone secretion data sets led to the development of a new measure known as ApEn (Approximate Entropy) (Pincus, 1991, 1995). This measure is now widely used to characterize and analyze not only biomedical data (Acharya et al., 2014; Ni, Cao, & Wang, 2014) but financial (Kristoufek & Vosvrda, 2014; Bhaduri, 2014) and seismic time series data (Kozuch & Wang, 2001).

Another measure that has come in to prominence is the Lempel-Ziv complexity (Lempel & Ziv, 1976). This is not to be confused with Lempel-Ziv lossless compression algorithm (Ziv & Lempel, 1977). This also has a wide range of applications including biomedical (Simons, Abasolo, & Hughes, 2015; Gomez-Pilar et al., 2013; Xia et al., 2014), genome data (Yu, He, & Yau, 2014) and speech analysis (Orozco-Arroyave et al., 2013).

After the advent of ApEn and LZ complexity measures, many different complexity measures similar to these were proposed. Some of them are sample entropy (Lake et al., 2002), multi-scale entropy (Humeau-Heurtier, 2015), symbolic entropy (Aziz & Arif, 2006), maximum approximate entropy (Restrepo, Schlotthauer, & Torres, 2014), permutation entropy (Bandt & Pompe, 2002; Rosso et al., 2001), multistate Lempel-Ziv (Sarlabous et al., 2009) and multiscale Lempel-Ziv (Ibáñez-Molina et al., 2015). Recently, a new complexity measure known as Effort-To-Compress (ETC) was proposed for time series analysis and classification (Nagaraj, Balasubramanian, & Dey, 2013). In this chapter, we restrict ourselves with the widely used ApEn and LZ complexity measures along with the newly proposed ETC measure.

Lempel-Ziv Complexity, Approximate Entropy, and Effort-To-Compress

We shall now briefly introduce three complexity measures – Lempel-Ziv complexity (LZ or LZC), Approximate Entropy (ApEn) and Effort-To-Compress (ETC). Subsequently, we shall employ these three complexity measures to determine the complexity of chaotic systems.

Lempel-Ziv Complexity (LZ or LZC)

Lempel-Ziv complexity is a popular measure in the field of biomedical data characterization (Gomez-Pilar et al., 2014; Xia et al., 2014). To compute the Lempel-Ziv complexity, the given data (if numerical) has to be first converted to a symbolic sequence. This symbolic sequence is then parsed from left to right to identify the number of distinct patterns present in the sequence. This method of parsing is proposed in the seminal work on Lempel-Ziv complexity (Lempel & Ziv, 1976). The very succinct description in (Hu, Gao & Principe, 2006) is reproduced here. Let $S = s1s2 \cdots sn$ denote a symbolic sequence; $S(i, j)$ denote a substring of S that starts at position i and ends at position j; $V(S)$ denote the set of all substrings ($S(i, j)$ for $i = 1, 2, \cdots n$; and $j \geq i$). For example, let $S = abc$, then $V(S) = \{a, b, c, ab, bc, abc\}$. The parsing mechanism involves a left-to-right scan of the symbolic sequence S. Start with $i = 1$ and $j = 1$. A substring $S(i, j)$ is compared with all strings in $V(S(i, j - 1))$ (Let $V(S(1,0)) = \{\}$, the empty set). If $S(i, j)$ is present in $V(S(1, j - 1))$, then increase j by 1 and repeat the process. If the substring is not present, then place a dot after $S(i, j)$ to indicate the end of a new component, set $i = j + 1$, increase j by 1, and the process continues. This parsing procedure continues until $j = n$, where n is the length of the symbolic sequence. For example, the sequence '*aacgacga*' is parsed as '*a.ac.g.acga.*'. By convention, a dot is placed after the last element of the symbolic sequence and the number of dots gives us the number of distinct words which is taken as the LZ complexity, denoted by $c(n)$. In this example, the number of distinct words (LZ complexity) is 4.

Since we may need to compare sequences of different lengths, a normalized measure is proposed and is denoted by C_{LZ} and expressed as:

$$C_{LZ} = \left(\frac{c(n)}{n}\right) \log_\alpha n.$$

where α denotes the number of unique symbols in the symbol set (Aboy et al., 2006).

Approximate Entropy (ApEn)

Approximate entropy is a complexity measure used to quantify regularity of time series, especially short and noisy sequences (Pincus, 1995). ApEn is a measure that monitors how much a set of patterns that are close together for a few observations, still retains its closeness on comparing the next few observations. Basically it checks for the convergence and divergence of patterns to check the complexity of the given sequence. If neighbouring patterns retain the same closeness, then we infer it to be a more regular pattern, with a concomitant lower ApEn value. The measure been defined in Pincus (1995) and we reproduce the definition here. Two input parameters, m and r, must be initially chosen for the computation of the measure - m being the length of the patterns we want to compare each time for closeness, and r being a tolerance factor for the regularity of the two sets of patterns being compared.

Given a sequence u of length N, we now define the complexity ApEn(m,r,N) as follows.

- Form vector sequences $x(1)$ through $x(N - m + 1)$ defined by $x(i) = [u(i), u(i + 1),...u(i + m - 1)]$, representing m consecutive u values, starting from the ith value.
- Define the distance $d[x(i), x(j)]$ between vectors $x(i)$ and $x(j)$ as the maximum difference in their respective scalar components.
- For each $i \leq N - m+1$, calculate the number of $j \leq N - m+1$ such that $d[x(i), x(j)] \leq r$ and call the number as $k(i)$.
- For each $i \leq N - m + 1$, calculate the parameters $Ci\, m(r) = k(i)/(N - m + 1)$. These parameters measure, within a tolerance r, the regularity or frequency of patterns similar to given pattern of length m.

Define:

$$\phi^m(r) = \frac{\sum_{i=1}^{N-m+1} \ln C_i^m(r)}{N - m + 1}$$

Using this, ApEn complexity measure is defined as:

$$ApEn(m, r, N) = \phi^m(r) - \phi^{m+1}(r).$$

It has been shown (Pincus, 1995) that for $m=1$ and 2, values of r between 0.1 to $0.25SD$(standard deviation) of the sequence provide good statistical validity of ApEn(m, r, N). In our analysis, we use $m=1$ and $r = 0.25SD$(standard deviation) of the sequence.

Effort-To-Compress (ETC)

Effort-To-Compress (ETC) is a recently proposed complexity measure that is based on the effort required by a lossless compression algorithm to compress a given sequence (Nagaraj, Balasubramanian, & Dey, 2013). The measure has been proposed using a lossless compression algorithm known as Non-sequential Recursive Pair Substitution (NSRPS). The algorithm for compressing a given sequence of symbols proceeds as follows. At the first iteration, that pair of symbols which has maximum number of occurrences is replaced with a new symbol. For example, the input sequence '11010010' is transformed into '12202' since the pair '10' has maximum number of occurrences compared to other pairs ('00', '01' and '11'). In the second iteration, '12202' is transformed to '3202' since '12' has maximum frequency (in fact all pairs are equally likely). The algorithm proceeds in this fashion until the length of the string is 1 or the string becomes a constant sequence (at which stage the entropy is zero and the algorithm halts). In this example, the algorithm transforms the input sequence '11010010' → '12202' → '3202' → '402' → '52' → '6'.

The ETC measure is defined as N, the number of iterations required for the input sequence to be transformed to a constant sequence through the usage of NSRPS algorithm. N is an integer that varies between 0 and $L - 1$, where L stands for the length of the input symbolic sequence. The normalized version of the measure is given by: $N/(L-1)$ (Note: $0 \leq N/(L-1) \leq 1$). See Nagaraj et al. (2013) for further details.

We shall now employ these three measures to measure the complexity of chaotic systems.

MEASURING COMPLEXITY OF CHAOTIC SYSTEMS

Many naturally occurring signals like heartbeat intervals and speech data are neither regular nor completely random and may display various kinds of non-linear behavior including chaos. Hence a study of the effectiveness of complexity measures on simulated chaotic and random data will give a good idea regarding its usefulness in characterizing real world signals. In this chapter we analyze the performance of ApEn, LZ and ETC complexity measures on data generated from various chaotic maps and flows. Noise analysis is also performed using additive Gaussian noise.

It is well known that most signals occurring in nature display a variety of behavior and are not restricted to just being periodic or random in nature. Common examples of such signals are ECG and speech signals. The nonlinear nature of these signals that causes various behaviour like periodicity and chaos are very well documented in (Goldberger, 1991; Teager & Teager, 1990). This being the case, it makes sense to generate synthetic data of various known complexities and do a preliminary analysis of the performance of complexity measures characterizing these signals before using real world signals. The goal of this section is to deal with complexity analysis of data of different complexities generated from chaotic maps, flows and stochastic systems.

Methodology

In the field of complexity analysis, automatic data classification deals with the ability of algorithms to identify the origin of a data sequence, given that it comes from a set of known sequences. Talbinejad, Tsoulfas & Musallam (2011) have done a basic complexity analysis of data from logistic map using LZ complexity measure while Pincus (1991) has used ApEn to analyse data from logistic map, Hénon map and Rössler system. They have shown that LZ and ApEn are able to distinguish between data complexities for sequences of different lengths but the analysis is done for data generated using a single initial value. This is not enough to claim that the measures are able to distinguish data of different complexities since different initial conditions will give rise to completely different sequences. We analyze the problem with multiple values of initial conditions and perform statistical hypothesis testing for differences in means to determine the minimum sequence length at which correct identification is achieved. This is performed for all the three measures namely ETC, LZ and ApEn and a comparative analysis is performed. This analysis is done for data generated using logistic map, tent map, Hénon map, Rössler system, Lorenz system and a stochastic system with Gaussian distribution. We also include uniform random sequence and check if the measures are able to distinguish it from chaotic data of different complexities.

In this work, we deal with data sequences of different complexities generated from the various chaotic maps and flows mentioned above. All the sequences produced consist of real numbers. While ApEn complexity measure is calculated directly using these values, LZ and ETC measures require that these be changed to symbols. Here we quantize the range of output values into equal sized bins, assigning a symbol to each bin and thus converting the string of real numbers into a symbolic sequence. The obtained symbolic sequences are then used for calculating LZ and ETC measures. Having generated these different sequences of varying lengths, complexity measures are applied and the results observed to see if there are marked statistically significant differences in the calculated complexity values.

Systems Description

We now describe the various maps and flows that have been used to generate data for our analysis. It is to be noted that along with data from each system, a uniformly distributed random sequence is also generated.

It is well know than that each system shows a range of behaviour corresponding to changes in a specific parameter value. Along with the mathematical description of the system, the parameter values that have been used to generate data of different complexities are also mentioned. Accordingly, the expected order of complexity for the generated data sets is provided. This can be used as a reference for understanding the results presented subsequently.

1. **Logistic Map**: As previously described, this is a second degree polynomial mapping that is used for modeling population dynamics. Mathematically, it is written as:

$$y_{n+1} = ay_n(1 - y_n).$$

Here a is the bifurcation parameter that controls the behaviour of the map. A bifurcation parameter of 3.83 produces a periodic sequence while $a = 3.9$ and $a = 4$ give rise to chaotic sequences with $a = 4$ displaying complete chaos (Alligood, 1997) with no attracting periodic orbits. Thus data generated with these values of a is expected to have complexities in the following order:

$$(a = 3.83) < (a = 3.9) < (a = 4) < \text{random sequence},$$

where "$A < B$" means that data generated for A is of lower complexity than data generated for B.

Figure 4. Logistic map (y_{n+1} vs. y_n)

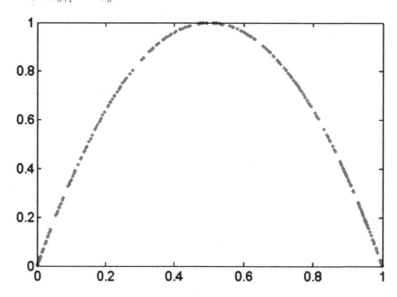

2. **Tent Map**: This is a first degree polynomial that can be mathematically written as:

$$y_{n+1} = \mu y_n, \qquad \text{for} \quad 0 \leq y_n < \tfrac{1}{2}.$$
$$= \mu(1 - y_n), \quad \text{for} \quad \tfrac{1}{2} \leq y_n < 1.$$

Here μ controls the nature of the sequence produced. From the expression of the Lyapunov exponent (a measure of the degree of chaos, see Alligood (1997)) of the tent map ($\lambda = ln \bmod (\mu)$), it can be inferred

Figure 5. Tent map (y_{n+1} vs. y_n)

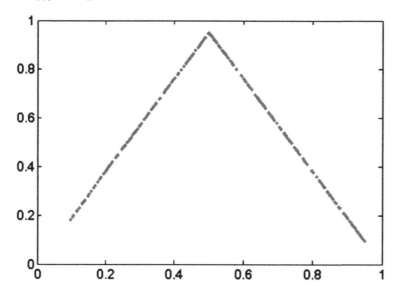

that the complexity of the sequence is directly related to μ. Higher the value of μ, higher is the complexity and vice versa. We have used $\mu = 1.5$, 1.8 and 1.9 for generating data with complexities as shown:

$$(\mu = 1.5) < (\mu = 1.8) < (\mu = 1.9) < \text{random sequence}.$$

3.   **Hénon Map**: It is a two dimensional map with quadratic nonlinearity that exhibits different phenomenon ranging from periodic to complete chaos. It can be modeled by the following two equations:

$$x_{n+1} = 1 - ax_n^2 + y_n,$$

$$y_{n+1} = bx_n.$$

Combining the two equations, we may write it as a single variable with two delays as:

$$x_{n+1} = 1 - ax_n^2 + bx_{n-1}.$$

Variation in the bifurcation parameters a and b produces data of different complexities. We fix the value of b at 0.3 and use three values of a (1.2, 1.3 and 1.4). Using $a = 1.3$ produces a period 6 orbit while $a = 1.2$ and 1.4 give rise to chaotic dynamics with $a = 1.4$ showing complete chaos (Strogatz, 2014). Thus the expected order of complexity is:

$$(a = 1.3) < (a = 1.2) < (a = 1.4) < \text{random sequence}.$$

Figure 6. Hénon Map (y_n vs. x_n)

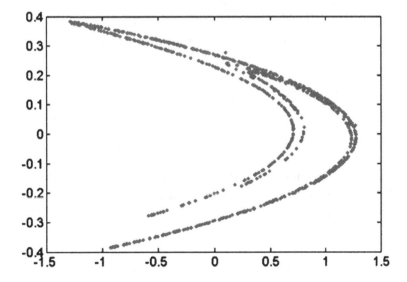

Figure 7. Rössler system ($x(t)$ vs. $y(t)$ vs. $z(t)$)

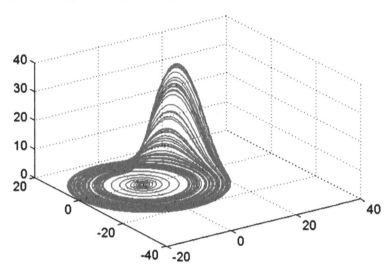

4. **Rössler System**: It is a continuous time dynamical system defined by three nonlinear differential equations capable of producing a range of behaviour including chaos. It is used for modeling different phenomenon, one being equilibrium in chemical reactions. The defining equations are as below:

$$\frac{dx}{dt} = -y - z,$$
$$\frac{dy}{dt} = x + ay,$$
$$\frac{dz}{dt} = b + Rz(x - c).$$

Pincus (1995) in his seminal paper on ApEn uses $a = 0.15$, $b = 0.2$ and $c = 5$ to generate time series data from the y values for analyzing the approximate entropy measure. Various sequences of different complexities have been generated using $R = 0.7$, 0.8 and 0.9 providing data with complexities in the given order:

$$(R = 0.7) < (R = 0.8) < (R = 0.9) < \text{random sequence}.$$

We generate similar data in order to perform our complexity analysis.

5. **Lorenz System**: It is a continuous time, three dimensional dynamical system, used for modelling weather conditions among other purposes. The model produces a rich set of dynamic behaviour. Mathematically, it is described as:

Figure 8. Lorenz system ($x(t)$ vs. $y(t)$ vs. $z(t)$) fig8.tiff

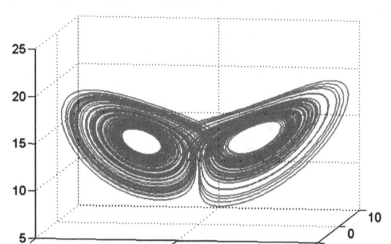

$$\frac{dx}{dt} = \sigma y - \sigma x,$$

$$\frac{dy}{dt} = \rho x - xz - y,$$

$$\frac{dz}{dt} = xy + \beta z.$$

With fixed values of $\sigma = 10$ and $\beta = 8/3$, the value of ρ is varied from 20 to 28 to get data of increasing order of complexity (Strogatz, 2014) as given below.

$(\rho = 20) < (\rho = 25) < (\rho = 28) <$ random sequence.

Similar to the analysis of the Rössler system, here also the *y* values are chosen for analysis.

6. **Stochastic System:** Along with the various maps and flows mentioned above, we also perform complexity analysis of data generated from a zero mean Gaussian distribution with a standard deviation of 0.1. Analysis is performed to check if the complexity of the data from Gaussian probability density function has lesser complexity as compared to a random signal (uniform probability density function).

Testing Procedure

For analysis purposes, data sequences of different complexities are generated from the various chaotic maps and flows described above. Using different values of the bifurcation parameters as given in the previous section, we obtain sequences of different complexities from each of the systems.

For each one of the systems, different sets of data sequences of various lengths between 10 and 200 were generated (ignoring the first 100 iterates and considering data from iterate 101 in order to get rid of any transient behaviour) and the three complexity measures (LZ, ApEn and ETC) were calculated for each. This was repeated 50 times, with data being generated using 50 different initial conditions chosen randomly. This generated 50 values of complexities for each data set for each of the data lengths for each of the systems.

Considering these 50 values as samples representing the corresponding complexity values of the original populations, we construct the interval plot of the mean showing 95% confidence interval for the mean complexity values. A single factor ANOVA with Tukey's test for pairwise comparisons of means is also performed for each to verify the results.

Results and Analysis

We first present the results obtained from data generated from logistic map and then give a summarized results got from all other systems. Figures 9 – 11 show the interval plots for the mean complexity values for logistic map data of length 15 using 4 bins, for the three measures LZ, ApEn and ETC respectively.

For the purpose of data classification, a particular measure is said to be successful only if it clearly distinguishes between all the data sets. Even if a single pair of data set is not being distinguished we need to mark the measure as a failure for that particular length. From the interval plots, it can be seen that LZ and ApEn measures are unable to distinguish between the complexities of different data sets. They show similar complexity values for $a=3.9$ and $a=4$. ETC on the other hand is able to correctly distinguish between all data sets.

Figure 9. 95% confidence interval for mean LZ complexity of 50 samples of logistic map data of length 15 using 4 bins

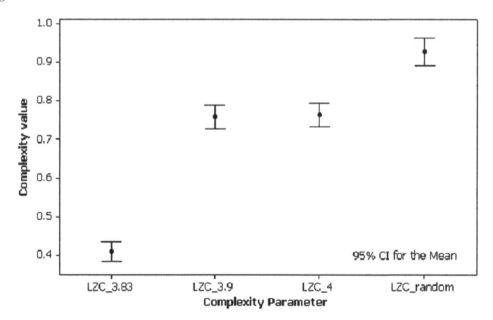

Figure 10. 95% confidence interval for mean ApEn complexity of 50 samples of logistic map data of length 15 using 4 bins

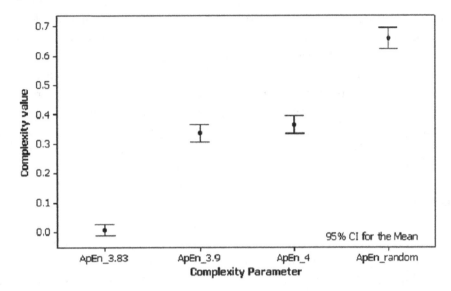

Figure 11. 95% confidence interval for mean ETC complexity of 50 samples of logistic map data of length 15 using 4 bins

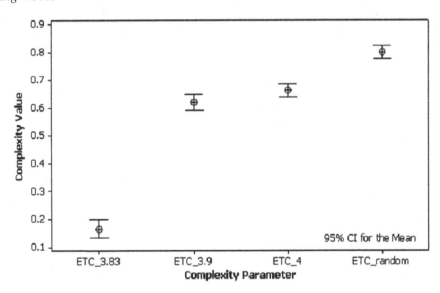

Similar analysis with data lengths of 20 and less showed that all the measures are able to correctly identify the order of complexity at lengths 20 while all the measures fail to work at data lengths shorter than 15. Hence, based on the sample data, at a 5% significance level (overall error rate) for the statistical test, there is sufficient evidence to conclude that the minimum data length required for ApEn and LZ complexity measures for correct classification of given logistic map data is 20 while the minimum length of data required for ETC measure is 15.

This analysis was repeated for all the systems and minimum data length required for each complexity measure for correct classification of data from each of the system was identified. Table 1 lists all the values so obtained. It is to be noted that a bin size of 8 was used for analyzing Rössler system while a bin size of 4 was used for all the other cases. This was done because, with a bin size of 4, ETC and LZ complexity measures could not characterize Rössler system data even for very large lengths.

With respect to the length of data required for classification, it can be seen that ETC works with minimum length data for logistic map. Recently, we have shown that ETC outperforms the celebrated Shannon entropy for characterizing dynamical complexity of short and noisy time series arising from chaotic dynamical systems as well as 2-state Markov chains (Nagaraj and Balasubramanian, 2017). Even though for other systems, ETC may not be the most efficient measure, but it is interesting to note that its performance is at least at par with either ApEn or LZ complexity measures for all the cases.

Effect of Noise

To study the effect of noise on the various systems, zero mean Gaussian noise with a standard deviation of 1 was added on to the signal and similar analysis was performed. To ensure that the noise doesn't override the signal itself, only a fraction of the noise output is added. In each of the cases, by trial and error, we found the signal to noise ratio (SNR) at which the performance of the measures was very close to the noise-free condition. Then for noise analysis, we considered noise with SNR that was around 15-20% less than the SNR at which the performance matches with the noise-free condition.

Table 2 shows the performance analysis of the different measures under the noisy conditions. It is evident that all measures undergo some performance degradation due to the presence of noise. (It is to be noted that stochastic system case is not considered since the system itself is Gaussian in nature and it doesn't add any value to analyze it by adding Gaussian noise).

It can be seen that difference in performance is significant in the case of ApEn while it is less for LZ and ETC measures for most of the cases. Thus we see that LZ and ETC complexity measures are more noise resistant than ApEn measure. It is possible that this is due to the fact that binning in LZ and

ETC may absorb the changes that the noise produces. In the case of ApEn measure, since it uses direct values and not the quantized values, effect of noise is relatively more pronounced.

In this section we analyzed the performance of ApEn, LZ and ETC complexity measures on data generated from various chaotic maps and flows. It has been shown that ETC measure can characterize better than the other two measures in the case of logistic map data. For data from other maps and systems,

Table 1. Minimum length of data required for correct classification of data from various maps and flows

System	ApEn	LZC	ETC
Logistic map	20	20	15
Tent map	40	30	30
Hénon map	50	30	30
Rössler system	175	65	65
Lorenz system	40	40	40
Stochastic system (Gaussian)	30	25	30

Table 2. Minimum length of data required for correct classification of data (in the presence of additive Gaussian noise with specified SNR (dB)) from various maps and flows. (SNR* denotes the SNR below which performance of the measure degrades and above which the measure is robust to noise and SNR$_{Anal}$ gives the SNR used for noise analysis)

System	SNR* (dB)	SNR$_{Anal}$ (dB)	ApEn (min. length)	LZC (min. length)	ETC (min. length)
Logistic map	70	58	85	30	20
Tent map	105	90	75	65	75
Hénon map	70	58	75	40	40
Rössler system	100	85	225	120	120
Lorenz system	140	125	160	90	60

though it may not be the best, it performs at par with either LZ or ApEn complexity measures. Further, in the presence of additive Gaussian noise, there is high performance degradation for ApEn while LZ and ETC complexity measures display higher noise rejection behaviour and are affected less by noise. This will have a big impact in analysis of data obtained from practical systems that would be invariably corrupted with noise. We now look at practical applications of these measures in cybernetics.

PRACTICAL APPLICATIONS IN CYBERNETICS

As discussed previously, human heart and brain exhibit chaos at various hierarchical levels of organization and functioning. Typical cybernetic applications involve monitoring and diagnosing physiological functions of the heart and the brain, with the aim of aiding clinical diagnosis. To this end, we shall consider three specific applications namely – analysis of a neuron firing model, intra-cranial pressure monitoring, and cardiac aging detection. We show the effectiveness of complexity measures (LZ, ApEn and ETC) in these applications.

Neuron Firing Model

Neurons form the basic information processing units in the central nervous system. Since there are billions of neurons working in unison, communication amongst themselves forms an important aspect of the nervous system functionality. This is made possible by electrical signals that are generated by electrons moving across neuronal membranes. On being stimulated (either internally or externally), neurons respond by firing different patterns of discrete 'action potentials' (short duration cell membrane potential spikes) that carry information about the stimuli (Vreeken et al., 2002, Gütig, 2014).

To investigate the dynamics of neuronal behaviour, different models have been proposed in literature. These have been used to simulate behaviour of single spiking neuron and spiking neuron networks with varying accuracy. 'Adaptive exponential integrate-and-fire' (AdEx) model, initially proposed by Brette and Gerstner (2005) is one commonly used model that is simple and realistic. It uses only two equations and a reset condition. The different firing patterns produced by the model are further detailed by Naud et al. (2008).

Adaptive Exponential Integrate-and-Fire Model

In this section, we reproduce the neuron model as described in Naud et al. (2008). The model shows the variation of membrane potential $V(t)$ due to injection of current $I(t)$. The two equations that characterize the model are:

$$C\frac{dV}{dt} = -g_L(V - E_L) + g_L\Delta_T \exp\left(\frac{V - V_T}{\Delta_T}\right) + I - w,$$

$$\tau_w\frac{dw}{dt} = a(V - E_L) - w.$$

There are nine parameters that define the variations of the membrane potential (V) and the adaptation current (w). They are: total capacitance (C), total leak conductance (g_L), effective rest potential (E_L), threshold slope factor (δ_T), effective threshold potential (V_T), conductance (a), time constant (τ_w), spike triggered adaptation (b) and reset potential (V_r).

When the current drives the voltage beyond the threshold value of V_T, the exponential term causes a sharp increase (upswing) in the action potential. The rise is stopped at reset threshold that has been fixed at 0 mV. The decrease (downswing) in the action potential is represented by the reset condition:

if $V > 0$ mV then $V \rightarrow V_r, w \rightarrow w_r$ where $w_r = w + b$.

It is to be noted that the nine parameters mentioned before can be modified to obtain various types of firing patterns as shown in Table 1 in Naud et al. (2008). Eight different firing patterns namely, tonic spiking, adaptation, initial burst, regular bursting, delayed accelerating, delayed regular bursting, transient spiking and irregular spiking are possible by changing the parameter values. In our work, we simulate the tonic and irregular spiking patterns and analyze if the complexity measures are able to distinguish between them. Readers interested in all the firing patterns are requested to refer to Naud et al. (2008) for complete details.

Firing Patterns Characterization Using Complexity Measures

Out of the eight different firing patterns possible with the AdEx model, we choose two of them for our analysis:

- Tonic spiking
- Irregular spiking

Tonic spiking as shown in Figure 12 is a firing pattern that produces spikes at regular intervals, while the interspike intervals in irregular spiking is aperiodic as shown in Figure 13. In fact, Naud et al. have shown in Naud et al. (2008) that irregular spiking is highly sensitive to initial conditions and is chaotic in nature. Thus analysis of these two cases is equivalent to analyzing periodic and chaotic signals. The obtained spike trains need to be first converted to a binary representation before we can proceed with the analysis. Amigo et al. (2004) have estimated the entropy rate of neuron spike trains. They use a similar spike train and divide the time axis into discrete bins and identify if at least one spike is present in each bin. If one or more spikes are present, then it is coded as1 else coded as 0. We also follow a similar procedure and divide the time axis in to bins of 1 millisec duration and check for spikes in the bins. Thus, the spike train is converted to a sequence of binary digits whose complexity is calculated using LZ, ETC and ApEn complexity measures. The complexity measures are calculated using a moving window of 50 millisec with 90% overlap. Figures 14 – 16 compare the tonic and irregular spike train analysis for LZ, ETC and ApEn complexity values respectively.

From Figures 14 and 15 it can be seen that LZ complexity measure shows similar variations across both the spike trains while in the case of ETC complexity measure, tonic spike train shows less varia-

Figure 12. Tonic spiking waveform showing periodic spikes

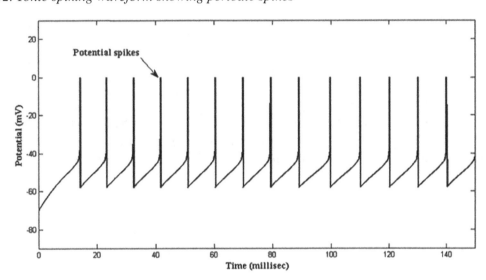

Figure 13. Irregular spiking waveform showing chaotic behavior

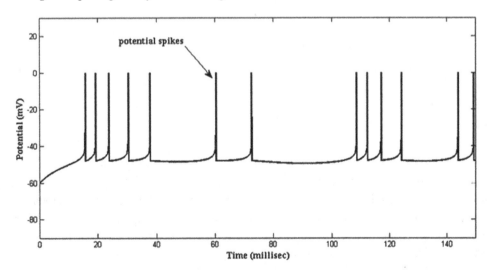

Figure 14. LZ complexity measures of tonic and irregular spiking using a moving window of 50 ms with 90% overlap. Similar variations are seen in both the graphs. The mean values of both are same, indicating the inability of LZ complexity measure to distinguish between the two spike trains

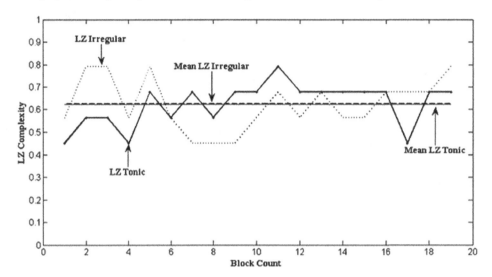

Figure 15. ETC complexity measures of tonic and irregular spiking using a moving window of 50 ms with 90% overlap. There is a clear difference in the variations of both graphs. The mean values of both are different, indicating that ETC complexity measure is able to distinguish between the two spike trains

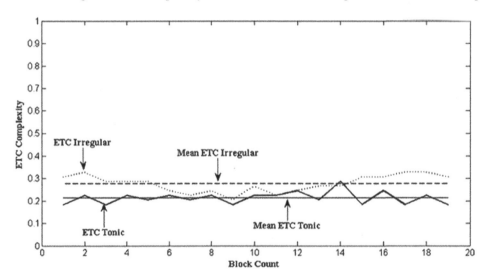

tions as compared to the irregular spike train. Further, the mean LZ complexity values of both the spike trains are (statistically) same while there is an appreciable statistical difference between the means of the spike trains using ETC complexity measure. This clearly shows that ETC complexity measure is able to characterize the periodic and chaotic nature of the tonic and irregular spike trains while LZ complexity measure fails to do so. Mean ApEn complexity measure values are higher for tonic than that of irregular spiking (Figure 16). This is not desirable and shows the limitation of the measure.

Figure 16. ApEn complexity measures of tonic and irregular spiking using a moving window of 50 ms with 90% overlap. Mean ApEn complexity measure values are higher for tonic than that of irregular spiking which is not desirable

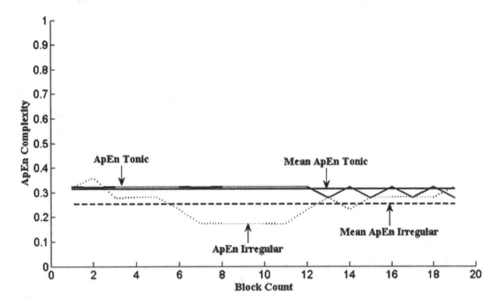

To further substantiate the results statistically, interval plots for mean LZ, ETC and ApEn complexity values were plotted and analyzed using complexity values calculated from each of the 50 ms windows as sample values. In addition to verifying using confidence interval plots, a '2 sample student's t-test' was also done to supplement the graphical analysis with the more formal hypothesis test and its associated numerical analysis. The t-test results may be summarized as follows:

- The mean LZ complexity of tonic spiking pattern (0.624 ± 0.095) is not significantly lesser ($t_{36} = 0$, $p = 0.5$) than that of irregular spiking pattern (0.624 ± 0.115).
- The mean ETC complexity of tonic spiking pattern (0.214 ± 0.028) is significantly lesser ($t_{36} = -5.84$, $p = 0$) than that of irregular spiking pattern (0.276 ± 0.038).
- The mean ApEn complexity of tonic spiking pattern (0.313 ± 0.018) is not significantly lesser ($t_{36} = 4.35$, $p = 1.000$) than that of irregular spiking pattern (0.252 ± 0.058).

Based on the sample data, at a 5% significance level (overall error rate) for the statistical test, there is sufficient evidence to conclude that the mean LZ and ApEn complexity measures of tonic spiking patterns are not significantly lesser than those of the corresponding irregular patterns, while the mean ETC complexity measure of tonic spiking pattern is significantly lesser than that of the irregular pattern. Thus we can confidently assert that ETC complexity measure is able to characteristically differentiate between the two neuron firing patterns, while LZ and ApEn complexity measures are unable to do so. In the future we would like to do an in-depth analysis of all the eight firing patterns and compare the relative performance of LZ, ApEn and ETC complexity measures in characterizing the same.

Why Complexity Analysis for Physiological Signals

Researchers in general tend to focus on either time domain analysis (mean, variances) or frequency domain based spectral analysis for physiologic signal analysis. Only in the past couple of decades, newer methods based on nonlinear dynamics involving chaos theory and complexity have come in to prominence (Valenza et al., 2013; Acharya et al., 2014). These dynamics based methods give us a different perspective to view the underlying physiologic control mechanisms. They are especially useful since most physiological signals are non-stationary in nature, which makes it difficult to apply conventional spectral analysis throughout the time series (Goldberger, 1996; Sanei & Chambers, 2013). In this section, we look at applications based on complexity analysis of intracranial pressure signals and inter-beat (RR) intervals time series data.

Intra-Cranial Pressure Monitoring

Intracranial pressure (ICP) is defined as the pressure inside the skull in the brain tissues and cerebrospinal fluids. The normal values of ICP vary with age of the person. For adults and older children, it is between 10-15 mmHg, for small children it ranges between 3-7 mmHg and for infants it can be anything between 1.5-6 mmHg (Rangel-Castillo, Gopinath, & Robertson, 2008). But in patients with traumatic brain injury, the pressure increases much beyond 25 mmHg, thus leading to a state of Intracranial Hypertension (ICH). During such episodes of ICH, the cardiovascular regulatory mechanisms get uncoupled as pointed out by Goldstein et al. (1993) and by Shlosberg et al. (2010). Another study on heart rate variability during ICH episodes (Kox et al., 2012) also is an indicator in the same direction. This leads us to surmise that the complex physiological functions undergo major changes during occurrences of ICH. This may have led Hornero et al. (2005) to hypothesize that complexity of the ICP signals would decrease during occurrences of ICH. To support the hypothesis, they have done complexity analysis of ICP signals using ApEn (Hornero et al., 2005, 2006) and Lempel-Ziv complexity measures (Aboy et al., 2006; Hornero, Aboy, & Abásolo, 2007) and have shown that the complexity values drop down rapidly during episodes of ICH and returns to pre-ICH level after the spike, thus identifying the onset of ICH. This shows the effectiveness of complexity measures in such cases. Similar analysis has been down using wavelet entropy by Xu et al. (2008). In our work, we show that ETC complexity measure also reduces drastically during ICH episodes and thus functions as a good tool to identify occurrences of ICH.

Complexity Analysis

Figure 17 shows an ICP signal of 3 minute duration collected from bedside ICU patient monitors by continuous invasive blood pressure measurement. The data was obtained from 'PhysioNet:Computers in Cardiology Challenge 2010 Test Set C' (Goldberger et al., 2000) and shows two possible ICH episodes, as seen by the sharp spikes in the graph.

Using a moving window of 5 seconds with 90% overlap, LZ, ApEn and ETC complexity values were calculated and Figure 18 shows the same. It can be clearly seen that all the complexity values show a sudden drop in values during episodes of ICH, thus lending credence to the fact that occurrence of ICH reduces the complexity of physiological functions. We see that our proposed ETC measure works as good as the other two measures and is equally capable of identifying the onset of ICH episodes.

Figure 17. Intracranial Pressure (ICP) signal showing two episodes of ICH (spikes)

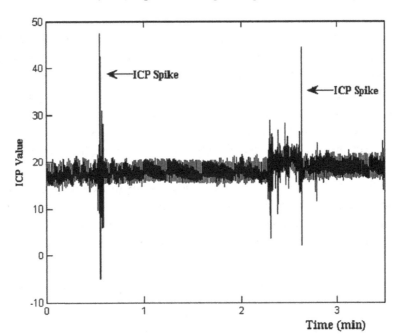

Figure 18. ApEn, LZ and ETC complexity measures applied on ICP signal. It can be seen clearly that all the complexity values decrease during ICH episodes

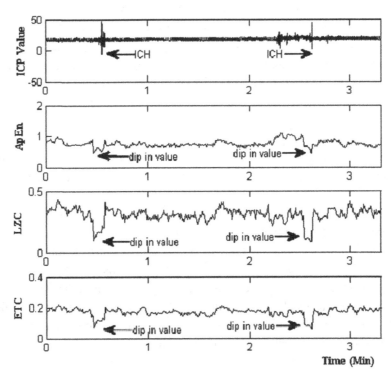

Cardiac Aging Detection

We have briefly described the chaotic nature of heart-rate variability in healthy human hearts. As we age, there are changes in the body and it results in reduction of complexity of physiological interactions between different control mechanisms. There is no longer a multitude of variations in the heart signal, but a settling down to more regular predictable dynamics. This leads to increase risk of cardiovascular diseases which are known to be number one cause of death globally. Cardiac signals being inherently non-linear, chaotic and non-stationary in nature, the complexity measures such as ApEn, LZ and ETC are good candidates to capture the reduction of complexity in the aging heart. Recently, we conducted a study of complexity analysis of beat-to-beat interval data from healthy young as well as healthy elderly subjects (Balasubramanian & Nagaraj, 2016). Our study reveals that complexity measures such as LZ and ETC are able to discriminate between beat-to-beat intervals of young and old subjects for lengths as short as 10 data samples, while ApEn is able to do so only for lengths greater than 15. This study paves the way for potential applications in detecting cardiac aging and could aid diagnosis.

SUMMARY AND FUTURE RESEARCH DIRECTIONS

Complex systems exhibit complex behavior owing to chaos. The underlying equations could be simple-looking non-linear deterministic equations, but lead to random-like behavior and exhibit sensitive dependence on initial conditions. Such behavior is seen everywhere – especially in biological systems such as the heart and the brain. In order to effectively monitor and control the behavior of such systems, it is imperative that we are able to firstly measure the complexity of the time series (measurements) arising out of such systems. This led us to briefly look at the various complexity measures in the literature (by no means exhaustive). Specifically, we described three complexity measures namely Lempel-Ziv complexity, Approximate Entropy and Effort-To-Compress. We simulated various chaotic systems (1D maps, as well as, flows) and studied the complexity of time series resulting from these systems using the aforementioned complexity measures. We have shown that these measures are indeed able to successfully classify chaotic systems.

One of the important domains of cybernetics is the field of biomedical applications. We have considered three specific applications namely analysis of a neuron firing model, intra-cranial pressure monitoring, and cardiac aging detection. We demonstrated the effectiveness of complexity measures (LZ, ApEn and ETC) in these applications.

Future research directions include investigating other complexity measures and not just the ones considered in this chapter. Also, the methods described in this chapter can be extended to other cybernetic applications and domains. Given that complex systems, especially chaotic ones, are all-pervasive, complexity measures continue to be useful for diverse applications. We have shown how complexity measures enable measuring, analyzing and classifying complex systems. However, complexity measures need not be limited to these tasks alone. It would be interesting to investigate the utility of such measures and methods in other aspects of cybernetics such as communication, feedback and control. This is definitely an area of future research work worth exploring.

ACKNOWLEDGMENT

We would like to thank Dept. of Biotechnology, Govt. of India for funding through the RGYI scheme which enabled the work on Effort-To-Compress complexity measure. We also gratefully acknowledge the help rendered by Gayathri R Prabhu (Indian institute of Technology (IIT), Chennai), Sutirth Dey (Indian institute of Science Educational and Research (IISER), Pune), Sriram Devanathan and Del Marshall (Amrita University) in this work. Much of the work in this chapter is a result of the doctoral research of KB and hence he would like to thank Amrita Vishwa Vidyapeetham for supporting this work.

REFERENCES

Aboy, M., Hornero, R., Abasolo, D., & Alvarez, D. (2006). Interpretation of the Lempel-Ziv Complexity Measure in the Context of Biomedical Signal Analysis. *IEEE Transactions on Bio-Medical Engineering*, *53*(11), 2282–2288. doi:10.1109/TBME.2006.883696 PMID:17073334

Acharya, U. R., Faust, O., Sree, V., Swapna, G., Martis, R. J., Kadri, N. A., & Suri, J. S. (2014). Linear and nonlinear analysis of normal and CAD-affected heart rate signals. *Computer Methods and Programs in Biomedicine*, *113*(1), 55–68. doi:10.1016/j.cmpb.2013.08.017 PMID:24119391

Alligood, K. T., Sauer, T. D., & Yorke, J. A. (2000). *Chaos: An introduction to dynamical systems*. Springer.

Amigó, J. M., Szczepański, J., Wajnryb, E., & Sanchez-Vives, M. V. (2004). Estimating the Entropy Rate of Spike Trains via Lempel-Ziv Complexity. *Neural Computation*, *16*(4), 717–736. doi:10.1162/089976604322860677 PMID:15025827

Azevedo, F. A., Carvalho, L. R., Grinberg, L. T., Farfel, J. M., Ferretti, R. E., Leite, R. E., & Herculano-Houzel, S. et al. (2009). Equal numbers of neuronal and nonneuronal cells make the human brain an isometrically scaled-up primate brain. *The Journal of Comparative Neurology*, *513*(5), 532–541. doi:10.1002/cne.21974 PMID:19226510

Aziz, W., & Arif, M. (2006). Complexity analysis of stride interval time series by threshold dependent symbolic entropy. *European Journal of Applied Physiology*, *98*(1), 30–40. doi:10.1007/s00421-006-0226-5 PMID:16841202

Balasubramanian, K., & Nagaraj, N. (2016). Aging and cardiovascular complexity: Effect of the length of RR tachograms. *PeerJ*, *4*, e2755. doi:10.7717/peerj.2755

Bandt, C., & Pompe, B. (2002). Permutation Entropy: A Natural Complexity Measure for Time Series. *Physical Review Letters*, *88*(17), 174102. doi:10.1103/PhysRevLett.88.174102 PMID:12005759

Benedetto, D., Caglioti, E., & Loreto, V. (2002). Language Trees and Zipping. *Physical Review Letters*, *88*(4), 048702. doi:10.1103/PhysRevLett.88.048702 PMID:11801178

Bennett, C. H. (1995). Logical Depth and Physical Complexity. *Computerkultur*, 207-235. doi:10.1007/978-3-7091-6597-3_8

Bhaduri, S. N. (2014). Applying Approximate Entropy (ApEn) to Speculative Bubble in the Stock Market. *Journal of Emerging Market Finance*, *13*(1), 43–68. doi:10.1177/0972652714534023

Brette, R., & Gerstner, W. (2005). Adaptive Exponential Integrate-and-Fire Model as an Effective Description of Neuronal Activity. *Journal of Neurophysiology*, *94*(5), 3637–3642. doi:10.1152/jn.00686.2005 PMID:16014787

Chaitin, G. (1974). Information-theoretic computation complexity. *IEEE Transactions on Information Theory*, *20*(1), 10–15. doi:10.1109/TIT.1974.1055172

Cover, T. M., & Thomas, J. A. (1991). *Elements of information theory*. New York: Wiley. doi:10.1002/0471200611

Devaney, R. L. (1989). *An introduction to chaotic dynamical systems*. London: Addison-Wesley.

Dugdale, J. S. (1996). *Entropy and its physical meaning*. London: Taylor & Francis. doi:10.4324/9780203211298

Ebeling, W., Steuer, R., & Titchener, M. R. (2001). Partition-based entropies of deterministic and stochastic maps. *Stochastics and Dynamics*, *01*(01), 45–61. doi:10.1142/S0219493701000047

Goldberger, A. (1996). Non-linear dynamics for clinicians: Chaos theory, fractals, and complexity at the bedside. *Lancet*, *347*(9011), 1312–1314. doi:10.1016/S0140-6736(96)90948-4 PMID:8622511

Goldberger, A. L. (1991). Is the normal heartbeat chaotic or homeostatic? *News in Physiological Sciences*, *6*(2), 87–91. PMID:11537649

Goldberger, A. L., Amaral, L. A., Glass, L., Hausdorff, J. M., Ivanov, P. C., Mark, R. G., & Stanley, H. E.. et al. (2000). PhysioBank, PhysioToolkit, and PhysioNet: Components of a New Research Resource for Complex Physiologic Signals. *Circulation*, *101*(23), e215–e220. doi:10.1161/01.CIR.101.23.e215 PMID:10851218

Goldstein, B., Deking, D., Delong, D. J., Kempski, M. H., Cox, C., Kelly, M. M., & Woolf, P. D. et al. (1993). Autonomic cardiovascular state after severe brain injury and brain death in children. *Critical Care Medicine*, *21*(2), 228–333. doi:10.1097/00003246-199302000-00014 PMID:8428474

Gomez-Pilar, J., Gutiérrez-Tobal, G. C., Álvarez, D., Del Campo, F., & Hornero, R. (2014). Classification Methods from Heart Rate Variability to Assist in SAHS Diagnosis. *IFMBE Proceedings*, *1825-1828*. doi:10.1007/978-3-319-00846-2_450

Gütig, R. (2014). To spike, or when to spike? *Current Opinion in Neurobiology*, *25*, 134–139. doi:10.1016/j.conb.2014.01.004 PMID:24468508

Hornero, R., Aboy, M., & Abásolo, D. (2007). Analysis of intracranial pressure during acute intracranial hypertension using Lempel–Ziv complexity: Further evidence. *Medical & Biological Engineering & Computing*, *45*(6), 617–620. doi:10.1007/s11517-007-0194-x PMID:17541667

Hornero, R., Aboy, M., Abasolo, D., McNames, J., & Goldstein, B. (2005). Interpretation of Approximate Entropy: Analysis of Intracranial Pressure Approximate Entropy During Acute Intracranial Hypertension. *IEEE Transactions on Bio-Medical Engineering*, *52*(10), 1671–1680. doi:10.1109/TBME.2005.855722 PMID:16235653

Hornero, R., Aboy, M., Abasolo, D., McNames, J., Wakeland, W., & Goldstein, B. (2006). Complex analysis of intracranial hypertension using approximate entropy. *Critical Care Medicine*, *34*(1), 87–95. doi:10.1097/01.CCM.0000190426.44782.F0 PMID:16374161

Hu, J., Gao, J., & Principe, J. (2006). Analysis of Biomedical Signals by the Lempel-Ziv Complexity: The Effect of Finite Data Size. *IEEE Transactions on Bio-Medical Engineering*, *53*(12), 2606–2609. doi:10.1109/TBME.2006.883825 PMID:17152441

Hu, J., Gao, J., & Principe, J. (2006). Analysis of Biomedical Signals by the Lempel-Ziv Complexity: The Effect of Finite Data Size. *IEEE Transactions on Bio-Medical Engineering*, *53*(12), 2606–2609. doi:10.1109/TBME.2006.883825 PMID:17152441

Humeau-Heurtier, A. (2015). The Multiscale Entropy Algorithm and Its Variants: A Review. *Entropy*, *17*(5), 3110–3123. doi:10.3390/e17053110

Ibáñez-Molina, A. J., Iglesias-Parro, S., Soriano, M. F., & Aznarte, J. I. (2015). Multiscale Lempel–Ziv complexity for EEG measures. *Clinical Neurophysiology*, *126*(3), 541–548. doi:10.1016/j.clinph.2014.07.012 PMID:25127707

Jiménez-Montaño, M. A. (1984). On the syntactic structure of protein sequences and the concept of grammar complexity. *Bulletin of Mathematical Biology*, *46*(4), 641–659. doi:10.1007/BF02459508

Korn, H., & Faure, P. (2003). Is there chaos in the brain? II. Experimental evidence and related models. *Comptes Rendus Biologies*, *326*(9), 787–840. doi:10.1016/j.crvi.2003.09.011 PMID:14694754

Kox, M., Vrouwenvelder, M. Q., Pompe, J. C., Van der Hoeven, J. G., Pickkers, P., & Hoedemaekers, C. W. (2012). The Effects of Brain Injury on Heart Rate Variability and the Innate Immune Response in Critically Ill Patients. *Journal of Neurotrauma*, *29*(5), 747–755. doi:10.1089/neu.2011.2035 PMID:22111862

Kozuch, M., & Wang, L. (2001). *Approximate entropy as a measure of irregularity in earthquake sequences*. Paper presented at AGU Fall Meeting.

Kristoufek, L., & Vosvrda, M. (2014). Measuring capital market efficiency: Long-term memory, fractal dimension and approximate entropy. *The European Physical Journal B*, *87*(7), 162. doi:10.1140/epjb/e2014-50113-6

Lake, D. E., Richman, J. S., Griffin, M. P., & Moorman, J. R. (2002). Sample entropy analysis of neonatal heart rate variability. *American Journal of Physiology. Regulatory, Integrative and Comparative Physiology*, *283*(3), R789–R797. doi:10.1152/ajpregu.00069.2002 PMID:12185014

Lempel, A., & Ziv, J. (1976). On the Complexity of Finite Sequences. *IEEE Transactions on Information Theory*, *22*(1), 75–81. doi:10.1109/TIT.1976.1055501

Li, T., & Yorke, J. A. (1975). Period Three Implies Chaos. *The American Mathematical Monthly*, *82*(10), 985. doi:10.2307/2318254

Lloyd, S. (2001). Measures of complexity: A nonexhaustive list. *IEEE Control Systems Magazine*, *21*(4), 7–8. doi:10.1109/MCS.2001.939938

Lloyd, S., & Pagels, H. (1988). Complexity as thermodynamic depth. *Annals of Physics*, *188*(1), 186–213. doi:10.1016/0003-4916(88)90094-2

MacKay, D. J. (2003). *Information theory, inference, and learning algorithms*. Cambridge, UK: Cambridge University Press.

Mandelbrot, B. (1967). How Long Is the Coast of Britain? Statistical Self-Similarity and Fractional Dimension. *Science*, *156*(3775), 636–638. doi:10.1126/science.156.3775.636 PMID:17837158

May, R. M. (1976). Simple mathematical models with very complicated dynamics. *Nature*, *261*(5560), 459–467. doi:10.1038/261459a0 PMID:934280

Nagaraj, N., & Balasubramanian, K. (2017). Dynamical Complexity of Short and Noisy Time Series: Compression-Complexity vs. Shannon Entropy. *The European Physical Journal. Special Topics*, 1–14. doi:10.1140/epjst/e2016-60397-x

Nagaraj, N., Balasubramanian, K., & Dey, S. (2013). A new complexity measure for time series analysis and classification. *The European Physical Journal. Special Topics*, *222*(3-4), 847–860. doi:10.1140/epjst/e2013-01888-9

Naud, R., Marcille, N., Clopath, C., & Gerstner, W. (2008). Firing patterns in the adaptive exponential integrate-and-fire model. *Biological Cybernetics*, *99*(4-5), 335–347. doi:10.1007/s00422-008-0264-7 PMID:19011922

Ni, L., Cao, J., & Wang, R. (2014). Time-Dependent Approximate and Sample Entropy Measures for Brain Death Diagnosis. *Advances in Cognitive Neurodynamics*, (4), 323-328. doi:10.1007/978-94-017-9548-7_46

Northrop, R. B. (2010). *Introduction to complexity and complex systems*. Boca Raton, FL: Taylor & Francis.

Orozco-Arroyave, J. R., Arias-Londoño, J. D., Vargas-Bonilla, J. F., & Nöth, E. (2013). Analysis of Speech from People with Parkinson's Disease through Nonlinear Dynamics. *Advances in Nonlinear Speech Processing*, 112-119. doi:10.1007/978-3-642-38847-7_15

Pincus, S. (1995). Approximate entropy (ApEn) as a complexity measure. *Chaos (Woodbury, N.Y.)*, *5*(1), 110–117. doi:10.1063/1.166092 PMID:12780163

Pincus, S. M. (1991). Approximate entropy as a measure of system complexity. *Proceedings of the National Academy of Sciences of the United States of America*, *88*(6), 2297–2301. doi:10.1073/pnas.88.6.2297 PMID:11607165

Rajendra Acharya, U., Faust, O., Adib Kadri, N., Suri, J. S., & Yu, W. (2013). Automated identification of normal and diabetes heart rate signals using nonlinear measures. *Computers in Biology and Medicine*, *43*(10), 1523–1529. doi:10.1016/j.compbiomed.2013.05.024 PMID:24034744

Rangel-Castillo, L., Gopinath, S., & Robertson, C. S. (2008). Management of Intracranial Hypertension. *Neurologic Clinics*, *26*(2), 521–541. doi:10.1016/j.ncl.2008.02.003 PMID:18514825

Rényi. (1961). *On Measures of Entropy and Information*. Alfréd: University of California Press.

Restrepo, J. F., Schlotthauer, G., & Torres, M. E. (2014). Maximum approximate entropy and threshold: A new approach for regularity changes detection. *Physica A: Statistical Mechanics and its Applications, 409*, 97-109. doi:10.1016/j.physa.2014.04.041

Rissanen, J. (1989). Stochastic Complexity in Statistical Inquiry (World Scientific series in computer science; v. 15). World Scientific.

Rosso, O. A., Blanco, S., Yordanova, J., Kolev, V., Figliola, A., Schürmann, M., & Başar, E. (2001). Wavelet entropy: A new tool for analysis of short duration brain electrical signals. *Journal of Neuroscience Methods, 105*(1), 65–75. doi:10.1016/S0165-0270(00)00356-3 PMID:11166367

Sanei, S., & Chambers, J. (2007). *EEG signal processing*. Chichester, UK: John Wiley & Sons. doi:10.1002/9780470511923

Sarlabous, L., Torres, A., Fiz, J., Gea, J., Galdiz, J., & Jane, R. (2009). Multistate Lempel-Ziv (MLZ) index interpretation as a measure of amplitude and complexity changes. *2009 Annual International Conference of the IEEE Engineering in Medicine and Biology Society*. doi:10.1109/IEMBS.2009.5333488

Shannon, C. E. (1948). A Mathematical Theory of Communication. *The Bell System Technical Journal, 27*(3), 379–423. doi:10.1002/j.1538-7305.1948.tb01338.x

Shlosberg, D., Benifla, M., Kaufer, D., & Friedman, A. (2010). Blood–brain barrier breakdown as a therapeutic target in traumatic brain injury. *Nature Reviews. Nephrology, 6*(7), 393–403. doi:10.1038/nrneurol.2010.74 PMID:20585319

Simons, S., Abasolo, D., & Hughes, M. (2015). Investigation of Alzheimers Disease EEG Frequency Components with Lempel-Ziv Complexity. *IFMBE Proceedings, 46-49*, 46–49. doi:10.1007/978-3-319-11128-5_12

Sokunbi, M. O. (2014). Sample entropy reveals high discriminative power between young and elderly adults in short fMRI data sets. *Frontiers in Neuroinformatics, 8*. doi:10.3389/fninf.2014.00069 PMID:25100988

Strogatz, S. H. (2000). *Nonlinear dynamics and chaos: With applications to physics, biology, chemistry, and engineering*. Cambridge, MA: Westview Press.

Talebinejad, M., Tsoulfas, G., & Musallam, S. (2011). *Lempel-ziv complexity for analysis of neural spikes. Canadian Medical and Biological Engineering Conference*, Toronto, Canada.

Teager, H. M., & Teager, S. M. (1990). Evidence for Nonlinear Sound Production Mechanisms in the Vocal Tract. *Speech Production and Speech Modelling*, 241-261. doi:10.1007/978-94-009-2037-8_10

Valenza, G., Citi, L., Lanata, A., Scilingo, E. P., & Barbieri, R. (2013). A nonlinear heartbeat dynamics model approach for personalized emotion recognition. *2013 35th Annual International Conference of the IEEE Engineering in Medicine and Biology Society (EMBC)*. doi:10.1109/embc.2013.6610067

Vreeken, J. (2003). *Spiking neural networks, an introduction*. Retrieved from Information and Computing Sciences website: http://eda.mmci.uni-saarland.de/pubs/2002/spiking_neural_networks_an_introduction-vreeken.pdf

Xia, D., Meng, Q., Chen, Y., & Zhang, Z. (2014). Classification of Ventricular Tachycardia and Fibrillation Based on the Lempel-Ziv Complexity and EMD. *Intelligent Computing in Bioinformatics*, 322-329. doi:10.1007/978-3-319-09330-7_39

Xu, P., Scalzo, F., Bergsneider, M., Vespa, P., Chad, M., & Hu, X. (2008). Wavelet entropy characterization of elevated intracranial pressure. *2008 30th Annual International Conference of the IEEE Engineering in Medicine and Biology Society*. doi:10.1109/iembs.2008.4649815

Yu, C., Lucy He, R., & Yau, S. S. (2014). Viral genome phylogeny based on Lempel–Ziv complexity and Hausdorff distance. *Journal of Theoretical Biology*, *348*, 12–20. doi:10.1016/j.jtbi.2014.01.022 PMID:24486229

Ziv, J., & Lempel, A. (1977). A universal algorithm for sequential data compression. *IEEE Transactions on Information Theory*, *23*(3), 337–343. doi:10.1109/TIT.1977.1055714

Chapter 16

Cyber–Physical Systems:
An Overview of Design Process, Applications, and Security

Lydia Ray
Columbus State University, USA

ABSTRACT

Pervasive computing has progressed significantly with a growth of embedded systems as a result of recent advances in digital electronics, wireless networking, sensors and RFID technology. These embedded systems are capable of producing enormous amount of data that cannot be handled by human brains. At the same time, there is a growing need for integrating these embedded devices into physical environment in order to achieve a far better capability, scalability, resiliency, safety, security and usability in important sectors such as healthcare, manufacturing, transportation, energy, agriculture, architecture and many more. The confluence of all these recent trends is the vision of distributed cyber-physical systems that will far exceed the performance of traditional embedded systems. Cyber-physical systems are emerging technology that require significant research in design and implementation with a few important challenges to overcome. The goal of this chapter is to present an overview of basic design and architecture of a cyber-physical system along with some specific applications and a brief description of the design process for developers. This chapter also presents a brief discussion of security and privacy issues, the most important challenge of cyber-physical systems.

1. INTRODUCTION

Advances in digital electronics throughout the last few decades have resulted in an explosive growth of embedded systems. There is a growing trend of systems with embedded wireless sensors and RFID (radio-frequency identification device) devices that can communicate with other systems such as smartphones over the Internet. These autonomous systems are capable of collecting and processing an enormous amount of data within a very short time. This characteristic is unmatched by a corresponding increase in human ability to consume information (Rajkumar et al., 2010). At the same time, there is a growing need for integrating these embedded devices into physical environment in order to achieve a far better

DOI: 10.4018/978-1-5225-2498-4.ch016

Figure 1. CPS in nutshell
(Source: Venkatasubramanian, 2009)

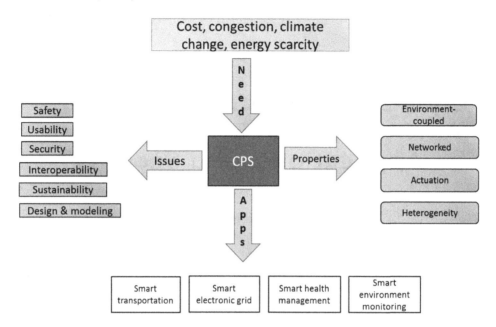

capability, scalability, resiliency, safety, security and usability in important sectors such as healthcare, manufacturing, transportation, energy, agriculture, architecture and many more. The confluence of all these recent trends is the vision of distributed cyber-physical information distillation and control systems of embedded devices that will far exceed the performance of traditional embedded systems (Cyber Physical Systems, n.d.; Lee & Sheshia, 2011; Rajkumar et al., 2010). Figure 1 demonstrates everything about CPS in a nutshell.

Cyber-physical systems (CPS) are "physical and engineered systems whose operations are monitored, coordinated, controlled and integrated by a computing and communication core", as defined by Rajkumar et al. (2010). As the name suggests, a cyber-physical system has two components: a physical component and a cyber component. The cyber part of the system consists of sensors, computers and network devices which monitor and control activity of the physical component with feedback loops (Cyber Physical Systems, n.d.). The goal for the CPS designers is to seamlessly integrate physical processes with software applications and networking, building on the existing technology of embedded systems.

Cyber-physical systems are emerging technology, which is currently in the development phase requiring significant research work for resolving a number of key challenges. Cyber-physical systems belong to the discipline of engineering and computer science with a strong foundation of mathematical abstractions. Mathematical abstractions have been used for modeling physical processes as well as for developing algorithms and programs for cyber applications for centuries. While mathematical abstractions for modeling physical processes focus on system dynamics, mathematical abstractions for algorithms and programs focus on processing data, abstracting away a few core physical properties such as passage of time. The key challenge of designing and implementing cyber-physical systems is to seamlessly integrate mathematical abstractions for physical processes and virtual (cyber) processes.

Cyber-physical systems have applications which are mission critical and/or safety critical. In fact, the need for mission-criticality and/or safety-criticality is one of the main aspirations for the vision of cyber-physical systems. However, because CPSs are distributed systems communicating over local area networks and the Internet, these systems are subject to many different cyber crimes and targeted cyber attacks, thus facing a great risk of performance and safety violations. A substantial amount of research has been done on cybersecurity and there exists well developed security mechanisms for digital devices. CPS researchers face the challenge to find ways to integrate these already existing security mechanisms in the design of a cyber-physical system.

The goal of this article is to provide a brief overview of cyber-physical systems with some important application areas, a brief overview of the design process of CPS and discuss security and privacy issues and mechanisms related to CPS. This article is organized in the following manner. The next section describes key features and characteristics of a cyber-physical system with some examples. Section 3 discusses some of the main application areas of CPS with examples. Section 4 describes the design process of a CPS. The security and privacy issues of CPS are described in section 5.

2. CYBER-PHYSICAL SYSTEMS: A BRIEF OVERVIEW

Cyber-physical systems monitor and control physical processes and uses feedback loops to adjust and improve performances continuously. These systems are adaptive, predictive, intelligent and real time and possibly include humans in the loop (Cyber Physical Systems, n.d.). What are the distinguishing features of a CPS? How does its system architecture look like? How does it function? This section provides answers to these questions.

Key Characteristics

A CPS typically has three key characteristics (Lee & Sheshia, 2011; Rajkumar et al., 2011; Venkatasubramanian, 2009):

- **Environment Coupling** : A CPS is very tightly coupled with the physical process it is part of. Any change in the process will instigate a change of behavior in the CPS and vice versa.
- **Components With Diverse Capabilities** : A CPS has components with different capabilities and different computing power. While typical embedded wireless sensors and RFID cards may have limited computing and communication power, these sensors may communicate and send data to a more powerful computer.
- **Networked** : Each component in CPS communicates with each other via internal or external networks.

Cyber-Physical System Architecture and Workflow

Figure 2 shows the general CPS structure that applies to any CPS. A CPS platform usually consists of sensors and actuators, and a distributed or centralized cyber controller with a communication stack, memory and a processing unit. Each CPS component consists of a sensing unit and control unit. Sensing

Figure 2. CPS architecture

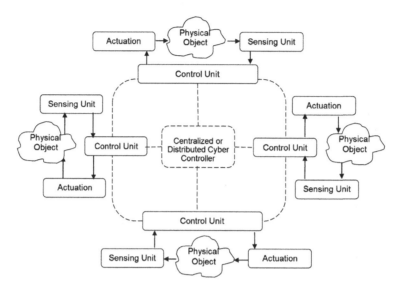

units provide feedback to control units which turns on actuation whenever necessary. All these components are networked and monitored by a centralized of a distributed cyber controller.

Cyber physical systems have three main functionalities:

- **Monitoring:** As an environment-coupled system, one of the most fundamental functions of a CPS is monitoring the environment. This task is accomplished by the sensing unit.
- **Processing:** The sensing unit collects data from the environment and sends data to the control unit to determine if that data satisfies a pre-defined criteria. The objective is to determine if there is any change in the environment that needs to be addressed.
- **Actuation:** After processing the collected data, the control unit determines if any action needs to be taken. An action may be changing the CPS's own behavior, or changing something in the physical environment. For example, a health monitoring system will deliver medicine to patient if there is sudden blood pressure drop, thereby changing the physical process.

A CPS can work in three different modes: passive, passively active and active.

- **Passive Mode:** A passive CPS only monitors an environment and collects and processes data.
- **Passively Active Mode:** In this mode, a CPS monitors the environment, and executes an indirect actuation by changing their own behavior in order to satisfy some pre-determined criteria of the physical process.
- **Active Mode:** An active CPS executes a direct actuation by modifying the behavior of the physical process in order to satisfy some pre-determined criteria of that process.

The examples given below will help us understand the key features.

Figure 3. A PHMS

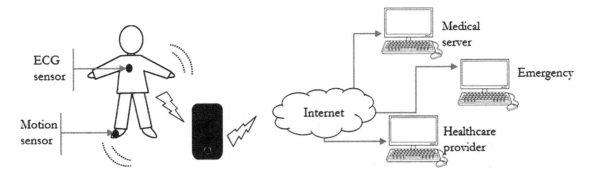

Pervasive Health Monitoring System

In order to understand the above characteristics, let's consider the following CPS as an example to explain some of the key characteristics of CPS. This is a Pervasive Health Monitoring System (PHMS) which consists of a number of wearable sensors that monitor different types of processes in human body and collect a variety of medical data such as blood pressure, heart rate, temperature, humidity etc. The collected data is then forwarded by these sensors through wireless medium to an entity called "base station". This base station can be a smart phone. The collection of sensors and the base station together is called Body Area Network (BAN) or Wireless Body Area Network (WBAN) (Jovanov et al., 2005). The base station forwards the collected and processed data to a more powerful entity (a computer) that organizes and stores this data as a structured electronic format, known as Electronic Patient Records (EPR) for future access of health care providers (Jovanov et al., 2005).

A PHMS *passively* monitors physiological processes such as heart activity, muscle activity, blood pressure, brain electrical activity, lungs activity etc. in a human body. It is tightly coupled with these physiological processes. Thus if there is a change in any of those physiological processes, for example if there is a sudden drop in the blood pressure, the base station will generate warning and will communicate with a healthcare provider.

In a PHMS, sensors that monitor the physiological processes are energy-constrained and thus have limited computing power. A base station, on the other hand, has more computing power and data processing ability. The base station sends pre-processed medical data to a computer which is more powerful than the base station. This explains how different components in a CPS have diverse capabilities.

Finally, all these components communicate via wireless medium. Sensors monitoring the physiological processes in a human body communicate with a smart phone in order to send the medical data. The smart phone generates a warning if there is any anomaly in the medical data obtained.

Smart Driveway Monitoring System

This system contains a sensor and a microcomputer. The wireless motion sensor monitors the driveway of a home and can detect arrival of a person or a car in the driveway. The sensor sends the signal to a microcomputer which processes this information and sends an alert to the home owner's smart phone over the Internet (Tew & Ray, 2016). Tightly coupled with the environment, the system *passively* monitors a driveway and detects existence of motion created by human or a vehicle.

Figure 4. A driveway monitoring system

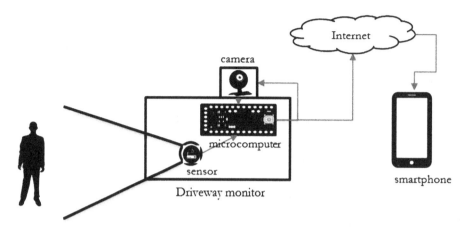

SCADA System

In a more complicated example, a large scale SCADA (Supervisory Control and Data Acquisition) system in an industry use sensors to monitor, collect and process data, control devices such as valves, pumps, motors, and more, which are connected through HMI (human-machine interface) software. A good example is water distribution plants. In these plants, the water tank levels, water pressure, temperature, filtration, sedimentation, chemical treatment etc. are all monitored and controlled by programmable logic controllers and workstations which are connected with each other via local area network and/or the Internet. A SCADA water distribution system, shown in Figure 5, uses a central computing system to monitor and control various pump stations in remote locations. This system works in an active mode and directly controls the operations of pump stations remotely using a technology called telemetry.

3. APPLICATIONS OF CYBER-PHYSICAL SYSTEMS

The need to reduce high medical costs, traffic congestion, to resolve problems with climate change and energy resources that are getting gradually scarce drives the emergence of cyber-physical systems. Thus, the main application domains of CPS are healthcare, transportation, energy, and large scale infrastructure. In this section, I will discuss a few selected most important application areas of CPS and explain how the distinguishing features of CPS can help fulfill the needs mentioned above. These application areas are selected from Cyber Physical Systems (n.d.).

CPS in Healthcare

Technology in healthcare has evolved from analog to digital to embedded systems over the last 20 years in the United States (Shnayber et al., 2005; Virone et al., 2006; Cyber Physical Systems, n.d.; NITRD, 2009; Haque, Aziz, & Rahman, 2014). Today sensors, actuators, microprocessor and software are used in healthcare devices in abundance. In hospitals, for example, medical devices with sensors monitor patient condition and send the data to a computer over wireless medium. The collected data, together with lab

Figure 5. A SCADA water distribution system
(Source: Watermatrix, n.d.)

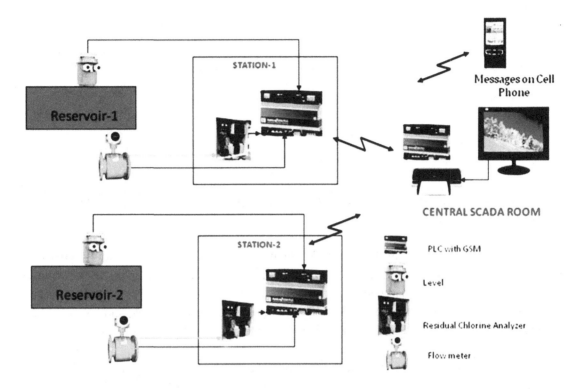

results are examined by health care providers to make a treatment decision for that patient. While these digital devices communicate with another computer (frequently called as "base station") via a wireless network, they operate somewhat in isolation in the sense that there is very limited communication among these devices (Cyber Physical Systems, n.d.; NITRD, 2009). The interoperability is very limited. Most embedded systems use only open-loop controllers which apply a single control effort with the assumption that desired result will be achieved. Since such systems do not get any feedback of the control effort, the result is loss of accuracy. There is no guarantee that the single control effort will have the desired result. Currently, there exist very few medical devices that use feedback loop to obtain better accuracy. Such devices include implantable cardioverter defibrillators (ICDs) and cochlear prosthetics (with soft operational deadlines) (NITRD, 2009).

With the advancement of ubiquitous computing and the recent trend of investment in CPS research, the future medical devices are likely to evolve as autonomous, patient-centric systems with ability to perform coordinated actions. Such devices will have the following benefits over existing healthcare technology:

- *Improved human-system interaction* will assist healthcare providers (and patients themselves) in critical decision making.
- A medical cyber physical system will be able to identify and demonstrate unknown system behavior and/or environment changes and evolve into better systems. Thus, a future medical CPS will be able to cope with a new and unreliable environment.

Figure 6. Workflow diagram of CPS based EMR

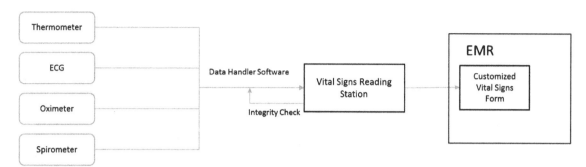

- A medical CPS will improve *response time* significantly due to faster processing and communication ability of sensors.

One such medical device is an Electronic Medical Records (EMR) system with a cyber-physical interface, described in Mendez and Ren (2012). An EMR is a system for storing patient information by health care providers. Traditionally, vital signs of a patient are recorded in an EMR manually, making the process error prone and time consuming. The solution proposed in Mendez and Ren (2012), is a cyber-physical interface that integrates the existing EMR system, vital sign reading station, software data handler and customized vital signs form.

There are many other CPS based medical devices that are being considered by researchers and manufacturers. Some of the challenges of design and implementation of CPS based medical devices include (but not limited to):

- There is a lack of development platforms to support seamless integration of hardware, software, human factors in CPS design;
- There is a need for an open-research community that includes both researchers and manufacturers "to create strategies for the development of end-to-end, principled, engineering-based design and development tools", according to NITRD (2009).
- Medical devices being safety-critical, security and privacy are significant concerns. Research is required for selecting and implementing appropriate security and privacy measures.

Smart Grid in Energy Management

An electric power transmission grid is one of the largest interconnected networks on earth. Currently, this electrical power grid uses a centralized approach in which a few power stations send electricity to consumers. Four major tasks are accomplished by this grid:

- **Electricity Generation** *:* Electricity is produced by harnessing forces of nature such as wind and water, or using nuclear reaction.
- **Transmission** *:* Electricity is transmitted via high voltage transmission lines.
- **Distribution**: Electricity is distributed to various buildings via transformer.

Figure 7. Electricity supply system

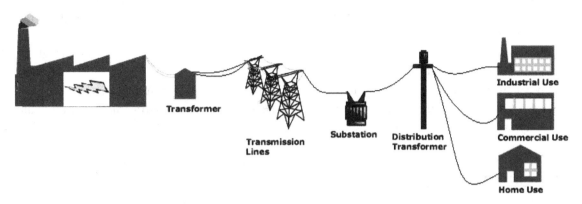

- **Consumption**: Electricity is consumed for home use, industrial use, commercial use and other purposes.

Due to a wide variety of usage of electricity and a diverse range of regulators, and a lack of communication among entities of this large grid, matching electricity generation with the demand is almost impossible. Therefore, in order to manage electricity outage, plants typically generate more electricity than required, thereby resulting in wastage and financial loss. Traditional electricity production process also generates the largest amount of greenhouse gases (EPA, n.d.). Lastly, information that may enable consumers to smartly determine when and how to energy in order to minimize wastage is not readily available.

The concept of smart grid has evolved to address these challenges. If various entities of the electric grid system are able to communicate with each other and also with consumers, the issues stated above can be handled effectively. A smart grid is envisioned to integrate physical and cyber systems (such as sensors, actuators, computers etc.) and exhibit the following characteristics as described in Karnouskos (2011):

- Integration of physical and virtual world that will lead to usage of feedback to continuously improve performance of the physical systems;
- Dynamic interaction among cyber and physical components via wired and wireless networks and parallel computing and distributed information processing in real-time that will allow the systems to hand time-critical situations effectively;
- Self-adaptation, self-organization and self-learning that will enable a smart grid to respond to faults, attacks and emergencies in a resilient and safe manner.

While smart grid is an excellent solution for today's energy problem, there are significant challenges to be overcome in order to implement this CPS in real world:

- **Architecture and Design:** The architecture and design of a smart grid must support communication between heterogeneous entities with different computing power.

- **Communication Technologies:** The existing communication technologies need to be improved in terms of packet drops, time delay, queuing delays and errors in order to be used in real-time dynamic environment of a smart grid.
- **Modeling and Simulation:** Modeling and simulation is important to ensure that a smart grid will operate effectively in a real environment.
- **Cyber Security:** As soon as a system gets connected to the Internet, it becomes subject to a variety of cyber-attacks. Smart grid being one of the most significant infrastructures in a country, safety and security is extremely important.

4. THE DESIGN PROCESS

Cyber physical systems are emerging technologies, with numerous challenges still unresolved.

The design process of cyber physical systems is not well developed and not well documented. Lee and Seshia, two leading researchers in this area, discuss the design process of any general CPS in their book *Introduction to Embedded Systems: A Cyber-Physical Systems Approach*. In this section, I will give a simple overview of a very general design process that describes how to go about designing and implementing cyber physical systems based on the book by Lee and Seshia.

As described in Lee et al. (2011), the design process of a CPS consists of three major tasks:

- **Modeling** *:* This is the starting point of a CPS design. A model is an imitation of a system. Model specifies, as demonstrated in Lee and Sheshia (2011), what a system does.
- **Design** *:* Design combines all parts together and builds the system. Design specifies, as described in Lee and Sheshia (2011), how a system does what it does.
- **Analysis** *:* Analysis of a system helps us gain a better understanding of the system's performance. In other words, it sheds light on why it does what it does, or why it fails to do what it is supposed to do.

Modeling

Lee and Seshia (2011) define a system as a combination of different components that work as a whole. A model for designing cyber-physical systems is defined by the following characteristics:

- It is a mathematical abstraction of a system. It omits a lot of details and only focuses on certain properties.
- It is said to have high fidelity if it describes the properties of a system accurately.

The dynamics of the system demonstrate how the system changes its state over time. The objective of modeling a system is to study the dynamics of the system.

A CPS being a hybrid system, there are two types of components: physical and logical. While a physical component consists of matters, a logical component is made of algorithms and programs. Moreover, the physical components are connected together by networking technology. Therefore, model of a cyber-physical system typically represents physical properties as well as computing and networking properties.

Figure 8. An actor model

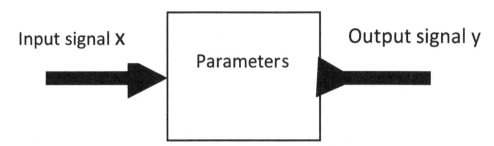

A physical process in a CPS is a combination of many things happening concurrently, in time continuum. The logical process, on the other hand, is sequential and step-by-step, thus discrete in nature. In order to create a CPS model that effectively unites a sequential process with a concurrent world, it is important to understand various modeling techniques for continuous and discrete system dynamics. There are many modeling techniques for studying dynamics of physical and logical systems. I will briefly describe a few techniques that are studied by Lee and Seshia in 2011.

For physical systems that are continuous in nature, Lee and Seshia introduce two distinct modeling techniques:

- **Newtonian Mechanics** *:* This technique uses differential or integral equations to relate input signals such as force or torque to output signals such as position, orientation or velocity.
- **Actor Model** *:* This technique models a continuous-time system as a box with an input port and an output port. A box is called an actor. Two actors can be combined to form cascade combination (see Figure 7).

Lee and Seshia demonstrate in Lee and Sheshia (2011) how different properties such as causality, memorylessness, linearity, time invariance, and stability of a physical system can be modeled using these techniques.

One important feature that characterizes a CPS is feedback control. A control system uses feedback control to increase reliability. A system with feedback control will measure the discrepancy between actual

Figure 9. A cascade combination of two actors

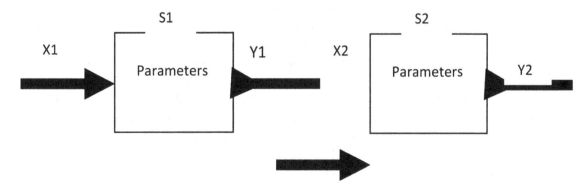

Figure 10. A simple finite state machine

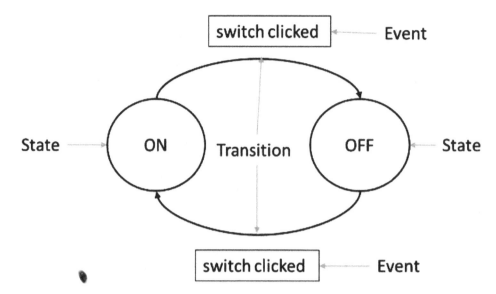

behavior and desired behavior and will use that information to correct the error. Feedback control is an essential part of embedded systems. It is a vast and complicated topic and out of scope of this chapter.

A discrete system is defined as a system that "operates in a sequence of discrete steps and is said to have discrete dynamics" (Lee & Sheshia, 2011). A discrete system is typically modeled using a state machine. In a state machine, a system moves from one state to another depending on the inputs and outputs. A state machine with a finite number of states is called a finite state machine. A finite state machine diagram is usually drawn with graphical notations. The set of states S is given by:

S = { S1, S2, S3 }

Transition from one state to another describes the discrete dynamics. Figure 8 demonstrates a simple finite state machines with two states "ON" and "OFF".

A finite state machine with a large number of states is difficult to draw. An extended finite state machine provides a solution for this problem by introducing variables that will characterize the transitions.

Lee and Seshia shows how to combine actor models and finite state machines to model physical and logical processes of a cyber-physical system and create a hybrid system model. In a hybrid system model, a finite state machine can be an actor that accepts continuous input signals.

Let's consider an example of a monitor system that uses a passive infrared sensor to detect the presence of a human in front of it. The sensor senses infrared energy emitted by humans. When there is a sudden increase in infrared energy, an alarm is sounded. This system can be modeled as a finite state machine with S = {humanPresent, humanAbsent}. The input is a continuous-time infrared energy τ: R R, where R is the set of all real numbers. $\tau(t)$ is the is the amount of energy at time t. Initial state in "humanAbsent". When $\tau(t)$ exceeds a pre-determined threshold m, the system detects a human and makes a transition to state "huamnPresent". The output are "alarmOn" and "alarmOff". We can model this system using a hybrid model shown in Figure 10.

The above example demonstrates that a hybrid system is modeled in a two-step process:

Figure 11. A hybrid model of a security system

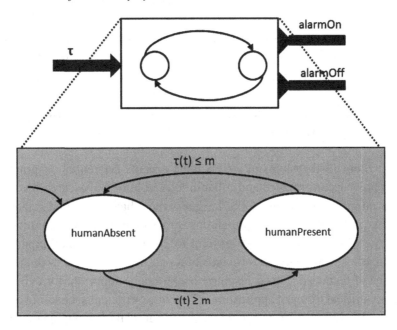

- First, the discrete system represented as a state machine gets embedded in a time base.
- Then a continuous refinement system is created to imitate the time-based behavior of the system.

Design

The design of a cyber-physical system consists of designing embedded systems and software. Lee and Seshia focuses on four key aspects of CPS design in Lee and Sheshia (2011).

- **Memory Architecture:** Memory system plays a key role in the performance of an embedded system. There are two types of memory: volatile and non-volatile. A volatile memory erases the contents as soon as the power is off. RAM (random access memory) of a traditional computer is an example of volatile memory. Contents are not lost in non-volatile memory system even when power goes off. A ROM (read-only memory) is an example of non-volatile storage. Any computing system typically requires a mix of volatile and non-volatile memory. An embedded system requires a mix of volatile and non-volatile memory. Also, a memory with larger capacity and/ or lower power consumption tends to be slower for reading and writing. In order to achieve good performance at a reasonable cost, it is important to use a hierarchical memory structure with an optimal mixture of volatile and non-volatile memory. Lee and Seshia (2011) is an excellent primary guide that gives CPS designers a good head start.
- **Input and Output:** In an embedded system, a sensor gets input from a physical process, sends it to a processor to process, collects the processed data and sends it to an actuator. The input/output technology for a cyber-physical system must be chosen very carefully for the following reasons:
  - CPS combines physical and logical processes together. While input/output of a physical process is analog, a software can process only digital i.e., discrete input and produces a discrete

output as well. Analog signals must be quantized carefully before software can operate on them.

    ◦   As Lee and Seshia describes, incorrect interaction between sequential operation of a software and concurrent events in physical world makes a system subject to failure.

    ◦   Incorrect use of parts leading to inaccurate input/output signals will cause system failure.

Clearly a CPS designer must have a solid knowledge of software and hardware mechanisms that can be used for input/output processing in an embedded system.

- **Multitasking:** Embedded systems in a CPS must execute sequential programs in a concurrent manner for improved performance and reliability. A volume of research has already been done on concurrent program executions. CPS designers must have solid understanding of processes, threads, message passing, interrupts, pipielining, program execution by multicore processors etc.
- **Scheduling:** A real-time system must respond to externally generated inputs within a specific time period. In other words, the performance of a real time system is evaluated by the output as well as the time of response. Timed response is extremely important for cyber-physical systems which are safety-critical for most applications. Therefore, efficient scheduling of tasks is of utmost importance for CPS design. CPS designer must have a good understanding of available scheduling mechanisms for real time tasks.

Lee and Seshia suggest that for an embedded system which is a component of a CPS, these four aspects of computing must be carefully considered by the designers. A customized design of hardware and software will save energy, which is a critical resource in most sensors.

Hardware and software, computing and physical processes are traditional abstraction layers in a system design. Lee and Seshia emphasize that such cross-layer thinking is extremely important for CPS designers to think across these traditional layers. For example, a developer who implements a software for a temperature sensor in PHMS (pervasive health monitoring system) must have solid knowledge of biological characteristics related to temperature of human body in order to implement a software that will work reliably and predictably under all types of real scenarios. A programmer who implements an automotive software, must know how processor features such as pipeline or cache can influence the execution times [10].

Analysis

Cyber-physical systems being safety-critical in their regular use, analysis of CPS is an extremely important process in order to evaluate the system and ensure that it meets all performance requirements. Lee and Seshia provide a few analysis techniques that will be particularly effective for comparing and analyzing system specifications, and analyzing the designs resulting from those specifications.

- **Temporal Logic:** As Lee and Seshia defines "temporal logic is a precise mathematical notation with associated rules for representing and reasoning about timing-related properties of systems." Lee and Seshia discuss the use of linear temporal logic (LTL) technique in order to describe property over a single, but arbitrary execution of a system. A few example properties that can be expressed using LTL are described below, according to Lee and Sheshia (2011):

- ○ Causal dependency and ordering of events: If event A happens during the execution of a system, then event B will always happen. Event A will always be following by an occurrence of event B.
- ○ Event A will always occur during an execution cycle of a system.

Using temporal logic many safety and liveness properties of CPS can be expressed.

- **Abstraction-Refinement Relation:** It is important to study these relations in order to determine whether and when a system can safely replace another, or whether a design can correctly implement a specification for system performance.
- **Reachability Analysis and Model Checking:** Reachability analysis helps determine the states of a system that are reachable. Model checking is a technique that helps determine whether a system satisfies a specification described by LTL. Lee and Seshia provides a number of basic algorithms for model checking and reachability analysis.
- **Quantitative Analysis:** Quantitative analysis is useful in evaluating a CPS performance with respect to any property that can be measured. For example, it helps ensure whether a home monitoring system will set on an alarm within a second of detecting a human presence. This technique can be used to perform a system's execution time analysis and analysis of any critical resource such as memory, power and energy.

5. SECURITY OF CYBER-PHYSICAL SYSTEMS

Applications of cyber-physical systems are all mission critical and/or safety critical in nature. In other words, cyber-physical systems monitor and control processes that are mission critical and/or safety critical. Therefore any security breach in a cyber-physical system can have devastating effect. Because of

Figure 12. Maroochy shire water sewerage system network architecture

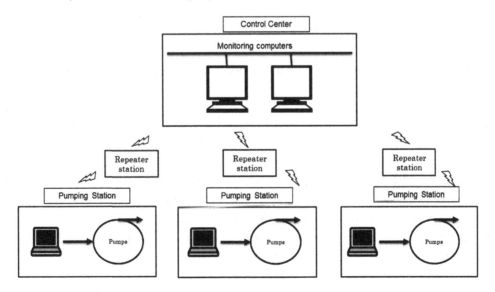

this fact cyber-physical systems are more likely to be subject of targeted attacks with potential of huge impact on human lives and economy. We will elaborate these points with two real life examples of CPS security breach.

The Maroochy Shire security breach that took place in 2000 helps us understand the importance of CPS security. Maroochy Shire Council in Queensland, Australia installed a SCADA (Supervisory Control and Data Acquisition) system for water sewerage. According to Abrams and Weiss (2008) this system consisted of 142 Sewage Pumping Stations. Each pumping station had a computer device that would send and receive instructions from a central control center and monitored and controlled the activities in the corresponding pumping station accordingly. In year 2000, a disgruntled ex-employee stealthily accessed some of these computers and changed electronic data in those computers causing serious malfunction in those pumping stations. The pumps did not work when they were supposed to. No alarm was issued to the central system. Connection between the central system and some of the pumping station computers were lost. More than 750 gallon of untreated water was released into various parts of the city jeopardizing marine and human lives and costing $200k for managing the aftermath. This is a great example that shows how catastrophic a CPS security breach can be.

Understanding the stake of CPS security compared to that of cybersecurity is also important. While breach of cybersecurity can cause financial damage, breach of CPS security can be potentially life threatening. Two hackers Miller and Valasek (Greenberg, 2015) remotely hacked a Chrysler jeep exploiting a vulnerability in Uconnect, an Internet-connected computer feature that controls the vehicle's entertainment and navigation. They were able to disable the brakes and send the car to a ditch.

Besides the targeted attacks like the two examples given above, there are privacy concerns as well. CPSs monitor physical processes they are embedded in. They contain and exchange detailed and sensitive information about the process. Privacy, confidentiality, and integrity of those information are essential.

We can conclude from the above examples that cybersecurity is a subset of CPS security. In addition to securing the cyber components in a CPS, security mechanisms are required for the physical components and for the networks of these components as well.

Principles of CPS Security

Like cyber-security, CPS security considers the six underlying principles of Perkerian Hexad (Andress, 2011), provided by Donn Parker in his book Fighting Computer Crime.

- **Confidentiality:** Data transmitted over a network by any component of a CPS must be prevented from unauthorized access.
- **Integrity:** Unauthorized and/or incorrect modification or fabrication of data must be prohibited using proper measures.
- **Availability:** Service a CPS must be available when needed.
- **Possession or Control:** This principle allows us to consider the physical state of the media in which data is stored. In a cyber-physical system, various components will have different storage media. Some of these storage media may be encrypted and others may not. The non-encrypted components will have both confidentiality and possession problem.
- **Authentication:** Any communication and/or transaction among CPS components via internal or external network must be strictly authenticated.

Figure 13. Six tenets of information security by Donn Parker (Andress, 2011)

Parkerian Hexad

Confidentiality	Availability	Integrity	Authenticatio	Possession	Utility

- **Utility:** This principle helps us determine the usefulness of a piece of information. Using utility security risk can be determined more accurately. For example, a compromised CPS component may have stored both encrypted and un-encrypted data. If the encryption keys are not compromised then that encrypted data would not be very useful to the attackers. Thus utility of that information will be much less than the data that is unencrypted from an attacker's perspective.

Lu et al. in 2015 add the following principles for cyber-physical systems:

- **Reliability:** Reliability is extremely important for a CPS because of its mission-critical and safety-critical nature. CPS users must be able to determine the reliability of the system periodically.
- **Robustness:** Robustness refers to the degree to which a system is able to function in the presence of a disruption. For a mission-critical cyber-physical system, robustness is an extremely important criteria.
- **Trustworthiness:** The data collected and/or generated by a CPS must be trustworthy. Measures of trustworthiness must be determined for a cyber-physical system based on specific application.

All of these principles will allow CPS security researchers to identify problem areas, develop necessary solutions using existing mechanism and develop various policies using cyber-physical systems.

Adversary Model

Cardenas et al. (2009) developed an adversary model in order to understand the scope of CPS security. According to Cardenas et al (2009), there are three categories of adversaries who present threats to cyber-physical systems.

- **Cybercriminals:** According to Cardenas et al (2009), cybercriminals attack any computer they find, typically using malware. A malware infected CPS may have serious impact on its users as reliability of the system will be violated. Confidentiality, availability and integrity can also be violated by malware with backdoors and ransomware.
- **Disgruntled Employees:** These attackers have a lot of insider knowledge and expertise to launch a devastating attack. Maroochy Shire incident (Abrams & Weiss, 2008) is an example of what a

Table 1. Categories and types of security attacks on cyber-physical systems

Category	Type	Description	Principles Violated
Passive	Information leakage	Unauthorized view/disclosure of information from a CPS	Confidentiality
	Traffic analysis	Finding information by sniffing data packets transmitted over a network	Confidentiality
Active	Replay attack	Previous messages / signals are recorded and then sent to a victim at a later time. Replayed message appear to come from the legitimate sender.	Authentication
	Masquerade attack	A message sent to a CPS by a spoofed sender.	Authentication, integrity
	Denial of service	The CPS is attacked in such a way that it stops responding to the legitimate users.	Availability
	Data modification	Signals, messages are intercepted, altered and sent to original destination (ARP poisoning, cache poisoning).	Integrity, confidentiality

disgruntled ex-employee is capable of doing. Disgruntled current employees can launch an attack from inside even if the exteriors of the system and the network are well protected.

- **Terrorists, Activists and Other Organized Criminal Groups:** These organized criminal groups can launch targeted attacks against cyber-physical systems with potentially dangerous impacts. Recent ransomware attacks against hospitals in US (Miliar, 2016) demonstrates potential dangers of targeted attacks on healthcare CPS. In each ransomware case in US, hospital authorities decided to pay the ransom demanded by the attackers in order to minimize the damage on the patients' health.
- **Nation States:** According to Gorman (2009), some national security officers claim that intrusion in US electric grid by spies took place. While such intrusions have been rare, it is quite possible that in near future enemy countries launch attack of smart infrastructures of a nation.

Types of Attacks

The attacks on cyber-physical systems can be categorized as passive and active (Northcutt, 2013). The following table, as described in Northcutt (2013), provides classification and description of different attack types under each category.

The attacks described above are typical for any traditional information system/embedded system. However, attackers may be able to launch new types of attacks based on the very unique nature of a cyber-physical system. One possible example is given by Cardenas et al (2009): *resonance attack*. In such an attack, a compromised sensor or controller will force the whole system to oscillate at its resonant frequency, according to Carddenas et al (2009). Significant research work is required to identify the unique attack models for cyber-physical systems.

Goals of CPS Security

Since cyber-physical system operations must involve the Internet, it is essentially impossible to provide a complete protection for these systems. Like cybersecurity, we have to focus on the following two key aspects:

Table 2. Common defense mechanisms at each layer between information asset and attack

External Network	Network Perimeter	Internal Network	Sensors and Physical Systems	Application Software	Data Layer
1. DMZ 2. VPN 3. Logging 4. Penetration testing 5. Vulnerability analysis	1. Firewall 2. Proxy 3. Logging 4. Auditing 5 Penetration testing 6. Vulnerability analysis	1. IPS 2. IDS 3. Logging 4. Auditing 5. Penetration testing 6. Vulnerability analysis	1. Authentication 2. Antivirus 3. Firewalls 4. IDS 5. IPS 6. Password 7. Hashing 8. Logging 9. Auditing 10. Penetration testing 11. Vulnerability analysis	1. SSO 2. Content 3. Filtering 4. Data validation 5. Auditing 6. Penetration testing 7. Vulnerability analysis	1. Encryption 2. Access 3. Controls 4. Backup 5. Penetration testing 6. Vulnerability analysis

- *Defense mechanisms* for minimizing risks of attacks
- *Detection and incident response mechanisms* to effectively deal with any attack

There already exists well-developed defense and detection mechanisms for network security and system security for computers and smart phones as well. Research is required to determine how to incorporate those mechanisms into CPS design in an application specific manner. In general, for information security a multilayer defense strategy called "defense in depth" is used. Similar approach should be taken for CPS security.

Let's discuss the layers first. Any cyber system contains at least one computing system and is connected to an internet network and an external network. Defense in depth strategy for information security implements defense mechanisms at the following layers:

- External network
- Network perimeter
- Internal network
- Host systems
- Applications
- Data layer

An attacker will have to counter defense mechanisms at each layer in order to finally reach an information asset stored in a system. The goal of a multi-layer defense strategy is to implement enough defense mechanisms so that there is enough time to detect and respond to an attack in progress. The following table demonstrates the typical defense mechanisms that are used in each layer for information security in a regular system (Northcutt, 2013). For a cyber-physical system, all or most of these measures must be in place.

While any typical computing system in a networked environment must have these security measures in place, actual implementation of these measures will vary from system to system depending on the type application, computing power, resources constraints etc. A cyber-physical system being a system of many different computing systems, such implementation is especially challenging. For example, SCADA systems that use wireless sensor network for data collection and dissemination use small resource constrained sensors with very limited computing power. Therefore traditional computing-intensive cryptographic mechanisms to protect confidentiality of data cannot be used. However, data collected by these small sensors will be transmitted to one more base stations which typically have more computing power. Hence these computing devices can use better cryptographic mechanisms. The CPS security researchers face the challenge of how to seamlessly integrate various security mechanisms into different components of a CPS and minimize the number of vulnerabilities.

In addition to *defense* and *detection* mechanisms, cyber-physical systems require *resiliency* and *deterrence*, according to [20]. Resiliency of a CPS refers to the ability of the CPS to survive and function reliably in the face of an attack. There are several security design principles that ensure resiliency of a computing system and can be applied to cyber-physical systems (Cardenas et al, 2009; Avizienis et al, 2004; Saltzer & Schroeder, 1975). Redundancy, for example, can provide resiliency against a single point failure. Principle of least privilege and principle of separation of duty, the two well-known computer security principles limit the area of damage by an attack. However, implementation of these principles in a cyber-physical system requires a lot of research and analysis. How will a separation principle work in a system with feedback loops to controller systems? How will traditional access control measures work in a CPS? Questions such as these must be addressed by research. Deterrence requires combination of effective laws and law enforcement officials to track crimes and criminals. According to Cardenas et al (2009) this is a promising area of research for CPS security researchers.

Before concluding the discussion on CPS security, we must mention that there are significant differences between traditional information technology (IT) security and CPS security. As recorded by Cardenas et al, (2009) these differences are as follows:

- In traditional IT systems, patching and updating software is an important security measure. In a CPS patching and updating a software can be very expensive. In 2008, reboot of a monitoring computer after a software update at a nuclear power plant reset data on control systems. This caused the safety systems wrongly interpret some data and the power plant was accidentally shut down.
- Availability in a cyber-physical system is more critical than availability in a traditional IT system. A CPS requires real-time availability, which requires careful implementation of security measures.
- Some components of cyber-physical system may require lightweight cryptographic solutions due to energy constraint, while other components may use traditional cryptographic mechanisms.

In conclusion, security in a cyber-physical system is extremely important. Security mechanisms must be integrated with the design of a CPS. Currently, such integration faces lots of challenge and requires a lot of research work. Since cyber-physical system designs vary widely from application to application, security mechanisms should also vary accordingly. Venkatasubramanian et al. (2009) and Venkatasubramanian, Mukherjee, and Gupta (2014) present some research on body area networks. Machado et al. (2013) present security research on vehicular networks.

6. SUMMARY

This chapter provides an overview of cyber-physical system, its applications and design process. Cyber-physical systems are future generation systems that have potential applications in important sectors such as healthcare, energy, transportation etc. If implemented correctly, cyber-physical systems will bring a permanent change in the way the world operates, by increasing connectivity and communication among heterogeneous entities via wired and wireless networking. However, there are significant challenges in design, implementation and use of cyber-physical systems. In a cyber-physical system, physical world and logical world of computing and networking must interact effectively and reliably. While physical world operates in time-continuum, logical computing is a sequential process of discrete steps, discrete inputs and outputs. Effective and safe interaction between physical and logical processes in a timely manner is the biggest challenge of CPS design. Implementation and use of a CPS face another major challenge of security and privacy. The moment a system uses the Internet for communication among various components of the system, it becomes subject to cyber threats and attacks. Extensive research is required to find effective solutions for security and privacy of a cyber-physical system. This chapter aims at providing the basic information on applications and design process of cyber-physical systems that will help potential researchers to form a basic idea about this technology.

REFERENCES

Abrams, M., & Weiss, J. (2008). *Malicious Control System Cyber Security Attack Case Study–Maroochy Water Services, Australia.* Retrieved from http://csrc.nist.gov/groups/SMA/fisma/ics/documents/Maroochy-Water-Services-Case-Study_report.pdf

Andress, J. (2011). *Basics of Information Security: Understanding the Fundamentals of InfoSec in Theory and Practice.* Syngress Press.

Avizienis, A., Laprie, J.-C., Randell, B., & Landwehr, C. (2004, January-March). Basic Concepts and Taxonomy of Dependable and Secure Computing. *IEEE Transactions on Dependable and Secure Computing, 1*(1), 11–32. doi:10.1109/TDSC.2004.2

Cardenas, A., Amin, S., Sinopoli, B., Giani, A., Perrig, A., & Sastry, S. (2009). Challenges for Securing Cyber Physical Systems. *Workshop on Future Directions in Cyber-physical Systems Security.*

Cardenas, Amin, Sinopoli, Giani, Perrig, & Sastry. (2009). *Challenges for Securing Cyber Physical Systems.* Retrieved from http://cimic.rutgers.edu/positionPapers/cps-security-challenges-Cardenas.pdf

Cyber Physical Systems. (n.d.). Retrieved from: http://cyberphysicalsystems.org/

Derler, L., & Sangiovanni-Vincentelli. (2012, January). Modeling Cyber-Physical Systems. *Proceedings of the IEEE.*

EPA. (n.d.). *Sources of Greenhouse Gas Emissions.* Retrieved from https://www3.epa.gov/climatechange/ghgemissions/sources.html

Gorman, S. (2009). *Electricity grid in the U.S. penetrated by spies.* Retrieved from http://www.wsj.com/articles/SB123914805204099085

Greenberg, A. (2015). Hackers Remotely Kill a Jeep on the Highway – With Me in It. *Wired*. Retrieved from: https://www.wired.com/2015/07/hackers-remotely-kill-jeep-highway/

Haque, S. A., Aziz, S. M., & Rahman, M. (2014, April). Review of Cyber-Physical System in Healthcare. *International Journal of Distributed Sensor Networks*, *10*(4), 217415. doi:10.1155/2014/217415

Jovanov, Milenkovic, Otto, & de Groen. (2005). A wireless body area network of intelligent motion sensors for computer assisted physical rehabilitation. *Journal of NeuroEngineering and Rehabilitation*, *2*(6).

Karnouskos. (2011). *Cyber-Physical Systems in the Smart Grid*. 9th IEEE International Conference on Industrial Informatics, Lisbon, Portugal.

Lee, E., & Sheshia, S. (2011). Introduction to Embedded Systems: A Cyber-Physical Systems Approach. LeeSeshia.org

Lu, T., Zhao, J., Zhao, L., Li, Y., & Zhang, X. (2015). Towards a Framework for Assuring Cyber Physical System Security. *International Journal of Security and Its Applications*, *9*(3), 25–40. doi:10.14257/ijsia.2015.9.3.04

Machado, R. G., & Venkatasubramanian, K. (2013). Short Paper: Establishing Trust in a Vehicular Network. *IEEE Vehicular Networking Conference*. doi:10.1109/VNC.2013.6737611

Mendez, E. O., & Ren, S. (2012). Design of Cyber-Physical Interface for Automated Vital Signs Reading in Electronic Medical Records Systems. *Electro/Information Technology (EIT), 2012 IEEE International Conference*. doi:10.1109/EIT.2012.6220696

Miliard, M. (2016). Two more hospitals struck by ransomware, in California and Indiana. *Healthcare IT News*. Retrieved from: http://www.healthcareitnews.com/news/two-more-hospitals-struck-ransomware-california-and-indiana

NITRD. (2009). *Networking and Information Technology Research and Development Program*. High-Confidence Medical Devices: Cyber-Physical Systems for 21st Century Health Care, A Research and Development Needs Report. Retrieved from https://www.nitrd.gov/About/MedDevice-FINAL1-web.pdf

Northcutt. (2013). Security of Cyber-Physical Systems: A Survey and Generalized Algorithm for Intrusion Detection and Determining Security Robustness of Cyber Physical Systems using Logical Truth Tables. *Vanderbilt Undergraduate Research Journal, 9*.

Rajkumar, R., Lee, L., Sha, L., & Stankovic, J. (2010). Cyber-physical systems: The next computing revolution. *Design Automation Conference (DAC), 2010 47th ACM/IEEE*.

Real Time Systems. (n.d.). Retrieved from http://www.cse.unsw.edu.au/~cs9242/08/lectures/09-realtimex2.pdf

Saltzer, J. H., & Schroeder, M. D. (1975, September). The Protection of Information in Computer Systems. *Proceedings of the IEEE*, *63*(9), 1278–1308. doi:10.1109/PROC.1975.9939

Shnayder, Chen, Lorincz, Fulford-Jones, & Welsh. (2005). *Sensor Networks for Medical Care*. Harvard University Technical Report.

Tew, J., & Ray, L. (2016). ADDSMART: Address Digitization and Smart Mailbox with RFID Technology. *IEEE UEMCON*. doi:10.1109/UEMCON.2016.7777879

Venkatasubramanian. (2009). *Security Solutions for Cyber-physical Systems* (Doctoral Dissertation). Arizona State University.

Venkatasubramanian, Mukherjee, & Gupta. (2014). CAAC - An Adaptive and Proactive Access Control Approach for Emergencies in Smart Infrastructures. *ACM Transactions on Autonomous and Adaptive Systems, 8*(4).

Virone, G., Wood, A., Selavo, L., Cao, Q., Fang, L., Doan, T., & Stankovic, J. et al. (2006). An assisted living oriented information system based on a residential wireless sensor network. *Proceedings of the Transdisciplinary Conference on Distributed Diagnosis and Home Healthcare*. doi:10.1109/DDHH.2006.1624806

WATERMATRIX Water Analysis and Waste Water Treatment. (n.d.). Retrieved from: http://www.watermatrix.net/Product.aspx?type=Automation

Wu, L., & Kaiser, G. (2013). *FARE: A Framework for Benchmarking Reliability of Cyber-Physical Systems. Columbia University Computer Science Technical Reports*. Columbia University.

Chapter 17
Scientometrics:
A Study of Scientific Parameters and Metrics

Sudeepa Roy Dey
PES Institute of Technology – Bangalore South, India

Gambhire Swati Sampatrao
PES Institute of Technology – Bangalore South, India

Archana Mathur
PES Institute of Technology – Bangalore South, India

Sandesh Sanjay Gade
University of Virginia, USA

Sai Prasanna
PES Institute of Technology – Bangalore South, India

ABSTRACT

The term "Scientometrics" emerges from two significant words –Science and Metrics. It is concerned with metrics used for quantitative analysis of researcher's contribution to various scientific domains. An effective medium to communicate scientific knowledge is via scholarly publications. It provides a platform to propagate research output within and across domains. Thus, there arise need to discover parameters which can measure a researcher's contribution to his field. The most significant metric to measure the impact of a scientific work is citations. The Citation Indexes are utilized as scientometric tool to measure the research output of authors, articles and journals. This book chapter explores the existence of many such scientific parameters at both journal and author level. Further, authors make an earnest attempt to use them to measure the internationality of peer-reviewed journals. They claim that already existing parameters alone are not sufficient for evaluation of internationality and explore new parameters for computing unbiased index both at journal and author level.

DOI: 10.4018/978-1-5225-2498-4.ch017

INTRODUCTION

Research activity cannot be performed in isolation. It involves utilization of scientific ideas and techniques established by scholars in a given domain. Researcher experiment with ideas and publish work mostly in peer reviewed scientific journals. Though there are various motivations to cite previous work, authors cite to acknowledge and give credits to the contribution that were already done to the subject matter. This provides insight to build and maintain citation-based indexes and to endorse all Scientists and researchers who made major contributions in the advancement of research and development. In any respect, most scientific parameters have originated from Eugene Garfield's concept of using bibliographic citations, Impact Factor being the most popular choice. While Impact Factor merely reflects number of citations per publication, H-index, another well known metric, incorporates both number of publications and number of citations in its influence computation. Although many prominent metrics are built using citation indexes, the research community often misuses these indexes and metrics by manipulating the citation count through practices like extensive self-citation, copious citation and at journal level, coercive citation. Researchers often suggest eliminating self-citations from total citation when computing influence. Arguably, self-citation cannot be labeled as unfair or unacceptable if an author choose to cite his related previous work. Copious citations is a practice in which multiple authors profusely cite each other with an intention to raise their h-index and similar influence-governing parameters. There have been similar cases of misuse, where Editor-in-Chief's of two high impact factor journals are seen publishing extensively not only in their own journals but also into each others'. The journals continue to demonstrate such practice till date hampering the dignity and integrity of the structure of scholarly publications.

Another notable trend, followed opportunistically is when editors of low ranked journals persuade authors to cite their journal with an inclination to push their impact factors. Even though most authors view coercive citation as inappropriate, few low-ranked authors do not mind adding unrelated references and return the favor to publishing journals. If one journal coerces, to improve its rank, others gravitate and this becomes a trend that contaminates the whole publication process. One possible solution could be penalizing the usage of self-citations which would reduce, if does not dethrone, the coercive motivation.

Although journal's prestige is reflected in its Impact factor, the overall framework of measuring "prestige" and for that matter its "internationality", demands clear understanding and usage of deep rooted parameters. Scientific indicators like I.F., raw citations, h-index, h5-index, g-index, i-10 index can work as instruments to measure prestige; when it comes to measuring "internationality", choosing a set of smart indicators and alternatively, defining new, unbiased ones become inevitable. There exist several vague definitions of the term "Internationality" which are based on including attributes like ISSN number, Editorial board members, reviewers, authors, Editors, Publishers and other associated entities of publishing community. Authors refute such definitions and claim that "internationality" should be defined as a quantifiable metric, which is devoid of any kind of misuse or manipulation, is unbiased towards origin of journal, author or article and calibrate journals on the basis of quality of research output it publishes.

The roadmap of the chapter is shown in Figure 1. The chapter is built on two pillars. The first cornerstone lay emphasis upon influence-measuring scientific parameters and examines in depth their merits and demerits. It defines 'internationality' of peer-reviewed journal and explores the capacity and degree to which these deep-rooted parameters contribute in computing 'internationality'. A comparison of new parameter with the existing ones is explained and appropriateness in using these novel parameters is illustrated by citing examples and case study. The chapter moves forward to describe Cobb Douglas

Figure 1. Road map "journal metrics"

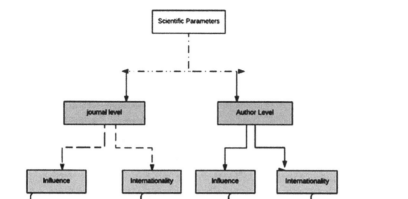

Model and mathematically proves its suitability for computing "internationality" of journals. Second pillar of the book chapter highlights the existing metric to measure scholastic influence and talk about new approaches toward author level metrics. It explores "influence" and "internationality" measuring metrics and moves ahead to explore the suitability of SIR and CISER model in their computation. In parallel, contribution of Citation Networks and Genealogy Tree in devising new indicators for author level metrics is also examined.

BACKGROUND

The increasing number of journals instigates a need for quantification mechanism to evaluate the quality of the published research articles. The research carried out on such lines are based only on the usage of term "international", without evaluating it without using appropriate measures or indices As a results, the literal definition of the word 'international' is used in its minimal sense (Buela-Casal et al, 2006).

Impact Factor, devised by Eugene Garfield is the most widely used method to measure Journal's influence. It's a value calculated over time, and is based on the number of citations received in the previous two year divided by the number of articles published in same years. For a journal, all its citations of previous n years should be available to calculate impact factor for year (n+1) implying the computation of impact factor involves significant overhead. In spite of its drawback, the Journal Impact Factor is a popular method to measure the scientific influence of journals. Most of its variants too require the citation data of the preceding few years from all the indexed journals.

The other popular measure is the Elsevier's Scopus which has a large collection of peer reviewed scholarly journals across various domains. Scopus utilizes its database to provide another type of journal metric to rank journals via SCImago Journal and Country Rank (SJR) portal. The SJR rank is a score evaluated by Scopus from the past five years' data addressing small number of journals. It is claimed that SCI, Thomson Reuters are little more selective than Scopus.

A lot of research is carried by researchers across the globe. Ali Uzun (Ali, 2004) surveyed an American journal and a few European journals and analyzed bibliographic data about foreign authors and their national affiliation from five years of publication. He has then used a simple linear regression analysis to show that 60% of variation in the proportion of foreign-authored articles in the set of five journals over the selected years could be explained by the percentage of foreign members on the editorial boards of the journals. PandelisPerakakis et.al (Buela-Casal et. al, 2006; Perakakis et.al, 2006) in two of the published works has proposed neuro-fuzzy system as a way to represent the problem of internationality. The neuro-fuzzy systems are the fuzzy sets of the weighted criteria linked by fuzzy rules in a multi-layer perceptron, whose output defuzzification gives measure of Journal Internationality Index akin to the Impact Factor for citations.

Aviles, Frank Pancho, Ramirez, IvonneSaidé (Aviles, Pancho, Ramirez, Ivonne, 2015) evaluated the internationality of several high visibility Library and information science journals by studying the permeation of international participation through the exploration of seven indicators: (1) the editorial and advisory boards, (2) peer review boards, (3) their database circulation, (4) authorship, (5) peer review evaluation criteria, (6) internationality of citations, (7) and citation impact.

NeelamJangid, SnehanshuSaha, Siddhant Gupta, Mukunda Rao J (Jangid et. al, 2015; Jangid et. al, 2014) introduced a new metric, Journal Influence Score (JIS), which is calculated by applying Principal Component Analysis (PCA) and multiple linear regression (MLR) on citation parameters, extracted and processed from various scholarly articles in different domains, to obtain a score that gauges a journals impact. The higher the score, more the journal is valued and accepted. Journals ranking results are compared with ranks of SJR, which internally uses Google's PageRank algorithm to calculate ranks. The results showed minimal error and the model performed reasonably well.

The general drawback in the above proposed models is that there is no common measure for the influence of journals across various domains. Also, there is a need to scrutinize the practices like self-citation which is the easiest way to increase the citation quotient of journals.Source Normalized Impact per Paper (SNIP) a measure proposed by Henk F. Moed (Henk, 2010) is the ratio of the journals citation count per paper and the citation potential in its subject field. It allows direct comparison of journals in different subject domains which is based on citation relationships. SNIP is based on citations from peer-reviewed papers to other peer-reviewed papers.

Minor modifications were done over the above mentioned method by Ludo Waltman et al (Waltman et. al, 2013). To correct the differences in citation practices, the source normalised approach is used. The benefit of this approach being, it does not require the classification of subject fields where the boundaries of fields are defined explicitly. There are some arguments around the original SNIP indicators' properties that may be considered counter-intuitive. For instance, it is possible that additional citation has a negative correlation with journals SNIP value. The revised SNIP indicator that they have introduced in this paper is defined to avoid these kinds of counter-intuitive behaviours.

Carl Bergstrom and Jewin West, in the year 2007, initiated a project called Eigenfactor Project (n.d.) which traces the routes in which the knowledge has passed down. They have framed citation networks which cater to the difference in standards of citation and different timelines in which the citations could occur. Their work claims that the probability of an article getting cited within a short span of time is very high. Thus it could be misleading if its importance is calculated based on the short time frame. Thus, the Eigen Score is calculated based on the citations obtained over a five year period.

Another major problem is the open access publishers who charge publication fees to authors and offer no editorial services. Such services offer an open gateway for the seekers of easy publication. Walt Crawford (Crawford, 2014) in 2014 has proposed the following steps to avoid predatory journals.

Step 1: To make a pertinent decision whether "The International Journal of A" is a good target, one must look for it in the Directory of Open Access Journals (doaj.org). If the journal is not in the directory, look for another journal in a similar subject category.

Step 2: If the journal is in DOAJ, explore its site, its APC policy, quality of English used, its editorial board members- whether they are real people. Otherwise start from step 1.

Step 3: Check whether article title over the past issues makes sense within the journal's scope or if any author show up repeatedly within the past few issues. If so, go to step 1 again.

However, it is observed that the method is more of a manual investigation and hence ungainly and elaborate. The above case studies clearly indicate that there is a need for a mechanism which offers to address the issue of internationality modelling and interface estimation of peer-reviewed journals in the fields of science and technology.

The concept of citation index, Impact Factor and SJR ranking provide limited respite to the above mentioned challenges of distinguishing and ranking legitimate publishers from the fake entities. This gives plenty of motivation and reason to work on proving a journal's credibility and integrity as well as ascertaining the quality, impact and influence of the publications.

"INFLUENCE" AS A METRIC: JOURNAL LEVEL

The evaluation of journals has been carried out extensively in the past century. A general interest in understanding the trends and patterns by assessing the journals has existed since the 1920's. However, the interests have varied persistently with respect to the context and paradigms of time. Academic institutions have been using publication information to evaluate their faculties during appraisals. The information mainly includes the impact factor (or influence) of the publishing journal. Higher the impact factor, more credible the scholar and his research is considered. However, it is important to gauge the integrity of journals which are pulling authors to publish. Recently, there are instances of predatory publishing that gained attention as well as worldwide criticism. Some illegitimate publishing houses charge authors with hefty publishing fee as they publish articles without providing any editorial service or peer-reviewing of the submitted article. Evaluation of a journal's influence thus, requires a close scrutiny from all perspectives.

Introduction to Scientific Parameters

This section presents some of the widely known scientific parameters that describe metrics used for the understanding of the calculation of Internationality as defined under differing contexts and assumptions. It is essential to understand that the parameters described in this section is not an exhaustive list, especially due to the emergence of several of these parameters which have evolved over the years to stay relevant in the digital age.

Impact Factor (IF)

The impact factor is one of the most important of all metrics that have been devised for understanding the international influence of a journal. This metric was put together by Eugene Garfield, the man who actively spearheaded research in the then newly-found area of Scientometrics and Bibliometrics back in the 1970's. Thomson Reuters acquired the Eugene Garfield founded Institute of Scientific Information and is generally accredited with the introduction of the widespread use of the Impact Factor as a metric in their annual publication of the Journal Citation Reports, listing the computed IF measures for popular journals that it followed.

Understanding the Impact Factor as a measure is simple. The IF can be defined as the arithmetic mean of citations received by an article published as part of a journal. The IF, as described by Eugene Garfield, considers the citations received over the span of three years from the current year.Hence,

$$IF_{2016}$$
$$= \frac{\textit{Number of citations received by journal from articles in 2016, 2015 and 2014}}{\textit{Total number of articles published by journalin 2016, 2015 and 2014}}$$

A minimum citation window of three years is taken into consideration to account for uniformity and maintain parity in trends of low impact as well as high impact research areas. This metric takes into account the articles which are assessed by a common panel through the process of peer-review of scholarly papers. This provides a fair impact measurement of the journal and diminishes the change of manipulation. The IF is subject to manipulation and this has led to heavy criticism by research scholars over the years. Regulations set by the editorial board of a journal can immensely influence the Impact Factor and this can be exploited to artificially boost index measures. Coercive citation, in particular, is a practice in which an editor coerces authors to add redundant citations for an article published by the corresponding journal. Activities such as this, while frowned upon, are still used to inflate a journal's impact factor. This makes Impact Factor weaker as an index because of a high possibility of it being operated in a journal's favor by altering citations to and from the journal. The impact factor was hailed as the pinnacle of metrics for understanding the influence of a journal tillcriticisms were discovered regarding articles of sub-par quality hijacking the impact factor of the journal and associating these values as their own. In this regards, it is important to understand that Impact factor does not reflect the average impactofthejournal.

h-index(hi)

The *h*-index was proposed by the Physicist Jorge E. Hirsch in the year 2005 as a measure which not only considers the quantity of citations but also their quality. The *h*-index addresses the concerns of other indicators and metrics usedin Scientometrics.

The *h*-index is defined as a metric, the value of which equals *h* when each of*h* published papers are cited at least *h* times by other articles. A simple algorithm to compute the *h*-index is as follows:-

Table 1. H-index computation

Article (published in journal)	A	B	C	D	E	F	G
Positional Index (P_i)	(i)	(ii)	(iii)	(iv)	(v)	(vi)	(vii)
Citations	14	11	9	6	3	1	0

Step 1: Sort the number of citations for each journal in a descending fashion and assign positional keys to each of the values.

Step 2: The *h*-index is the last positional key in the sorted structure from **Step 1** such that the value corresponding to the key is greater than or equal to the positional key.

The mathematical representation of the *h*-index is as follows:-

$$h - index(f) = \max_i \min(f(i), i) h - index(f) = \max_i \min(f(i), i)$$

The Impact Factor impact considers the entire spectrum of articles within a journal. While this accounts for the quantity of citations considered in the calculation of the metric, it overlooks quality of scientific publications. Impact Factor considers the total number of articles published in a journal as mentioned in previous section.This cannot possibly account for a good representation of the quality of articles. It is fallacious to assume that the entire population of articles in a journal represents "good" or "impactful". *h*-index considers a subset of this population by keeping in view the selection of number of articles that are greater than or equal to a positional index for computing this metric. For instance, consider for a journal a pattern of publication shown in Table 1.

For this journal, the *h*-index would be 4 since this is the minimum case where the number of citations is either greater than or equal to the number of papers in that journal. This does reflect the fact that the computation of the *h*-index keeps in mind highly cited articles only, making it a much easier metric to calculate in comparison to the Impact Factor.

While, *h*-index is a relatively beneficial metric for usage, it does have some limitations. First and foremost, it does not account for citations across fields of a domain. Citations within and across domains could potentially reveal moreinformation about its quality. This is not considered for the computation of the *h*-index and poses as a major disadvantage. *h*-index can be exploited by using unfair practices like self-citations. Consider a scenario where articles published in a journal practice self-citations. In doing so, the citation count for these articles would increase. It is also likely that this citation count would also increase in value over the positional index, thereby increasing the *h*-index. Ideally, this does not capture the essence of "quality" that makes *h*-index an improvement over the Impact Factor metric.

There exists a variation of the *h*-index that was introduced by Google as part of the indicators developed for use on Google Scholar. Primarily referred to as *h5*-index, it places a restriction of considering a complete 5-year period worth of journal citation data for calculating the index as defined earlier. The benefit of *h*-index is readily apparent as shown in the following case study.

CASE STUDY

Source: Journal Metrics, SCImago Journal Rank, Google Scholar websites for data captured until 2014.

Journal Name; Journal of Clinical Oncology
Country Name: United States
Subject Area: Biochemistry, Genetics and Molecular Biology, Medicine
Publisher: American Society of Clinical Oncology
ISSN: 0732183X, 15277755
Impact Factor: 12.408
h-index: 402
h5-index: 202

Hence it can be observed that the *h5*-index presents a better representation of the metric since it only considers citations from five years prior to the publication of the journal.

SCImago Journal Rank (SJR)

The development of the SJR indicator was a turning point in the study of scientometrics and was actively spearheaded at the University of Extremadura by Professor Félix de Moya in 2009. The key principle that sets SJR apart from other parameters is its inherent acknowledgment of the fact that citations are dynamic in nature and that no two citations are the same. In a long list of parameters including the ones described above, it is evident that the quantity of citations of a scholarly publication is not independently sufficient as a measure to understand the influence of a journal. Hence, several metrics also take into account the quality of these citations when evaluating the impact of a journal. The SJR metric is defined as a size-independent indicator of a journal's scientific prestige [journalmetrics.com/sjr.php].It ranks journals by assigning weights to citations as well as by utilizing concept of eigenvector centrality derived from network theory. The *size-independent* nature of the SJR metric has been attributed to the PageRank algorithm which provides a computational model that could be used to efficiently address the issues of dealing with large scale networks such as the Scopus database. The use of PageRank thus, holstered the SJR metric with the prowess to deal with the extremely large and heterogeneous journal citation networks for assessing the quality of citations. [doi:10.1016/j.joi.2010.03.002] SJR employs the PageRank algorithm for iterative weighing of citations. Since SJR does not only take into account the number of citations received by a journal but also the source from where the citations are received. The reputation of the journals for in comingcitations is factored into the computation of the SJR.

SJR uses a citation window of three years and restricts self-citations to one-third of the inbound citations in order to curtail the artificial inflation of a journal's value. Journals are then ranked in order of their *"average prestige per article"*.

Methodology to Compute Prestige SJR

The Prestige SJR (PSJR) is calculated in two phases: Phase 1 is a size-dependent metric that reflects the prestige of whole journals. Phase 2 is a size independent metric that reflects journal to journal prestige.

Phase One

1. Assign an identical amount of prestige to each journal (1/n).
2. The prestige is redistributed in an iterative process where each iteration assigns new prestige values to each journal that meet the following three criteria:
    a. Let X=A minimum prestige value for a journalif it is included in the database.
    b. Let Y= A publication prestige given by the number of papers included in the database for a journal.
    c. Z=A citation prestige given by the number and "importance" of the citations received from other journals whereby journals transfer their attained prestige to each other.
3. Compute Prestige SJR= X+Y+Z.

$$
PSJR_i = \overbrace{\frac{(1-d-e)}{N}}^{1} + \overbrace{e \cdot \frac{Art_i}{\sum\limits_{j=1}^{N} Art_j}}^{2} + d \overbrace{\left[\sum_{j=1}^{N} C_{ji} \cdot \frac{PSJR_j}{C_j} \cdot CF + \frac{Art_i}{\sum\limits_{j=1}^{N} Art_j} \cdot \sum_{k \in DN} PSJR_k \right]}^{3} \dots \quad (1)
$$

The components 1 and 2 in the above equation of SJR are simple as they calculate the journal's prestige by computing number of publications and citations made by that journal. The values remain constant throughout the iteration process. The difficult task is to calculate the last component because it considers prestige transferred to a journal *by* the number of the citations received from other journals. To achieve this, each citation is compared by the prestige achieved by the citing journal in the previous iteration divided by the number of references found in that journal. The important aspectis,since citations up to the three-year window are used to distribute journal prestige, a procedure is defined to avoid losing the prestige value corresponding to the remaining citations. For this a correction factor is incorporated that spreads the undistributed prestige over all the journals to their accumulated prestige proportionally. Finally the sum of the prestige values of all the journals in the database is normalized to unity. The iterative process terminates when the difference between the corresponding prestige values of the journals in two consecutive iterations is no longer significant.

Phase Two

Phase 1 highlighted the prestige of a whole journal but it fails to calculate the journal to journal comparison. As a result larger journals have greater prestige value. Phase 2 addresses the above problem. It normalizes prestige value of each journal by number of articles, reviews and conference papers it has published. Finally these normalized values are increased proportionally so that a score is obtained.

SCImago is an average value per article. So it does not indicate the importance of the journal—a big journal may have the same SCImago value as smaller ones. SCImago is a portal that provides information on journals and country scientific indicators devised from Scopus database. There are a total of 13 parameters taken into account to calculate the score. Next section discusses JIS (Saha et al, 2016), a relatively new metric to counteract this by reducing the number of parameters to five. This reduces the overhead of storage and the complexity of the process.

Figure 2. Detailed design for JIS computation

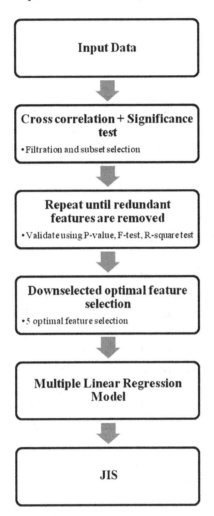

JIS (Journal Influence Score)

The emergence of JIS is attributed to the fact that unlike SJR, JIS is conceptually lightweight. It does not require any storage of data and is computationally faster. JIS is calculated using the following methodology.

As depicted in Figure 2, the JIS computation methodology uses initial 12 parameters from SCImago Journal and Country Rank portal. Since "quarter" of a year is crucial in terms of influence, it is taken as additional 13th parameter. Using cross correlation and multiple linear regression, the number of input parameters are reduced from 13 to final 5. The 5 optimal features selected are quarter, H-index, total number of documents in a year, total references, cites/doc in previous two years. Regression is run on these final 5 parameters to obtain regression statistics which is used in the equation below -

The Multiple Linear Regression formed is:

Journal Influence Score = 0.513322- (0.14076 *Quarter) + (0.004716 * H index) + (0.000131 * Total Documents for Current Year) - (8.3E-06 * Total References) + (0.301404 *Cites/Doc. in previous 2 years)

Where 0.513322 is the base score of the journal.

JIS offers a novel approach in calculating the influence score of a journal without having to bear the overhead of storing data that is synonym with SJR. Also as compared to SJR which is an iterative process, JIS is lightweight in approach.The database size is insignificant and also time complexity is much less. The number of input variables used is only five which is a significant step towards reduction of dimensions

INTERNATIONALITY: AT JOURNAL LEVEL

The previous section throws light on usage of popular scientific indicators to determine impact of research across domains. Because of the associated demerits, the research on journal ranking based only on influence is apparently inadequate and thus opens a scope to develop unbiased ranking mechanism that integrate journal's influence as well as "internationality". The "Internationality" in real sense is the measure of research impact that crosses demographic boundaries and is devoid of any kind of local influence. The local influence could be due to reciprocity of citations within a peer group, within a genealogy tree of authors or among Editor-in-chief's of leading Journals.

Defining Internationality is an open problem to the scientometric community. Various definitions have been stated in past wherein journal's internationality is gauged by insignificant attributes like ISSN number, language of publications, constitution of editorial board, reputation of Editors, country of publication etc. While defining internationality, authors do not consider using any of these parameters, since authors believe that journals cannot be marked as "International" on grounds of their structure and composition like members of editorial Board, reviewers and author. An "international" journal, according to authors is one that facilitates dispersion of Science and knowledge seamlessly across national as well as international boundaries. Therefore, definition of "internationality" must involve all unbiased attributes which are immune to manipulations while judging journal's credibility. The need to discover such unbiased metrics has led many scholars into this field wherein new dimensions are defined and existing dimensions are debated upon. This section introduces few such approaches and lists out the possible metrics used to generate it.

Definition: "Internationality of a journal" is defined as measure of influence across boundaries and across network of journals. It calibrates quality of publications in terms of originality, authenticity, the transformation it brings to and impact it makes on current research within its community. It is observed that, journals receive citations mostly from their local group. Authors, Editor-in-chief's cite themselves extensively for their own gains. A need is realized to develop a transparent and reliable metric destitute of such local impacts, that takes into consideration quality of published-work and national and international spectrum of subscribing readers, authors and reviewers for influence computation.Since almost all existing metrics involves citation count, their live a risk of coercive and copious citations. Also each of the above metrics alone cannot define Internationality in true sense. With intense conviction, the authors introduce a list of modified metrics for computation of internationality of a journal:

1. International Collaboration Ratio(ICR)
2. Non Local Influence Quotient (NLIQ)
3. Source –Normalized Impact per paper(SNIP)
4. Other Citations Quotient

1. International Collaboration Ratio or ICR

ICR (Ginde et al, 2016) of a journal is given by a measure which compares nationality/affiliation of authors with the publishing journal's country and evaluates the level to which the research is 'international'. It ensures a heterogeneous mix of authors from different countries who collaborate for intrinsic research activities and publish their work across boundaries. ICR is computed by considering the following parameters:

a. Country information of the source Journal
b. Authors and co-authors affiliation and country name for each article
c. Weights assigned to different combinations of author's affiliation and of the journal. Example: Consider a journal J which belongs to a country C. The articles in the journal J are - A1, A2, and A3.

The following cases are considered to calculate the weights assigned to journals:

i. Weight is assigned '1' when all authors of an article are from different countries and none of them has nationality same as J's. (considering this as truly 'international')
ii. Weight is '0.5' when half of the authors are from countries different from J's.
iii. Weight is '0' when authors and journal originate from same country. (since no research traversed the national boundaries)

ICR is computed as a ratio of sum of weights of all authors who published in journal J and the total number of authors.

2. Non Local Influence Quotient

Definition of "Internationality" embeds the usage of all influence measuring factors which are free from any kind of localized effect. For this reason, a new metric NLIQ (Ginde et al, 2016) is included as one of parameters for computing internationality. It tries to reduce and eliminate all local manipulations in terms of citations whether they are across peer groups or across journals. The metric does not leave room to any strategic maneuver to extract citations whether it is coercive or cohesive, at journal level or author level. Before defining NLIQ, it is important to throw some light at different 'Journal Collaborations' which hints on how journals may unite in an attempt to manipulate citations, to increase influence and thereby ranking

As indicated in Figure 3, consider two journals J1 and J2. The journals have articles A1 A2 A3 and B1 B2 B3 respectively. The arrows or link represent the citations. All connections between the journals and within the journals can be termed as Journal collaboration. Hence in other words, A2->A3, A3->A1

Figure 3. Inter-journal/intra-journal collaboration

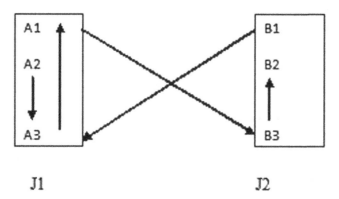

are intra journal collaboration while all links from J1->J2 or vice versa are inter journal collaboration. This indicates the relationship between journals and within a journal in terms of the citations made.

a. **Inter-Journal Collaboration**: A cycle formed when authors of highly prestigious journals, due to their citation tendency, cite papers of journals that are of higher or same rank. When a citation graph of such journals is constructed, a dense loop is seen which indicates a strong collaboration between them. These associations are due to the fallacy that authors who publish in high ranking journals are cited more often than others. This pattern imprudently increases the prestige of journals due to the increased citation count.

b. **Intra-Journal Collaboration**: A cycle formed when published papers of a journal cite papers of the same journal (termed as journal's self citation). Trend is often witnessed when authors are forced by Editor-in-chief's to cite papers of their journal so as to inflate their citation count. Coercive citation artificially boosts impact and rank of journals.

$$Journals\ self-citation rate\ =\frac{No.\ of\ journals\ self-citation\ in\ a\ year}{Total\ number\ of\ citations\ in\ a\ year}^{*}100$$

NLIQ (Non local influence quotient) a new metric eliminates the concern of coercive citation and self-citation mentioned above. The novelty of NLIQ is that it favors inter journal collaboration over intra journal collaboration thereby ruling out all citations that is made from within the journal. It is the ratio of number of citations made from one paper in a given journal to articles published in different journals divided by total number of citations of papers in a journal. The term non local refers to number of external citations received by papers of a journal and hence higher the count; greater will be the NLIQ value.

As indicated in Figure 4, consider a journal 'x' that has 'n' number of total citations made by all its papers.The articles A1, A2 A6 have citations to other journals namely y, z and w. So NLIQ of 'x' for a particular year in this case:

$$is\ given\ by =\frac{Number\ of\ citations\ made\ by'\ x'\ to\ other\ journals}{Total\ number\ of\ citation\ of\ x}$$

Figure 4. NLIQ

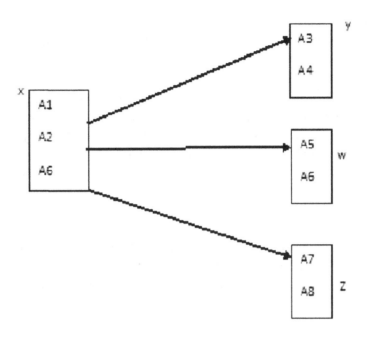

NLIQ qualifies as a novel metric to calculate internationality as it indicates the spectrum of the journal in terms of the citations which are non-local. Every journal that claims to be international must exhibit a high value of NLIQ indicative of diffused local impact. Greater the quotient, lesser is the local manipulation.

3. Source Normalized Impact per Paper (SNIP)

Citation practices can vary across subject fields (Henk, 2010). For example, domains like Biochemistry or Life Sciences may have articles containing 50 references whereas a Mathematical article may have just 10 articles in its reference list. When measuring journal's impact, this difference in citation behavior creates disparity across subject fields as citation count of some journals would be less even though the research quality and productivity would be high. SNIP removes the discrepancy by dividing the Raw Impact per Paper (RIP) with the citation potential of that subject field. RIP (a variant of ISI impact factor) is the average number of citations a journal receives in a given year from the articles of preceding three years. Citation potential is the count of only cited references published in indexed journals. This normalizes the discrepancy between subject fields and allows comparing journals belonging to two different domains. SNIP is thus a good indicator of unprejudiced, unbiased influence computation and can be utilized as a potential parameter in computing "internationality" of journals

4. Other Citation Quotient

OCQ (Ginde et al, 2016) is calculated by taking the complement of self-citation divided by total citations. The key to calculate this is to calculate self-citations and then see if at least one author is common between citing and cited paper. This factor ensures that any coercive citations or self-citations are negated and unnatural boost to journal influence is not taken into account. The other citations are prompted to give a fair basis of judging work. To award a high internationality score the ratio of self-citation to total citation must be less. Also if this ratio is found to be equal to that of total citations of the journal then, zero must be the internationality score.

All these metrics are used together as input to Cobb Douglas model for computation of internationality of journals and thereby ensuring a fair ranking scheme. The next section explores the econometric model and explains relationship between inputs and outputs and the amount of inputs that can produce a given output. The model is used for the first time to compute internationality of journals where the values of above mentioned parameters are extracted and fed to the model.

COBB DOUGLAS MODEL

Cobb Douglas production function is widely used in economics to represent the relationship of outputs and inputs. Given the set of independent variables as above discussed parameters, the Cobb Douglas function is used to calculate the internationality of a journal. Notice the formula with respect to Y which is the internationality score;

$$Y = A\prod_{i=1}^{N} x_i^{ai}$$

When the function Y is implemented, the variables x_i will be those extracted from various algorithms in the previous sections and α_i is the elasticity coefficients. Here values of x_i are as follows.

X_1 : Other Citation Quotients
X_2 : International Collaboration Ratio
$X3$: SNIP
X_4 : Non-Local influence Quotient

Proof of Concept

So far we have discussed the Cobb Douglas formula and how it can be used to calculate the internationality score. Now we further explain how maximum score will be obtained at decreasing return to scale when $\alpha < 1\alpha < 1.$.

Lemma 1: Maximum score at decreasing return to scale which is true when:

$$\sum_{i=1}^{n} \alpha_1 < 1$$

Where α_i is the elasticity of input variable x_i. Consider the production function:

$$Y = \prod_{i=1}^{n} kx_i^{x_i}$$

To prove: $\sum_{i=1}^{n} \alpha_i < 1$

Considering a profit function

$$\pi_n = \prod_{i=1}^{n} kx^a - \sum_{i=1}^{n} wx$$

We know profit maximization is achieved at:

$$p\frac{\alpha_y}{\alpha_x} = wi$$

So to derive conditions for optimization

$$pk\frac{\alpha_1}{x_1}\prod_{i=1}^{n} x_{i}^{ai} = w_1$$

$$pk\frac{\alpha_1}{x_1}\prod_{i=1}^{n} x_{i}^{ai} = w_2$$

$$pk\frac{\alpha_1}{x_1}\prod_{i=1}^{n} x_{i}^{ai} = w_3$$

Multiplying these equations with x_i, we get the following equations:-

$$p\alpha 1\prod_{i=1}^{n} kx_i^{ai} = w_1 x_1 => p\alpha_1 y = w_1 x_1 p\alpha 1\prod_{i=1}^{n} kx_i^{ai} = w_1 x_1 => p\alpha_1 y = w_1 x_1 \tag{4}$$

$$p\alpha_2\prod_{i=1}^{n} kx_i^{ai} = w_2 x_2 => p\alpha_2 y = w_2 x_2 p\alpha_2\prod_{i=1}^{n} kx_i^{ai} = w_2 x_2 => p\alpha_2 y = w_2 x_2 \tag{5}$$

Similarly $p\alpha_n\prod_{i=1}^{n} kx_i^{ai} = w_n x_n => p\alpha_n y = w_n x_n p\alpha_n\prod_{i=1}^{n} kx_i^{ai} = w_n x_n => p\alpha_n y = w_n x_n$ (6)

Dividing equations (5) to (6) by (4) we obtain the following values of x_2, x_3, x_n

$$x_2 = \frac{\alpha_2}{\alpha_1}\frac{w_1}{w_2}x_1$$

$$x_{n-1} = \frac{\alpha_{n-1}}{\alpha_1}\frac{w_1}{w_{n-1}}x_1$$

Substituting these values of x_i in equation (1) and using them in the production function it is observed that Y increases in price of its output and decreases in prices of its input when the following conditions are true.

$$\sum_{i=1}^{n} \alpha_i < 1$$

Therefore decreasing returns to scale is validated.

Concavity of Cobb-Douglas Function Using Hessian Matrix

Cobb-Douglas production model is concave in nature and the maximum value is achieved by giving some factors as input. To prove the concavity of a function, Hessian matrix is used.

Definition

Suppose fϵc^2 which is a class of continuous and second order differential functions. *U is an open curve set then f can be defined as U is a subset of R$_n$ ->RR$_n$->R.*

1. f is concave iff the hessian matrix D^{2}F(X)=H is negative semi definite for all x that belong to U.
2. Given a convex set: $x_1 x_2 x_1 x_2$ be any two points in S, then a function f is concave if

$$(1 - \lambda)f(x1) + \lambda f(x2) \leq (f(1 - \lambda)x1 + \lambda x2) \; \lambda \; belongs \, [0,1]$$

Decreasing returns to scale result in increase in output with addition of an input but at a lower rate.

Implications

1. Cobb-Douglas function is concave for conditions on elasticity. For these values of elasticity the Hessian matrix of the function is negative semi-definite
2. The extrema of the function f(x,y)is used as the model to calculate the internationality score. It achieves global maximal values that suggest the levels of internationality.
3. For f($x_1 x_2$)it is concave if $\alpha \geq 0, \beta \geq 0, \alpha + \beta \leq 1$

The above section discussed internationality and its impact on journal ranking in detail. The problems of the existing metrics are suitably argued and new dimensions to calculate influence score are introduced. But in the world of research and scholars another problem which is growing exponentially is to efficiently rank authors based on their scholarly publication and calculate the influence of a scholar. The next section suitably introduces the term "Scholastic Measure" in terms of existing metrics like h-index and i-10 and then gradually progresses towards new metrics that make use epidemiological models and genealogy tree.

SCHOLASTIC MEASURES

Definition: It is a metric to calculate the "internationality" and "influence" of an author or scholar in a particular domain.

Existing Approach: The current author ranking metrics are based on number of citations received by an author in a time period. The most commonly used author ranking metrics is H-index that is based on the set of the researchers most cited papers and the number of citations that they have received in other publications. H-index reflects both the number of publications and the number of citations perpublication. The index is designed to improve upon simpler measures such as the total number of citations or publications. People judge authors on the h-index value but there are major limitations to it:

- H-index can be largely manipulated by self citations and coercive citations.
- H-index does not account for citations across fields of a domain.
- Note that each database may determine a different H-index for the same individual as the content in each database is unique and different.

The g-index is an alternative for h-index, which is different from h index as it does not average the numbers of citations. As we know H-index only requires a minimum of n citations for the least-cited article from a list of papers and thus ignores the citation count of very highly cited papers. Roughly, the effect is that h is the number of papers of a quality threshold that rises as h rises whereas g-index allows citations from higher-cited papers to be used to bolster lower-cited papers in meeting this threshold. Therefore, in all cases g is at least h, and is in most cases higher. Apart from h-index and g index, another metric which is commonly used to measure the authors influence is i-10 which was invented by google scholar. It counts the number of publications of an author with at least 10 citations. One of the major limitations of i-10 is:-

- It is used only in google scholar.
- Largely dependent on publication count of an author

All these metrics purely rely on total number of citations received by an author which raises a lot of open ended questions like-

1. Is citation count alone sufficient to measure a researcher's innovation and impact?
2. Citations can only go up and are subject dependant.
3. The influence of the knowledge area in the citation volume seems important, because not all subjects have the same citation opportunities. It is known that articles in Social Sciences, Engineering and Humanities receive fewer citations and these also have a higher half-life as compared to life sciences', while journals on Health sciences receive more citations. Different research types have different citation profiles so it is important to understand how can this be normalized?
4. Most importantly, how to tackle problems of manipulating citations like self citations and copious citations.

New Dimensions to Measuring Scholastic Impact

Defining "Internationality of an author" has been a debatable subject as all author level metrics have ranked authors purely on citation count and publications made in a time period of 5-10 years. The consequences of which are not appreciable enough and are frequently biased and manipulated. Lot of researchers have attempted the problem and have got suitably better results. This section focuses on new scientific parameters that measure "Internationality" and "Influence" of an author.

1. NLIQ (Non local Influence quotient): Authors receive citations for the published work. These received citations are either from local community e.g. peers, supervisors, within a journal, self citations. These are called Intra Citations. The other source is non local community e.g.: external sources or citations that are from authors apart from the intra citation. The actual impact of an author is suitably established only when the citations are counted of the external community instead of total citations received. This justifies the term "Non local" and truly signifies the "internationality". To Measure NLIQ the tools required are:

1. Genealogy Citation Tree
2. Citation Network

1. Genealogy Citation Tree

A Genealogy Tree is used to study the citation pattern and see how an author grows in his or her peer network. Genealogy Tree and graph is also helpful in finding self citations and local citations that is further important to trace the citation genealogy ratio to measure NLIQ. Genealogy graph can help trace the sibling citations as well. The tree is created with each node containing the following fields: Name, Institute, ID and weight. This model will work effectively for cases like:

*   **Unique Name Case**: A dictionary is defined with author name as key and lists of ids associated with name as values. Finally frequency based on author name is calculated. Unique name case is considered when number of values associated with input author name in the dictionary structure is greater than one.
*   **Multiple Name Case**: This case arises when input author name has more than one value associated in the dictionary structure. This requires performing unique name case for each id.
*   **Two Advisor Case**: This case depicts a scenario where an author has two advisors. This requires back traversing each node and assign weights 1 and 2.The citations count is done by traversing one hop above for advisor having weight one and for advisor having weight two count citations from one hop above and below till the advisee nodes.
*   **Multiple Name Case and Two Advisor Case**: This case checks the dictionary structure and for each ids it finds out if its value is one

Also the following matrices are suitably created to implement the above cases like the all author matrix Aij, two advisor matrix (nx2) where n is the number of authors having two advisors and two advisee matrix (n x m) where n is the total number of authors having two advisors and m maximum number of advisee of authors having two advisors. Finally CGR is computed as follows:-

$$CGR = \frac{y - x}{Y}$$

y - Total number of citations of an author

x - Genealogy Citations (two hops above and below)

NLIQ is hence measured as

Non-Genealogy Citations =Total citations - Genealogy Citations

2. Citation Network

Meaning of citation is "a quotation from or reference to a book, paper, or author, especially in a scholarly work". Earlier, the citations were used to reflect the linkages to trace the original work done by scientists; they are now used as a tool to evaluate the quality of scientific publications and also to monitor progress in the respective scientific fields.

Researchers often want to understand the pattern in which science evolves and knowledge grows. To perceive in what capacity research has progressed, network of research fields and its interactions is created. One such network that demonstrates the crucial relationship between papers and their citations is a Citation Network. A citation network is an interconnection of nodes and edges, where nodes represent articles and edges indicate a citation from one article to another. Different variants of citation networks are co-citation network, bibliographic coupling and co-authorship network. These are discussed as follows.

- **Citation Network**: A network arises from scientific publications formed by citations between articles can be shown by a timeline arrow as depicted in the Figure 5.
- **Co-Citation:** It refers to the frequency with which two articles are cited together by other articles. This gives an indication of the extent to which the two articles are related. The construction of co-citation network over a research field can make bibliometricians understand the evolution of scientific knowledge in a particular domain. Figure 6 shows a Co-citation Network
- **Bibliographic Coupling:** It refers to the number of articles that are sharing one or more references in their bibliographic section. It is an indicator of socio-cognitive structure of a research domain. The co-citation analysis and bibliographic coupling is based on the assumption that if some articles are strongly co-cited, it may represent the subject relatedness of these scientific literatures and may also uncover the irregularities of citation pattern within and across different fields. Figure 7 is showing a Bibliographic Coupling

Figure 5. Citation pattern (courtesy Sergei Maslov, Citerank Images)

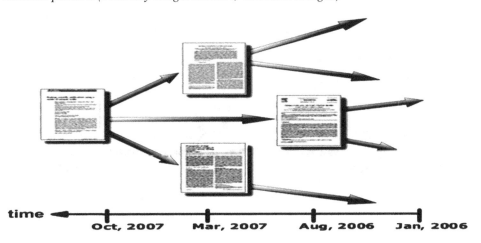

Figure 6. Co-citation network (courtesy The Scholarly Kitchen)

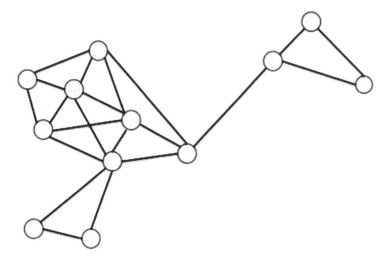

- **Co-Authorship Network**: Research scholars with different interest and background contribute at different levels and reconcile their work to bring into existence a well-documented scientific literature as publication. Co-authorship (Figure 8) determines the level of participation in a research team. Research is on to evaluate the relationship between co-authorship and the research output. Findings show that a strong co-authorship leads to a maximized output and larger frequency of publications.

Figure 7. Bibliographic coupling (courtesy Tethne documentation)

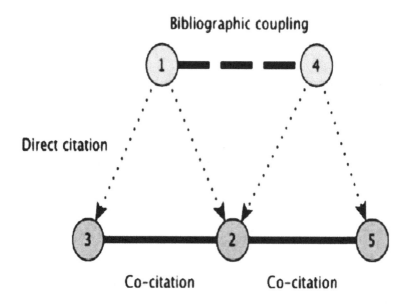

Figure 8. Co-authorship network (courtesy Cyberinfrastructure for Network Science Center)

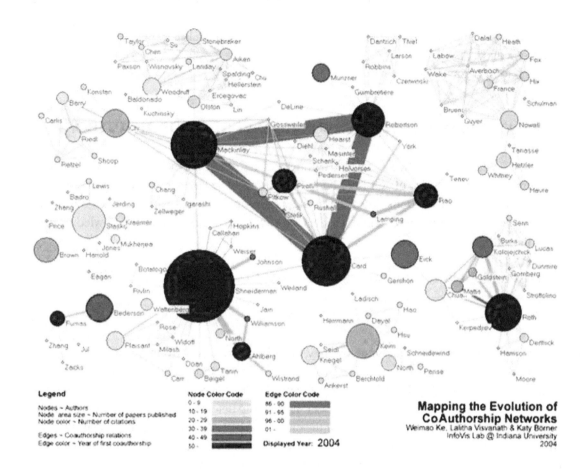

INTERNATIONAL COLLABORATION

Research is a collaborative effort. An author must work with scholars who bring in their share of demographic knowledge and ideas. This will not only enhance the research work but also diffuse the impact. To study this ratio a new metric called International collaboration ratio is introduced. This metric uses matrix of each author and his articles along with the citation count. It also establishes a relationship between how many co authors are associated with that article and their affiliation as well. A co- authorship network is created and weights are assigned for each edge between the two nodes. The above steps are elaborated in the algorithm below.

Algorithm

1. Initialize author A with list of articles in a matrix A[j] and citation count. Also initialize co-authors list as a[c].
2. Fetch authors' affiliation and co-authors affiliation for each article.

3.   Create a graph with nodes as author affiliation and co-authors affiliation and edge if same article/
     path
4.   If there exist an edge has all co authors of same country assign weight=0
5.   Else if no edge assign 1
6.   Calculate total ratio weight

OTHER CITATIONS QUOTIENT: MEASURING DIVERSITY OF AN AUTHOR

Self-citation is defined as a citation where the citing and the cited paper share at least one author. Other-Citation is the complement of self-citation/total citations. The key to computing Other-Citations Quotient is to calculate self-citations. To observe the citation pattern and various states of an author epidemiology models are introduced. These models highlight the diffusion rate of knowledge and the diversity in the authors.

Deterministic Models for Infectious Diseases: SI, SIR, SIER, and CISER

SIR Model

SIR model (shown in Figure 9) is an epidemiology model that studies the rate of infected people in a closed population over a fixed time period. The model compartments three stages namely S is the number susceptible, I is the number of infectious, and R is the number recovered (immune).Citation patterns of an author and its growth will be based on this model. It will help determine the rate at which authors get citations and what is the recoverability chance of the citation. SEIR Model has an additional state called Exposed. This is the population that gets exposed due to infection. The behavior of all these models can be utilized to understand the pattern of citations received by an author.

Figure 9. SIR

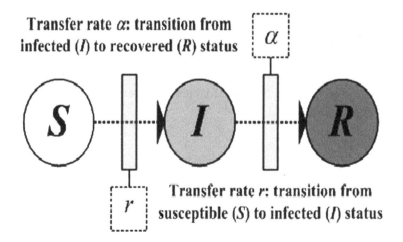

CISER Model

The derivation of the epidemiological dynamics of amoebiasis through the population is based on the following premise. The population under consideration is grouped into five epidemiological classifications where at any time t of the period of the disease outbreak, the individual in the population should be classified in one of the following classes:

- **Susceptible**: Class of s individuals in the population who are not yet infected.
- **Exposed**: Infected class but level of infection is small
- **Infective**: Infected and suffering class
- **Carrier**: Host to the disease
- **Removed**: They fought and recovered or die

Underlying Model Assumptions:

1. All authors are in S state as they are highly likely to receive Citation.
2. The Number of citation received from other authors is the rate of infection that takes an author from S->I or Exposed state. Exposed state is citations are few and chances of increasing are high.
3. Carrier state of an author is when author is an host to citations
4. R is the number of citations that recovered after removing self and copious citations.
5. The rate of transfers of citations are denoted in the diagram (Figure 10) and they refer to the transmission rates and threshold. If it crosses the threshold value E->I

Figure 10. CISER MODEL

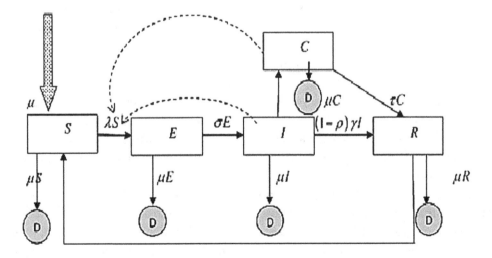

CONCLUSION

Chapter has historically established the evolution of Scientometrics as a field of study. It has clearly brought out the fact that unless metrics defining the worthiness of literary articles, are based on mathematical and conceptual grounds, the research as a whole will suffer a huge challenge in progressing further and research phenomenon will become dogmatic and may not breed justifying results.

Terms like Scientometrics and Bibliometrics are a many times used interchangeably in research world. As a matter of fact, Scientometrics deals with measuring scientific contents and its impact on science community whereas bibliometrics deal with analyzing the communication system of science vis-à-vis, citation count of scholarly publications. The chapter establishes an understanding that the gloomy definitions of already in-place indicators cannot cater to the need of measuring scholarly articles and authors from all viewpoints. Thus, there exist undeniable needs to explore and build new parameters which can modularize, classify and set apart good research from bad. Instigated by this, authors explored a gamut of new metrics to measure advances in science and technology. It is well explored that the novel parameters discussed here, like NLIQ, Other's citation and SNIP are capable of handling the complexities that are bred because of usage of used parameters like impact factor, H-index and many more.

It is quite apparent that, since JIF computation is based on 2 year citation window, an irrefutable pressure gets build on Journal's Editor-In-chief to accrue citations. Intending to improve their impact factor and raise their rank, they coerce authors to cite articles, thereby hampering the integrity of publication process. NLIQ as discussed in the chapter can handle this to large extend by computing quotient that is devoid of local effect. Examples of editors of two different journals citing one another (copious citation) and publishing in each others' journals are evident. Ji-Huan He, the founder and editor-in-chief of IJNSNS (the International Journal of Nonlinear Science and Numerical Simulation) is also an editor of CSF (Chaos, Solitons and Fractals). El Naschie is one of the two co-editors of IJNSNS. Ji-Huan and El Naschie, both, publish copiously, not only in their own journals but also in each other's. They are noticed citing one other frequently. Evidently, IJNSNS had the highest impact factor in the category "Mathematics, Applied", and in the Thomson Reuters category "Mathematics, Interdisciplinary Applications," CSF was ranked number 2. "Cognizant citations", wherein Editors of high ranking journal are involved in boosting their citation count at individual and at journal level, raise serious doubts on using impact factor as one of the parameters in influence computation exercise.

Another case of journal mischief became evident, when a computer generated research paper, with suitable usage of grammar and vocabulary and completely free from scientific content was sent to 'The Open Information Science Journal' (TOISCIJ). Four months later, the paper was accepted for publication and authors were notified to pay the article processing fee (Crawford, 2014). Multiple such cases were brought into limelight indicative of fact that the whole mechanism of judging scientific quality needs phenomenal change.

Giving definition to 'internationality' and choosing parameters to tackle the challenge of defining internationality in true spirit, have been taken after much of research and thorough introspection. International collaboration ratio (ICR) is an indicator that takes into account number of authors originating from different countries for collaborative research and impact that creates across demographic boundaries. This aspect should mandatorily be considered in computation of the internationality of Journals. Similarly Other-citation Quotient captures influence received in the form of citation from outside the Journal, annihilates the effect of local influence, and reduces the impact of coercive and copious citation.

Darwin's universal theory of "survival of the fittest" must be applicable in the field of research as well. With the exponential growth in publication field, the authenticity and credibility of true scholar is hard to determine. The book chapter explores certain fair and unbiased approach to appraise scientists and journals. Certain important questions are raised about citation parameters and their working and how to normalize them since not all citations are equal. Normalization is hence seen as a process of benchmarking that is needed to enhance comparability across diverse scientists, fields, papers, time periods, and so forth. The new Metrics discussed in above sections like NLIQ (non local influence quotient) which is calculated using genealogy tree and citation networks will be able to curb the problems addressed and present an optimal solution to the ongoing debate of efficiently ranking researchers. Along with" Internationality" and "Influence" the chapter also introduces "Diversity" as an author ranking metrics that is a qualitative parameter which takes inspiration from epidemiological models like SIR, SIER and CISER.

Thus the endeavor brought up in this book chapter, to introduce and use the newly defined metrics for influence and 'internationality' computation, goes a long way in pumping fresh vigor and transparency in the domain of scientific research.

REFERENCES

Aviles, Ramirez, & Saidé. (2015). Evaluating the Internationality of Scholarly Communications in Information Science Publications. *iConference 2015 Proceedings*. Retrieved from http://hdl.handle.net/2142/73769

Buela-Casal, G., Perakakis, P., Taylor, M., & Checa, P. (2006). Measuring internationality: Reflections and perspectives on academic journals. *Scientometrics*, *67*(1), 45–65. doi:10.1007/s11192-006-0050-z

Crawford, W. (2014). Journals, 'Journals' and Wannabes: Investigating The List. *Cites & Insights, 14*(7).

Factor, E. (n.d.). Retrieved from: www.Eigenfactor.com

Ginde, G., Saha, S., Mathur, A., & Sagar, B. S. D. (2016, May). ScientoBASE: A Framework and Model for Computing Scholastic Indicators of non-local influence of Journals via Native Data Acquisition algorithms. *Scientometrics*, *108*(3), 1479–1529. doi:10.1007/s11192-016-2006-2

Jangid, Saha, Gupta, & J. (2014). Ranking of Journals in Science and Technology Domain: A Novel And Computationally Lightweight Approach. *IERI Procedia, 10,* 5762. doi:10.1016/j.ieri.2014.09.091

Jangid, Saha, Narasimhamurthy, & Mathur. (2015). *Computing the Prestige of a journal: A Revised Multiple Linear Regression Approach*. WCI-ACM Digital library.

Moed, H. F. (2010, July). Measuring contextual citation impact of scientific journals. *Journal of Informetrics Volume*, *4*(3), 265–277. doi:10.1016/j.joi.2010.01.002

Perakakis, P., Taylor, M., Buela-Casal, P., & Checa, P. (2006). A neuro-fuzzy system to calculate a journal internationality index. *Proceedings CEDI symposium*. Retrieved from http://damir.iem.csic.es/~michael/OA/perakakis_et_al_2005.pdf

Saha, Jangid, Mathur, & Anand. (2016). DSRS: Estimation and Forecasting of Journal Influence in the Science and Technology Domain via a Lightweight Quantitative Approach. *Collnet Journal of Scientometrics and Information Management*.

Uzun, A. (2004). Assessing internationality of scholarly journals through foreign authorship patterns: The case of major journals in information science, and Scientometrics. *Scientometrics, 61*(3), 457–465. doi:10.1023/B:SCIE.0000045121.26810.35

Waltman, van Eck, Thed, van Leeuwen, & Visser. (2013). Some modifications to the SNIP journal impact indicator. *Journal of Informetrics, 7,* 272-285.

Zupanc, G. K. H. (2014). Impact beyond the impact factor. *Journal of Comparative Physiology. A, Neuroethology, Sensory, Neural, and Behavioral Physiology, 200*(2), 113116. doi:10.1007/s00359-013-0863-1 PMID:24264238

Chapter 18
Design of Assistive Speller Machine Based on Brain Computer Interfacing

Suryoday Basak
PESIT – Bangalore South, India

ABSTRACT

Machine Learning (ML) has assumed a central role in data assimilation and data analysis in the last decade. Many methods exist that cater to the different kinds of data centric applications in terms of complexity and domain. Machine Learning methods have been derived from classical Artificial Intelligence (AI) models but are a lot more reliant on statistical methods. However, ML is a lot broader than inferential statistics. Recent advances in computational neuroscience has identified Electroencephalography (EEG) based Brain Computer Interface (BCI) as one of the key agents for a variety of medical and nonmedical applications. However, efficiency in analysing EEG signals is tremendously difficult to achieve because of three reasons: size of data, extent of computation and poor spatial resolution. The book chapter discusses the Machine Learning based methods employed by the author to classify EEG signals for potentials observed based on varying levels of a subject's attention, measured using a NeuroSky Mindwave Mobile. It reports challenges faced in developing BCIs based on available hardware, signal processing methods and classification methods.

1. INTRODUCTION

A *Brain Computer Interface* (BCI) is any system that does not rely on the conventional communication routines for a user to interact with a computer such as a mouse, keyboard, touchpad, etc. Instead, it utilizes signals from the brain to control a computer. Based on an imagined action, thought, or perception, signals are generated in specific regions of the brain and in turn, these signals may be used to control computers. Consequently, a BCI does not require physical motion of a user. The primary goal of any BCI, hence, is to provide an appropriate control interface, without requiring the usual communication

DOI: 10.4018/978-1-5225-2498-4.ch018

pathways, such as gestures, voice, button clicks, etc.; the patient is required to be still, relaxed, and focussed on a single mental task, or a series of mental tasks.

In the recent years, hype has surrounded the study of Brain Computer Interfaces as its indispensable usefulness in many scenarios opens up a world of possibilities: many users are unable to communicate with people, or with computers due to various physiological conditions, such as amyotrophic lateral sclerosis (ALS), locked-in syndrome (LIS) or severe paralysis. For them, life becomes a burden; the inability to communicate and convey one's wishes to others is extremely daunting. BCI poses numerous solutions that may allow them to live better lives and communicate effectively. Over the past decade, scientists have developed voice translators that can translate thoughts to speech, wheelchairs, exoskeletons and games that work on the basis of imagined motion, amongst many other things. Such developments are on the rise and show promise to provide for better communication mechanisms in people who are unable to communicate.

Among the possible methods of acquiring signals from the brain are electroencephalography (EEG), magnetoencephalography (MEG) and functional magnetic resonance imaging (fMRI). The most popular signal acquiring method for Brain Computer Interfaces in use today is EEG, primarily due to its low cost, ease of setup and good temporal resolution; in contrast, MEG and fMRI are relatively expensive to setup, and are primarily used for medical research and diagnosis but this does not undermine their potential as acquisition systems for BCIs. The origin of the word *electroencephalography* is as follows: *electro*: denoting the electrical signals, *encephalo*: which refers to a phenomenon of the brain, and *graphy*: which denotes a drawing or a representation of a quantifiable phenomenon. EEG was discovered by Richard Canton (1842–1926). He experimented on rabbits and monkeys, and presented his findings of electrical activities of their brains. The first EEG recording of a human was presented by Hans Berger in 1942. EEG has seen innumerable uses in medical science, and researchers have tried to use EEG to understand the roots of epileptic seizures, analyse comas, etc. As an EEG recording would reflect the mental state of a subject, the EEG of a subject is altered by neurological conditions, disorders, drowsiness, drug actions, etc. EEG, due to its low cost, is also popular in numerous non-medical applications (a BCI is generally a non-medical application).

It is but natural for the reader to ponder that just like all other biological traits, even the electrical activity in the brain must be unique to each individual. Such is the case, and for a system to discern intentions from different brain signals of different subjects, Machine Learning (ML) techniques are employed. Machine Learning has its roots in classical Artificial Intelligence (AI) approaches, where the goal is to make a computer learn trends and discerning features in data (one of the prime differences between AI and ML is that AI generally refers to a replication of human abilities, whereas ML is used in data analytics across a broad spectrum of domains). However, ML techniques are more reliant on statistical measures. In a typical BCI setup, data corresponding to different *intentions* for each subject is collected several times, over multiple recording sessions. The author defines *intention* or *intent* in the current context to be any action that the user of a BCI would want the computer to perform, corresponding to a single and unique mental state. This will be further explained later in this section. The duration of each recording session is specific to each application. Once an adequate amount of data is collected for each intention, appropriate signal processing and machine learning approaches are used to teach the system the characteristics of the signals corresponding to each intention. In this chapter, the signal processing techniques that are featured are the *Wavelet Transform*, and *Common Spatial Patterns* (CSP). The Wavelet Transform essentially finds regions of maximum correlation of a signal to a wavelet, which is a small wave; the CSP algorithm is used to find spatial patterns in the processed data after the Wavelet Transform.

The CSP is a *dimensionality reduction* algorithm, that is, it helps us to find the discriminatory features in the data, which may be used to optimally differentiate between data from different classes. The ML algorithms featured in this chapter are *Decision Trees, Random Forests, Support Vector Machines* and *k-Nearest Neighbours*. The popularity of ML and the resurgence of AI, surrounding *Deep Learning* is because of the large volume data in the world today. In many digital repositories all over the world, a lot of data is stored from the research of many scientists, and to effectively extract information from this data, Machine Learning, Data Mining, etc. have been encompassed comprehensively under the generic domain of *Data Analytics*. Data Analytics provides refers to trend analysis and predictive analysis in numerous fields as business, astronomy, biology, etc.

Machine Learning approaches are further classified as supervised and unsupervised methods.

- **Supervised Methods:** In supervised methods, *class labels* are associated with data, so that the system can understand the features associated with every class of data present in the dataset. The prediction from any supervised learning method, or classification, is essentially the class label of the class that the system thinks that the input data would belong to.

- **Unsupervised Methods:** Contrary to supervised methods, data without associated class labels is used in unsupervised methods. The task of the system here is to *identify classes* that may exist in the data, based on *similarity* of features in the data. In the current work, supervised learning methods are used. The class labels in the data correspond to the intention of the user. The ML techniques used in the current work is briefly explained below:

- **Decision Trees:** Decision trees use tree data structures to model decisions. These can be used for classification or regression; for the task of classification, it takes labelled data for training. Each *split* at a node is based on a feature (attribute) of the data set, the first node is called the *root node*, which can be any important feature and hence considered as best predictor. Every other node of the tree is then split into child nodes based on certain splitting criteria or decision rule, which identify the belongingness of the particular object (data entity) to the feature class. The leaf nodes represent *pure nodes*, and each entity in a leaf node is assigned the class label of the corresponding node. Typically, an impurity measure is defined for each node and the criterion for splitting a node is based on increase in purity of child nodes as compared to the parent node i.e. splits that produce child nodes which have significantly less impurity as compared to the parent node are favoured. The *Gini index* and *entropy* are two popular impurity measures. Entropy may be interpreted as a descriptor of information gain from that node. One significant advantage of decision trees is that both categorical and numerical data can be handled; a disadvantage is that decision trees tend to over fit the training data.

- **Random Forests:** Classifiers may be combined in order to improve the classification results from each classifier. Systems which use combinations of classifiers are called *ensemble learning systems*. A Random Forest classifier is an ensemble of multiple decision trees, where the features are sampled from the set of all features in a given dataset. Each tree enunciates a classification and decision is taken based upon majority voting for the task of classification. When a new object from the dataset needs to be classified, data is classified using each of the trees. Classification implies a tree voting for the corresponding object. Random forest works efficiently with large datasets. It gives accurate results even in the cases of missing data. As an illustrative example, consider that we have a dataset with a feature-set $S = \{\theta_1, \theta_2, ..., \theta_n\}$. Decision trees are constructed with a feature set S', and $|S'| < n$. This process is repeated many times and at the end of every iteration, the predicted outcome for each instance of certain test data is accumulated. At the end of k iterations, the most recurring outcome for each instance of the test data is selected as the corresponding class label.

- **Support Vector Machine:** SVM classifiers are candidate classifiers for binary class discrimination. The basic formulation is designed for the linear classification problem; the algorithm yields an optimal hyperplane i.e. one that maintains largest minimum distance from the training data, defined as the *margin*. It can also perform non-linear classification via the use of kernels, which involves the computation of inner products of all pairs of data in the feature space; this implicitly transforms the data into a different space where a separating hyperplane can be found. One advantage of the SVM is that the optimization problem is convex. The result may not be transparent always which is a drawback of this method. The significant challenges in analysing the EEG signals are low signal-noise ratio: they are prone to internal and external noise, and volume conduction: the activation of different regions of the brain for the same thought, leading to redundant data. In addition, as the number of mental states to be classified increases, we need to build intelligent algorithms that learn the most discriminatory features.
- **k-Nearest Neighbours:** The kNN classifiers work on the basis of the maximum similarity to a class of data amongst the k nearest neighbours. The parameter k is fed to the classifier and in the classification process. For classifying any arbitrary test sample, the k closest neighbours are considered. Out of these k closest neighbours, the class pertaining to the highest number of occurrences is assigned as the class of the respective test data. For example, for $k = 7$, and for a data set with two classes, *Class1* and *Class2*, if four out of the seven closest neighbours belong to *Class1* and three out of the seven closest neighbours belong to *Class2*, then the test data is classified as a member of *Class1*; likewise, if a larger fraction of the nearest neighbours belong to *Class2*, then the instance of the test data is classified as a member of *Class2*.

Much of the work involving research in BCI involves setups with multiple electrodes. In the current work, the hardware interface used is the NeuroSky Mindwave Mobile. The said device has a single electrode placed on the forehead and an ear-clip. The device measures the potential difference between the two points. The inspiration to use a smaller device is from the fact that with any technological appliance, the trend is to reduce the form-factor optimally. With an optimal form factor, the ease of use increases, thus attracting more users of any given system. The NeuroSky Mindwave Mobile is easy to use and transmits data using Bluetooth. The protocol used by the Mindwave is provided by the company NeuroSky, as a part of the Thinkgear bundle. An open-source python library exists for the Mindwave, under the name of NeuroPy; it uses callback functions to receive data over Bluetooth. Callback functions are event driven functions that operate asynchronously in their own threads.

The chapter explains an architecture for a brain-controlled speller machine. The proposed system displays a letters from the English alphabet and allows the user to select characters which are displayed. A cursor moves over individual letters, allowing the user to select an appropriate character at any given time. Characters may be used to form words, and words may be used to form sentences. The *intention* of a user in this context is binary in nature: a positive intent would result in the selection of a character, and appending it to a string of words, whereas a negative intent would overlook a character when the cursor indicates it. By progressively building up meaningful words and sentences this way, a patient who is suffering from ALS or LIS may be effectively communicate with others around her. Although, the current system is not robust in itself, it provides insights to how such a system may be designed and developed. This application was developed to make the process of signal acquisition corresponding to every intent easier.

In Section 2, the underlying principles of developing a Brain Computer Interface are briefly explained. The development of a Brain Computer Interface depends on various factors such as the subject for whom it is being developed, the region of the brain from which the signals are to be acquired, the task that is to be performed by the system, etc. Through Section 3, the methods used by the author are explained: signal acquisition, signal processing, data classification. Results are reported as a part of Section 3.4 which provides insights to the challenges faced by engineers who work in the field and the required sophistication that is required to develop an acceptable BCI that may be used for the simplest of tasks. This section and the conclusion following it are important as a naïve reader may be illusioned in many ways about how Brain Computer Interfaces are developed and need some solid evidence of the shortcomings of *consumer grade* signal acquisition devices.

This chapter targeted serves as a primer for those interested in Brain Computer Interfaces. The illustrations of signal processing and machine learning algorithms are for naïve readers, assumed to have no background in the same.

2. BCI DESIGN PRINCIPLES

BCI research is a young and eclectic field of research. Researchers from various backgrounds such as engineering, science, mathematics, neuroscience and biology are involved in developing Brain Computer Interfaces of the future. The reason for this is that since a BCI involves an interaction of a subject with a computer by means of signals from the brain. Hence, it is important to incorporate elements from all the mentioned fields to acquire signals that can be used to develop a control system.

2.1. Types of BCI

The hardware interface for BCI systems may be broadly classified into invasive and non-invasive methods.

- **Invasive:** Invasive Brain Computer Interfaces require an electrode to be surgically implanted inside the brain of a subject. Invasive methods provide the best signal-to-noise ratio, but the involved risks are profound. This method poses many dangers due to the formation of scar tissues around the electrode as it is a foreign body, or impairment of certain neurological functions. Although cochlear implants for hearing has gained popularity in the recent years, it does not eradicate the many hazards involved in having a foreign body in the brain.
- **Non-Invasive:** Non-invasive Brain Computer Interfaces do not require an electrode implant inside the brain. It utilizes signals appearing on the scalp. The bulk of tissues and skull bone interceding the surface of the brain from the electrode in this case reduces the efficacy of this method, resulting in more noise. The advantage, of course, is that it is a much safer alternative to invasive methods, and cheaper, too.

An intermediate to the above mentioned genres of hardware is to use a partially invasive electrode: one that is placed inside the skull, but not hampering the brain. This method reduces the risk of damage to the brain, but nonetheless, requires a surgical procedure for implanting. Though non-invasive methods incorporate a larger amount of noise in the acquired signals, it is preferred when experimenting on humans. Invasive methods are often employed when the experiments performed on animals such as rats, rabbits or monkeys. Other methods of signal acquisition include magnetoencephalography (MEG) and functional magnetic resonance imaging (fMRI).

2.2. Non-Invasive EEG Based BCI

In methods that use Non-Invasive EEG based BCI, EEG recordings are done as a subject performs a mental task. The nature of the task may be any of these, but not restricted to:

1. **Motor Imagery:** This type of task involves imagining the movement of an appendage (Mohanachandra, Saha & Deshmukh, 2014)
2. **Steady State Visually Evoked Potentials (SSVEP):** In this genre of task, potentials in the visual cortex are stimulated by flickering lights at different wavelengths and flickering frequencies.
3. **Subvocalization:** This involves a subject saying out a word in her mind, without articulation (Mohanchandra & Saha, 2016).

A lot of data for each unique task is collected over multiple sessions, usually spanning days. Once an adequate amount of data is collected, the signals are pre-processed and dimensionality reduced, before ML techniques are applied to associate EEG signals with specific intents of the subject.

Figure 1. The standard 10-20 system of electrode placement (top-view of head)

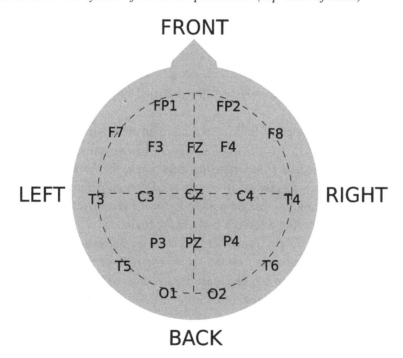

Table 1. The different frequency bands of EEG signals and their corresponding mental states

EEG Bands	Frequency (Hz)	Distribution	State of Mind
Delta	0.5-4	Central cerebrum and parietal lobes	Deep sleep, non-REM sleep
Theta	4-8	Frontal, parietal and temporal lobes	Drowsiness, first stage of sleep
Alpha	8-13	Most prominent at occipital and parietal lobe	Relaxed wakefulness with eyes closed
Mu	8-12	Central electrodes, over motor and somatosensory cortex	Shows rest state motor neurons
Beta	13-30	Frontal and central regions	Highly alert and focused
Gamma	>30	Very localized	Higher mental activity, including perception and consciousness

For the purpose of standardization, there exists a system of electrode placement called the 10-20 system of electrode placement. The '10' and '20' represent 10% or 20% respectively of the distance between electrodes, as the distance between the front-to-back or right-to-left distance of the skull of the subject. The diagram below shows the standard positions of electrodes in the various lobes of the skull.

The table above shows the different frequency bands of EEG signals and their significance. In multichannel EEG systems, the number of electrodes employed may be up to about 256. As the electrodes in the non-invasive system are present on the surface of the scalp, they are called *dry* electrodes, and are generally made of silver chloride. To facilitate conduction, an electrode gel is used. Though the NeuroSky Mindwave Mobile device does not require an electrode gel, its electrode is made of silver chloride. The tasks mentioned earlier in this section may be used to appropriately alter the EEG and these signals can then be used to control a computer.

2.3. NeuroSky Mindwave Mobile

The signals are acquired from the Neurosky Mindwave Mobile device. The Thinkgear bundle is comprised of the sensors and a chip to process signals. The device has capabilities to send packets of data over Bluetooth. The Radio Frequency Communication (RFCOMM) protocol is used to establish a link between the device and a computer. The RFCOMM protocol serially transfers data by emulating a serial cable line setting and the status of an RS-232 serial port. The RFCOMM connects to lower layers of the Bluetooth stack through the Logical Link Control and Adaption Protocol (L2CAP) layer. The L2CAP layer is used within the Bluetooth stack, and passes data to a Host Controller Interface (HCI). In our case, the HCI is the computer which records the data, and the device is the Mindwave Mobile.

The RFCOMM protocol finds wide use in devices that need to communicate serially, such as Bluetooth robotics projects, keyboards, etc., and is supported by all major Operating Systems. A link between the device and a Linux computer is set up by using the rfcomm command, and by specifying the device's address, port number and number of channels.

The format of the command to establish the link between the Linux Computer and the Mindwave device is

```
sudo rfcomm bind <device index> <physical address> <channel>
```

The device index is a unique number used to recognize a Bluetooth device that is bound to the computer. The physical address is the Mindwave's physical address. The default value of channel is 1; it is an optional argument. An example of the command in use is:

sudo rfcomm bind 0 20:68:9D:88:C0:C6   1

Following this, raw data is sampled from the device at 512 Hz, using the NeuroPy module for Python, which uses *callbacks* to receive data asynchronously.

2.4. Supplementary Target BCI Applications

Researchers have experimented with the NeuroSky Mindwave Mobile to develop brain computer interfaces. Much of the related work is directed towards developing games for mobile platforms, or interfaces for robots. Anupama H. S. et al. (2014) have proposed a design of a wheelchair using the same device, which is based on using the values of attention and meditation returned by the device as features for an associated action. Along the same lines, Nilay Yildirm et al. (2015) have developed a game similar to the popular mobile phone game Flappy Bird, utilizing values of attention and meditation. In his Master of Science in Computer Science thesis, Erik Andreas Larsen (2011) has attempted to build a game by classifying mental states using a Neural Network, based on values of alpha, beta, delta, theta and gamma, and eye blinks returned from the device; classification and detection of eye blinks yielded a 91% accuracy, but classification of mental states yielded a 60% accuracy.

Despite all the shortcomings of the device, its merits are low cost and ease of use. Classification of EEG signals becomes more difficult as the number of electrodes reduces. The current work, the author used minimal hardware and proposes a method to classify EEG signals.

Figure 2. Flow of data in the experimental setup

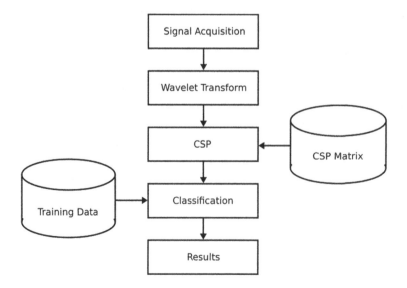

2.5. Overview of the Proposed System

The flowchart above describes the setup of the proposed system, based on the author's experiments.

1. The data is acquired from the NeuroSky Mindwave Mobile device.
2. The data is pruned appropriately and the *Wavelet Transform* is applied, by considering segments of length 1024 values.
3. CSP is applied to the data; the CSP Matrices are calculated from the training data.
4. Once the inter-class variance is increased between classes, the response is classified.
5. Based on the classification, the appropriate action is performed by the computer.

3. METHODOLOGY

3.1. User Interface

A graphical interface for the device was built using the *pygame* module in Python 2.7. The interface consists of English alphabets, and two special characters for space and clear. All the characters are displayed in rows of seven characters. While recording the test data, the subject is shown a colour coded cursor-box: red denoting that the subject's response should be negative; for a positive response yellow is an indicator for the subject to get ready, following which, a green box denotes that a positive response is being recorded. After a positive response to a row, only the characters from that row are displayed and recorded with; the responses on a character may be positive or negative. Upon a negative response to a row, the cursor moves to the next row in sequence. The colour indicator of the cursor is generated randomly.

A recording session comprised of about twenty to twenty five recordings, each individual recording lasting thirteen seconds, including time for the subject to get ready for a positive or negative response. Between each individual recording, a 10s break is provided. For each subject, about 200 recordings have been done, 100 for each class of response. Once recorded, the data is pruned from the end appropriately.

Figure 3. Selection of a group of characters

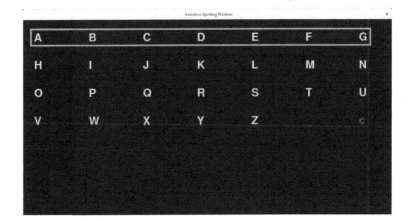

Figure 4. Selection of a single character from a group of characters

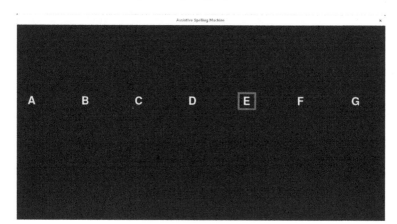

3.2. Feature Extraction

In the current work, a combination of methods for signal pre-processing and feature extraction is explored to achieve best possible results using minimal hardware. The performance and accuracy of the classifiers are quantitatively measured. The primary focus of the present work is to develop a prototype of a system that may assist in communication of subjects who are incapable of speech or gesture communication. In this section, the underlying principles of the methods used to extract features from the acquired signals are explained. Reiterating, the text is targeted towards naïve readers looking for a gentle introduction to the subject. Norms and sequences are explained: although they are not of direct consequence, they are used in Wavelet Transforms. Having an idea of the same is necessary and hence these topics are introduced as a part of this section.

3.2.1. Norms

In mathematics, a norm is a function that gives us an index of the *size* or *magnitude* of a vector or a matrix. For a vector v, the norm is generally represented as ‖v‖. Norms for vectors and matrices are explained below.

3.2.1.1. Vector Norms

The most commonly used norm for vectors is the Euclidean norm. Consider a vector u_{in} a two-dimensional Euclidean vector space.

Here, and $W = u \sin \theta$, by considering the vector components.

The norm of u, given as ‖u‖ $= H^2 + W^2$, which is the *length* of u, by Pythagoras' Theorem. Expanding the above equation by substituting for H and W,

Figure 5. A vector making an angle θ θ in a two-dimensional space

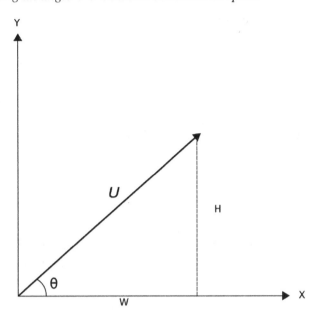

$$\| u \| = \sqrt{(u\cos\theta)^2 + (u\sin\theta)^2}$$
$$= \sqrt{u^2\cos\theta^2 + u^2\sin\theta^2}$$
$$= \sqrt{u^2(\cos\theta^2 + \sin\theta^2)}$$
$$= \sqrt{u^2}$$

Thus, in a two dimensional Euclidean space, $\| u \| = \sqrt{u^2}$. Similarly, if a vector is a resultant of n vectors u_1, u_2, ..., u_n the norm of v is given as $\| v \| = \sqrt{u_1^2 + u_2^2 + ... + u_n^2}$. The 2D Euclidean norm is a very specific case of vector norms. There are different norms that exist that provide a measure of distance in various circumstances. Some of the commonly used norms are explained below. For each of these, we assume a vector v to be a resultant of n vectors, u_1, u_2, ..., u_n.

1. **1-norm:**

    The **1-norm** is defined as the *sum* of the *absolute values of all the vector components*.

$$\| v \|_1 = | u_1 | + | u_2 | + ... + | u_n |$$

2. **2-norm:**

    The **2-norm** is the special case of *Euclidean norm*.

$$\| v \| = \sqrt{u_1^2 + u_2^2 + ... + u_n^2}$$

3. **p-norm**:

The **p-norm** is the most general case of norms, defined as follows:

$$|| v ||_p = (u_1^{\ p} + u_2^{\ p} + ... + u_n^{\ p})^{\frac{1}{p}}$$

4. **Infinity Norm**:

The *infinity norm* is defined as the maximum of the absolute values of the components of vector *v*.

$$|| v ||_\infty = \max\{| u_1 |, | u_2 |, ..., | u_n |\}$$

3.2.1.2. Matrix Norms

The concept of vector norms can be extended to matrices. The fundamental properties of norms does not change for matrices: a matrix norm is an index of *size* or *magnitude*. In this section, we describe norms for two-dimensional matrices.

1. **The 1-norm**

The 1-norm in the case of matrices is the maximum of the column sums.

$$|| A ||_1 = \max_{1 \le j \le n} \left(\sum_{i=1}^{n} | a_{ij} | \right)$$

2. **The Frobenius Norm**

The Frobenius norm is analogous to the *Euclidian* norm for vectors. It is the *square root* of all *squares* of all the elements in a matrix.

$$|| A ||_F = \sqrt{\sum_{i=1}^{m} \sum_{j=1}^{n} (a_{ij})^2}$$

3. **p,q-Norm**

The *p,q-Norm* in matrices is analogous to the *p-Norm* in vectors. Here, the values of the symbols *p* and *q* may or may not be the same, and generally, the indices *i* and *j* are treated differently (rephrase) The *p,q-norm* is defined as:

$$|| A ||_{p,q} = \left[\sum_{j=1}^{n} \left(\sum_{i=1}^{m} | a_{ij} | \right)^{\frac{q}{p}} \right]^{\frac{1}{q}}$$

4. ***Infinity Norm***

   The infinity norm in the case of matrices is similar to the infinity norm for vectors. It is the greatest of all the row sums in a matrix.

$$\| A \|_{\infty} = \max_{1 \leq i \leq m} \sum_{j=1}^{n} (a_{ij})$$

3.2.1.3. Properties of Norms

Let F F represent a field of real or complex values. Let $F^{m \times n}$ $F^{m \times n}$ denote the vector space of all $m \times n$ $m \times n$ matrices.

1. $\| A \| = 0$, *iff* A = 0, else ||A|| > 0
2. $\| A \| = | \alpha | . \| A \|$ for all $\alpha \in \mathbb{R}$ and all matrices in $F^{m \times n}$
3. $\| A + B \| = \| A \| + \| B \|$, for all matrices A and B in $F^{m \times n}$
4. $\| AB \| = \| A \| . \| B \|$ for all matrices A and B in $F^{m \times n}$, where m = n. This is not satisfied by all matrices; the matrices which satisfy this relation are said to be in the *submultiplicative form*.

3.2.2. Sequences

In Mathematics, a sequence is a set of ordered objects. For example, the following is a sequence:

1, 2, 3, 4, 5…

Sequence (1)

   Another example of a sequence:

$$1, \frac{1}{2}, \frac{1}{3}, \frac{1}{4}, \dots$$

Sequence (2)

   Numerical sequences are generally denoted by an expression of the ith term. The sequences above may be represented as $a_i = i$ and $a_i = \frac{1}{i}$, respectively, for $i \geq 1$.

   A very popular example of sequences is the *Fibonacci* sequence. The elements of the Fibonacci sequence are:

0, 1, 1, 2, 3, 5, 8, 13, 21, …

   The elements in the Fibonacci sequence are given as:

$$a_i = a_{i-1} + a_{i-2}$$
$$a_0 = 0$$
$$a_1 = 1$$

3.2.2.1. Convergence and Divergence of Sequences

A sequence, whose i^{th} element is given as a_i is said to *converge* if for an arbitrarily large i, the corresponding element is defined. In other words, a sequence is said to be *convergent* if it has a defined limit. Else, it is *divergent*.

Consider *Sequence (1)*. Here, the ith element is given as $a_i = i$ for $i \geq 1$. Hence, the limit is given as:

$$\lim_{i \to \infty} a_i = \lim_{i \to \infty} i = \infty$$

This is a *divergent* sequence as it does not have a well-defined limit. The larger the value of i, the greater the value of a_i. Hence, for an arbitrarily large value of i, the ith element in the sequence is not defined.

Consider *Sequence (2)*. Here, the ith element is given as $a_i = \frac{1}{i}$, for $i > 1$. Hence,

$$\lim_{i \to \infty} \frac{1}{a_i} = \lim_{i \to \infty} \frac{1}{i} = 0$$

This is a *convergent* sequence as for an arbitrarily large i, the value of a_i tends to zero. In this sequence, the larger the value of i, the smaller the value of a_i, and as it progressively nears zero, we say it is convergent.

3.2.3. Wavelet Transform

3.2.3.1. The Fourier Transform and its Limitations

The Fourier Transform of a time-series signal decomposes it into its corresponding frequency components. In the 19th century, Joseph Fourier proved that any signal can be represented as a summation of sinusoidal signals, thus laying the foundation for representing a signal using sines and cosines only.

The Fourier Transform of a signal is:

$$X(f) = \int_{-\infty}^{\infty} x(t)e^{-2\pi ift} dt$$

Here, X is in hertz (Hz) and x is in seconds. The signal, which is a function of time, is transformed to its frequency components. The inverse Fourier Transform is given as:

$$x(f) = \int\limits_{-\infty}^{\infty} X(t)e^{2\pi ift} df$$

The Fourier Transform is one of the most important transformations in the fields of Mathematics, Signal Processing and Electrical Engineering. In brief, some of the applications are finding the *fundamental frequency* and *harmonics* in musical notes, electrical supply mains, voice, etc. In the field of Machine Learning, the Fourier Transform is widely used to extract the fundamental frequency and harmonics, and to use them as features for classification, clustering, etc.

However, the Fourier Transform suffers from some limitations.

1. Time - Frequency Resolution Trade-off

In the Fourier Transform, once we have information about the frequencies for a signal, or for a part of a signal, we cannot say with certainty where in time each frequency component occurs. This is illustrated with an example.

Consider two signals *S1* and *S2* as shown in Figure 6. As illustrated, the characteristics of *S1* and *S2*, such as amplitude at different points, frequency are different. The frequency components of *S1* and *S2* are also illustrated below the respective plots of the signals. The frequency components are also distinct, and are found using the Fourier Transform. For *S1*, the most prominent peaks occur at around 3Hz and 10Hz, whereas for *S2*, the peaks occur at around 10Hz and 30Hz, ignoring the components of lesser importance, which make the plots look jagged. The frequency components are found by using the Fourier Transform.

Now consider two signals *Signal-1* and *Signal-2*, which are constructed using *S1* and *S2* in series. *Signal-1* is constructed such that the first five seconds are comprise of *S1*, and the last five seconds comprise of *S2*. *Signal-2* is constructed such that the first five seconds comprise of *S2*, and the last five seconds comprise of *S1*.

Figure 6. Two signals $S1$ $S1$ *and* $S2$ $S2$ *, and their corresponding frequency components*

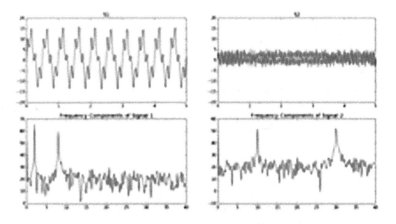

Figure 7. Two signals $Signal-1$ $Signal-1$ *and* $Signal-2$ $Signal-2$ *comprising of* $S1$ $S1$ *and* $S2$ $S2$ *and their corresponding frequency components*

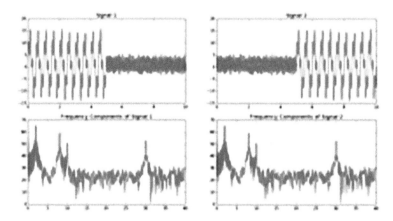

Signal-1 and *Signal-2* are shown in Figure 7. However, the frequency components of *Signal-1* and *Signal-2*, as found by the Fourier Transform, are the same. So based on the Fourier Transform, the characteristic frequencies of *Signal-1* and *Signal-2* are the same, whereas the signals themselves are not the same.

This is in fact a consequence of *Heisenberg's Uncertainty Principle*, which states that the position and the velocity of a body cannot be accurately determined simultaneously; if we can determine the velocity of a body with a high degree of certainty, we will be unable to determine its position accurately and vice versa. Applied to the context of time-frequency transformations, if we can resolve the signal in time with a high degree of certainty, we lose information about the frequency components of the signal, and vice versa.

One method to overcome the limitations of the Fourier Transform is to divide the signal into *bins* occurring at regular intervals from the starting point of the signal, and then applying the Fourier Transform to each bin. This approach results in the *Short Term Fourier Transform* (STFT). The trade-off here is that while the higher frequencies will be adequately detected, any frequency component that is larger than the size of a *bin* will not be adequately detected.

2. Sinusoidal Basis Vectors

The basis vectors in Fourier transform are always sinusoidal in nature, that is a signal is always decomposed into its *sine* and *cosine* components. This is a limitation as the Fourier Transform does not allow the usage of any other vectors as basis functions. The usage of sinusoidal basis functions only returns the components in the signal that are sinusoidal in nature.

3.2.3.2. Wavelets

The term *wavelet* refers to *a small wave*. Wavelets occur in various fields of study, including signal processing, mathematics etc. Generally, a wavelet is a wave that spans over a short period of time. The wavelet *Daubechis-4* ('db4') is illustrated below. The *x* axis represents time, and the *y* axis represents amplitude.

Figure 8. The Daubechis-4 Wavelet

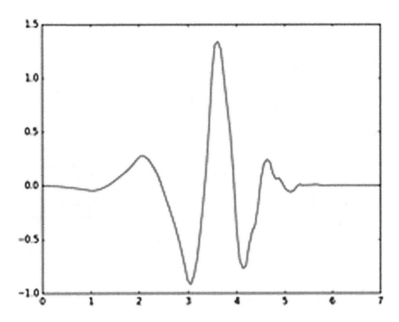

In the Wavelet Transform, the wavelets form the *basis vectors* for the decomposition of a signal, which is a function of time. The advantage of this is that signals need not be approximated by their sine and cosine components only. Depending on the application, a wavelet may be selected appropriately for signal decomposition. Since a wavelet has a finite duration, the time and frequency resolutions are improved - a sinusoidal wave, as used in the Fourier Transform, is infinite, and hence approximating a signal using a sinusoidal wave of frequency f would return how strongly the signal can be approximated to that signal, but not the *instances in time* where the frequency f occurs.

In the Wavelet Transform of a signal, a wavelet is selected as the *mother wavelet*, and is *dilated* over successive iterations of approximating the signal. Based on how well the signal correlates to the mother wavelet, or to a dilated wavelet at different instances, we can find out the instances in time where a certain frequency occurs.

3.2.3.3. The Continuous Wavelet Transform

The idea of the Continuous Wavelet Transform (CWT) arises from *Multiresolution Analysis* (MRA). MRA provides a better time resolution and poor frequency resolution at high frequencies, and better frequency resolution and poor time resolution at lower frequencies.

In the case of the CWT, this is achieved by *dilating* the wavelet. In the wavelet transform, this process is called the *scaling* of the wavelet. The CWT is calculated using the following using:

$$\psi = \frac{1}{\sqrt{|s|}} \int_{-\infty}^{\infty} x(t)\overline{\varphi}\left(\frac{t-\tau}{s}\right) dt$$

Figure 9. The wavelet transform applied to Signal-1 and Signal-2 and their corresponding wavelet plots

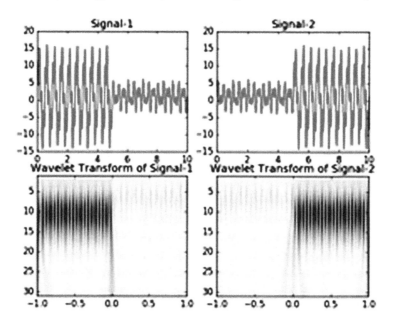

Here ψ denotes the transformation and *x(t)* is the original signal, which is a function of time. $\varphi(t)$ represents the mother wavelet, which is *scaled* using the scaling factor *s*, and *translated* using the translation factor τ over the entire signal. The *translation* may be thought of as similar to applying the Fourier Transform for a *bin* as in the case of the STFT.

Consider the same signals, *Signal-1* and *Signal-2*, used in explaining the limitations of the Fourier Transform in section 3.2.3.1. Now, the wavelet transform is applied using the *Mexican Hat* wavelet, and the results are illustrated in Figure 8. The darker regions in the corresponding wavelet plots represent regions of better correlation with the wavelet, and the *y-axis* represents the iteration of dilation of the mother wavelet. Without going into the intricate details of the plot, it can be noticed that the darker regions for both the signals occur in different regions, unlike in the case of the Fourier Transform, which in essence, signifies that better correlations occur in different regions of the signal. In this case, the wavelet is better correlated with the *S1* component.

How do we guess the characteristic components? The mother wavelet has certain characteristic features, and the more correlated a region of the signal is to the wavelet in any iteration, using the characteristics of the mother wavelet, we can guess the characteristic features in different regions of the signal.

3.2.3.4. The Discrete Wavelet Transform

A discrete wavelet transform is any wavelet transform for which the wavelets are sampled discretely. Wavelets characterised by a low pass and a high pass filter bank is a feature extraction method applied in the current work. Daubechies wavelet of type 17 is used for feature extraction in the current work. The signal is decomposed as approximation *A* and detail *D* components and analysed in the 15-30Hz frequency band. The decomposition can be described as:

$$A_j = A_{j+1} + D_{j+1}$$

Figure 10. The filter bank structure of the DWT

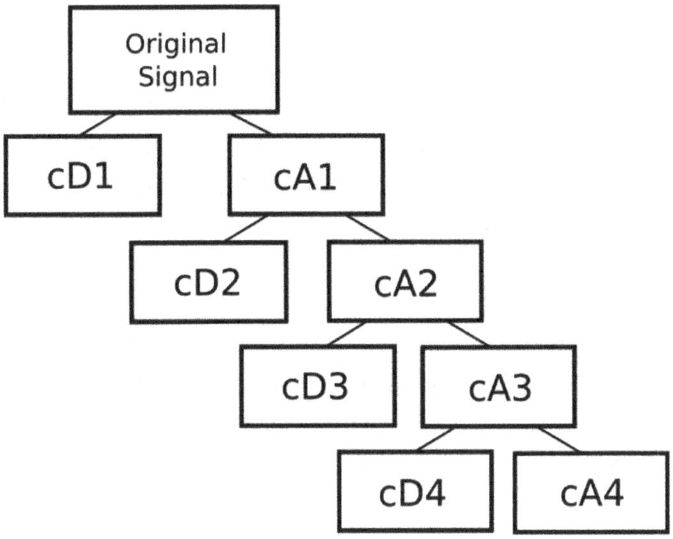

where the approximation is again decomposed into approximation and detail.

The decomposition may be done more than once for a better frequency resolution. The approximation coefficients are further decomposed with low pass and high pass filters. This may be represented as a binary tree where the approximation at each level is decomposed into the approximation and detail of the next level. Each node has a different frequency localization. This structure is called a *filter bank*.

3.2.4. *Common Spatial Patterns*

Common Spatial Patterns (CSP) is used to further increase the inter-class variance (Mohanachandra & Saha, 2016). In essence, the wavelet transform measures the correlation between a wavelet at every time instance of the acquired signal, and CSP maximizes the separation between classes by increasing the variance of one class and simultaneously minimizing the variance associated with the other class. The CSP algorithm is commonly used in optimal channel selection from two classes of data, to reduce dimensions. Its working is based on simultaneous diagonalization of two covariance matrices.

Let *ch* represent the number of channels and *t* be the number of recorded samples per channel. Then the size of the data acquired from one trial will have a size of $h \times t$. The data from one trial may be represented as $E_n \in R^{ch \times t} \xrightarrow{transforms} X_n \in R^d$. A set of feature vectors can be represented as a matrix $X \in R^{d \times n}$.

The CSP Algorithm projects E_n to a *spatial filter* S such that $S = W^T E$ where $W \in R^{d \times ch}$ and $S \in S^{d \times t}$.

The selection of appropriate weights using the characteristic values and characteristic weights can be done using $W^T \sum W$, such that $W^T(\sum_1 + \sum_2) = I$.

The projection matrix W is computed by the simultaneous diagonalization of two the covariance matrices from the two classes. The covariance matrices $\sum_1$ and $\sum_2$ are calculated in the following way:

$$\Sigma = \frac{XX^T}{trace(XX^T)} \tag{1}$$

for the corresponding class as Σ_i where X^T represents the transpose of the matrix X, and $trace(XX^T)$ gives the sum of the diagonal elements of the matrix XX^T. The average covariance matrices $\overline{\Sigma_1}$ and $\overline{\Sigma_2}$ of multiple trials is computed for each class. Following this, the *eigen value decomposition* is performed on composite covariance matrix Σ_c using:

$$\Sigma_c = \overline{\Sigma_1} + \overline{\Sigma_2} = UDU^T \tag{2}$$

U is a matrix of normalized eigenvectors, such that $UU^T = I$ and D is the corresponding matrix of eigenvalues. The obtained eigenvalues are sorted in ascending order. Following this, the whitening transform is performed using:

$$P = D^{-\frac{1}{2}}U^T \tag{3}$$

The matrix P transforms the average covariance matrix for fast convergence. The whitening transformation is applied to the original covariance matrices of the two classes as shown below. The matrix P transforms the average covariance matrix to $\widehat{\Sigma_1}$ and $\widehat{\Sigma_2}$ as shown:

$$\widehat{\Sigma} = P\Sigma P^T \tag{4}$$

The steps in the whitening transform are shown below.

$$
\begin{aligned}
P &= D^{-\frac{1}{2}}U^T \\
&\Rightarrow D^{-\frac{1}{2}}P = U^T \\
&\Rightarrow P^T(D^{-\frac{1}{2}})^T = U \\
&\Rightarrow P^T = UD^{-\frac{1}{2}}
\end{aligned}
\tag{5}
$$

Thus,

$$\widehat{\Sigma_1} = P\Sigma_1 P^T \Rightarrow \widehat{\Sigma_1} = D^{-\frac{1}{2}}U^T\Sigma_1 UD^{-\frac{1}{2}} \tag{6}$$

and,

$$\widehat{\Sigma_2} = P\Sigma_2 P^T \Rightarrow \widehat{\Sigma_2} = D^{-\frac{1}{2}}U^T\Sigma_2 UD^{-\frac{1}{2}} \tag{7}$$

Therefore, from Equations 2, 6 and 7,

$$\widehat{\Sigma_1} + \widehat{\Sigma_2} = D^{-\frac{1}{2}}U^T\Sigma_1 UD^{-\frac{1}{2}} + D^{-\frac{1}{2}}U^T\Sigma_2 UD^{-\frac{1}{2}}$$

$$\Rightarrow \widehat{\Sigma_1} + \widehat{\Sigma_2} = D^{-\frac{1}{2}}U^T(\Sigma_1 + \Sigma_2)UD^{-\frac{1}{2}}$$

$$\Rightarrow \widehat{\Sigma_1} + \widehat{\Sigma_2} = D^{-\frac{1}{2}}U^T(UDU^T)UD^{-\frac{1}{2}}$$

$$\Rightarrow \widehat{\Sigma_1} + \widehat{\Sigma_2} = D^{-\frac{1}{2}}(U^TU)D^{\frac{1}{2}}D^{\frac{1}{2}}(U^TU)D^{-\frac{1}{2}}$$

$$\Rightarrow \widehat{\Sigma_1} + \widehat{\Sigma_2} = D^{-\frac{1}{2}}ID^{\frac{1}{2}}D^{\frac{1}{2}}ID^{-\frac{1}{2}} \qquad (8)$$

$$\Rightarrow \widehat{\Sigma_1} + \widehat{\Sigma_2} = D^{-\frac{1}{2}}D^{\frac{1}{2}}D^{\frac{1}{2}}D^{-\frac{1}{2}}$$

$$\Rightarrow \widehat{\Sigma_1} + \widehat{\Sigma_2} = (D^{-\frac{1}{2}}D^{\frac{1}{2}})(D^{\frac{1}{2}}D^{-\frac{1}{2}})$$

$$\Rightarrow \widehat{\Sigma_1} + \widehat{\Sigma_2} = (I)(I)$$

$$\Rightarrow \widehat{\Sigma_1} + \widehat{\Sigma_2} = I$$

Hence, any orthonormal matrix I will obey:

$$V^T(\Sigma_1 + \Sigma_2)V = I \qquad (9)$$

Following this, CSP is formulated as an optimization problem using sequential programming. Using the theory of the Hessian matrix, the local minima is found from the covariance matrices.

$$\min_{w_i}(1-\alpha)\left(\sum_{i=m+1}^{2m} w_i\Sigma_1 w_i + \sum_{i=1}^{m} w_i\Sigma_2 w_i\right) + r \qquad (10)$$

where,

$$r = \alpha\sum_{i=1}^{2m}\frac{||w_i||}{||w_i||_1 + ||w_i||_p} \qquad (11)$$

is the regularization term, used to induce sparsity.
Here,

$$w_i(\Sigma_1 + \Sigma_2)w_j^T = 1; i,j = \{1,2,...,2m\}, 0 \le \alpha \le 1, p = 0.5 \qquad (12)$$

Σ_1 and Σ_2 are the covariance matrices of *Class1* and *Class2* of our data. The weights w_i are computed using Equation 12, such that $w_i \in R^{1\times n}$, $i = 1,2,...,2m$. w_i represents the first and last m rows of the CSP projection matrix, denoting m largest characteristic values of Λ_1 and Λ_2, where Λ_1 and Λ_2 are the diagonal matrices of *Class1* and *Class2* respectively. The characteristic values are ordered in descending order. The optimal value of α is found from the local or global minima of the convex optimization problem.

Lastly,

$$
\begin{aligned}
\hat{\Sigma}_1 &= V\Lambda_1 V^T \\
\hat{\Sigma}_2 &= V\Lambda_2 V^T
\end{aligned}
\tag{13}
$$

where V is a set of characteristic vectors. The CSP projection matrix W is computed as shown in Equation 14. The rows of W are the spatial filters and the columns of W^{-1} are the common spatial patterns.

$$
W = P^T V
\tag{14}
$$

The original EEG trial is transformed into uncorrelated, linearly independent components with the projection matrix W from Equation 14 as $S = W^T E$.

3.3. Classification Methods

3.3.1. Decision Tree

Decision trees use a tree data structures to model decisions and predict outcomes. Decision trees are helpful in cases where one decision leads to a series of choices. When we deal with a lot of data, there may be certain feature points which may be used as boundaries that help us to separate one type of data from another.

As an illustrative example, let us consider a student's dinner habits. We have the data for two weeks of her attendance to the dining hall of her hostel. On the days she doesn't have dinner at the hostel, she eats out. We are trying to relate her attendance based on what is served for dinner: the main course, the side dish and the dessert. The following table shows all the data.

The data for the days from 1 to 14 are the *training set*. Based on observations from the training set, we will predict her attendance on day 15.

On the whole, we observe that she had dinner at the hostel on 8 out of the 14 days, and she ate out on the remaining 6 days.

We represent the root node of our decision tree as the blue box. We have also enlisted the days that she ate at the hostel in green colour, and the days she did not eat in hostel in red colour, beneath the box.

Just based on the number of days that she ate at the hostel, we will be unable to predict with a high level of certainty if she will eat on day 15 or not. So as our first *split point*, i.e the feature that we will use to predict the next level of outcomes, let us consider the *main course*. We extend branches in the tree, based on it.

As we can see in the above tree, that under each of the nodes, there are still *uncertainties*. Hence, these nodes are called *impure nodes* or *impure sets*. So to make our prediction more robust, let us also include the attribute of *side dish* and extend our decision tree further.

When we further add nodes branching from *Pasta*, we see that for the attributes *Meat* and *Veg Salad*, all the decisions are true, whereas for the attribute *Mashed Potatoes*, all the decisions are false. All the

Table 2. A student's dinner habits based on her food preference

Day	Main Course	Side Dish	Dessert	Action
1	Pasta	Meat	Ice Cream	YES
2	Rice	Mashed Potatoes	Custard	NO
3	Bread	Mashed Potatoes	Chocolates	NO
4	Bread	Veg Salad	Ice Cream	YES
5	Pasta	Mashed Potatoes	Chocolates	NO
6	Bread	Mashed Potatoes	Ice Cream	YES
7	Rice	Veg Salad	Chocolates	NO
8	Bread	Meat	Custard	YES
9	Rice	Veg Salad	Ice Cream	NO
10	Pasta	Veg Salad	Custard	YES
11	Pasta	Mashed Potatoes	Custard	NO
12	Rice	Meat	Custard	YES
13	Bread	Meat	Chocolates	YES
14	Pasta	Meat	Custard	YES
15	Bread	Veg Salad	Chocolates	?

Figure 11. Days when the student had and did not have dinner in her hostel dining hall

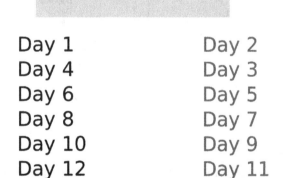

pure nodes, wherein she ate at the hostel are coloured green, and all the pure nodes wherein she ate outside are coloured red. Hence, these two *leaf nodes* are *pure* sets. This means that whenever pasta was served with meat or veg salad, the student ate at the hostel's dining hall, and whenever pasta was served with mashed potatoes, she ate out. Similarly, we branch out the tree from the nodes *Rice* and *Bread*, and get the tree below.

Figure 12. Growing the decision tree based on main course only

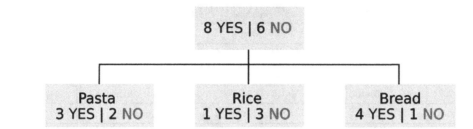

Figure 13. Growing the tree further by considering the side dish attribute

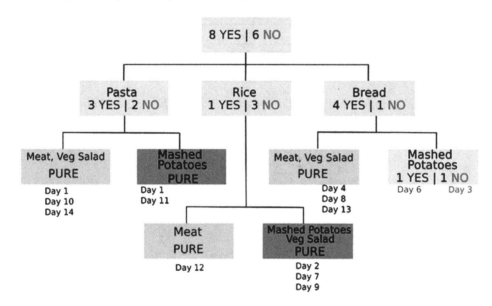

But when we look at the node *Bread* and its branch *Mashed Potatoes*, we see that the set isn't *pure*. Hence, under this attribute, we extend the tree further, by considering the *Dessert* attributes.

Now, all the nodes in the tree are *pure*. This is a necessary condition for a decision tree to be used.

We can now predict if the student will be present on day 15. Looking at the table, we see that on day 15, the *Main Course* is *Bread*, the side dish is *Veg Salad* and the *Dessert* is *Chocolates*. Tracing these attributes in the tree, we observe that whenever *Bread* was served with *Veg Salad*, the student dined at her hostel. So according to this decision tree, the prediction is that she will eat at her hostel dining hall on day 15.

In the above example, the choice of the *split points* is not necessarily optimized. For all practical cases, the data is a lot more than this! Some of the most popular algorithms for selecting split points and generating decision trees are:

Figure 14. Fully grown decision tree, incorporating all attributes

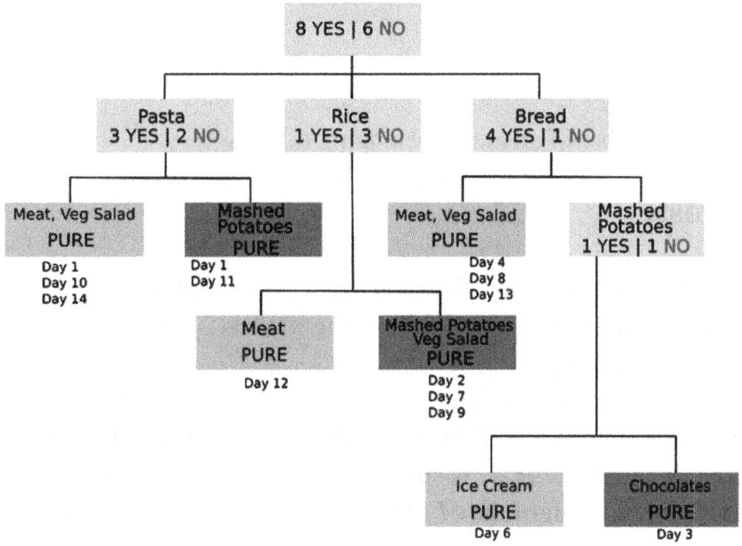

1. ID2
2. C4.5
3. CART
4. Best First Tree
5. SLIQ
6. SPRINT

Generally, the optimization of all learning approaches involves minimization of an error term. By minimizing an error, the algorithm ensures better classification accuracy, and yields better results. One of the most popular measures of impurity or error is the *Gini Impurity* (Duda, Hart, Stork, 2001). For the task of classification, it is given as:

$$i(N) = \sum_i P(\omega_i)P(1 - \omega_i)$$

where $i(N)$ represents impurity at a node N

ω_i represents an element from class i

The Gini Impurity index is calculated by considering the probability of the elements from a class i occurring at a node N. The probability of ω_i ω_i at a node would be given by:

$$Gini = \frac{N(i)}{\sum_{j}^{n} N(j)}$$

where $N(i)$ represents the number of elements belonging to class i.

3.3.2. Random Forests

A Random Forest is an ensemble of many Decision Trees. The purpose of doing this is to increase accuracy, as the prediction from a combination of learning models is generally better than single-model paradigms (Duda, Hart, Stork, 2001).

A *random forest algorithm* works as a large correlation of decorrelated decision trees. If we are presented with N training samples, then we sample n cases from the original data at random, with repetition. If there are M attributes, a number $m < M$ is specified such that in each smaller tree that is created, m attributes are selected at random out of the M and the best *split points* on these m are used to split the node. The value of m is held constant during the forest growing and each tree in the forest is grown to the largest extent possible.

Let us consider the following matrix S, with M columns, and N rows.

$$S = \begin{bmatrix} a_1 & a_2 & a_3 & \dots & a_M \\ b_1 & b_2 & b_3 & \dots & b_M \\ c_1 & c_2 & c_3 & \dots & c_M \\ \dots & \dots & \dots & \dots & \dots \\ N_1 & N_2 & N_3 & \dots & N_M \end{bmatrix}$$

The Random Forest algorithm will generate subsets of S, having m columns and n rows. For example, let us assume that the following matrices are generated.

$$S_1 = \begin{bmatrix} a_4 & a_7 & a_{11} & \dots & a_{m_1} \\ b_4 & b_7 & b_{11} & \dots & b_{m_1} \\ c_4 & c_7 & c_{11} & \dots & c_{m_1} \\ \dots & \dots & \dots & \dots & \dots \\ n_4 & n_7 & n_{11} & \dots & n_{m_1} \end{bmatrix}$$

$$S_2 = \begin{bmatrix} a_2 & a_5 & a_{14} & \dots & a_{m_2} \\ b_2 & b_5 & b_{14} & \dots & b_{m_2} \\ c_2 & c_5 & c_{14} & \dots & c_{m_2} \\ \dots & \dots & \dots & \dots & \dots \\ n_2 & n_5 & n_{14} & \dots & n_{m_2} \end{bmatrix}$$

$$S_3 = \begin{bmatrix} a_5 & a_9 & a_{14} & \cdots & a_{m_3} \\ b_5 & b_9 & b_{14} & \cdots & b_{m_3} \\ c_5 & c_9 & c_{14} & \cdots & c_{m_3} \\ \cdots & \cdots & \cdots & \cdots & \cdots \\ n_5 & n_9 & n_{14} & \cdots & n_{m_3} \end{bmatrix}$$

From each of the above subsets, a corresponding decision tree is constructed, and the *test data* is passed as an input to all the decision trees. The outcomes from each tree is recorded, and the outcome with the most occurrence is assumed to be the correct output. Each decision tree *votes* for a certain outcome, and the outcome with the higher number of votes is assigned as the class label of the test data.

3.3.3. Support Vector Machine

Watson and Nadaraya introduced *kernel methods* for predictive learning in 1964. Based on a training dataset or a predictor dataset, the estimated response variable for a given input is defined as the weighted average of the training response. A vector space **V** is spanned by the predictor variables and their location and the weight kernel is assigned to each response variable, defining the weights and is called the kernel function. The kernel function is often represented as a monotonic decreasing function of some scaled parameter and distance, weights being adaptive, aiding the kernel value to diminish with distance between points.

Kernel methods suffer from two major drawbacks: model insufficiency and statistical inaccuracy. Since the kernel function is not explicitly defined, the method lacks a detailed explanation of the dependence of the kernel function on the predictor variables. Each prediction requires scanning the entire database rendering the computation time intensive for large datasets. If the distance function is not chosen carefully, the regression model performs inadequately, inducing sparsity in extremely large datasets but a handful of predictor variables.

Support Vector Machines is one of the more recent kernel methods and overcomes some of the critical limitations of elementary kernel methods. Define $y = f(x)$, where $x \in R^d$, f is a non-linear map and unknown $y \in R$; the training dataset (x_i, y_i); $i = \{1, 2, ..., m\}$ is the only interpretation available. The model is *regression-like*, except for the fact f is not known. The problem definition resembles a traditional inferential statistics problem. However unlike an inference problem, parametric structure (linear or otherwise) in learning from the training data is absent. Also, SVM doesn't rely on SSE and MLE since the default assumption of stochastic data being normally distributed is not encouraged.

The dataset in the exercise of classification of mental states, following the Wavelet Transform is multidimensional and the underlying relation or mapping is not very smooth. Therefore, regression models or assumptions about normality in data are not favoured. Kernel based methods like SVM, which constructs a *hyperplane* to separate two classes and may be extended later to discriminate among multiple classes, prove to be extremely useful for this kind of problem problem (Mohanachandra et al., 2014; Mohanachandra, Saha and Murthy, 2014).

So how does an SVM work? Let us consider linearly separable binary datasets with features x_1 and x_2 (easily extensible to $x_1, x_2, x_3, ..., x_n$). The task is to classify the elements shown in Figure 15.

But consider the following case (Figure 16):

In this case, both the hyperplanes classify all the data points correctly but the best hyperplane is the one which leaves a maximum margin from both classes. Now, what is a *margin*?

A *margin* is the distance between the hyperplane and the *closest element* (data point) (Manning, Raghavan & Schütze, 2008)

Figure 15. The use of a hyperplane in SVM

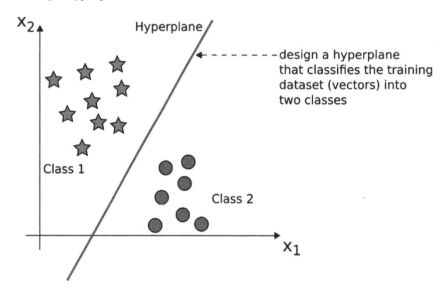

Figure 16. Multiple hyperplanes constructed to segregate two classes

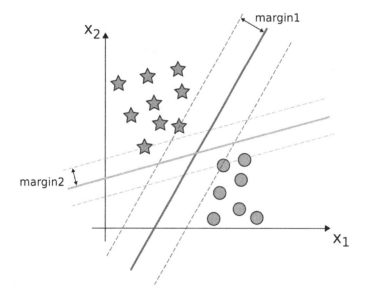

. As observed from Figure 2, *margin1* is larger than *margin2* and hence is the best candidate hyperplane among the two. Going back to Figure 1, a hyperplane is mathematically represented as:

$$g(x) = w^T x + w_0 \tag{15}$$

where, w is the weight vector; and

x is the training dataset

The hyperplane is scaled such that

$$g(x) = \begin{cases} \geq 1, \forall x \in Class1 \\ \leq 1, \forall x \in Class2 \end{cases}$$

and the distance (margin), z is computed by:

$$z = \frac{|g(x)|}{\|w\|} = \frac{|\pm 1|}{\|w\|} = \frac{1}{\|w\|}$$

such that the total margin becomes $\dfrac{2}{\|w\|}$.

This implies that the classification problem is an optimization exercise where the margin w has to be minimized for maximum separability.

This implies,

$$\min \sum_{i=0}^{n} w_i \lambda_i y_i$$

subject to the constraints

$$\sum_{i=0}^{n} \lambda_i y_i = 0$$

This method is known as the *Lagrangian Multiplier* method.

As a simple example, let us consider the following two data points. The green dot represents the point (5,3.5) and the blue dot represents the point (11,12) in the coordinate system. We have to classify these two points into two separate classes and accordingly, find the best hyperplane to do so.

Here, we have:

$$w = (11,12) - (5,3.5) \equiv (6a, 8.5a)$$

From the above equation, we arrive at (from Equation 15):

$$11a + 102a + w_0 = -1$$
$$30a + 51a + w_0 = 1$$

$$\Rightarrow a = -\frac{1}{16}; w_0 = \frac{97}{16} \tag{16}$$

Therefore, the best hyperplane may be defined by:

$$g(x) = -\frac{3}{8} x_1 - \frac{17}{32} x_2 + \frac{97}{16} \tag{17}$$

From the above equations (Equations 16 and 17), we arrive at:

g(5,3.5) = -1 ~Class1

g(11,12) = 1 ~Class2

The classification task in the current work involved a binary classification, that is, classification into two classes. Thus, the above approach was used to classify data into two classes, based on the levels of attention.

Figure 17. Selecting optimal hyperplane between the two given points

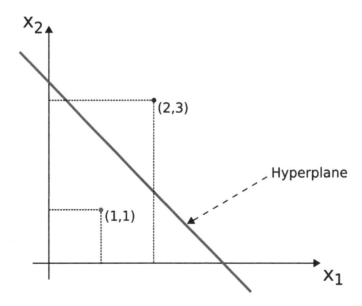

3.3.4. K Nearest Neighbours

The k-NN is a vector classification technique that classifies feature vectors based on the nearest training samples in a feature space. The advantage of the k-NN method over other learning methods is its ability to deal with multiple class problems (Yazdani, Ebrahimi & Hoffmann, 2009). The algorithm is robust to noisy data as it averages the k nearest neighbours. The vector is classified by a majority vote of its neighbours. Typically, the value of k is chosen as a small positive integer in order to make the boundaries between various classes in the feature space more distinct.

In the training phase, the feature vectors are assigned a corresponding class label. The training samples are vectors in a multidimensional vector space, each with an assigned class label. In the classification phase, an unclassified vector is assigned the label as that of the k nearest neighbours.

As an example, from (the above) figure, the test sample (colour: blue) should be assigned the same label as the class represented by red stars or green circles. The test sample is assigned the same label of the class represented by red stars when $k = 3$, as it looks only for the three nearest neighbours. If $k = 5$, the same test sample looks for the five nearest neighbours and is assigned the label as the class represented by the green squares.

3.4. Results and Discussion

The proposed system was tested on four healthy subjects. The results from each classifier is given below: mean accuracy, sensitivity and specificity. In each case, the accuracy varies from subject to subject, as the signals obtained depends on the test subject as well as the test case. Each subject had approximately a hundred trials of each task, contributing to a total of 200 trials for two mental states of each subject. For every subject, the dataset was divided in the ratio of 4:4:2 of each task: The first 40% of the data

Figure 18. Classification using the k Nearest Neighbours approach

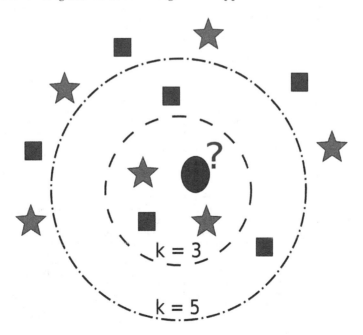

was used to generate the spatial filters for the CSP algorithm. This, along with the next 40% were used to generate training data from the spatial filters. The last 20% for each iteration was the training data and was used to evaluate the results from each classifier. A total of 1000 iterations were performed for each subject for each classifier.

The results of the experiment show that the sophistication required to develop a well-functioning Brain Computer Interface is far beyond a single electrode system, with the electrode placed on the forehead. As for existing work which have made used of the NeuroSky Mindwave devices: most of them rely on a *level* of attention to perform a simple task, not the different classes of attention. While this popularization of BCI is useful to attract attention towards the study of the field, a system like this is not particularly useful in itself.

The results of the experiment reflect almost a random experiment where success is as likely as failure. With only Subject 1 the results are close to 70% accuracy: this is encouraging. However, this accuracy is far less than what can be achieved using sophisticated signal acquisition devices like the Skull Cap.

Table 3. Results from random forests classifier

Subject	Mean Accuracy(%)	Maximum Accuracy(%) (in one iteration)	Minimum Accuracy(%) (in one iteration)	Sensitivity	Specificity
1	68.210	100.0	22.22	0.772	0.582
2	54.111	100.0	10.0	0.766	0.317
3	52.509	100.0	7.143	0.692	0.366
4	51.931	93.75	8.33	0.760	0.286

Table 4. Results from support vector machines classifier

Subject	Mean Accuracy(%)	Maximum Accuracy(%) (in one iteration)	Minimum Accuracy(%) (in one iteration)	Sensitivity	Specificity
1	60.447	100.0	16.667	0.884	0.288
2	49.746	93.75	6.667	0.933	0.066
3	51.775	90.909	7.692	0.847	0.204
4	49.481	100	6.25	0.914	0.088

Table 5. Results from k-nearest neighbours classifier

Subject	Mean Accuracy(%)	Maximum Accuracy(%) (in one iteration)	Minimum Accuracy(%) (in one iteration)	Sensitivity	Specificity
1	68.193	100.0	21.429	0.743	0.612
2	53.041	94.737	0.0	0.708	0.354
3	47.985	92.857	7.692	0.620	0.347
4	50.883	92.308	10.0	0.722	0.303

4. FUTURE RESEARCH DIRECTIONS

With time, technology becomes smaller and more compact. We can appreciate this by comparing the first generation computers to the computers of the present: today, our machines are much smaller, portable, cheap, and are more powerful than the *supercomputers* of previous generations. Such is the trend with any technological application. In BCI as well, with time, headsets and applications have become more compact, and this is triggered by developments at the hardware end as well as the analyses' end. This chapter provides insights about attempts at making EEG hardware cheaper and with a more effective form factor. The author's research involved using this hardware to analyze subjects' mental states based on their level of attention.

Subjects need to be adequately trained for tasks pertaining to interaction with computers based on brain waves. Even with the best of the current technology, subjects need to be still, relaxed and focused on a certain task. It is particularly difficult to classify mental states based on attention alone: more popular approaches include motor imagery, visually evoked potentials and subvocalization. Motor imagery is based on imagined motion of certain body parts such as an arm, or a leg; subvocalization is the act of silently pronouncing a word in the mind, without actually saying it out loud; Steady State Visually Evoked Potentials (SSVEP) is an approach where brainwaves are triggered by visual cues, such as flickering lights of different frequencies. These approaches are preferred as the related tasks activate certain regions of the brain, and based on which regions are activated, a brain-computer interface may be effectively developed. The key direction in which the development of more compact hardware must be driven is to utilize specific genres of mental tasks, such as motor imagery, subvocalization, SSVEP or other similar approaches.

While the classification accuracy achieved in the present work is not very high, the results show promise to drive research in the fields of non-medical applications, using portable hardware with less electrodes to reduce the cumbersome nature of traditional BCI setups. Other headsets like the Emotiv EPOC and the Muse headbands should also be experimented with. When the number of electrodes in a BCI setup is reduced, the placement of the electrodes in the appropriate positions over a subject's scalp is of foremost importance. This is one of the major limitations of the aforementioned EEG headsets: the positions of the electrodes are fixed.

The direction of work following this would be to increase the flexibility of usage in EEG headsets, and to better analyse the signals acquired from subjects. The current setup serves as a prototype which may be extended to various applications such as games and other entertainment for locked-in or paralyzed patients.

5. CONCLUSION

The greatest challenges of EEG based Brain Computer Interfaces are their non-stationarity, low signal-to-noise ratio and the variety of noise resources such as muscle artefacts, eye blinks, etc. A demand for robust signal and data processing methods subsists, to obtain accurate results in and other cognitive tasks, wherein no external stimulus is used to enhance the signal amplitude. In the current work, different methods of signal pre-processing (*wavelet transform, CSP*) and classification (*Decision Trees, Random Forests, SVM, kNN*) are used, and their performance accordingly evaluated, using statistical parameters. Test subjects need to be rigorously trained in order to be able to perform the necessary mental tasks, and give good results. A lack of concentration, or muscle artefacts may lead to more noise and as a result, may affect the quality of the result. Research must also be driven to develop smaller, more usable and more robust hardware devices that may pertain to specific needs as per a user's requirements. Better hardware, developed with time, such as better quality electrodes, wiring, amplifiers, etc. will also play a significant part in the development of BCI in the future.

The priority of methods according to their capability is difficult to acclaim as each method has significant advantages and shortcomings for specific applications. The findings of the current work may be extended to drive an object, provided the appropriate interface, or be used with a system with more electrodes and be implemented as a full-fledged speller machine.

REFERENCES

Anupama, H. S., Cauvery, N. K., & Lingaraju, G. M. (2014). Brain Controlled Wheelchair for Disabled. *International Journal on Computer Science and Engineering*, 4(2), 157–166.

Duda, R. O., Hart, P. E., & Stork, D. G. (2001). *Pattern Classification*. Wiley doi:10.1109/NER.2009.5109299

Larsen, E. A. (2011). *Classification of EEG Signals in a Brain-Computer Interface System* (Unpublished masters' dissertation). Norwegian University of Science and Technology (NTNU).

Manning, C. D., Raghavan, P., & Schütze, H. (2008). *Introduction to Information Retrieval*. Cambridge University Press.

Mohanchandra, Saha, & Murthy. (2014). *EEG based Brain Computer Interface using Wavelets and SVM*. Paper presented at Grace Hopper Conference India (GHCI), Bangalore. Karnataka, India.

Mohanchandra, K., & Saha, S. (2014). Optimal Channel Selection for Robust EEG Single-trial Analysis. *AASRI Conference on Circuit and Signal Processing*. doi:10.1016/j.aasri.2014.09.012

Mohanchandra, K., & Saha, S. (2016). *A Communication Paradigm Using Subvocalized Speech, Augmented Human Research*. Springer Singapore.

Mohanchandra, K., Saha, S., & Deshmukh, R. (2014). *Twofold Classification of Motor Imagery using Common Spatial Pattern*. Paper presented at the International Conference on Contemporary Computing and Informatics, Mysore, Karnataka, India doi:10.1109/IC3I.2014.7019636

Mohanchandra, K., Saha, S., Murthy, K. S., & Lingaraju, G. M. (2014). Distinct adoption of k-nearest neighbour and support vector machine in classifying EEG signals of mental tasks. *International Journal of Intelligent Engineering Informatics*, 3(4), 313–329. doi:10.1504/IJIEI.2015.073064

Theodoridis, S., & Koutroumbas, K. (2009). *Pattern Recognition*. Academic Press.

Yazdani, A., Ebrahimi, T., & Hoffmann, U. (2009). Classification of EEG Signals Using Dempster Shafer Theory and a K-Nearest Neighbor Classifier. Paper presented at the International IEEE EMBS Conference on Neural Engineering, Antalya, Turkey.

Yildirim, N., Ulas, M., & Varol, A. (2015). A Game Development for Android Devices Based on Brain Computer Interface: Flying Brain. *Proc. of the Intl. Conf. on Advances in Applied science and Environmental Technology*, 77-81.

Compilation of References

Abhayaratne, C., & Bhowmik, D. (2013). Scalable watermark extraction for real-time authentication of JPEG 2000 images. *Journal of Real-Time Image Processing*, *8*(3), 307–325. doi:10.1007/s11554-011-0218-5

Aboy, M., Hornero, R., Abasolo, D., & Alvarez, D. (2006). Interpretation of the Lempel-Ziv Complexity Measure in the Context of Biomedical Signal Analysis. *IEEE Transactions on Bio-Medical Engineering*, *53*(11), 2282–2288. doi:10.1109/TBME.2006.883696 PMID:17073334

Abrams, M., & Weiss, J. (2008). *Malicious Control System Cyber Security Attack Case Study–Maroochy Water Services, Australia*. Retrieved from http://csrc.nist.gov/groups/SMA/fisma/ics/documents/Maroochy-Water-Services-Case-Study_report.pdf

Acharya, U. R., Faust, O., Sree, V., Swapna, G., Martis, R. J., Kadri, N. A., & Suri, J. S. (2014). Linear and nonlinear analysis of normal and CAD-affected heart rate signals. *Computer Methods and Programs in Biomedicine*, *113*(1), 55–68. doi:10.1016/j.cmpb.2013.08.017 PMID:24119391

Adelsbach, A., Katzenbeisser, S., & Sadeghi, A. R. (2004). Cryptography meets watermarking: Detecting watermarks with minimal or zero knowledge disclosure.*Proc. European Signal Processing Conference (EUSIPCO)*, *1*, 446–449.

Alaeiyan, M., Asadpour, J., & Mojarad, R. (2013). A Numerical Method for MEC Polynomial and MEC Index of One-Pentagonal Carbon Nanocones. Fullerenes, Nanotubes and Carbon Nanostructures, 21(10), 825-835.

Algorithm ontology. (n.d.). Retrieved March 31, 2016, from http://www.opentox.org/dev/apis/api-1.1/Algorithms

Algorithmia - Open Marketplace for Algorithms. (n.d.). Retrieved March 31, 2016, from https://algorithmia.com/

Ali, A., & Aggarwal, J. K. (2001). Segmentation and recognition of continuous human activity.*Proc. IEEE Workshop on Detection and Recognition of Events in Video*, 28–35. doi:10.1109/EVENT.2001.938863

Alizadeh, Y., Iranmanesh, A., Doslić, T., & Azari, M. (2014). The edge Wiener index of suspensions, bottlenecks, and thorny graphs. *Glasnik Matematicki Series III*, *49*(69), 1–12. doi:10.3336/gm.49.1.01

Alligood, K. T., Sauer, T. D., & Yorke, J. A. (2000). *Chaos: An introduction to dynamical systems*. Springer.

Aly̆uz, Dibekliŏglu, C̨eliktutan, G̈okberk, Sankur, & Akarun. (2008). Bosphorus database for 3D face analysis. Biometrics and Identity Management, 5372, 47–56.

Amigó, J. M., Szczepański, J., Wajnryb, E., & Sanchez-Vives, M. V. (2004). Estimating the Entropy Rate of Spike Trains via Lempel-Ziv Complexity. *Neural Computation*, *16*(4), 717–736. doi:10.1162/089976604322860677 PMID:15025827

Andress, J. (2011). *Basics of Information Security: Understanding the Fundamentals of InfoSec in Theory and Practice*. Syngress Press.

Andrews, S., Tsochantaridis, I., & Hofmann, T. (2002). Support vector machines for multiple-instance learning. *Advances in Neural Information Processing Systems, 15.*

Anupama, H. S., Cauvery, N. K., & Lingaraju, G. M. (2014). Brain Controlled Wheelchair for Disabled. *International Journal on Computer Science and Engineering, 4*(2), 157–166.

Aramaki, E., Imai, T., Miyo, K., & Ohe, K. (2006, November). Automatic deidentification by using sentence features and label consistency. In *i2b2 Workshop on Challenges in Natural Language Processing for Clinical Data* (pp. 10-11).

Aronson, A. R. (2001). Effective mapping of biomedical text to the UMLS Metathesaurus: the MetaMap program. In *Proceedings of the AMIA Symposium* (p.17). American Medical Informatics Association.

Arulampalam, M. S., Maskell, S., Gordon, N., & Clapp, T. (2002). A tutorial on particle filters for online nonlinear/non-Gaussian Bayesian tracking. *IEEE Transactions on Signal Processing, 50*(2), 174–188. doi:10.1109/78.978374

Ashrafi, A. R., Ghorbani, M., & Hossein-Zadeh, M. A. (2011). The eccentric connectivity polynomial of some graph operations. *Serdica Journal of Computing, 5*, 101–116.

Ashrafi, A. R., & Ghorbani, M. (2010). A Study of fullerenes by MEC polynomials. *Electronic Materials Letters, 6*(2), 87–90.

Asikuzzaman, M., Alam, M. J., Lambert, A. J., & Pickering, M. R. (2014). Imperceptible and robust blind video watermarking using chrominance embedding: A set of approaches in the DT CWT domain. *IEEE Transactions on Information Forensics and Security, 9*(9), 1502–1517. doi:10.1109/TIFS.2014.2338274

ATLAS. (n.d.). *Trigger and Data Acquisition System.* Available: http://atlas.cern/discover/detector/trigger-daq

Auer, B. F., & Bisseling, R. H. (2012). Graph coarsening and clustering on the GPU. *Graph Partitioning and Graph Clustering, 588*, 223–240. doi:10.1090/conm/588/11706

Avidan, S. (2004). Support vector tracking. *IEEE Transactions on Pattern Analysis and Machine Intelligence, 26*(8), 1064–1072. doi:10.1109/TPAMI.2004.53 PMID:15641735

Aviles, Ramirez, & Saidé. (2015). Evaluating the Internationality of Scholarly Communications in Information Science Publications. *iConference 2015 Proceedings.* Retrieved from http://hdl.handle.net/2142/73769

Avizienis, A., Laprie, J.-C., Randell, B., & Landwehr, C. (2004, January-March). Basic Concepts and Taxonomy of Dependable and Secure Computing. *IEEE Transactions on Dependable and Secure Computing, 1*(1), 11–32. doi:10.1109/TDSC.2004.2

Avron, H., Maymounkov, P., & Toledo, S. (2010). Blendenpik: Supercharging LAPACKs least-squares solver. *SIAM Journal on Scientific Computing, 32*(3), 1217–1236. doi:10.1137/090767911

Axeda Machine Cloud | PTC. (n.d.). Retrieved March 31, 2016, from http://www.ptc.com/axeda/product/iot-platform

Aydemir, O., & Kayikcioglu, T. (2014). Decision tree structure based classification of EEG signals recorded during two dimensional cursor movement imagery. *Journal of Neuroscience Methods, 229*, 68–75. doi:10.1016/j.jneumeth.2014.04.007 PMID:24751647

Azevedo, F. A., Carvalho, L. R., Grinberg, L. T., Farfel, J. M., Ferretti, R. E., Leite, R. E., & Herculano-Houzel, S. et al. (2009). Equal numbers of neuronal and nonneuronal cells make the human brain an isometrically scaled-up primate brain. *The Journal of Comparative Neurology, 513*(5), 532–541. doi:10.1002/cne.21974 PMID:19226510

Aziz, W., & Arif, M. (2006). Complexity analysis of stride interval time series by threshold dependent symbolic entropy. *European Journal of Applied Physiology, 98*(1), 30–40. doi:10.1007/s00421-006-0226-5 PMID:16841202

Babenko, B. (2008). *Multiple instance learning: algorithms and applications. Technical report.* San Diego, CA: University of California.

Bache, K., & Lichman, M. (2013). *UCI machine learning repository.* Retrieved from http://archive.ics.uci.edu/ml

Bae, S. H., Halperin, D., West, J., Rosvall, M., & Howe, B. (2013, December). Scalable flow-based community detection for large-scale network analysis. In *2013 IEEE 13th International Conference on Data Mining Workshops* (pp. 303-310). IEEE. doi:10.1109/ICDMW.2013.138

Balakrishnama, S., & Ganapathiraju, A. (1998). *Linear Discriminant Analysis- A brief tutorial.* Retrieved on 04-05-16 from https://www.isip.piconepress.com/publications/reports/1998/isip/lda/lda_theory.pdf

Balasubramanian, K., & Nagaraj, N. (2016). *Cardiac Aging Detection Using Complexity Measures.* Retrieved from http://arxiv.org/abs/1603.00817

Ball & Brunner. (2010). *Overview of Data Mining and Machine Learning methods.* Retrieved on 25-04-16, from http://ned.ipac.caltech.edu/level5/March11/Ball/Ball2.html

Bandt, C., & Pompe, B. (2002). Permutation Entropy: A Natural Complexity Measure for Time Series. *Physical Review Letters, 88*(17), 174102. doi:10.1103/PhysRevLett.88.174102 PMID:12005759

Barni & Bartolini. (2004). *Watermarking Systems Engineering (Signal Processing and Communications, 21).* Boca Raton, FL: CRC Press, Inc.

Barni, M., Bartolini, F., & Piva, A. (2001). Improved wavelet-based watermarking through pixel-wise masking. *IEEE Transactions on Image Processing, 10*(5), 783–791. doi:10.1109/83.918570 PMID:18249667

Bar-Shalom, Y., & Foreman, T. (1988). *Tracking and Data Association.* Academic Press Inc.

Beauchamp, M. (2005). See me, hear me, touch me: Multisensory integration in lateral occipital - temporal cortex. *Current Opinion in Neurobiology, 15*(2), 145–153. doi:10.1016/j.conb.2005.03.011 PMID:15831395

Beck, T., Gollapudi, S., Brunak, S., Graf, N., Lemke, H. U., Dash, D., & Brookes, A. J. et al. (2012). Knowledge engineering for health: A new discipline required to bridge the ICT gap between research and healthcare. *Human Mutation, 33*(5), 797–802. doi:10.1002/humu.22066 PMID:22392843

Beckwith, B. A., Mahaadevan, R., Balis, U. J., & Kuo, F. (2006). Development and evaluation of an open source software tool for deidentification of pathology reports. *BMC Medical Informatics and Decision Making, 6*(1), 1. doi:10.1186/1472-6947-6-12 PMID:16515714

Belkin, M., Niyogi, P., & Sindhwani, V. (2006). Manifold regularization: A geometric framework for learning from labeled and unlabeled examples. *Journal of Machine Learning Research, 7*, 2399–2434.

Benedetto, D., Caglioti, E., & Loreto, V. (2002). Language Trees and Zipping. *Physical Review Letters, 88*(4), 048702. doi:10.1103/PhysRevLett.88.048702 PMID:11801178

Benjamini, Y., & Hochberg, Y. (1995). Controlling the false discovery rate: A practical and powerful approach to multiple testing. *Journal of the Royal Statistical Society. Series B. Methodological, 57*, 289–300.

Bennett, C. H. (1995). Logical Depth and Physical Complexity. *Computerkultur,* 207-235. doi:10.1007/978-3-7091-6597-3_8

Berner, E. S., Detmer, D. E., & Simborg, D. (2005). Will the wave finally break? A brief view of the adoption of electronic medical records in the United States. *Journal of the American Medical Informatics Association, 12*(1), 3–7. doi:10.1197/jamia.M1664 PMID:15492029

Besl, P. J., & McKay, N. D. (1992). A method for registration of 3-D shapes. *IEEE Transactions on Pattern Analysis and Machine Intelligence*, *14*(2), 239–256. doi:10.1109/34.121791

Bhaduri, S. N. (2014). Applying Approximate Entropy (ApEn) to Speculative Bubble in the Stock Market. *Journal of Emerging Market Finance*, *13*(1), 43–68. doi:10.1177/0972652714534023

Bhatnagar, G., Wuand, Q. M. J., & Raman, B. (2012). Robust gray-scale logo watermarking in wavelet domain. *Computers & Electrical Engineering*, *38*(5), 1164–1176. doi:10.1016/j.compeleceng.2012.02.002

Bhowmick, S., & Srinivasan, S. (2013). A template for parallelizing the louvain method for modularity maximization. In *Dynamics On and Of Complex Networks* (Vol. 2, pp. 111–124). Springer New York. doi:10.1007/978-1-4614-6729-8_6

Bhowmik, D., & Abhayaratne, C. (2007). Morphological wavelet domain image watermarking.*Proc. European Signal Processing Conference (EUSIPCO)*, 2539–2543.

Bhowmik, D., & Abhayaratne, C. (2008). A generalised model for distortion performance analysis of wavelet based watermarking. In *Digital Watermarking* (pp. 363–378). Springer.

Bhowmik, D., & Abhayaratne, C. (2014). On Robustness Against JPEG2000: A Performance Evaluation of Wavelet-Based Watermarking Techniques. *Multimedia Systems*, *20*(2), 239–252. doi:10.1007/s00530-013-0334-0

Bhowmik, D., & Abhayaratne, C. (2009). Embedding distortion modeling for non-orthonormal wavelet based watermarking schemes. *Proc. SPIE Wavelet App. in Industrial Processing VI, 7248*. doi:10.1117/12.810719

Bhuiyan, H., Chen, J., Khan, M., & Marathe, M. V. (2014). Fast Parallel Algorithms for Edge-Switching to Achieve a Target Visit Rate in Heterogeneous Graphs. *Parallel Processing (ICPP), 2014 43rd International Conference on IEEE*, 60–69.

Bi, J., & Liang, J. (2007).Multiple instance learning of pulmonary embolism detection with geodesic distance along vascular structure.*Proceedings of IEEE Conference on Computer Vision and Pattern Recognition.* doi:10.1109/CVPR.2007.383141

Bi, J., Wu, D., & Boyer, K. (2009). A min-max framework of cascaded classifier with multiple instance learning for computer aided diagnosis.*Proceedings of IEEE International Conference on Computer Vision and Pattern Recognition.*

Bi, J., & Liang, J. (2010). *Method of multiple instance learning and classification with correlations in object detection.* US Patent No. US7822252 B2.

Bian, H., Ma, X., & Vumar, E. (2012). The Wiener-type indices of the corona of two graphs. *Ars Combinatoria*, *107*, 193–199.

Bianchi, T., & Piva, A. (2013). Secure watermarking for multimedia content protection: A review of its benefits and open issues. *IEEE Signal Processing Magazine*, *30*(2), 87–96. doi:10.1109/MSP.2012.2228342

BioASQ. (n.d.). *BioASQ project, Data.* Retrieved January 07, 2015, from http://www.bioasq.org/participate/data

Blackman, S. S. (2004). Multiple hypothesis tracking for multiple target tracking. *IEEE Aerospace and Electronic Systems Magazine*, *19*(1), 5–18. doi:10.1109/MAES.2004.1263228

Blackstock, M., & Lea, R. (2012). IoT Mashups with the WoTKit. In *Internet of Things (IOT), 3rd International Conference on the. IEEE*, (pp. 159–166). doi:10.1109/IOT.2012.6402318

Blankenberg, D., Kuster, G. V., Coraor, N., Ananda, G., Lazarus, R., Mangan, M.,... Taylor, J. (2010). Galaxy: a web-based genome analysis tool for experimentalists. In Current protocols in molecular biology (pp. 19–10). doi:10.1002/0471142727.mb1910s89

Blondel, V. D., Guillaume, J. L., Lambiotte, R., & Lefebvre, E. (2008). Fast unfolding of communities in large networks. *Journal of Statistical Mechanics*, *2008*(10), P10008. doi:10.1088/1742-5468/2008/10/P10008

Bonchev, D., & Klein, D. J. (2002). On the Wiener number of thorn trees, stars, rings, and rods. *Croatica Chemica Acta*, *75*, 613–620.

Boser, B. E., Guyon, I. M., & Vapnik, V. N. (1992). A training algorithm for optimal margin classifiers.*Proc. Fifth Annual Workshop on Computational Learning Theory, COLT '92*, 144–152. doi:10.1145/130385.130401

Botts, M., & Robin, A. (2007). *OpenGIS sensor model language (SensorML) implementation specification*. OpenGIS Implementation Specification OGC, 7(000).

Botts, M., Percivall, G., Reed, C., & Davidson, J. (2006). OGC® sensor web enablement: Overview and high level architecture. In GeoSensor networks (pp. 175-190). Springer Berlin Heidelberg.

Bowman, F. D. (2007). Spatiotemporal models for region of interest analyses of functional neuroimaging data. *Journal of the American Statistical Association*, *102*(478), 442–453. doi:10.1198/016214506000001347

Bowman, A. W. (1984). An alternative method of cross-validation for the smoothing of density estimates. *Biometrika*, *71*(2), 353–360. doi:10.1093/biomet/71.2.353

Boykov, Y., & Funka-Lea, G. (2006). Graph cuts and efficient N-D image segmentation. *International Journal of Computer Vision*, *70*(2), 109–131. doi:10.1007/s11263-006-7934-5

Brandes, U., Delling, D., Gaertler, M., Gorke, R., Hoefer, M., Nikoloski, Z., & Wagner, D. (2008). On modularity clustering. *IEEE Transactions on Knowledge and Data Engineering*, *20*(2), 172–188. doi:10.1109/TKDE.2007.190689

Breiman, L., Friedman, J. H., Olshem, R. A., & Stone, C. J. (1984). *Classification and Regression Trees*. London: CRC Press.

Breiman, L. (2001). Random forests. *Machine Learning*, *45*(1), 5–32. doi:10.1023/A:1010933404324

Brette, R., & Gerstner, W. (2005). Adaptive Exponential Integrate-and-Fire Model as an Effective Description of Neuronal Activity. *Journal of Neurophysiology*, *94*(5), 3637–3642. doi:10.1152/jn.00686.2005 PMID:16014787

Brodal, P. (1992). *The Central Nervous System: Structure and Function*. New York: Oxford University Press.

Broida, T. J., & Chellappa, R. (1986). Estimation of object motion parameters from noisy images. *IEEE Transactions on Pattern Analysis and Machine Intelligence*, *PAMI-8*(1), 90–99. doi:10.1109/TPAMI.1986.4767755 PMID:21869326

Bronstein, A. M., Bronstein, M. M., & Kimmel, R. (2005). Three-dimensional face recognition. *International Journal of Computer Vision*, *64*(1), 5–30. doi:10.1007/s11263-005-1085-y

Browne, M. W., Cudeck, R., Bollen, K. A., & Long, J. S. (1993). Alternative ways of assessing model fit. *Sage Focus Editions*, *154*, 136–136.

Bruce, I. P., Karaman, M. M., & Rowe, D. B. (2011). A statistical examination of SENSE image reconstruction via an isomorphism representation. *NeuroImage*, *29*, 1267–1287. PMID:21908127

Buela-Casal, G., Perakakis, P., Taylor, M., & Checa, P. (2006). Measuring internationality: Reflections and perspectives on academic journals. *Scientometrics*, *67*(1), 45–65. doi:10.1007/s11192-006-0050-z

Burges, C. J. (1998). A tutorial on support vector machines for pattern recognition. *Data Mining and Knowledge Discovery*, *2*(2), 121–167. doi:10.1023/A:1009715923555

Buxhoeveden, D., & Casanova, M. (2002). The Minicolumn and the Evolution of the Brain. *Brain, Behavior and Evolution, 60*(3), 125–151. doi:10.1159/000065935 PMID:12417819

Buxhoeveden, D., & Casanova, M. (2002). The minicolumn hypothesis in neuroscience. *Brain, 125*(5), 935–951. doi:10.1093/brain/awf110 PMID:11960884

Buzun, N., Korshunov, A., Avanesov, V., Filonenko, I., Kozlov, I., Turdakov, D., & Kim, H. (2014, December). Egolp: Fast and distributed community detection in billion-node social networks. In *2014 IEEE International Conference on Data Mining Workshop* (pp. 533-540). IEEE. doi:10.1109/ICDMW.2014.158

Cain, F. (2016). *What are the Different Kinds of Supernovae?* Retrieved on 20-04-2016, from http://www.universetoday.com/127865/what-are-the-different-kinds-of-supernovae/

Campisi, P. (2005). Video watermarking in the 3D-DWT domain using quantization-based methods. *Multimedia Signal Processing, IEEE 7th Workshop on*, 1–4.

Canny, J. (1986). A computational approach to edge detection. *IEEE Transactions on Pattern Analysis and Machine Intelligence, PAMI-8*(6), 679–698. doi:10.1109/TPAMI.1986.4767851 PMID:21869365

Cappelleri, D. J., Frecker, M. I., Simpson, T. W., & Snyder, A. (2002). Design of a PZT Bimorph Actuator Using a Metamodel-Based Approach. *ASME Journal of Mechanical Design, 124*(2), 354–357. doi:10.1115/1.1446866

Cardenas, A., Amin, S., Sinopoli, B., Giani, A., Perrig, A., & Sastry, S. (2009). Challenges for Securing Cyber Physical Systems. *Workshop on Future Directions in Cyber-physical Systems Security.*

Cardenas, Amin, Sinopoli, Giani, Perrig, & Sastry. (2009). *Challenges for Securing Cyber Physical Systems.* Retrieved from http://cimic.rutgers.edu/positionPapers/cps-security-challenges-Cardenas.pdf

Carlsson, G. (2009). Toploogy and Data. *Bulletin (New Series) of the American Mathematical Society, 46*(2), 255–308.

Chaitin, G. (1974). Information-theoretic computation complexity. *IEEE Transactions on Information Theory, 20*(1), 10–15. doi:10.1109/TIT.1974.1055172

Chan, H. T., Hwang, W. J., & Cheng, C. J. (2015). Digital hologram authentication using a hadamard-based reversible fragile watermarking algorithm. *Journal of Display Technology, 11*(2), 193–203. doi:10.1109/JDT.2014.2367528

Chapelle, O., Chi, M., & Zien, A. (2006). A continuation method for semi-supervised SVMs. *Proceedings of the 23rd International Conference on Machine Learning*, 185–192.

Chapelle, O., Schölkopf, B., & Zien, A. (Eds.). (2006). *Semi-Supervised Learning*. MIT Press. Retrieved from http://www.kyb.tuebingen.mpg.de/ssl-book

Chen & Woods. (2004). Bidirectional MC-EZBC with lifting implementation. *Circuits and Systems for Video Technology. IEEE Transactions on, 14*(10), 1183–1194.

Chen, T.-S., Chen, J., & Chen, J.-G. (2003). A simple and efficient watermarking technique based on JPEG2000 codec. *Proc. Int'l Symp. on Multimedia Software Eng.*, 80–87. doi:10.1109/MMSE.2003.1254425

Chen, M., Liu, S., & Szymanski, B. K. (2014, September). Parallel toolkit for measuring the quality of network community structure. In *Network Intelligence Conference (ENIC), 2014 European* (pp. 22-29). IEEE.

Chen, C. P., & Zhang, C.-Y. (2014). Data-intensive applications, challenges, techniques and technologies: A survey on Big Data. *Information Sciences, 275*, 314–347. doi:10.1016/j.ins.2014.01.015

Chen, X., & Xie, M. G. (2014). A split-and-conquer approach for analysis of extraordinarily large data. *Statistica Sinica*, 1655–1684.

Cheong, C. Y., Huynh, H. P., Lo, D., & Goh, R. S. M. (2013, August). Hierarchical parallel algorithm for modularity-based community detection using GPUs. In *European Conference on Parallel Processing* (pp. 775-787). Springer Berlin Heidelberg. doi:10.1007/978-3-642-40047-6_77

Chinchor. (2001, January 12). *Named Entity Scores– English, in: Message Understanding Conference Proceedings.* Retrieved January 06, 2015, from http://www.itl.nist.gov/iaui/894.02/related_projects/muc/proceedings/ne_english_score_report.html

Clauset, A., Newman, M. E., & Moore, C. (2004). Finding community structure in very large networks. *Physical Review E: Statistical, Nonlinear, and Soft Matter Physics*, *70*(6), 066111. doi:10.1103/PhysRevE.70.066111 PMID:15697438

Cole, D. M., Smith, S. M., & Beckmann, C. F. (2010). Advances and pitfalls in the analysis and interpretation of resting-state FMRI data. *Frontiers in Systems Neuroscience*, *4*, 1–15. PMID:20407579

Comaniciu, D., & Meer, P. (2002). Mean shift: A robust approach toward feature space analysis. *IEEE Transactions on Pattern Analysis and Machine Intelligence*, *24*(5), 603–619. doi:10.1109/34.1000236

Comaniciu, D., Ramesh, V., & Meer, P. (2003). Kernel-based object tracking. *IEEE Transactions on Pattern Analysis and Machine Intelligence*, *25*(5), 564–577. doi:10.1109/TPAMI.2003.1195991

Compton, M., Barnaghi, P., Bermudez, L., García-Castro, R., Corcho, O., Cox, S., & Taylor, K. et al. (2012). The SSN ontology of the W3C semantic sensor network incubator group. *Web Semantics: Science, Services, and Agents on the World Wide Web*, *17*, 25–32. doi:10.1016/j.websem.2012.05.003

Cooper, D. B., & Freeman, J. H. (1970). On the asymptotic improvement in the out-come of supervised learning provided by additional nonsupervised learning. *IEEE Transactions on Computers*, *100*(11), 1055–1063. doi:10.1109/T-C.1970.222832

Coorevits, P., Sundgren, M., Klein, G. O., Bahr, A., Claerhout, B., Daniel, C., & De, et al.. (2013). Electronic health records: New opportunities for clinical research. *The Association for the Publication of the Journal of Internal Medicine*, *274*(6), 547–560. doi:10.1111/joim.12119 PMID:23952476

Corcho, O., & García-Castro, R. (2010). Five challenges for the semantic sensor web. In Semantic Web (vol. 1, no. 1, pp. 121–125).

Courtot, M., Juty, N., Knupfer, C., Waltemath, D., Zhukova, A., Drager, A., & Hastings, J. et al. (2011). Controlled vocabularies and semantics in systems biology. *Molecular Systems Biology*, *7*(1), 543. doi:10.1038/msb.2011.77 PMID:22027554

Cover, T. M., & Thomas, J. A. (1991). *Elements of information theory*. New York: Wiley. doi:10.1002/0471200611

Cox, I. J., Kilian, J., Leighton, F. T., & Shamoon, T. (1997). Secure spread spectrum watermarking for multimedia. *IEEE Transactions on Image Processing*, *6*(12), 1673–1687. doi:10.1109/83.650120 PMID:18285237

Cox, I. J., Miller, M. L., & Bloom, J. A. (2002). *Digital watermarking*. San Francisco, CA: Morgan Kaufmann Publishers Inc.

Cox, I. J., Miller, M. L., & Bloom, J. A. (2002). Watermarking applications and their properties. *Information Technology: Coding and Computing, 2000. Proceedings. International Conference on*, 6–10.

Crawford, W. (2014). Journals, 'Journals' and Wannabes: Investigating The List. *Cites & Insights, 14*(7).

Cressie, N. A. (1993). *Statistics for Spatial Data*. New York: Wiley.

Cristianini, N., & Shawe-Taylor, J. (2000). *An Introduction to Support Vector Machines*. Cambridge University Press.

Culp, M. (2011a). On propagated scoring for semisupervised additive models. *Journal of the American Statistical Association, 106*(493), 248–259. doi:10.1198/jasa.2011.tm09316

Culp, M. (2011b). spa: A semi-supervised R package for semi-parametric graph-based estimation. *Journal of Statistical Software, 40*(10), 1–29. doi:10.18637/jss.v040.i10

Culp, M. V., & Ryan, K. J. (2013). Joint harmonic functions and their supervised connections. *Journal of Machine Learning Research, 14*, 3721–3752.

Culp, M. V., Ryan, K. J., & Banerjee, P. (2016). On safe semi-supervised learning. *IEEE Pattern Analysis and Machine Intelligence.*

Culp, M., & Michailidis, G. (2008). Graph-based semisupervised learning. *IEEE Transactions on Pattern Analysis and Machine Intelligence, 30*(1), 174–179. doi:10.1109/TPAMI.2007.70765 PMID:18000333

Currin, C., Mitchell, T. J., Morris, M. D., & Ylvisaker, D. (1991). Bayesian Prediction of Deterministic Functions, with Applications to the Design and Analysis of Computer Experiments. *Journal of the American Statistical Association, 86*(416), 953–963. doi:10.1080/01621459.1991.10475138

Cyber Physical Systems. (n.d.). Retrieved from: http://cyberphysicalsystems.org/

Dalal, N., & Triggs, B. (2005). Histograms of oriented gradients for human detection.*Proc. IEEE CVPR, 1*, 886–893. doi:10.1109/CVPR.2005.177

Dankelmann, P., Goddard, W., & Swart, C. S. (2004). The average eccentricity of a graph and its subgraphs. *Utilitas Mathematica, 65*, 41–51.

Das, K. C., & Trinajstić, N. (2011) Relationship between the eccentric connectivity index and Zagreb indices. *Computers & Mathematics with Applications (Oxford, England), 62*(4), 1758–1764. doi:10.1016/j.camwa.2011.06.017

Davis, T. M., Mortsell, E., Sollerman, J., Becker, A. C., Blondin, S., Challis, P., & Zenteno, A. et al. (2007). Scrutinizing Exotic Cosmological Models Using ESSENCE Supernova Data Combined with Other Cosmological Probes. *The Astrophysical Journal, 666*(2), 716–725. doi:10.1086/519988

De, N., Nayeem, S. M. A., & Pal, A. (2014). Bounds for modified eccentric connectivity index. *Advanced Modeling and Optimization, 16*(1), 133–142.

De, N., Nayeem, S. M. A., & Pal, A. (2014). Computing modified eccentric connectivity index and connective eccentric index of V-phenylenic nanotorus. *Studia Universitatis Babes-Bolyai Chemia, 59*(4), 129–137.

De, N., Nayeem, S. M. A., & Pal, A. (2014). Connective eccentricity index of some thorny Graphs. *Annals of Pure and Applied Mathematics, 7*(1), 59–64.

De, N., Nayeem, S. M. A., & Pal, A. (2014). Modified Eccentric Connectivity of Generalized Thorn Graphs. *International Journal of Computer Mathematics, 2014*, 1–8. doi:10.1155/2014/436140

De, N., Nayeem, S. M. A., & Pal, A. (2014). Total eccentricity index of the generalized hierarchical product of graphs. *International Journal of Applied and Computational Mathematics, 1*. doi:10.1007/s40819-014-0016-4

De, N., Nayeem, S. M. A., & Pal, A. (2015). Modified eccentric connectivity index and polynomial of Corona product of graphs. *International Journal of Computers and Applications, 132*(9), 1–5. doi:10.5120/ijca2015907536

De, N., Pal, A., & Nayeem, S. M. A. (2014). On some bounds and exact formulae for connective eccentric indices of graphs under some graph operations. *International Journal of Combinatorics, 2014*, 1–5. doi:10.1155/2014/579257

De, N., Pal, A., & Nayeem, S. M. A. (2015). Total eccentricity index of some composite graphs. *Malaya Journal of Matematik, 3*(4), 523–529.

De, N. (2012). Augmented Eccentric Connectivity Index of Some Thorn Graphs. *International Journal of Applied Mathematical Research, 1*(4), 671–680. doi:10.14419/ijamr.v1i4.326

De, N. (2012). Bounds for connective eccentric index. *International Journal of Contemporary Mathematical Sciences, 7*(44), 2161–2166.

De, N. (2012). On eccentric connectivity index and polynomial of thorn graph. *Applications of Mathematics, 3,* 931–934.

Deb, K., Pratap, A., Agarwal, S., & Meyarivan, T. (2002). A fast and elitist multiobjective genetic algorithm: Nsga-ii. *IEEE Transactions on Evolutionary Computation, 6*(2), 182–197. doi:10.1109/4235.996017

Deb, K. (2001). *Multi-objective optimization using evolutionary algorithms*. John Wiley and Sons.

Decision Trees. (2015). Retrieved on 03-05-16 from www.uni-weimar.de/medien/.../unit-en-decision-trees-algorithms.pdf

Dehghan, A., Kovacevic, A., Karystianis, G., Keane, J. A., & Nenadic, G. (2015). Combining knowledge-and data-driven methods for de-identification of clinical narratives. *Journal of Biomedical Informatics, 58,* S53–S59. doi:10.1016/j.jbi.2015.06.029 PMID:26210359

Deleger, L., Molnar, K., Savova, G., Xia, F., Lingren, T., Li, Q., & Solti, I. et al. (2013). Large-scale evaluation of automated clinical note de-identification and its impact on information extraction. *Journal of the American Medical Informatics Association, 20*(1), 84–94. doi:10.1136/amiajnl-2012-001012 PMID:22859645

Dempster, A. P., Laird, N. M., & Rubin, D. B. (1977). Maximum likelihood from incomplete data via the EM algorithm. *Journal of the Royal Statistical Society. Series B. Methodological,* 1–38.

Deng, L., Li, J., Huang, J., Yao, K., Yu, D., Seide, F., & Acero, A. et al. (2013). Recent advances in deep learning for speech research at Microsoft. *IEEE International Conference on Acoustics, Speech, and Signal Processing (ICASSP),* 8604–8608. doi:10.1109/ICASSP.2013.6639345

Deng, X., Hung, Y., & Lin, C. D. (2015). Design for Computer Experiments with Qualitative and Quantitative Factors. *Statistica Sinica, 25,* 1567–1581.

Deng, X., Lin, C. D., Liu, K. W., & Rowe, R. K. (2016). Additive Gaussian Pro- cess for Computer Models with Qualitative and Quantitative Factors. *Technometrics, 0.* doi:10.1080/00401706.2016.1211554

Derler, L., & Sangiovanni-Vincentelli. (2012, January). Modeling Cyber-Physical Systems. *Proceedings of the IEEE.*

Devaney, R. L. (1989). *An introduction to chaotic dynamical systems*. London: Addison-Wesley.

Dey, N., Pal, M., & Das, A. (2012). A session based blind watermarking technique within the ROI of retinal fundus images for authentication using dwt, spread spectrum and harris corner detection. *International Journal of Modern Engineering Research, 2,* 749–757.

Dey, S., Jaiswal, D., Dasgupta, R., & Mukherjee, A. (2015). Organization and Management of Semantic Sensor Information using SSN Ontology: Energy Meter Use Case.*Proceedings of the 7th IEEE International Conference on Sensing Technology.* doi:10.1109/ICSensT.2015.7438444

Dey, S., Jaiswal, D., Pal, H. S., & Mukherjee, A. (2015). A Semantic Algorithm Repository and Workflow Designer Tool: Signal Processing Use Case. In *International Conference on IoT as a Service,IoT360 Summit, Rome.*

Dey, S., Dasgupta, R., Pal, A., & Misra, P. (2013). Semantic Web Challenge Competition ISWC. *Sensxplore: A tool for sensor discovery using semantics with focus on smart metering*. Retrieved March 31, 2016, from http://challenge. semanticweb.org/2013/submissions/swc2013_submission_8.pdf

DG INFSO & EPoSS. (2008). Internet of things in 2020: Roadmap for the future. INFSO D, 4.

Diamond, M., Scheibel, A., & Elson, L. (1985). *The Human Brain Coloring Book*. New York: Barnes and Noble Books.

Dibeklioǧglu, Gˇ okberk, & Akarun. (2009). Nasal region-based 3D face recognition under pose and expression variations. *3rd International Conference on Advances in Biometrics*, 309–318.

Dietterich, T. G., Lathrop, R. H., & Lozano-Perez, T. (1997). Solving the multiple-instance problem with axis-parallel rectangles. *Artificial Intelligence*, *89*(1-2), 31–71. doi:10.1016/S0004-3702(96)00034-3

Digital Watermarking Alliance. (2016). Retrieved from www.digitalwatermarkingalliance.org/applications.asp

Dijkstra, E. W. (1959). A note on two problems in connexion with graphs. *Numerische Mathematik*, *1*(1), 269–271. doi:10.1007/BF01386390

Djorgovski, S. G., Mahabal, A. A., Donalek, C., Graham, M. J., Drak, A. J., Moghaddam, B., & Turmon, M. (2012). *Flashes in a Star Stream: Automated Classification of Astronomical Transient Events*. Retrieved from https://arxiv.org/ftp/arxiv/papers/1209/1209.1681.pdf

Došlić, T., Saheli, M., & Vukičević, D. (2010). Eccentric connectivity index: Extremal graphs and Values. *Iranian Journal of Mathematical Chemistry*, *1*, 45–56.

Doslić, T., & Saheli, M. (2014). Eccentric connectivity index of composite graphs. *Utilitas Mathematica*, *95*, 3–22.

Drineas, P., Magdon-Ismail, M., Mahoney, M. W., & Woodruff, D. P. (2012). Fast approximation of matrix coherence and statistical leverage. *Journal of Machine Learning Research*, *13*, 3475–3506.

Drineas, P., Mahoney, M. W., & Muthukrishnan, S. 2006. Sampling algorithms for l2 regression and applications. *Proceedings of the seventeenth annual ACM-SIAM symposium on Discrete algorithm*, 1127-1136. doi:10.1145/1109557.1109682

Drineas, P., Mahoney, M. W., Muthukrishnan, S., & Sarl, S. (2011). Faster least squares approximation. *Numerische Mathematik*, *117*(2), 219–249. doi:10.1007/s00211-010-0331-6

Drira, H., Amor, B. B., Daoudi, M., & Srivastava, A. (2009). Nasal region contribution in 3D face biometrics using shape analysis framework. *3rd International Conference on Advances in Biometrics*, 357–366. doi:10.1007/978-3-642-01793-3_37

Duda, R. O., Hart, P. E., & Stork, D. G. (2001). *Pattern Classification*. Wiley doi:10.1109/NER.2009.5109299

Dufour, R. M., Miller, E. L., & Galatsanos, N. P. (2002). Template matching based object recognition with unknown geometric parameters. *IEEE Transactions on Image Processing*, *11*(12), 1385–1396. doi:10.1109/TIP.2002.806245 PMID:18249707

Dugdale, J. S. (1996). *Entropy and its physical meaning*. London: Taylor & Francis. doi:10.4324/9780203211298

DUL. (n.d.). Retrieved March 31, 2016, http://www.loa-cnr.it/ontologies/DUL.owl

Dureja, H., & Madan, A. K. (2007). Superaugmented eccentric connectivity indices: New generation highly discriminating topological descriptors for QSAR/QSPR modeling. *Medicinal Chemistry Research*, *16*(7-9), 331–341. doi:10.1007/s00044-007-9032-9

Ebeling, W., Steuer, R., & Titchener, M. R. (2001). Partition-based entropies of deterministic and stochastic maps. *Stochastics and Dynamics*, *01*(01), 45–61. doi:10.1142/S0219493701000047

Edelsbrunner, H., Letscher, D., & Zomorodian, . (2002). A. Topological persistence and Simplification. *Discrete & Computational Geometry, 28*(4), 511–533. doi:10.1007/s00454-002-2885-2

Edwards, G. J., Taylor, C. J., & Cootes, T. F. (1998). Interpreting face images using active appearance models.*Proc. IEEE International Conference on Automatic Face and Gesture Recognition*, 300–305. doi:10.1109/AFGR.1998.670965

Efron, B., & Tibshirani, R. J. (1998). *An Introduction to the Bootstrap.* Boca Raton, FL: Chapman & Hall/CRC Press.

Efron, B. (1979). Bootstrap methods: Another look at the jackknife. *Annals of Statistics, 7*(1), 1–26. doi:10.1214/aos/1176344552

Efron, B. (1983). Estimating the error rate of a prediction rule: Improvement on cross-validation. *Journal of the American Statistical Association, 78*(382), 316–331. doi:10.1080/01621459.1983.10477973

Eid, M., Liscano, R., & El Saddik, A. (2007). *A universal ontology for sensor networks data.* doi:10.1109/CIMSA.2007.4362539

Emambakhsh, M., Evans, A. N., & Smith, M. (2013). Using nasal curves matching for expression robust 3D nose recognition.*6th IEEE International Conference on Biometrics: Theory, Applications and Systems (BTAS)*, 1–6. doi:10.1109/BTAS.2013.6712732

EPA. (n.d.). *Sources of Greenhouse Gas Emissions.* Retrieved from https://www3.epa.gov/climatechange/ghgemissions/sources.html

Everitt, B., & Hothorn, T. (2011). *An Introduction to Applied Multivariate Analysis with R.* Springer Science & Business Media. doi:10.1007/978-1-4419-9650-3

Facebook users worldwide. (2016, April 15). Retrieved from http://www.statista.com/statistics/264810/number-of-monthly-active-facebook-users-worldwide/

Factor, E. (n.d.). Retrieved from: www.Eigenfactor.com

Fallahpour, M., Shirmohammadi, S., Semsarzadeh, M., & Zhao, J. (2014). Tampering detection in compressed digital video using watermarking. *IEEE Transactions on Instrumentation and Measurement, 63*(5), 1057–1072. doi:10.1109/TIM.2014.2299371

Fang, K. T., Li, R., & Sudjianto, A. (2006). *Design and Modeling for Computer Experiments.* New York: CRC Press.

Faraway, J. (2016). *Faraway: Functions and Datasets for Books by Julian Faraway.* Retrieved from https://CRAN.R-project.org/package=faraway

Fathalikhani, K., Faramarzi, H., & Yousefi-Azari, H. (2014). Total eccentricity of some graph operations. *Electronic Notes in Discrete Mathematics, 45*, 125–131. doi:10.1016/j.endm.2013.11.025

Feng, X. C., & Yang, Y. (2005). A new watermarking method based on DWT. *Proc. Int'l Conf. on Computational Intelligence and Security, Lect. Notes in Comp. Sci. (LNCS), 3802*, 1122–1126. doi:10.1007/11596981_168

Fingelkurts, A., Fingelkurts, A., & Kähkönen, S. (2005). Functional connectivity in the brain – is it an elusive concept? *Neuroscience and Biobehavioral Reviews, 28*(8), 827–836. doi:10.1016/j.neubiorev.2004.10.009 PMID:15642624

Fisher, R. A. (1950). *Statistical Methods for Research Workers* (11th ed.). London: Oliver and Boyd.

Forman, S. D., Cohen, J. D., Fitzgerald, M., Eddy, W. F., Mintun, M. A., & Noll, D. C. (1995). Improved assessment of significant change in functional magnetic resonance imaging (fMRI): Use of a cluster size threshold. *Magnetic Resonance in Medicine, 33*(5), 636–647. doi:10.1002/mrm.1910330508 PMID:7596267

Fortunato, S. (2010). Community detection in graphs. *Physics Reports*, *486*(3), 75–174. doi:10.1016/j.physrep.2009.11.002

Fox, M. D., & Raichle, M. E. (2007). Spontaneous fluctuations in brain activity observed with functional magnetic resonance imaging. *Nature Reviews. Neuroscience*, *8*(9), 700–711. doi:10.1038/nrn2201 PMID:17704812

Freund, Y., & Schapire, R. E. (1997). A decision-theoretic generalization of on-line learning and an application to boosting. *Journal of Computer and System Sciences*, *55*(1), 119–139. doi:10.1006/jcss.1997.1504

Fridrich, J., Goljan, M., & Baldoza, A. C. (2000). New fragile authentication watermark for images.*Proc. IEEE ICIP*, *1*, 446 –449.

Friedman, C., Shagina, L., Socratous, S. A., & Zeng, X. (1996). A WEB-based version of MedLEE: A medical language extraction and encoding system. In *Proceedings of the AMIA Annual Fall Symposium* (p. 938). American Medical Informatics Association.

Friston, K. J. (2011). Functional and effective connectivity: A review. *Brain Connectivity*, *1*(1), 13–36. doi:10.1089/brain.2011.0008 PMID:22432952

Friston, K. (2005). A Theory of cortical responses. *Phil. Trans. R. Soc. B.*, *360*(1456), 815–836. doi:10.1098/rstb.2005.1622 PMID:15937014

Friston, K. (2010). The free-energy principle: A unified brain theory? *Nature Reviews. Neuroscience*, *11*(2), 127–138. doi:10.1038/nrn2787 PMID:20068583

Fulton, W. (1995). *Algebraic Topology: A First Course. Graduate Texts in Mathematics*. New York: Springer. doi:10.1007/978-1-4612-4180-5

Fung, G., Dundar, M., Krishnapuram, B., & Rao, R. B. (2007). Multiple instance learning for computer aided diagnosis. Advances in Neural Information Processing Systems.

Gai, K., & Li, S. 2012. Towards cloud computing: a literature review on cloud computing and its development trends. *2012 Fourth International Conference on Multimedia Information Networking and Security*, 142-146. doi:10.1109/MINES.2012.240

Genovese, C. R., Freeman, P., Wasserman, L., Nichol, R. C., & Miller, C. (2009). Inference for the Dark Energy equation of state using Type Ia Supernova data. *The Annals of Applied Statistics*, *3*(1), 144–178. doi:10.1214/08-AOAS229

Genovese, C. R., Lazar, N. A., & Nichols, T. E. (2002). Thresholding of statistical maps in functional neuroimaging using the false discovery rate. *NeuroImage*, *15*(4), 870–878. doi:10.1006/nimg.2001.1037 PMID:11906227

Ghorbani, M., & Hemmasi, M. (2009). Eccentric connectivity polynomial of C_{12n+4} fullerenes. *Digest Journal of Nanomaterials and Biostructures*, *4*, 545–547.

Ghorbani, M., & Malekjani, K. (2012). A new method for computing the eccentric connectivity index of fullerenes. *Serdica Journal of Computing*, *6*, 299–308.

Ghorbani, M. (2011). Connective Eccentric Index of Fullerenes. *Journal of Mathematical Nanoscience*, *1*, 43–52.

Ginde, G., Saha, S., Mathur, A., & Sagar, B. S. D. (2016, May). ScientoBASE: A Framework and Model for Computing Scholastic Indicators of non-local influence of Journals via Native Data Acquisition algorithms. *Scientometrics*, *108*(3), 1479–1529. doi:10.1007/s11192-016-2006-2

Gittens, A., & Mahoney, M. W. (2013). Revisiting the Nystrom method for improved large-scale machine learning. *ICML*, *28*(3), 567–575.

Goeuriot, L., Jones, G.J., Kelly, L., Leveling, J., Hanbury, A., Müller, H., Salantera, S., Suominen, H. and Zuccon, G. (2013). ShARe/CLEF eHealth Evaluation Lab 2013, Task 3: Information retrieval to address patients' questions when reading clinical reports. *CLEF 2013 Online Working Notes, 8138.*

Goldberger, A. L., Amaral, L. A., Glass, L., Hausdorff, J. M., Ivanov, P. C., Mark, R. G., & Stanley, H. E. et al. (2000). PhysioBank, PhysioToolkit, and PhysioNet: Components of a New Research Resource for Complex Physiologic Signals. *Circulation, 101*(23), e215–e220. doi:10.1161/01.CIR.101.23.e215 PMID:10851218

Goldberger, A. L. (1991). Is the normal heartbeat chaotic or homeostatic? *News in Physiological Sciences, 6*(2), 87–91. PMID:11537649

Goldberger, A. (1996). Non-linear dynamics for clinicians: Chaos theory, fractals, and complexity at the bedside. *Lancet, 347*(9011), 1312–1314. doi:10.1016/S0140-6736(96)90948-4 PMID:8622511

Goldstein, B., Deking, D., Delong, D. J., Kempski, M. H., Cox, C., Kelly, M. M., & Woolf, P. D. et al. (1993). Autonomic cardiovascular state after severe brain injury and brain death in children. *Critical Care Medicine, 21*(2), 228–333. doi:10.1097/00003246-199302000-00014 PMID:8428474

Golub, G. H., & Van Loan, C. F. (2012). *Matrix computations.* JHU Press.

Gomez-Pilar, J., Gutiérrez-Tobal, G. C., Álvarez, D., Del Campo, F., & Hornero, R. (2014). Classification Methods from Heart Rate Variability to Assist in SAHS Diagnosis. *IFMBE Proceedings, 1825-1828.* doi:10.1007/978-3-319-00846-2_450

Gorman, S. (2009). *Electricity grid in the U.S. penetrated by spies.* Retrieved from http://www.wsj.com/articles/SB123914805204099085

Greenberg, A. (2015). Hackers Remotely Kill a Jeep on the Highway – With Me in It. *Wired.* Retrieved from: https://www.wired.com/2015/07/hackers-remotely-kill-jeep-highway/

Gross, N. (1999). *21st Century Internet, Bloomberg Business Week.* Retrieved March 31, 2016, from http://www.businessweek.com/1999/99_35/b3644024.htm

Grossberg, S. (2003). *How Does The Cerebral Cortex Work? Development, Learning, Attention and 3D Vision by Laminar Circuits of Visual Cortex.* Technical Report TR-2003-005, Boston University, CAS/CS.

Grossberg, S., & Seitz, A. (2003). *Laminar Development of Receptive Fields, Maps, and Columns in Visual Cortex: The Coordinating Role of the Subplate.* Technical Report 02-006, Boston University, CAS/CS.

Gupta, S., Singh, M., & Madan, A. K. (2000). Connective eccentricity Index: A novel topological descriptor for predicting biological activity. *Journal of Molecular Graphics & Modelling, 18*(1), 18–25. doi:10.1016/S1093-3263(00)00027-9 PMID:10935202

Gütig, R. (2014). To spike, or when to spike? *Current Opinion in Neurobiology, 25,* 134–139. doi:10.1016/j.conb.2014.01.004 PMID:24468508

Gutman, I. (1998). Distance in thorny graph. *Publ. Inst. Math. (Beograd), 63,* 31–36.

Haering, N., Venetianer, P. L., & Lipton, A. (2008). The evolution of video surveillance: An overview. *Machine Vision and Applications, 19*(5-6), 279–290. doi:10.1007/s00138-008-0152-0

Han, G., Santner, T. J., Notz, W. I., & Bartel, D. L. (2009). Prediction for Computer Experiments Having Quantitative and Qualitative Input Variables. *Technometrics, 51*(3), 278–288. doi:10.1198/tech.2009.07132

Haque, S. A., Aziz, S. M., & Rahman, M. (2014, April). Review of Cyber-Physical System in Healthcare. *International Journal of Distributed Sensor Networks, 10*(4), 217415. doi:10.1155/2014/217415

Hara, K. (2006, November). Applying a SVM based Chunker and a text classifier to the deid challenge. In *i2b2 Workshop on challenges in natural language processing for clinical data* (pp. 10-11).

Harary, F. (1969). *Graph Theory*. Addison-Wesely.

Harris, C., & Stephens, M. (1988). A combined corner and edge detector. *Proc. of Fourth Alvey Vision Conference*, 147–151.

Hartung, F., & Girod, B. (1998). Watermarking of uncompressed and compressed video. *Signal Processing*, *66*(3), 283–301. doi:10.1016/S0165-1684(98)00011-5

Hashemi, R. H., Bradley, W. G., & Lisanti, C. J. (2004). *MRI: The Basics* (2nd ed.). Philadelphia, PA: Lippincott Williams & Wilkins.

Hastie, T., Tibshirani, R., & Friedman, J. (Eds.). (2009). The Elements of Statistical Learning (Data Mining, Inference and Prediction, Second Edition). Springer.

He, B., Guan, Y., Cheng, J., Cen, K., & Hua, W. (2015). CRFs based de-identification of medical records. *Journal of Biomedical Informatics*, 58. PMID:26315662

Health Insurance Portability and Accountability Act. P.L. 104e191, 42 U.S.C. 1996.

Heckman, G. (1995). *Harmonic Analysis and Special Functions on Symmetric Spaces*. Academic Press.

Hedayat, A. S., Sloane, N. J. A., & Stufken, J. (1999). *Orthogonal Arrays: Theory and Applications*. New York: Springer. doi:10.1007/978-1-4612-1478-6

Hein, M., Audibert, J., & von Luxburg, U. (2005). From graphs to manifolds–weak and strong point- wise consistency of graph Laplacians. In *Proceedings of the 18th Annual Conference on Learning Theory*, (pp. 470–485). New York, NY: Springer. doi:10.1007/11503415_32

Helwig, N. E., & Ma, P. (2016). *Smoothing spline ANOVA for super-large samples: scalable computation via rounding parameters*. arXiv preprint arXiv:1602.05208

Herrold, C., Palomero-Gallagher, N., Hellman, B., Kröner, S., Theiss, C., Güntürkün, O., & Zilles, K. (2011). The receptor architecture of the pigeons nidopalladium caudolaterale: And avian analague to the mammalian prefrontal cortex. *Brain Structure & Function*, *216*(3), 239–254. doi:10.1007/s00429-011-0301-5 PMID:21293877

He, Y., Lin, C. D., & Sun, F. (2016). On Construction of Marginally Coupled De- signs. *Statistica Sinica*.

Heydari, A., & Gutman, I. (2010). On the terminal Wiener index of thorn graphs. *Kragujevac Journal of Mathematics*, *32*, 57–64.

Higdon, D., Gattiker, J., Williams, B., & Rightley, M. (2008). Computer Model Calibration Using High-Dimensional Output. *Journal of the American Statistical Association*, *103*(482), 570–583. doi:10.1198/016214507000000888

Hirschman, L., Yeh, A., Blaschke, C., & Valencia, A. (2005). Overview of BioCreAtIvE: Critical assessment of information extraction for biology. *BMC Bioinformatics*, *6*(Suppl 1), S1. doi:10.1186/1471-2105-6-S1-S1 PMID:15960821

Horn, B. K. P., & Schunck, B. G. (1981). Determining optical flow. *Artificial Intelligence*, *17*(1-3), 185–203. doi:10.1016/0004-3702(81)90024-2

Hornero, R., Aboy, M., Abasolo, D., McNames, J., & Goldstein, B. (2005). Interpretation of Approximate Entropy: Analysis of Intracranial Pressure Approximate Entropy During Acute Intracranial Hypertension. *IEEE Transactions on Bio-Medical Engineering*, *52*(10), 1671–1680. doi:10.1109/TBME.2005.855722 PMID:16235653

Hornero, R., Aboy, M., Abasolo, D., McNames, J., Wakeland, W., & Goldstein, B. (2006). Complex analysis of intracranial hypertension using approximate entropy. *Critical Care Medicine*, *34*(1), 87–95. doi:10.1097/01.CCM.0000190426.44782. F0 PMID:16374161

Hornero, R., Aboy, M., & Abásolo, D. (2007). Analysis of intracranial pressure during acute intracranial hypertension using Lempel–Ziv complexity: Further evidence. *Medical & Biological Engineering & Computing*, *45*(6), 617–620. doi:10.1007/s11517-007-0194-x PMID:17541667

Horton, J., & Adams, D. (2005). The cortical column: A structure without a function. *Phil. Trans. Royal Society B*, *360*(1456), 837–862. doi:10.1098/rstb.2005.1623 PMID:15937015

Hosmer, D. W. Jr. (1973). A comparison of iterative maximum likelihood estimates of the parameters of a mixture of two normal distributions under three different types of sample. *Biometrics*, *29*(4), 761–770. doi:10.2307/2529141

Hsu, C. W., & Lin, C. J. (2002). 'A comparison of methods for multiclass support vector machines'. *Neural Networks. IEEE Transactions on*, *13*(2), 415–425.

Hsu, Chang, & Lin. (2000). *A practical guide to support vector classification*. Academic Press.

Hu, J., Gao, J., & Principe, J. (2006). Analysis of Biomedical Signals by the Lempel-Ziv Complexity: The Effect of Finite Data Size. *IEEE Transactions on Bio-Medical Engineering*, *53*(12), 2606–2609. doi:10.1109/TBME.2006.883825 PMID:17152441

Huang, F., Niranjan, U. N., Hakeem, M. U., & Anandkumar, A. (2013). *Fast detection of overlapping communities via online tensor methods*. arXiv preprint arXiv:1309.0787

Huettel, S. A., Song, A. W., & McCarthy, G. (2004). *Functional Magnetic Resonance Imaging*. Sunderland, MA: Sinauer.

Hui, P., Crowcroft, J., & Yoneki, E. (2011). Bubble rap: Social-based forwarding in delay-tolerant networks. *IEEE Transactions on Mobile Computing*, *10*(11), 1576–1589. doi:10.1109/TMC.2010.246

Humeau-Heurtier, A. (2015). The Multiscale Entropy Algorithm and Its Variants: A Review. *Entropy*, *17*(5), 3110–3123. doi:10.3390/e17053110

Hung, Y. (2011). Adaptive Probability-Based Latin Hypercube Designs. *Journal of the American Statistical Association*, *106*(493), 213–219. doi:10.1198/jasa.2011.tm10337

Hung, Y. (2011b). Penalized Blind Kriging in Computer Experiments. *Statistica Sinica*, *21*(3), 1171–1190. doi:10.5705/ss.2009.226

Hung, Y., Amemiya, Y., & Wu, C. F. J. (2010). Probability-Based Latin Hypercube Design. *Biometrika*, *97*(4), 961–968. doi:10.1093/biomet/asq051

Huo, F., & Gao, X. (2006). A wavelet based image watermarking scheme. *Proc. IEEE ICIP*, 2573–2576.

Husz, Z. L., Wallace, A. M., & Green, P. R. (2011). Tracking with a hierarchical partitioned particle filter and movement modelling. *IEEE Transactions on Systems, Man, and Cybernetics. Part B, Cybernetics*, *41*(6), 1571–1584. doi:10.1109/TSMCB.2011.2157680 PMID:21724518

Ibáñez-Molina, A. J., Iglesias-Parro, S., Soriano, M. F., & Aznarte, J. I. (2015). Multiscale Lempel–Ziv complexity for EEG measures. *Clinical Neurophysiology*, *126*(3), 541–548. doi:10.1016/j.clinph.2014.07.012 PMID:25127707

IBM Bluemix is the cloud platform that helps developers rapidly build, manage and run web and mobile applications. (n.d.). Retrieved March 31, 2016, from www.ibm.com/software/bluemix/welcome/solutions2.html

Iman, R. L., & Conover, W. J. (1982). A Distribution-Free Approach to Inducing Rank Correlation Among Input Variables. *Communications in Statistics Part B-Simulation and Computation, 11*(3), 311–334. doi:10.1080/03610918208812265

Ishida, E. E. O. (2012). Kernel PCA for Supernovae Photometric Classification. *Proceedings of the International Astronomical Union, 10*(H16), 683–684. doi:10.1017/S1743921314012897

Jain, A. K., Ross, A., & Pankanti, S. (2006). Biometrics: A tool for information security. *IEEE Transactions on Information Forensics and Security, 1*(2), 125–143. doi:10.1109/TIFS.2006.873653

Jain, A. N., Ross, A., & Prabhakar, S. (2004). An introduction to biometric recognition. *IEEE Transactions on Circuits and Systems for Video Technology, 14*(1), 4–20. doi:10.1109/TCSVT.2003.818349

Jangid, Saha, Gupta, & J. (2014). Ranking of Journals in Science and Technology Domain: A Novel And Computationally Lightweight Approach. *IERI Procedia, 10,* 5762. doi:10.1016/j.ieri.2014.09.091

Jangid, Saha, Narasimhamurthy, & Mathur. (2015). *Computing the Prestige of a journal: A Revised Multiple Linear Regression Approach.* WCI-ACM Digital library.

Janowicz, K., & Compton, M. (2010, November). The stimulus-sensor-observation ontology design pattern and its integration into the semantic sensor network ontology. In *Proceedings of the 3rd International Conference on Semantic Sensor Networks* (vol. 668, pp. 64-78). CEUR-WS. org.

Jiang, H. J., Deng, X., Lopez, V., & Hamann, H. (2015). Online Updating of Computer Model Output Using Real-time Sensor Data. *Technometrics*.

Ji, J., Shao, F., Sun, R., Zhang, N., & Liu, G. (2008). A TSVM based semi-supervised approach to SAR image segmentation. *IEEE International Workshop on Education Technology and Training and International Workshop on Geoscience and Remote Sensing, 1,* 495–498. doi:10.1109/ETTandGRS.2008.13

Jiménez-Montaño, M. A. (1984). On the syntactic structure of protein sequences and the concept of grammar complexity. *Bulletin of Mathematical Biology, 46*(4), 641–659. doi:10.1007/BF02459508

Jin, R., Chen, W., & Simpson, T. (2001). Comparative Studies of Metamodeling Techniques under Multiple Modeling Criteria. *Journal of Structural and Multidisciplinary Optimization, 23,* 1–13.

Jin, R., Chen, W., & Sudjianto, A. (2005). An Efficient Algorithm for Construct- ing Optimal Design of Computer Experiments. *Journal of Statistical Planning and Inference, 134*(1), 268–287. doi:10.1016/j.jspi.2004.02.014

Joachims, T. (1999). *Transductive inference for text classification using support vector machines* (Vol. 99). ICML.

Johnson, C. R. (1970). Positive definite matrices. *The American Mathematical Monthly, 77*(3), 259–264. doi:10.2307/2317709

Johnson, M., Moore, L., & Ylvisaker, D. (1990). Minimax and Maximin Distance Design. *Journal of Statistical Planning and Inference, 26*(2), 131–148. doi:10.1016/0378-3758(90)90122-B

Joseph, V. R. (2006). Limit Kriging. *Technometrics, 48*(4), 458–466. doi:10.1198/004017006000000011

Joseph, V. R. (2016). Space-Filling Designs for Computer Experiments: A Review, (with discussions and rejoinder). *Quality Engineering, 28*(1), 28–44. doi:10.1080/08982112.2015.1100447

Joseph, V. R., & Delaney, J. D. (2007). Functionally Induced Priors for the Analysis of Experiments. *Technometrics, 49*(1), 1–11. doi:10.1198/004017006000000372

Joseph, V. R., Gul, E., & Ba, S. (2015). Maximum Projection Designs for Computer Experiments. *Biometrika, 102*(2), 371–380. doi:10.1093/biomet/asv002

Joseph, V. R., & Hung, Y. (2008). Orthogonal-Maximin Latin Hypercube Designs. *Statistica Sinica, 18*, 171–186.

Joseph, V. R., Hung, Y., & Sudjianto, A. (2008). Blind Kriging: A New Method for Developing Metamodels. *ASME Journal of Mechanical Design, 130*(3), 031102-1–8. doi:10.1115/1.2829873

Jovanov, Milenkovic, Otto, & de Groen. (2005). A wireless body area network of intelligent motion sensors for computer assisted physical rehabilitation. *Journal of NeuroEngineering and Rehabilitation, 2*(6).

Kaczynski, T., Mischaikow, K., & Mrozek, M. (2004). *Computational Homology*. Springer. doi:10.1007/b97315

Kang, Cohen, & Medioni. (2004). Object reacquisition using invariant appearance model. *Proc. of International Conference on Pattern Recognition (ICPR), 4*, 759–762.

Kao, M.-H., Mandal, A., Lazar, N., & Stufken, J. (2009). Multi-objective optimal experimental design for event-related fMRI studies. *NeuroImage, 44*(3), 849–856. doi:10.1016/j.neuroimage.2008.09.025 PMID:18948212

Karlen, M., Weston, J., Erkan, A., & Collobert, R. (2008). Large scale manifold transduction. In *Proceedings of the 25th International Conference on Machine Learning*, (pp. 448–455). ACM.

Karnouskos. (2011). *Cyber-Physical Systems in the Smart Grid*. 9th IEEE International Conference on Industrial Informatics, Lisbon, Portugal.

Karpenka, N. V., Feroz, F., & Hobson, M. P. (2013). *A simple and robust method for automated photometric classification of supernovae using neural networks*. MNRAS429,1278–1285. Retrieved from http://arxiv.org/find/astro-ph/1/au:+Souza_R/0/1/0/all/0/1

Kennedy, M. C., & OHagan, A. (2000). Predicting the Output from a Complex Computer Code when Fast Approximations are Available. *Biometrika, 87*(1), 1–13. doi:10.1093/biomet/87.1.1

Kim, J. D., Ohta, T., Pyysalo, S., Kano, Y., & Tsujii, J. I. (2009, June). Overview of BioNLP'09 shared task on event extraction. In *Proceedings of the Workshop on Current Trends in Biomedical Natural Language Processing: Shared Task* (pp. 1-9). Association for Computational Linguistics. doi:10.3115/1572340.1572342

Kim, J. R., & Moon, Y. S. (1999). A robust wavelet-based digital watermarking using level-adaptive thresholding.*Proc. IEEE ICIP, 2*, 226–230.

Kim, Lee, Moon, Cho, Lim, Kwon, & Lee. (2004). A new digital video watermarking using the dual watermark images and 3D DWT. TENCON 2004. IEEE Region 10 Conference, 291–294.

Kleinberg, J. M. (1999). Authoritative sources in a hyperlinked environment. *Journal of the ACM, 46*(5), 604–632. doi:10.1145/324133.324140

Korn, H., & Faure, P. (2003). Is there chaos in the brain? II. Experimental evidence and related models. *Comptes Rendus Biologies, 326*(9), 787–840. doi:10.1016/j.crvi.2003.09.011 PMID:14694754

Kotsiantis, S. B., Zaharakis, I. D., & Pintelas, P. E. (2007). *Supervised machine learning: A review of classification techniques. Frontiers in Artificial Intelligence and Applications, Emerging Artificial Intelligence Applications in Computer Engineering: Real Word AI Systems with Applications in EHealth, HCI, Information Retrieval and Pervasive Technologies* (Vol. 160). IOS Press.

Koumaras, H. G. (2008). *Subjective video quality assessment methods for multimedia applications*. Technical Report ITU-R BT.500-11, Geneva, Switzerland.

Kox, M., Vrouwenvelder, M. Q., Pompe, J. C., Van der Hoeven, J. G., Pickkers, P., & Hoedemaekers, C. W. (2012). The Effects of Brain Injury on Heart Rate Variability and the Innate Immune Response in Critically Ill Patients. *Journal of Neurotrauma*, *29*(5), 747–755. doi:10.1089/neu.2011.2035 PMID:22111862

Koz, A., & Alatan, A. A. (2008). Oblivious spatio-temporal watermarking of digital video by exploiting the human visual system. *IEEE Transactions on Circuits and Systems for Video Technology*, *18*(3), 326–337. doi:10.1109/TCSVT.2008.918446

Kozuch, M., & Wang, L. (2001). *Approximate entropy as a measure of irregularity in earthquake sequences*. Paper presented at AGU Fall Meeting.

Krishnapuram, B., Raykar, V. C., Dundar, M., & Bharat Rao, R. (2009). *System and method for multiple-instance learning for computer aided diagnosis*. US Patent No. US20090080731 A1.

Kristoufek, L., & Vosvrda, M. (2014). Measuring capital market efficiency: Long-term memory, fractal dimension and approximate entropy. *The European Physical Journal B*, *87*(7), 162. doi:10.1140/epjb/e2014-50113-6

Kundur, D., & Hatzinakos, D. (2004). Toward robust logo watermarking using multiresolution image fusion principles. *IEEE Transactions on Multimedia*, *6*(1), 185–198. doi:10.1109/TMM.2003.819747

Kung, S. Y., Mak, M. W., & Lin, S. H. (2005). *Biometric Authentication: A Machine Learning Approach*. Prentice Hall Professional Technical Reference.

Kuzmin, K., Shah, S. Y., & Szymanski, B. K. (2013, September). Parallel overlapping community detection with SLPA. In *Social Computing (SocialCom), 2013 International Conference on* (pp. 204-212). IEEE. doi:10.1109/SocialCom.2013.37

Kwon, O., & Lee, C. (2001). Objective method for assessment of video quality using wavelets.*Proc. IEEE Int'l Symp. on Industrial Electronics (ISIE 2001)*, *1*, 292–295.

Lafferty, J., McCallum, A., & Pereira, F. C. (2001). *Conditional random fields: Probabilistic models for segmenting and labeling sequence data*. Academic Press.

Lafferty, J., & Wasserman, L. (2008). *Statistical analysis of semi-supervised regression*. In J. C. Platt, D. Koller, Y. Singer, & S. T. Roweis (Eds.), Advances in Neural Information Processing Systems (Vol. 20, pp. 801–808). Curran Associates, Inc.

Lafon, S., & Lee, A. (2006). Diffusion Maps and Coarse-Graining: A Unifed Framework for Dimensionality Reduction, Graph Partitioning, and Data Set Parameterization. *IEEE Transactions on Pattern Analysis and Machine Intelligence*, *28*(9), 1393–1403. doi:10.1109/TPAMI.2006.184 PMID:16929727

Lake, D. E., Richman, J. S., Griffin, M. P., & Moorman, J. R. (2002). Sample entropy analysis of neonatal heart rate variability. *American Journal of Physiology. Regulatory, Integrative and Comparative Physiology*, *283*(3), R789–R797. doi:10.1152/ajpregu.00069.2002 PMID:12185014

Lao, Z., Shen, D., Xue, Z., Karacali, B., Resnick, S. M., & Davatzikos, C. (2004). Morphological classification of brains via high-dimensional shape transformations and machine learning methods. *NeuroImage*, *21*(1), 46–57. doi:10.1016/j.neuroimage.2003.09.027 PMID:14741641

Larsen, E. A. (2011). *Classification of EEG Signals in a Brain-Computer Interface System* (Unpublished masters' dissertation). Norwegian University of Science and Technology (NTNU).

LaSalle, D., & Karypis, G. (2013, May). Multi-threaded graph partitioning. In *Parallel & Distributed Processing (IPDPS), 2013 IEEE 27th International Symposium on* (pp. 225-236). IEEE. doi:10.1109/IPDPS.2013.50

Laslett, G. M. (1994). Kriging and Splines: An Empirical Comparison of Their Pre- dictive Performance in Some Applications. *Journal of the American Statistical Association*, *89*(426), 391–400. doi:10.1080/01621459.1994.10476759

Laws, K. (1980). *Textured image segmentation* (PhD Thesis). Electrical Engineering, University of Southern California.

Lazar, N. A., Luna, B., Sweeney, J. A., & Eddy, W. F. (2002). Combining brains: A survey of methods for statistical pooling of information. *NeuroImage, 16*(2), 538–550. doi:10.1006/nimg.2002.1107 PMID:12030836

Le Martelot, E., & Hankin, C. (2013). Fast multi-scale detection of relevant communities in large-scale networks. *The Computer Journal.*

Lee, E., & Sheshia, S. (2011). Introduction to Embedded Systems: A Cyber-Physical Systems Approach. LeeSeshia.org

Lempel, A., & Ziv, J. (1976). On the Complexity of Finite Sequences. *IEEE Transactions on Information Theory, 22*(1), 75–81. doi:10.1109/TIT.1976.1055501

Leskovec, J., Lang, K. J., & Mahoney, M. (2010, April). Empirical comparison of algorithms for network community detection. In *Proceedings of the 19th international conference on World wide web* (pp. 631-640). ACM. doi:10.1145/1772690.1772755

Levy & Stager. (2012). *Digital watermarking applications.* US Patent App. 13/590,940.

Li, S. (2011). Zagreb polynomials of thorn graphs. *Kragujevac Journal of Science, 33*, 33–38.

Li, T., & Yorke, J. A. (1975). Period Three Implies Chaos. *The American Mathematical Monthly, 82*(10), 985. doi:10.2307/2318254

Li, X., Xie, Z., & Yi, D. (2012). A Fast Algorithm for Constructing Topological Structure in Large Data. Homology. *Homotopy and Applications, 1*(14), 221–238. doi:10.4310/HHA.2012.v14.n1.a11

Lichman, M. (2013). *UCI machine learning repository.* Retrieved from http://archive.ics.uci.edu/ml

Li, J., Jiang, H., & Wong, W. H. (2010). Modeling non-uniformity in short-read rates in RNA-Seq data. *Genome Biology, 11*(5), 1–11. doi:10.1186/gb-2010-11-5-r50 PMID:20459815

Limprasert, W., Wallace, A., & Michaelson, G. (2013). Real-time people tracking in a camera network. *IEEE Journal on Emerging and Selected Topics in Circuits and Systems, 3*(2), 263–271. doi:10.1109/JETCAS.2013.2256820

Lin, C. Y., & Chang, S. F. (2000). Semifragile watermarking for authenticating JPEG visual content. *Proc. SPIE Security, Steganography, and Watermarking of Multimedia Contents, 3971*, 140–151.

Linkletter, C. D., Bingham, D., Hengartner, N., Higdon, D., & Ye, K. Q. (2006). Vari- able Selection for Gaussian Process Models in Computer Experiments. *Technometrics, 48*(4), 478–490. doi:10.1198/004017006000000228

Lin, N., & Xi, R. (2011). Aggregated estimating equation estimation. *Statistics and Its Interface, 4*(1), 73–83. doi:10.4310/SII.2011.v4.n1.a8

Li, R., Lin, D. K., & Li, B. (2013). Statistical inference in massive data sets. *Applied Stochastic Models in Business and Industry, 29*, 399–409.

Li, R., & Sudjianto, A. (2005). Analysis of Computer Experiments Using Penalized Likelihood in Gaussian Kriging Models. *Technometrics, 47*(2), 111–120. doi:10.1198/004017004000000671

Liu, H., Lussier, Y. A., & Friedman, C. (2001). Disambiguating ambiguous biomedical terms in biomedical narrative text: An unsupervised method. *Journal of Biomedical Informatics, 34*(4), 249–261. doi:10.1006/jbin.2001.1023 PMID:11977807

Liu, Z., Chen, Y., Tang, B., Wang, X., Chen, Q., Li, H., & Zhu, S. et al. (2015). Automatic de-identification of electronic medical records using token-level and character-level conditional random fields. *Journal of Biomedical Informatics, 58.* PMID:26122526

Liu, Y., & Zheng, Y. F. (2005, August). One-against-all multi-class SVM classification using reliability measures. In *Neural Networks, 2005. IJCNN'05. Proceedings. 2005 IEEE International Joint Conference on* (Vol. 2, pp. 849-854). IEEE.

Liu, K.-W., & Rowe, R. K. (2015). Numerical Study of the Effects of Geosynthetic Reinforcement Viscosity on Behaviour of Embankments Supported by Deep-mixing- method (DMM) Columns. *Geotextiles and Geomembranes, 43*(6), 567–578. doi:10.1016/j.geotexmem.2015.04.020

Liu, W., He, J., & Chang, S. (2010). Large graph construction for scalable semi-supervised learning. *Proceedings of the 27th International Conference on Machine Learning*, 679– 687.

Li, Y. F., Kwok, J. T., & Zhou, Z. H. (2010). Cost-sensitive semi-supervised support vector machine. *Proceedings of the National Conference on Artificial Intelligence, 1*, 500.

Lloyd, S., & Pagels, H. (1988). Complexity as thermodynamic depth. *Annals of Physics, 188*(1), 186–213. doi:10.1016/0003-4916(88)90094-2

Lloyd, S. (2001). Measures of complexity: A nonexhaustive list. *IEEE Control Systems Magazine, 21*(4), 7–8. doi:10.1109/MCS.2001.939938

Loeppky, J. L., Sacks, J., & Welch, W. J. (2009). Choosing the Sample Size of a Computer Experiment: A Practical Guide. *Technometrics, 51*(4), 366–376. doi:10.1198/TECH.2009.08040

Lowe, D. G. (2004). Distinctive image features from scale-invariant keypoints. *International Journal of Computer Vision, 60*(2), 91–110. doi:10.1023/B:VISI.0000029664.99615.94

Lu, T., Zhao, J., Zhao, L., Li, Y., & Zhang, X. (2015). Towards a Framework for Assuring Cyber Physical System Security. *International Journal of Security and Its Applications, 9*(3), 25–40. doi:10.14257/ijsia.2015.9.3.04

Lu, H., Halappanavar, M., & Kalyanaraman, A. (2015). Parallel heuristics for scalable community detection. *Parallel Computing, 47*, 19–37. doi:10.1016/j.parco.2015.03.003

Luo, Z., & Wu, J. (2014). Zagreb eccentricity indices of the generalized hierarchical product graphs and their applications. *Journal of Applied Mathematics, 2014*, 1–8. doi:10.1155/2014/241712

Machado, R. G., & Venkatasubramanian, K. (2013). Short Paper: Establishing Trust in a Vehicular Network. *IEEE Vehicular Networking Conference*. doi:10.1109/VNC.2013.6737611

MacKay, D. J. (2003). *Information theory, inference, and learning algorithms*. Cambridge, UK: Cambridge University Press.

Mahoney, M. W. (2011). Randomized algorithms for matrices and data. *Foundations and Trends® in Machine Learning, 3*, 123-224.

Mahoney, M. W., & Drineas, P. (2009). CUR matrix decompositions for improved data analysis. *Proceedings of the National Academy of Sciences of the United States of America, 106*(3), 697–702. doi:10.1073/pnas.0803205106 PMID:19139392

Maia, T., & Frank, M. (2011). From reinforcement learning models to psychiatric and neurological disorders. *Nature Neuroscience, 14*(2), 154–162. doi:10.1038/nn.2723 PMID:21270784

Mallat, S. G. (1989). A theory for multiresolution signal decomposition: The wavelet representation. *IEEE Transactions on Pattern Analysis and Machine Intelligence, 11*(7), 674–693. doi:10.1109/34.192463

Malliaros, F. D., & Vazirgiannis, M. (2013). Clustering and community detection in directed networks: A survey. *Physics Reports, 533*(4), 95–142. doi:10.1016/j.physrep.2013.08.002

Mandelbrot, B. (1967). How Long Is the Coast of Britain? Statistical Self-Similarity and Fractional Dimension. *Science, 156*(3775), 636–638. doi:10.1126/science.156.3775.636 PMID:17837158

Manning, C. D., Raghavan, P., & Schütze, H. (2008). *Introduction to Information Retrieval.* Cambridge University Press.

Ma, P., Mahoney, M. W., & Yu, B. (2015). A statistical perspective on algorithmic leveraging. *Journal of Machine Learning Research, 16*, 861–911.

Ma, P., Mahoney, M., & Yu, B. (2014). A Statistical Perspective on Algorithmic Leveraging. *JMLR: Workshop and Conference Proceedings, 32*, 91-99.

Ma, P., & Sun, X. (2015). Leveraging for big data regression. *Wiley Interdisciplinary Reviews: Computational Statistics, 7*(1), 70–76. doi:10.1002/wics.1324

Maron, O., & Lozano-Perez, T. (1998). A framework for multiple-instance learning. Advances in Neural Information Processing Systems, 10.

Martelot, E. L., & Hankin, C. (2013). *Fast multi-scale community detection based on local criteria within a multi-threaded algorithm.* arXiv preprint arXiv:1301.0955

Martin, J. D., & Simpson, T. W. (2005). On the Use of Kriging Models to Approxi- mate Deterministic Computer Models. *AIAA Journal, 43*(4), 853–863. doi:10.2514/1.8650

Marusic, Tay, Deng, & Palaniswami. (2003). A study of biorthogonal wavelets in digital watermarking. *Proceedings of International Conference on Image Processing, 2*, II–463. doi:10.1109/ICIP.2003.1246717

Mat'ern, B. (1986). *Spatial Variation* (2nd ed.). New York: Springer. doi:10.1007/978-1-4615-7892-5

May, R. M. (1976). Simple mathematical models with very complicated dynamics. *Nature, 261*(5560), 459–467. doi:10.1038/261459a0 PMID:934280

McCallum, A., Freitag, D., & Pereira, F. C. (2000, June). *Maximum Entropy Markov Models for Information Extraction and Segmentation* (Vol. 17). ICML.

McKay, M. D., Beckman, R. J., & Conover, W. J. (1979). A Comparison of Three Methods for Selecting Values of Input Variables in the Analysis of Output From a Computer Code. *Technometrics, 21*, 239–245.

McLachlan, G. J., & Ganesalingam, S. (1982). Updating a discriminant function on the basis of un classified data. *Communications in Statistics–Simulation and Computation, 11*(6), 753–767. doi:10.1080/03610918208812293

McMillian, N. J., Sacks, J., Welch, W. J., & Gao, F. (1999). Analysis of Protein Activity Data by Gaussian Stochastic Process Models. *Journal of Biopharmaceutical Statistics, 9*(1), 145–160. doi:10.1081/BIP-100101005 PMID:10091915

Mendez, E. O., & Ren, S. (2012). Design of Cyber-Physical Interface for Automated Vital Signs Reading in Electronic Medical Records Systems. *Electro/Information Technology (EIT),2012IEEE International Conference.* doi:10.1109/EIT.2012.6220696

Meng, X., Saunders, M. A., & Mahoney, M. W. (2014). LSRN: A parallel iterative solver for strongly over-or underdetermined systems. *SIAM Journal on Scientific Computing, 36*(2), C95–C118. doi:10.1137/120866580 PMID:25419094

Menzel, R. (2012). The honeybee as a model for understanding the basis of cognition. *Nature Reviews. Neuroscience, 13*(11), 758–768. doi:10.1038/nrn3357 PMID:23080415

Merzenich, M. (2001). Cortical Plasticity Contributing to Child Development. In J. McClelland & R. Siegler (Eds.), *Mechanisms of Cognitive Development: Behavioral and Neural Perspectives* (pp. 67–96). Lawrence Erlbaum Associates, Publishers.

Meystre, S. M., Friedlin, F. J., South, B. R., Shen, S., & Samore, M. H. (2010). Automatic de-identification of textual documents in the electronic health record: A review of recent research. *BMC Med Res Methodol BMC Medical Research Methodology*, *10*(1), 70. doi:10.1186/1471-2288-10-70 PMID:20678228

Mian, Bennamoun, & Owens. (2007). An efficient multimodal 2D-3D hybrid approach to automatic face recognition. *Pattern Analysis and Machine Intelligence, IEEE Transactions on, 29*(11), 1927–1943.

Miliard, M. (2016). Two more hospitals struck by ransomware, in California and Indiana. *Healthcare IT News*. Retrieved from: http://www.healthcareitnews.com/news/two-more-hospitals-struck-ransomware-california-and-indiana

Miličević, A., & Trinajstić, N. (2006). Combinatorial enumeration in chemistry. In A. Hincliffe (Ed.), *Chemical Modelling: Applications and Theory* (Vol. 4). Cambridge, UK: RSC Publishing.

Moed, H. F. (2010, July). Measuring contextual citation impact of scientific journals. *Journal of InformetricsVolume*, *4*(3), 265–277. doi:10.1016/j.joi.2010.01.002

Mohanchandra, K., Saha, S., & Deshmukh, R. (2014). Twofold classification of motor imagery using common spatial pattern. *International Conference on Contemporary Computing and Informatics (IC3I), IEEE, 2014*, 434 - 439. doi:10.1109/IC3I.2014.7019636

Mohanchandra, K., Saha, S., & Lingaraju, G. M. (2015). *EEG based brain computer interface for speech communication: principles and applications. Intelligent Systems Reference Library, Brain-Computer Interfaces: Current Trends and Applications* (Vol. 74). Berlin: Springer-Verlag GmbH; doi:10.1007/978-3-319-10978-7

Mohanchandra, K., Saha, S., Murthy, K. S., & Lingaraju, G. M. (2014). Distinct adoption of k-nearest neighbour and support vector machine in classifying EEG signals of mental tasks. *International Journal of Intelligent Engineering Informatics*, *3*(4), 313–329. doi:10.1504/IJIEI.2015.073064

Mohanchandra, K., & Saha, S. (2014). Optimal Channel Selection for Robust EEG Single-trial Analysis. *AASRI Conference on Circuit and Signal Processing (CSP 2014)*, 9, 64-71. doi:10.1016/j.aasri.2014.09.012

Mohanchandra, K., & Saha, S. (2016). *A Communication Paradigm Using Subvocalized Speech, Augmented Human Research*. Springer Singapore.

Mohanchandra, Saha, & Murthy. (2014). *EEG based Brain Computer Interface using Wavelets and SVM*. Paper presented at Grace Hopper Conference India (GHCI), Bangalore. Karnataka, India.

Mohanchandra, Saha, Murthy, & Lingaraju. (2015). Distinct adoption of k-nearest neighbour and support vector machine in classifying EEG signals of mental tasks. *International Journal of Intelligent Engineering Informatics,3*(4), 313-329.

Moorhouse, A., Evans, A. N., Atkinson, G. A., Sun, J., & Smith, M. L. (2009). The nose on your face may not be so plain: Using the nose as a biometric.*3rd IET International Conference on Crime Detection and Prevention (ICDP)*, 1–6. doi:10.1049/ic.2009.0231

Moroz, L., Kocot, K., Citarella, M., Dosung, S., Norekian, T., Povolotskaya, I., & Kohn, A. et al. (2014). The ctenophore genome and the evolutionary origins of neural systems. *Nature*, *510*(7503), 109–120. doi:10.1038/nature13400 PMID:24847885

Morris, M. D., & Mitchell, T. J. (1995). Exploratory Designs for Computer Experi- ments. *Journal of Statistical Planning and Inference*, *43*(3), 381–402. doi:10.1016/0378-3758(94)00035-T

Mortazavi, A., Williams, B. A., Mccue, K., Schaeffer, L., & Wold, B. (2008). Mapping and quantifying mammalian transcriptomes by RNA-Seq. *Nature Methods*, *5*(7), 621–628. doi:10.1038/nmeth.1226 PMID:18516045

Nagalakshmi, U., Wang, Z., Waern, K., Shou, C., Raha, D., Gerstein, M., & Snyder, M. (2008). The transcriptional landscape of the yeast genome defined by RNA sequencing. *Science*, *320*(5881), 1344–1349. doi:10.1126/science.1158441 PMID:18451266

Nagaraj, N., Balasubramanian, K., & Dey, S. (2013). A new complexity measure for time series analysis and classification. *The European Physical Journal. Special Topics*, *222*(3-4), 847–860. doi:10.1140/epjst/e2013-01888-9

Nascimento, M. A., Sander, J., & Pound, J. (2003). Analysis of SIGMODs co-authorship graph. *SIGMOD Record*, *32*(3), 8–10. doi:10.1145/945721.945722

Naud, R., Marcille, N., Clopath, C., & Gerstner, W. (2008). Firing patterns in the adaptive exponential integrate-and-fire model. *Biological Cybernetics*, *99*(4-5), 335–347. doi:10.1007/s00422-008-0264-7 PMID:19011922

Nédellec, C., Bossy, R., Kim, J. D., Kim, J. J., Ohta, T., Pyysalo, S., & Zweigenbaum, P. (2013, August). Overview of BioNLP shared task 2013. In *Proceedings of the BioNLP Shared Task 2013 Workshop* (pp. 1-7).

Nelken, I. (2004). Processing of complex stimuli and natural scences in the auditory cortex. *Current Opinion in Neurobiology*, *14*(4), 474–480. doi:10.1016/j.conb.2004.06.005 PMID:15321068

Nencka, A. S., Hahn, A. D., & Rowe, D. B. (2009). A Mathematical Model for Understanding the Statistical effects of k-space (AMMUST-k) preprocessing on observed voxel measurements in fcMRI and fMRI. *Journal of Neuroscience Methods*, *181*(2), 268–282. doi:10.1016/j.jneumeth.2009.05.007 PMID:19463854

Nesterov, Y. (2005). Smooth minimization of non-smooth functions. *Mathematical Programming*, *103*(1), 127–152. doi:10.1007/s10107-004-0552-5

Newman, M. E., & Girvan, M. (2004). Finding and evaluating community structure in networks. *Physical Review E: Statistical, Nonlinear, and Soft Matter Physics*, *69*(2), 026113. doi:10.1103/PhysRevE.69.026113 PMID:14995526

Nezhadarya, E., Wang, Z. J., & Ward, R. K. (2009). Image quality monitoring using spread spectrum watermarking. *Proc. IEEE ICIP*, 2233–2236. doi:10.1109/ICIP.2009.5413955

Ni, L., Cao, J., & Wang, R. (2014). Time-Dependent Approximate and Sample Entropy Measures for Brain Death Diagnosis. *Advances in Cognitive Neurodynamics*, (4), 323-328. doi:10.1007/978-94-017-9548-7_46

Niles, I., & Pease, A. (2001). Towards a standard upper ontology. In *Proceedings of the international conference on Formal Ontology in Information Systems*. ACM.

NITRD. (2009). *Networking and Information Technology Research and Development Program*. High-Confidence Medical Devices: Cyber-Physical Systems for 21st Century Health Care, A Research and Development Needs Report. Retrieved from https://www.nitrd.gov/About/MedDevice-FINAL1-web.pdf

nobelprize.org. (n.d.). *The Nobel Prize in Physics 2013*. Available: http://www.nobelprize.org/nobel_prizes/physics/laureates/2013/

NodeRED. (n.d.). Retrieved March 31, 2016, from http://nodered.org/

Nolte. J., (2002). *The Human Brain: An Introduction to Its Functional Anatomy*. Mosby, A Division of Elsevier Science.

Northcutt. (2013). Security of Cyber-Physical Systems: A Survey and Generalized Algorithm for Intrusion Detection and Determining Security Robustness of Cyber Physical Systems using Logical Truth Tables. *Vanderbilt Undergraduate Research Journal, 9.*

Northrop, R. B. (2010). *Introduction to complexity and complex systems*. Boca Raton, FL: Taylor & Francis.

Oakley, J., & OHagan, A. (2002). Bayesian Inference for the Uncertainty Distribu- tion of Computer Model Outputs. *Biometrika*, *89*(4), 769–784. doi:10.1093/biomet/89.4.769

OASIS – Organization for the Advancement of Structured Information Standards. (n.d.). Retrieved March 31, 2016, from https://www.oasis-open.org/

Ojala, T., Pietikainen, M., & Maenpaa, T. (2002). Multiresolution gray-scale and rotation invariant texture classification with local binary patterns. *IEEE Transactions on Pattern Analysis and Machine Intelligence*, *24*(7), 971–987. doi:10.1109/TPAMI.2002.1017623

Orozco-Arroyave, J. R., Arias-Londoño, J. D., Vargas-Bonilla, J. F., & Nöth, E. (2013). Analysis of Speech from People with Parkinson's Disease through Nonlinear Dynamics. *Advances in Nonlinear Speech Processing*, 112-119. doi:10.1007/978-3-642-38847-7_15

Owen, A. (1992). Orthogonal Arrays for Computer Experiments, Integration and Vi- sualization. *Statistica Sinica*, *2*, 439–452.

Owen, A. (1994). Controlling Correlations in Latin Hypercube Samples. *Journal of the American Statistical Association*, *89*(428), 1517–1522. doi:10.1080/01621459.1994.10476891

Pacheco, J. E., Amon, C. H., & Finger, S. (2003). Bayesian Surrogates Applied to Conceptual Stages of the Engineering Design Process. *ASME Journal of Mechanical Design*, *125*(4), 664–672. doi:10.1115/1.1631580

Page, L., Brin, S., Motwani, R., & Winograd, T. (1999). *The PageRank citation ranking: Bringing order to the web*. Academic Press.

Pal, A., Mukherjee, A., & Balamuralidhar, P. (2014). Model Driven Development for Internet of Things: Towards Easing the Concerns of Application Developers.*International Conference on IoT as a Service,IoT360 Summit*.

Palaniappan, R., & Mandic, D. P. (2007). Biometrics from brain electrical activity: A machine learning approach. *IEEE Transactions on Pattern Analysis and Machine Intelligence*, *29*(4), 738–742. doi:10.1109/TPAMI.2007.1013 PMID:17299228

Palla, G., Derényi, I., Farkas, I., & Vicsek, T. (2005). Uncovering the overlapping community structure of complex networks in nature and society. *Nature*, *435*(7043), 814–818. doi:10.1038/nature03607 PMID:15944704

Papadopoulos, S., Kompatsiaris, Y., Vakali, A., & Spyridonos, P. (2012). Community detection in social media. *Data Mining and Knowledge Discovery*, *24*(3), 515–554. doi:10.1007/s10618-011-0224-z

Paragios, N., & Deriche, R. (2002). Geodesic active regions and level set methods for supervised texture segmentation. *International Journal of Computer Vision*, *46*(3), 223–247. doi:10.1023/A:1014080923068

Park, J. S. (1994). Optimal Latin-Hypercube Designs for Computer Experiments. *Journal of Statistical Planning and Inference*, *39*(1), 95–111. doi:10.1016/0378-3758(94)90115-5

Pattabiraman, K., & Kandan, P. (2014). Weighted PI index of corona product of graphs. *Discrete Mathematics. Algorithms and Applications*, *06*. doi:10.1142/S1793830914500554

Paxton, N. C., Russell, S., Moskowitz, I. S., & Hyden, P. (2015). A Survey of Community Detection Algorithms Based On Analysis-Intent. In *Cyber Warfare* (pp. 237–263). Springer International Publishing. doi:10.1007/978-3-319-14039-1_12

Perakakis, P., Taylor, M., Buela-Casal, P., & Checa, P. (2006). A neuro-fuzzy system to calculate a journal internationality index. *Proceedings CEDI symposium*. Retrieved from http://damir.iem.csic.es/~michael/OA/perakakis_et_al_2005.pdf

Perkins, C. E. (2001). *Ad hoc networking* (Vol. 1). Reading, MA: Addison-wesley.

Peterson J. (in press). *Zombies, Predatory Wasps and Consciousness*. Academic Press.

Peterson, J., Kesson, A. M., & King, N. J. C. (in press). *Viral Infections and Central Nervous System Infection Models*. Academic Press.

Peterson, J. (2015a). Computation In Networks. *Computational Cognitive Science, 1*(1), 1. doi:10.1186/s40469-015-0003-z

Peterson, J. (2015b). Nodal Computation Approximations in Asynchronous Cognitive Models. *Computational Cognitive Science, 1*(1), 4. doi:10.1186/s40469-015-0004-y

Peterson, J. (2016). *BioInformation Processing: A Primer On Computational Cognitive Science*. Singapore: Springer Series on Cognitive Science and Technology. doi:10.1007/978-981-287-871-7

Phillips, P. J., Flynn, P. J., Scruggs, T., Bowyer, K. W., Jin Chang, K., Hoffman, J., … Worek, W. (2005). Overview of the face recognition grand challenge. *IEEE Conference on Computer Vision and Pattern Recognition (CVPR)*, 947– 954. doi:10.1109/CVPR.2005.268

Phillips. (1993). Article. *Astrophys. J., 413*, L105.

Phyu, T. N. (2009). Survey of classification techniques in data mining. *Proceedings of the International MultiConference of Engineers and Computer Scientists,* 1, 18-20.

Pincus, S. M. (1991). Approximate entropy as a measure of system complexity. *Proceedings of the National Academy of Sciences of the United States of America, 88*(6), 2297–2301. doi:10.1073/pnas.88.6.2297 PMID:11607165

Pincus, S. (1995). Approximate entropy (ApEn) as a complexity measure. *Chaos (Woodbury, N.Y.), 5*(1), 110–117. doi:10.1063/1.166092 PMID:12780163

Pinheiro, J. C., & Bates, D. M. (1996). Unconstrained Parametrizations for Variance- Covariance Matrices. *Statistics and Computing, 6*(3), 289–296. doi:10.1007/BF00140873

Piper, A., Safavi-Naini, R., & Mertins, A. (2005). Resolution and quality scalable spread spectrum image watermarking. *Proceedings of the 7th workshop on Multimedia and security*, 79–90. doi:10.1145/1073170.1073186

Plantié, M., & Crampes, M. (2013). Survey on social community detection. In *Social media retrieval* (pp. 65–85). Springer London. doi:10.1007/978-1-4471-4555-4_4

Pong & Bowden. (2002). An improved adaptive background mixture model for real-time tracking with shadow detection. In P. Remagnino, G. A. Jones, N. Paragios, & C. S. Regazzoni (Eds.), *Video-Based Surveillance Systems* (pp. 135–144). Springer, US.

Pratas, F., Trancoso, P., Sousa, L., Stamatakis, A., Shi, G., & Kindratenko, V. (2012). Fine-grain parallelism using multi-core, Cell/BE, and GPU Systems. *Parallel Computing, 38*(8), 365–390. doi:10.1016/j.parco.2011.08.002

Press Release. Gartner. (2014). *Gartner Says 4.9 Billion Connected Things Will Be in Use in 2015*. Retrieved March 31, 2016, from http://www.gartner.com/newsroom/id/2905717

Pronzato, L., & Mller, W. G. (2012). Design of Computer Experiments: Space Filling and Beyond. *Statistics and Computing, 22*(3), 681–701. doi:10.1007/s11222-011-9242-3

Pudil, P., & Novovičová, J. (1998). Novel methods for feature subset selection with respect to problem knowledge. In Feature Extraction, Construction and Selection, (pp. 101–116). Springer. doi:10.1007/978-1-4615-5725-8_7

Pyysalo, S., Ohta, T., Rak, R., Sullivan, D., Mao, C., Wang, C., & Ananiadou, S. et al. (2012). Overview of the ID, EPI and REL tasks of BioNLP Shared Task 2011. *BMC Bioinformatics*, *13*(11), 1. PMID:22759456

Qian, P. Z. G. (2009). Nested Latin Hypercube Designs. *Biometrika*, *96*(4), 957–970. doi:10.1093/biomet/asp045

Qian, P. Z. G. (2012). Sliced Latin Hypercube Designs. *Journal of the American Statistical Association*, *107*(497), 393–399. doi:10.1080/01621459.2011.644132

Qian, P. Z. G., & Wu, C. F. J. (2008). Bayesian Hierarchical Modeling for Integrating Low-Accuracy and High-Accuracy Experiments. *Technometrics*, *50*(2), 192–204. doi:10.1198/004017008000000082

Qian, P. Z. G., & Wu, C. F. J. (2009). Sliced Space-Filling Designs. *Biometrika*, *96*(4), 945–956. doi:10.1093/biomet/asp044

Qian, P. Z. G., Wu, H., & Wu, C. F. J. (2008). Gaussian Process Models for Computer Experiments with Qualitative and Quantitative Factors. *Technometrics*, *50*(3), 383–396. doi:10.1198/004017008000000262

Qian, Z., Seepersad, C., Joseph, R., Allen, J., & Wu, C. F. J. (2006). Building Surrogate Models with Detailed and Approximate Simulations. *ASME Journal of Mechanical Design*, *128*(4), 668–677. doi:10.1115/1.2179459

Que, X., Checconi, F., Petrini, F., Wang, T., & Yu, W. (2013). *Lightning-fast community detection in social media: A scalable implementation of the louvain algorithm.* Department of Computer Science and Software Engineering, Auburn University, Tech. Rep. AU-CSSE-PASL/13-TR01.

Raghavan, U. N., Albert, R., & Kumara, S. (2007). Near linear time algorithm to detect community structures in large-scale networks. *Physical Review E: Statistical, Nonlinear, and Soft Matter Physics*, *76*(3), 036106. doi:10.1103/PhysRevE.76.036106 PMID:17930305

Raizada, R., & Grossberg, S. (2003). Towards a theory of the laminar architecture of cerebral cortex: Computational clues from the visual system. *Cerebral Cortex*, *13*(1), 100–113. doi:10.1093/cercor/13.1.100 PMID:12466221

Rajendra Acharya, U., Faust, O., Adib Kadri, N., Suri, J. S., & Yu, W. (2013). Automated identification of normal and diabetes heart rate signals using nonlinear measures. *Computers in Biology and Medicine*, *43*(10), 1523–1529. doi:10.1016/j.compbiomed.2013.05.024 PMID:24034744

Rajkumar, R., Lee, L., Sha, L., & Stankovic, J. (2010). Cyber-physical systems: The next computing revolution. *Design Automation Conference (DAC), 201047th ACM/IEEE.*

Rangel-Castillo, L., Gopinath, S., & Robertson, C. S. (2008). Management of Intracranial Hypertension. *Neurologic Clinics*, *26*(2), 521–541. doi:10.1016/j.ncl.2008.02.003 PMID:18514825

Rao, Dundar, Krishnapuram, & Fung. (1998). *System and method for multiple instance learning for computer aided detection.* US Patent No. US7986827 B2.

Ratsaby, J., & Venkatesh, S. S. (1995). Learning from a mixture of labeled and unlabeled examples with parametric side information. In *Proceedings of the Eighth Annual Conference on Computational Learning Theory*, (pp. 412–417). ACM. doi:10.1145/225298.225348

Real Time Systems. (n.d.). Retrieved from http://www.cse.unsw.edu.au/~cs9242/08/lectures/09-realtimex2.pdf

Rebonato, R., & Jackel, P. (1999). The Most General Methodology for Creating a Valid Correlation Matrix for Risk Management and Option Pricing Purposes. *The Journal of Risk*, *2*(2), 17–27. doi:10.21314/JOR.2000.023

Rényi. (1961). *On Measures of Entropy and Information.* Alfréd: University of California Press.

Restrepo, J. F., Schlotthauer, G., & Torres, M. E. (2014). Maximum approximate entropy and threshold: A new approach for regularity changes detection. *Physica A: Statistical Mechanics and its Applications, 409*, 97-109. doi:10.1016/j.physa.2014.04.041

Reyes-Aldasoro, C. C., Griffiths, M. K., Savas, D., & Tozer, G. M. (2011). Caiman: An online algorithm repository for cancer image analysis. *Computer Methods and Programs in Biomedicine, 103*(2), 97–103. doi:10.1016/j.cmpb.2010.07.007 PMID:20691494

Richards, Homrighausen, Freeman, Schafer, Poznanski. (2012). Semi-supervised learning for Photometric Supernova Classification. *Monthly Notices of the Royal Astronomical Society, 419*, 1121–1135. doi:10.1111/j.1365-2966.2011.19768.x

Richiardi, J., Achard, S., Bunke, H., & Van De Ville, D. (2013). Machine learning with brain graphs: Predictive modeling approaches for functional imaging in systems neuroscience. *IEEE Signal Processing Magazine, 30*(3), 58–70. doi:10.1109/MSP.2012.2233865

Riedel, T., Yordanov, D., Fantana, N., Scholz, M., & Decker, C. (2010, June). A model driven internet of things. In *Networked Sensing Systems (INSS), 2010 Seventh International Conference on* (pp. 265-268). IEEE. doi:10.1109/INSS.2010.5573154

Riedy, E. J., Meyerhenke, H., Ediger, D., & Bader, D. A. (2011, September). Parallel community detection for massive graphs. In *International Conference on Parallel Processing and Applied Mathematics* (pp. 286-296). Springer Berlin Heidelberg.

Riedy, J., Bader, D. A., & Meyerhenke, H. (2012, May). Scalable multi-threaded community detection in social networks. In *Parallel and Distributed Processing Symposium Workshops & PhD Forum (IPDPSW), 2012 IEEE 26th International* (pp. 1619-1628). IEEE. doi:10.1109/IPDPSW.2012.203

Riess, , Strolger, L.-G., Casertano, S., Ferguson, H. C., Mobasher, B., Gold, B., & Stern, D. et al. (2007). New Hubble Space Telescope Discoveries of Type Ia Supernovae at z > 1: Narrowing Constraints on the Early Behavior of Dark Energy. *The Astrophysical Journal, 659*(1), 98–121. doi:10.1086/510378

Rissanen, J. (1989). Stochastic Complexity in Statistical Inquiry (World Scientific series in computer science; v. 15). World Scientific.

Rosso, O. A., Blanco, S., Yordanova, J., Kolev, V., Figliola, A., Schürmann, M., & Başar, E. (2001). Wavelet entropy: A new tool for analysis of short duration brain electrical signals. *Journal of Neuroscience Methods, 105*(1), 65–75. doi:10.1016/S0165-0270(00)00356-3 PMID:11166367

Rosvall, M., & Bergstrom, C. T. (2007). An information-theoretic framework for resolving community structure in complex networks. *Proceedings of the National Academy of Sciences of the United States of America, 104*(18), 7327–7331. doi:10.1073/pnas.0611034104 PMID:17452639

Rot, A., & von Andrian, U. (2004). Chemokines in innate and adaptive host defense: Basic chemokinese grammar for immune cells. *Annual Review of Immunology, 22*, 891–928.

Rovelli, C., & Vidotto, F. (2013). *An Elementary introduciton to Quantum Gravity and Spinfoam Theory.* Retrieved from http://www.cpt.univ-mrs.fr/~rovelli/IntroductionLQG.pdf

Rowe, D. B., Hahn, A. D., & Nencka, A. S. (2009). Functional magnetic resonance imaging brain activation directly from k-space. *Magnetic Resonance Imaging, 27*(10), 1370–1381. doi:10.1016/j.mri.2009.05.048 PMID:19608365

Rowe, R. K., & Liu, K.-W. (2015). 3D Finite Element Modeling of a Full-scale Geosynthetic-Reinforced, Pile-supported Embankment. *Canadian Geotechnical Journal.* doi:10.1139/cgj-2014-0506

Russo, S., & Nestler, E. (2013). The brain reward circuitry in mood disorders. *Nature Reviews. Neuroscience, 14*(9), 609–625. doi:10.1038/nrn3381 PMID:23942470

Russomanno, D. J., Kothari, C., & Thomas, O. (2005). Sensor ontologies: from shallow to deep models. In *System Theory, SSST'05.Proceedings of the Thirty-Seventh Southeastern Symposium on* (pp. 107–112). doi:10.1109/SSST.2005.1460887

Ryan, K. J., & Culp, M. V. (2015). On semi-supervised linear regression in covariate shift problems. *Journal of Machine Learning Research, 16*, 3183–3217. Retrieved from http://jmlr.org/papers/v16/ryan15a.html

Sacks, J., Welch, W. J., Mitchell, T. J., & Wynn, H. P. (1989). Design and Analysis of Computer Experiments. *Statistical Science, 4*(4), 409–423. doi:10.1214/ss/1177012413

Saha, Jangid, Mathur, & Anand. (2016). DSRS: Estimation and Forecasting of Journal Influence in the Science and Technology Domain via a Lightweight Quantitative Approach. *Collnet Journal of Scientometrics and Information Management.*

Saltzer, J. H., & Schroeder, M. D. (1975, September). The Protection of Information in Computer Systems. *Proceedings of the IEEE, 63*(9), 1278–1308. doi:10.1109/PROC.1975.9939

Sanei, S., & Chambers, J. (2007). *EEG signal processing.* Chichester, UK: John Wiley & Sons. doi:10.1002/9780470511923

Sanes, J., & Zipursky, S. (2010). Design Principles of Insect and Vertebrate Visual Systems. *Neuron, 66*(1), 15–36. doi:10.1016/j.neuron.2010.01.018 PMID:20399726

Santner, T. J., Williams, B. J., & Notz, W. I. (2003). *The Design and Analysis of Computer Experiments.* New York: Springer. doi:10.1007/978-1-4757-3799-8

Sarlabous, L., Torres, A., Fiz, J., Gea, J., Galdiz, J., & Jane, R. (2009). Multistate Lempel-Ziv (MLZ) index interpretation as a measure of amplitude and complexity changes. *2009 Annual International Conference of the IEEE Engineering in Medicine and Biology Society.* doi:10.1109/IEMBS.2009.5333488

Savova, G. K., Masanz, J. J., Ogren, P. V., Zheng, J., Sohn, S., Kipper-Schuler, K. C., & Chute, C. G. (2010). Mayo clinical Text Analysis and Knowledge Extraction System (cTAKES): Architecture, component evaluation and applications. *Journal of the American Medical Informatics Association, 17*(5), 507–513. doi:10.1136/jamia.2009.001560 PMID:20819853

Scannicchio, D. (2010). ATLAS trigger and data acquisition: Capabilities and commissioning. *Nuclear Instruments & Methods in Physics Research. Section A, Accelerators, Spectrometers, Detectors and Associated Equipment, 617*(1-3), 306–309. doi:10.1016/j.nima.2009.06.114

Scheirer, W. J., de Rezende Rocha, A., Sapkota, A., & Boult, T. E. (2013). Toward open set recognition. *IEEE Transactions on Pattern Analysis and Machine Intelligence, 35*(7), 1757–1772. doi:10.1109/TPAMI.2012.256 PMID:23682001

Schlief, F., & Tino, P. (2004). Indefinity Proximity Learning: A Review. *Neural Computation, 27*(10), 2039–2096. doi:10.1162/NECO_a_00770

Schmidt, R. R., Cruz, E. E., & Iyengar, M. K. (2005). Challenges of Data Center Thermal Management. *IBM Journal of Research and Development, 49*(4.5), 709–723. doi:10.1147/rd.494.0709

Schwarz, L. A., Mkhitaryan, A., Mateus, D., & Navab, N. (2012). Human skeleton tracking from depth data using geodesic distances and optical flow. *Image and Vision Computing, 30*(3), 217–226. doi:10.1016/j.imavis.2011.12.001

Scopus. (2016). Retrieved from www.scopus.com

Scudder, H. J. (1965). Probability of error of some adaptive pattern-recognition machines. *IEEE Transactions on Information Theory, 11*(3), 363–371. doi:10.1109/TIT.1965.1053799

Sebastiani, F. (2002). Machine learning in automated text categorization. *ACM Computing Surveys*, *34*(1), 1–47. doi:10.1145/505282.505283

Segundo, Silva, Bellon, & Queirolo. (2010). Automatic face segmentation and facial landmark detection in range images. *Systems, Man, and Cybernetics, Part B: Cybernetics, IEEE Transactions on, 40*(5),1319–1330.

Serby, D., Meier, E. K., & Van Gool, L. (2004). Probabilistic object tracking using multiple features.*Proc. International Conference on Pattern Recognition, 2*, 184–187.

Shannon, C. E. (1948). A Mathematical Theory of Communication. *The Bell System Technical Journal*, *27*(3), 379–423. doi:10.1002/j.1538-7305.1948.tb01338.x

Shao, J., & Tu, D. (2012). *The jackknife and bootstrap*. Springer Science & Business Media.

Sharma, V., Goswami, R., & Madan, A. K. (1997). Eccentric connectivity index: A novel highly discriminating topological descriptor for structure-property and structure-activity studies. *Journal of Chemical Information and Modeling*, *37*, 273–282.

Sherman, S. (2004). Interneurons and triadic circuitry of the thalamus. *Trends in Neurosciences*, *27*(11), 670–675. doi:10.1016/j.tins.2004.08.003 PMID:15474167

Shi, J., & Tomasi, C. (1994). Good features to track.*Proc. IEEE CVPR*, 593–600.

Shlosberg, D., Benifla, M., Kaufer, D., & Friedman, A. (2010). Blood–brain barrier breakdown as a therapeutic target in traumatic brain injury. *Nature Reviews. Nephrology*, *6*(7), 393–403. doi:10.1038/nrneurol.2010.74 PMID:20585319

Shnayder, Chen, Lorincz, Fulford-Jones, & Welsh. (2005). *Sensor Networks for Medical Care*. Harvard University Technical Report.

Shotton, J., Winn, J., Rother, C., & Criminisi, A. (2009). TextonBoost for image understanding: Multi-class object recognition and segmentation by jointly modeling texture, layout, and context. *International Journal of Computer Vision*, *81*(1), 2–23. doi:10.1007/s11263-007-0109-1

Simons, S., Abasolo, D., & Hughes, M. (2015). Investigation of Alzheimers Disease EEG Frequency Components with Lempel-Ziv Complexity. *IFMBE Proceedings*, *46-49*, 46–49. doi:10.1007/978-3-319-11128-5_12

Singh, G., Memoli, F., Ishkhanov, T., Sapiro, G., Carlsson, G., & Ringach, D. (2008). Topological analysis of population activity in visual cortex. *Journal of Vision (Charlottesville, Va.)*, *8*(8), 1–18. doi:10.1167/8.8.11 PMID:18831634

Singh, A., Nowak, R., & Zhu, X. (2009). *Unlabeled data: Now it helps, now it doesn't*. In D. Koller, D. Schuurmans, Y. Bengio, & L. Bottou (Eds.), Advances in Neural Information Processing Systems (Vol. 21, pp. 1513–1520). Curran Associates, Inc.

Skiena, S. (1999). Who is interested in algorithms and why? Lessons from the stony brook algorithms repository. ACM SIGACT News, 30(3), 65–74.

Soheili, M. R. (2010). Blind Wavelet Based Logo Watermarking Resisting to Cropping. *Proc. 20Th International Conference on Pattern Recognition*, 1449–1452. doi:10.1109/ICPR.2010.358

Sokunbi, M. O. (2014). Sample entropy reveals high discriminative power between young and elderly adults in short fMRI data sets. *Frontiers in Neuroinformatics*, *8*. doi:10.3389/fninf.2014.00069 PMID:25100988

Soman, J., & Narang, A. (2011, May). Fast community detection algorithm with gpus and multicore architectures. In *Parallel & Distributed Processing Symposium (IPDPS), 2011 IEEE International* (pp. 568-579). IEEE. doi:10.1109/IPDPS.2011.61

Sprecher, S., & Reichert, H. (2003). The urbilaterian brain: Developmental insights into the evolutionary origin of the brain in insects and vertebrates. *Arthropod Structure & Development*, *32*(1), 141–156. doi:10.1016/S1467-8039(03)00007-0 PMID:18089000

Staudt, C. L., & Meyerhenke, H. (2013, October). Engineering high-performance community detection heuristics for massive graphs. In *2013 42nd International Conference on Parallel Processing* (pp. 180-189). IEEE. doi:10.1109/ICPP.2013.27

Stevenson, G. G., Knox, S., Dobson, S., & Nixon, P. (2009). Ontonym: a collection of upper ontologies for developing pervasive systems. In *Proceedings of the 1st Workshop on Context, Information and Ontologies*. ACM. doi:10.1145/1552262.1552271

Strogatz, S. H. (2000). *Nonlinear dynamics and chaos: With applications to physics, biology, chemistry, and engineering*. Cambridge, MA: Westview Press.

Sttz, T., Autrusseau, F., & Uhl, A. (2014). Non-blind structure-preserving substitution watermarking of h.264/cavlc inter-frames. *IEEE Transactions on Multimedia*, *16*(5), 1337–1349. doi:10.1109/TMM.2014.2310595

Stubbs, A., Kotfila, C., & Uzuner, Ö. (2015). Automated systems for the de-identification of longitudinal clinical narratives: Overview of 2014 i2b2/UTHealth shared task Track 1. *Journal of Biomedical Informatics*, *58*, S11–S19. doi:10.1016/j.jbi.2015.06.007 PMID:26225918

Suen, C. Y. (1989). Some Resolvable Orthogonal Arrays with Two Symbols. *Communications in Statistics. Theory and Methods*, *18*(10), 3875–3881. doi:10.1080/03610928908830128

Sundheim, B. M. (1996, May). Overview of results of the MUC-6 evaluation. In *Proceedings of a workshop on held at Vienna, Virginia* (pp. 423-442). Association for Computational Linguistics. doi:10.3115/1119018.1119073

Supernovae and Gamma-Ray Bursts. (2013). Dept. of Astrophysics, University of Oxford. Retrieved from http://www-astro.physics.ox.ac.uk/~podsi/sn_podsi.pdf

SWE-OGC. (2013). *Sensorml, o&m and tml standard*. Retrieved March 31, 2016, from http://www.opengeospatial.org/standards/

Swiler, L. P., Hough, P. D., Qian, P., Xu, X., Storlie, C., & Lee, H. (2014). Surrogate Models for Mixed Discrete-Continuous Variables. In *Constraint Programming and Decision Making* (pp. 181–202). Springer International Publishing. doi:10.1007/978-3-319-04280-0_21

Szarvas, G., Farkas, R., & Busa-Fekete, R. (2007). State-of-the-art anonymization of medical records using an iterative machine learning framework. *Journal of the American Medical Informatics Association*, *14*(5), 574–580. doi:10.1197/jamia.M2441 PMID:17823086

Talebinejad, M., Tsoulfas, G., & Musallam, S. (2011). *Lempel-ziv complexity for analysis of neural spikes. Canadian Medical and Biological Engineering Conference*, Toronto, Canada.

Tang, B. (1993). Orthogonal Array-Based Latin Hypercubes. *Journal of the American Statistical Association*, *88*(424), 1392–1397. doi:10.1080/01621459.1993.10476423

Tang, B. (1998). Selecting Latin Hypercubes Using Correlation Criteria. *Statistica Sinica*, *8*, 965–978.

Taubman, D. S., & Marcellin, M. W. (2002). *JPEG2000 Image Compression Fundamentals, Standards and Practice*. Springer. doi:10.1007/978-1-4615-0799-4

Teager, H. M., & Teager, S. M. (1990). Evidence for Nonlinear Sound Production Mechanisms in the Vocal Tract. *Speech Production and Speech Modelling*, 241-261. doi:10.1007/978-94-009-2037-8_10

Tew, J., & Ray, L. (2016). ADDSMART: Address Digitization and Smart Mailbox with RFID Technology. *IEEE UEM-CON*. doi:10.1109/UEMCON.2016.7777879

The Data Explosion in 2014. (2016, April 15). Retrieved from http://aci.info/2014/07/12/the-data-explosion-in-2014-minute-by-minute-infographic/

Theodoridis, S., & Koutroumbas, K. (2009). *Pattern Recognition*. Academic Press.

ThingWorx I ThingWorx. (n.d.). Retrieved March 31, 2016, from http://www.thingworx.com/

top500.org. (2014). *June 2014*. Available at: https://www.top500.org/lists/2014/06/

Torii, M., Fan, J. W., Yang, W. L., Lee, T., Wiley, M. T., Zisook, D., & Huang, Y. (2014, November). De-identification and risk factor detection in medical records. Seventh i2b2 Shared Task and Workshop: Challenges in Natural Language Processing for Clinical Data.

TOSCA - Topology and Orchestration Specification for Cloud Applications. V1.0. (2013). Retrieved March 31, 2016, from http://docs.oasis-open.org/tosca/TOSCA/v1.0/os/TOSCA-v1.0-os.html

Tryon. (1939). *Cluster analysis: Correlation profile and orthometric (factor) analysis for the isolation of unities in mind and personality*. Edwards Brother, Incorporated, Lithoprinters and Publishers.

Tsai, J.-M., Chen, I.-T., Huang, Y.-F., & Lin, C.-C. (2015). Watermarking technique for improved management of digital medical images. *Journal of Discrete Mathematical Sciences and Cryptography*, *18*(6), 785–799. doi:10.1080/0972052 9.2015.1023532

Tyler, J. R., Wilkinson, D. M., & Huberman, B. A. (2005). E-mail as spectroscopy: Automated discovery of community structure within organizations. *The Information Society*, *21*(2), 143–153. doi:10.1080/01972240590925348

Type I and Type II Supernovae. (2016). Retrieved from http://hyperphysics.phy-astr.gsu.edu/hbase/astro/snovcn.html#c3

Type Ia supernova data used by Davis, Mörtsell, Sollerman, et al. (2007). Retrieved from http://dark.dark-cosmology.dk/~tamarad/SN/

Uehira, K., Suzuki, K., & Ikeda, H. (2016). Does optoelectronic watermark technology migrate into business and industry in the near future? applications of optoelectronic watermarking technology to new business and industry systems utilizing flat-panel displays and smart devices. *IEEE Transactions on Industry Applications*, *52*(1), 511–520. doi:10.1109/TIA.2015.2480769

Underbrink, A., Witt, K., Stanley, J., & Mandl, D. (2008). Autonomous mission operations for sensor webs, In *AGU Fall Meeting Abstracts* (vol. 1, 2008, p. 05).

Uzun, A. (2004). Assessing internationality of scholarly journals through foreign authorship patterns: The case of major journals in information science, and Scientometrics. *Scientometrics*, *61*(3), 457–465. doi:10.1023/B:SCIE.0000045121.26810.35

Uzuner, Ö., Solti, I., & Cadag, E. (2010). Extracting medication information from clinical text. *Journal of the American Medical Informatics Association*, *17*(5), 514–518. doi:10.1136/jamia.2010.003947 PMID:20819854

Uzuner, Ö., South, B. R., Shen, S., & DuVall, S. L. (2011). 2010 i2b2/VA challenge on concepts, assertions, and relations in clinical text. *Journal of the American Medical Informatics Association*, *18*(5), 552–556. doi:10.1136/ami-ajnl-2011-000203 PMID:21685143

Valenza, G., Citi, L., Lanata, A., Scilingo, E. P., & Barbieri, R. (2013). A nonlinear heartbeat dynamics model approach for personalized emotion recognition. *2013 35th Annual International Conference of the IEEE Engineering in Medicine and Biology Society (EMBC)*. doi:10.1109/embc.2013.6610067

Van der Weken, D., Nachtegael, M., & Kerre, E. E. (2004). Using similarity measures and homogeneity for the comparison of images. *Image and Vision Computing, 22*(9), 695–702. doi:10.1016/j.imavis.2004.03.002

Vapnik. (2011). *Statistical Learning Theory.* John Wiley & Sons.

Vapnik, V. N., & Chervonenkis, A. Y. (1974). *Theory of Pattern Recognition* [in Russian]. Nauka.

Veenman, C. J., Reinders, M. J. T., & Backer, E. (2001). Resolving motion correspondence for densely moving points. *IEEE Transactions on Pattern Analysis and Machine Intelligence, 23*(1), 54–72. doi:10.1109/34.899946

Veksler, O. (2013). *k Nearest Neigbors.* Retrieved on 04-05-16 from www.csd.uwo.ca/courses/CS9840a/Lecture2_knn.pdf

Venkatasubramanian, Mukherjee, & Gupta. (2014). CAAC - An Adaptive and Proactive Access Control Approach for Emergencies in Smart Infrastructures. *ACM Transactions on Autonomous and Adaptive Systems, 8*(4).

Venkatasubramanian. (2009). *Security Solutions for Cyber-physical Systems* (Doctoral Dissertation). Arizona State University.

Vinod & Bora. (2006). Motion-compensated inter-frame collusion attack on video watermarking and a countermeasure. *IEE Proceedings-Information Security, 153*(2), 61–73.

Viola, P., Platt, J. C., & Zhang, C. (2006). Multiple instance boosting for object detection. Advances in Neural Information Processing Systems, 18.

Virone, G., Wood, A., Selavo, L., Cao, Q., Fang, L., Doan, T., & Stankovic, J. et al. (2006). An assisted living oriented information system based on a residential wireless sensor network. *Proceedings of the Transdisciplinary Conference on Distributed Diagnosis and Home Healthcare.* doi:10.1109/DDHH.2006.1624806

Vo, B.-N., & Ma, W.-K. (2006). The Gaussian mixture probability hypothesis density filter. *IEEE Transactions on Signal Processing, 54*(11), 4091–4104. doi:10.1109/TSP.2006.881190

Vreeken, J. (2003). *Spiking neural networks, an introduction.* Retrieved from Information and Computing Sciences website: http://eda.mmci.uni-saarland.de/pubs/2002/spiking_neural_networks_an_introduction-vreeken.pdf

Vukičević, D., Zhou, B., & Trinajstić, N. (2007). Altered Wiener Indices of Thorn Trees. *Croatica Chemica Acta, 80,* 283–285.

Vukiþeviü, D., Nikoliü, S., & Trinajstiü, N. (2005). On the Schultz Index of Thorn Graphs, Internet Electron. J. Mol. Des., 4, 501-514.

Walikar, H. B., Ramane, H. S., Sindagi, L., Shirakol, S. S., & Gutman, I. (2006). Hosoya polynomial of thorn trees, rods, rings, and stars. *Kragujevac Journal of Science, 28,* 47–56.

Waltman, van Eck, Thed, van Leeuwen, & Visser. (2013). Some modifications to the SNIP journal impact indicator. *Journal of Informetrics, 7,* 272-285.

Wang, J., & Zucker, J.-D. (2000). Solving the multiple instance problem - a lazy learning approach. *17th International Conference on Machine Learning.*

Wang, S., Zheng, D., Zhao, J., Tam, W. J., & Speranza, F. (2007). An image quality evaluation method based on digital watermarking. *IEEE Transactions on Circuits and Systems for Video Technology, 17*(1), 98–105. doi:10.1109/TCSVT.2006.887086

Wang, Y., Brzozowsha-Prechtl, A., & Karten, H. (2010). Laminary and columnar auditory cortex in avian brain. *Proceedings of the National Academy of Sciences of the United States of America, 107*(28), 12676–12681. doi:10.1073/pnas.1006645107 PMID:20616034

Wang, Z., Bovik, A. C., Sheikh, H. R., & Simoncelli, E. P. (2004). Image quality assessment: From error visibility to structural similarity. *IEEE Transactions on Image Processing, 13*(4), 600–612. doi:10.1109/TIP.2003.819861 PMID:15376593

Wang, T., Qian, X., & Wang, X. (2015, September). HLPA: A hybrid label propagation algorithm to find communities in large-scale networks. In *2015 IEEE 7th International Conference on Awareness Science and Technology (iCAST)* (pp. 135-140). IEEE. doi:10.1109/ICAwST.2015.7314035

WATERMATRIX Water Analysis and Waste Water Treatment. (n.d.). Retrieved from: http://www.watermatrix.net/Product.aspx?type=Automation

Watson, A. B. (1993). Visual optimization of dct quantization matrices for individual images. Proc. American Institute of Aeronautics and Astronautics (AIAA) Computing in Aerospace, 9, 286–291. doi:10.2514/6.1993-4512

Watts, D. J., & Strogatz, S. H. (1998). Collective dynamics of 'small-world'networks. *Nature, 393*(6684), 440-442.

Weisberg, S. (2005). *Applied linear regression.* John Wiley & Sons. doi:10.1002/0471704091

Welch, W. J., Buck, R. J., Sacks, J., Wynn, H. P., Mitchell, T. J., & Morris, M. D. (1992). Screening, Predicting, and Computer Experiments. *Technometrics, 34*(1), 15–25. doi:10.2307/1269548

Wellner, B., Huyck, M., Mardis, S., Aberdeen, J., Morgan, A., Peshkin, L., & Hirschman, L. et al. (2007). Rapidly Retargetable Approaches to De-identification in Medical Records. *Journal of the American Medical Informatics Association, 14*(5), 564–573. doi:10.1197/jamia.M2435 PMID:17600096

Wickramaarachchi, C., Frincu, M., Small, P., & Prasanna, V. K. (2014, September). Fast parallel algorithm for unfolding of communities in large graphs. In *High Performance Extreme Computing Conference (HPEC)*, (pp. 1-6). IEEE. doi:10.1109/HPEC.2014.7040973

Wiener, H. (1947). Structural determination of paraffin boiling points. *Journal of the American Chemical Society, 69*(1), 17–20. doi:10.1021/ja01193a005 PMID:20291038

Williams, R. J., & Martinez, N. D. (2000). Simple rules yield complex food webs. *Nature, 404*(6774), 180–183. doi:10.1038/35004572 PMID:10724169

Wolf, M. S., & Bennett, C. L. (2006). Local perspective of the impact of the HIPAA privacy rule on research. *Cancer, 106*(2), 474–479. doi:10.1002/cncr.21599 PMID:16342254

Wolpert, D. H. (1992). Stacked generalization. *Neural Networks, 5*(2), 241–259. doi:10.1016/S0893-6080(05)80023-1

Wood-Vassey, . (2007). Observational Constraints on the Nature of the Dark Energy: First Cosmological Results from the ESSENCE Supernova Survey. *The Astrophysical Journal, 666*(2), 694–715. doi:10.1086/518642

Worsley, K. J., & Friston, K. J. (1995). Analysis of fMRI time-series revisited again. *NeuroImage, 2*(3), 173–181. doi:10.1006/nimg.1995.1023 PMID:9343600

Worsley, K. J. (2003). Detecting activation in fMRI data. *Statistical Methods in Medical Research, 12*(5), 401–418. doi:10.1191/0962280203sm340ra PMID:14599003

Wu, L., & Kaiser, G. (2013). *FARE: A Framework for Benchmarking Reliability of Cyber-Physical Systems. Columbia University Computer Science Technical Reports.* Columbia University.

Wu, C.-F. J. (1986). Jackknife, bootstrap and other resampling methods in regression analysis. *the Annals of Statistics*, 1261-1295.

Wu, C. F. J., & Hamada, M. (2009). *Experiments: Planning, Analysis, and Parameter Design Optimization* (2nd ed.). New York: Wiley.

Xia, X., Boncelet, C. G., & Arce, G. R. (1998). Wavelet transform based watermark for digital images. *Optics Express*, *3*(12), 497–511. doi:10.1364/OE.3.000497 PMID:19384401

Xia, D., Meng, Q., Chen, Y., & Zhang, Z. (2014). Classification of Ventricular Tachycardia and Fibrillation Based on the Lempel-Ziv Complexity and EMD. *Intelligent Computing in Bioinformatics*, 322-329. doi:10.1007/978-3-319-09330-7_39

Xie, L., & Arce, G. R. (1998). Joint wavelet compression and authentication watermarking. *Proc. IEEE ICIP*, 2, 427–431.

Xie, J., Kelley, S., & Szymanski, B. K. (2013). Overlapping community detection in networks: The state-of-the-art and comparative study. *ACM Computing Surveys*, *45*(4), 43. doi:10.1145/2501654.2501657

Xu, H., Stenner, S. P., Doan, S., Johnson, K. B., Waitman, L. R., & Denny, J. C. (2010). MedEx: A medication information extraction system for clinical narratives. *Journal of the American Medical Informatics Association*, *17*(1), 19–24. doi:10.1197/jamia.M3378 PMID:20064797

Xu, C., Zhang, Y., & Li, R. (2015). *On the Feasibility of Distributed Kernel Regression for Big Data.* arXiv preprint arXiv:1505.00869

Xu, P., Scalzo, F., Bergsneider, M., Vespa, P., Chad, M., & Hu, X. (2008). Wavelet entropy characterization of elevated intracranial pressure. *2008 30th Annual International Conference of the IEEE Engineering in Medicine and Biology Society*. doi:10.1109/iembs.2008.4649815

Xue, H., Chen, S., & Yang, Q. (2008). Structural support vector machine. *Advances in Neural Networks-ISNN, 2008*, 501–511.

Yamada, T., Maeta, M., & Mizushima, F. (2016). Video watermark application for embedding recipient id in real-time-encoding vod server. *Journal of Real-Time Image Processing*, *11*(1), 211–222. doi:10.1007/s11554-013-0335-4

Yang, H., & Garibaldi, J. M. (2015). Automatic detection of protected health information from clinic narratives. *Journal of Biomedical Informatics*, 58. PMID:26231070

Yang, H., Shao, L., Zheng, F., Wang, L., & Song, Z. (2011). Recent advances and trends in visual tracking: A review. *Neurocomputing*, *74*(18), 3823–3831. doi:10.1016/j.neucom.2011.07.024

Yang, J., & Xia, F. (2010). The Eccentric Connectivity Index of Dendrimers. *International Journal of Contemporary Mathematical Sciences*, *5*, 2231–2236.

Yang, J., Ren, Y., Chen, Y., & Chuah, M. C. (2010). A social community based approach for reducing the propagation of infectious diseases in healthcare. *Mobile Computing and Communications Review*, *14*(3), 7–9. doi:10.1145/1923641.1923645

Yarahmadi, Z., & Ashrafi, A. R. (2012). The Szeged, Vertex PI, first and second Zagreb Indices of corona Product of Graphs. *Filomat*, *26*(3), 467–472. doi:10.2298/FIL1203467Y

Yazdani, A., Ebrahimi, T., & Hoffmann, U. (2009). Classification of EEG signals using Dempster Shafer theory and a k-nearest neighbor classifier. *NER 2009: 4th International Conference on Neural Engineering*, 327-330. doi:10.1109/NER.2009.5109299

Yazdani, A., Ebrahimi, T., & Hoffmann, U. (2009). Classification of EEG Signals Using Dempster Shafer Theory and a K-Nearest Neighbor Classifier. Paper presented at the International IEEE EMBS Conference on Neural Engineering, Antalya, Turkey.

Ye, J., Lazar, N. A., & Li, Y. (2009). Geostatistical analysis in clustering fMRI time series. *Statistics in Medicine*, *28*(19), 2490–2508. doi:10.1002/sim.3626 PMID:19521974

Ye, K. Q. (1998). Orthogonal Column Latin Hypercubes and their Application in Com- puter Experiments. *Journal of the American Statistical Association*, *93*(444), 1430–1439. doi:10.1080/01621459.1998.10473803

Ye, K. Q., Li, W., & Sudjianto, A. (2000). Algorithmic Construction of Optimal Symmetric Latin Hypercube Designs. *Journal of Statistical Planning and Inference*, *90*(1), 145–159. doi:10.1016/S0378-3758(00)00105-1

Yildirim, N., Ulas, M., & Varol, A. (2015). A Game Development for Android Devices Based on Brain Computer Interface: Flying Brain. *Proc. of the Intl. Conf. on Advances in Applied science and Environmental Technology*, 77-81.

Yilmaz, A., Javed, O., & Shah, M. (2006). Object tracking: A survey. *ACM Computing Surveys*, *38*(4), 13, es. doi:10.1145/1177352.1177355

Yilmaz, A., Xin Li, , & Shah, M. (2004). Contour-based object tracking with occlusion handling in video acquired using mobile cameras. *IEEE Transactions on Pattern Analysis and Machine Intelligence*, *26*(11), 1531–1536. doi:10.1109/TPAMI.2004.96 PMID:15521500

Yu, C., Lucy He, R., & Yau, S. S. (2014). Viral genome phylogeny based on Lempel–Ziv complexity and Hausdorff distance. *Journal of Theoretical Biology*, *348*, 12–20. doi:10.1016/j.jtbi.2014.01.022 PMID:24486229

Yu, G., & Feng, L. (2013). On Connective Eccentricity Index of Graphs. MATCH Communications in Mathematical and in Computer Chemistry, 69, 611-628.

Zafeiriou, S., Hansen, M., Atkinson, G., Argyriou, V., Petrou, M., Smith, M., & Smith, L. (2011). The Photoface database. *IEEE Conference on Computer Vision and Pattern Recognition Workshops (CVPRW)*, 132–139.

Zeng, J., & Yu, H. (2015, September). Parallel Modularity-based Community Detection on Large-scale Graphs. In *2015 IEEE International Conference on Cluster Computing* (pp. 1-10). IEEE. doi:10.1109/CLUSTER.2015.11

Zhang, H., Berg, A. C., Maire, M., & Malik, J. (2006). SVM-KNN: Discriminative nearest neighbor classification for visual category recognition. *Computer Society Conference on Computer Vision and Pattern Recognition*, 2, 2126-2136. doi:10.1109/CVPR.2006.301

Zhang, H., Shu, H., Coatrieux, G., Zhu, J., Wu, Q. M. J., Zhang, Y., & Luo, L. et al. (2011). Affine legendre moment invariants for image watermarking robust to geometric distortions. *IEEE Transactions on Image Processing*, *20*(8), 2189–2199. doi:10.1109/TIP.2011.2118216 PMID:21342852

Zhang, L., & Hua, H. (2010). The Eccentric Connectivity Index of Unicyclic Graphs. *International Journal of Contemporary Mathematical Sciences*, *5*, 2257–2262.

Zhang, M.-L., & Zhou, Z.-H. (2009). Multi-instance clustering with applications to multi-instance predic-tion. *Applied Intelligence*, *31*(1), 47–68. doi:10.1007/s10489-007-0111-x

Zhang, Z., & Mo, Y. L. (2001). Embedding strategy of image watermarking in wavelet transform domain.*Proc. SPIE Image Compression and Encryption Tech.*, 4551-1, 127–131. doi:10.1117/12.442900

Zhang, B., Cheng, X., Bie, R., & Chen, D. (2012, November). A community based vaccination strategy over mobile phone records. In *Proceedings of the Second ACM Workshop on Mobile Systems, Applications, and Services for HealthCare* (p. 2). ACM doi:10.1145/2396276.2396279

Zhang, Q., Qirong, Q., & Guo, K. (2015, August). Parallel overlapping community discovery based on grey relational analysis. In *2015 IEEE International Conference on Grey Systems and Intelligent Services (GSIS)* (pp. 151-156). IEEE. doi:10.1109/GSIS.2015.7301846

Zhang, Y., & Notz, W. I. (2015). Computer Experiments with Qualitative and Quan- titative Variables: A Review and Reexamination. *Quality Engineering*, *27*(1), 2–13. doi:10.1080/08982112.2015.968039

Zhang, Y., Wang, J., Wang, Y., & Zhou, L. (2009, June). Parallel community detection on large networks with propinquity dynamics. In *Proceedings of the 15th ACM SIGKDD international conference on Knowledge discovery and data mining* (pp. 997-1006). ACM. doi:10.1145/1557019.1557127

Zhou, B., & Du, Z. (2010). On eccentric connectivity index. *MATCH Communications in Mathematical and in Computer Chemistry*, *63*(1), 181–198.

Zhou, B., & Vukičević, D. (2009). On Wiener-type polynomials of thorn graphs. *Journal of Chemometrics*, *23*(12), 600–604. doi:10.1002/cem.1258

Zhou, B. (2005). On modified Wiener indices of thorn trees. *Kragujevac Journal of Science*, *27*, 5–9.

Zhou, Z.-H., & Zhang, M.-L. (2007). Solving multi-instance problems with classifier ensemble based on constructive clustering. *Knowledge and Information Systems*, *11*(2), 155–170. doi:10.1007/s10115-006-0029-3

Zhou. (2004). *Multi-instance learning: A survey. Technical report*. Nanjing University.

Zhou, D., Bousquet, O., Lal, T. N., Weston, J., & Schölkopf, B. (2004). Learning with local and global consistency. *Advances in Neural Information Processing Systems*, *16*(16), 321–328.

Zhou, Q., Qian, P. Z. G., & Zhou, S. (2011). A Simple Approach to Emulation for Computer Models With Qualitative and Quantitative Factors. *Technometrics*, *53*(3), 266–273. doi:10.1198/TECH.2011.10025

Zhu, X., Ding, J., Dong, H., Hu, K., & Zhang, X. (2014). Normalized correlation-based quantization modulation for robust watermarking. *IEEE Transactions on Multimedia*, *16*(7), 1888–1904. doi:10.1109/TMM.2014.2340695

Zhu, X., Ghahramani, Z., & Lafferty, J. (2003). *Semi-supervised learning using Gaussian fields and harmonic functions* (Vol. 3). ICML.

Ziv, J., & Lempel, A. (1977). A universal algorithm for sequential data compression. *IEEE Transactions on Information Theory*, *23*(3), 337–343. doi:10.1109/TIT.1977.1055714

Zivkovic, Z., & van der Heijden, F. (2006). Efficient adaptive density estimation per image pixel for the task of background subtraction. *Pattern Recognition Letters*, *27*(7), 773–780. doi:10.1016/j.patrec.2005.11.005

Zupanc, G. K. H. (2014). Impact beyond the impact factor. *Journal of Comparative Physiology. A, Neuroethology, Sensory, Neural, and Behavioral Physiology*, *200*(2), 113116. doi:10.1007/s00359-013-0863-1 PMID:24264238

About the Contributors

Snehanshu Saha received MS degree in Mathematics from the Clemson University, USA, in 2003. He obtained his PhD in Mathematics from University of Texas at Arlington in 2008. He is currently working as Professor in the Department of Computer Science and Engineering and & Head- Center for Applied Mathematical Modeling & Simulation, PESIT South-Bangalore. His research interests include Brain-Computer interface/Big Data analytics/ Mathematical Modeling/ Theory of Differential Equations/ Astro-informatics. He has served as an invited speaker for many international conferences in Indian and abroad. He serves as the reviewer for many journals like Computational Cognitive Science, Springer, International Journal of Innovative Information and Electrical Engineering (IJIIEE), etc. He is a senior member of the IEEE.

Abhyuday Mandal is an Associate Professor at University of Georgia, USA. He received his bachelor's and master's degrees from Indian Statistical Institute, Kolkata, another master's degree from University of Michigan and Ph.D. in 2005 from Georgia Institute of Technology. His research interests include design of experiments, optimization and genetic algorithms, drug discovery and fMRI data analysis. Currently he is an Associate Editor of *Statistics and Probability Letters and Sankhya - Series B.*

* * *

Surbhi Agrawal works as an Assistant Professor in CSE Department, PESIT-BSC.

Karthi Balasubramanian received his Bachelor of Technology degree from Netaji Subhas Institute of Technology (formerly known as Delhi Institute of Technology), New Delhi, India in 1999 and M.A.Sc degree from Simon Fraser University, Burnaby, Canada in 2002. Later, he obtained his doctorate degree from Amrita University for his work on 'A new complexity measure for time series analysis and classification'. Currently he is working as an Assistant Professor in the department of electronics and communication at Amrita University. Prior to joining the university, he has experience working as a chip design engineer at companies like Cogent Chipware Inc. and PMC-Sierra. His areas of interest include nonlinear dynamics, information theory and complex systems with application in genomics and EEG/ECG signal processing.

Prithish Banerjee received his Ph.D. in Computational Statistics from West Virginia University in 2016. He is currently a Post Doctoral Research Associate at Wayne State University in the School of Medicine. His fields of interest are Statistical Machine Learning, Graph-Based Learning, and Missing Data Problems.

Suryoday Basak is a research associate in the Center of Applied Mathematical Modeling and Simulation (CAMMS). His research interests include AstroInformatics and Brain Computer Interfaces.

Pushpak Bhattacharyya is Professor of Computer Science and Engineering at IIT Bombay. He was a Visiting research fellow in Massachusetts Institute of Technology in 1990. He is well known for his contributions to natural language processing and has several distinctions in that field. He has also currently been appointed as Vijay and Sita Vashee Chair Professor. A highly recognised researcher, Prof. Bhattacharyya is a member of National Knowledge Commission. For his outstanding contribution to computer science, he has received many accolades including IBM Innovation award (2007), Yahoo Faculty Award (2011), P. K. Patwardhan Award for Technology Development (2008), and VNMM Award of IIT Roorkee (2014). Prof. Bhattacharyya specializes in Natural Language Processing (NLP), Machine Learning (ML), Machine Translation (MT), Cross Lingual IR (CLIR) and Information Extraction (IE). Recently his text book "Machine Translation" has been published by CRC Press, Taylor and Francis Group, USA. Students of MT, NLP and ML, with interest in Indian Languages should find this book very helpful.

Deepayan Bhowmik received the B.E. in Electronics Engineering from Visvesvaraya National Institute of Technology, Nagpur, India in 2003, the MSc. in Electronics and Information Technology from Sheffield Hallam University, UK in 2006 and the Ph.D. from the University of Sheffield, UK in 2011. Previously he worked as a research associate at Heriot-Watt University, Edinburgh \& the University of Sheffield, UK and a system engineer in ABB Ltd., India. Currently he is working as a Lecturer in Computing at Sheffield Hallam University, Sheffield, UK. Dr. Bhowmik received UK Engineering and Physical Sciences Research Council (EPSRC) Dorothy Hodgkin Postgraduate Award (DHPA) in 2006-2010 and a Digital Catapult-EPSRC fellowship in 2016-2017 to conduct research on multimedia security. His research interests include multimedia forensics and security, computer vision and embedded image processing hardware.

Sobin C. C. received the BTech degree in Information Technology from the College of Engineering, Thalassery, Kerala (affiliated to Cochin University, Kerala), in 2004, and the M.Tech degree in Computer Science and Engineering from Indian Institute of Technology(IIT), Madras in 2010. He is currently doing his PhD in Computer Science from Indian Institute of Technology(IIT), Roorkee. He worked as an Assistant Professor in MES Engineering College, Kerala, before joining for PhD in IIT Roorkee. His research interests include routing in Delay Tolerant Networks, mathematical modelling, Internet-of Things. He is a student member of the IEEE.

Mark Vere Culp received his Ph.D. in Statistics from The University of Michigan in 2007. He joined West Virginia University in 2007, where he is currently an Associate Professor of Statistics. His research interests are in the areas of machine learning, data mining, and data science. He has published in several journals including The Journal of Computational and Graphical Statistics, The Journal of the American Statistical Association, and The Journal of Machine Learning Research. This work was supported by the NSF CAREER/DMS-1255045 grant.

Nilanjan De received the M.Sc. degree in Applied Mathematics from Kalyani University, in 1997, and the M.Tech degree from Jadavpur University. He obtained his PhD in Mathematics from National Institute of Technology, Durgapur. He is currently working as Teacher In Charge and Assistant Professor in the Department of Basic Sciences and Humanities, Calcutta Institute of Engineering and Management, Kolkata. His research interests include Discrete Mathematics/Combinatorics/Graph Theory.

Sounak Dey completed his B.Sc. (Physics) from Serampore College under Calcutta University and his Master's degree in Computer Application from BIT Mesra, Ranchi. On completion of education (and a small stint at AMI Industries, Mumbai thereafter), Sounak has joined at Kolkata office of UshaComm Pvt. Ltd. which is a telecomm billing product company headquartered at London. During his two years at UshaComm, he has chance to interact with several telecom service providers across the world including ScanCom, Vartec Telecom, MultiLinks etc. At the end of 2005, he joined Tata Consultancy Services and is working there till date in the same group that evolved as Innovation Labs around 2010. At TCS, he was involved in various R&D projects in domains like Video Conferencing solutions, Smart TV applications, Distance Education application over TV and internet etc. His recent area of work involves semantic technologies in the context of Internet of Things.

Sudeepa Roy Dey is working as assistant professor in department of computer science and Engineering, PESIT_BSC. She is a Bachelors and Masters degree holder in Computer Science and Engineering. She has eight years of teaching and research experience. Her research areas are Machine learning, Cloud Computing and Optimization techniques.

Asif Ekbal received the M.Tech and Ph.D. degrees in Computer Science & Engineering from Jadavpur University, Kolkata, India, in 2004 and 2009, respectively. He is currently a faculty member in the department of Computer Science and Engineering, Indian Institute of Technology Patna, India. He has authored or coauthored more than 100 papers. His current research interests include Natural Language Processing, Data Mining and Machine Learning Applications, Information Extraction, Bio-text Mining and Machine Learning in Social Networks. His h-index is 20 and total citation count of his papers is 1189 (according to Google scholar).

Mehryar Emambakhsh was awarded a PhD in Electronic and Electrical Engineering from the University of Bath in 2015, researching the potential of the 3D shape of the nose for biometric authentication. He has been a Post-Doctoral Research Associate (PDRA) in big data science at Aston University and is currently a PDRA in RADAR and video data fusion for autonomous vehicles at Heriot- Watt University. His research interests are in 3D object recognition and data mining.

Sandesh Sanjay Gade is a research associate at PES Institute of Technology, Bangalore South Campus. He completed his bachelor's degree in Computer Science & Engineering and is pursuing graduate studies currently. An avid programmer and developer, Sandesh's area of interests is in the fields of bioinformatics, distributed computing, machine learning, graph databases and web technologies.

Swati Sampatrao Gambhire, Faculty, PESIT-BSC, holds Bachelors and Masters degree in Computer Science and Engineering. She has a teaching experience of 6 years in various technical institutions. Her research areas include Cloud Computing, Machine Learning and Optimization.

Dibyanshu Jaiswal has completed his Bachelors in Computer Science from Dr. B. C. Roy Engineering College, Durgapur, West Bengal in 2011 and Master of Engineering in Computer Science from Jadavpur University, Kolkata West Bengal in 2013. He joined Innovation Labs of Tata Consultancy Services in September 2013 and is currently working as Researcher. Dibyanshu's research mainly involves working with distributed computing systems and semantic web of data in the context of Internet of Things.

Vandana M. Ladwani holds a Master's Degree in Computer Science and Engineering from RTM Nagpur University. She is working as Assistant Professor in PES Institute of Technology Bangalore South Campus and has 10 years of teaching and research experience in academics. She is pursuing PhD in Signal Processing and Machine Learning.

Sai Prasanna M. S., Faculty, PESIT-BSC has B.E. and M.Tech degrees in Computer Science and Engineering. She has teaching experience of two years. Her primary research interest is cloud Computing and Optimization.

Archana Mathur is a working as Assistant Professor in PESIT Bangalore South Campus. She is pursuing PhD from VTU in domain of Scientometrics. She has done Masters from Bangalore University in Web Technologies. Her research interest includes: Scientometrics, Machine Learning and Semantic Web.

Arijit Mukherjee completed his Bachelors and Master's degree in Computer Science from reputed universities in India. After completion of the Master's degree, Arijit worked in the software industry (namely Tata Consultancy Services and Verizon) for about five years till 2002 in various projects for telecommunication giants such as Bell Atlantic, Nokia, and Siemens. His major projects were related to Residential Broadband, Intelligent Network, Corporate GSM and Data Network Management Systems. In May 2002 Arijit joined the School of Computing Science, Newcastle University, UK as a Research Associate and started working with evolving Grid technologies and service orientation. He was one of the main researchers in the internationally acclaimed my Grid, OGSA-DAI and OGSA-DQP projects which contributed to the development of W3C standards for Web Services/SOA. His special interest was in dynamic service provisioning within the context of distributed databases on which he completed his PhD in 2008. From June 2008, Arijit worked as a lead researcher at Connectiva Systems (I) Pvt. Ltd., a telecommunications revenue assurance product company in Kolkata, India, for three years. He joined the Innovation Labs of Tata Consultancy Services in September 2011 and is currently working as a Senior Scientist. Arijit's research involves massively parallel processing, distributed systems and cognitive computing in the context of Internet of Things.

Nithin Nagaraj has Bachelors in Electrical and Electronics Engineering from National Institute of Technology Karnataka (1999), Masters in Electrical Engineering from Rensselaer Polytechnic Institute, Troy, New York (2001) and Ph.D. from National Institute of Advanced Studies (NIAS, 2010). After a short stint as a visiting faculty in Mathematics at IISER Pune, he joined as Assistant Professor at the Department of Electronics and Communication Engineering, Amrita University, Kerala for the period 2009-2013. He has worked as Research Scientist and Lead Scientist at GE Global Research Center at Bengaluru in the area of biomedical signal and image analysis (2001-2004, 2013-2015) before joining the Consciousness Studies Programme at NIAS in October 2015. His research interests have spanned information and coding theory, cryptography, wavelets, compressed sensing, chaos theory and its applications, modeling of complex systems, and scientific theories of consciousness. He has co-authored 14 peer-reviewed international journal publications, over 35 national and international conference presentations, with a total of 650+ Google Scholar citations. He is a co-inventor of 8 U.S. patent applications (2 granted). He is an invited reviewer of several international journals such as IEEE Transactions on Image Processing, Chaos (American Institute of Physics), CNSNS (Elsevier), Acta Applicandae Mathematicae, IEEE Transactions on Information Forensics & Security, EURASIP Journal of Information Security, Computers and Mathematics with Applications (Elsevier), Journal of Theoretical Biology and others.

Hima Patel is data scientist at Shell Technology Centre, Bangalore. Prior to joining Shell, she was associated with GE Global Research and GE Healthcare. In her ten years of experience, she has worked on a large number of industrial research problems leading to both patents and transitions to working products. Her research interests are in the fields of machine learning, computer vision and data mining. She received her B.E.in Computer Engineering and M Tech in Information and Communication Technologies in 2004 and 2006 respectively.

Parth Pahtak is currently working as Research Lead at ezDI, his main focus is on NLP and NLP inclined Machine Learning. He has 5 years of experience in healthcare domain with main focus being clinical NLP, Big Data and Predictive Analysis.

James Peterson received his Ph.D. in mathematics in 1980 from Colorado State University. His research involves a fusion of mathematics, computation and science in fields such as immunology and cognitive models.

Vaskar Raychoudhury received the BTech degree in Information Technology from the B.P. Poddar Institute of Management & Technology, Kolkata (affiliated to The University of Kalyani, West Bengal), in 2003, and the MS degree in Information Technology from the School of Information Technology, Indian Institute of Technology, Kharagpur in 2006. He obtained his PhD in Computer Science from The Hong Kong Polytechnic University in 2010. Later he continued his post doctoral research in the same university for a year before moving to the the Institut Telecom SudParis, in France where he worked for another year as a post-doctoral research fellow. He is currently an Assistant Professor in the Department of Computer Science and Engineering, Indian Institute of Technology Roorkee. His research interests include mobile and pervasive computing, context awareness, and (Mobile) social networks, and he keeps publishing high-quality journals and conference papers in these areas. He has served as program committee member in ASE/IEEE Socialcom, ICDCN, and many others. He serves in the capacity of the reviewer for many top IEEE and Elsevier journals. He is a member of the ACM, the IEEE, the IEEE Computer Society, and the IEEE Communication Society.

Kenneth J. Ryan earned a Ph.D. in Statistics from Iowa State University in 2001. He is currently an Associate Professor in the Department of Statistics at West Virginia University.

Sriparna Saha received the M.Tech and Ph.D. degrees in computer science from Indian Statistical Institute Kolkata, Kolkata, India, in 2005 and 2011, respectively. She is currently a Faculty Member in the Department of Computer Science and Engineering, Indian Institute of Technology Patna, Patna, India. She is the author of a book published by Springer-Verlag. She has authored or coauthored more than 100 papers. Her current research interests include pattern recognition, multiobjective optimization and biomedical information extraction. Her h-index is 15 and total citation count of her papers is 1336 (according to Google scholar). She is the recipient of the Lt Rashi Roy Memorial Gold Medal from the Indian Statistical Institute for outstanding performance in MTech (computer science). She is the recipient of the Google India Women in Engineering Award,2008. She is the recipient of Junior Humboldt Research Fellowship. She had also received India4EU fellowship of the European Union to work as a Post-doctoral Research Fellow in the University of Trento, Italy from September 2010-January 2011. She was also the recipient of Erasmus Mundus Mobility with Asia (EMMA) fellowship of the European Union to work as a Post-doctoral Research Fellow in the Heidelberg University, Germany from September 2009-June 2010. She won the best paper award in International Conference on Advances in Computing, Communications and Informatics (ICACCI 2012). One of her papers in the journal "Data and Knowledge Engineering" titled "Combining multiple classifiers using vote based classifier ensemble technique for named entity recognition" received the tag of "most downloaded article".

Manisha Srivastava is a machine learning scientist at Amazon Customer Service team where she uses NLP techniques to help improve the customer experience. Prior to Amazon she worked as a machine learning engineer at TripAdvisor where she worked on improving the quality of business listings by building models to detect duplicate listings, permanently closed business etc. She received her masters degree in Computer Engineering from Texas A&M University, College Station. Before this she worked as data scientist at General Electric Research lab, India where she applied predictive analytics in domains like healthcare, oil & gas, and wind energy. She did her undergraduate studies at Indian Institute of Technology, Guwahati.

Ramasubramanian (Ramsu) Sundararajan is a Principal with the Operations Research group of Sabre Airline Solutions in Bangalore, India. He holds a bachelor's degree in Information Systems from the Birla Institute of Technology & Science, Pilani, India, and a doctorate in Information Systems from the Indian Institute of Management, Kolkata, India. Ramsu has over 13 years of experience in applying machine learning / data mining techniques to a variety of problems in the area of finance, healthcare, energy and aviation, first at GE Global Research between 2003-14 and now at Sabre since August 2014.

Shweta Yadav received the B.Tech and M.Tech degree in Computer Science & Engineering from the Punjab Technical University, India and Punjabi University, India in 2011 and 2013, respectively. She is currently working towards the PhD. degree in the Department of Computer Science & Engineering at the Indian Institute of Technology Patna, India. Her current research interests include: Bio-medical Text Mining, Clinical Text Mining, Evolutionary Multi-Objective Optimization, and Particle Swarm Optimization in general.

Ye Yang is a PhD Student in the Department of Statistics, University of Georgia.

Index

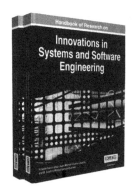